CALVIN COOLIDGE

THE MAN FROM VERMONT

CALVIN COOLIDGE

The Man from Vermont

By
CLAUDE M. FUESS

ARCHON BOOKS
Hamden, Connecticut
1965

LIBRARY OF CONGRESS CATALOG CARD NUMBER: 65-19595
PRINTED IN THE UNITED STATES OF AMERICA

Introduction

WHEN, in the summer of 1932, I had an informal conversation with Mr. Coolidge at Plymouth, Vermont, regarding his possible biography, he finally said drily, "Better wait till I'm dead," and changed the subject to the much pleasanter one of Amherst College. Within a few months he was in his grave, and I was unexpectedly at work on this book. The preparation of the manuscript has been delayed by matters beyond my own control, particularly by the fact that new material was constantly being found. It seems unlikely, however, that many more of Coolidge's private letters will be brought to light or will greatly alter verdicts already formed.

Mrs. Coolidge has generously permitted me to examine a large number of letters written by Coolidge to his father and stepmother from his schoolboy days until Colonel Coolidge's death in 1926 — letters which the latter had carefully preserved in a large mahogany cigar humidor. Furthermore she has enabled me to have access to some other important documents and has answered many questions. It must be emphasized, however, that this is, in no sense, an "official" biography, and that Mrs. Coolidge is not a sponsor for it or for the views expressed herein. Mr. Frank W. Stearns, before his death on March 6, 1939, had opened up all his personal files and allowed me to quote as I pleased from his correspondence. I have had the advantage of long talks with him and his intimate associate, Mr. Benjamin F. Felt, who has advised me on various details. To Mrs. Coolidge, Mr. Stearns, and Mr. Felt, I am deeply indebted.

In the course of my researches, I have, of course, spent much time at Plymouth and Northampton, visiting places and people connected with Coolidge. The Amherst College chapter was written *con amore*, as must always be the case when a graduate deals with his Alma Mater. I have been fortunate in being able to consult four of Coolidge's secretaries, — Henry F. Long, Everett Sanders, Harry Ross, and the late Edward T. Clark, — as well as several of those who knew him best, including Miss Aurora Pierce, former Governor Channing H. Cox, the late Judge Henry P. Field, Bruce Barton, Charles A. Andrews, and Coolidge's law partner, Ralph

Hemenway. Robert M. Washburn, Coolidge's first biographer, has called my attention to many significant points and has shown an unfailing interest in my project.

Among those who have furnished material or read chapters have been Mrs. Sarah Pollard, Herbert L. Moore, Miss Florence Cilley, former Attorney General J. Garibaldi Sargent, Justice Harlan F. Stone, Frederick S. Allis, Alfred E. Stearns, Grosvenor H. Backus, Lucius R. Eastman, John P. Deering, Charles T. Burnett, James B. Cauthers, C. Green Brainard, the late Dwight W. Morrow, President Stanley King of Amherst College, Thomas Cochran, Frank W. Buxton, Charles H. Taylor, Andrew J. Peters, Herbert Parker, Robert Lincoln O'Brien, William F. Whiting, William M. Butler, Henry L. Stoddard, William C. Endicott, Nicholas Murray Butler, Wallace McCamant, General Edward L. Logan, Edward D. Duffield, Clarence S. Brigham, William A. Macdonald, Charles M. Davenport, Mrs. Alexandra Carlisle Pfeiffer, Roger L. Scaife, Senator David I. Walsh, Morgan B. Brainard, Howard D. French, Charles K. Bolton, Mark A. De Wolfe Howe, Charles S. Hopkinson, Frederick C. Nichols, Albert P. Wadleigh, President Harold W. Dodds, Foster W. Stearns, James A. Nelson, Robert W. Maynard, George F. Booth, Louis H. Warner, Colonel Robert F. Goodwin, William V. Hodges, Roy A. Young, and many others. Henry L. Stimson and Joseph C. Grew were of much assistance on the chapter dealing with foreign relations under the Coolidge administration. A complete list of the persons who have sent me letters or contributed anecdotes would fill several pages.

Mr. William Allen White's *A Puritan in Babylon* appeared just before the completion of my manuscript, and I have profited by it, although, as will be seen, I am far from agreeing with him in some of his judgments and conclusions.

It has been essential, of course, to spend much time in examining the rich Coolidge collection in the Forbes Library, in Northampton, where Mr. Harrison, the Librarian, has placed its treasures at my disposal. The Boston Athenaeum, as usual, has been a delightful place for leisurely study, especially the consultation of newspapers, and Miss Gregory and her staff have been uniformly courteous and helpful. To Charles J. Dean, of Northampton, Mrs. Guy W. Hersey, of Peterborough, New Hampshire, Miss Helen G. Moore, Mr. Stearns's personal secretary, and my own secretaries, Miss Rosamond Greenwood and Miss Nettie I. Crosby, I am obligated for much patient and tiresome copying and compilation.

Through the kindness of Mr. and Mrs. Frederick J. Manning I

have been allowed to consult the Taft papers and to use excerpts which have to do with Coolidge and his administration.

To Edward A. Weeks, one of the most tolerant and patient of editors, I am profoundly grateful. His advice has been sound, and his suggestions have been wise.

My wife, who has listened uncomplainingly to the reading of most of the chapters, has kept me from numerous *faux pas,* both in style and in substance. Her share in the book is so large that she has seemed to me a partner in its production.

No one can complete a volume which has occupied his time for almost six years without being conscious of his and its inadequacies. But I have never deviated from my original purpose of seeking the truth and following it, wherever it led. Calvin Coolidge deserves fair treatment, free from prejudice or cynicism, and this I have tried to give him without overwhelming him with indiscriminate eulogy. I can only add that he has amply repaid the labor. Some statesmen diminish in size and importance under microscopic study. Coolidge, on the other hand, has seemed to me to grow more interesting. I finish this biography with the conviction that he was not only a useful public servant but a great and good man.

C. M. F.

August 25, 1939
DUBLIN, NEW HAMPSHIRE

CONTENTS

ILLUSTRATIONS

CALVIN COOLIDGE

THE MAN FROM VERMONT

I

Yankee Ancestry and Vermont Environment

On the late afternoon of September 21, 1928, President Calvin Coolidge, standing on the rear platform of a train which had stopped for a few minutes at Bennington, in southern Vermont, delivered, perhaps extemporaneously, a short address so rhythmic that it falls easily into verse form — indeed has often been so printed — and seems a spontaneous overflow of powerful emotion. Veteran newspapermen not unaccustomed to surprises found themselves listening intently to these introductory sentences : —

> Vermont is a state I love.
> I could not look
> Upon the peaks
> Of Ascutney, Killington,
> Mansfield, and Equinox,
> Without being moved
> In a way that no other scene
> Could move me.
>
> It was here
> That I first saw
> The light of day;
> Here I received my bride,
> Here my dead lie,
> Pillowed on the loving breast
> Of our everlasting hills.

After a summer spent in Wisconsin, Coolidge had been traveling by special train through Vermont, examining the damage caused by recent floods and everywhere being greeted by old friends. He had persistently refused to make speeches along the route; but as he was leaving his native state the impulse to say something was evidently irresistible.

At no moment in his career did Calvin Coolidge publicly display deeper feeling. It is true that his customary reticence could usually be dissipated by a reference to Vermont [1] and that his letters from the White House to his father were often tinged with nostalgia; but he was rarely stirred to poetic expression even on this subject. That it should have been homesickness which aroused him thus to unusual eloquence may seem amazing. It must be remembered, however, that no American statesman has been more closely identified with one special section of the country. Theodore Roosevelt, William H. Taft, Woodrow Wilson, were of a different type, and very few could say offhand where they were born. Calhoun, on the other hand, was always the South Carolinian, and Harding typified the Middle West. So Coolidge, even in Washington, bore the unmistakable stamp of the provincial, the perfect Yankee.[2] No well-traveled American could possibly have attributed that nasal twang to Georgia or Indiana or Minnesota. He was a New Englander in every gesture and quaint turn of phrase — and proud of it. He could assume successfully for a time the manner and tailoring of the cosmopolitan, but when the emergency was over he liked to relax in surroundings where he was comfortable. He was born in New England, educated in New England, rose to distinction in New England. In his soul was, I believe, a spirit like that voiced by Amy Lowell in her poem "Lilacs": —

> Lilacs in me because I am New England,
> Because my roots are in it,
> Because my leaves are of it,
> Because my flowers are for it;
> Because it is my country
> And I speak to it of itself,
> And sing of it with my own voice
> Since certainly it is mine.

This biography, then, will be inevitably an interpretation of New England — but not the cultured, somewhat frigid Back Bay of the Adamses and Lawrences and Lowells and Cabots, of Marquand's *The Late George Apley* and Santayana's *The Last Puri-*

---

[1] E. G. Lowry, *Washington Close-ups*, 26.

[2] Something of this provinciality is suggested, I think deliberately, by Charles Hopkinson in his portrait of Coolidge now hanging in the front hall of the White House. Even when he was President he had a keen interest in the little details of farm life at Plymouth, and asked his father questions about cattle and crops. John Spargo, speaking on January 17, 1933, before the Joint Assembly of the Legislature of Vermont, said of Coolidge, "He was Vermont incarnate." The Washington correspondent of the London *Times* for January 12, 1933, wrote, "He [Coolidge] was racy of New England; was New England incarnate, in his speech, his habit of mind, even his appearance, the New England which — like Boston as a city — is not only a region but a state of mind."

tan; [3] not the scholarly Cambridge of Longfellow and Charles Eliot Norton and William James and Barrett Wendell; not the mystical Concord of Emerson and Thoreau, or the "cold roast Boston" of Nahant and Beverly Farms and Bar Harbor. The New England of Calvin Coolidge was that of the countryside, of the rural simplicity of *Snow-Bound,* of *Ethan Frome,* of *North of Boston,* of Margaret Deland and Dorothy Canfield Fisher and Edwin Arlington Robinson. Although his prowess as a dirt farmer may have been exaggerated for political purposes, he was undeniably close to the soil, and his membership in the Algonquin Club did not transform him into the boon companion of Beacon Street Brahmins. Nor was he much affected by the alien elements in New England — the Irish and Italians of Boston, the French Canadians of the mill cities, the Poles in the tobacco and onion fields of the Connecticut Valley. His folks were Yankees, who lived and died away from congested centres of population. The small farm, the country store, the village church and school — all these exerted their influence on the growing boy. And supplementing these environmental forces was the subtle, still only half-explicable, power of heredity. A Yankee ancestry began what a New England countryside completed.

In Calvin Coolidge, then, we have the Yankee,[4] untainted and unashamed, with his wiry, nervous body, his laconic speech, his thrift, his industry, his conservative distrust of foreigners and innovations, and his native dignity. When, at the close of his pilgrimage from Plymouth to the White House, after he had entertained monarchs and been the guest of captains of industry, he returned to Vermont, it was as if he had never gone away. The ex-President, rocking ceaselessly while curious visitors drove up, stared, and departed, sat on his porch, wearing a last year's hat and rather seedy clothes, watching the late afternoon slip by as his father and grandfather after middle age had done before him, and, despite all his honors, looking like part of the landscape. He had never seen London or Paris, the Acropolis or the Pyramids; he was unfamiliar with cotillions and grand opera. He had been, it is true, Governor and President, and had sat in high places; but those hours

---

[3] "I come from Boston," said a rather effusive lady once to President Coolidge. "Yes, and you'll never get over it," was the unexpected reply. Even when he had risen to political heights, Coolidge had few friends among what is called the "upper crust" of Boston society. The more aristocratic branch of the Coolidge family always regarded him with suspicion.

[4] The word "Yankee" has been derived from various sources, but it is probably an Indian corruption of the word *anglais.* The typical New England Yankee has by no means disappeared, as those who spend their summers in New Hampshire or Vermont have reason to know.

were gone now, and he was getting past his prime, and he was back in Plymouth, where he belonged, among friends who understood him and would not ask too many questions.

So we, to understand him, must begin with Vermont, for there we shall find the clue to what Broadway and Pennsylvania Avenue thought to be his enigmatical utterances. Even then, unless we have Vermont affiliations, we shall miss significant details. We must not sentimentalize or be misguided by a craving for the picturesque. We must seek only the truth, and in so doing hope to clarify what has been fatuously called the mystery of Calvin Coolidge. He was no more mysterious than Abraham Lincoln or Grover Cleveland or any other figure who, emerging from obscure origins, has fabricated for himself a notable career.

Vermont, with its area of but 9564 square miles, is a very tiny state, from one end of which to the other a motorist may travel comfortably in a few hours. It has no important waterways except the Connecticut River on its eastern boundary and Lake Champlain to the west; and only a relatively insignificant proportion of arable land. It is called the Green Mountain State, and wherever one enters it there are verdant hills — hills covered to their summits with maples and beeches and birches, hemlocks and spruces and pines. Although the agriculturist and the manufacturer have to struggle against difficulties, marble and granite can be cut in nearly every section.

The population of the state in 1930 was only 359,611, and it has no large city, only fourteen communities having more than 2500 inhabitants. Vermont has grown very little in sixty years. Indeed its total population in 1870, just before Coolidge was born, was 330,551, of whom 47,155 were not natives. The Anglo-Saxon element still predominates, for there was little in the remote Green Mountains to tempt the Germans, Scandinavians, and Irish who landed in such numbers on our shores in the 1850's, and the Latins and Slavs who began their great migration towards the close of the last century.

Vermont was not one of the thirteen original colonies. The section now constituting the state was claimed by both New York and New Hampshire during the French and Indian Wars, and the controversy over the so-called New Hampshire Grants was assuming all the aspects of a bloody feud when the Revolution broke out and gave the Green Mountain Boys another outlet for their energies. Only after prolonged disputation did the inhabitants of that district, assembled at Windsor in June 1777, proclaim an independent state, under the name of Vermont. Officers were chosen in March 1778, the first governor being Thomas Chittenden, and the state was formally admitted to the Union by Congress on March 4, 1791.

In all Vermont few townships were, in 1872, the year of Calvin Coolidge's birth, more isolated than Plymouth, in Windsor County, in the eastern part of the state. In its original charter, signed by Governor Benning Wentworth of New Hampshire in 1751, the township was called Saltash, and it was still Saltash when, in 1777, a certain John Mudge made the first settlement within its boundaries. At this period the only safe means of penetrating the almost unbroken wilderness was over the military road cut by General Jeffrey Amherst in the 1750's from Fort Number Four — now Charlestown, New Hampshire — on the Connecticut River, northwest to Crown Point and Fort Ticonderoga. This highway can still be traced through the southern part of the township. It was apparently in 1781 that Calvin Coolidge's great-great-grandfather, John Coolidge (1756–1822), who had been a captain in the Revolutionary forces, located a farm along this military road, on a height of land rising westward from the Black River.[5] Covered as it was with evergreen and hardwood trees, it had to be cleared before it would support any vegetation, and even then the soil was thin and rocky, yielding a living only to those who kept everlastingly at it. Why Captain Coolidge left the relatively fertile Massachusetts land and sought this sterile section is difficult to explain except on the assumption that he craved "more elbowroom."

Plymouth Township was not formally organized until 1787;[6] and at the earliest recorded town meeting, in March 1789, Captain Coolidge was chosen as one of the three selectmen. In the Vermont census of 1790, he appears as the head of a family consisting of one male of sixteen years, three males under sixteen, and three females. To each of his five children Captain Coolidge gave a farm in the neighborhood, the one belonging to his eldest son being that in Plymouth Notch eventually inherited by President Coolidge. Captain Coolidge was the first of the family to be buried in the cemetery at the Notch. Meanwhile along the ridges and in the

[5] Captain Coolidge came to Saltash from Lancaster, Massachusetts. His original farm, west of Frog City, is now known locally as the McWain Place.

[6] Why it was named Plymouth I have been unable to ascertain. The pioneer settlers in New England displayed no originality in christening their settlements. For example, there is a Plymouth in every New England state except Rhode Island. Plymouth, Vermont, is now one of the twenty-four townships in Windsor County, and is bounded on the north by Bridgewater, on the east by Reading, on the south by Ludlow, and on the west by Rutland County. It is approximately 140 miles from Boston.

river valleys little hamlets were springing up with such picturesque names as Kingdom, Frog City, Five Corners, Pinney Hollow, Tyson Furnace, and Nineveh. Of all these settlements, Plymouth Union, on the Black River, was probably the least obscure, and became the place where town meetings were usually held. From the Union the road to the east rises sharply for a short distance to a height of land and then drops in more gradual fashion into a broad, irregularly shaped bowl, where nestles Plymouth Notch, about fourteen hundred feet above sea level. The Union was, in some degree, a manufacturing community, whose sophisticated residents scorned the Notch folks as "rubes" and "hayseeds"; and the rivalry between the two hamlets occasionally quickened into violent encounters. From the Notch the road winds eastward through the forest down a long slope to Bridgewater Corners and then along the Ottauquechee River to Woodstock, the shire village, and its shaded green, about eleven miles away. The highway from the Union south follows the Black River down the valley along the western shore of some of the loveliest lakes in New England until it reaches Ludlow, another trading centre for the Plymouth people.

Plymouth Notch, where Calvin Coolidge was born and spent his childhood days, included in its period of maximum prosperity six or seven farmhouses, a church, a store, a schoolhouse, a cemetery, and some miscellaneous sheds and outbuildings. Here the farmers from the encircling hillsides did their marketing and gossiping when they had no time to drive to Woodstock or to Ludlow. The railroad, which had reached both Ludlow and Woodstock in the mid-century, did not penetrate to the Union, and only with the spread of the automobile have it and the Notch become easily accessible to the outside world.

In 1850 the township of Plymouth claimed 1400 inhabitants, who possessed 275 horses, 1739 cattle, and 8144 swine. Within its limits were thirteen sawmills, three gristmills, two stores, two taverns, and two hotels. The mineral resources, especially the limestone, had already been somewhat exploited; and to-day abandoned kilns of field stone may be noticed along the roadside. Colonel John C. Coolidge, Calvin's father, earned his first hundred dollars burning out lime at one dollar and a quarter a hogshead. Marble was being cut as early as 1834; iron was smelted at Tyson Furnace; and a placer miner at Five Corners in the 1860's created a local "boom" by taking out several thousand dollars' worth of gold dust. But the residents had to live by the soil; and after the Civil War, those Vermont soldiers who had been stationed in such pleasant

territory as the Ohio Valley came to recognize the relative un-
productiveness of their own unfruitful acres and wandered away to
richer lands. Plymouth, removed from the main arteries of transportation, with none of the luxuries and few of the conveniences of
modern civilization, could not hold ambitious men. There the snow
fell early and lingered long.

> Roaring snows, downsweeping from the uplands,
> Bury the still valleys, drift them deep.

"Everything in Vermont," says John Cotton Dana, "looks toward
winter." The houses were built close to the highway so that long
walks through the snow could be avoided. The laborer wore himself
out for a meagre reward. It is not astonishing that the sons of
Plymouth scattered to the far corners of the nation, often leaving
their old homesteads to fall into ruin. In 1870, the population had
diminished to 1285. To-day on Plymouth's 22,249 acres dwell only
a few more than three hundred inhabitants, and the number will
probably never again be as large as it was when Calvin Coolidge
was born.[7]

Despite this decline, Plymouth Notch in the twentieth century
looks superficially much as it did in 1872 — an unimpressive huddle
of buildings tucked away among the hills. Saltash Mountain, over
three thousand feet high, is within easy climbing distance, but
cannot be seen from the hamlet itself. Life was extremely simple
and, by urban standards, uncomfortable. Not a house in the Notch
had gas lamps, coal fires, or running water. Even after Calvin
Coolidge became President his homestead contained no "newfangled
plumbing." Each bedroom had its commode, washbowl, and pitcher,
and the sanitary facilities had not altered since 1800. In the winter
every Notch boy was up long before the sun, dressed in an un-
heated chamber, and, lighting his lantern, groped his way to the
less arctic kitchen to wash hurriedly in ice-cold water. Plymouth
houses had no Hepplewhite chairs or Duncan Phyfe tables. The
parlor, seldom used except for ceremonial occasions, was customarily furnished in "store furniture," of heavy and sombre
walnut, upholstered with black haircloth. The centre of the home
was the kitchen, the source of supplies, where everybody assembled
when work time was over. But the barn, after all, was the most
necessary structure. Built large and stormproof, it was usually, for

[7] Land to-day in Plymouth can frequently be bought for less than ten dollars
an acre, and farms are sold because they are not worth the payment of the accumulated taxes. A tax valuation of three or four dollars an acre is not uncommon.

convenience, attached to the house. Without it, life on the farm would have had to cease.

The spirit of independence characteristic of Stark and the Green Mountain Boys had by no means disappeared. The Notch was a self-contained community where, if a farmer needed an implement, he or one of his more skillful neighbors manufactured it. The days of mail-order houses and of rapid transit by the Ford Model T had not yet arrived, and necessity actually became the mother of invention. Colonel John C. Coolidge once explored the jumbled attic of the Coolidge homestead and there resurrected the farm tools of five generations — a stonemason's hammer, a mattock, a bush scythe, a loom and flax wheel, a reel, a swift, a log beehive, a sap yoke, a wooden fan for winnowing the chaff from the wheat, hetchels and bobbins and jack planes.[8] The routine farmer's day was packed with physical labor, and bodily strength and endurance were highly regarded. A boy on a Plymouth farm became accustomed early to hard work. Even when he was a child, Calvin Coolidge filled the wood box, led the cattle to and from pasture, fed the chickens and the pigs, dropped seed potatoes, and drove the mowing machine and horse rake. At fourteen or fifteen he was ready to pitch hay with the men. It seems to us like drudgery, but it was a healthful existence, spent largely in the open air, and not likely to produce neuroses. On the women, however, the strain was often unendurable, for their lives were confined, and the monotony frequently resulted in melancholy and even in insanity.

Living under these conditions, the people of Plymouth preserved what Edmund Burke called a "fierce spirit of liberty," keeping themselves rugged, self-reliant, and proud. To strangers they were uncommunicative, and visitors regarded them as angular and taciturn. They were able to take care of themselves, and few of them had mortgages on their farms or failed to meet their notes promptly at the Ludlow Bank. While they possessed few books, most of them read a newspaper — the weekly *Woodstock Standard,* the weekly *Vermont Tribune* published at Ludlow, or the *Rutland Herald,* a daily.[9] They remained, and still remain, conservative — Vermont was one of the two states carried by Taft in 1912 — and impatient with radicalism. In accordance with the Puritan tradition brought by the original settlers from Massachusetts, they regarded

[8] On one much publicized occasion the President presented to Henry Ford an ancient sap bucket, saying, as he took it from his father and handed it to Mr. Ford, "My father had it, then I had it, and now you've got it." See the illustration facing page 352.

[9] Nine daily newspapers are published in Vermont, two of them in Burlington.

frivolity as a misdemeanor and idleness as a sin, and stressed the virtues of thrift, industry, and honesty. They were pleased with Calvin Coolidge's record, but did not consider it in any sense remarkable that one of their type should have become President of the United States. He himself, as we shall see, retained, even in the White House, the habits acquired during his childhood at Plymouth Notch.[10]

Judged by the culture of Boston, or even of Brattleboro, Plymouth Notch was, and is, a primitive and uncultured community. The buildings at their best are commonplace, and the fine arts are little cultivated. But where nature is unspoiled by man, the stretches of woodland are very beautiful. Hills rise one after the other, — Mount Tom, Old Notch, Mount Ambrose, South Hudus Mountain, and Blueberry Hill, — until Mount Killington is reached, 4241 feet high, towering over the Rutland Valley. Down the hollows in the slopes dash countless rippling brooks — Farmer, Great Roaring, Tinker, Buffalo, Money, and many others. His early associations made Calvin Coolidge peculiarly sensitive to the charms of the Vermont countryside. When he was Governor of Massachusetts he was asked, "Do you ever think that you would like some day to return to Plymouth to live?" After the customary few seconds of thought, he replied, "I love the hills." He was not generally regarded as a sentimental man. But he had a passion for his native state, thought of it when he was away, and was eager to return to it. Once he said: —

Vermont is my birthright. Here one gets close to nature, in the mountains, in the brooks, the waters of which hurry to the sea; in the lakes, shining like silver in their green setting; fields tilled, not by machinery, but by the brain and hand of man. My folks are happy and contented. They belong to themselves, live within their incomes, and fear no man.

He spent the last summer of his life, during the Presidential campaign of 1932, in the old homestead, close to the scenes of his childhood. We cannot doubt that he felt there

> The peace that lives beneath the starry sky,
> The sleep that dwells among the lonely hills.

[10] Irwin H. ("Ike") Hoover, in his *Forty-two Years in the White House,* points out that Coolidge as President slept on an average eleven hours a day, going to bed always before ten o'clock, getting up early in the morning, and taking a nap in the afternoon, in the manner of his farmer ancestors. It was his habit before retiring to go to the White House kitchens to investigate the larder, as he had done as a boy in Plymouth.

The influence of environment on Calvin Coolidge was very powerful, but no less potent than that of heredity. Most of the American Coolidges trace their line back to John Coolidge, who died in Watertown, Massachusetts, August 22, 1691, at the age of eighty-seven. John Coolidge was probably born in Cambridge, England, in 1604, came to New England about 1630, and is first mentioned in the Watertown records in 1636.[11] A man of property, he left a competence to each of the five sons who survived him; and each one of them — John, Simon, Stephen, Nathaniel, and Jonathan — founded a dynasty of some distinction. John, the oldest, was the progenitor of the so-called Sherborn-Natick branch of the family, of which the late Louis A. Coolidge (1861–1925), the Boston author and publicist, was a member. Nathaniel, the fourth son, became the ancestor of Henry D. Coolidge, clerk of the Massachusetts Senate, and of the David Hill Coolidge family of Boston, from which Charles A. Coolidge, the architect, is descended. The youngest brother, Jonathan, had a great-great-great-grandson, Joseph Coolidge (1798–1879), who married in 1825 Eleanor Wayles Randolph, granddaughter of Thomas Jefferson, assumed a prominent position in the aristocracy of Boston, and became himself the grandfather of some unusually able men, including John Gardner Coolidge (1863–1936), the diplomat, Archibald C. Coolidge (1866–1928), the historian, and Julian Lowell Coolidge, the Master of Lowell House at Harvard University. Still another of Jonathan's descendants, Joseph Coolidge (1773–1840), married his second cousin once removed, Elizabeth Bulfinch, sister of the architect, Charles Bulfinch. It was from him and his large estate that Coolidge Corner, in Brookline, Massachusetts, took its name. On the whole, the descendants of Jonathan Coolidge constituted the most famous branch of the family until Calvin Coolidge appeared and surpassed his kin. The family in all its ramifications is one of the most distinguished of those dating from colonial times in America.

Calvin Coolidge came down direct from John Coolidge of Watertown, through the latter's second son, Simon.[12] The names of

---

[11] See *Records of the Governor and Company of the Massachusetts Bay*, Vol. I, p. 372, under date of May 25, 1636, when John Coolidge was made a freeman of the Colony. See also the *New England Historical and Genealogical Register*, October 1926, 401ff. The Coolidge family has been traced as far back as the fifteenth century, with variant spellings, such as Coledge, Colledge, Cullege, Cooledge, Coallage, Cowledge, College, and many others. The Christian name of John Coolidge's wife was Mary, but her family has not yet been ascertained. John Coolidge was a deputy to the Great and General Court of the Massachusetts Bay Colony and a selectman of Watertown.

[12] Judge Henry P. Field, of Northampton, Massachusetts, told of a drive which he took with Governor Coolidge, at a time when the latter was much troubled, to

the President's American forbears, beginning with John, are as follows: John, Simon, Obadiah, Obadiah, Josiah, John, Calvin, Calvin Galusha, and John Calvin — good old New England names, harsh and Biblical and unromantic. With one or two exceptions, they did not move far from their original home. They lacked as a family the pioneer instinct which drove so many New Englanders westward, beyond the Hudson, then across the Mississippi, and finally through the Rockies to the Pacific. They were practical Yankees, who wasted no time dreaming of "something lost behind the ranges."

The Coolidges were indubitably a tough-fibred and robust stock. Of the nine male heads of families in direct succession down to Calvin Coolidge the recorded ages were 87, 61, 42, 44, 62, 66, 73, 63, and 81, the average duration of life being a little over 64. Over three centuries the number of children to a family gradually diminished: John had eight, Simon seven, and Obadiah eleven, while the three most recent generations have had but two each. No one of Calvin Coolidge's direct ancestors attained any eminence in his state; nor, on the other hand, was any one of them convicted of a misdemeanor or a crime. Most of them were farmers, and among them were no clergymen, no physicians, no teachers, no judges. They were substantial citizens who paid their bills promptly, held minor offices in the community, were content with little, did the day's work faithfully, and died with characters unstained. The adjectives which their contemporaries applied to them were "respectable," "virtuous," "reliable," "good." They had no discernible interest in music, art, or literature. One or two did some soldiering, but for the most part they led tame lives, undisturbed by emotional complexes or frustrations. They married into sound stock, — Barrons, Rogerses, Rouses, Goddards, Priests, Thompsons, Brewers, — and occasionally a lively wife would introduce a lighter strain into the more sluggish Coolidge blood. But the Coolidge attributes persisted and appeared in Calvin Coolidge. Up to the hour when he became a national figure, however, the Coolidges of his branch of the family had been prudent, law-abiding, steady-going, without evidence of unusual ability.

Mention has been made of Captain John Coolidge, who, in 1781, shortly after his marriage to Hannah Priest and the birth of his eldest son, Calvin (1780–1853), settled in Plymouth, later

---

Watertown, when he hunted out the old cemetery down a country lane, led Field to a crumbling tombstone bearing the names of John and Mary Coolidge, and said simply, "These are my first ancestors in this country." See *Good Housekeeping*, March 1935.

bringing there also his younger brother, Obadiah. Captain John, six feet and a half tall, had had much military experience, first as a private in Captain Howe's company at Lexington, later in Captain Longley's company at Cambridge, and finally in Captain David Moore's company, serving in Rhode Island towards the close of the war. To his son Calvin he gave, when the boy was twenty-one, the present Coolidge farm at Plymouth Notch, but beyond this fact we have no information regarding him. Calvin's oldest and only sur-viving son, Calvin Galusha Coolidge (1815–1878), is still remem-bered in that vicinity as a tall, spare man, with a fondness for prac-tical jokes. His popularity is attested by the many offices which he held — constable, justice of the peace, representative in the legis-lature, and agent of the town.[13] His grandson remembered that Calvin Galusha wore around home a blue woolen frock, cut like a shirt, with flaps reaching to the knees — a useful though not beautiful garment which Calvin Coolidge occasionally donned at Plymouth, to the amazement of newspapermen from city pave-ments.

When he was nearly thirty, Calvin Galusha Coolidge — known locally as "Galoosh" — married, March 4, 1844, Sarah Almeda Brewer (1823–1906),[14] a direct descendant of John Putnam, who came to the colonies about 1640. The Brewers had some traces of Indian blood, and Sarah's aunt, whom little Calvin was once taken to visit, fascinated the lad by smoking a pipe. It was to this some-what attenuated relationship that the President whimsically re-ferred when he declared that he had Indian blood in his veins. "Aunt Mede," as she was called by everybody, young or old, in the vicinity, was a vigorous personality, possessing an instinctive knowl-edge of herbs and simples and exceptional skill as a midwife. She spun woolen yarn, from which she knitted stockings and mittens, and she never lost the art of spinning and weaving sheets and table-cloths. She read books to her grandchildren, taught classes in the Notch Sunday School, and was a living exponent of practical Christianity. She died at the age of eighty-three, just after her grandson had married Grace Goodhue.

Calvin Coolidge's grandparents undoubtedly made much of

[13] In the *Vermont Register* for 1872, Calvin G. Coolidge is mentioned as agent for Plymouth and as a justice of the peace. Hiram Dunlap Moor, Calvin Coolidge's other grandfather, was then postmaster, and the merchants named were D. P. Wilder and John C. Coolidge.

[14] Sarah Almeda Brewer's father and mother — Israel C. Brewer (1797–1873) and Sally C. Brewer (1801–1884) — are buried at Sun Prairie, Columbia County, Wisconsin. Calvin Coolidge's great-grandmother was alive until the boy was twelve years old, but probably never saw him.

CALVIN GALUSHA COOLIDGE

SARAH ALMEDA BREWER COOLIDGE

CALVIN COOLIDGE'S GRANDFATHER AND GRANDMOTHER

their only grandson; and if modern theories of heredity are correct, many of his characteristics must have been inherited from them. During his last illness Calvin G. Coolidge deeded to his grandson the property known as the Lime Kiln lot — forty acres of no great value, which Calvin Coolidge always retained. "Aunt Mede" watched over his education. In his library was a copy of *The Green Mountain Boys,* with the inscription, "Presented to John Calvin Coolidge, by his Grandmother, Sarah A. Coolidge, December 24, 1882." Many other books were gifts to him from her.

Calvin Galusha Coolidge was a farmer by occupation, but he had certain recognized avocations, such as politics and raising and trading horses. He had two sons: Julius Caesar Coolidge, the younger, who died in 1870, in his twentieth year; and John Calvin Coolidge (1845–1926), who, after studying in the Notch school and polishing off his education with a few terms at Black River Academy, in Ludlow, worked for the village wheelwright, settled down on his father's farm, even taught for a short period in the district school at Pinney Hollow, and finally, in 1868, married and became a storekeeper. As a youth he had done chores around the farm, but he had also learned how to lay bricks and had become fairly proficient as a carpenter, a mason, and a carriage maker. In his *Autobiography* Calvin Coolidge says of his father, "If there was any physical requirement of country life which he could not perform, I do not know what it was." He pitched the hay on to the oxcart; he owned and knew how to use the tools for mending water pipes and tinware; he could even help a blacksmith at the forge. A visitor to Plymouth once remarked to Colonel John, "You appear to have been everything in this town except the undertaker." The reply was, "As a boy in the wheelwright's shop I used to make coffins, and we thought in those days that to use anything but hard wood for coffins was a cheat." As he grew older, his common sense won the confidence of his neighbors and, because the Notch had no lawyer, he was often called upon to draft wills, settle estates, and play Sir Oracle for the countryside. When he began to operate the Notch store — to-day known as the Cilley store [15] — he rented the building for forty dollars a year and made a profit of about one hundred dollars a month, an income which, in that community, established its recipient as a plutocrat. Gradually he became a lead-

[15] Miss Florence L. Cilley, who now manages the Notch store, is a mine of information on Plymouth affairs. The room in which Calvin Coolidge was born adjoins her general store, and business has been brisk in the summertime ever since the spot has become a place of pilgrimage.

ing citizen, an Admirable Crichton, with a hand in every important local enterprise. In 1875 he formed a partnership with his wife's brother, F. C. Moor, and a year later, after the birth of a daughter, he bought a house across the road, — the one known as the homestead, in which his son Calvin was later to take the oath as President of the United States, — with two acres of land and several barns and sheds, as well as a blacksmith shop. The price which he paid was reported to be $375. Two years later, when his father died, John C. Coolidge inherited some property and promptly sold out his share in the store to his partner, who continued as the local merchant.

John C. Coolidge was popular in a rather large circle in Vermont. When he was a schoolteacher, families were willing to pay twenty-five cents a week for the privilege of boarding him. While he was active in his store, he took trips to Boston every spring and fall to buy goods, and he often drove to various cities in his own state. After his appointment in 1900 on the staff of Governor William W. Stickney, he was regularly called Colonel Coolidge and rather enjoyed the title, although he was no warrior in appearance. His positions of trust were numerous. In 1880, he was town superintendent of schools in Plymouth; and in 1884 it is officially recorded that he received the sum of $11.40 "for superintending the schools for the year." He represented Plymouth three times in the Vermont House of Representatives, and even had, in 1910, a term in the State Senate. At different periods he served as selectman, tax collector, road commissioner, constable, deputy sheriff, and school commissioner. Of the approximately 250 registered voters in Plymouth, nine tenths were Republican, but the community was divided on local issues into Coolidgeites and anti-Coolidgeites, with the former usually in the lead. The decisive battle was waged annually at the March town meeting, held at the Union in Levi Green's hall, the floor of which had been liberally sprinkled with sawdust to meet the requirements of the tobacco users. From attending these gatherings as a youngster, Calvin Coolidge absorbed what he described as "a working knowledge of the practical side of government," including taxation, court procedure, and parliamentary law. Colonel Coolidge was an inveterate politician, whose shrewdness and discretion were transmitted to his son.

Calvin Coolidge's mother, whom he resembled in features and physique, was Victoria Josephine Moor (1846–1885), the daughter of Hiram Dunlap Moor, who owned the large farm across the road

from the Notch store, a farm now known as the Wilder Place.[16]
The ancestry of Hiram D. Moor is still in dispute; but he married,
December 5, 1838, Abigail Franklin, daughter of Luther Franklin
and Priscilla Pinney — the latter a member of the family for
which Pinney Hollow, two miles northeast of the Notch, was
named. Victoria Josephine Moor,[17] born on March 14, 1846, in
Pinney Hollow, was one of six children, two of whom lived to an
advanced age.[18] When she was about three years old, her father
moved to the Notch, where she and John C. Coolidge were playmates. They were married at Plymouth on May 6, 1868, when she
was twenty-two and he was a year older, and spent their brief
honeymoon in Woodstock.

It is a pity that we cannot learn more of Victoria Coolidge's
personality, for her face as shown in her pictures is most appealing.
A quaint daguerreotype of her and two of her sisters reveals her
in the Age of Innocence, with a starched white collar and cuffs,
and guileless eyes, like a Vermont Elaine. She was depicted by her
son as having "a very light and fair complexion with a rich growth
of brown hair that had a tint of gold in it"; and he added that
"her hands and features were regularly and finely formed." Mrs.
Pollard, her oldest sister, described her as "quiet, refined, orderly,
conscientious, even in her disposition, and a model housekeeper."
Evidently she had a touch of mysticism alien to the more practical
Coolidge temperament; and the deep vein of sentiment which undoubtedly existed in Calvin Coolidge came to him from her. She
liked to plant flowers and watch sunsets and stroll along woodland
paths. Her formal education ended with the grammar school and a
year at Black River Academy in Ludlow, but she always read good
books. Possibly she was a shade too fastidious for the rather
primitive life of the Notch. At any rate, her health gave way shortly

---

[16] This house was originally constructed as an inn, and, although it is now very
much in disrepair, the old barroom and dance hall can still be discerned.

[17] For the ancestry of Victoria Josephine Moor, see Vol. LXXVI, p. 303,
New England Historical and Genealogical Register (1923). Luther Franklin's
mother was Sarah Starr, who came to Guilford from Thompson, Connecticut, in
1777. Her husband, Jabez Franklin, came to Vermont in the same year from Scit-
uate, Rhode Island.

[18] The Moor family consisted of four girls and two boys. One son, Franklin,
married a Sawyer and succeeded John C. Coolidge as owner and operator of the
Notch store. The other son, Farmer, lived long in Louisiana. One daughter (Priscilla) was killed tragically, when very young, by a falling tree. Another, Gratia
Ellen, married a man named John J. Wilder, and long occupied the Moor house at
the Notch. The remaining sister, Sarah Jane, who married Don C. Pollard, died in
the summer of 1935, at Proctorsville, Vermont, three miles east of Ludlow. She was
a delightful old lady, full of reminiscences of the Moor and Coolidge families.

after her marriage and she became a chronic invalid, probably from some form of tuberculosis. She was too feeble and died too young to have an abiding influence on her son's character; but from her he inherited qualities which seem to his biographer very important.

Once again, to complete the background, we must return to environment. There is hardly a level acre within the borders of Plymouth Township. The triangle enclosed by roads from the Notch to Bridgewater Corners, then to West Bridgewater, and south to Plymouth Union, is a wild bit of mountain country, impassable except on foot and including areas of dense forest. Such farms as still exist lie on the slopes of the hills, where the soil is constantly being washed away, revealing an uninspiring crop of boulders. Only here and there along the little brooks is the land at all fertile. Nature seems everywhere to be closing in on man. Walter Hard says of his Mountain Pioneer: —

> Gone is the house he built.
> Gone are the fields he cleared and tilled.
> He was a victor for just a moment;
> Then, with the slow and stealthy step of time,
> Back came the unconquered forest.

Only courageous and hardy men and women could have settled here, or remained to fight against the wilderness. Everywhere are hills, one low range after another, with the roads cut out where the passage is easiest, usually where streams have first found their way. To the casual wanderer it is charming — the sudden vistas, the unexpected glimpses of water through the trees, the lichened boulders, the patches of pasture land in the midst of maples and birches. It is essentially romantic. But to those who struggled there, it had — and has — its cruel aspects. Nature is much the same from generation to generation.

The Plymouth of to-day is not precisely that of the 1870's. Some of the country along the Woodstock road near Pinney Hollow has been cleared by the Civilian Conservation Corps and transformed into the Calvin Coolidge Park, a thickly wooded reservation in the heart of the Green Mountains. Dams have been constructed, roads have been cut, and the underbrush has been removed. The forest has been preserved without the loss of beauty. But many of the farmhouses are slowly disintegrating, and nobody cares about restoring them. The more ambitious young people have departed. The hillsides around the Notch are dotted with deserted barns, crumbling cellar holes, and abandoned pastures.

VIRGINIA JOSEPHINE MOOR COOLIDGE   JOHN CALVIN COOLIDGE

CALVIN COOLIDGE'S MOTHER AND FATHER

Weeds are growing between the worn stones
That lead to a door which gives no welcome.

So far as industry is concerned the place will probably never recover. Even summer tourists, or city people seeking refuge from noise and smoke, are not likely to choose this section. Fortunately the beauties of nature do not diminish when it runs wild. Not even the vendors of hooked rugs and maple sugar, not even the parasitic capitalizers of the Coolidge tradition who infest the vicinity of the homestead, can altogether destroy the charm of the Notch. But it has ceased to be a place of hope, and over it all is "a haunting mist of memory."

II

Birth and Boyhood

ON Thursday, July 4, 1872, — Independence Day, — Mrs. John C. Coolidge, after being married for over four years, gave birth to a son. No record exists of the precise hour of day or night when the future President came into the world, and the event was not mentioned in any newspaper. The attending physician was apparently Dr. Rodman, of Bridgewater, the usual Coolidge doctor; but "Aunt Mede," John C. Coolidge's mother, who knew the rudiments of midwifery, was doubtless on hand. The birth took place in the building then used by John C. Coolidge both as residence and as store, in a small chamber, exactly twelve feet by eight in size and seven and one-half feet high, with but one window and its only door opening directly on the kitchen. Although the room itself has been somewhat altered since 1872 and a bay window has been added, it is not difficult to trace the original outlines. The bed in which the mother lay was constructed very simply of maple, with plain posts, and was long ago relegated to a back bedroom in the homestead across the street. Calvin Coolidge was not born in a log cabin. That would have seemed romantic. But the place of his birth was drab and rather dismal. The delicate Victoria Josephine Moor Coolidge, bearing the names of two empresses, with her frail body and sensitive mind, must have suffered on that uncomfortably hot day in midsummer. The only beauty in her surroundings was that of nature, in her own flower garden and on those green hillsides of which she could catch just a glimpse from her window.

It was a period when politics in the United States were seething with partisanship. The Republican voters of the Notch, constituting virtually its entire male adult population, had viewed with alarm the nomination on the preceding May 3 of Horace Greeley, Sage of Chappaqua, for the Presidency by the Liberal Republicans, meeting at Cincinnati, and had approved the action of the Republican Old Guard, who, assembling at Philadelphia a month later, had renominated Ulysses S. Grant. Preparations were being completed for the Democratic National Convention, which was to open on July 9 and, with sublime fatuity, was to endorse the nomination of Greeley. The World Peace Jubilee and International Music Festival was going on during the first week in July in the Boston Coliseum; and there, on July 3, an audience of more than twenty thousand greeted and cheered Horace Greeley. The Geneva Tribunal was about to make its award of $15,500,000 to be paid by England to the United States for depredations committed on our commerce during the Civil War by the *Alabama, Florida,* and *Shenandoah.* Sumner, Conkling, and Blaine were national figures. The revolt against President Grant was at its height, but the resentment at the Crédit Mobilier and other financial scandals was yet to come. In short, it was that decade of the 1870's in which American politics and government were certainly not at their best.

Reading the pages of the Vermont newspapers for 1872, especially those in Rutland, Ludlow, and Woodstock, we can reproduce the mood of Plymouth Notch, even though the news reported from that settlement itself is meagre. The only important political contests were local ones, for Vermont was solidly Republican, and John C. Coolidge's son was brought up in an atmosphere of party orthodoxy. Julius Converse, an elderly but ambitious resident of Woodstock, had just received the honor which he had coveted all his life, and was soon to be governor of the state, succeeding John W. Stewart. The United States Senators were two distinguished statesmen, — George F. Edmunds and Justin S. Morrill, — each about to begin his long career of usefulness as a legislator. The state's lone Congressman was Charles W. Willard. John C. Coolidge had met all these celebrities, and they knew him. The possibility that Vermont would ever in a national election cast more than 56,000 votes for a Democrat — as it did in 1932 — would have seemed fantastic. But even when the Republican Party fell on evil days, Vermont did not succumb entirely to the new heresy. The state has never since the Civil War gone anything but Republican on national issues.

During that first week of July, 1872, John C. Coolidge might have followed in the newspapers the trial of the notorious Stokes for the murder of "Jim" Fisk on the steps of the Grand Central Hotel. He noticed, perhaps, that Ira Sumner, son of William Sumner, of Plymouth, "caught a bear in a trap on the mountain," and that Mr. Robert Wallace, a student from Madison University, had been engaged to preach at Liberty Hall, in Plymouth, on Sundays during the summer months. If he went through the papers thoroughly, he read of the virtue of Vinegar Bitters, — a "great blood purifier," — of Jurubera, — the marvelous South American remedy, — and countless other proprietary medicines. New York Central was selling at about 98, Erie Common at 57, Western Union at 75, Government 5's at 113 and 6's at about 117. Engineers were surveying the new railroad from Montpelier to Barre, and some gold had just been discovered near Jayville. The Civil War was over and since then not much had happened.

Calvin Coolidge's published *Autobiography* is altogether too general, too lacking in details, to please an inquisitive biographer. We do not know by whom he was christened or where the ceremony took place — if, indeed, it took place at all. His cradle and the first baby carriage in which he ever rode are in Henry Ford's "Coolidge Collection" at Dearborn, Michigan. We do know that he was named John Calvin Coolidge, after his father, and that his parents called him Calvin, or "Cal." In the school records he appears as J. Calvin Coolidge, John C. Coolidge, Jr., Calvin G. Coolidge, and even Calvin J. Coolidge. Not until he left college did he discard the John and start fresh with the world as Calvin Coolidge.

We know almost nothing about his babyhood, his teething, his infant illnesses, except that he broke his arm when he was about three years old by falling from a horse. His father reported later that Calvin had few childish ailments. His mother, in spite of her chronic invalidism, acted as his nurse and taught him his letters from a set of wooden blocks. On April 15, 1875, Calvin's sister, Abigail Gratia Coolidge, named for her Grandmother Moor, was born, and the two children naturally grew up as playmates. When Calvin was only a little over three years old, his Grandfather Coolidge took his mother and him to Montpelier to visit John C. Coolidge, then serving his second term in the legislature. The small boy's most vivid memory was of a stuffed catamount, or wildcat, in the capitol museum.

John C. Coolidge was getting on in the world. When he bought his new home in 1876, some black-walnut furniture was purchased in Boston for the parlor and sitting room. Later a piazza was added — decidedly a luxury. His service in the legislature gave him prestige, and he had accumulated some property, which was increased in 1878, when his father died. On his trips to Rutland, Montpelier, and Boston, he had become accustomed to wearing "store clothes," — a business suit with a white shirt, linen collar and cuffs, — and he continued this habit in Plymouth, except when he was doing farm work. In the Coolidge home there were always a "hired girl" and a "hired man," who were treated, however, as equals, almost as members of the family. Calvin Coolidge wrote later, "Whatever was needed never failed to be provided." The family lived during cool weather in the kitchen, near the stove, as did all of the farmers of that region. The most important event of the daily life of Plymouth was the appearance of the Bridge-water-Ludlow stage, with its magnificent horses wearing bells to herald their approach.

Although John C. Coolidge was not strictly a farmer in the sense that he made his living from the land, there were "chores" to be done around the place, and Calvin was expected to perform his share of them, like the other boys in the vicinity. In the first week or two of April he helped joyfully with the making of the maple syrup. As the season advanced, he mended fences, did the spring planting, harvested and threshed the grain, cut and husked the corn, dug potatoes, picked apples, and stored wood for the winter. He was able, by the time he was twelve, to plow alone, without assistance from the "hired man."

It was a very democratic community, without either paupers or aristocracy. Although his father had been in the legislature and was the local magnate, Calvin carried apples and popcorn balls to town meeting and sold them, as his ancestors had done before him. His first long trousers were cut down from a discarded pair of his Grandfather Coolidge's; and he earned his first spending money by sawing a cord of four-foot wood twice in two, for which he received the magnificent sum of fifty cents. The Coolidges were regarded by their neighbors as "comfortably fixed," but extravagance was frowned upon in Plymouth as a major vice. Calvin, according to his own confession, had a boyish ambition to keep a store, as his father had done, but nothing came of it.

A boy on a farm is bound to have a close companionship with his parents, and young Calvin Coolidge was thrown a great deal with his father. In after years the President said, "My father had qualities that were greater than any I possess. He was a man of untiring industry and great tenacity of purpose. . . . It always seemed possible for him to form an unerring judgment of men and things. I cannot recall that I ever knew of his doing a wrong thing. He would be classed as decidedly a man of character." [1] Calvin's mother

---

[1] The judgment of John C. Coolidge's neighbors was not always so eulogistic, and he was regarded by some of them as unreasonably "near." For a story of his uncommunicativeness, see Walter Hard's "A Coolidge Note," in his book of sketches called *Vermont Vintage*.

died when he was twelve years old, when she had reached her thirty-ninth birthday; and he and his sister were called to her bedside in her very last hours to receive her blessing. As a result of an accident caused by a runaway horse, she had been seriously wounded, and the wound never fully healed. Many years later Calvin took his wife to the spot where the disaster occurred, on one of the side roads near the Notch. In his *Autobiography* he wrote of his mother, "We laid her away in the blustering snows of March. The greatest grief that can come to a boy came to me. Life was never to seem the same again." On August 3, 1923, before the President set out on his journey to Washington, he walked to the Plymouth cemetery and stood for a moment or two reflective before his mother's grave.

I have read assiduously all the available material about Calvin as a boy and can find almost nothing to distinguish him markedly from his playmates. Some of the stories are obviously apocryphal, deliberately concocted after he became famous. Once Bruce Barton asked him whether it ever occurred to him as a child that he would become President, and he replied whimsically, "If my mother had any such notion she kept it to herself, and the remarks of my father rather indicated that he thought if I did not change my ways I would come on the town. He kept up admonitions of that character until I had entered public life." Calvin was actually a normal country boy whose potentialities were not at the time evident to his friends. Like the others, he spoke pieces, acted in amateur plays, and even was cast in the part of end man at the local minstrel show. He never received a "licking," although there is a vague legend that one of his teachers gave him "a real shaking-up," so that buttons were dislodged from his coat. At the age of ten he made a patchwork quilt, which is still to be seen in the Plymouth farmhouse.

He himself always felt that he was a shy youngster; and in middle age, in one of his rare confidential moods, he said to a friend: —

Do you know, I've never really grown up? It's a hard thing for me to play this game. In politics, one must meet people, and that's not easy for me. . . . When I was a little fellow, as long ago as I can remember, I would go into a panic if I heard strange voices in the kitchen. I felt I just couldn't meet the people and shake hands with them. Most of the visitors would sit with Father and Mother in the kitchen, and the hardest thing in the world was to have to go through the kitchen door and give them a greeting. I was almost ten before I realized I couldn't go on that way. And by fighting hard I used to manage to get through that door. I'm all right with old friends, but every time I meet a stranger, I've got to go through the old kitchen door, back home, and it's not easy.[2]

Out of these inhibitions, or mild phobias, a psychologist might conceivably build up an elaborate theory of Coolidge's abnormal personality, based on the influence of his mother. But it does not appear that as a boy he was regarded as exceptionally taciturn, or in any sense peculiar. His shyness was not pathological. In the long winters, with their heavy falls of snow, he and the other children used to coast on a bobsled down the steep slope at the Five Corners, sometimes being thrown off hilariously at the curve in the road near the schoolhouse. There was skating on the mill pond, and once in a while an energetic organizer would arrange for a strawride in a pung piled high with hay, into which the boys and girls burrowed; and they would drive behind sturdy Morgan horses to the jingling music of the sleigh bells down the valley to the Union and beyond. Indoors in the winter there were husking bees, candy pulls, singing schools, and now and then a local entertainment. His house had no fireplaces, but everybody in the evening sat around the wood stove, played backgammon or checkers, or talked over the events of the day. As he wrote, "The whole stream of life moved leisurely, so that there was time to observe and think." Calvin was with girls as much as with boys, but no one has ever hinted that he had any adolescent romance, or produced an authentic childhood sweetheart for him, or even suggested a fondness for kissing games, such as Post Office and Drop the Handkerchief. A biographer who limits himself to the truth,— as every respectable biographer should do — can uncover no secrets or scandals. Life on the farm at Plymouth was simple, wholesome, and unfurtive.

In the summer the boys and girls were outdoors from dawn until dusk, and although everyone had his chores to do, recreation was not lacking. Perhaps Calvin's most alluring haunts were two caverns in the limestone region at the northwest end of the township, on a hillside not far from the highway up Black River Valley. One had six compartments and was almost as mysterious as that in which Tom Sawyer was once lost. Fishing was a favorite pastime, and young Calvin, like the others, would occasionally dig a can of worms, shoulder a crude rod cut and trimmed from a tree, and follow the narrow stream which flows through the Brown and Wilder farms.

[2] This statement, originally made to Frank W. Stearns, is quoted from *Calvin Coolidge, His First Biography*, by Robert M. Washburn. It is the most illuminating confession that Coolidge ever made.

Professor Bliss Perry has drawn upon himself the wrath of anglers by his essay *In Defense of Fishing with Worms;* but Calvin Coolidge was indifferent to the contempt of devotees of the dry fly. The youngsters of Plymouth were after trout, and, if they could be successful with angleworms, they were content.

The annual Sunday School picnic held at one of the many lakes in the vicinity was a holiday for both young and old. An extant photograph of such an affair in the summer of 1887 shows the future President in a group of sixty or seventy people, of both sexes and all ages, on pleasure bent. When the circus paused for a day at Ludlow or Rutland, the children were often allowed to go, and set out at three in the morning in the horse-and-buggy days in order to arrive for the parade. In the autumn came the Windsor County Fair, at Woodstock, where farm products were exhibited and horse races — trotting and pacing — were held. Thanksgiving was a family festival, much more significant than Christmas.

Kitchen and square dances, now almost forgotten except for a sporadic revival, were popular pastimes among the young people of Plymouth. The Money Musk, the Virginia Reel, and the Lancers were rather vigorous diversions, quite different from the languorous and more intimate dances of a later generation but much relished by the brawny sons and buxom daughters of the countryside. Calvin Coolidge, however, did not care for recreation of this type. If it is true that his Grandmother Brewer once gave him a dollar for not attending a dance, he earned the money very easily, and without suffering.

Calvin's religious and moral training came chiefly from his mother and from his sturdy grandmother, "Aunt Mede." When he did not obey his grandmother, she sometimes shut him up in the attic, in a room without windows and dusty with spiderwebs. He never had to be incarcerated for the same offense twice. A church had been built at the Notch, but there was no organized congregation and the pulpit was supplied by itinerant or occasional preachers. Calvin himself was not made a church member when he was a boy and did not formally unite with any religious body until after he became President. Even Sunday School, so influential with many people of that period, seems to have been intermittent at Plymouth, and the lad's knowledge of the Bible was derived from lessons read at home. "My Grandmother Coolidge read a chapter in the Bible nearly every day and was constantly referring to it in her talk," wrote Coolidge in 1932.

In a much publicized interview which President Coolidge somewhat unexpectedly gave to Bruce Barton on September 23, 1926, he said regarding his religious life: —

I have always attended church regularly when I could, but there being no organized church in our town when I was a boy, I did not join a church. After I became President the First Congregational Church of Washington, without consulting me, voted to make me a member. I was pleased that they took such action and of course accepted the election to membership which they offered me. . . . It would be difficult for me to conceive of anyone being able to administer the duties of a great office like the Presidency without a belief in the guidance of a divine providence. Unless the President is sustained by an abiding faith in a divine power which is working for the good of humanity, I cannot understand how he would have the courage to attempt to meet the various problems that constantly pour in upon him from all parts of the earth.

Calvin Coolidge began going to school on December 17, 1877, in his sixth year, in District Number 9, at Plymouth Notch, in a schoolhouse only a few yards from his front door. Plymouth Township was then divided into several districts, in each of which was maintained a small school of the "ungraded variety" — that is, without any set classes. The two terms — one in the fall and one in the winter — were arranged at periods when the boys and girls were not badly needed for farm work. The teachers, paid only a pittance, seldom taught more than two terms in succession in the same school. The buildings were usually small frame structures, with seats made of spruce boards crudely put together. In the middle of the room was a big wood-burning box stove, around which the children huddled in zero weather. There was, of course, no running water, and the toilet facilities were primitive — although similar to those to which the children were accustomed in their own homes. Most of the pupils brought their luncheons in tin pails, and the noon hour was a period of merriment.

The Notch schoolhouse in 1877 was constructed of field stone cut from an adjacent quarry and split into fairly smooth slabs. At that time there were twenty families in the Notch District, with twenty-three pupils, ranging from five to eighteen, attending the school, the youngest being Calvin. The textbooks used were Webb's *Word Method,* the *New American Reader and Speller,* French's *Arithmetic,* Greenleaf's *Algebra,* Anderson's *United States History,* Alden's *Civil Government,* Hall's *Geography and History of Vermont,* Conant's *Parsing and Drill Book,* and *Spencerian Writing.*

The boy was seldom tardy, and his conduct was regularly reported as "Good." [3]

In the winter term of 1884–1885, the teacher at the Notch was Ernest C. Carpenter, who has carefully preserved the Vermont School Registers of District Number 9 for that period and has also supplied some interesting reminiscences. The winter term opened on December 1, 1884, and closed on February 20, 1885. Among the pupils were seven Moores, five Kavanaughs, and four Wilders, as well as Calvin Coolidge, who was in his thirteenth year, and his sister Abbie, who was nine. The oldest student during that term was eighteen, the youngest seven. The amount paid to the teachers for two terms was $159.70, including board for thirty weeks, which was figured at $37.70.

In describing his own education, Calvin Coolidge confessed that few, if any, of his teachers reached the standard required to-day by any public grammar or high school. Any prospective instructor was required to qualify by an examination before the town superintendent, but the demands were not exacting. Calvin himself took and passed this test at the age of thirteen, and his clever sister, Abbie, not only passed it at the age of twelve but actually a few months later taught a term of school in a neighboring town. Ordinarily the instructors in District Number 9 were women, but in the winter a man was sometimes appointed, as in the case of Mr. Carpenter. Writing from actual experience, Mr. Ernest S. Kavanaugh has said: —

Schoolteachers were chosen as much for their ability to maintain discipline as to impart knowledge, and if perchance the teacher were a man, to keep order, he had early to demonstrate his ability to thrash any boy in school, and woe to him who could not. The life of a woman teacher was no sinecure, and unless she assumed command early in the term and maintained it throughout, life for her was anything but a bed of roses.

The recollections of Calvin's schoolmates contribute very little to our understanding of him. He was not noticeably reticent, but was always inclined to debate any subject at length. Mr. Kavanaugh says that he was just "one of the gang, more studious and a better scholar, but otherwise with little to differentiate him from the crowd." The journalist Joe Toye once interviewed Calvin's early

[3] Much of the material regarding Calvin Coolidge's early education is taken from *The Boyhood Days of President Calvin Coolidge*, by Ernest C. Carpenter (The Tuttle Company, Rutland, Vermont, 1926). I have also consulted several of his former schoolmates and have myself frequently visited the site of the old Notch schoolhouse and walked about the surrounding country.

schoolmate, Albert A. Sargent, who said of him, "He wasn't particularly brilliant or otherwise at school. He was neither popular nor unpopular. . . . He wasn't a leader in anything." Certainly he was no youthful prodigy. In a school of about thirty he usually ranked among the first half dozen, — never at the top, — and he was methodical, faithful to the tasks assigned, and punctual at his duties. Several have recalled that he never loafed or loitered, and seemed to "work on a schedule." He was as mischievous as any normal youngster, and had a fondness for teasing small children, especially girls. One of the Kavanaugh sisters has not forgotten how, when he once persisted in throwing snow down her neck, she turned on him and gave him a sound thrashing. Occasionally he made droll remarks. Jennie Chamberlain, who worked in the Coolidge household, remembered that when he was asked to wash his face and hands he replied, "I don't know about that. I've known people to get drowned in water." But from all the reminiscences of this period not one sign of future distinction emerges. He was just an ordinary boy, who seemed likely to end his days on the farm or in the village store.

One story was told by President Coolidge in 1924 regarding the Garfield-Hancock Presidential campaign of 1880: —

It was during that campaign that I, a small boy, approached my father, who was a very good businessman, with the proposition that he should furnish me with a penny to buy some candy. He told me that we were in the midst of a political campaign, and there was a probability, a possibility at least, that we were going to elect a Democrat for President. Such an action, he said, would undoubtedly be followed by hard times and therefore it was necessary to economize.

That was good, sound doctrine, I think. Anyhow, it had to do for me. But I recall that next morning after the election, and as soon as the news reached our town that James A. Garfield had been chosen President, I went to my father and told him the result indicated we were to continue a Republican administration, and with that prospect in view I was able to secure the advance of the sum I asked.

Coolidge's school training did not markedly influence his reading. His early interest turned to history and biography. The first real book he could remember was *The Rangers; or the Tory's Daughter*. Fortunately, however, his mother had excellent taste in literature and taught him to enjoy Tennyson and Scott, from whose poems he could recite long passages. His Grandmother Coolidge, a strong, resolute woman with deep religious convictions, read to him, as we have seen, from the Bible; and she also gave him a complete set of Shakespeare, which he carried with him to college. It was she who introduced him not only to *The Green Mountain Boys* but also to such popular historical works as *Napoleon and His Marshals* and *Washington and His Generals*. "Books were anything but plentiful in our neighborhood," he once wrote. Calvin liked Burns and Whittier, principally because they portrayed the kind of life which he knew as a boy; and he regarded *Snow-bound* as "a complete description of what is best in rural New England." In an article entitled "Books of My Boyhood," Coolidge once listed certain volumes which he remembered, among them being, besides those already mentioned, *Men of Our Times* (Harriet Beecher Stowe), *From Canal Boy to President* (a biography of James A. Garfield), *Livingstone Lost and Found,* Hilliard's *Sixth Reader, Choice Poems and Lyrics, Captain John Brown, History of the Indian Wars, The Young People's Bible History, The New Testament, Life and State Papers of Lincoln* (Henry J. Raymond), and *The Orations of Cicero*. But in the Coolidge home the library was very small. His father confined his reading to the daily newspapers and to the law treatises which he was obliged to consult. "Evenings and rainy days," he said, "were about all the time it was thought well to devote to books in our town." The household was in no sense bookish, compared, for example, with the homes in which Henry Cabot Lodge or Woodrow Wilson grew up. In later days, Coolidge said to Bruce Barton: —

I have little time to read books and magazines, except those that bear on problems that are before me for solution. . . . I have little time for current fiction. I much prefer biography and history. Of the books of the Bible, I have found the writings of Saint Paul the most interesting to me.

It is illuminating to have Coolidge say, "It was not until I came to read the Orations of Cicero in my Latin course that I began to have any realization of the value of literature for its own sake."

After the death of his mother when he was only twelve years old, the boy went through a period of despondency, which troubled the family. He did, however, continue at school in District Number 9 for another year. From April 1, 1885, until April 1, 1886, the record shows that J. Calvin Coolidge attended school 48½ days in the fall term, 40 days in the winter term, and 59 days in the spring term, with no tardy marks and good deportment. By this time he had advanced as far as he could go in the little stone schoolhouse. He had received already as much formal education as most adults in the community. It was time for him to move on.

III

Preparing for College

BLACK RIVER ACADEMY, — known locally as B.R.A., — in Ludlow, was familiar to the Coolidges, for Calvin's mother and father, as well as his Grandmother Coolidge, had attended it for brief periods, and John C. Coolidge was one of its twenty-four Trustees. Opened in the spring of 1835, it had long been popular as a "finishing school" for sons and daughters of the farmers of eastern Vermont. Although it had a charter from the state legislature, it was actually in its course of study not far above an ordinary high school; but it had prestige because of its support by the Baptist Church, and several distinguished men were among its graduates. On August 24–25, 1885, it had observed its fiftieth anniversary, amid a torrent of oratory which had stirred the surrounding countryside.[1]

Ludlow itself lies a thousand feet above sea level, at the foot of the main range of the Green Mountains and on the Rutland Division of the Central Vermont Railroad. The catalogue of Black River Academy in the 1880's announced: "The high elevation and mountain air insure a healthful climate; and the village is exceptionally free from low places of amusement, so that the moral atmosphere is also very good." Many of the houses are relics of the most depressing period of American architecture; and the original academy building, comprising a few recitation rooms, some offices, and an assembly hall, stood in unmitigated ugliness on a bluff above the Black River. In the autumn of 1887, shortly after Calvin Coolidge had enrolled, this was damaged by fire and then demolished, and a new structure, more commodious but hardly more beautiful, was erected.

[1] The centennial of the academy, held June 23–25, 1935, was marked by almost incessant eulogy of Calvin Coolidge. Among other famous former students have been John G. Sargent, Attorney General of the United States under President Coolidge; Paul Harris, Chicago attorney and founder of Rotary International; William W. Stickney, Governor of Vermont; Redfield Proctor, United States Senator and Secretary of State under Harrison; and Ernest W. Gibson, another United States Senator.

In the late winter of 1886, when the temperature was thirty below zero, father and son, having jointly reached a decision, drove the twelve miles to Ludlow in an open sleigh, or cutter, containing not only the lad's two small handbags but also a calf which was being shipped to market. As he dropped the youngster in Ludlow, the father said drily, "Calvin, if you study hard and are a good boy, maybe some time you'll go to Boston too; but the calf will get there first." It was Calvin's first great adventure, his earliest break with the past and entrance into a new field, and he remembered it later when he moved by successive steps into other enterprises.

Because the school had no dormitories, students not living at home had to find board and lodging in the village. Calvin had quarters with a friend named Herbert L. Moore, at the home of Charles Parker, on the broad, elm-shaded main street. Later he seems to have moved to "Mrs. Sherwin's" and to have roomed with a boy named Coburn, and finally with a certain Hicks, of whom he wrote, "I believe he is from Perkinsville, but I am not sure I like him very well." Young Coolidge never went out in the evening. After supper, he and his friends would walk together around the park and then go back to the house, where he would study by the light of an oil lamp or read one of the volumes in the small Parker library. It was an uneventful existence, but Calvin was not accustomed to much excitement. Herbert L. Moore, in an interview given in 1926, said : —

Cal always was a student. Unlike most of us who had to work hard on the farm and could not get away for any long periods, he always went to school. He didn't play ball or skate, nor did he hunt, swim, fish, or go in for any sports, except that he walked a great deal. When he was in the academy, he went to the public library every day, and I think he read every book in it.

The Principal in 1886 was John Pickard, and his associates were Miss Rowena A. Pollard, Preceptress, and Miss Clara L. Prior, Assistant. Of the approximately 125 pupils, only a few were preparing for college. Entering in the middle of the academic year, Calvin continued English grammar and began algebra, besides taking a course in civil government which introduced him to the Constitution of the United States. As textbooks he used Wells's famous *Algebra* and Kellogg's *Rhetoric*. In the following autumn he was initiated into the mysteries of Latin and during the next year — 1887–1888 — into Greek, two languages now seldom taught in the rural schools of Vermont. The youngster was fairly well drilled in the ancient classics and retained for Greek and Latin a partiality which was expressed in his later addresses on education. His own speeches showed traces of Ciceronian influence. In mathematics he was less successful. One of his classmates said of him: —

He used to come to my room in the evening for help. I remember one night as he came in he said to the housekeeper, "Well, I've come down to help Henry do his algebra again." He said it so solemnly that she asked me afterwards if I was falling behind in my algebra.

He also studied French, joining a class in the middle of the year and making up the back work by rising at three in the morning. Other subjects which he pursued were ancient history, rhetoric, and American literature. While he was no more than an average student, he had little difficulty in keeping up with his companions.

The few letters still extant from this period were written to his sister, his father, and his grandmother, and are largely in a matter-of-fact tone. The earliest document in his own hand that I have discovered is a letter to his sister, dated "Nov. 29," presumably in 1886, from Ludlow and reading as follows: —

I have received Grandmas letter today and all right. I am not very well as I have a bad cold though it is not so bad as it was when I went from home. I shall expect my cards tomorrow. When papa comes down send me my other coat, a bible, and some wood in chunks.

Pinney did not come on the down mail expect him tonight on the five o'clock.

Miss Chellis took Rendall's place at school, Miss Prior Miss Chellis's and Jennie (Lealand) Walker Miss Prior's.

I am going to a set of 4 lectures commenceing next friday. I got a half ticket which cost 50 cts they are illustrated by the magic lantern including scenes in all the wonderland of the world. I wish you could be here.

J. C. C.

P.S. Send down my ring by papa, and I would like a picture or two to hang up in my room the rest of the boys have got some.

J. C. C.

Calvin was frequently homesick and, for a time, rather unhappy. Although he was only twelve miles from Plymouth, he asked many questions as to how things were going along on the farm. On February 3, 1887, he wrote to Abbie: —

I suppose you are having a good time fact is I know you are having a better time than you will ever have down here though you do not probably see it in that light.

In the following autumn George Sherman, a young graduate of Amherst College, was engaged as Principal, with Miss M. Belle Chellis as Preceptress. Sherman evidently injected a new spirit into the institution and had a beneficial influence on Coolidge. Within a few weeks plans were approved for a new schoolhouse, and, on October 8, 1887, Calvin wrote to his father: —

I suppose I have been to school in the old Academy building for the last time. We now move out and up to Whitcomb and Atherton's hall. . . . Rev. Ora Taymor was at school yesterday morning; and made a prayer, probably the last one that will ever be made in the old building, although perhaps there was one last night as they had a gathering of old students there.

The new structure, dedicated on August 27, 1889, was used by the school during Calvin's senior year.

While in the retrospect Coolidge confessed that Black River Academy "had much to be desired in organization and equipment," he felt that it "possessed a sturdy spirit and a wholesome regard for truth." With few exceptions the pupils were earnest boys and girls sincerely desirous of making progress; for, as he said, "their coming had meant too much sacrifice at home not to be taken seriously." The cost of education at the school seems to us to-day ridiculously low — seven dollars a term for tuition and about three dollars a week for room and board. Calvin estimated that his schooling in Ludlow cost his father about $150 a year. But even this to a thrifty Vermonter was no trivial sum, and Calvin tried to help out. On Saturdays he sometimes did piece work in the Ludlow carriage shop, where he learned how to fabricate toys and perambulators and earned a little spare cash. Whatever he accumulated was placed by his father to the boy's account in the Ludlow Savings Bank. During the long vacation, lasting from the middle of May until early September, he was back in Plymouth, doing a full day's labor in the fields. He was thus brought up to understand the energy which must go into the earning of a dollar and the necessity of being prudent with what had come so hard.

But Calvin, like the other boys around him, had plenty of fun. Although he was healthy, he was no athlete, being rather more slender than most lads of his age; furthermore, organized athletics did not exist, and the only games were a kind of primitive baseball and the customary outdoor sports of swimming, skating, and coasting. Some legends persist of boisterous pranks and nocturnal escapades, such as are inevitable when normal youngsters are herded

Ludlow Vt. Feb 3d 1887.

Dear Abbie

I wrote to Grandma the other day and rec. a letter from her the same day I sent the letter. I have not herd from you for quite a while as I only saw papa a few minutes the other day.

I suppose you are in a hurry to have school close well so am I. I do not expect to pass in Algebra but still have a faint hope that I may squeak through with about 71% but if I do not do better than that I shall go into another class next term and do better so I can feel that I do know something about it.

I suppose you are having a good time fact is I know you are having a better time than you will ever have down here though you do not probaly see it in that light Do you know whether you will come in the spring or not yet. I guess you had not better what do you think?

It is now just 8 oclock so you may know just what you were

FACSIMILE OF ONE OF THE EARLIEST LETTERS WRITTEN BY
CALVIN COOLIDGE

together. In one of his letters, October 8, 1887, he says, "I went down to the ox roast at Perkinsville with Hicks last Wednesday." In a letter to his sister Abbie, March 2, 1887, we find an amusing passage: —

I shall come home next Fri if I can so if you know of any body coming down let me know.

I have the dearest little darling for a best girl that you ever saw.

My roommate is the best in town.

These last 3 lines were written by some of the boys while I was at dinner. I room with Colburn this term.

In after years Mrs. Asa Barney Chapman, a member of the class of 1889 at Black River Academy, maintained that she was the first girl whom Calvin Coolidge ever took to a dance; but it was a Leap Year dance, in 1888. During the Presidential election of that year, Coolidge sided with Harrison and helped celebrate the Republican victory with a torchlight parade.

Often when he needed recreation Calvin walked to Cavendish Gorge, where the Black River has cut a channel between solid walls of limestone, gneiss, and mica shist, in places sixty feet deep. He sometimes spent a week-end with his mother's elder sister, Mrs. Don C. Pollard, — whom he called "Aunt Sarah," — at Proctorsville, three miles down the Black River. Now and then in good weather he walked home to Plymouth on Friday afternoon, past Echo Lake and along the valley to the Union, and then up the final steep hill to the Notch. Frequently he would carry with him a volume or two from the Academy library of 125 books.

Calvin's sister, Abigail, three years younger than he, had continued in school at District Number 9, but he was eager to have her with him at Black River Academy. On February 1, 1887, he wrote to his grandmother, "Do you think Abby will come down here to school this spring? Aunt Sarah thinks it would be a good plan." A day or two later he wrote to Abbie herself, "When are you coming down to see about coming to school of course you will come down some time." On January 29, 1888, he pursued the subject more insistently, writing to his father: —

What do you think about Abbie's coming to school here this spring? I think she had better, if you want she should commence a course here next fall. . . . If you decide to have her come I think you can get her boarded here. Mrs. Morgan too wants some boarders.

Abbie was a lively, affectionate girl, with flaming red hair, who was full of energy and impressed everybody by her personality. When she actually did enter Black River Academy in the autumn of 1888, she made a brilliant record. In March 1890, she was attacked suddenly in Ludlow by what was then diagnosed as inflammation of the bowels, — unquestionably our modern appendicitis, — was carried back to Plymouth, and there, despite all that medical care could do, died within a week. She was only fifteen. Calvin was at her bedside in her last hours, and her loss was a source of grief to him to the very end of his days. He and his father were now left together, with no women relatives, to take care of one another. He wrote his father from Ludlow, April 19, 1890, "It is lonesome here without Abbie."

Calvin Coolidge's development while he was at Black River Academy was entirely normal, free from inhibitions, frustrations, and complexes. More introspective and dreamy than some people have thought, he nevertheless had learned to face his world realistically, without troubling others. If he had any period of *Sturm und Drang,* he kept it to himself. If he fell in and out of any childish love affair, he left no record of it. He did speak of his delight in long solitary horseback rambles among the hills around the Notch; and one sentence, "The silences of Nature have a discipline all their own," throws a vague light on his temperament. He did not brood, he did not scribble Byronic verses, he did not muse more extensively on the universe than most boys — but he thought to good purpose, achieved a kind of independence, and, without being too much aware of it at the moment, was formulating his individual creed and philosophy. He was definitely growing up.

In one eloquent paragraph of his *Autobiography* Coolidge pays a tribute to Mr. Sherman and Miss Chellis [2] for guiding him through Greek and Latin, for giving him a vision of the world when it was young and showing him how it developed, for telling him "of the glory and grandeur of the ancient civilization that grew up around the Mediterranean and in Mesopotamia." It was this phase of his instruction that apparently lingered longest with him, and for which he was the most grateful.

Calvin Coolidge was graduated from Black River Academy in the spring of 1890, in a class of five boys and four girls. The Baccalaureate Sermon was preached on Sunday, May 16, by the Reverend Evan Thomas, and the Commencement exercises came

---

[2] Both Mr. Sherman and Miss Chellis lived to see Calvin Coolidge President of the United States and sent him letters of congratulation.

at two-thirty on the afternoon of Friday, May 23. The President of the class was Albert A. Sargent, later an attorney at Barre, Vermont; the Vice President was Leslie Armington; and the Secretary was J. Calvin Coolidge. We are fortunate in having not only the printed program but also an excellent account published in the *Vermont Tribune*. We know that the sky was clear, that the air was springlike and invigorating, and that Hammond Hall was decorated beautifully with potted plants and flowers as the class marched down the aisle and took seats on the stage of the new auditorium. The Reverend J. B. Reardon, of the Universalist Church, offered prayer, and then Albert Asa Sargent delivered the Salutatory. Sixth on the long program was J. Calvin Coolidge, who spoke on "Oratory in History." [3] For the first time the name of Calvin Coolidge appeared in the public press when the *Tribune* said: —

Calvin Coolidge gave an historical résumé of the influence of oratory in the formation of public opinion and in the great movements of history. It was the master spirit of both the nations of antiquity. When the Commons of Rome were ground to the dust beneath the load of debts which they owed to their patrician creditors, the oratory of an old man, imprisoned for debt, broke the shackles which bound him and caused a change of laws. The eloquence of Brutus was potent in driving the Tarquin from Rome. Down the ages he came with a swift but sure tread and naming the men who, by silvery and impetuous speech, had swayed the people, — Cicero confounding Cataline, Peter the Hermit spurring the people on to drive back the Crescent, Luther giving birth to the Protestant Reformation, Cobden and Bright in securing the repeal of the obnoxious Corn Laws were cited as instances. In American History illustrations were not wanting. James Otis in 1761, Patrick Henry in the first American Congress, Webster in defending the Constitution, Garrison and Phillips in overturning slavery were notable instances. This oration was masterly in its conception and arrangement.

Other speakers followed Coolidge — Clara S. Pollard, with a recitation quaintly entitled, "There is a Lion in the Way"; Rufus N. Hemenway, in what was described as a "ringing address" on "National Pride"; and then the Valedictory, by Jessie Armington.

[3] Coolidge wrote his father on April 19, 1890, "My oration is all done and about learned. The subject is 'Oratory in History.' Mr. Sherman told me it was the best one he had seen but I suppose he was flattering me. Would you be willing that I should get a suit of clothes this spring? Those that I have I have worn every day for almost two terms and do not look hardly fit to wear for best. Those I got to graduate in I cannot wear until then."

The concluding event was the awarding of diplomas by G. L. Armington of the Trustees, who remarked, "The end of education is attainment. Energy is a better endowment than natural talents." He dwelt for a few moments on the class motto, *Jam tempus agi res;* and the exercises closed with the benediction. In the evening came a Commencement concert by the Temple Quartette of Boston, assisted by Miss Ella Chamberlain, Whistling Soloist. It was a big day for Ludlow and for Calvin Coolidge.

In June 1901, Coolidge, then a Northampton lawyer, returned to Black River Academy as a Commencement speaker, and his remarks were reported in part as follows: —

I too am glad to see so many here, and I am glad to see and feel the expression of interest we all have in the institution we represent. Black River Academy has changed greatly since my decade. I know the changes have been for the better. But there is one thing that has never seemed to change and that is the loyal spirit which the students past and present always manifest in the old Academy; and however loyal its friends may be in the future, however illustrious its graduates may become, and however much they may advance its interests, they can never exceed in kindly solicitude and watchful care, such friends as it has had in the past, among whom we all recall Dr. Lane, Judge Walker, and many others who contribute time and money in all the surrounding country. And I think we ought to be especially grateful for the aid received from Ludlow and Ludlow Village, an arrangement of mutual advantage to the Academy and the citizens of the Town. And while, as I say, the loyalty of its friends cannot increase, I do hope to see their numbers increase, and a still larger field of usefulness be opened to Black River Academy.[4]

All the available evidence indicates that nobody in Plymouth or Ludlow regarded the boy, Calvin Coolidge, as a prodigy. No village sage or phrenologist predicted that he would become President. No one dreamed that he would ever attract much attention from biographers. That even he had any visions of fame seems improbable. But he was scholastically ambitious, and he had thought of asking his father to let him have an additional preparatory year at Andover or Exeter and go from there to college. It was Principal George Sherman, the first well-educated person with whom Calvin had come in contact, who pointed out the virtues of his own Alma Mater, Amherst, and suggested that the boy might enter there direct from Black River Academy. It must be remembered that no member

---

[4] For some years Black River Academy has functioned virtually as a public high school, and a new school building was completed in 1938. The original corporation of the Academy cooperates with the local school board.

of the Plymouth branch of the Coolidges had had a college education and that college graduates in that section of Vermont were scarce. John Garibaldi Sargent — known locally as "Garry" — had been graduated from Tufts College in 1887, but Calvin was not then well acquainted with him. As for Amherst, it had a reputation for sound learning and safe, conservative doctrine. The name of its statesman-president, Julius H. Seelye, had penetrated even to Plymouth. Furthermore it was not far away, and it was inexpensive.

It was a crucial moment in Calvin Coolidge's career when it was decided that he could and ought to go to college.[5] It is possible that he would have achieved fame if he had remained in Plymouth; but I do not believe it. Destiny could not have fulfilled itself without first removing him from his restricted environment. College transported him into that larger geographical and intellectual world with which his ancestors had been unacquainted, taught him what lay outside of Plymouth Notch and even of Vermont, and offered him his opportunity.

Black River Academy did not enjoy college-certificate privileges. Accordingly, in the autumn of 1890, after the usual summer of hoeing and haying on the farm, with some reading in the evenings, the eighteen-year-old, russet-haired youth set out for Amherst to take the prescribed entrance examinations in Greek, Latin, English, and mathematics. His father drove him in a buggy to Ludlow, where all alone he boarded a train on the Rutland Railroad for Bellows Falls. At this junction he transferred to the Central Vermont Railroad, running south through Northfield, Millers Falls, Montague, Leverett, and Cushman, to Amherst, along a route which is to-day decidedly "off the main line." Probably Calvin alighted at the old Central Vermont station in Amherst and walked from there carrying his portmanteau up Main Street to the Common and

---

[5] The determining factor in the decision was the influence of Principal George Sherman, who recognized the potentialities of his pupil. John C. Coolidge was not the man to reach such a conclusion by himself. Dr. George D. Olds, of Amherst, speaking at an Amherst Dinner in New York in 1925, recounted the following anecdote: —

"When Mr. Coolidge was inaugurated as Vice President four years ago, I rode on the train from Springfield to Washington with Colonel John C. Coolidge, his father, and with his two sons. It was as difficult to draw out John as it is Calvin, and I understand now where the President gets his taciturnity. In the end, Colonel Coolidge warmed up and told me that when Calvin was fifteen years old, it was a serious question whether or not he should go to college.

"Colonel Coolidge said that he was not sure his son was the right type, and that he finally decided he had better apprentice him to a pharmacist in a neighboring drugstore. At that time all drugstores had liquor in stock, and after the Colonel told Calvin of his decision, his son thought for a minute or two, and then said: 'Father! Sell rum?' That ended it."

the College. Where he took a room and what he did are nowhere recorded. But he was not there very long. On the trip down he contracted a cold which, growing rapidly worse, interfered with his examinations and eventually forced him home to Plymouth, where he was ill, as he says, "for a considerable time." He did not fully recuperate until early winter, and for a while apparently abandoned the idea of going to college. The story is interesting but vague in details, and the reader must use his imagination if he wishes to picture the homesick, discouraged lad and his melancholy return to the Vermont hills.

In the late winter Coolidge sufficiently recovered his strength to go back for a few weeks to his old school in Ludlow; but as spring approached, with Mr. Sherman to encourage him, he entered St. Johnsbury Academy,[6] then the leading preparatory school in the state, lying about eighty miles north of Plymouth. The Principal was Dr. Charles E. Putney (1840–1920), a graduate of Dartmouth in the class of 1870 — a remarkable man who had served three years in the Union Army, going afterwards to college when he was twenty-six years old and winning Phi Beta Kappa standing. He was described by Coolidge as "a fine drill-master, a very exact scholar, and an excellent disciplinarian." The Vice Principal from 1883 to 1895 was Audubon L. Hardy,[7] a classmate of George Sherman's at Amherst in 1879. Most of the work covered by Coolidge was review, Dr. Putney taking him in Greek and Latin and Mr. Hardy in mathematics.[8] He was not a candidate for the school diploma and, according to Mr. Hardy, did not enter into the activities of his class. He was registered as J. Calvin Coolidge and engaged room and board at 4 Main Street, with L. W. Rowell, a job

[6] Coolidge wrote his father, April 3, 1891, "Professor Sherman thinks it would be a good plan for me to go to St. Johnsbury this spring term if I could enter the Senior class there and graduate, thus I could get into Amherst all right on a certificate. I have not heard from Amherst yet. Sherman has not heard from St. J. yet but he has written to see what I could do. . . . It is one of the best fitting schools in New England and would give me a high standing in college."

[7] Mr. Hardy, later Superintendent of Schools in Amherst from 1898 to 1915, is now retired, but still a resident of Amherst. He has been most helpful in giving me vivid recollections of Calvin Coolidge as a student at St. Johnsbury Academy.

[8] Coolidge arrived at St. Johnsbury on April 4, 1891, and consulted Dr. Putney, who wrote him on April 7, "As to giving you a certificate to Amherst I will say that we are careful not to certify any of our pupils who have not done satisfactory work and are not likely to sustain the reputation of the Academy as a good fitting school. . . . If at the end of the term you are up to the standards which entitle our pupils to certificates, we will give you one. . . . If you come, we shall do the just and right thing by you." On May 27, Coolidge wrote his father, "I am getting along all right in school. Mr. Putney told me he had never had any one come into his class so late that did so well as I have." On May 31, he wrote, "Mr. Putney told me Friday that he should give me a certificate."

printer, in a building now used as a boys' dormitory. Of the impression which he made, Mr. Hardy has written: —

He was just the same kind of a boy that I have known him as a man, quiet, faithful, studious, dependable, doing the day's work and doing it well, staying on the job until it was done. Probably no one thought that he would be President of the United States, but we who knew him best knew that he was the stuff out of which great men are made.

Just ten years before, St. Johnsbury had had another interesting student, Charles Edward Russell, later a well-known socialist and reformer, the precise antithesis of Calvin Coolidge in his economic and political philosophy. From Russell's autobiography, *Bare Hands and Stone Walls,* we get a neatly drawn sketch of the attractive Vermont village as he saw it.

It was a beautiful place, notably beautiful even in a region plethoric in natural charm. The wide streets, lined with rows or double rows of great awesome elms; the faultless precision of the trimmed and garnished lawns; the houses, often in excellent colonial, all kept and gleaming as if new tricked in paint; the ordered avoidance of the least maculation; the air of a settled, approved, and durable competence, — you are to imagine what impression all this would make on one raw from the helter-skelter and catch-as-catch-can of the prairies.

Russell discovered, however, that the community "reeked with piety; aggressive, militant, grim, implacable. . . . The dead weight of the intensive and, as it seemed to me, smug religious formalism," he added, "drove me into violent revolt." He was particularly horrified at the tyranny exercised by the Fairbanks oligarchy: —

The baronial family lived in the castle on the height; the townspeople kowtowed below. The place was the site of the Fairbanks scale factory; members of the Fairbanks family were the barons; in effect their word was law.

Pondering on the situation, Russell reached the conclusion that "the root of the evil was the accursed tariff." On Calvin Coolidge, deposited in St. Johnsbury for only a few weeks, his surroundings had little influence. He pored assiduously over his books, made almost no acquaintances, engaged in no speculations on the local feudal system, and certainly did not investigate the iniquity of the tariff. For the moment he was concerned solely with getting into Amherst College.

Nevertheless Coolidge did not altogether forget St. Johnsbury.

His references to it in his *Autobiography* are cursory; but in 1916, at an Amherst Alumni dinner in Boston when he was Lieutenant Governor, he mentioned appreciatively his one term in St. Johnsbury and then, turning to Mr. Hardy, said, "My teacher in mathematics does not agree with me. I had him in algebra, and I had no use for the subject, but I am glad that he let me through."

In 1932, Mr. Hardy suggested to the St. Johnsbury Trustees that it might be appropriate to grant Coolidge an honorary diploma, and the sheepskin was regularly voted at Commencement of that year. At the Academy graduation exercises in 1934, two elm trees from the Coolidge homestead at Plymouth were planted and a bronze tablet was placed on a small boulder to commemorate the event. Mr. Hardy made the dedicatory speech.

What Calvin Coolidge actually earned from St. Johnsbury Academy in the spring of 1891 was a certificate entitling him to admission to Amherst College without entrance examinations. His review work had been satisfactory and he was now adequately prepared for college.

Again Calvin Coolidge spent a summer on the Plymouth farm. The culminating event of the vacation was a trip with his father to the dedication at Bennington of the Battle Monument, the tall stone obelisk which towers to a height of three hundred feet beneath the shadow of Mount Anthony. It was a brilliant occasion, with appropriate patriotic speeches in profusion, including an address by President Benjamin Harrison. "I wondered," wrote Coolidge in his *Autobiography,* thinking of the President, "how it felt to bear so much responsibility and little thought that I should ever know."

On September 9, Colonel John C. Coolidge, who had been a widower for more than six years, married Carrie A. Brown, a Plymouth spinster whom young Calvin had known all his life. The match was in every way suitable. Colonel John, in his forty-seventh year, was sure to be lonely with his son away at college; his new wife was thirty-four, a graduate of Kimball Union Academy and a successful schoolteacher. She liked books and music and filled the place of a real mother to Calvin. In fact her influence upon both her husband and her stepson was entirely beneficial. Many of Calvin Coolidge's letters in later days were written to her. "For thirty years," said Coolidge, "she watched over me and loved me, welcoming me when I went home, writing me often when I was away, and encouraging me in all my efforts." She did not die until 1920, just before his nomination for the Vice Presidency.

IV

Amherst College

THROUGHOUT Calvin Coolidge's mature life his college was in his mind and its influence on him persisted. Astute Washington matrons discovered that he could be induced to talk about it when even his other favorite topics, Vermont and agriculture, were exhausted. At Amherst many of Coolidge's ideas, perhaps his entire political philosophy, took shape. He returned frequently, though unostentatiously, to class reunions and spoke at alumni gatherings. At Commencement in 1919, he announced, "I should fail in my duty and neglect my deep conviction if I did not declare that in my day there was no better place to educate a young man." When, on May 28, 1921, he was elected a life Trustee, he felt greatly honored. If any position could have tempted him in his retirement after 1929, it was the presidency of Amherst.[1] At the close of my last conversation with him, August 6, 1932, he said, "Amherst's a good college." From him that was superlative praise.

The Amherst of the 1890's was a small, closely knit community in which each undergraduate was known to the others by his nickname and the professors could differentiate their students from one another without too much guesswork. The enrollment in 1891–1892 was 336, of whom 139 were from Massachusetts and 259 from New England and New York combined. It was, however, growing perceptibly, and increased to 392 in 1892–1893, 435 in 1893–1894, and 439 in Coolidge's senior year. The faculty numbered approximately thirty, of whom twenty-five were full or associate professors. The undergraduates were largely sons of professional men, from

---

[1] Shortly after the resignation of Arthur Stanley Pease as President of Amherst, Frederick S. Allis was at Coolidge's home in Northampton on business. Coolidge asked, "Who is being considered for President?" Allis replied that one of the names he had heard mentioned most was that of Calvin Coolidge. Coolidge smiled and said, "No, it is bad enough to have Congress on your hands without having a college faculty." Mrs. Coolidge later said to Mr. Allis, "Mr. Coolidge would not have made a good college president. He had his own ideas of education, and he could carry them out with his own boys, but not with an undergraduate body, and I think he realized that."

well-to-do but not wealthy families, and rural rather than urban in their antecedents. A considerable number were receiving financial aid or working their way through college. Sophisticated youths were conspicuous through their rarity.

Amherst itself was an attractive village with a population of less than four thousand, of whom very few were factory or mill workers and nearly all were of Anglo-Saxon stock. It was seven miles from Northampton — known to the college as "Hamp" — and a trifle more to South Hadley. Smith and Mount Holyoke, with their feminine allurements, were not as quickly accessible to Amherst men as they are to-day. The glory of the town was its Common, not level and smooth-shaven like a Cambridge lawn, but irregular in contour and dotted with noble elms. At the south end on a knoll the college had developed, founded in 1821 as the result of a community movement — "a classical institution for the education of indigent young men of piety and talents for the Christian ministry." The first President, the Reverend Zephaniah Swift Moore, had been at the head of Williams College and had brought with him fifteen Williams undergraduates as a nucleus for the new society of scholars in the Connecticut Valley. Although its originators had been Calvinistic in their theology, Amherst had broadened over the years and was not regarded in the 1890's as notably sectarian. Prayers, however, were still held each morning, but not before breakfast as in the early days, and the students were obliged to attend two church services on Sunday.

In that pre-Ford period Amherst was a delightfully isolated and self-sufficient spot, where the young men did not take extended week-ends but stayed on the campus, formed intimate relationships among themselves, and chattered beyond midnight and even until dawn about the universe and its problems. It was also a singing college, where little groups went arm in arm melodiously down the street or sat on the historic fence through spring evenings making "close harmony." But the life was not all talk and song. The teaching was stimulating; the intellectual atmosphere was genuine; a spirit of freedom and self-reliance flourished among the students. It was not entirely accidental that Amherst produced in that decade a number of graduates who became leaders in law and government — Harlan F. Stone, Dwight W. Morrow, Bertrand H. Snell, and Calvin Coolidge, not to mention others who attained distinguished positions in various arts and professions. The song which hails Amherst as the "mother of mighty men" has factual truth as well as sentimental verity.

In the spring of 1890 the venerable President Julius H. Seelye, one of the outstanding figures of his era in American education, resigned at the age of sixty-six, after a prosperous administration of fourteen years. His successor was the Reverend Merrill Edwards Gates, who came to Amherst at forty-three, well recommended from Rutgers, and was formally inaugurated at Commencement in 1891. Coolidge's characterization of Gates as a person "of brilliant intellect and fascinating personality" was kind, but certainly not the whole picture. In the autumn of 1891, when Calvin Coolidge matriculated, Gates, superficially prepossessing, was regarded as urbane, cultured, and scholarly, with unusual gifts as an orator, but before many months had passed he was suspected of being pompous, showy, and unreliable, and he did not long retain the confidence of those around him. Unnecessarily autocratic and narrowly pietistic, he fell inevitably into difficulties. The crucial episode was his quarrel with the College Senate, — a representative undergraduate committee established by President Seelye, — through which he incurred the contempt, both veiled and open, of the abler students. The months which followed were marked by recrimination, irritation, and lack of harmony in the college, culminating in Gates's resignation in the spring of 1898. Coolidge saw him only at a distance and usually on a platform, was never entertained in the President's house, and owed very little to him.[2] The obscure rustic from Plymouth, Vermont, was not likely to appeal to Gates, who enjoyed boasting to his classes of his intimacy with the great.

On Thursday, September 17, 1891, Amherst opened for its seventy-first year; and John Calvin Coolidge, having brought with him this time a certificate from St. Johnsbury Academy, was ex-

[2] On November 13, 1892, Coolidge wrote his father, "Pres. Gates preached to us this morning, his text, 'As a man thinketh, so is he.' He discussed it from a psychological point of view and urged upon us the importance of keeping our thoughts centered along strong and profitable lines. It was not an exhortation to work harder on our studies but rather to keep before us some great and noble thoughts around which our whole personality might center not as a narrow specialist but as a broad and liberal cultured man. Without wishing to be egotistical or to say anything derogatory to the head of this Christian institution I must say that I think I and Prexy Gates agree there." On February 22, 1894, in the midst of the Senate controversy, Coolidge said in a letter to his father, "President Gates is not growing popular here, and I understand that the Trustees are getting unsatisfied with him. I am not looking for his removal very soon but think it will come in time if he does not change his policy. He is narrowing down continually the breadth of principle that has characterized Amherst in the years past; he is narrowing down the liberal principles of ex-President Seelye to the methods of a preparatory school; he has encroached upon the famous system of self-government that has made this college an example that we pointed to with pride, — in short, the management of the college since he became its head has 'progressed backward,' and only the high place we have taken in athletics and our former reputation have increased our numbers and advanced the college."

cused from entrance examinations and duly registered as a freshman. The two old dormitories, North and South Colleges, dating back to the 1820's, although not entirely abandoned, had fallen into disrepair, and most undergraduates roomed either in fraternity houses or in lodgings in the village. Coolidge secured a room at "Mr. Trott's" — a comfortable brick building still standing a little back from the road on South Pleasant Street, with peculiar pointed windows which attract the attention of the passing pedestrian or motorist.[3] Seventeen other Vermonters were registered that year in Amherst; indeed the only other student living at "Mr. Trott's" was Alfred Turner, from Rutland, only twenty-five miles from Plymouth. But of the eighty-five members of his class recorded in the catalogue, young Coolidge had probably not met a single one before coming to Amherst.

For his room Coolidge paid $60 a year, with twenty-five cents a week for care. He had to furnish his own wood and the oil for his lamp. He engaged his board at a house on Pleasant Street, at a cost of three dollars and a half a week — a sum which seemed exorbitant to the young Vermonter accustomed to country prices. Among those who sat at his table were Dwight W. Morrow, — nicknamed speedily "Kid" because of his small stature and youthful appearance, — and "Charlie" Andrews, now the Treasurer of Amherst College. One anecdote of this period has survived and has been often related in different versions. A big black cat occasionally prowled around the dining room. On one evening the principal dish was hash, a dish familiar to Coolidge as to all native New Englanders. When Calvin was served, he examined his plate critically for a few seconds and then called to the waiter, a classmate named Albert M. Tibbetts, better known as "Bitts." As "Bitts" drew near, Coolidge said, "Bring me the cat." The animal was produced, spitting and clawing, and Coolidge, taking a long look at her, simply murmured, "Thank you," and then — but not until then — began to eat his hash.

From the *Students' Hand-Book,* or "Freshman Bible," distributed by the Young Men's Christian Association to all newcomers, Coolidge gathered some information about his college — its history, its equipment, its alumni, its social life. One section described walks or drives to the "Orient," to Whately Glen, to Mount Holyoke and Mount Toby. A page or two of "Freshman Pointers" urged him to secure his gymnasium locker at once and

[3] This house is now (1938) occupied by Professor Charles W. Cobb, of the Amherst College faculty, and is owned by the College.

to attend all the athletic contests, incidentally drawing his attention to the merits of Glynn, the tailor, and Blodgett & Clark, student furnishers. Especially was he requested not to miss the first Thursday evening prayer meeting of the term or to fail, at the very outset of his career as an undergraduate, to "show himself a Christian." A paragraph or two on the Greek-letter fraternities described them as "the most unique feature of Amherst life" and declared that they were "strongly recommended by the members of the faculty."

Amherst was then as now a fraternity college, with nine different secret societies ranging from Alpha Delta Phi, established at Amherst in 1836, to Phi Delta Theta, which had come as recently as 1888. Unfortunately neither Principal Sherman nor Mr. Hardy had been a fraternity man, and no one else was available to sponsor the modest and inconspicuous freshman from Plymouth. He was the type of yearling ordinarily characterized by sophomores as "green." He had no superficial smoothness, no parlor tricks, none of the fluency calculated to appeal to a "Rushing Committee." Coolidge was by no means unimpressed by fraternities and what they had to offer. In the spring of 1890 he had written to his father from Black River Academy : —

Dick Lane thinks he and I had better go down to Amherst some time this spring to see about getting me into a society there. The societies are a great factor of Amherst and of course I want to join one if I can. It means something to get into a good society at Amherst; they don't take in everybody. I may not get a chance to join but Dick thinks I can if we scheme enough.

This letter reveals something of young Calvin's inner self and explains in some degree his loneliness at Amherst. Lane, the son of the Coolidge family physician, was somewhat older than Calvin and had graduated in 1889 from Middlebury College, where he was a "Deke" — a member of Delta Kappa Epsilon. Unfortunately his influence, if he exercised it, was not sufficiently potent. During the busy "rushing season" covering the opening week of the fall term tired freshmen were led from one fraternity house to another for a half hour in each and then "pledged" if they seemed desirable. But no upperclassmen spent sleepless nights meditating on young Coolidge's qualifications for Alpha Delta Phi or Delta Kappa Epsilon. When the elections were over, "Bert" Pratt and "Gussie" Post had been taken by "Alpha Delt," "Charlie" Burnett by "Psi U," Jay Stocking by "Deke," "Kid" Morrow and Lucius Eastman by "Beta Thet," and "Charlie" Andrews by "Phi Delt"; but the unsponsored Coolidge was an "Ouden," a "Barbarian," a non-fraternity man in a college where fraternity affiliations somewhat determined a man's status. There is something pathetically reticent in a sentence from a letter which he wrote home, October 15, 1891, "I don't seem to get acquainted very fast." On January 6, 1892, after returning from his first Christmas vacation, he wrote, "Every time I get home I hate to go away worse than before and I don't feel so well here now as the first day I came here last fall but suppose I will be all right in a day or two." Two days later, he wrote again, "I feel quite reconciled to being here tonight but felt awful mean yesterday and the day before, I don't know why, I never was homesick any before." But sensitive though he was, he did not brood over his disappointment. Instead he went quietly at his immediate duty, which he considered to be acquiring an education. His heart was never worn on his sleeve.

His new life was far from dull. He attended the entertainments of the Amherst College Lecture Association, including a concert by the Boston Symphony Orchestral Club, lectures by Dr. Truman J. Backus on "Alexander Hamilton," by Max O'Rell on "America As Seen through French Spectacles," by the Reverend Russell H. Conwell on "The Silver Crown; or Born a King," and by C. E. Bolton on "Lands of the Midnight Sun." As spring drew near, he displayed much interest in the coming Presidential campaign, and wrote his father, February 28, 1892: —

We are going to have a Republican National Convention in College Hall March 15 for the benefit of the Baseball Association; so I have sent you a Convention Herald containing the names of the delegates.

A great many of the boys have signs hung out on their houses eight or ten feet square bearing the name of their state and such devices as "Women's Rights and Free Cider," "Free Silver and Non-Compulsory Church," and many other such.

The candidates are Blaine and Harrison, and the boys go about the street at night in bands singing for their respective candidates, so we are having quite an interesting time just now.

Back in Plymouth young Calvin Coolidge was by no means the unappreciated figure that he was in Amherst. When he returned home from college at the close of his freshman year, he was invited to deliver the Independence Day address in his native town and thus had an opportunity to exhibit before a sympathetic audience what he had learned of declamation. His speech on "Freedom" was burning with fervor, replete with denunciation of Proud Albion, and rich was the glorification of our Revolutionary heroes. Never again was Calvin Coolidge so florid as on that July morning. It was the beginning of his career as a public orator, and this was the earliest of a long succession of appearances before his fellow countrymen.

After a summer spent on the farm, Coolidge went back to Amherst as a sophomore, still rooming at "Mr. Trott's," with Turner as the only other collegian in the house. He wrote to his father, September 25, 1892: —

I cannot tell much about my work yet whether it will be hard or easy, but do not expect it to be such drudgery as last year's work was. Not but that it will be just as hard and perhaps harder but not so exacting and more interesting, and we shall have closer relations with our instructors. Then we are not regarded with so much distrust and so have more freedom from the discipline the Freshman instructors feel it their duty to impose upon us. . . .

I like my new boarding place pretty well. It is not so good as board was here, but they say they are going to give better board soon. They are coons. The old man told one of the boys, "You jes' wait until nex' month when we get a little money ahead, and we will give good respectable board."

The Amherst of those days had no college dining hall, and the undergraduates usually boarded with landladies in the village. At different periods Coolidge ate at "Morse's," — now the house just south of the President's home and once occupied by the late Professor Frederic L. Thompson, — at "Collins's," at "Huntress's," and possibly at one or two others not now identifiable. In his junior year he moved his headquarters to "Mrs. Avery's," a house on Prospect Street, where he roomed with John Percival Deering, of Saco, Maine, whom he had grown to know well. There were students from other classes in this house: "Ned" Capen, '94, a member of Psi Upsilon and a prominent person on the campus; Morton D. Dunning, '96, another "Psi U"; and Alexander H. Backus, '97, an "Alpha Delt." By this date a large proportion of Coolidge's classmates were settled in their respective fraternity houses.

In their senior year Coolidge and Deering moved next door, to "Dr. Paige's," where they occupied the two rooms to the right on the second floor.[4] Dr. Henry E. Paige, a veterinarian, became

[4] Letter from John P. Deering, February 2, 1933. I myself roomed on the ground floor of Dr. Paige's house in 1901–02, directly under the suite occupied by Coolidge and Deering; but Coolidge had not then started up the ladder to fame, and the very commonplace-looking residence certainly attracted little attention.

very fond of the silent young Vermonter and often took him with him on professional visits to farms in the neighborhood. Dr. Paige was a brother of Theodore L. Paige, who kept the famous livery stable in Amherst and who, in the Gay Nineties, was well known to all the collegians with sporting proclivities. It was of him that Frederick J. E. Woodbridge, '89, later Dean of Columbia and a Trustee of Amherst, wrote in the plaintive ballad so dear to every Amherst alumnus: —

> Paige's horse is in the snowdrift,
>   Paige's sleigh is upside down;
> And my head goes reeling, reeling,
>   As I stagger into town.
>
> Let the student's lamp be burning,
>   Shed its gleams across the snow;
> So that I, from Hamp returning,
>   May find my way to go.

But Calvin Coolidge did not indulge in any such ribaldry. Indeed he did not associate with the group who were likely to patronize Paige's stable. During his first two years at Amherst he was, to say the least, an inconspicuous member of the class of 1895. One of his classmates writes me, "A drabber, more colorless boy I never knew than Calvin Coolidge when he came to Amherst. He was a perfect enigma to us all. He attended class regularly, but did not show any very great interest." Early in the freshman mathematics course Professor Olds, who had sandy hair, looked over the victims in front of him and then called on "My red-headed brother in the second row." This was Coolidge; and this is also one of the few authentic incidents which can be rescued from the oblivion of his first two years in college. He did not make a practice of calling on his professors; he did not sing on the Glee Club or strum the mandolin; he had no "girl," either in Amherst or in "Hamp." He did not join the Y.M.C.A. or the college church. He took no part in athletics, although he did in his letters comment on intercollegiate contests. In later life, when reporters tried to enliven the monotony of his past, he confessed that in games he did "hold the stakes." He did not enter into competition for the editorial board of the *Student*, the undergraduate newspaper. On January 7, 1892, he wrote his father, "I want to do careful work but many men in my class have strength, preparation, inclination, and ability to do much more than myself." All of the more explosive manifestations of youthful ebullition had no attraction for him.

A few of his acquaintances called him "Cooley" or "Cal" or "Red," but he was little known to most members of the class. When he had become President of the United States, several of his college mates recalled in him qualities which they certainly did not perceive when he was a sophomore. The fact is that he displayed few traits which could encourage prophecy. If he had dropped out of Amherst in the spring of 1893, he would hardly have been missed.

It was the more serious aspects of college life which appealed to him most. Even before he arrived in Amherst he wrote his father : —

Of course to learn anything it will be necessary for me to associate with those who can teach me something. I have not the training of a man from a school like St. Johnsbury, Saxton's River, or Phillips Exeter, but I hope I have the ability yet to receive it, though not having it would cause me some embarrassment.

He was at college not to be a playboy, not to sow his wild oats, but to secure an education. Accordingly he attended faithfully to his studies and spent a normal amount of time in reading and thinking. In his first letter home, September 27, 1891, he said, "I do not think my studies are going to crowd me any after I get started, and have hopes that I shall have time to do good thorough work in class room and get time for study and reading outside the regular work. Everything connected with the college is all it could be desired and I am looking forward to a pleasant and profitable course here." On January 14, 1892, when he received his first report, he wrote to his father : —

I have just got my marks for all last term's work. They are 2, scale of 5. I knew that would be so. That is the average. They would call it 2 if it were 2.9 so it is not very definite. Probably not a man in the class got a 4. The marks seem pretty low, don't they?

When he was finally recognized, however, it was not because of high scholarship, but because his intrinsic character and ready wit had at last become apparent; and even then he did not become in any sense a leader. Every year at Amherst, as at the other small New England colleges, there are lads who resemble Calvin Coolidge — self-respecting, earnest, persistent, but unschooled in the social graces. They sometimes come into their own, after college is over, and at the twenty-five-year reunions they occasionally return with all the outward marks of prosperity and distinction. But many of them also remain in comparative obscurity and are seldom heard of again.

Coolidge's first collegiate success came when he was more than halfway through his course and in an unexpected fashion. One of the cherished privileges of juniors at Amherst was the right to wear a silk hat and frock coat and carry a cane. These resplendent articles of apparel Calvin Coolidge purchased. The attainment of social maturity was celebrated early in the fall term by what was styled the "Plug Hat Race," in which the members of the class, each adorned with "topper" and stick, sprinted the length of Pratt Athletic Field, the last seven men to cross the line being obligated to provide a supper for the others. In a ludicrous contest Coolidge was one of the losers. The ensuing banquet, held on November 23, 1893, in Hitchcock Hall, consisted chiefly of oyster stew and beer. Russell E. Prentiss, a prominent "Psi U," the last man to cross the line,[5] was toastmaster, and the topic assigned to John C. Coolidge was "Why I Got Stuck." In his remarks he first in pantomime turned his pockets inside out to show that his expenditure as host had left him "broke." He went on, "You wouldn't expect a plow horse to make time on the race track or a follower of the plow to be a Mercury." He explained that pitching hay was poor preparation for success as a sprinter, and ended, "Remember, boys, the Good Book says that the first shall be last and the last shall be first" — a statement in which, it has been asserted, "the occult might hear the voice of prophecy." No one heard the prophetic voice at that moment; but Coolidge's little speech did win him a respect which he had hitherto not enjoyed, and his classmates from that moment thought of him as a wit. A photograph taken on the spot shows the seven losers,[6] four sitting in front, the other three standing, all elegantly attired like ushers at a wedding. In this picture Calvin Coolidge looks very little like a lad from a Vermont farm.

The fraternity question had for Coolidge a belated but satisfactory solution. According to Charles M. Stebbins, '92, he and his classmate, Robert Clark, discussed with Coolidge in the spring of 1892 the possibility of starting at Amherst a chapter of Phi Gamma Delta, a leading national fraternity into which Clark had previously been initiated at Colgate. When Stebbins and Clark had finished their preliminary explanation, in an interview which took place at Huntress's boarding house, they asked Coolidge bluntly whether he would care to join. Although he replied cautiously, "I

---

[5] Mr. Prentiss writes me, February 22, 1935, "I remember I got laughing so at the rest that I stopped in the middle of the field, and could only walk in, a bad last place."
[6] See "'Cal' Coolidge at Amherst," in the *Boston Post,* by Professor Henry W. Lawrence, Ph.D., of Connecticut State College.

AS A BOY OF EIGHT

AS A YOUTH OF SEVENTEEN

AS AN AMHERST UNDER-
GRADUATE

AS A NORTHAMPTON LAWYER

don't know but I would," the plan was not then carried further. In the autumn of 1893 one of the better-known fraternities offered a "bid" to Deering, Coolidge's roommate, who refused it unless Coolidge could be taken also. Several in the group were unenthusiastic about the suggestion, and Deering, because of his loyalty to his friend, was left out.

The Phi Gamma Delta project was, however, only temporarily interrupted. In December 1894, Harry Otto Rhodes, who had previously been a member of the Sigma Chapter of Phi Gamma Delta in Wittenberg College, Springfield, Ohio, and had later transferred to Amherst, formed there the Alpha Chi Chapter of his fraternity. Inevitably and platitudinously known as "Dusty," Rhodes was popular and had little difficulty in securing nine other men as charter members, among them being Deering. It was an audacious undertaking, for the college was already amply supplied with fraternities, but the new chapter flourished from its inception. On January 15, 1895, probably at Deering's suggestion, Calvin Coolidge was formally elected, and a committee consisting of Rhodes and James B. Cauthers, '96, extended the invitation. They employed no persuasion, entered into no arguments, but merely asked him point-blank whether he would care to join. He answered with a prompt and laconic "Yes," was initiated almost at once, and attended his first meeting on January 22.[7] He wrote to his father, January 20, 1895: —

The term will cost me more than I expected when I came back. Being in a society will cost considerable, I cannot tell how much, perhaps $75, though not all this term. This expense would naturally come at the beginning of the course, but did not in my case. I know you must be short of money this winter, and I am perfectly willing to pay this extra expense myself. I will send you an order on the Rutland Trust Company and you can send my book over and get the money for me.

Coolidge was an active and devoted fraternity man. He did not smoke or dance or play cards like most of the brothers, and he did not join in the "wild parties" occasionally held, but he was on hand at all the formal social functions. Cauthers, who was intimately associated with him in "Fiji" affairs, has said of him: —

He took a deep interest in the chapter, was most faithful in attending "goat" and committee meetings, and while he did not live at the house, he passed considerable time there. We soon began to rely upon

[7] See letter of James B. Cauthers to the author, October 8, 1937. Cauthers took part in the initiation as an officer of the chapter.

his counsel and judgment, and he was a distinct help to us in many serious problems we had to meet at that time.

As a matter of fact, only three members of the senior delegation — Rhodes, Dunbar, and Ray — roomed in the Phi Gamma Delta House. Coolidge's photograph taken with his fraternity brothers of 1894–1895 shows a dignified, gentlemanly-looking youth, in a tall, stiff linen collar and white bow tie, with a handkerchief projecting from his outer coat pocket and the "Delta's" star upon his breast, sitting in the front row of the group with Cauthers at his right and Benjamin E. Ray, '95, at his left.

After Coolidge had graduated from Amherst and settled in the neighboring Northampton, he still kept in touch with the active chapter and held frequent conferences with Cauthers regarding its needs. In 1903, when it was decided to purchase a house, Cauthers, after some negotiations, gave his note for $2000, which Coolidge himself endorsed and put through his own bank. Later, after the property had been acquired, Coolidge acted as attorney for the chapter, arranged for a substantial loan, and formed the corporation which held the legal title to the house and grounds. Whenever the chapter required a lawyer, Coolidge served in that capacity — without compensation. Sometimes he would visit the chapter house after the boys had left and go over it from cellar to garret to make sure that everything was in order. When he was nominated for Vice President in June 1920, he was at the twenty-fifth reunion of his class in Amherst. A reception was hastily arranged at the Phi Gamma Delta House and fifteen hundred people filed by him there. He had planned to attend the Diamond Jubilee of the fraternity at Pittsburgh in September 1923, but President Harding's death and his own promotion to the office of chief executive changed his plans.

While he was in the White House, Coolidge was especially gracious in extending fraternal courtesies to his brother "Fijis." His older son, John, was pledged and initiated into Phi Gamma Delta at Amherst in the autumn of 1924, as a freshman; and on May 1, 1926, the President became one of six charter members of an organization called "Fiji Sires and Sons," and the other five had luncheon with Mrs. Coolidge and him. C. Green Brainard, '96, recalls that long after he had reached high political station "Brother" Coolidge would go to the Phi Gamma Delta House from Northampton at Commencement and sit on the porch for hours with some of his friends back for reunion. He contributed generously to the restoration of the fraternity house in 1929. On February 20, 1929, his portrait by the artist Cartotto was presented to the Phi Gamma Delta Club in New York City; and on that occasion Mr. Cauthers spoke briefly of his intimacy with the President and the latter's affection for the fraternity. Enough has been said to indicate that his association with Phi Gamma Delta was altogether happy and that he did not forget it, even in the midst of public duties. It was his only fraternal tie, for he never joined the Masons, the Elks, the Odd Fellows, or any other brotherhood.

We must now turn to the intellectual training which Coolidge received at Amherst. As a freshman, he was compelled to take Greek, Latin, and mathematics for three terms each, with declamation and rhetoric for two. The Greek, under the quaint, old-fashioned, and conscientious Professor Levi Elwell, included the *Odyssey,* the *Alcestis,* and selections from Herodotus. Elwell's features, after assiduous cultivation of the beard, had come to resemble those of Socrates, whose bust, obviously for purposes of agreeable comparison, stood beside the Professor's desk. His peculiarities were the delight of his pupils, who encouraged him to deliver his famous lecture, "Why My Desk Faces the Rising Sun!" and at intervals blackened the eyes of the bust and crowned the stately head with a silk hat, mainly in order to provoke the wrath of the outraged teacher. In Latin, under the caustic and unpopular "Eph" Wood, Coolidge covered portions of Cicero's letters and essays, Livy, and Horace. Mathematics, including geometry, algebra, and trigonometry, was taught by Professor George D. Olds, a young recent addition to the faculty who was soon, because of his popularity, to be elected an honorary member of the class of 1895. "Georgie," as he was universally called, was a brisk, imaginative, and inspiring instructor who made a lasting impression even on those of his pupils who disliked the subject. Short, frail, and bespectacled, he looked hardly older than his students, but he had a keen mind and unbounded enthusiasm, and Coolidge was fond of him then and later.[8] In his scholarship for his freshman year Coolidge had an average of approximately seventy — a respectable "gentleman's grade."

Coolidge's frank comment on his progress, inserted in his *Autobiography,* is as follows : —

---

[8] Later "Georgie" was Dean, Acting President, and finally, in 1924, President of Amherst College, succeeding Dr. Alexander Meiklejohn. In November 1923, President and Mrs. Olds spent nearly a week at the White House with Dr. Olds's former and most famous pupil, then President of the United States.

During my first two years at Amherst I studied hard but my marks were only fair. It needed some encouragement from my father for me to continue. In Junior year, however, my powers began to improve. . . . In the latter part of my course my scholarship had improved, so that I was graduated *cum laude*.

As a sophomore, Coolidge elected Greek for two more terms. His was the last class to read the *Oration on the Crown* [9] under the venerable Professor William S. Tyler, — "Old Ty," — who had graduated from Amherst in 1830 and had been a teacher there since 1836, who had written a history of his college and had outlived nearly all his contemporaries. The Amherst *Olio*, the college year book, commemorated one classroom incident in the following lines by an anonymous contributor : —

> The class in Greek was going on :
> Old Ty a lecture read, —
> And in the row in front there shone
> Fair Coolidge's golden head.

> His pate was bent upon the seat
> In front of him ; his hair
> Old Tyler's feeble gaze did meet,
> With fierce and ruddy glare.

> O'ercome by mystic sense of dread,
> Old Ty his talk did lull, —
> "Coolidge, I wish you'd raise your head,
> I can't talk through your skull!"

Coolidge had one sophomore term of Latin under the cultured, sensitive, sympathetic Professor William L. Cowles, known as "Billy" to the Amherst men of many generations. He continued mathematics through differential and integral calculus without any special distinction, took three terms each of French, German, and Italian without learning to speak or write any one of these languages very well, and had two terms of physics, in one of which he received a "D," the lowest mark of his college career. He had no failures against his name, and he did get an occasional "A" — for one term in rhetoric, for two terms in French, and for two terms in history. His general average for the four years was 78.71, somewhat short of that required for Phi Beta Kappa, but still creditable.

[9] On January 15, 1893, Coolidge wrote, "We are reading the speech of Demosthenes on the crown in Greek this term. It is called the greatest speech of the greatest orator in the world and was delivered in 330 B.C. Eloquence does not seem to grow very fast if after 2200 years we can produce nothing to rival this speech."

It is apparent that Coolidge had what would be called to-day a "scholastic aptitude" rather above that of the normal undergraduate, and a decided bent for languages rather than for science. His active interest in intellectual matters was not, however, really aroused until, as a junior, he elected history and philosophy. The course in history at Amherst then covered virtually the entire junior and senior years, beginning with an outline of ancient history and coming down to the Reconstruction Period in the United States. The teacher was Anson Daniel Morse,[10] a tall, thin, wiry man, slightly stooped in the shoulders, with a scanty moustache and beard which he plucked reflectively as he paced restlessly up and down the platform. He was subject to frequent attacks of illness, particularly in the winter, and was never really robust. Temperamentally fastidious, meditative, and cautious, he was assiduous in the pursuit of facts and judicial in his interpretation of them. His deliberate manner was due in part to the necessity of conserving energy but also to his passion for discriminating judgments. In the 1890's he was in the full maturity of his powers and his distinctive personality affected profoundly such receptive and vigorous scholars as Dwight W. Morrow and Harlan F. Stone. Those who were willing to yield to his suggestions — as Calvin Coolidge was — were infected with his accuracy and thoroughness. Of Morse's senior course in United States history Coolidge wrote: —

It was a thesis on good citizenship and good government. Those who took it came to a clearer comprehension not only of their rights and liberties but of their duties and responsibilities.

"It has always seemed to me that all our other studies were in the nature of a preparation for the course in philosophy," said Coolidge in his *Autobiography*. This was given by Professor Charles E. Garman, the most famous and mysterious of Amherst teachers, around whose romantic personality legends gathered even during his lifetime. Garman, who had graduated from Amherst in 1872, one year after Morse, had been called back in 1880 to his college, where through what must be called his genius he gradually acquired over his students an influence as enduring as it was impressive. Although he lived in an unpretentious and somewhat secluded dwelling at 10 Gray Street, he understood the value of dramatic appearances. In his conventional black frock coat and bow tie he looked grimly

[10] Morse, after graduating from Amherst in 1871 and engaging for some years in research and instructional work in other institutions, returned to Amherst in 1876 and remained there until his death in 1916, although he was made Professor Emeritus in 1907.

ministerial; but his pale face, piercing coal-black eyes, and gleaming white teeth made him resemble even more a middle-aged Hamlet. A confirmed valetudinarian, he shunned physical exercise, was morbidly susceptible to drafts, kept his study and lecture room like a hothouse, and even on warm spring days wrapped his delicate throat in a muffler. A lesser man might have been suspected of posing, but Garman, with all his peculiar habits, was genuine at heart.

Garman's course, as Coolidge knew it, covered four terms — the spring term of the junior year and the entire senior year — and dealt successively with psychology, philosophy, and ethics. His unusual technique had been developed in the 1880's and was thereafter little changed. He employed no textbooks, but distributed to his classes thin pamphlets which he and his negro servant, William Glasgow, printed in his cellar on a small hand press; and, with a mystic ceremony savoring of a secret order, he exacted a pledge that his pupils would return them to him and not show them to anybody outside their own section. At heart and by training a devout and rather orthodox New England Congregationalist, Garman early adopted the Socratic method and a policy of setting up one theory after another, each of which he in turn demolished until he and his listeners had reached the truth. He insisted at each stage that they weigh the evidence and, through reason alone, arrive at a logical and irrefutable conclusion — Christianity. At intermediate stages in the evolution of this philosophical instruction, many of his pupils fancied themselves agnostics and atheists and, in their zeal, not only talked among themselves far into the night but even sought out their mentor in the evening to ask his guidance. One of the Amherst Trustees would not let his son take Garman because he was afraid the boy's religious faith would be undermined. In the 1890's Garman was regarded in some quarters with suspicion and even fear, and the college finally, by conferring on him the degree of Doctor of Divinity, put its stamp of approval on his teaching. Although foolish men occasionally suspected Garman of heresy, he had given his classes before the course was ended a foundation for a firm religious conviction. A few radical undergraduates were more skeptical and less docile under Garman's authority, but his influence was tremendous and amazingly beneficial to practically all of his students. To the great majority who admired him he was a model of intellectual curiosity, tolerance, fairness, and idealism. One alumnus has described him as "a scholar with a keenly analytical mind, a masterly power of synthesis, and an ardent love of truth." Garman published almost nothing. He was too busy teaching. But the class of 1908 placed on his tablet in the College Church the words, "He chose to write on living men's hearts." Coolidge said of him, "We looked upon Garman as a man who walked with God." [11]

In paying his tribute to this distinguished teacher Coolidge stressed the moral and religious implications of his course in philosophy. "He believed in the Bible," said Coolidge, "and constantly quoted it to illustrate his position." But he also drew his analogies from economics and sociology and science, and the political issues of the day, thus making philosophy seem to be a practical guide to conduct and not merely an abstract study. "He contrived," says Walter A. Dyer, "to make philosophy a matter of vital importance to the average young man." Another estimate, by Dr. Arthur H. Pierce, is worth quoting: —

He left his students not so much a doctrine as that rarer and more precious gift, a philosophic temper, with its ever present spirit of inquiry and its love for philosophy as the path of truth.

Many of Garman's pet phrases became bywords on the campus: "Carry all questions back to fundamental principles"; "Weigh the evidence"; "The question *how* answers the question *what*"; "Process not product." From the creed and attitude built up in that Amherst lecture room Calvin Coolidge never receded. In his *Autobiography* he says of Garman and his teaching: —

His course was a demonstration of the existence of a personal God, of our power to know Him, of the Divine immanence, and of the complete dependence of all the universe on Him as the Creator and Father "in whom we live and move and have our being." Every reaction in the universe is a manifestation of His Presence. . . . No doubt there are those who think they can demonstrate that this teaching was not correct. With them I have no argument. I know that in experience it has worked. In time of crisis my belief that people can know the truth, that when it is presented to them they must accept it, has saved me from many of the counsels of expediency. The spiritual nature of man has a power of its own that is manifest in every great emergency from Runnymede to Marston Moor, from the Declaration of Independence to the abolition of slavery.

Coolidge, as these words indicate, remained throughout his life

[11] See *Garman of Amherst*, by Walter A. Dyer, '00, reprinted from the *Sewanee Review*, April 1935. A *Memorial Volume* published after his death contains essays by several of his more brilliant followers, and his *Letters, Lectures, and Addresses* were later collected by Mrs. Garman. The excellent sketch of him in the *Dictionary of American Biography* is by William L. Raub, '93, Professor of Philosophy in Knox College.

an orthodox and earnest Christian, with an unquenchable faith both in humanity and in the divine and openly manifest power of an omniscient and all-ruling personal God. To him the church was an indispensable element in a good social order.[12] These beliefs were, of course, part of his early training, but they were intensified by what he learned from the lips of Garman; and the disciple recognized privately and publicly his debt to his master. Professor Burnett rightly maintains that a discerning person can read in Coolidge's speeches, and indeed in his almost every act, the philosophy of Garman. By the time that Coolidge had started his march to fame, Garman was dead; but the opinions of the teacher lived on in the achievements of his pupil. Still another quotation from the *Autobiography* will indicate how lasting was Garman's influence: —

In ethics he taught us that there is a standard of righteousness, that might does not make right, that the end does not justify the means, and that expediency as a working principle is bound to fail. The only hope of perfecting human relationship is in accordance with that law of service under which men are not so solicitous about what they shall get as about what they shall give. . . . To Garman was given a power which took his class up into a high mountain of spiritual life and left them alone with God. . . . What he revealed to us of the nature of God and man will stand. Against it "the gates of hell shall not prevail."

Although Coolidge did some work in public speaking under the capable Professor Henry A. Frink, he did not regard it as having much affected his own oratorical method. Frink, a survival of classical tradition of Webster and Everett, was rather florid and expansive and addicted to sweeping formal gestures; while Coolidge himself moved more and more in the direction of simplicity, directness, and brevity. He was like Herbert Spencer in his conviction that the best style is marked by economy of words. Nevertheless his grade during three terms of debating under Frink was consistently "B"; and it has been alleged by one of his classmates that during the debates of the junior year he was never defeated. The records of these debates are unfortunately not available; but the Reverend Jay T. Stocking, who knew him well at Amherst and often spoke against him, once wrote: —

[12] Attendance at both church and chapel exercises was then compulsory at Amherst, and Coolidge later as Trustee strongly favored upholding this policy. In his *Autobiography* he said, "If attendance on these religious services ever harmed any of the men of my time, I have never been informed of it. The good it did I believe was infinite."

It was in his junior year that we discovered Coolidge. In that year we began debating, and in the debates we found that he could talk. It was as if a new and gifted man had joined the class.

On November 2, 1893, Coolidge wrote home: "In view of the fact that yesterday I put up a debate said to be the best heard on the floor of the chapel this term . . . can you send me $25?" On January 14, 1894, he continued: "I had a debate yesterday as to whether a Presidential or Parliamentary form of government is the better. I had the Parliamentary side which is not particularly popular inasmuch as it is really to show England's government is better than our own, and I spoke against Pratt of Brooklyn, who is a very good debater, being captain of our football team. But the Parliamentary side won by a large majority when the question was decided."

In the last term of his junior year, by vote of the students taking public speaking, the J. Wesley Ladd prize for the best oration was divided between Coolidge and H. L. Williston. Coolidge's subject was "The Story of the Cid and Its Meaning" — a topic rather more literary than one would have expected him to select. His marks for two terms of public speaking were "B" and "C"; and for one term of what was called declamation his grade was "B." Coolidge's first senior debate was on October 23, 1894, against Charles T. Burnett on the question, "Do the United States Owe More to England than to Holland?" I find in the Amherst *Student* a note regarding a debate on May 18, 1895, between Bridgman and Coolidge on the topic, "From present indications is the Northern Immigrant a greater menace to our country than the Southern negro?" In neither case can I discover the winner or the winning side. The evidence indicates, however, that Coolidge was considered to be a formidable opponent in debate.

Coolidge took only one course in English literature, and it was clearly not a subject which stirred his real interest. His taste in poetry was never discriminating, his favorites being authors like Eugene Field, James Whitcomb Riley, and Rudyard Kipling. While he was ill at home in the autumn of 1890 he read and memorized much of Scott's poetry. He did at one time read Shakespeare and Milton, — not, I think, with much appreciation, — but he does not mention or quote from Wordsworth, Shelley, Keats, Tennyson, or Browning, and his preference was for verse of a didactic or ethical trend, like Longfellow's "The Psalm of Life" or Whittier's *Snow-bound*. Once in the White House when the conversation drifted towards poetry the President made his contribution to the discussion by observing drily, "There was a man named Smith in my time at Amherst who used to write some verse." When he was advised by well-meaning friends to emulate Theodore Roosevelt and entertain distinguished poets at luncheon in the White House, the only contemporary he could suggest was a genial and sentimental Irish-American bard, Denis F. MacCarthy, whom he had met in Boston. Coolidge's prose reading in his college days, and later, was chiefly in the orators and historians — Macaulay, Carlyle, Webster, and Rhodes.

On one occasion, however, he experimented in the field of romanticism. To the Amherst *Literary Monthly* for October 1894 he contributed under the signature of J. Calvin Coolidge a tale called "Margaret's Mist," dealing with a legend of Ausable Chasm, a deep gorge near Keeseville, New York, on the outskirts of the Adirondacks and a place which Coolidge had visited during the preceding summer. Briefly it concerns Margaret Meldon, "a maiden just blossoming into womanhood," who is the daughter of the proprietor of an inn near Ausable Falls. Attracted by the flattery of Waldo Martin, who poses as a student of geology from London, the simple country lass becomes his promised bride. On the eve of the nuptials, which were to be solemnized "on Wednesday evening, at eight o'clock, October 23," a stranger, "a woodsman tall and brawny," arrives at the inn and later joins Martin in holding up the government stagecoach, killing the driver, and making off with a considerable sum of money. Margaret subsequently discovers the two villains at Table Rock dividing their spoils, reveals herself dramatically, and in the stilted language of the heroines of Mrs. Southworth or Mary J. Holmes denounces her peccant lover: —

"Waldo Martin," said the emotionless Margaret, "I need no explanation. I know now. How I have loved you! How I've trusted you! Robber! Murderer! Betrayer! Yet I cannot expose you. I love you still. Go over the earth in freedom. Expiate your crime. I plead for you before a Higher Tribunal."

While speaking, she had moved towards the pool, and, with her eyes still fixed upon the man she had loved, she plunged beneath its eddies. The black water closing over her buried the sorrowing maiden forever beneath its bosom.

The stolid and outwardly unperturbed Martin seems to have made no effort to rescue his sweetheart; but that night a wild storm sweeping over the Champlain Valley must have wrecked his boat in the middle of the lake and brought upon him a just retribution. The story closes in an appropriate strain of pathos: —

Ever since that day, when the western sun kisses the rippling lake good night, the mystic cloud so long known as Margaret's Mist appears at the bend over Table Rock to mark the tragic spot and signify the purity of the soul so long ago gone out beneath its shadow.

Weakly imitative of Scott, of Hawthorne, and of the Victorian sentimentalists at their worst, "Margaret's Mist" is perhaps the last story which the prosaic Coolidge might have been expected to write. It was his only venture into mysticism, his first and only attempt at fiction. For the remainder of his career he was to be dealing principally with facts.

When the class of 1895 cast its statistical votes, the three most popular professors were Garman, with twenty supporters, Olds, with fifteen, and Morse, with eight. The best course in college was declared to be psychology, by a vote of forty-three. These figures represent a fair judgment of the Amherst faculty in the 1890's. Coolidge himself wrote many years later : —

As I look back upon the college I am more and more impressed with the strength of its faculty, with their power for good. Perhaps it has men now with a broader preliminary training, though they then were profound scholars, perhaps it has men of keener intellects, though they then were very exact in their reasoning, but the great distinguishing mark of all of them was that they were men of character.

Coolidge's class graduated seventy-six men, the youngest being barely twenty and the oldest thirty-one. Politically, on their own confession, forty-five were Republican, eight Democratic, and thirteen Independent, with several unwilling to commit themselves. The class agreed that Amherst's greatest need was a new college hall. For the most popular man Dwight W. Morrow received twenty-four votes against fourteen for Charles T. Burnett, his nearest rival; and Morrow was also voted "the most likely to succeed." [13] The story that Morrow himself voted for Coolidge as "the most likely to succeed" has often been printed, but unfortunately cannot be verified by any official record. Mrs. Morrow, however, has been willing to vouch for its authenticity, and it would seem to be a pity, under the circumstances, to cast doubt on so respectable a tradition.[14] But Mrs. Morrow and Mrs. Coolidge have

[13] These figures, taken from the *Student* for June 25, 1895, differ slightly from those in the 1895 *Classbook*. Coolidge's only committee appointment at Commencement was as a member of the Statistics Committee.

[14] Charles A. Andrews writes: "Dwight himself told me at about the time Calvin was nominated for the Vice Presidency or actually became President that in the voting where most of the fellows voted for him (Dwight) as most likely to

the impression that their husbands were "not intimate friends while they were at Amherst College."

Even as a senior Coolidge was a quiet, reserved, and apparently studious undergraduate who came and went with the rank and file without displaying any gift for leadership. His roommate, Deering, has described him as "an ordinary American boy," who occasionally indulged in silly pranks like peppering Professor Morse's gardener with an air gun. The phrases used by his classmates regarding him are rather noncommittal: "unostentatious in the extreme"; "not a fluent conversationalist, but rather a good listener"; "a man of character, both shrewd and straightforward"; "eminently methodical, and got things done without the appearance of haste"; "constant in application, determined, simple, and independent." These are not the glowing words which mature men apply to a boyhood companion who early aroused their admiration and held their hearts. It is true that the Reverend Jay T. Stocking later said of him, "I never knew a man who seemed more content to be himself, to go his own way no matter what the impulse of the crowd"; but this comment was made after Coolidge had become a personage. Lucius R. Eastman says, "We all of us came to like Coolidge as a comfortable table companion, but I do not think any of us rated him very high until the end of senior year. I think it would be stretching the facts a little to say that, other than having a high regard for him personally and recognizing his ability for quiet humor, we expected much from him, for we did not." [15] Frederick S. Fales, '96, writes, "Coolidge was a very retiring, silent individual, with few friends, and not at all an outstanding figure, even in his class." [16] Another intimate friend declares, "He remained through his college course the same quiet, faithful, unpretentious figure that he was as President." Dr. Robert B. Osgood has pointed out that in the class pictures taken on the steps of Walker Hall during his freshman and senior years, Coolidge is to be seen standing at the foot of the same column, book under his arm. Osgood's comment was, "He sticks to his post."

Even in his senior year, then, Coolidge showed little promise of future eminence. Harlan F. Stone, Bertrand H. Snell, Dwight W.

become famous he (Dwight) voted for Calvin." The Reverend Jay T. Stocking adds corroborative evidence. On the other hand Lucius R. Eastman believes "that this particular story has had much more currency and has assumed an importance that is out of proportion." Eastman feels certain that Morrow did not begin to think highly of Coolidge until after 1915. Several members of the class who do not wish their names to be used have told me that it is improbable, under the circumstances, that Morrow voted for Coolidge.

[15] Letter to the author, January 27, 1933.
[16] Letter to the author, February 2, 1933.

Morrow, Alfred E. Stearns, — all in college with Coolidge, — were leaders there as they were to become in life. Coolidge, however, was no better and no worse than the average of those around him. He was a slender young man, clearly very much like his mother, and his photographs give him a delicate appearance. As an upperclassman he was neat in his dress, and his reddish hair was carefully smoothed down and parted. Neither wealthy nor poor, neither brilliant nor dull, neither pious nor dissipated, he aroused little comment from teachers or undergraduates.

At the very close of his college career, however, he did attract some attention. On September 21, 1894, principally because of his reputation as an excellent debater, he was elected by his classmates as Grove Orator, with the duty of addressing them at the Class Day exercises and making the audience laugh. Coolidge's letter to his father at the time indicates that he was very proud of the honor [17] — the first of his many elective offices — and he certainly prepared himself with much care. The Baccalaureate Sermon was preached on Sunday, June 23, by the Reverend Henry A. Stimson. The Hardy Prize Debate, a traditional feature of the Commencement program, was participated in by Andrews, Hardy, Morrow, Stocking, Bishop, Little, Ray, and Tibbetts, and Morrow took first prize. The competitors in the Hyde Prize Speaking were Bishop, Colby, Roelker, Bryant, Noyes, and Stocking; and again Coolidge was not one of them. On Tuesday morning, near the College Church, Edwin J. Bishop delivered the Ivy Oration and William J. Boardman the Ivy Poem. In the afternoon, in College Hall, Morrow gave the Class Oration, — an unusually able defense of idealism, — and Charles T. Burnett read the Class Poem, entitled "The Seven Sleepers of Ephesus," in sonorous blank verse. Following this indoor program the class and their guests assembled in the College Grove, lighted their corncob pipes as many generations of seniors had done before them, and then lay back on the grass to hear Calvin Coolidge as he began: —

The mantle of truth falls upon the Grove Orator on condition he wear it wrong side out. For the Grove Oration is intended to give a glimpse of the only true side of college life — the inside. And how can this be displayed but by turning things wrong side out?

Now college life has three relations — the relation to the class, the relation to the faculty, and the relation to other things. The class relation

---

[17] He wrote: "Class elections went very well. There are three orators and poets, — class, Ivy, and grove, — making six men. Two places went to Vermont, — Boardman of Barnet is Ivy Poet, I am grove orator. I put more work into it than Alfred did into Freeman's meeting and was elected on the first ballot, 53 to 18, against a man from Brooklyn, Bridgman."

begins with a cane rush where the undergraduates use Anglo-Saxon and ends with a diploma where the faculty use Latin — if it does not end before by a communication from the President in just plain English.

Like every Grove Orator he was heckled, but continued imperturbably, pausing now and then to reply scathingly to some ribald comment. His witty sallies aroused shouts of laughter, and when the audience demanded the repetition of a clever sentence, he spoke it again in precisely the same words and with the same solemn, almost stern expression. The oration was packed with what would to-day be called "wisecracks," many of them sarcastic observations on members of the faculty — remarks which, although good-natured in tone and intention, had nevertheless something of a bite. Professor Olds remembered it as "wisdom touched with whimsical humor." The specimens quoted from the oration may seem to a reader more than forty years after the event to be unremarkable; but the speech pleased the crowd and fitted the occasion. Many of Coolidge's classmates have told me that it was at this time, after living near him and with him for nearly four years, that they first recognized the superior quality of his mind. He closed with a direct address to his fellows : —

Gentlemen of the Class of '95: Oh! you need not look so alarmed. I am not going to work off any song and dance about the cold, cruel world. It may not be such a misfortune to be out of college. It is not positive proof that a diploma is a wolf because it comes to you in sheep's clothing. No one in business will have to pay Professor Tyler two dollars for an extra examination.

Wherever we go, whatever we are, scientific or classical, degreed or disagreed, we are going to be Amherst men. And whoever sees a purple and white button marked with '95 shall see the emblem of a class spirit that will say, "Old Amherst, doubtless always right, but right or wrong, Old Amherst!"

In commenting on this incident in his *Autobiography* Coolidge said : —

While my effort was not without some success I very soon learned that making fun of people in a public way was not a good method to secure friends, or likely to lead to much advancement, and I have scrupulously avoided it.

That Coolidge's chief fame among his mates should have come from the Plug Hat Speech and the Grove Oration, both deliberately humorous, will not seem strange to those who knew him well. Despite his usual serious manner and superficial austerity, he had a keen sense of the ridiculous which frequently found expression in laconic and witty observations the more startling because they were so unexpected. His fondness for a mild type of practical joke was familiar to all the White House attendants, who were constantly on their guard.

The Grove Oration was followed by the Grove Poem, recited by Charles A. Andrews. It is perhaps significant that although in his rhymes Andrews mentioned many of his classmates by name he did not refer to Calvin Coolidge, who was later to become one of his close friends.

On Wednesday, June 26, Coolidge marched into College Hall with his class to the seventy-fourth annual Commencement, listened to the eight seniors who had been selected to speak on the platform, — among them being Burnett, Morrow, and Stocking, — and received his sheepskin from President Gates. While he did graduate *cum laude,* he did not, like Andrews, Morrow, and Stocking, make Phi Beta Kappa — to which society, however, he was elected as an honorary member in 1921. Sixty-two men received the degree of Bachelor of Arts and fourteen that of Bachelor of Science. Following these exercises came the Alumni Luncheon, devoted mainly to addresses in praise of the recently deceased President Seelye. The program for the week closed with a reception in the evening at the President's House.

In filling out the questionnaire submitted to each member of his class, Coolidge answered the query, "What do you plan to do next year?" by writing, "Nothing, I reckon. Must rest after these four hard years." On January 7, 1895, in a significant letter, he wrote his father : —

I have not decided what I shall do next year, shall probably go into the store or go to a law school at Boston or New York. That is about as far as I can get, and think you will have to decide which I shall do. I do not see as I have much of any preference now but may have later. I expect to sell out the present in terms of the future and am not in any hurry to get rich. I should like to live where I can be of some use to the world and not simply where I should get a few dollars together.

Dr. Jay T. Stocking recalled that Coolidge said to him as they parted, "I'm only sure of one thing — that I'm a Republican." He had recorded himself among the twelve members of the class who intended to study law, but where and how he was still uncertain.[18]

[18] On March 12, 1893, he wrote to his father : "I wonder what you will do with the farm when grandmother goes away. Indeed I have often wondered if it would not be an elephant on somebody's hands when she did not want to live there any more. Perhaps I shall want it to live on when I am done going to school."

Probably he and his father slipped quietly away and took the train for Plymouth, where he settled down for his last working summer on the farm.

Perhaps this is the place for continuing the Amherst story a little further. At the class dinner on June 17, 1895, at the Cooley House, in Springfield, Ernest W. Hardy had been Toastmaster, and the list of orators had included Deering, Colby, Andrews, Rhodes, and Stocking — but not Coolidge or Morrow. Ten years afterward, at his decennial reunion, Coolidge, although Chairman of the Republican City Committee in Northampton, was still relatively obscure. He attended the reunion events, but no one thought of asking him to deliver an address. The presiding officer at the banquet was his former roommate, Deering, then a judge of the municipal court of Saco, Maine, and the speakers included Burnett, Stocking, Hardy, Pratt, Osgood, and others — all of them presumably on the road to success. At the large Commencement Dinner, Dwight W. Morrow represented the class, pointing with pride to their one "real live Congressman, Charles Blakeslee Law, of the Fourth New York District." In the *Decennial Classbook* Coolidge's name is not mentioned except under the roll call of the members. He was still plodding along without attracting more than local attention in Northampton.

How the situation had changed at the twenty-fifth reunion in 1920! In the booklet, *Famous Men of a Famous Class*, prepared by Frederick Houk Law, — who had become a teacher of English, — Coolidge's picture was the frontispiece. Andrews was the prosperous treasurer of a business corporation; Morrow had become a banker and a partner in Morgan and Company; Eastman was a substantial merchant; "Gussie" Post had been a pioneer in aviation; Burnett was a professor of Psychology in Bowdoin College; Osgood was a distinguished surgeon; Stocking was a well-known preacher; Deering, a lawyer at Biddeford, was being mentioned as a possibility for Governor of Maine; William S. Tyler was a lawyer in New York City. But Calvin Coolidge, the obscure undergraduate, was Governor of the Commonwealth of Massachusetts, a national figure because of his attitude towards the Boston Police Strike, and Republican candidate for Vice President of the United States. The comment on him and his career in the volume reads in part as follows : —

Coolidge has made a great number of brilliantly epigrammatical speeches, founded, as all Amherst men know, solidly on the good old Amherst spirit, and on the truths taught by Professor Garman. The hills and classrooms of old Amherst echo in his speeches.

At the fortieth reunion, both Coolidge and Morrow were dead, and their portraits were in Amherst's Hall of Fame.

One of Coolidge's distinguished successes in Amherst was not made public until after he had graduated. In the Amherst *Student* for November 24, 1894, appeared an announcement of a prize of a silver medal offered by the National Society of Sons of the American Revolution to a senior in Amherst who should write the best essay on the subject, "The Principles Fought for in the War of the American Revolution." Only undergraduates who had taken five terms of history were eligible. The winner of the silver medal at Amherst was to have his essay submitted in competition for a gold medal worth $150, offered for the winning essay on the same subject from any American college. Coolidge confided to no one his intention of entering the contest, but his essay was ready before April 1, 1895, for the Amherst Department of History to read. It was awarded the silver medal at Amherst, evidently without any public announcement, and then submitted in the national competition. Just before Christmas, when Coolidge was studying law in Northampton, in the office of Hammond and Field, the news arrived that he was the winner. Judge Field learned of his clerk's success from the columns of the *Springfield Republican*. "Is this item true?" asked Judge Field. "Yes, here's the medal," replied Coolidge, reaching into his desk and drawing it out. "Have you told your father?" asked Field. "No, do you think I'd better?" was the answering query.

When Calvin Coolidge had become President of the United States, everything relating to him was naturally of interest, and this prize essay was included in a volume of his speeches entitled *The Price of Freedom* (1924). Even in juxtaposition to his later and more mature addresses it brought him no discredit. While it lacked the terseness and compactness of his gubernatorial and presidential style, it showed the fondness for short sentences and the closeness of reasoning which were to become so characteristic of his writing. It merited attention in 1924 because of its reiteration of the principle that "sovereignty is always finally vested in the people" and that, even under a tyranny, "the people will realize more and more that the sovereignty is with them and will finally assert it."

It is demonstrable that Calvin Coolidge's political philosophy, although inevitably modified as advancing age and political associations turned him more conservative, was formed under Morse and Garman, and that the doctrines of which he was to become the symbol may be traced back to his teachers. He thought deeply on the ideas that these Amherst professors imparted to their classes; he quoted them in political discussions, even employing their precise language. On November 2, 1894, he wrote: —

The nineteenth century is slipping away. We are to live in the scientific age of the 20th century and must prepare for it now. There are millions who can only be hands and only a few who can be heads. I believe it is an age where culture and education are going to be more in demand than ever. I believe it will be the age of the college man.

More than the average alumnus he was directly influenced by his college training; thus the part played by Amherst in his intellectual and spiritual development cannot be too much stressed. Coolidge's conception as a Trustee of what his Alma Mater should be was stated by President King in 1933: —

He made no pretense of expertness in the field of education. He emphasized his point of view that Amherst should continue to be a small college with a relatively simple curriculum, devoting herself exclusively to cultural education as distinguished from vocational or professional training. He aspired to have at the college teachers of unusual ability, and he continued to emphasize that it was a part of the duty of the college by precept and practice to develop sound character and deep religious feeling.

In this discussion of Coolidge's college days we have left untouched some of the events which seemed at the time to matter most: the Cane Rush; the Yale-Harvard football game at Springfield in the autumn of 1891, when Yale won by a score of 10–0 and Coolidge saw more people than he had ever seen at a circus; the "Cider Meet" in the autumn of 1892, when the sophomores crushed the freshmen ignominiously; the great football season of 1892, when Captain George D. Pratt, '93, and his eleven defeated Dartmouth, 30–2, and Williams, 60–0; and the almost equally great baseball season of 1893, when "Al" Stearns, '94, headed a nine which won three times each from Williams and Dartmouth. We have said nothing of the sorrowful record of Coolidge's senior year, when Amherst reached her nadir in athletics, losing to her rivals in virtually every sport.[19] We have talked little about warm spring evenings on the verandah of the Phi Gamma Delta House, about bonfires and songs and cheers, about walks on Sunday after-

[19] On November 20, 1892, Coolidge wrote home, "We pride ourselves here that we keep athletics in its proper place and make scholarship the chiefest and foremost consideration and also that the men who win our victories are not all brutes but scholarly athletes who contend for the love of Amherst and not as hired professionals merely represent us in name." College loyalty could go no further.

noons, about the Freshman River and the Pelham Hills and Sugar-
loaf Mountain and the serrated peaks of the Holyoke Range. All
these were part of college life and must have lingered in Calvin
Coolidge's memory. As it turned out, his permanent anchorage was
to be in Northampton, within easy reach of his college environment.
The valley of the Connecticut was to continue to be his home.

It is clear from Coolidge's later remarks that he was, during
his first two years at Amherst, acutely conscious of his slow progress.
His ambitions had been thwarted; he had failed to make a fraternity,
he was unnoticed by those around him, his marks were only
mediocre, and he had no compensating successes. Nevertheless he
was learning the lesson of the value of hard and faithful work, and
he schooled himself to abide the outcome. In his *Autobiography*
he wrote: —

In the development of every boy who is going to amount to anything there comes a time when he emerges from his immature ways
and by the greater precision of his thought and action realizes that he
has begun to find himself. Such a transition finally came to me. It was
not accidentally but the result of hard work. If I had permitted my
failures, or what seemed to me at the time a lack of success, to dis-
courage me, I cannot see any way in which I would ever have made
progress.

It must be repeated that there was nothing superficially brilliant
or attractive about young Coolidge. He was aware that he was not
facile or fluent or magnetic, and would have to earn the respect of
others through more substantial qualities — through persistence,
faithfulness, integrity, and the confidence which sound character
inspires. This he did in college as later in the legislature, in fact
throughout his political life. At first unimpressive in strange surroundings, he slowly gained the attention of those people who
counted.

Yet in Amherst his one extraordinary talent lay entirely dormant.
Dr. Stocking, in writing about Coolidge, has said: —

I was not one of those who expected Coolidge to have any spectacular
career. I did not think he would become famous. The last place in the
world I should have expected him to succeed was politics. He lacked
small talk, and he was never known, I suspect, to slap a man on the
back. He rarely laughed. He was anything but a mixer. The few who got
in personal contact with him had to go the whole way.

Here, then, was a man who was by temperament precisely the
opposite of a political leader like Franklin Delano Roosevelt. A

person who runs for elective office in the United States ordinarily has to be a "good fellow," with ease and charm of manner — qualities which Coolidge certainly did not reveal at Amherst. Yet this same Coolidge, by one of human nature's miracles, became perhaps the best vote-getter in American history — one of our few Presidents who, without question, could have had three terms in the White House. And when this happened there was not one of his classmates, possibly excepting Morrow, who could honestly say, "I told you so!"

V

Early Days in Northampton

CALVIN COOLIDGE's association with Northampton, Massachusetts, of which he was a citizen from 1895 until his death in 1933, was originally a matter of chance. Before his college course was ended he had made up his mind that the law was "the highest of the professions," in which, he felt, "the duties would be congenial and the opportunities for service large." A poorly authenticated story avers that when he and "Kid" Morrow confided to one another their intention of becoming lawyers and Morrow asked where Coolidge planned to settle, the latter replied, "Northampton's the nearest courthouse!" The fact is that, after receiving his Amherst diploma and returning to Plymouth for the' summer, he talked over with his father his plans for the future. It was possible to enroll in one of the better-known law schools, such as those at Columbia, Harvard, or New York University, but the expense was more than the thrifty Calvin wished to incur. On the other hand, the old-fashioned process of "reading law" in an office, thus undergoing a practical and inexpensive apprenticeship to the profession, was still in vogue, and, being customary in rural Vermont, was more readily approved by Colonel Coolidge. Accordingly Calvin wrote former Governor William P. Dillingham,[1] of Montpelier, Vermont, on August 30, 1895, as follows: —

If I could get into a good office I am thinking of reading there for some time, or perhaps finishing my preparation for the bar, rather than going to law school. Is there a vacancy with your firm?

If there is any hope of your considering the proposition favorably I should be pleased to go up to the city to talk with you or you can

---

[1] William Paul Dillingham (1843–1923), born in Waterbury, Vermont, attended Kimball Union Academy, studied law, and was admitted to the bar in 1867. He had been Governor from 1888 to 1890, and later succeeded Justin S. Morrill as United States Senator in 1900. In 1895, when Coolidge wrote him, he was temporarily out of public affairs. He was in the Senate until his death and sat under Coolidge as presiding officer when the latter was Vice President.

advise me by mail as to the terms you would make if you ever bother with students.

I am just out of college and am somewhat undecided between the school and the office. Can you give me any suggestion? Could you take me after I had spent some time, say a year or two, in a school?

It will be noticed that the young man made no mention of his father or the latter's acquaintance with Dillingham. He wished to stand on his own feet. At the moment Dillingham was absent from his city on business, and the reply to Coolidge's letter was necessarily delayed. Before the answer did arrive, offering him a place in the Montpelier office, Coolidge was accepted as a clerk with Hammond and Field, the leading law firm of Northampton, and wrote to Dillingham, October 19, 1895: —

You see I am settled for the present. I should perhaps prefer Vermont, but I could not better my place anywhere else out of the shadow of the green hills.

The story of how Coolidge started his legal career has too frequently been embellished by the imaginative pencils of journalists. In early September following his graduation, responding to an invitation from his classmate, Ernest W. Hardy, Coolidge went to Northampton and was escorted by him to Hammond and Field's office in the old and now demolished First National Bank Building on the corner of Main and King streets. Hardy, who had been known in college as "Fat" or "Chipmunk," was a jovial, talkative person, the direct opposite of Coolidge in temperament, and his garrulity and easy-going characteristics frequently got him into difficulties.[2] According to the clear remembrance of Field, the junior partner, Hardy spoke effusively in praise of his college friend; while Coolidge, after an introductory "Good morning," lapsed into patient silence, merely standing impassive with slightly bowed head and hands crossed in front of him holding his derby hat. Field, just back from Europe, explained that he would have little time to devote to a student but that Coolidge might sit at a desk, read as much as he wished, and learn what he could. The result was noted in the *Daily Hampshire Gazette* for September 17, 1895: —

[2] Hardy studied law in the office of Richard W. Irwin and later formed the firm of Irwin and Hardy. His partner, Irwin, was eighteen years older and had been educated in the public schools and Boston University Law School. He was an influential figure in Northampton politics and was eventually in 1911 appointed by Governor Foss as Justice of the Superior Court. He retired as Judge in 1929 and died March 9, 1932, some months before Coolidge. Irwin was a shrewd observer, familiar with practical politics, and was at times very helpful to Coolidge.

THE BIRTHPLACE OF CALVIN COOLIDGE AT
PLYMOUTH NOTCH, VERMONT

THE BURIAL PLACE OF CALVIN COOLIDGE

J. Calvin Coolidge, of Plymouth, Vt. and a graduate of Amherst, class, '95, is to take a position in the law office of Hammond and Field.

In all Massachusetts Calvin Coolidge could not have found a place more to his liking. Both John C. Hammond and Henry P. Field were Amherst graduates, the former in the class of 1865 and the latter in that of 1880; and Hammond, at his fortieth reunion the preceding June, had been much amused at Coolidge's witty Grove Oration. Hammond was a massive and rugged personality of high principles, sterling character, and fine community spirit, to whom Amherst in 1925 awarded the degree of Doctor of Laws. Field, with whom Hammond formed a partnership in 1888, was quick and clever of mind, with mirth-making gifts as a raconteur and a memory for gossip and anecdote which was unfailing to the end of his days. After his appointment in 1919 as Judge of Probate for Hampshire County, he was universally known as Judge Field. No Amherst gathering in the vicinity was complete without him, and at his death in 1937 his modest fortune was left to his fraternity, Psi Upsilon, and to his college.[3]

Both Mr. Hammond and Judge Field were identified throughout their mature lives with Northampton and were familiar with its history and people. Often called the "Meadow City," it had been settled in 1654 by pioneers from Springfield and Windsor further down the Connecticut, who chose as a site for their village the low ridge to the west of the great bend of the river just north of Mount Holyoke and Mount Tom — a location described by Edmund Clarence Stedman in his lines: —

> There still the giant warders stand
> And watch the currents downward flow,
> And westward still, with steady hand,
> The river bends her silver bow.

Geologically it was probably once the bed of a vast lake the banks of which are now the low hills encircling the city. The settlers, having purchased the land from the aborigines, soon changed the

---

[3] Judge Field was a rich and accurate source of information regarding Coolidge, especially his Northampton period, and gave me much aid in the preparation of this biography. Only a month before his death I was with him for a week at the Lord Jeffrey Inn, in Amherst, and took copious notes of conversations which often lasted far into the August night — for he hated to go to bed. Judge Field always declined to use his influence with Coolidge for his own or anyone else's advantage. He once remarked to the President, "One thing I'm proud of. I never asked you for anything." "Yes, you did," was the unexpected reply. "You asked me to veto the Bonus Bill, and I did."

Indian name of Nonotuck to that of the English city which some of them could recall. Although the first cabins were hastily erected along what is now Pleasant Street, later dwellings inevitably clustered around Meeting House Hill, in the very heart of the present municipality. In the seventeenth century Northampton suffered from redskin marauders, and in 1676 successfully repulsed an organized attack. The names of many of the early citizens, Elder John Strong and Medad Pomeroy, Reverend Solomon Stoddard and William Clarke, are still honored; and among the other notable figures have been the stern Jonathan Edwards, minister in the Congregational Church from 1727 until his dismissal in 1750; Joseph Hawley and Seth Pomeroy, sturdy heroes of the French and Indian Wars; the Federalist Caleb Strong (1745–1819), Governor of Massachusetts for eleven years, longer than any other man; four United States Senators including, besides Strong, Isaac C. Bates, Elijah Hunt Mills, and Eli P. Ashmun; and George Bancroft, the historian, who, with J. G. Cogswell, conducted a famous school on Round Hill from 1823 to 1834. Local pride was a prevailing mood with every Northampton citizen.

The settlement spread out gradually over low, rolling hills, which are less conspicuous to-day than they were two centuries ago. The central section of the city is now shaped not unlike a tree, the bent trunk being represented by Bridge and Main streets, rising slightly to Smith College at the western end, with avenues branching off on either side at irregular intervals — Pleasant Street and King Street, Gothic Street, South Street, and State Street, and finally West Street and Elm Street, which virtually encircle Smith College. Main Street is a wide, impressive boulevard, on which are located the Hampshire County Courthouse, the City Hall, the Edwards Church, the Memorial Hall, the Academy of Music, and many of the better office buildings. As yet the tallest block is only four stories high, and the place resembles a shire town, close to the surrounding agricultural land. The streets are, for the most part, comfortably broad and bordered with elms and maples.

In 1895, Northampton, although nominally a city, was actually a trading and industrial centre drawing patronage from several hamlets within its legal jurisdiction — Bay State Village, Florence, and Leeds, the last being the most remote. The population of about 15,000 was mostly native Yankee, with a few Irish, destined to increase rapidly in numbers and influence through Calvin Coolidge's lifetime. The French, Poles, and Lithuanians now so picturesquely ubiquitous in Northampton and the other settlements in the fertile

Connecticut intervale were, in 1895, scarcely evident. The unique feature of the city was Smith College for young women, opened there in 1875 with the scholarly L. Clark Seelye as President. The most attractive area in Northampton was that which the Smith Trustees had been farsighted enough to acquire between Elm and West streets and Mill River, including the section where the stream widens into Paradise, the lake resort for Smith College girls. Northampton was literally an educational centre, for within a few miles of its City Hall were Amherst College and Massachusetts Agricultural College, Mount Holyoke College, Williston Seminary, and many other institutions, including the Capen-Burnham School and the Clarke Institute for the Deaf, both in Northampton itself. Smith College was an important factor in Northampton affairs, and its property increased substantially in extent and value from 1895 to 1933. Largely because of it, the city was attractive as a residential community, whose people enjoyed the advantages of excellent concerts, lectures, and plays. Like most college towns its society was reasonably free from the menace of the ostentatious rich. Its churches and schools were good. It was small enough so that a newcomer, without prestige or powerful friends, would not be altogether overwhelmed. It was large enough so that he could find the opportunity which he desired.

Obviously it was a place in which everybody was aware of everybody else. Before long most of the population of Northampton knew that Hammond and Field had a new, sandy-haired student who had just graduated from Amherst College but in spite of that was a "queer duck," an "odd stick," very shy and uncommunicative. After two or three years he could walk out of his front door west to Main Street, then along past the Edwards Church down Main Street to his office, nodding to friends as he went along, well informed about the bank account of each, familiar with their idiosyncrasies and with the domestic problems and general reliability of them all. A man has to be sound in character to defy the close scrutiny of his neighbors in a spot like Northampton. In a metropolis one's minor vices or flaws of temper may escape attention; but in Northampton each man soon becomes known for what he is — "just a little shady," "too fond of his toddy," "too much away from his office," "so tight he squeaks." No one in such an environment can long "put on side" or pretend to be richer or better than he is. If he runs up bills and does not pay them, people soon hear about it and begin to whisper. Coolidge bore this ordeal well. He was not vulnerable to petty gossip. He could be trusted. No one ever uncovered in his life even a suspicion of scandal. And it was observed that he minded his own business and let others mind theirs.

Calvin Coolidge could easily have found for himself some legitimate recreation, but his mind was fixed first on the law and second on politics. His days were spent in mastering his profession; in the evenings he was likely to read a little history. Judge Field said that Calvin did not overwork. Often he would turn in his swivel chair at the black walnut desk and stare for long minutes out the window — perhaps thinking. He could not be persuaded even by the members of the firm to go to the football and baseball games at Amherst. He joined the Wishton-Wish Canoe Club, at Hockanum, in Hadley, but seldom used its privileges except on Sunday afternoon. Undoubtedly he craved companionship, but he did not always know how to make himself companionable. He did, however, find jovial company in "Dick" Irwin, Ernest Hardy, and one or two others who lunched regularly at Rahar's Inn.[4] Those who were acquainted with him say that he did not accept invitations to dinner, that he avoided formal entertainments, and that he seemed quite content to "sit around." Judge Field once confided to Hammond, "I guess we've added the Sphinx to our staff." Coolidge seemed to have no craving for excitement, no passion for exploration, no wish to break the routine. It was noticed, however, that he seemed to get along well with tradesmen, with clerks in the stores, with streetcar conductors, with people who liked to talk politics. One is reminded of Paul Leicester Ford's novel, *The Honorable Peter Stirling*, the hero of which was a young lawyer who rose to be governor because so many of the common people trusted him.

With commendable ambition Coolidge devoted himself to qualifying as a lawyer. The only other student in the musty office was Edward A. Shaw; and the two clerks together learned by experience how to prepare writs, deeds, wills, contracts, and the ordinary legal documents. The Superior Court sat in Northampton for three civil and two criminal sessions each year, and Coolidge then observed

---

[4] Rahar's Inn, presided over by the picturesque "Dick" Rahar, was a resort much frequented by Amherst undergraduates, especially on Saturday evenings in the spring and fall. It was also a place where many local politicians met for luncheon. Coolidge's habits were sufficiently abstemious. He never took a drink in the daytime, but in the evening would occasionally indulge himself in a cocktail or a glass of beer. One night after dinner Coolidge passed the office desk as Rahar was putting away two five-dollar gold pieces, and asked a question about them. Rahar explained that he followed the custom of giving Mrs. Rahar, for her personal use, all the gold coins that came in. "Nice custom," said Calvin, and went out. At the end of the month, however, Coolidge and his two friends, Irwin and Hardy, came up to the desk to pay their bills and each pulled out five five-dollar gold pieces — seventy-five dollars in all. Calvin Coolidge had had his pleasant joke, and Mrs. Rahar did get the money.

its procedure and became acquainted with the practical as well as the theoretical aspects of trial work. He and Shaw were soon being called upon to prepare briefs and hunt out evidence. Judge Field never maintained that Coolidge was at his desk earlier or lingered longer than anyone else in the office, but he did not fail in diligence, and, to quote his own words, "was soon conversant with contracts, torts, evidence, and real property, with some knowledge of Massachusetts pleading."

On June 29, 1897, when he had been a student for twenty months, he appeared before a County Committee consisting of Mr. Hammond, Judge William G. Bassett, and Judge William P. Strickland. The motion for his admission to the bar was presented by Mr. Field; and Calvin Coolidge, after having been duly questioned, was admitted to practice in the Massachusetts courts. It was only a few days before his twenty-fifth birthday. His accomplishment had been in no respect exceptional, for his two friends, Hardy and Shaw, who had started with him, were admitted to the bar at the same time.[5]

By this date Coolidge was recognized as having distinctive qualities which made him different from other young men in Northampton. His scorn of normal exercise and recreation, his regular habits, his devotion to his law books — these made him seem like one of Benjamin Franklin's industrious apprentices. When he took a vacation, he announced solemnly that he was "going up to Plymouth to shoot woodchucks," and he was back almost before the news of his departure had spread. Tales were whispered around about him. In 1896, Orville Prouty, Selectman of Hadley, climbed to the office of Hammond and Field to inquire whether he, in his legal capacity, could move the body of a man who had been killed while rowing on a near-by lake. Mr. Prouty, finding the two partners out, reluctantly explained his quandary to a slender youth who was reading at a small desk. The stranger, after listening intently, said simply, "Can move body," and returned to his book. Somewhat annoyed at his informant's abnormal reticence, Mr. Prouty said, "Are you sure?" only to receive again the laconic reply, "Yes, can move body." On the way downstairs Prouty met Hammond and inquired, "Who the devil is that tongue-tied blond you've got up there? Doesn't he ever get excited?" Hammond answered, "That young chap isn't much on gab but he's a hog for

[5] Dwight W. Morrow had studied eight months in a law office in Pittsburgh and had then entered Columbia Law School, graduating in June 1899, two years after Coolidge was admitted to the bar. Coolidge and Morrow did not meet for some years after leaving college.

work. If he tells you the body can be moved, you can bet your life it can. He's only been in the office a few months, but I've found out that when he says a thing is so, it is." [6]

In a small community like Northampton incidents of this kind lose nothing in the reporting. Coolidge's reputation for discreet silence — one of the most valuable of his political assets — was established during those early months in Hammond and Field's office. After his admission to the bar Coolidge was uncertain where to hang out his shingle. He considered a possible opening in Great Barrington and even meditated emigrating to Boston. Finally he opened an office of his own, on February 1, 1898, in the Masonic Building on the north side of Main Street. He had two rooms on the second floor, for which he paid a rental of $200 a year. The outer room had but two windows, looking out on Main Street; the inner one had no window, but offered a secluded place, under artificial light, for confidential discussion. He furnished his quarters with some money inherited from his Grandfather Moor and was soon equipped fully as well as most of the young attorneys in the city. His earnings during his first year were slightly over $500. It was not much, but he could live on it; and at last he had the satisfaction of knowing that he was completely self-supporting and need no longer call upon his father for part of his expenses. In 1899, he was appointed counsel for the Nonotuck Savings Bank, of which some years afterwards he became President.[7] His fees for his second year of practice amounted to $1400.

Coolidge did not in those days or later have an extensive trial practice nor did he become in any sense a leader of the bar. His advice was frequently sought, and he wisely urged a settlement out of court whenever that was practicable. Like most young lawyers he accepted some collection business, managed real estate, did mortgage and title work for the bank, and settled estates. In his *Autobiography* he said: —

People began to feel that they could consult me with some safety and without the danger of being involved needlessly in long and costly litigation in court. Very few of my clients ever had to pay a bill of costs. . . . This course did not give me much experience in the trial of cases, so I never became very proficient in that art, but it brought me a satisfactory practice and a fair income.

[6] This now famous story, quoted in Horace Green, *Life of Calvin Coolidge,* pp. 36ff., from Arnold D. Prince, is apparently authentic, at least in substance. It is retold in the *Daily Hampshire Gazette,* September 20, 1920.

[7] Coolidge was elected President of the Nonotuck Savings Bank on November 27, 1918, and retired on August 31, 1921. He remained on the Board of Corporators until his death.

Despite his intermittent excursions into local politics, Coolidge's primary thought was to improve himself in the profession by which he proposed to earn a livelihood. He built up his balance in the bank, and his credit improved each year. It was important, as he saw it, that he should always be at his desk when he was needed; and there he sat day after day, his feet usually on the shelf of his new oak roll-top desk, sometimes reading or making notes, sometimes just looking out the window at the passers-by. If he had any dreams of greatness, he kept them to himself. In his *Autobiography* he wrote, "I fully expected to become the kind of country lawyer I saw around me, spending my life in the profession, with perhaps a final place on the bench."

When Coolidge first arrived in Northampton he lived, according to a well-authenticated report, in the Lyman House at 63 Center Street, in an upstairs room. Soon, however, he engaged an apartment on Round Hill, in the home of Robert N. Weir, steward of the Clarke Institute for the Deaf. Round Hill, a street rising rapidly to the northeast from Elm Street, is a popular residential district, dominated by Clarke Institute. There Coolidge lived until his marriage, a voter in the aristocratic Ward Two, which included Smith College and most of the culture of the city. It was, to make it even more congenial to him, strongly Republican.

As we have seen, Coolidge had learned the language of politics from his office-holding father and had eagerly followed campaigns as a college undergraduate. His first appearance as a practical politician was in the autumn of 1895, when he assisted his "boss," Henry P. Field, then a candidate for Mayor, and handed out ballots at a meeting in Ward Six. Field was elected on December 3 by a comfortable margin, and Coolidge had his earliest experience of being connected with a victorious party. In the following year he was an alternate delegate to a Republican convention at Chester, called to nominate a State Senator.

The national campaign of 1896 was tremendously exciting, especially after the nomination on July 10 of William Jennings Bryan as the Democratic candidate for President on a "Free Silver" platform. To Republicans and even to conservative Democrats he was no "Modern Moses," but rather a demagogue who was rallying all the hosts of radicalism and must be curbed at any cost. In the *Easthampton News* John B. O'Donnell, a Democrat who had been Mayor of Northampton, published an open letter defending Bryan's attitude on the silver question. At Field's instigation, Coolidge undertook a reply, which appeared in the Northampton *Daily Gazette* for August 5, 1896, and is probably his earliest contribution to political controversy. It was prefaced by an editorial note: —

A vigorous discussion of the silver question is the article of J. Calvin Coolidge on the second page of this issue, and even Mayor O'Donnell will be compelled to admit that his young opponent writes in a way which shows that he knows what he is talking about. It's a decidedly able communication, and will well repay careful perusal.

What Coolidge did was to make a survey of O'Donnell's letter paragraph by paragraph, answering each of the latter's points. He began: —

Not being familiar with the money question, I have been for some time seeking information, especially on the free coinage side. In that spirit, and not as an advocate of any doctrine, I read ex-Mayor O'Donnell's letter in the *Easthampton News*. I studied it and was disappointed; it does not seem that the author has done himself justice.

It is unnecessary here to pursue Coolidge's refutation of O'Donnell's rather lame analysis of "Free Silver" doctrine, but his final paragraph shows him to be a plausible controversialist: —

And finally we come to that most specious device of the advocate. All discussion of the merits of free silver is dropped, and we are asked to content ourselves with reading testimony to the character of its prime agitator. His private virtues are so attractive! And what are they? Merely a few conventional decencies which all the funeral orations since the memory of man have claimed as the attributes of each departed spirit. William J. Bryan is accused of financial heresy and we are told that his morals are orthodox. He is censured for an attempt to debauch the monetary system of America and the defense is "a personal character as pure as a woman." He is charged with desiring to pollute the sacred shrine of the public credit, and we are calmly informed that he says his prayers every night.

During that summer while Coolidge was home on a short vacation he pleased his father by supporting the gold standard in a local debate at Plymouth Union. In November McKinley was elected, and Coolidge was vindicated at the ballot box. Soon he became an active worker for the Republican Party. The municipal government of Northampton was composed of seven words, each of which chose an Alderman and three Councilmen; thus the Board of Aldermen consisted of seven and the Common Council of twenty-one. The two boards together made up the City Council, over which the Mayor presided, and these officers were elected annually, in December of each year. The Republican City Committee, responsible for picking the candidates, consisted of thirty-five voters, five from each ward. An aspirant for political office naturally started at the bottom and, if he showed promise, moved on up. Sooner or later Coolidge, with his interest in government, was bound to be drawn into politics; and as a resident of the safely Republican Ward Two, he could secure a footing rather easily. In addition he had the encouragement of Hammond, who was elected District Attorney in the autumn of 1895, and of Field, who was Mayor and in some respects the most influential Republican in the city.

In 1897, Coolidge was placed upon the Republican City Committee for Ward Two and sat among his associates in unassuming fashion, inconspicuous and silent, looking about him and learning. In October 1898, he was a delegate from Ward Two to a Republican convention at South Deerfield, at which John C. Hammond was renominated for District Attorney. On December 7, 1898, he was elected as one of the three Councilmen from Ward Two, receiving 207 votes to 236 for Allen N. Clark and 206 for Harry W. Kidder. The highest of the three contesting Democrats had only 148 votes. At the same time John L. Mather, another Republican, was elected Mayor to succeed Henry P. Field. At the first meeting of the Council for the year, Coolidge was placed on three committees — on Claims, on Military Affairs, and on Rules, Orders, and Ordinances. The position of Councilor paid no salary and was not generally regarded as important, but it did widen Coolidge's acquaintance and experience. Almost his first act was to move a resolution of respect upon the death of an Irish Democratic colleague — a courtesy which won him the friendly regard of the Democratic group on the Council. All his life Coolidge insisted that a vote captured from Democrats really counted as two, and in his Northampton days he never antagonized unnecessarily any members of the opposition party. During his service on the Council the only matter of significance in his record was his effort to have an armory built for the local military company on its return from the Spanish War.

On November 16, 1899, the *Daily Hampshire Gazette* published an item under the heading of "City Politics" : —

Calvin Coolidge has filed with the City Clerk his declination of the Republican nomination for Councilman from Ward Two.

Coolidge had made up his mind to be a candidate for the office of City Solicitor, which paid a salary of $600 and did not involve very heavy responsibilities. "I wanted to be City Solicitor because

I believed it would make me a better lawyer," he said in his *Auto-biography*. Actually the City Solicitor, who was the legal adviser to the City Council, was elected by that body at one of its early meetings; and Coolidge, already known to most of the members, was chosen by a comfortable margin. This success introduces one of the earliest authentic Coolidge anecdotes — the story of the supporter of a defeated candidate who, after the decision of the Council, said to Coolidge, "I don't know now how you won. I didn't vote for you"; to which the new City Solicitor replied drily, "Somebody did!"

The close-mouthed young attorney was rapidly mastering the fine art of personal solicitation of voters. He did not draw cigars from his vest pocket, he did not slap men on the back, he did not buttonhole them unctuously on street corners or in hotel lobbies. He seemed to defy all traditions as to the qualities of popular politicians. Although a few intimate friends hailed him as "Cal," he had no nickname, and no one could have called him a "mixer." And yet he did get along with people, mainly because he had what Kipling had styled the "common touch." Something about him inspired confidence. He never promised more than he could perform or let himself be drawn into an overstatement. He was a polite listener, even to Democrats; and when he spoke, he said something. Perhaps the very strangeness of his tactics was appealing to voters who were weary of the customary pre-election flattery.

Among his friends at this period was James Lucey, an Irishman from County Kerry, who kept a cobbler's shop in a basement room on Gothic Street, a favorite haunt for a group of his Democratic compatriots. Coolidge, who had met him first as a sophomore in Amherst, occasionally dropped in at the shop for a chat and subsequently won the support of the picturesque old gentleman, who advised his cronies to vote for Lawyer Coolidge even though he was a Republican. Newspapermen later found Lucey a colorful source of copy and made the most of his stories. His genius as a philosopher was undoubtedly exaggerated, but he was a self-respecting, loyal, volatile Celt, who exerted some political influence in certain quarters.[8] With persons of this type Calvin Coolidge always got along well, possibly because he understood them.

In 1901 Coolidge was reëlected as City Solicitor and wrote his

[8] The *Literary Digest* for December 10, 1927, had an interview with Lucey headed, "The Shoemaker Who Made Coolidge President," containing some interesting stories of their friendship. Lucey's daughter was a secretary in the office of Judge Henry P. Field, and Coolidge used his influence to secure for her a scholarship at Smith College.

father a letter, dated January 28, a few sentences from which
deserve quotation: —

I was duly reëlected to the office of City Solicitor. There were a couple
of Irishmen after the job. They made me some trouble but they did
not secure votes enough. I have business enough to get a fair living,
but there is no money in the practice of the law. You are fortunate that
you are not still having me to support. If I ever get a woman some one
will have to support her, but I see no need of a wife so long as I have
my health.

In January 1902, Coolidge received his first political setback
when Theobald M. Connor, a Democrat, defeated him for a third
term as City Solicitor. The newspaper account states that all the
Democrats and two Republicans on the City Council voted for
Connor. In presenting his candidate Councilman Stevens spoke
of Coolidge's faithful service to the city and thought him worthy to
be continued in office; but the principle of rotation was too firmly
established to be thus broken.

As City Solicitor, Coolidge undertook law cases for the municipality and once prevailed against Mr. Hammond in what he described as "an unimportant case in the Supreme Court." It was a
period when he was also widening his private practice, but his fees
were not large and he was making only a modest living. We have
few letters of this period, but one sent to his grandmother at Christmas time is characteristically whimsical in tone: —

I am sending you a little box which was made from sumach wood
by a man over ninety years old I believe. It is not good for anything
but will come in handy for you to put away and forget about it.

I wish you a very happy Christmas. The first Christmas I can remember I spent at your house and besides the Leslie family and Steve
there was also goose to eat. We had a Christmas tree at night, and I
got a fine sled with a red top, and green runners striped with white.
It was a mighty handsome thing but not very strong and when I left it
in the walk at night where father fell over it he used to break it, but
Hen Willis could mend it with iron and glue.

I have looked at the Law some but do not yet find that you can get
a pension, so do not make any arrangements at present to spend the
money.

The *Gazette* for June 4, 1903, carried half a column under the
heading, "Clerk Calvin Coolidge. Able and Popular Lawyer Appointed Clerk of Courts *pro tem.*" William H. Clapp, for many years
Clerk of the Courts for Hampshire County, had recently died, leav-

ing vacant a position which paid a salary of $2300 and was regarded as one of the coveted political "plums" in Western Massachusetts. Coolidge was appointed by Judge Maynard to fill the vacancy, but kept his head and announced on June 6 that he did not intend to run for the office in November.[9] On July 28 he wrote his father in part as follows: —

I should think you better get a hired girl if my Mother don't want one. It is better than doctors. I don't know when I can get away. I suppose I might go one time as well as another, — my salary goes on.

I am not a candidate for Clerk of the Courts. I could not practice and I had rather stay at the bar. There is more money at the bar for a man really fit for Clerk. I could have the nomination with no opposition if I had wished but I shall stay at the bar. My successor will probably take office after the Nov. election about Jan. 1, 1904.

I have happened to have good luck with all the cases I have been in for the last year, but I do not try many cases. Three in the District Court, two in the Probate Court, four in the Superior Court, one before Auditor and one in Supreme Court and all decided in my favor. Probably next year it will be all the other way, the law is uncertain, one or two of counsel on the other side have found that out.

During his short incumbency Coolidge learned much about the Superior and Supreme Judicial Courts, but he was glad enough on January 1, 1904, to return to a profession which, as he said, "might be more precarious, but also had more possibilities." He was being attracted more and more by a political career and did not intend to let himself be entombed in a sinecure position. He was willing to wait until the right psychological moment and meanwhile work faithfully for the party.

Coolidge's Republicanism, as we have seen, was inherited and traditional and he was never tempted to become a mugwump. He always believed that effectiveness in government is dependent on the responsibility of one party or another for legislation. It must be emphasized also that he did not wait for the office to seek the man. When an opening was presented of which he wished to take advantage, he had no hesitation about publicizing his qualifications. Judge Field pointed out that Coolidge in those early days preferred to run his own campaigns and usually did it very efficiently. There was no sentimental nonsense about him in his political relation-

[9] Daniel Webster in 1805 had to make precisely the same decision when, as a struggling law apprentice in the office of Christopher Gore, in Boston, he was offered a position as Clerk of the Court of Common Pleas for Hillsborough County, New Hampshire, at a salary of at least $1500 a year from fees. Webster declined the offer and moved on to prosperity and fame.

ships. If he desired an office, he indulged in no coy gestures or
false humility, but made his wishes evident.

When he retired as Clerk of Courts, Coolidge was promptly
chosen Chairman of the Republican City Committee and found himself much occupied in a Presidential year. The Roosevelt ticket
swept the country against the feeble candidacy of the Democratic
Alton B. Parker; but locally the Republican candidate for Mayor,
running for the fourth time, was defeated by eighty votes. In
commenting on the result Coolidge said later: —

We made the mistake of talking too much about the deficiencies of
our opponents and not enough about the merits of our own candidates.
I have never again fallen into that error.

Calvin Coolidge was now regarded as a rising young man and
an eligible bachelor. In the winter of 1904–1905 he was still rooming in the same house with Mr. Weir on Round Hill and taking most
of his meals at Rahar's Inn. Weir, who has been described as
"something of a character around town," was a genial, loquacious,
light-hearted man with irrepressible social instincts, well acquainted
with the Clarke School faculty, and did not fail to meet Miss Grace
Goodhue,[10] who came to Northampton in the autumn of 1903 to
take a training course which would enable her to teach the deaf.
Weir introduced Miss Goodhue to Coolidge, and his interest in her
was soon aroused. She was the only young lady who had ever attracted his attention.

The comments in Northampton when the supposed misogynist,
Lawyer Coolidge, appeared at public functions with the animated
and charming Miss Goodhue were amusing, and she was the victim
of considerable banter from her friends. Calvin's first gift to her,
and the earliest indication that he was a possible suitor, was a
porcelain plaque of Mount Tom, which he purchased on a trip
with her to its summit. He had taken dancing lessons while he
was in Amherst, but Miss Goodhue would not waltz with him, telling
him that if he danced as badly as he skated, the experience would
not be a pleasant one. He was not a romantic wooer, and Miss

[10] Grace Anna Goodhue was born in Burlington, Vermont, the daughter of
Andrew I. Goodhue and his wife, Elmira. Andrew Goodhue was a mechanic who
became a steamboat inspector on Lake Champlain. Miss Goodhue graduated from
Burlington High School in 1897 and entered the University of Vermont, where she
displayed marked theatrical talent, also singing in the Glee Club and winning election to Phi Beta Kappa. Through Miss Caroline Yale, Principal of the Clarke
School and a family friend of the Goodhues, she was offered a position in Northampton. She was vivacious, witty, gregarious, fond of a good time, and in most
respects the temperamental opposite of Calvin Coolidge.

Goodhue, who was popular in other quarters also, was in little danger of being swept from her feet by his impetuosity. During the celebration by Northampton in 1904 of its 250th anniversary, she attended with him a reception given by the Daughters of the American Revolution in the City Hall and they sat down in some vacant chairs, only to be ousted by an usher who explained that those particular seats were reserved for Governor and Mrs. Bates. Fourteen years later, when his election as Governor was announced as certain, he turned to his wife and said, "Well, Grace, even the Daughters of the American Revolution can't put us out of the Governor's chairs now."

Numerous anecdotes about the courtship have appeared in the papers, many of them manufactured but a few of them authentic. According to one legend, Lucey, the shoemaker, gave the young lawyer some excellent practical advice on how to plead his cause.[11] The intimacy must have been developing, for early in the summer of 1905 Miss Goodhue was invited to Plymouth, where Calvin's grandmother, "Aunt Mede," said to him, "That's a likely gal. Why don't you marry her?" "Mebbe I will, Grandma," was the only reply. A few days later, when Grace Goodhue had gone to Burlington on her vacation, Lawyer Coolidge took a few days off and appeared unexpectedly at the Goodhue home. Several versions of what followed have been printed, the most plausible maintaining that, when Mr. Goodhue entered his living room and found Coolidge there reading a magazine, he said, "Hello, Calvin, what are you doing in Burlington? Got some business here?" "No," was the reply. "Came up to marry Grace." "Why, have you spoken to her yet?" "No, I can wait a few days if it's any convenience to you."

Somehow things did get settled, and an understanding was reached. Miss Goodhue then asked Calvin to accompany her on a drive of eight miles to the home of a college friend. He appeared dressed with scrupulous care in a new and well-tailored blue serge suit, a derby hat, and patent-leather shoes with very wide silk shoelaces, and at the last moment placed a whisk broom in the back of the carriage. When they arrived, Coolidge drove the horse into the back yard and hitched him carefully to a ring in the corner of the barn. Then he took out the whisk broom and brushed the dust and horsehairs from his clothing and went very deliberately inside to be introduced. The conversation went along in halting fashion, Coolidge contributing nothing until he could bear the ordeal no longer and, arising, said with a smile, "We'll be going now." As

[11] Green, 60–61.

he disappeared to get the horse, Miss Goodhue's friend said, "My land, Grace, I'd be afraid of him!" As they drove homeward, Miss Goodhue protested, "Now, why did you act like that? She thinks that you are a perfect stick and said she'd be afraid of you." His only reply was, "She'll find I'm human."

Mrs. Goodhue wished her daughter to resign from teaching and come home for a year before she was married, but Coolidge took the position that he was able to support a wife and there was no reason for postponement. He had his way, and the ceremony was set for October 4, 1905. Coolidge went to Burlington on the previous afternoon with his best man, Dr. A. H. McCormick. The wedding itself was a quiet house affair, with only about fifteen people present, including Colonel and Mrs. John C. Coolidge and Calvin's aunt, Mrs. Pollard, with her husband. The officiating clergyman was the Reverend Edward Hungerford. The day was rainy, and someone remarked on the bad omen. Calvin replied, "I don't mind the weather if I get the girl."

The couple spent their honeymoon in Montreal, intending to be gone a fortnight. But when the first week was up they had seen all the sights and gone to all the theatres they could find, and Coolidge said one morning, "Guess we'd better be going back." He made the excuse that he wished to show off his bride, but Mrs. Coolidge knew very well that he was restless over an impending election for School Committeeman and eager to be back in the fray. For three weeks they lived at the Norwood, then Northampton's leading hotel, only a short distance from his office. Then they rented for the winter a small dwelling from a professor in Smith College and started housekeeping with one maid in the simple fashion to which both of them had been accustomed. The Norwood was about to close up, and Mrs. Coolidge purchased a large part of her domestic supplies from its stock. For years her sheets and pillow-cases, her table linen and plated silver, bore the mark, "Norwood Hotel."

Mrs. Coolidge has described gleefully one of her first lessons in domesticity. One afternoon she saw her husband coming home from his office carrying an odd-looking and ancient russet-colored bag. When opened, it was full of men's socks, fifty-two pairs in all, every one in need of mending. Later she asked him if he had married her to get his stockings darned, and he answered, "No, but I find it mighty handy."

By a strange irony Coolidge's marriage was followed by the only defeat at the polls that he ever experienced. He had been duly nominated for School Committeeman, an office with no pay but which would keep him in the public eye for possible further advancement. Another Republican, S. D. Drury, also took out nomination papers, to Coolidge's disgust, with the result that, on December 5, John J. Kennedy, the Democratic candidate, was elected by 934 votes to 840 for Coolidge and 762 for Drury. During the campaign Kennedy met him on the street and said jokingly, "Calvin, I think I've got you beaten." "Well," he answered, "either way they'll have a good man." Some weeks afterward, Coolidge was told by a Republican neighbor that he had voted for Kennedy, giving as a reason his conviction that members of the School Committee should have children in the public schools. Coolidge's only response was, "Might give me time!"

In August 1906, the Coolidges rented one half of a double house at 21 Massasoit Street, for which they paid $27 a month and which was to be their home even while they were temporarily residents of Washington. In his *Autobiography* Coolidge wrote, "We like the house where our children came to us and the neighbors who were so kind. When we could have had a more pretentious home we still clung to it." The other half was occupied for several years by Miss Imogene Prindle and her mother and later, after 1918, by Dr. F. W. Plummer, Principal of the Northampton High School. On the first floor were a front hall, a parlor, — with three bay windows, — a dining room, a kitchen and pantry, and a corridor leading to the cellar stairs. On the second floor, besides the large central hall, were three bedrooms and a bathroom, with stairs up to an attic chamber. Massasoit Street, running east from Elm Street for about one third of a mile to Prospect Street, is lined with maples which in summer afford abundant shade and mitigate the plainness of the dwellings, the architecture of which, although diversified, is certainly not distinguished. The Coolidges lived in the seventh house on the right from Elm Street — a house which is little different from thousands of middle-class homes across the continent. As neighbors they had some of the men and women who made up the substantial citizenry of the city, — the postmaster, a clergyman or two, a small manufacturer, a florist, some teachers, — all of them living on modest incomes. The Coolidges also kept within their means and had only moderate desires. Of this period Coolidge wrote in later days: —

Of course my expenses increased, and I had to plan very carefully for a time to live within my income. I know very well what it means to awake in the night and realize that the rent is coming due, wondering where the money is coming from with which to pay it. The only way I know of to escape from that constant tragedy is to keep running expenses low enough so that something may be saved to meet the day when earnings may be small.

The Coolidges did manage very economically. Their telephone was a party line. They owned no automobile or other vehicle until Coolidge became Vice President and did very little traveling or entertaining. Coolidge stoked his own furnace, like every other male householder on the street. There was always a maidservant in the house. Mrs. Reckahn, who came about 1916, was called a housekeeper, but she did virtually everything — cooking, making beds, sweeping, and washing clothes. They seldom went out to the theatre or to concerts, and although Mrs. Coolidge enjoyed card games, he did not play them. In Northampton it was said, "Grace Coolidge always made the best of things," but there were moments when her burden must have seemed far from light. It took her some time, as she confesses, to get acquainted with her husband's peculiarities. Early in her married life, having learned indirectly that Mr. Coolidge was to speak that evening at some church gathering, she appeared at the door with her hat and coat on prepared to accompany him. "Where you going?" he asked. "I just thought I'd go out and hear you talk." "Better not," was the comment. And she didn't!

Mrs. Coolidge likes to tell the story of her first attempt at producing an apple pie "such as mother used to make." The pie was tough, and neither one of them could make an impression on it at dinner. Later in the evening, when two of Mrs. Coolidge's Clarke School friends dropped in, Mr. Coolidge insisted that they should have some pie, and somehow they managed to eat it to the last morsel. Then Coolidge said, quite seriously, "Don't you think the Road Commissioner would be willing to pay my wife something for her recipe for piecrust?"

The best-known anecdote of this period, however, is that of the time when Mrs. Coolidge, as a bride, was inveigled by a book salesman into paying eight dollars for *Our Family Physician,* a volume of medical information. It cost more money than she could afford, and therefore she said nothing to her husband about the matter, but merely left the volume on the parlor table. One day she glanced inside and found on the flyleaf, in a handwriting which she knew well, these words, "This work suggests no cure for a sucker." There was no signature.

Judge Field, a pewholder in the famous Edwards Congregational Church past which Coolidge walked nearly every day of his life, had invited him to occupy his pew; and Mrs. Coolidge, after her marriage, transferred her membership to it. Although Coolidge was not then a church member, he attended Sunday services with fair regularity and was especially active in the Edwards Church Men's Club. He was not regarded as notably devout, but he had a respect for the church and its function in any well-organized social system. He was not a "joiner" and when urged by friends to become a Mason or an Odd Fellow or a Red Man, he quietly declined. "Dick" Irwin, who was watching Coolidge's political progress, was often in despair because his protégé would not play the game in the orthodox fashion. What happened was that Coolidge accumulated no fraternal obligations and therefore all the lodges were for him. He had the good sense not to identify himself with one to the exclusion of others.

Mrs. Coolidge soon had enough to keep her occupied at home, for their elder child, John, was born on September 7, 1906. Three days later Coolidge wrote to his stepmother, who was then on a visit to Michigan: —

Can't you come back here from Albany and see your grandson? He came Sept. 7th just as the clocks were striking six. Grace had little pains all day, but not very severe until four o'clock. She went to bed about five. She had a very easy time of it. The boy is real white and was born hungry. His hair is dark, but his eyes are blue and his mouth is like mine they say. His name is John, and he has Coolidge hands. I told Grace I should call a girl Carrie because you had no little girl.

Grace and John send love to Grandma.

And so Calvin Coolidge became a family man and could be regarded as having settled down. Neither he nor Mrs. Coolidge was disturbed because she sometimes had to do the washing and cooking and take care of the baby. From their viewpoint these were functions which a wife should gladly perform, as part of her recognized duties, just as a husband should be the "provider." And they were very happy. In his *Autobiography* Calvin Coolidge wrote of their marriage, "We thought we were made for each other. For almost a quarter of a century she has borne with my infirmities, and I have rejoiced in her graces."

Ten years had now passed since Calvin Coolidge had settled in Northampton. In that decade he had established a reputation for probity, industry, thrift, and reticence, for being "on the job every day and all day." William Allen White has expressed it well by saying, "His master passion seemed to be to do the day's work so well that he might do to-morrow's work better." He was regarded as a serious-minded young fellow, sensible rather than brilliant, and yet just a trifle queer — according to Judge Field, "an inscrutable little devil." He had been successively City Councilman, City Solicitor, Clerk of Courts, and Chairman of the Republican City Committee. Although not rated by his acquaintances as magnetic or eloquent, he had managed to come out well on election day. He had formed the habit of calling on his constituents in their homes and saying simply, "I want your vote. I need it. I shall appreciate it." He had loyal supporters among persons with some political influence : Cobbler Lucey, in his basement shop on Gothic Street; "Phil" Gleason, the blacksmith, who had converted several Irish Democrats to his cause; Johnny Dewey, the tavern keeper; Ed Lynch, the brickmason; Jim Maloney, the baker; Cliff Lyman, from Bridgman's bookshop; and numerous small tradesmen and clerks and schoolteachers, the men and women to whom he nodded as he walked to his office each morning. He often gathered with other aspiring young politicians and some veterans in the drugstore of Clark and Parsons to talk over the situation. In Northampton in 1905 Calvin Coolidge was known as a shrewd politician, a good vote-getter, a chap who might possibly become Mayor or even go to Congress — a good man to watch.

VI

The Horizon Widens

DURING the winter and spring following his defeat for the School Committee Coolidge was inactive politically, but devoted himself to the law and fell readily into the familiar routine. The local party managers had their eyes on him, however, and would not permit such a seductive vote-getter to stay in private life. On September 15, 1906, the *Daily Hampshire Gazette* published an item under the heading "Calvin Coolidge Willing but Not Anxious": —

But seven days remain in which candidates for the Republican nomination for representative can file their petitions with Chairman Louis Warner of the city committee, and he is beginning to get anxious, as they are not forthcoming. Calvin Coolidge has shed the most light on the situation by saying that he would consider the nomination. He says he should like to go to the legislature sometime. At present, he thinks, because of business conditions, he would prefer to wait, but adds that probably there always will be something of that kind, so that perhaps now would be as favorable for him as any time. He says he does not care enough about it to fight for the nomination, and that if some prominent party men such as ex-mayors Hallett or Mather want the nomination he would gladly stay out and put his shoulder to the wheel. And even then, if he doesn't have to fight for the nomination, he adds that he cannot now say whether he would accept. "If the party wants me, however, I will consider the matter," says Mr. Coolidge. If he don't get some candidate soon Chairman Warner says he will begin to do some real deep thinking.

This fairly obvious "feeler" having met with a satisfactory response, the *Gazette* announced three days later that Lawyer Coolidge would be the Republican candidate for Representative. Papers were at once circulated for securing the necessary thirty-five signatures to a petition asking that his name be placed on a ballot to be cast at the party caucus; and there being no opposition, he was duly nominated on September 25. Moses Bassett, a Democrat, was seeking reëlection, but was regarded as a vulnerable adversary, and Coolidge had convinced himself, or had allowed himself to be convinced, that it was the right psychological moment for venturing another step up the political ladder.

The lower branch of the Massachusetts General Court — as the bicameral legislative body is called under the Constitution — is not usually composed of great orators or even of professional politicians. Often a popular doctor or farmer or real-estate agent will be accorded a term in the House by his district in recognition of his prestige among his neighbors. It consisted in 1907 of a membership of 240, of whom four were allotted to Hampshire County. The salary was only $750 a year, with mileage, — certainly not enough to tempt anyone by its financial reward, — but the legislature sat only from January to June, and even when it was in session, a representative could escape for week-ends at home. Most important of all, a member of the General Court could make the acquaintance and, if he was fortunate, enjoy the friendship of those party leaders whose influence was paramount in the Commonwealth. An apprenticeship in the General Court is almost essential for a fledgling statesman seeking advancement in Massachusetts.

Coolidge proved himself to be a vigorous campaigner. The *Gazette* printed on September 26 a column on him and his record, with his photograph and one interesting but hardly accurate sentence, "Mr. Coolidge has acquired considerable real estate since he came to Northampton and is now one of the large taxpayers." He asked Mr. Field to prepare a brief biography of him to be mailed to every Northampton voter. On October 26 he presided at a Republican rally in the City Hall, introducing Curtis Guild, Jr., the Republican nominee for Governor, Frederick H. Gillett, the Congressional candidate, and other office seekers. He began, "The frost may be on the pumpkin but it does not seem to be in City Hall," and continued in a most felicitous address, the first campaign speech of any significance in his career. During the final weeks he carried on an intensive house-to-house canvass, directed especially at the Irish Democrats, and it was said of him that he talked personally with every voter in the city. Coolidge in his *Autobiography* maintained that he attracted a considerable number of Democratic voters, many of whom never thereafter deserted him. To the astonishment of some of the corner-drugstore prophets, he received on November 7 a vote of 1329 as against Bassett's 1065, a majority of 264 and a large Republican gain over the previous year. The friendly *Gazette* in commenting on these figures said : —

Until about a week ago it was thought Bassett would be reëlected, but the work put in by Coolidge's friends turned the tide. The defeat of Bassett, however, is believed to be due to the work of the friends of Michael J. McCarthy, who was one of the candidates last year for Representative, and was badly cut by the friends of Bassett. . . . For some reason not fully explained many of the members of the labor organizations are said to have voted for Coolidge. The vote of the railroad men which was claimed for Bassett did not materialize apparently.

Before setting out for Boston in January, Coolidge obtained from "Dick" Irwin, who had been a Senator and was well known on Beacon Hill, a letter of introduction to John N. Cole,[1] of Andover, Speaker of the House of Representatives. Although it has often been reproduced, this note will bear reprinting as good contemporary evidence not only of current local opinion regarding Coolidge but also of the latter's astuteness in finding influential sponsors : —

DEAR JOHN, —

This will introduce to you the new member-elect from my town, Calvin Coolidge. Like the singed cat, he is better than he looks. He wishes to talk with you about committees. Anything you can do for him will be appreciated.

Sincerely yours,
DICK

When the hour of departure came, Coolidge was accompanied to Boston by Henry P. Field, a man well versed in political procedure, who escorted him to the headquarters of the Republican State Committee and introduced him to the inner circle. Later one of these leaders remarked to Field, "I shook hands with your friend and he gave me a cold"; and another in brief comment asked, "What in hell can a chap like that do down here?" Most of the members of the General Court from Western Massachusetts lived during the session in the Adams House, a famous hostelry on Washington Street.

[1] John Newmarch Cole (1863–1922), of Andover, one of the ablest men in the Commonwealth, gained recognition first through the *Andover Townsman*, of which he was both owner and editor. In 1906, 1907, and 1908 he was Speaker of the House and seemed likely to go much higher; but enemies blocked his nomination for Lieutenant Governor, and he returned to private life until Governor McCall in 1916 appointed him to the Commission on Waterways and Public Lands; and Governor Coolidge in 1919 made him Commissioner of Public Works. Cole was a first-rate presiding officer. I have seen him on the floor of the Andover Town Meeting untangle a parliamentary snarl so that even his bitterest opponents — and he had many — were moved to grudging admiration. He was a resolute, blunt, courageous, and dominating figure, a tireless worker, and a dangerous foe. He was of valued assistance to Coolidge while the latter was in the State House.

Coolidge engaged a "dollar bedroom," with no bath and only a washbowl of hot and cold running water, on the third floor, its only daylight coming from a half-sized window facing on an inner court. It was uncomfortable and badly furnished, but it was the best that Coolidge thought he could afford; furthermore he was neither accustomed to luxury nor sensitive to aesthetic deficiencies. In the evenings when he was alone, — and he was seldom invited elsewhere in those days, — he sat by himself in the central dining room at the table by the looking glass, third from the corner. Occasionally he would pause for a short chat with Frank Hall, the proprietor, in the hotel office. After dinner before going to sleep he would read under the sickly gas jet in his room — sometimes the *Manual for the General Court,* occasionally a history of the United States, and always the *Evening Transcript.*

The proprietor of the Adams House had made available to the Western Massachusetts Club a large room on the second story of the Mason Street addition, which was used by the members for playing cards, reading, and talking. Here many of the legislators would discuss affairs of the day and Coolidge, although usually silent, would occasionally interject a dry remark which attracted attention. Now and then they would adjourn to the Mason Street café for sandwiches and beer. Coolidge, although he was not a teetotaler, would usually say, "Bring me a pot of green tea." When the western members held their organization meeting on January 10, Commissioner John H. Manning, of Pittsfield, was made Permanent President and Representative Coolidge was elected Secretary. Several dinners were held during the winter, and Coolidge learned to know well his colleagues from his own section.

Coolidge soon became a familiar figure on the Boston and Maine train leaving the capital from the North Station at 4.09 on Friday or Saturday afternoon and arriving in Northampton at 7.25. There were no Pullmans, and he ordinarily chose a smoking car. Even when the car was almost empty, he preferred to sit down with some fellow traveler, but his conversation was unreliable in amount. He customarily boarded the 7.40 back to Boston on Monday morning, reaching the North Station at 10.50. Most of his Sundays were thus spent at home.

In Boston he led an unexciting existence, devoted principally to legislative business. He actually studied bills, attended dull committee meetings and hearings, seldom left the floor during sessions, and was nearly always recorded as voting. He was an obscure member of the House; his name rarely appeared in the Boston newspapers except on a roll call; but he soon acquired a reputation for faithfulness and reliability. In the morning he walked briskly and unobtrusively across the Common to the State House; he had luncheon frequently at the Bellevue Hotel, for he had no idea of joining a club; he merely did the day's work systematically and thoroughly. He did not care for the theatre or enjoy symphony concerts, and he must have had some lonesome evenings. But after all it was what had happened at college. He was a slow starter and was quite willing to wait. And he did have some acquaintances to keep him company. His habits, meanwhile, were impeccable, and his wildest dissipation was a glass of very much diluted whiskey — very rarely a glass of light beer.[2]

On January 7 the General Court convened, and Calvin Coolidge took his oath of office in the Bulfinch State House with which he was to be so intimately associated. He was assigned seat 59, in the fourth row at the Speaker's left, between Lorenzo D. Baker, Jr., of Barnstable, and Clesson Kenney, of Worcester. Among his associates were several gentlemen who were later to become conspicuous in Massachusetts affairs: Elias B. Bishop, of Middlesex, Grafton D. Cushing, of Suffolk, William F. Garcelon, of Newton, Eugene C. Hultman, of Quincy, Robert Luce, of Middlesex, Edwin T. McKnight, of Suffolk, Malcolm E. Nichols, of Suffolk, and Joseph Walker, of Brookline. It was Martin W. Lomasney, of Suffolk, one of the most picturesque and powerful of the Democratic group, who said to his neighbor, after looking Coolidge over, "Either a schoolteacher or an undertaker." Charles V. Blanchard, of West Somerville, became one of his closest friends and is rumored to have taught Coolidge how to garb himself appropriately for various occasions. Robert M. Washburn, who became his first biographer, was not a member of the House until 1908.

Even after reading Irwin's letter of introduction, Speaker Cole was not sufficiently impressed to give the newcomer any important appointments, but did place him on the Committee for Mercantile Affairs and later on that on Constitutional Amendments. On the first day of the session Coolidge proposed a bill to limit the speed of automobiles, providing that no automobile or motorcycle should

---

[2] Attorney Hugh P. Drysdale, of North Adams, recalls one occasion when Coolidge drank rye whiskey. At a dinner in the Algonquin Club, the waiters were English, and one of them leaned over Coolidge's shoulder and asked, "What will you have for a liqueur, sir?" Coolidge looked up and said, "Huh?" and the flunkey repeated the question. Coolidge then turned to Drysdale and asked, "What is he saying, Hugh?" Drysdale explained, and Coolidge said to the waiter, "Bring me a little rye." "I confess," writes Drysdale, "that this was a new cordial to me, and I didn't notice whether he poured water in it or drank it straight."

THE LEGISLATOR

be licensed until the licensing authorities had satisfied themselves that it did not "have a speed capacity of more than twenty miles an hour when running over a level macadam highway." What was the motive behind this measure I cannot discover, but it does indicate a conservative tendency. The bill was strongly opposed by Colonel Charles L. Young, of Springfield, and on February 28, the Committee on Roads and Bridges "voted to report leave to withdraw on the petition." Coolidge's first effort at legislation was unsuccessful.

During Coolidge's first term in the House he spoke only once on the floor and then in connection with a bill introduced by him to prevent unfair discrimination in the theatrical business. In his speech Coolidge declared that the theatrical syndicates in New York City prevented the production of the best plays at "one-night stands" unless the local managers entered into an agreement to take no other attraction without permission of the syndicates. He stated that in 1906, when Madame Bernhardt appeared at the Academy of Music in Northampton, a syndicate canceled all the other bookings. In the course of the debate Mr. Vittum, of Beverly, asked, "Is it not true that the trouble at Northampton was because an old fuddy-dud of a trustee wouldn't allow the performance of leg shows?" Coolidge replied that he assumed the gentleman referred to was President Seelye, of Smith College, who had under his care young ladies from all parts of the country and not unnaturally had a regard for the character of the performances they might attend. The bill was eventually referred to the next General Court.

But Coolidge did play a large part in drafting a measure to prevent discriminatory price-fixing by corporations. Petitions providing for unrestricted competition in the manufacture and scale of articles in common use had been presented to the Committee on Mercantile Affairs, and Coolidge was instructed to draw up a bill combining the wishes of all the petitioners. The result was a measure of great length and detail, which was ultimately lost in the Senate. During the session Coolidge voted for the direct election of United States Senators and for woman suffrage — in both cases on the losing side. In those days he would have been classified as a liberal rather than a conservative. On the other hand, the most important new friend that he made that winter was Senator Winthrop Murray Crane,[3]

[3] Winthrop Murray Crane (1853–1920), born in Dalton, Berkshire County, Massachusetts, attended Wilbraham Academy and Williston Seminary, and then, entering the family business of paper manufacturing, built up a large fortune. He was a delegate-at-large to six political conventions; was Lieutenant-Governor (1897–1899) and Governor (1900–1902), and succeeded George F. Hoar as United

of Dalton, who was certainly no revolutionary. Crane and Coolidge were much alike in their reticence and caution, and the younger man came to have the same views on most questions as his older adviser. Of him Coolidge wrote, "I did not come into personal relation with him until I had entered public life in Boston. The more I saw of him the more I came to admire him." Again and again in Calvin Coolidge's career we shall find him guided and guarded by the sagacious counsel of Murray Crane.

During this session Coolidge was a silent member; but he became well acquainted with the Hall of Representatives — its white mahogany paneling, its stately Corinthian pillars supporting the gallery, its famous codfish cut from pine and hanging opposite the Speaker's desk, its frieze on which were carved the names of fifty-three sons of Massachusetts, including the Adamses, Webster, Everett, Choate, and many others distinguished in their respective fields. The room was not an ancient one, — it had been occupied first in 1895, — but the State House in its original form with its red brick Bulfinch front and shining golden dome erected in the late eighteenth century had great traditions, and Calvin Coolidge had a profound respect for its past. Before twenty years had gone by his own portrait was to adorn the State House walls,[4] and he was to be named among the notable figures in the Commonwealth.

When the General Court prorogued on June 29, Coolidge returned to Northampton to resume his somewhat disrupted law practice. But he also found himself faced with the problem of winning a reëlection. His Democratic opponent was Alfred J. Preece, an Alderman of the city, who was not considered by the Republicans to be dangerous. On October 19, the Republicans held a reception at the new Draper Hotel for Guild and Draper, the party standard-bearers; and Coolidge presided later in the evening over a large gathering in the City Hall. He had been accused of being unfriendly to the workingman, and in his speech he answered the charge without evasion, summarizing the measures passed by the General Court appropriating money for the direct benefit of working people and providing for the protection of health and life, all of them being bills which had his support. In commenting on this record he said: —

States Senator, serving from 1904 until 1913, when at his own wish he retired from office. Crane was a "boss" in the Republican Party, and his influence on Massachusetts politics, though often concealed, was decisive. President Coolidge wrote on August 4, 1925, a foreword to a biography of Crane by Solomon Bulkley Griffin.
    [4] A life-sized portrait of Coolidge by Edmund C. Tarbell, in the south gallery of the Senate Chamber, was unveiled on May 20, 1926.

If there are any body of our citizens who ought to feel satisfied with my efforts in their behalf, it is our working people. I have no doubt they are. I have never heard a word of complaint from a union man. It has all come from someone who desires to ride into office through their dissatisfaction. I have no doubt the workingmen of Northampton are too well informed to be caught by misrepresentation.

The *Gazette* expressed the opinion that Coolidge would be elected by a safe majority — "as he deserves to be." At the polls on November 6, however, he had a narrow escape, securing a majority of only 63 over Preece. Guild was reëlected as Governor and Treadway as State Senator. Treadway and Coolidge often spoke during this campaign from the same platform and became close friends. When both had been elected, Treadway, the proprietor of the Red Lion Inn at Stockbridge, gave an elaborate dinner. But Coolidge ate nothing, apparently not tempted by the rare and delicious dishes. Treadway inquired, "Calvin, aren't you feeling well?" "Yes, I'm all right." "But isn't there anything on the menu I can have brought to you?" "Well, if you insist, I'd like some dry toast and a cup of weak tea."

During the summer of 1907, before the autumn campaign, Coolidge took his family to Plymouth for a vacation — his first real relaxation since his marriage. On September 19, after his return to Northampton, he wrote his father: —

John creeps up on his knees now and goes up stairs and runs all over the house.

I hope mother is steadily gaining. We are thinking what a nice time we had at home and are coming again next summer, — with another baby.

Just before election time John N. Cole had paid a visit to Northampton and had spent the night at 21 Massasoit Street. The Speaker now knew the quality of the Representative from Northampton and appointed him early in 1908 on two excellent committees — the Judiciary and Banks and Banking. As a member of the Judiciary Committee he was offered the opportunity of drafting and taking charge of a so-called Anti-Monopoly Bill. His speeches in its favor attracted attention in the press, and when the measure became law, he was assigned some of the credit for it. He fought hard for a bill to reimburse cities and towns for the cost of transportation of state paupers to the hospital at Tewksbury, — a measure obviously favorable to the section west of the Connecticut, — and brought it safely through legislative complications. He helped to defeat a bill abolishing sittings of the Supreme Court in the counties of Hampshire, Franklin, and Berkshire. Possibly his best speech during the session was made in support of a bill modifying the law regarding injunctions so that an injunction could not be issued in a labor dispute to prevent one employer's seeking by fair means to induce a workman to leave his job. The *Northampton Daily Herald* said in connection with these and other bills which Coolidge had supported: —

Mr. Coolidge is entitled to the thanks of the wage laborers of his district for his manly defense of their interests.

During this session a Representative made a very long and wearisome speech, in the course of which he began many successive paragraphs with "Mr. Speaker, it is . . ." After he had sat down, Coolidge drew himself out of his chair and said, "Mr. Speaker, it is not!" Everybody laughed, and the measure was killed.

No hostile comment was aroused by his vote, on April 23, to raise the salaries of legislators in the General Court.

Edward E. Whiting, in his book *President Coolidge,* presents an interesting summary of the labor measures for which Coolidge voted during his two terms in the Lower House — bills to place surgical equipment in all factories, to make obligatory one day's rest in seven, to increase the number of playgrounds for children, to provide special low railway fares for workingmen and half fares for their children, and to prevent cheating in the sale of small lots of coal. In the years 1907 and 1908 the espousal of such elementary measures for the laboring man's safety, health, and comfort was regarded as indicating a progressive trend; and it is clear from all the available evidence that he regarded himself in those days as a liberal thinker. Although later events focused attention on his conservatism, he was never a "standpatter," and the desirability of orderly and cumulative advancement towards improved economic and social conditions was always part of his political philosophy. From experience he gradually became more and more suspicious of radical thinkers who wished to overturn the foundations of our civilization in order to put their reforms into operation. He never believed in burning down the barn in order to get rid of the rats. But like W. Murray Crane, his mentor, he was a man of sympathy and vision.

When the General Court broke up on June 13, Coolidge's legislative experience was interrupted for several years. It was not customary for a Representative to seek more than two terms; and although he could probably have been renominated, he did not offer himself as a candidate in the autumn of 1908, but watched the Presidential campaign as a citizen no longer active in the field of politics. He did, however, allow himself to be appointed as Republican Chairman in Ward Two. His experience on Beacon Hill had made him a better lawyer, had enlarged his acquaintance and added to his reputation. Well aware that it is a mistake to press fortune too hard, he was content to bide his time. He did, at a political rally in November, defend himself against the charge that he had tried to bribe a man named Arthur J. Lamontagne to vote the Republican ticket by telling him that if he could induce the French voters to support Mayor Clapp, Lamontagne might expect to be appointed as a member of the Board of License Commissioners. Coolidge declared that the allegation was false, the product of a slanderous mind. As a matter of fact, he had been asked to be a candidate for Mayor, but according to the *Gazette* had announced that he could not afford to give more time to public service.

Meanwhile his family had been enlarged. In April, he missed two meetings of the Judiciary Committee and when he finally did appear on a Wednesday, his colleagues slily intimated that he had been on a "bender." "No," he replied, "I just had a boy born." "Why in hell didn't you tell us?" said one of his friends. "Didn't think you'd be interested," was the answer. This son, Calvin Coolidge, Jr., was born on Monday, April 13, 1908. More money was required for the expenses of the Coolidge home, and the head of the household was glad to return to his law office and build up his practice.

For the following winter and spring he was very busy. On February 10, 1909, he appeared before the Committee on Judiciary at the State House as counsel for Thomas L. Hisgen, to argue in favor of a bill to prohibit discrimination in commercial dealings. What Coolidge did was to attack the practice of large corporations in underselling small competitors. He insisted that a statute should be passed forbidding "large aggregations of capital" to sell more cheaply in one place than in another. "You forbid a labor union to injure a man's business," he said, "but a giant corporation can do exactly the same thing." It is interesting to remember that he declared on this occasion, "Havoc, spoil, and ruin follow these 'aggregations of capital.' "

Later in the spring Coolidge made a trip to Arizona to hold a corporation meeting and had his first glimpse of the West. He traveled very economically, using day coaches all the way. For a short period in the summer his family and he were back again in

Plymouth. And then in the autumn of 1909 came once more the temptation to get into politics. The Democratic Mayor of Northampton, James W. O'Brien, was retiring at the close of 1909, and Coolidge was told that he was the man to bring the city government back to the Republican Party. At a meeting of the Republican City Committee held early in November, with more than seventy present, Coolidge was unanimously endorsed as the candidate. In reply he said that he would not have entered a contest for the nomination, but that as no one else wished to run, he would accept, even though it would involve a sacrifice of his professional interests and of his home life. On November 20, the *Gazette* published in his behalf an extended account of his career, declaring that the nomination which had come to him had been "won fairly by hard work" and adding that he had not "spared himself as a private in the ranks."

His Democratic opponent, Henry E. Bicknell, was a popular merchant of the city whom everybody knew and respected. Unfortunately for his success, however, Bicknell, out of sheer good nature, had allowed himself to espouse, in a debate at the Edwards Congregational Church, the cause of the "drys." Coolidge, on the other hand, was the attorney for the Springfield Brewery. Ordinarily the Democratic nominee would have had an initial advantage, but the "wets," including many of the Irish and French voters, lined up against him. Coolidge did not indulge in personalities. The *Gazette* said : —

There is one thing that we like about Candidate Coolidge ; he does not say anything about the other candidate. At the Democratic rallies they keep telling what a poor man Coolidge is, how little he ever did that was good and how much he has done that is bad. . . . Mr. Coolidge, we notice, does not say anything about the other candidate directly or indirectly, but he and his speakers set out their own claims to public support the best they can and then quit.

Of his methods of campaigning Coolidge wrote, "I called on many of the voters personally, sent out many letters, spoke at many ward rallies, and kept my poise." The literature sent out in his behalf stressed his "training, experience, and equipment" and pointed out that his advice was being "continually sought by the business and banking interests of the city." He certainly did not cease his wooing of the Irish Catholics, many of whom were enthusiastic for him. Typical of his speeches was one delivered on December 2 in Florence, — part of Ward Six in Northampton, — in which he closed as follows : —

It is a great honor to be selected as a candidate for Mayor of Northampton, an honor which we cannot all attain. But there is a higher honor yet, for which we may all be candidates, the honor of being upright, worthy, decent citizens. I want to be a perpetual candidate on that ticket. I want my campaign run on that principle. There has been some complaint about the methods of my campaign. I am sorry. I never could satisfy the other party. They seem like the British at the battle of Bennington who complained that the Green Mountain boys took aim in battle. . . . It is of great consequence when the campaign is over, whatever the result, that my fellow citizens may say of me, "He has conducted a clean, honorable campaign and borne himself like a man."

Coolidge's election on December 5 by a small majority of 187 votes was decidedly a personal triumph,[5] but it was whispered around the city by the gossips that his victory was made possible by Rum and Religion. What he felt on the matter may be gathered from a letter to his father, dated December 10: —

I did not have to reply to the *Herald* attack, for everybody knew it was not true. Folks know I do not go into saloons, and I never bought a drink during the campaign.

I have got to have an overcoat, a business suit, an evening suit, and a cutaway suit. Grace has got to have a suit, a dress, an evening dress, an evening wrap, and a dress hat and street hat, total about $300 or more.

The nearer I got to my house or office the better I ran, and it was the opposite with the other fellow. At least 400 Democrats voted for me. Their leaders can't see why they did it. I know why. They knew I had done things for them, bless their honest Irish hearts.

On December 25 Coolidge went into further detail in another letter to his father: —

Your generous Christmas letter is just received. We are very thankful for it. I could not have been Mayor without your help. The salary is $800, they may raise it to $1200. It just about pays the extra expense the office makes one. Mr. Bicknell is a merchant, — boots & shoes & gents furnishings, lives in Ward 2 on the edge of 5 same as I do, business in Ward 1 on the edge of 4, mine is Ward 1 on the edge of 3. 1 and five are strong Democrat wards. 1 is about 100 and last year 5 went 175. You see I cut 1 to 20 and 5 to 75 and got a big majority in 2, 3, & 4. Ward 6 is about even, but there is a row on out there so no Republican can get only one faction of the Republican strength

---

[5] One of his classmates back for his fifteenth reunion in 1910 joked him about his political career. "Say, Cooley, I hear you're Mayor of Northampton! How did you ever land that job?" "Oh, just by keeping my mouth shut so they wouldn't know what a fool I was!"

in that ward. Ward 7 is Democrat by about 40. I got all the Italians, Jews, Polish, most of the French and hundreds of Irish. Mr. Bicknell is a nice fellow and belongs to everything, — usually he is President. . . . What pleases Grace most is three free seats to me as the Mayor as one of the Trustees of the Academy of Music, — our opera house.

When Calvin Coolidge took the oath of office as Mayor on January 3, 1910, he began a period of continuous officeholding which did not terminate until March 4, 1929, at the close of his Presidential term and in the course of which he moved steadily on and up with amazing regularity and certainty. His heart, he has said, was in the law, but the lure of public service was stronger. William Allen White has said of him, very accurately: —

He made his living out of law. He has made his life out of politics. . . . Politics, to which he has devoted himself earnestly, taught him how to be useful and gave him fame.

After 1910 Coolidge virtually relegated his profession to second place in his activities and became the servant of the public. While he was Mayor he continued to keep his law office open, but actually the city business demanded much of his time. It is never easy to uncover in any man the motives which determine his conduct, and the problem is even more insoluble in the case of so uncommunicative a person as Calvin Coolidge. It may be that as early as 1910 he was laying his plans far ahead. After all, the desire for fame exists in most normal human beings, and Coolidge was not exempt from it. But nowhere in his letters does one find this desire expressed. Later in his career, when a persistent woman asked him what his hobby was, he replied, "Holding office." But I am sure that with him the wish to be of service to the community was strong, and that he never regarded officeholding merely as a means of advancement.

The Mayor in any city is a person of importance, and Coolidge was now a prominent citizen in Northampton. When he was about to take his seat to preside at the first meeting of the Board of Aldermen, he found eleven cents in the chair. As he displayed the money to his associates he said laconically, "Probably left there by some office seeker." As Mayor he received a salary of $800. The preceding City Council had voted to raise the compensation to $1000, but Coolidge, although he would have been glad of the extra money, had refused to accept the increase. As Mayor, he was *ex officio* Chairman of the Committees on Finance, on Printing, and on Highways, Streets, Street Sprinkling, and Bridges. He went every

weekday to his office on the ground floor of the City Hall, —
quarters now occupied by the Tax Commissioner, — and kept appointments faithfully from ten to twelve, often returning in the
afternoon for special engagements. The position does not offer a
large opportunity for spectacular service; furthermore the city
affairs had been previously well administered, and there was little
genuine need for reform. Towards the close of his first term, however, the *Gazette,* in summarizing what had been accomplished, gave
an impressive list of achievements: the reducing of the city debt
by $30,000 and the lowering of the tax rate from $17 to $16.50; the
increase to some extent of teachers' salaries; a faithful enforcement
of the license laws; increased efficiency in the fire and police departments; and several improvements in roads. "Law and order have
never been better maintained," said the *Gazette,* "and the city's interests have been safeguarded at every point." This is probably the
first time that the phrase "law and order," later to be so much
associated with Coolidge's record, was used in connection with him.

On June 25 Coolidge wrote from his office in the City Hall to
congratulate his father on his nomination for the position of Vermont
State Senator: —

I congratulate you most heartily on your nomination. I am sure you
will find the Senate interesting, if not very profitable. I am very glad
you are to have the satisfaction of serving in it. John and Calvin will
be pleased when they know about such things as I am now.

I wish you would come down for a little while on the 4th. It is a
long time since you were here. You can come just as well now as any
time. After Oct. you will be in Montpelier. Grace and the boys want
to see you and might go home with you. I wish Mother would come
also. I should like you to visit me while I am Mayor and you may not
have another chance.

I shall try to go to Montpelier while you are there. I have not been
there since you were in the House. I can remember the catamount
stuffed and sitting in the Governor's chair. I reached for the red ink
bottle and grandfather scrabbled me out.

On September 6, Calvin sent his father some excellent advice: —

When this reaches you I suppose you will be duly chosen a Senator
for Vermont.

You will I am sure find it a very interesting experience and unless the
members there are much better than ours you will not find any one at
Montpelier who is better qualified to legislate for the State than you
are. You need not hesitate to give the other members your views on any
subject that arises. It is much more important to kill bad bills than to

pass good ones, and better to spend your time on your own committee work than to be bothering with any bills of your own except in some measure that your own county or some other persons may want you to introduce for them.

See that the bills you recommend from your committee are so worded that they will do just what they intend and not a great deal more that is undesirable. Most bills can't stand that test. It will usually be a good plan to see what the Mass. statute is on the point.

It won't make any difference what you wear.

Little John will be four years old when you get this. I think he is worthy to bear your name.

At the close of Coolidge's first term he was renominated, and early in December was reëlected by a plurality of 256, against Bicknell, his Democratic opponent of the previous year. On December 3, in an interview with a *Gazette* reporter, he stated that he was confident. "Only a little ginger from now on," he added, "and we are winners." After his victory, he set out with his family to visit Montpelier, where his father was in the Vermont Senate, and allowed himself to be quoted as follows: —

We have had a victory. That is all. I shall not qualify it as either party or personal. It was a victory of our citizens, working together for what they believed was right. My friends have placed me under obligations which I shall never forget, although I know I shall never be able to repay. God bless Northampton.

Coolidge's second term as Mayor was uneventful, and he himself was busy with plans for his future. The Honorable Allen T. Treadway,[6] who had been the Senator from the Berkshire-Hampden-Hampshire district and was the President of the Senate in 1910 and 1911, had planned to withdraw from that office in the autumn of 1910, after three years at the State House; but his friends urged him to continue for another term. Treadway reminded them that there was "a young man from Northampton" who was in line for the Senatorship and who must be seen. Treadway then called Coolidge by telephone and explained the situation, adding, "If you say the word, I won't accept a renomination." "Allen," answered Coolidge, "I want to go to the Senate sometime, but I don't care when. When you are all through, let me know." The incident did

[6] Allen Towner Treadway, born in 1867 in Stockbridge, Massachusetts, was graduated from Amherst in 1886, a member of Alpha Delta Phi, and engaged for some years in the hotel business. He was in the Lower House of the General Court in 1904 and in the State Senate from 1908 to 1911. Since March 4, 1913, he has been a member of Congress, serving with steadily increasing influence on important committees.

not injure Coolidge in the minds of Treadway's many friends and supporters.

Early in 1911, Coolidge was mentioned by the *Boston Record* as a possibility for the Republican nomination for Secretary of State. This was a compliment, for the office was an important one, paying a salary of $5000, but Coolidge evidently ignored the rumor. In writing to his father on January 2, he said: —

I was inaugurated again this morning. I shall not run again. While it helps me in a way, it costs a good deal to do the things a Mayor has to do and takes much time. I wanted to gratify you. . . .

Are you sending anything to Aunt Sarah? You know you boarded me a good deal on her when I was at Ludlow. I think you saved enough on that so you can make her a remembrance. Shall I buy something here and take it up for you & mother?

As soon as it became known that Treadway was running for Congress, Coolidge announced his candidacy for the Senate and received the Republican nomination, equivalent in that district to an election. The district comprised seventeen towns in Berkshire County, thirteen in Hampshire, and ten in Hampden, the number of legal voters in 1911 being 16,093. The Democratic candidate was Coolidge's former opponent, Alfred J. Preece, who had meanwhile succeeded Coolidge as Representative. The gubernatorial contest between Eugene N. Foss,[7] then a Democrat, and Louis A. Frothingham, a Republican, was bitterly fought, but Foss was reëlected, and the Massachusetts Republicans were again steeped in gloom. Coolidge, however, won over Preece by 5541 votes to 4061. Coolidge wrote on December 6 to his stepmother: —

We were able to elect a Republican for mayor yesterday so the city is safe for another year.

I have been summoned to appear before the General Court for January third, or rather to appear in it. . . .

You and father can come down and spend Christmas week with us and go to Boston to see the Governor inaugurated if you will.

On his own confession Coolidge was not altogether happy during the first months of his return to Boston and the Adams House and Beacon Hill — all of it now familiar territory to him. It was

[7] Eugene Noble Foss (1858–1939), born in Berkshire, Vermont, after attending the University of Vermont, became a manufacturer, married his employer's daughter, and ultimately became President of the Company. Elected to the 61st Congress, March 22, 1919, to fill out an unexpired term, he was Democratic Governor of Massachusetts for three terms, from 1910 to 1913, but was defeated in 1913 for reelection.

never easy for him to adjust himself to a new group, and the small
Senate Chamber, with only forty members, was quite different
from the larger Lower House. He was assigned seat number 3
on the left of the President, who was Levi H. Greenwood.[8] During the 1912 session he was Chairman of the Joint Committee on
Legal Affairs and a member of the Committee on Cities. As Chairman of the Committee on Agriculture he was compelled to face
some urgent problems connected with the milk business and the
dairymen. Coolidge was insistent that a special commission should
be appointed to investigate and report an orderly plan for solving
the difficulties. When his proposal was rejected, he opposed each
of the various bills up for consideration and by his influence had
them all defeated. His letters indicate that he had little leisure. On
January 16 he wrote, "We are just beginning active work on our
2000 or so bills." On January 22, he wrote: —

I was intending to go to the Amherst dinner this evening, but I
feel so tired I think I shall go early to bed.
We are very busy in committee work now, and sometimes I have
three going at once.

Again on January 31, he was saying: —

I have a great deal of work to do in the Senate. So much I do not
have time to attend to all of it.

On January 1, 1912, in the Lawrence Duck Mill at Lawrence,
a strike broke out which was to involve twelve mills and set the
polyglot population of the textile centre into furious excitement.
The ostensible cause was a law passed on May 27, 1911, prohibiting
the employment of young persons under eighteen years for more than
fifty-four hours a week. The companies refused to pay the current
wage for fifty-six hours a week for fifty-four hours of work. The
main outbreak came on Friday, January 12, during one of the
coldest periods in New England weather history; and "Joe" Ettor,
an outside agitator, appeared at this crisis to keep matters stirred
up. Early in February a conciliation committee was appointed consisting of three Senators and five Representatives, and Coolidge was
chosen chairman. This committee held almost daily sessions with
representatives of the American Woolen Company, and pressed the

[8] Levi Henry Greenwood (1872–1930), born in Gardner, Massachusetts, attended St. Paul's School and Harvard College and became a manufacturer and
newspaper publisher. He was a member of the State Senate from 1909 until 1913,
and President of that body in 1912 and 1913.

manufacturers rather hard in an effort to secure terms of a satisfactory settlement. On February 14, Coolidge wrote his stepmother: —

I am chairman of the Committee to see if any conciliation can be brought about at Lawrence. The leaders there are socialists and anarchists, and they do not want anybody to work for wages. The trouble is not about the amount of wages; it is a small attempt to destroy all authority whether of any church or government.

As conditions grew more serious and children were being sent away, it was apparent that both employers and employees were in a bitter mood. Because of the widespread publicity given to the strike by the newspapers, the nation was watching and waiting for the outcome. Coolidge, as chairman, was calm and unprejudiced; but eventually his committee effected a settlement agreeable to both sides. A wage increase was granted; the men nearly all resumed work on March 15; and Coolidge gained the respect of both labor and capital.

During the summer of 1912 Coolidge was busy on a recess committee, of which he was chairman, the function of which was to secure better transportation facilities for rural communities west of the Connecticut. It was a Presidential year, and the split in the Republican Party between conservatives and progressives, Taft men and Roosevelt men, was spreading confusion. In the Commonwealth, the irrepressible Eugene N. Foss was running for his third term as Governor against Joseph Walker, the regular Republican candidate, and Charles Sumner Bird, the Progressive. Calvin Coolidge was, of course, for Taft and Walker. His own opponent for the Senatorship was Herbert C. Joyner, of Great Barrington, whose only argument was that the people were ready for a change.

At a Republican rally on October 19, Coolidge spoke at some length in condemnation of the Roosevelt doctrine of the recall of judicial decisions. At a second gathering, on October 30, the Taft Clubs of Amherst College and Massachusetts "Aggie" paraded with fireworks and bands. But eloquence and illuminations were impotent for the Republicans in 1912. Woodrow Wilson was elected President, the first Democrat to hold that office since Cleveland; Foss rode exultantly to his third consecutive victory; and Calvin Coolidge was fortunate to win over his rival by a vote of 6211 to 4222 — a majority of 1989.

The session of the General Court which convened on New Year's Day, 1913, has been described by Coolidge as the most enjoyable

he ever spent with any legislative body. President Greenwood, of
the Senate, made him chairman of the standing Joint Committee on
Railroads, and also placed him on the very important Committee
on Rules as well as that on the Municipal Finance. His special committee, after their summer's research, reported a measure transforming the Railroad Commission into a Public Service Commission — a measure eventually passed over the Governor's veto;
and another bill permitting trolley roads in Western Massachusetts
was also passed in spite of the gubernatorial opposition. It has been
asserted that every report of Coolidge's Committee on Railroads
during the session was accepted by the Senate — an almost unprecedented record. In January when a United States Senator was
to be elected by the General Court, the candidates were Samuel
W. McCall and John W. Weeks; Coolidge, after casting a complimentary vote on the first ballot for his friend, Allen T. Treadway,
supported Weeks. The defeat was a tragic blow to McCall. In the
committee rooms as well as on the floor itself Coolidge had become a real force. It is interesting to find him writing to his father
on March 14, in a tone quite unusual for him up to that moment: —

For two or three days I have not been feeling very well, but think
I shall get rested over Sunday. I have been placed in a position of great
influence this year, being one of the three leaders and not the least of
them. I am sure you would be gratified if you saw the place I hold here.

In his *Autobiography* Coolidge again stressed the gain in self-
confidence which came to him at this stage of his career: —

It was in my second term in the Senate that I began to be a force
in the Massachusetts Legislature. . . . I made progress because I
studied subjects sufficiently to know a little more about them than any
one else on the floor. I did not often speak but talked much with the
Senators personally and came in contact with many of the business men
of the state. The Boston Democrats came to be my friends and were
a great help to me in later times.

It was at this period that he first displayed the instinct for
politics, the acute judgment, the familiarity with human motives,
which were so marked in his later life. He was swayed by reason,
not by emotion, and was incapable of playing the demagogue.
Perhaps this is why people seemed to trust him.

Coolidge's colleagues in the Senate were not, except in a few
instances, men of unusual gifts, and his passion for detail, his
thoroughness, and his common sense made him stand out among

legislators who did not take their responsibilities as seriously as he. The *Springfield Republican,* in reviewing the sessions, said: —

Senator Coolidge is serving his second term in the Senate, and his conspicuous service has been in connection with the railroad control bill. He has been on the sub-committee to frame the measure, as well as a member of the large committee, and he has been close to the inside of all the progress and conferences over the bill. He is one of the most cautious men in the Senate, and he is one of the most quiet. He is not of a sort to make a demonstration over a matter of even the highest importance. He gives the impression of being a secretive man. . . . He attends to his duties diligently, and he gives the impression that he is always looking out for the details of his bills and not letting anything slip by him which ought to go in, or omitting anything which should not be left out.

As this summary indicates, Coolidge presided over the committee sessions when the perennial problems of the New Haven Railroad were being discussed. When Robert M. Washburn, who had remained in the House and was also on the Joint Committee on Railroads, made some tactical error in connection with the committee program, Coolidge scribbled a note, "Sand your tracks, you're slipping," and handed it to him. His silences did not trouble Washburn, who thought that when Coolidge appeared cold, he was really diffident. Washburn wrote: —

No man understands Calvin Coolidge unless he recognizes his silence. No man understands his silence unless he recognizes as its original cause his original diffidence. . . . On the inside he is warm.

By the summer of 1913, then, Calvin Coolidge had begun to find himself. He had proved himself capable of assuming and holding leadership, and the sensation was a pleasant one. Not brilliant or showy, he had made his way chiefly through the confidence he inspired. With few of the attributes of the orator, he had impressed others by his knowledge, his parliamentary skill, his quiet patience, and his sagacity. A member with such efficiency is always sure to be respected in the General Court, and Calvin Coolidge was now among the leaders. He had few enemies and many loyal friends. If he perpetrated no blunders, he was on his road to higher things.

VII

Up the Political Ladder

EXCEPT when conditions were unusual it had been customary for the State Senator from the Berkshire-Hampden-Hampshire District to retire at the close of his second term and make way for another deserving party worker. Coolidge, however, knew that Levi H. Greenwood, who had been President of the Senate for two terms, was considering the announcement of his candidacy for Lieutenant Governor; consequently he perceived an opportunity of succeeding Greenwood as presiding officer of the Senate. He explained his embarrassing situation to the Republican leaders in Northampton, found them ready to comply with his desires, and, when he offered himself for a third term, met with only negligible opposition. Meanwhile he had discreetly canvassed his legislative colleagues and had modestly discussed his ambitions with the influential Senator W. Murray Crane. And then, to his dismay, Greenwood, who suspected that it would be a poor Republican year, decided not to run for Lieutenant Governor.

It looked for a week as if all Coolidge's deep-laid plans and quiet labor were to be wasted. On November 4, however, came the election. The division in the Republican Party had not yet healed, and David I. Walsh, of Fitchburg, was elected Governor, carrying with him for the first time in many years the entire Democratic state ticket. The victory was the more astounding because Walsh was an Irish Roman Catholic. Fully as amazing, moreover, was the defeat of Greenwood. He had been an ultraconservative, a violent opponent of votes for women, and the suffragists succeeded in beating him at the polls by coming out unitedly in favor of his opponent, Edward Sibley. As for Coolidge, he had upset the "rotation system" and had won by an even larger margin than he had expected. The news of Greenwood's disaster reached Northampton on Tuesday evening. On Wednesday morning Greenwood came to Boston, cleaned out his desk, and withdrew from the State House in undisguised irritation. Coolidge was also on his way to the capital, reaching there before noon on Wednesday and going at once into action. First of all he saw "Uncle Murray" Crane, and the two between them, by use of the telephone, had obtained within twenty-four hours a sufficient number of pledges to ensure Coolidge's election as President of the Senate. It was a good stroke of political strategy, made possible by the "lucky break" of Greenwood's defeat, and was the first of several incidents which led discerning party managers to regard Coolidge as the Child of Fortune. Coolidge himself simply maintained that he was ready when the opportunity arrived.

The story of the events of the next few days, as reported in the press, has dramatic aspects. On November 6, 1913, after noting that the new Senate would be composed of twenty-one Republicans, seventeen Democrats, and two Progressives, the *Boston Herald* continued: —

Three men are now in the field for the Presidency of the Senate on the Republican side, — Calvin Coolidge, of Northampton, W. A. Bazeley, of Uxbridge, and Lombard Williams, of Dedham.

On November 11, the *Herald,* now better informed, declared that Coolidge had been securing pledges and definitely making headway. On the next day the *Hampshire Gazette,* possibly inspired, printed the following note: —

Senator Calvin Coolidge of Northampton has a clear majority, eleven, of the 21 Republican members-elect of the Senate of 1914 pledged to him in writing for the presidency of that body. . . . It is also claimed that all the Republican candidates who have been mentioned for the presidency of the State Senate except one had joined Senator Coolidge, and that one is expected to do so before night.

On the thirteenth the *Boston Herald,* under the heading "Coolidge Leads in Contest for Head of Senate," printed his picture — the first time that it had appeared in a Boston newspaper — and announced that he held pledges from sixteen Senators.[1] On the following morning it continued: —

Senator William A. Bazeley took himself out of the Senate Presidency field yesterday, and Senator Calvin Coolidge now has no opposition for the Republican nomination.

[1] On November 17, Coolidge wrote to Benjamin F. Felt, "Evidently the *Journal* does not know all the Republican Senators have chosen to give me written pledges." This use of the word *choose* is strangely anticipatory of Coolidge's famous statement in 1927.

The situation was summed up by the *Boston Sunday Globe* in these words: —

The presidency of the Senate is settled, and Calvin Coolidge of Northampton will preside over its deliberations for the year 1914. Coolidge came to town last Wednesday and showed his fellow Republicans that while some of them were talking through their hats, he could lay down 16 out of the 22 Republican votes in the upper branch of the legislature, and the other candidates and near candidates tumbled all over themselves to get out of the way of the steam-roller.

Coolidge will make a good presiding officer. He doesn't need to consult a specialist when anything bobs up that requires nerve. He can state a humorous legislative proposition without smiling. As to the political advisability of selecting Coolidge, that's a question on which there is a difference of opinion among Republicans.

The *Springfield Republican's* correspondent said of Coolidge's triumph, "It was nothing short of wonderful the way he walked right into the ring and took the prize before the public could realize there was a contest." A clever move had been accomplished by Coolidge and his friends, and he had reason to be elated. Some of the gossips objected to having the office of President of the Senate go so soon again to the district which Allen T. Treadway had represented when he held that office. A few of the more progressive Republicans did not like Coolidge's attitude on the Western Trolley Bill and the Railroad Merger Bill. But generally speaking the Republicans were satisfied. This incident was for Coolidge of immense importance. From that time on he was material for any state office. He had won his spurs.

It has been alleged by persons supposedly "on the inside" that Coolidge's election as President of the Senate was brought about by the machinations of certain powerful lobbyists for large corporations who thought that he would, in return, do anything "to stand in with people who could take care of him when he got out of politics, as he must inevitably do." According to the gossip, one political manipulator, hearing late on Tuesday evening of Greenwood's defeat, gathered his cohorts about him, decided on a program, and, while Calvin Coolidge was calmly sleeping in Northampton, had lined up a positive majority for him in the Senate. He then telephoned Coolidge to come to Boston by the first train on Wednesday, and met him with the news that the Presidency of the Senate was his. This story, like others purporting to show that Coolidge was subservient to large financial interests in New England, has been whispered around Boston in various forms for many years.

There can be no doubt that many lobbyists did support Coolidge on this and other occasions, well aware that it pays to be on the side of a winner. It is equally true that he treated them courteously, did not ignore them or decline their proffered aid, and sometimes helped them, as he helped others, when their requests were legitimate. But the allegation that lobbyists by themselves made Coolidge President of the Senate has little to support it. Coolidge was at the time the ablest Senator on the floor, the obvious candidate when Greenwood was eliminated. It is possible that the midnight meeting did take place as described, and that the little group of wire-pullers did find it advantageous to cry, "We did it!" But the preponderance of testimony indicates that Coolidge took the initiative and, with the help of W. Murray Crane, managed his own affairs on that fateful Wednesday morning.

The matter would deserve little space if it were not crucial in the interpretation of Coolidge's character and motives. If he was controlled then and later by large corporations which watched out for his political progress, this biography is inconsistent, unharmonious, and false. Coolidge, like the practical man that he was, saw no reason for refusing to meet lobbyists or for declining to listen to their suggestions; but he also kept his independence and made his own decisions. It is significant that, in spite of the most persistent search by his political foes, nothing has ever been discovered to his discredit. The influence of the lobbyists — whom everybody acquainted with political affairs in Massachusetts could name — was always less than they thought it was, and gossip has greatly exaggerated it. Their magical resourcefulness was familiar to Senator Coolidge, who was no prude in such matters, but he was also aware of their sinister methods, and he had no intention of touching pitch and being defiled. If this is not the correct interpretation, it is the duty of the defamers of Calvin Coolidge to prove their case.

Shortly after his return to Northampton, Coolidge's younger son, Calvin, Jr., was taken suddenly ill with pneumonia and was for a few days very ill indeed. His father wrote to Colonel John C. Coolidge on December 7, "He is very thin and weak, but you would be proud to see how much courage he has. He is a thoroughbred." He soon had to undergo an operation but was convalescent by Christmas. Mrs. Coolidge then went to Burlington for a short rest from her troubles, but her husband remained in Northampton making his plans for the winter.

At 11.05 on the morning of Wednesday, January 7, 1914, Clerk

Henry D. Coolidge, who had held his position since 1889, called the Senate to order, and James P. Timilty, the senior Senator present, took the chair. Governor Foss then read the oath of office. When the balloting for President took place, Coolidge received thirty-one votes against five for Francis J. Horgan, a Democrat, and two for Charles M. Cox, a Progressive. He took his place on the rostrum with what the *Boston Herald* described as "little fuss and feathers" and then delivered his inaugural address — an address which, in the retrospect, seems remarkable not only for its brevity but also for its clarity and saneness, and which voiced a political philosophy formed by thought and experience. In it may be found most of the principles on which Coolidge during his career in public service conducted the people's business. The keynote of it all lay, perhaps, in the sentences, "Don't hurry to legislate. Give administration a chance to catch up with legislation." This important idea, new to most legislative chambers, was expressed in other terms: "The people cannot look to legislation generally for success. Industry, thrift, character, are not conferred by Act or Resolve. Government cannot relieve from toil; it can provide no substitute for the rewards of service." Coolidge was advocating a doctrine of self-reliance, announcing his conviction that man must learn to depend chiefly on himself, that he "has a right that is founded upon the constitution of the universe to have property that is his own." He went so far in his justification of the capitalistic system as to assert that "it may be that the fostering and protection of large aggregations of wealth are the only foundation upon which to build the prosperity of the whole people." Compact though this address was, it had a ringing eloquence, as those who heard it were aware; and they were especially stirred by its noble peroration : —

Statutes must appeal to more than material welfare. Wages won't satisfy, be they never so large. Nor houses; nor land; nor coupons, though they fall thick as the leaves of autumn. Man has a spiritual nature. Touch it, and it must respond as the magnet responds to the pole. To that, not to selfishness, let the laws of the Commonwealth appeal. Recognize the immortal worth and dignity of man. Let the laws of Massachusetts proclaim to the humblest citizen, performing the most menial task, the recognition of his manhood, the recognition that all men are peers, the humblest with the most exalted, the recognition that all work is glorified. Such is the path to equality before the law. Such is the sublime revelation of man's relation to man — democracy.

In his *Autobiography* Coolidge was very frank regarding his motive for delivering such a speech at such a time. He had been fearful that the radical spirit which he had observed at close quarters during the Lawrence strike might undermine the national morale. He had noticed that, during the previous session of the General Court, many bills had been introduced aimed at helping the employee by impairing the property of the employer. Coolidge himself could not then have been accused of caring for money or possessions. In choosing to serve the public he had deliberately abandoned the possibility of accumulating wealth, and his own manner of living was simple to the verge of frugality. But he believed, as his ancestors had believed, in the right of man to save his earnings and keep them. For him the solution of most sociological problems lay in keeping busy. Accordingly he resolved to appeal "to the conservative spirit of the people." Thus it was that he urged them to "have faith in Massachusetts" and to "do the day's work."

In this connection, Mr. Frank W. Stearns recalls that during his earliest conversation of any length with Coolidge, in 1915, the latter spoke substantially as follows: —

When I first went to the Legislature I was a very young man. I suppose those who voted for me considered me a Radical or a Liberal. I had only been a member of the Legislature a few months when I made up my mind that Massachusetts at any rate was legislating faster than it could administer and that the sane thing was to call halt for the time being. I had not changed my views on these questions, but I had entirely changed my views as to what it was wise to do at the minute, and I changed my position and was probably called a conservative. I remember thinking at the time that neither the so-called liberals nor the so-called conservatives would understand me. Perhaps both would think I was dishonest or at least not firm in my convictions, and my career would end with that session of the Legislature. . . . Apparently they had more faith in me than I thought they would have.

The hour was to come, even before his death, when radical young men were to ridicule Coolidge's political philosophy. The mood of the world has changed immeasurably in the quarter of a century since Coolidge declared that "large profits mean large pay rolls." Perhaps he did not take sufficiently into account the fact that periods recur, even under a democracy, when the most self-reliant and ambitious man may be unable to get work which pays a living wage; when government interference may be necessary if industrial slavery is to be avoided; when "large aggregations of wealth" may be so protected that they become tyrannical. But in Coolidge's creed there is much that is still sound, and one paragraph is frequently quoted: —

Do the day's work. If it be to protect the rights of the weak, whoever objects, do it. If it be to help a powerful corporation better to serve the people, do that. Expect to be called a standpatter, but don't be a standpatter. Expect to be called a demagogue, but don't be a demagogue. Don't hesitate to be as revolutionary as science. Don't hesitate to be as reactionary as the multiplication table. Don't expect to build up the weak by pulling down the strong.

Colonel John C. Coolidge wrote to his wife early in January, "You would be surprised to see the power Calvin seems to have. Every one seems ready to carry out his wishes when he makes them known." Oddly enough, however, the address aroused very little attention in the newspapers at the time of its delivery. The *Transcript* and other papers printed short paragraphs from it, but no one of them mentioned it editorially until January 15, when the *Herald,* in a leading article headed "Calvin Coolidge's Quaint Philosophy," said : —

In originality of statement, in courageousness of expression, in a philosophic poise rarely found in political addresses, it is decidedly conspicuous.

The unusual quality of this address coincided with his arrival, at the age of forty-two, in a position which made him one of the outstanding personages in the Commonwealth. The Presidency of the Senate was indeed, as he described it, a place "of great dignity and power." Through it he had "come into the possession of an influence reaching beyond the confines of my own party which I was to retain as long as I remained in public life." Because the Governor, David I. Walsh, was a Democrat, Coolidge was conceded the legislative domination of the Republican Party. He was responsible for the appointment of committees, could reward his friends and conciliate potential foes. What was thought of him may be gathered from a note in the *Boston Globe* "State House Gossip" : —

Those who have been at the State House in recent years say that the President of the Senate, Mr. Coolidge, is one of the keenest men who have filled that chair in a long time. When he first came to the Legislature, his nasal twang and other peculiarities made some of his Eastern colleagues laugh, and they used to call him — behind his back — David Harum.

David was himself a pretty shrewd Yankee, and so is Mr. Coolidge. It did not take him long to make an impression in the Legislature, and his path to the present high position which he holds has been a comparatively easy one. If it is not injudicious to apply the word "countryman" to a man who is a graduate of Amherst College and has been Mayor of Northampton, that word might be used to describe the President of the Senate at first impressions.

That resemblance to David Harum may bring Mr. Coolidge still higher honors if he cares for them and the times are ripe. The Republicans have not had since the days of George D. Robinson a candidate for Governor whose manner of speech appealed to the men who live outside the big cities of the state. Republican nominations for the governorship are not worth much just now, but a number of men have, nevertheless, been mentioned for that honor in the past few days. The ability to appeal to the people who work the plough is an asset not to be disregarded. Mr. Coolidge has that.

So far as I have been able to ascertain, this is the earliest mention of Calvin Coolidge as a possible Governor of the Commonwealth. Unquestionably he had arrived.

After a stormy battle the aristocratic Grafton D. Cushing[2] was elected on the fourth ballot Speaker of the House. On Thursday morning, after a long delay due to a debate in the House over Cushing's right to name committees, Coolidge administered the oath of office to the new Governor, David I. Walsh. Soon Coolidge announced his appointments, giving the Democrats two chairmanships and two full committees. Then the General Court settled down to business for the winter, and Calvin Coolidge took his place in his new quarters in the State House. Although he had warned his colleagues against excessive legislation, a new record was established on January 17 for the number of bills filed, 1700 having been reported. Committee hearings and the usual undramatic routine duties occupied the legislators for some weeks, during which Coolidge spent evening after evening in studying details. The newspapers had other matters to fill their pages: the eloquent "Jim" Curley was elected Mayor of Boston and was inaugurated on February 1; Joseph Conrad's *Chance* appeared and was duly praised by the

[2] Grafton Dulany Cushing, born in Boston, August 4, 1864, was graduated at Harvard in 1885, studied law, and practised in Boston. He was a member of the House of Representatives from 1906 to 1914, and Speaker for three terms, 1912–1914. He was elected Lieutenant Governor in 1915. Tall, dignified, and handsome, he dressed with sartorial elegance while in public office. When B. Loring Young, a Boston lawyer, called on Vice President Coolidge in the New Willard Hotel garbed in the conventional morning coat, striped trousers, silk hat, and walking stick, Mr. Coolidge surveyed him from head to foot and then asked in his nasal twang, "Hello, Loring, seen Grafton Cushing lately?" When Coolidge, as Lieutenant Governor, was reviewing a parade of State Guard troops, he saw Cushing marching as a private in the rear rank with a musket on his shoulder, and said to Major Wolcott, "Well, Major, I'm glad to see that Grafton can walk without his cane." Cushing, after having long been out of politics, died on May 31, 1939, in New York City.

critics; Dr. Richard C. Cabot's *What Men Live By* was approved by the discriminating; the Boston Athenaeum, the private library on Beacon Street opposite the Bellevue Hotel, was being reconstructed. The world was on the verge of the most terrible war in history, but no one seemed to sense what was coming.

Coolidge's daily program changed but little. His private office as President of the Senate was on the third floor of the State House opening off the Senate Reading Room and close to the Senate Chamber, in a small, high-ceilinged room from which he could look out on a balcony and the open space to the north of the east wing of the State House. It had only one window, a desk, and a sofa, and in it Coolidge could be very much secluded if he wished. Its mahogany paneling made it seem ornate, but dignified. Along the corridors and up and down the stairways when the General Court was in session were the usual little groups of lobbyists, political hangers-on, and loafers waiting to see somebody of influence. Coolidge arrived early at the desk and attended strictly to business, seldom leaving the State House except for luncheon at the Bellevue or the Parker House. He continued to occupy Room 60 at the Adams House and to go back to Northampton for week ends. That he was conscious of his success, proud of his high position, could not have been detected in his manner, but his letters to his father and stepmother contain little items showing what he really felt. On March 5, for example, he wrote his father: —

I met Mr. Taft twice and what he said was so much like what I had said that I sent him a copy of my address. He sent me the enclosed letter which you may return to me, also an autograph copy of his book on Popular Government. He was at Smith College February 23, where I sat on the platform with him. The neighbors must laugh to hear mother reading letters to them.

As a presiding officer he was calm and fair-minded. He had a thorough acquaintance with parliamentary procedure and was sound in his rulings. When Senator Walter E. McLane, told by an indignant colleague to go to hell, protested, Coolidge replied, "Senator, I've examined the Constitution and the Senate rules, and there's nothing in them that compels you to go."

The session of 1914 was exceptionally long and busy, and the General Court did not prorogue until July 7. During a winter when large appropriations for relief were made necessary, Coolidge cooperated with Governor Walsh in seeing that the state business was carried on with a minimum of dispute between the two political parties. The President of the Senate need not vote unless he wishes to do so, but he can control lawmaking by merely a casual remark, and Coolidge never hesitated to use his power. Although a strong party man, he was never a blind and bigoted partisan, and his relations with the Democrats were uniformly friendly. He did not seek the limelight, nor was he accorded much publicity in the newspapers. After his election as President of the Senate, the reporters left him alone, finding that he was not sufficiently spectacular. Mayor Curley offered them far more spicy material. Characteristic of Coolidge's methods of expediting business was a letter sent from his office, dated March 30, 1914, headed in large letters "ALARM": —

There are 706 items on the Bulletin upon which hearings have been closed and reports have not been made, and there are 908 still unreported. I hope that you will undertake during this week to call and attend as many executive sessions as possible and report on everything you can possibly decide.

I suggest that hearings begin at 10 o'clock in the morning and that you proceed to make reports whether a quorum of the committee is present or not. It will help if you will be on time at committee meetings.

Occasionally he took the floor himself, and his words had the force of authority.

Early in August the World War broke out, and the United States, without realizing it, was about to enter upon a new adventure. As we look back upon that summer, we can see that it marked a turning point in the evolution of civilization. An era of calm and peace was rapidly passing away. At the moment it seemed impossible that Massachusetts could ever be involved in what looked like an exclusively European dispute; but more and more the catastrophe across the water assumed world-wide proportions and our participation eventually became inevitable. If this biography during those early days of the war seems to be concerned with local and trivial matters, it is because the full significance of what was going on did not strike home until 1917.

The Republican convention in Worcester that autumn was more enthusiastic and optimistic than any since before the schism of 1912. Coolidge, as Chairman of the Resolutions Committee, drafted the platform, a document thoroughly liberal in tone, pledging the party to various plans for social welfare, including reasonable hours of work for laborers, health measures, workingmen's compensation, urban sanitation, city planning, and the care and protection of children. The gubernatorial nominee, Samuel W. McCall, was an admirable choice. It is true that Walsh was reëlected early in November by a small plurality, but the Republicans carried the remainder of the state ticket, and the party was ready again to present a united front. Calvin Coolidge, running against Ralph A. Staab, — the candidate of both Democrats and Progressives, — received 6381 votes for Senator against his opponent's 3596. The *Daily Hampshire Gazette*, commenting on the result, said: —

Calvin Coolidge got the largest vote in this city of any candidate. . . . Senator Coolidge is the best vote getter in the state, and he will be heard from later.

When the Senate convened in January 1915, it was made up of thirty-three Republicans and seven Democrats, all but one of the latter from Boston. Coolidge was the unanimous choice of the Senate for President, this being a genuine tribute to his popularity; and Channing H. Cox, then just beginning his distinguished career, was made Speaker of the House. Coolidge's speech at the opening of the Senate in 1915 was eagerly awaited, for people had not forgotten his brilliant address of the year before. But instead of trying to outdo his earlier effort, he uttered only forty-four words: —

Honorable Senators: My sincerest thanks I offer you. Conserve the firm foundations of our institutions. Do your work with the spirit of a soldier in the public service. Be loyal to the Commonwealth and to yourselves and be brief; above all things, be brief.

In his *Autobiography* Coolidge expressed the concern which he felt in 1915 over "the great complication of laws and restrictive regulations, from a multiplicity of Boards and Commissions, which had reached about one hundred, and from a large increase in the number of people on the public pay rolls." He was troubled over the waste of money and effort and the rapidly rising taxes necessary to support luxuries; and he did what he could, as chairman of a legislative group, to remedy these evils. While he was President of the Senate the volume of legislation was considerably diminished; indeed the spirit of the Upper House while he was in control was much different from what it had been. His influence, which was fully recognized, was exerted for economy and efficiency, and he secured and held the confidence of his fellow Senators. He himself expressed the transformation by saying that the citizens "were becoming tired of agitation, criticism, and destructive policies and wished to return to constructive methods."

What was Calvin Coolidge like in 1915, in his forty-third year?

Physically he was slender, about five feet nine inches tall, and weighing little over one hundred and fifty pounds. His sandy hair was getting scanty, and his forehead was high. His blue eyes were deepset above a nose which in profile seemed unusually prominent with a slight downward turn at the end. His lips were thin, slightly slanting, and pressed close together, and his chin was pointed and rather long. His features were delicate and refined, giving him in certain aspects a very youthful appearance, for the tired wrinkles of middle age had not appeared around the eyes. Seen at a reception, he was insignificant, but studied closely he revealed an expression which indicated that he was no ordinary man.

Coolidge's voice was nasal, and words issued from his mouth with a peculiar ring or twang easily imitated by those who wished to ridicule him. Robert M. Washburn remembers that once when a Senator went down to the Lower Chamber, Coolidge burst out, "What's he maousin' raound the Haouse for?" His version of such words as *rule* and *constitution* was certainly unusual and helped him to win the farmer vote.

In his dress Coolidge was neat and immaculate, usually wearing an inconspicuous suit of blue serge made by his tailor since his college days, William K. Staab, of Northampton. He preferred a turndown collar, with a striped cravat of neutral colors. He had lost the rustic air which he had in Amherst and now could move in any gathering like a man of the world.

He had not yet reached a position where his peculiarities were an asset. The day was to come when his reticence, his dry humor, his quaint turns of phrase, were to lend him individuality; when he was to be as picturesque as Mark Twain or "Uncle Joe" Cannon or Vice President Garner; when story after story was to be invented and attributed to him; when he was to become an American myth. In 1915 he was just a Yankee in politics. To many of his acquaintances he seemed unresponsive, harsh of voice, angular of soul, cautious and unemotional. But behind that expressionless, rather bored countenance were the play of feeling and the operation of a shrewd and vigorous mind.

Coolidge's character must be reserved for discussion until it has been more fully developed. We have seen how many of his traits originated — his passion for economy, his disgust at waste, his taciturnity, his dislike of impulsiveness, his positive hatred of ostentation. We have dwelt at some length on his habits of industry, his zeal for routine work, his apparent lack of imagination, his disinclination for sports, his obvious provincialism. His Puritan nature abhorred graft and extravagance and immorality. His tastes were simple to the point of drabness, and he cared nothing whatever for luxury. He was the very embodiment of common sense, the antithesis of what was eccentric or fantastical or irregular.

While Coolidge was never attracted by socialism or by any conception of a socialized state, he did believe that government must aim at improving the lot of the common man. He felt that some better process should be devised through which the wage earner could share the prosperity of his employer. He advocated vigorously many forms of legislation for the benefit of the poor and under-privileged. By nature he was no aristocrat; indeed his sympathies were with the majority of people who have to toil hard for a living. On the other hand, he had no patience with agitators or revolution-ists. His liberalism did not lead him to favor violent protests, for instinctively he preferred orderly gradual change and peaceful evolution.

At this period Coolidge was probably not looking forward to the White House. When the presidency of the Senate suddenly opened before him, he must have realized that the governorship might be his — with a little good fortune. Before very long he had to make another decision. Many a fine man in Massachusetts politics had gone as far as he and then moved on into Congress, like Allen T. Treadway. Others had reached the position of President of the Senate and then retired, voluntarily or involuntarily, to private life, like William D. Chapple or Levi H. Greenwood. Coolidge has himself written, "When I went home at the end of the 1915 session it was with the intention of remaining in private life and giving all my attention to the law." He was not the man to work consciously with promotion in view. What he needed most was a sponsor, — somebody with fixity of purpose, influence, money, — to foster his interests and smooth his path. Calvin Coolidge was lucky. But his greatest stroke of luck was the friendship of Frank Waterman Stearns, the perfect model of the King Maker — a persistent, self-effacing, altruistic hero-worshiper. It was owing to Stearns that within a few months Coolidge was involved in a new contest and another triumph.

VIII

A Friend Appears

OF all the external factors which affected Calvin Coolidge's career the most potent and unexpected was Frank Stearns. Mark Hanna, who acted as Providence for William McKinley, sought and received his reward in the Senatorship from Ohio. Harry M. Daugherty claimed and deserved the credit for placing Warren G. Harding in the White House — and became Attorney General of the United States. But Frank W. Stearns asked nothing and secured nothing from Coolidge. He proposed no bargain, implied or defined. He exacted no *quid pro quo*. He was, of course, a hero-worshiper, but deep in his heart was the conviction that in helping Coolidge he was doing well by his country. Coolidge, who had had few close friends, never quite understood why Stearns was so devoted to him, but he accepted the gift of generous affection and was as grateful as it was possible for a man of his undemonstrative temperament to be. Of Stearns, Coolidge wrote: —

He never obtruded or sought any favor for himself or any other person, but his whole effort was always disinterested and entirely devoted to assisting me when I indicated I wished him to do so. It is doubtful if any other public man ever had so valuable and unselfish a friend.

Frank Waterman Stearns was born, November 8, 1856, in Boston of good Mayflower stock, the son of Richard Hall Stearns, who in 1847 had established the drygoods firm of R. H. Stearns and Company, now on Tremont Street, opposite Boston Common. After attending Noble's School, he went to Amherst College, was a member of the Chi Psi fraternity, and was graduated in the class of 1878. He entered at once into his father's store, eventually becoming its president and building up a considerable fortune as well as a reputation as a kind and just employer. In 1880 he married Emily Williston Clark, by whom he had three children. Always devoted to his college, Mr. Stearns was in 1908 chosen an alumni Trustee of Amherst for a term of five years, and in 1916 he was elected a permanent member of the Board. He was identified with numerous philanthropic organizations and movements and was a model citizen of Boston. He died on March 6, 1939, of pneumonia, having been active almost to the end.

Mr. Stearns was in 1915 a rugged, thick-set man, rather below average height, with grayish hair and moustache, phlegmatic but dignified in bearing and impressive because of his searching eyes, strong jaw, and firm lips. He was steady and reliable and had the assured manner of a person unaccustomed to failure; but he was also simple and sincere, and he possessed not only a singular modesty and evenness of disposition, but also an optimism based on faith and courage. He cared nothing whatever for the trappings of wealth or for publicity, and was one of those rare persons who refuse to say the inevitable "few words" at dinners — and mean it. Practical in his business dealings, endowed with both sagacity and common sense, he had also in his nature a deep vein of idealism. He was friendly and democratic, and loved to light his cigar and talk, not egotistically, but in a self-deprecatory tone, of his experiences. People laughed at Mr. Stearns for his unalterable and reiterated opinion that Calvin Coolidge was reserved for great things. But he was imperturbable, patient, and stubbornly persistent. Some dogged quality in his character drove him on in spite of ridicule and hostility until the hour arrived when he could say to his critics, "You'll have to admit now that I was right."

As a boy Mr. Stearns had heard his father speak in the State House, where he was for two terms a Representative, and had later been interested mildly in current events in both state and nation. But he had almost nothing to do actively with politics until he was nearly sixty, and then emerged as a type utterly incomprehensible to such professionals as W. Murray Crane and Henry Cabot Lodge. Again and again the bosses asked one another, "What's Stearns's game? What's he getting out of it?" Such altruism was new in their experience. Among the very practical Republican leaders Mr. Stearns had all the irresistible enthusiasm of a single-minded fanatic, unwilling to compromise or even to admit the possibility of defeat. For fifteen years nothing mattered to him except the progress of Calvin Coolidge. To insure this he raised and spent money freely,[1]

---

[1] Mr. Benjamin F. Felt points out that Mr. Stearns accomplished remarkable things for a relatively moderate personal expenditure. The money was always the lesser part of his contribution.

Frank Waterman Stearns

WARREN'S
OLDE STYLE

put his business affairs in charge of others, and buttonholed every man who could be of help in his personal crusade. He also gave Coolidge all the facilities of his private office and made him generous gifts of money when the need was evident. That is why in the copy of his syndicated articles which Mr. Coolidge presented to Mr. Stearns in 1931 is the inscription, "To Frank W. Stearns, who really brought me to a position making this book possible." When Mr. Stearns received these two handsome bound volumes, he wrote the ex-President a letter which has hitherto never been published and is here printed through Mr. Stearns's courtesy: —

It is not possible to let that inscription in "your" book pass without telling you (which I could not to your face) how much it means to me and to mine, and I cannot think of anyone in the history of this country who has anything so much to be prized, unless by chance either George Washington or Abraham Lincoln saw fit to say something of a similar kind to some devoted friend of his.

Of course I am not admitting this is true, but I have a clear conscience that I did put into the cause all the energy and thought and devotion that I am possessed of. That much is true. After all, I guess all I can say is thank you.

Mr. Stearns's earliest relationship with Calvin Coolidge was in the spring of 1912. H. W. Kidder, Treasurer of Amherst College, wrote to Stearns as a Trustee, setting forth at some length certain objections to a bill pending in the General Court in regard to a system of sewage disposal in the town of Amherst and expressing his fears that, under its provisions, unjust financial obligations might be put upon the college. In his letter, Kidder said: —

I asked Calvin Coolidge, a graduate of the college in the class of '95 who is now in the Senate, — from Northampton, — to keep watch of this thing and let me know when anything could be done, but I have not heard from him as to any hearings on the bill.

Mr. Stearns, who at this time had never heard of Coolidge, asked his Amherst classmate, Arthur H. Wellman, a well-known Boston lawyer, to look into the matter. After seeing Senator Coolidge on March 11, 1912, Wellman wrote Kidder, "I have interviewed Senator Coolidge, who seemed to have entirely forgotten the matter and apparently had never read the bill." Mr. Kidder thought at the moment that Coolidge was reserved and rather cool in his manner, and Mr. Stearns was consequently much annoyed; but the hearings on the bill had closed in the previous January and it was still in the

House, where a Senator would naturally not have known much about it. Under the circumstances Coolidge thought that it would be difficult to secure any amendment and so expressed himself, perhaps rather curtly, to Mr. Wellman, who was obliged to agree with him. The measure was passed, signed by the Governor on April 13, 1912, and proved to be unobjectionable. The incident is trivial except that it was Mr. Stearns's first impression that Coolidge made little effort to be ingratiating, even to a representative of the Trustees of Amherst College.[2]

Early in 1915 Dwight W. Morrow [3] said to Stearns, "I have a classmate in Boston who is quite a fellow — man named Coolidge. Do you know him?" Stearns replied, "No." Morrow said, "You ought to — I will tell him that he ought to know you." Shortly afterwards, at a dinner at the Algonquin Club, Stearns, remembering Morrow's suggestion, spoke to Coolidge, who merely extended a cold hand and muttered, "How-d'-do" — nothing more. When the meal was over, however, he came by Stearns's seat and said, "Ever anything you want up on the Hill come up and see me." A little later Stearns, although he had nothing which he wished in the way of legislation, did call at the Senate Chamber during a busy session. Coolidge noticed him, invited him to sit with him on the rostrum, and explained to him briefly what was going on. Mr. Stearns's account of the incident continues : —

It was evidently a day on which they were rushing through bills for final action, and the whole business was droning along. Behind the chair of the President of the Senate was a corridor, separated from the rostrum by portieres. While I sat there, three different Senators, one after another, stuck their heads through the opening in the portieres, saying, "Mr. President, I think we ought to do so-and-so." In each case he answered, "No," and the Senator simply said, "All right, just as you say." This entire absence of effort to impress me was different from the action of any politician that I had ever met, and it finally interested me so much that I began to look him up.

On his return to his office Stearns wrote Coolidge a note asking for his photograph and commenting on the latter's efficiency as presiding officer. To this Coolidge responded in what is apparently the first of his letters to Stearns : —

[2] This story is told from information supplied by both Mr. Stearns and Mr. Wellman, who agree on the essentials. It has also appeared in more highly colored and exaggerated forms.

[3] Morrow had from time to time seen Coolidge at the latter's office in Northampton, and at the class's fifteenth reunion in 1910 had been much impressed by Coolidge's growth in achievement and prestige.

My dear Sir:

Please accept my thanks for your very kind letter.

I am ordering some photographs and I shall be very pleased to send you one when they come.

I trust you will let me know any time you have any ideas of how we can better serve the Commonwealth.

Cordially yours,

Calvin Coolidge

Some weeks later Mr. Henry P. Field and Mr. Stearns had a conversation regarding the possibility of bringing their college more to the front in Boston. Stearns, who had been pleased with what he had learned of Coolidge's record, thought it might be beneficial for the President of the Senate and therefore for Amherst if a complimentary dinner could be arranged for him by a group of representative Amherst graduates and their friends. Thus an Amherst conspiracy was hatched — fortunately of a non-indictable sort. First Stearns wrote Coolidge for one hundred reprints of his speech on assuming the presidency of the Senate in 1914, and distributed them where he thought seed should be sown. Then he had an invitation prepared and signed by a number of influential gentlemen, reading as follows: —

Dear Senator Coolidge:

A number of your Amherst College friends have watched with interest the work you are doing for the Commonwealth, and will be pleased if you will accept the invitation to be present at a dinner in your honor, which seems the best way they can make you know their interest and appreciation.

Some of us feel that the duty of good citizens is not wholly met by using care in the selection of proper candidates for the Legislature and by voting for them at election time. We have the feeling that perhaps it would be acceptable to our Senators and Representatives if they could be in real touch with citizens in various walks of life, — teachers, clergymen, doctors, lawyers, business men, — and that if such acquaintance were more common, it would work to the advantage of the state.

Perhaps at this dinner you will say something that will help us, if we are right in this idea, to make it effective. We suggest as a place for the dinner the Algonquin Club, and for time, May 12th at 7 o'clock.

Among the names attached to this document were Arthur B. Chapin, who presided at the dinner; Charles A. Andrews, of Coolidge's Amherst class; President Meiklejohn, Professor Olds, and Professor Churchill, of the Amherst faculty; Channing H. Cox, Galen L. Stone, Richard W. Irwin, and one or two other non-

Amherst men; and Judge Alden P. White, Robert W. Maynard, Robert J. Bottomly, and other Amherst graduates well-known in Boston and vicinity. Seventy-seven signed the invitation and sixty-seven were actually present at the banquet. The committee invited Colonel John C. Coolidge to attend and even sent him railroad transportation, but he merely replied, "Gentlemen: Can't come. Thank you. JOHN C. COOLIDGE." The dinner was a notable affair, in spite of Coolidge's refusal to be introduced as a candidate for Lieutenant Governor, and he emerged with credit from a trying ordeal. The speakers were Professor Olds, Dwight W. Morrow, Channing H. Cox, and Coolidge. The Amherst '95 *Bulletin,* in describing the affair, said, "If Calvin believes all the nice things said about him he is already buying a larger hat." On the following morning Coolidge wrote his father: —

We had a very nice dinner last night. About 65 were present. Mr. Stearns, of R. H. Stearns Co., whose letter I showed to you, got it up. They read your letter there and called it a characteristic Coolidge letter. I am sure you would have been proud of the character of the men who came to honor me.

All this was done without any noisy propaganda, and nothing whatever was said about the affair in the newspapers. Meanwhile Coolidge had expressed himself fully on at least one current question. On March 29 the *Boston Journal* printed an interview with him on the subject of employment, in the course of which he said, "If any man is out of a job it's his own fault. . . . The State is responsible for sending Democrats to Washington who have arranged the tariff laws with very harmful results. . . . The State is not warranted in furnishing employment for anybody so that that person may have work. Anybody who is not capable of supporting himself is not fit for self-government. If people can't support themselves, we'll have to give up self-government." When asked to suggest a remedy for the evils of unemployment, Coolidge merely said, "Yes, I have a plan. My plan is for a Republican administration to enact adequate tariff laws to open the shops and factories so that things will take care of themselves." Evidently Coolidge's panacea for unemployment in 1915 was to have citizens vote the straight Republican ticket. It reads to-day like a reactionary utterance which might have done him harm, but no one seems to have paid any attention to it.

Mention of him for Lieutenant Governor became so frequent by the beginning of May that Coolidge wrote to his stepmother: —

I have been too busy to read the papers and so saw nothing of what you mention. I have never thought of running for Lieut. Governor myself. I have all I can attend to looking after my duties as President of the Senate. A good many people have spoken to me about it. I have no plans except to try to do what is given me to do. I have been in office about as long as I feel I want.

The Senate members gave a dinner for him at a Boston hotel in mid-May and passed resolutions recording their appreciation of his services as presiding officer. He was not even aroused when Guy A. Ham, a Boston lawyer and a gifted speaker, announced his candidacy for the Republican nomination. On June 3, Stearns wrote Coolidge: —

I brought Mr. Garcelon in in the automobile with me this morning. I do not know how wise a man he is, but he is an enthusiast and knows what is going on pretty well. I knew he felt under some obligation to Mr. Greenwood, in case Mr. Greenwood should decide to be a candidate for Lieutenant-Governor. Mr. Garcelon says that Mr. Greenwood will not run and that he, Garcelon, is enthusiastically and permanently for you.

Will you please be frank with me and let me know if I am doing any harm by my talk whenever I get a chance? The style of my talk is that I do not know, and I think nobody knows, whether you can be persuaded to run, but if you can, you are the man we want. If that is harmful at this stage of the game, please be frank and say so, but please do not tell me until you are fully ready to have it known whether or not you intend to run. I would much rather be in a position to say that I do not know.

To this very candid letter, Coolidge replied on the same day: —

At the present time I have no plans for the coming year. It is gratifying to me that a man of your standing should be interested in me and should take the pains to speak well of me. I am sure that anything you may say will be a help to me and no harm to me or the party.

I am a little embarrassed to have you doing so much without knowing that I can ever supplement your efforts and think I ought to warn you that your energy may be thrown away so far as any political developments are concerned.

He had apparently at this time not made up his mind as to his future plans. The story is told, on the authority of Civil Service Commissioner Green, that Coolidge during the spring asked a few of his friends to urge Governor Walsh to appoint him as a member of the Department of Public Utilities; that they called as a group at the executive offices only to be told that Walsh had named a man for the vacancy just fifteen minutes before. If they had arrived earlier, Coolidge might conceivably have remained a minor office holder in Massachusetts all his life.[4] This is only one additional bit of evidence of the way in which some mysterious force seems to have been driving Coolidge, almost in spite of himself, on the road to Washington.

In June the General Court prorogued, and still Coolidge had given no intimation of his decision. The Coolidges had planned to go to the Panama Exposition, Mrs. Coolidge starting on June 30 and he himself following in order to arrive on July 18. The newspapers, meanwhile, were discussing him more and more frequently as the logical candidate for Lieutenant Governor. The Boston correspondent of the *Springfield Republican* spoke on June 2 very favorably on the subject: —

President Coolidge of the Senate has been mentioned for the second place on the Republican state ticket this year. Since the retirement of Clinton White from the Public Service Commission, his name has been one of those which has seemed to fit the need of a representative of the public who has a large and strong grasp of business principles, who is politically sound and is true to the interests of the general public, and at the same time a safeguard for the corporate interests which are always more or less under attack by the public, which is as selfish from its point of view as the capitalists are from theirs. Whenever the President has been before the public, his superior intellectual equipment has been evident in the calm, dignified, concise, and broad statements of his principles and facts. If his record in the House and Senate be studied, it will be found to be remarkably radical for a man who has a reputation of being so conservative. This balance makes it the more probable that he tries to strike a just medium between the capitalists and the public. His administration has been business-like and without any fireworks.

Coolidge returned to Northampton for a few days, consulted with a few of his advisers, including Mr. Field, did some quiet thinking, and then went back to Boston, dined with Mr. Stearns at the Algonquin Club, — the precise date cannot be ascertained, but it must have been about June 20, — and there handed him a small slip of paper evidently torn hastily from an envelope on which he had scribbled the words, "I am a candidate for Lieutenant Governor,

[4] Letter of Frank W. Buxton, editor of the *Boston Herald*, to the author, March 27, 1936. The story is confirmed by Senator Walsh himself in a letter to me dated March 30, 1938. He, however, says, "My recollection is that I felt the appointment ought to go to a Democrat as the Democrats had a minority representation on the Commission, so I tendered the name of a Democrat for confirmation."

Calvin Coolidge," and said, "You can send that to the papers if you want to." On July 5, he wrote to his stepmother : —

Grace is in San Francisco today. I gave up my trip to look after my campaign. I expect to be nominated but nothing is certain now when 200,000 or more are to make the selection. I thought I might as well try it.

Nothing in Coolidge's correspondence at this period creates the impression that he was planning for a distant and distinguished future. Rather he appears like a half-reluctant figure responding to the pressure of a *deus ex machina,* Mr. Stearns. Stearns actually wrote Morrow about the possibility of having Amherst give Coolidge an LL.D. that June, but Morrow demurred, saying, "Have degrees been conferred upon Lawrence and Gillett? If not I should think that there might be a feeling that Coolidge should perhaps wait until he has a little further proving in politics."

When Stearns asked him, not unnaturally, why he had wasted so much time in reaching his decision, he replied, "I was President of the Senate. Legislation was well in hand. If I had announced myself for a higher office while the Legislature was in session, legislation would have been in a mess. I should have lost control of the Senate, and most of the other thirty-nine members would have been candidates for my place as President of the Senate. Can you not see that it would not have been right for me to have done any differently? Now we will go to it and see what we can do." [5]

Now that he had Coolidge's expressed coöperation, Stearns moved into action with all his dynamic energy. Soon he was mailing letters out all over the state from his private office at the R. H. Stearns Company. Typical is a note which he sent to Principal Alfred E. Stearns of Phillips Academy, a member of the class of 1894 at Amherst, in the last paragraph of which he said : —

You have probably noticed in the papers that our friend, Calvin Coolidge, has announced himself as a candidate for the nomination for Lieutenant Governor. I know that such people as George Lawrence, '80, and Senator Crane, hold a very high opinion of him and believe that for the good of the State he should be kept in public office and in a high place. I think you will be interested to read the speech which Coolidge made a year ago this winter when he was first elected President of the Massachusetts Senate, a copy of which I enclose. I am very much interested in helping him to get a large vote in the primaries. I hope his candidacy may appeal to you.

[5] Memorandum furnished me by Mr. Frank W. Stearns.

Coolidge himself did his share of letter-writing and also sent a note to Principal Stearns, the conventional tone of which is amusing when it is remembered that "Al" Stearns was one of the two or three outstanding Amherst undergraduates of Coolidge's day in college: —

DEAR SIR:

As you and I were in Amherst about the same time, it occurs to me that you might be interested to know that I am a candidate for Lieutenant-Governor.

Everyone has an influence on public affairs if he will take the trouble to exert it. You can be of assistance to me by speaking or writing to your friends or telling your local newspaper about me.

I should be pleased if you could do anything along these lines.

Very truly yours,
CALVIN COOLIDGE

Primaries September 21

Before very long a committee was formed to take charge of the Coolidge campaign, with Frank W. Stearns as Chairman, Arthur B. Chapin, Amherst, '89, as Treasurer, Senator James F. Cavanagh, of Everett, as Secretary, together with Congressman Augustus P. Gardner and Oscar O. La Montagne, a Holyoke attorney. The group never held a stated meeting, but the individual members, especially Mr. Stearns, worked very hard.[6] When this technical question of management was adjusted, Coolidge wrote Mr. Stearns in an attempt to keep him from overdoing: —

All seems going well. I hope you will not take politics too seriously. I figured it out that it was worth while for me to be a candidate even

[6] In discussing the matter of personnel, Stearns wrote Coolidge on June 26, 1915: "As I see it, I work best outside of Committees. I can shout pretty loud and pretty persistently when I am deeply interested and I certainly am this time. All I want to do is to do the best for you. Please do not think for a moment that I do not feel greatly honored that you so strongly want me on the Committee, because I do. You will know me better as time goes on. One of my ways of making myself effective where I have a strong admiration and belief in a person, especially a young person, is to put them in the fore-front and back them up in every conceivable way that I know how. I am doing that with regard to Mr. Maynard in the business. I shall take more pride in seeing him go ahead and make a position in the community than in anything I could possibly do myself. So far as the business is concerned, he takes the place of a son, — my son not caring to go into the business. Now here is a chance for you to have a laugh if you want to. You will think that for an old codger like me, I am getting sentimental. Never mind, a little sentiment does not hurt once in a while, but I feel just the same way with regard to your political future that I do with regard to Maynard's business future. This is personal and it is also because I believe that it is for the great good of the State, and later of the country, that it should be so. If later it shall develop that my relations to you are confidential and more than ordinarily friendly, I shall feel that I have received still another degree, which I shall value very greatly."

if I do not get it. I want you to know you have done me a great benefit by encouraging me to run whatever the result, — but I shall win.

Now I do not want you to be troubled with any details or responsible for any particular thing. There will be no meetings of the committee or anything like that for you to bother with. I would like the use of your name and to have people know you believe in me, — that is the best asset I have.

There are no formal duties in politics. People will judge of me by the men who are willing to be known as my supporters. That is the great help of a committee..

But Stearns had already reached the point where he had no inhibitions when Coolidge's career was concerned. He solicited financial aid from anybody who seemed likely to be interested, including Dwight W. Morrow, who wrote him, "I shall be very glad to contribute to Coolidge's campaign fund, for I feel about it just as you do, but I do not want to make a contribution which would place Coolidge in the position that he feels under an obligation to anybody." Several men of wealth joined Mr. Stearns in defraying the expenses of the autumn campaign. Stearns wrote to Professor Olds, of Amherst, on July 23 : —

Just now, in addition to what little an old man can do for the dry goods business, I am spending all my spare time working for Calvin Coolidge. You know I never go half way on anything and I have become convinced that the salvation of the Commonwealth and the country demands that Calvin Coolidge should be kept in active public life and as near the top as possible. Just for the minute it does not seem best to push him for anything higher than Lieutenant-Governor of Massachusetts, but later, of course, he must be Governor and still later President. Just think what a time we will have at Commencement when the President of the United States, a graduate of your Class, '95, comes back to Commencement. There is one thing sure — if he comes back and makes a speech, nobody will have any doubt what he intends to say. It won't be much, but it will be clear.

Coolidge obviously did not know Mr. Stearns well at this time and apparently regarded him as a well-meaning "angel" who could not be expected to get into the hurly-burly of a campaign. But Stearns on his part sent him a notable letter, dated August 5, 1915, in which he made his position much clearer : —

I am going to speak very frankly. I have become very attached to you and your future, strictly as a business matter.

I also believe, as I believe anything, that the State of Massachusetts cannot afford not to have you in high public office. Mind you, I am not trying to throw bouquets, — we are talking business. For both these reasons, I am anxious to do everything I can, and I am not in the least afraid of work, and certainly am not afraid to have my name (whatever that is worth) attached to your fortunes. As a matter of fact I take a pride in having it so attached.

I shall not in any way be burdened by any work that you want me to do, if it does not involve public speaking, and I certainly shall not begrudge any time that is required for committee meetings, but shall be delighted to attend them. I did have a fear that you, being impressed by the enthusiasm that I have put into this matter, over-estimated the value of my position in the community, — at any rate, so far as it could be effective for you, — and I did shrink from taking so responsible a position because I know that I am not a good committee man, and I was afraid that I might just rattle around in the place and so block the doing of the best that could be done in your interest, and this last is my reason for thinking that someone else had better be Chairman of the Committee.

I hope the Committee can meet frequently and plan the thing out with great care.

I realize that in politics we cannot always hope to get the ideal. Under all the circumstances I am for Mr. McCall for Governor, not because I think it is ideal, but because I think it is practically the best thing to do now. I believe the ideal thing right now would be for both candidates for Governor to withdraw and heartily support you for that place.

It is not difficult to deduce from this letter that Mr. Stearns had no misgivings regarding the qualifications of his protégé. Before the campaign was well started, Mr. Robert W. Maynard, of the Amherst class of 1902, one of Mr. Stearns's younger associates in his store, said to him, "I belong to a group of men, about fourteen in all, who have dinner together nearly every evening. They will all probably vote for Coolidge because they know little about the candidates and trust your judgment; but they ask a great many questions, and I don't know how to answer them." Mr. Stearns promptly dictated a letter to Mr. Maynard and asked him to read it to his friends, who found it so acceptable and convincing that he had a large number of copies printed for distribution. Whenever he heard of anyone who wanted information about his candidate, Mr. Stearns sent him a pleasant note enclosing a copy of the "Maynard Letter," which thus had a wide circulation. He also addressed a similar communication to Coolidge, declaring that he had been attracted to him by his public record and that the latter's experience in the legislature and in the government of Northampton qualified him in a special way for the place of Lieutenant Governor.[7]

The Republican primary elections were to be held on September 21, the aspirants for the gubernatorial nomination being Samuel W. McCall,[8] Grafton D. Cushing, and the irrepressible Eugene N. Foss. Coolidge's opponent, Ham, was indefatigable as a campaigner and an orator of the florid, expansive type.[9] When Coolidge began to make speeches, Mr. Stearns was much disturbed because his candidate had such a quiet, undramatic style of talking, with no conception of the value of climaxes; but as he listened at the door to the comments of the audience as they came out, he discovered that they were discussing what Coolidge had said as if they were interested. Possibly with design, Coolidge matched the rolling sonorous periods of Ham with an effective kind of understatement. Again and again with his penetrating nasal twang he said, "You will expect me to promise that if we Republicans are given power once more we will reduce taxes. I hold out no hope that we can reduce taxes. That is a hard thing to do, and I don't want to deceive anyone; but I do promise that if we are put in power we will try very hard not to increase taxes, and I promise you that we will get one hundred cents of value for the Commonwealth for every dollar expended."

As the primary campaign developed it was clear that the best ticket strategically would be McCall and Coolidge — as the *Boston Herald* said, "the linking of Greater Boston and the Connecticut Valley." Coolidge had a distinct advantage in the fact that he possessed the respect of his colleagues in the General Court, many of whom were likely to be controlling figures in their respective districts. Furthermore the party leaders felt that McCall, who had had very little experience in state affairs, needed a running mate who was thoroughly familiar with them. Coolidge himself seems to have been confident from the beginning. The newspapers made much of a dialogue on August 20 between a well-known political reporter and Coolidge in the lobby of Young's Hotel. "Are you going to be nominated for Lieutenant Governor, President Coolidge?" asked the representa-

[7] See the Northampton *Gazette,* August 24, 1915.
[8] Samuel Walker McCall (1851–1923), born in Pennsylvania, graduated from Dartmouth College in 1874, read law in Nashua and Worcester, and made his home eventually in Winchester, Mass. Elected to Congress in 1892, he represented the 8th District for twenty consecutive years. In 1913 he was defeated for the Republican nomination for Senator by John W. Weeks. He was a scholar and wrote excellent biographies of Thaddeus Stevens and Thomas B. Reed. See *Publications of the Mass. Hist. Soc.,* Vol. 57, for a Memoir by Lawrence S. Mayo.
[9] From some aspects the contest for the Lieutenant Governorship was a battle between representatives of Amherst and Dartmouth, both of which had strong alumni contingents in Boston.

tive of the press. "Yes," was the laconic reply. "I am going to quote you, Mr. President," warned the reporter. "You may," was the answer. "I am talking seriously. I am going to secure the nomination." This, according to the witnesses, was the first time in Coolidge's career in the legislature that he had allowed himself to make a direct statement to a newspaperman. "Quick curtain," was the only comment made by the editor of the *Gazette*.

Coolidge spoke in many places, improving in his delivery and his fluency as the summer drew to a close, but never more effectively than on September 4, at an Essex County barbecue held on the estate of Congressman Augustus P. Gardner. After condemning the overcrowding of state institutions for the sick, poor, and insane, he continued with emotion unusual for him : —

I feel the time has come when the people must assert themselves and show that they will tolerate no delay and no parsimony in the care of our unfortunates. Restore the fame of our state in the handling of these problems to its former lustre.

I repeat that this is not partisan. I am not criticizing individuals. I am denouncing a system. When you substitute patronage for patriotism, administration breaks down. We need more of the Office Desk and less of the Show Window in politics. Let men in office substitute the midnight oil for the limelight.

It is clear that Coolidge gained in self-confidence, in forcefulness, and in logical utterance as he moved from one platform to another, and that his audience liked his simple, unpretentious ways. On September 18, when the campaign was almost over, he wrote to his father : —

The campaign is coming to a close and while it is impossible to tell what is going to happen the outlook seems to be good. I think I have been making very large gains in the past two weeks. Every newspaper of importance in the state is supporting me. The business interests also appear to be on my side. Whatever the outcome may be my support has been such that I am very proud of it and feel that I shall be a gainer by having been a candidate even if I am not nominated.

On the morning of September 21 the *Boston Herald* printed an editorial, "For Calvin Coolidge," in which it mentioned various prominent men who were sponsoring that candidate, including, of course, Mr. Stearns. The result of the primary election was to make McCall the Republican choice for Governor by 65,942 votes against 59,799 for Cushing and 9775 for Foss. Coolidge defeated Ham by

74,592 to 50,401 — a majority which was gratifyingly decisive. On the following morning the *Herald* commented: —

From a political standpoint the nomination of Mr. Coolidge was the sensational event of the day. The Coolidge campaign has only been in existence six weeks. The Ham campaign has been running more than a year. There were some brave spirits in the political world who surmised that Coolidge might win, but they were not overboisterous in making their beliefs known. Coolidge in the popular judgment was due to be swept out of sight in Boston and to close the day with only a moderate showing in the western part of the state.

Coolidge received the results of the primaries in Northampton and, when victory was assured, made a graceful statement for the local *Gazette*. Much pleased at his success in his first campaign throughout the Commonwealth, he went for a few days to Burlington to meet his wife and visit her mother, who had been ill. To that place Mr. Stearns sent him the first of what was to be a long succession of congratulatory letters. Describing the result as "a remarkable personal victory" for Coolidge, he went on: —

I have been receiving congratulations all day. To a small extent I deserve them, because I have worked hard and I think reasonably intelligently, but the thing that has produced the result, outside of the character and attainments of the candidate, is the fact that in a wonderful degree the best people in the community, from every class in the community, have quickly responded and been willing not only to vote for you but to work for you. The other candidate may still be able to call more people by their first name in this section than you are, but I doubt whether it is right to say now that he is better known in this part of the State than you are. . . .

To this letter Coolidge replied on September 23 in a note concluding: —

Now you know you need some rest as well as I. I shall be in by Monday A.M. I feel sure.
You will know how much I appreciate your help if I do not say much of it. I should not have been where I am had it not been for you.

On the same day Stearns wrote his brother, Richard: —

I hope you have read in the papers the result of the Primaries. I was perfectly astonished. I thought McCall would be nominated but I did not feel sure of it. The result shows that it was a very close thing.
With regard to Coolidge, he got into the campaign so late that I could not help feeling nervous, although he seemed to be confident that

we would be nominated. I don't believe he had any notion that he would get such a tremendous vote. If he did, I did not. It certainly is a splendid result and will give him great prominence for other places later on. You saw him and had a talk with him, but only once; you will have to see him several times before you begin to realize what a powerful man he is. Often when I meet him, he will sit still for half an hour without opening his mouth, but he evidently has a great power of getting there.

On Sunday Coolidge was back in Northampton, where after church he was knocked down by a Ford runabout on Main Street and narrowly escaped serious injuries. He was carrying an open umbrella and did not observe the approaching machine until it was too late. He was on his feet in a few seconds after being hit and then accepted the invitation of the driver to take him home. In the afternoon Coolidge was off for Boston, flatly refusing to disclose the identity of the man whose car had struck him.

On October 2, in Tremont Temple, at the Republican State Convention, Grafton D. Cushing presided, and the dove of peace spread out his wings. Even the Progressives returned to the temple after their pursuit of strange gods, and harmony was almost oppressively prevalent. Coolidge's speech of acceptance, which was hailed with tremendous enthusiasm, condemned particularly "the ruthless exercise of the removing power" on the part of the existing administration and the "petty tyranny" which was being exercised over the great industries of Massachusetts through the attitude of supervising commissions. "We are face to face," he declared, "with a system of administration not for the public good but for the dispensation of public contracts." He continued: —

The majority of the voters of this Commonwealth are opposed to a continuation of these conditions. They have secured a start here because we have met defeat in the past through a division of our forces. We are reuniting now through the exercise of wiser counsels — wiser counsels which are by no means confined to either one of our past divisions.

And so the final phase of the prolonged campaign was opened. Again he started on a round of speeches arranged by the party managers, moving from city to city in accordance with a schedule. His theme, developed in several different ways, was humanitarian legislation, designed to build up character, to establish independence, not pauperism. Especially he dwelt on the plank in the Republican platform advocating social insurance. As a warning, however, he said again and again: —

It ought to be understood that there can be no remedy for lack of industry and thrift secured by law. It ought to be understood that no scheme of insurance and no scheme of government aid is likely to make us all prosperous. And above all these remedies must go forward on the firm foundation of an independent, self-supporting, self-governing people. . . . To those who fear we are turning socialists, and to those who think we are withholding just and desirable public aid and support, I say that government under the Republican Party will continue in the future to be so administered as to breed not mendicants but men.

Speech after speech gave Coolidge's interpretation of what the party policy was to be. The Republicans, with candidates who inspired confidence, had little doubt of success. On October 10, Coolidge wrote his stepmother : —

My hardest work is over. I think there is little doubt of my election. I would not be surprised if I get the most votes of anyone on the ticket. There were 27 towns where I got all the votes for nomination; in the largest of these I got 62 votes. I carried all the counties but two.

I shall be speaking all the time but that is all. The State and local committees look after the work now which I was having to do myself through my committee in the primary contest. I got a very handsome endorsement which you and father may well be proud of.

McCall's opponent was David I. Walsh,[10] one of the ablest vote-getters in the Commonwealth, and the result was sure to be close. Coolidge's competitor was Edward P. Barry,[11] who had already served one term as Lieutenant Governor with no unusual distinction. During the closing weeks of the campaign McCall and Coolidge made virtually a complete tour of the Commonwealth, speaking from automobiles during the day at outdoor mass meetings and in halls in the evening. In a very short period the two candidates spoke in such manufacturing centres as Attleboro, Beverly, Everett, Fall River, Framingham, Haverhill, Lawrence, Lynn, New Bedford, Newburyport, Pittsfield, Quincy, Salem, Springfield, Taunton, Waltham, and Worcester, appealing for the votes of the working-men. At one significant gathering in Lowell both Warren G. Hard-

[10] David Ignatius Walsh (1872–), born in Leominster, Mass., graduated from Holy Cross College in 1893 and from Boston University Law School in 1897. He was in the Massachusetts House of Representatives in 1900–1901. In 1907 he settled in Fitchburg. Defeated in 1911 for Lieutenant Governor, he was elected in 1913, and was Governor in 1914 and 1915. In 1919 he was elected U. S. Senator and still holds that office. He has been delegate-at-large to six National Democratic Conventions.

[11] Edward P. Barry (1864–1937), born in South Boston and trained at the Boston University Law School, was admitted to the bar in 1904, after having been a reporter on the *Boston Herald*. He was on the Governor's Council, 1907–1909.

ing, then a Senator from Ohio, and Nicholas Longworth, a Congressman from the same state, spoke for McCall and Coolidge. Of Coolidge's work as a "stump speaker" the *Herald* said on October 19, in an editorial: —

Political reporters who have accompanied the Republican campaigners through the western part of the state note that Calvin Coolidge, nominee for Lieutenant-Governor, is not only proving an exceedingly effective speaker, but that he does all the speaking for McCall and none for himself. He can well afford to do this. On his own election over Edward P. Barry he may count with absolute certainty.

Coolidge learned much about campaigning from this arduous experience. When he was President of the United States, a group of apprehensive Republican leaders went to the White House to seek his counsel on how to win certain impending state elections.

"Funny," said the President after listening in unflustered silence to the unfolding of difficulties, "what a lot of trouble you fellows have getting elected. [Slight pause.] I don't."

James W. Wadsworth, Jr., then United States Senator from New York and facing a hard contest for reëlection, sought explicit advice, saying, "Just what would you do, Mr. President?"

"When you going home?"

"Very soon."

"Then," said Mr. Coolidge, "hitch up a buggy and drive around the state."

The harmony and concentration of the Republicans were at last beginning to show results. In late October Coolidge wrote his father from the Adams House: —

Campaign is practically over. I shall be elected, — probably by a large majority. Mr. McCall will probably win. He may have a large majority but it is likely to be close. I have been making fifteen speeches some days for the past three weeks.

On the same day the *Hampshire Gazette* printed an anonymous ballad entitled "Shout for 'Cal,'" beginning: —

> Now for Coolidge we will sing,
> Honest "Cal" must have his fling;
> Loud for him our praises ring,
> "Cal" was born to be a king.

Fortunately these verses did not much damage the candidate's prospects. Election morning, November 2, dawned cool and fair; and when the stars came out that evening it was evident that the Massachusetts Republicans, for the first time in five years, were in control of all branches of the state government. On the next day the *Herald* said: —

> The election has given the Republican Party a new leader in its Lieutenant-Governor-elect, Calvin Coolidge, of Northampton. . . . Going into the western hill towns where the Democrats thought they were firmly lodged through their professed interest in the farmers, Coolidge swept away their claims with his calm, business-like, persuasive argument. In gestures and flights of oratory he nowhere measured up to the picturesque Mr. Barry, but he won the confidence of the people and won their votes. . . . It is shown clearly that Coolidge has developed into a party leader of the first rank.

The official count showed that McCall had won by 6313 votes and Coolidge by 52,204. It was indeed a glorious victory, but Coolidge was probably right when he told his father, "I have no doubt that my being on the ticket elected Mr. McCall." On the other hand, McCall had a much more formidable opponent and altogether a harder task. For Coolidge this campaign of 1915 was crucial. If he had been beaten either for the nomination or for the election, the door of opportunity would have been closed to him for a long period, perhaps forever, as has been the case with so many young Massachusetts statesmen who have made their way a certain distance along the road to success only to be thwarted by a defeat. A man's reputation in politics depends on many factors. An error in judgment as to the proper occasion for announcing a candidacy may be irretrievable. Such a blunder Coolidge never made.

Grateful though Coolidge was for Mr. Stearns's friendship, he was still somewhat puzzled by it. The advent of this powerful backer, so unselfish, so avowedly without political ambition, was a mysterious phenomenon, not explicable by the laws which ordinarily actuate human conduct. After the election, with characteristic thoughtfulness, Stearns wrote Mrs. Coolidge: —

> You and I have one thing in common, at any rate. You picked out Calvin Coolidge some years ago and gave him your endorsement; more recently I picked him out and gave him the most emphatic endorsement I knew how to. Of course many others can claim to have picked him out, but amongst them all I think we can shake hands over the proposition that yours was the most important endorsement and mine comes next.

On his part, Coolidge wrote to Stearns a somewhat more formal letter, intended to express as a matter of record his own sense of deep obligation: —

You have been taking a leading and active part in an historical campaign. Had it not been for your work during the summer and before the election, we could not have secured our victorious result. The party is very much beholden to you.

In so far as my own fortunes could be shaped by anyone but myself, you are responsible for my nomination and election, above all my nomination. It was your endorsement that made my candidacy accepted at its face value. If my public services are hereafter of any value, the credit should be shared with you.

I trust you are having an opportunity to attend to some of your own affairs.

To this letter Stearns replied, on November 13: —

Your very kind letter has been received. I shall treasure it. Not that I can accept all that you say as to the importance of anything that I did, but I did my best. As you said in a previous letter after the Primaries, "You will have to read between the lines." I cannot say all that I would like to. I will gladly share with you interest in everything you do but your "public services" are more distinctly your own than is the case with most public men and no one has a right to any share in the good you do.

As I look at it, your campaigns have only had an auspicious opening. They are in their early stages as yet. As long as I have health and strength, you can count on me. If I could feel that it was right for me to take to myself even a portion of what you suggest as to the value of my work, I should feel that I had made good a part of the work in the public service which I have always felt I ought to do and never have done. I am almost staggered by the realization that every step now must be taken with great care, because the opportunity is wonderful and the need is almost beyond words.

Coolidge's real gratefulness was perhaps indicated better in less stilted fashion in some casual "thank you" notes. In writing to acknowledge a gift, he said to Stearns: —

Please accept our thanks for remembering us at Thanksgiving and for the very many things you have done for us. I have often wondered why the greatest merchant in Boston was giving so much attention to my welfare.

On December 23, Coolidge sent another note, of Christmas greeting: —

When you reach home Christmas eve I hope you will find this to wish you and Mrs. Stearns a very Merry Christmas.

I am sure the past year has been very different for me than it would have been but for your affectionate regard and your helpful influence. I trust you have found some compensation in seeing your efforts successful, and some in my assurance of appreciation.

Again, as the New Year approached, he evidently thought it right to say a word of caution so that Stearns might not be too painfully disillusioned: —

At the risk of seeming only to reiterate I must take this holiday season to thank you again for your many favors during the year. Your continued help and approval has made me feel very proud. I hope you will keep in mind that political action is very uncertain and not so set your heart on it that it can seriously disappoint.

It is the process that is important, let the result be what it may. I want to join you in such action that you and I can feel that we have taken the correct course whether others happen to approve or no.

During that summer and autumn Stearns was studying Coolidge in his astute, clear-visioned manner, hoping that his intuition would be justified by experience. He was troubled intermittently by Coolidge's extraordinary reticence and amateurish manner as a public speaker. "For some time," he wrote, August 16, 1916, regarding Coolidge, "I wondered whether his disinclination to talk was a pose. Since then I have become well acquainted with his father and have listened to accounts of his grandfather, and have become convinced that it is an inherited difficulty, if you call it a difficulty." With regard to the platform problem, Stearns added: —

As to Coolidge's ability as a speaker, I do not know that there is much to be said. Of course his voice is not strong, and he has none of the "style" of the professional orator. But his manner is always dignified, and its very lack of sensationalism creates an impression of reserve power in the man. Furthermore his delivery is steadily improving, as he gains in experience and self-confidence. . . . He has, of course, none of the graces of oratory. There has been some discussion as to whether it was wise to make him give a little attention to such matters. Personally I do not think it would be wise. He has a carefully thought out method in all his work. It is his own. It comes to him from a long line of ancestry, and I think we should run great risks if we tried to change it. . . .

In an article in the *American Magazine* for November 1929, Mrs. Coolidge expressed her view of the relationship between Mr. Stearns and her husband: —

Here I pause to pay tribute to one of the most beautiful friendships I have ever known. I have carefully avoided personalities, feeling strongly that we have a tendency to deal too much and too lightly with them. This is my one lapse. In the early days of my husband's Presidency much was said and written about a short, somewhat stocky friend of his, that he was this one or that one of the Administration, likening him to close advisers of former Presidents.

This friend went his quiet way, noting these comparisons, regretting them but giving no sign. He mingled with the newspaper men around the executive offices, joked with them, talked with them of things in general, won their admiration and affection, and told them that as an administration adviser he was a good floorwalker. As time went on they became convinced that he told them the truth.

No one ought to question Mr. Stearns's statement that his chief motive in backing Coolidge was "to see Massachusetts affairs in competent, honest, and courageous hands." The *Boston Herald* described him editorially at the time of his death as a man "who perceived things which were veiled from others and gave himself without limit to the honorable attainment of a great ideal." He enjoyed being a power in politics, being consulted on party matters, being brought into intimate contact with the party leaders. He had been successful in business, and liked being equally successful in governmental affairs. He discerned very clearly also that Coolidge was not the man to let anyone else direct or dominate him — that he was not likely to be a puppet statesman with some master to pull the strings. But this made no difference to him. To Stearns, Calvin Coolidge seemed in 1915 to be the man in Massachusetts public life whose thought and work were most constructive. That he also came to love him with a deep affection must be obvious to those who read the full story.

IX

Lieutenant Governor

SUCCESSFUL though he had been in the eyes of his neighbors in Plymouth or Northampton, Coolidge was not yet among the notabilities of the nation. In the edition of *Who's Who in America* for 1916–1917 were the names and records of nine other Coolidges, but not that of Calvin. Professors Archibald C. Coolidge and Julian L. Coolidge, distinguished members of the Harvard University faculty; Charles A. Coolidge and J. Randolph Coolidge, well-known architects; Dane Coolidge, a novelist; Emelyn Lincoln Coolidge, a physician; John Gardner Coolidge, a diplomat; and Louis A. Coolidge, a Massachusetts Republican leader living in Milton — all these were then on excellent authority more famous than the Lieutenant Governor of the Commonwealth. Probably he had never been mentioned up to that time in any newspapers outside of New England and New York. Nevertheless in Massachusetts he was a recognized personality, and his lean face and crackling voice were familiar to thousands of voters from Cape Cod to the Berkshires.

At the inauguration ceremonies on January 6, 1916, he aroused no small amount of curiosity. For the first time since 1909 the Republicans had control of the Executive and both branches of the General Court; and when Coolidge administered the oath to his new chief, Governor McCall, they both received an ovation. The House chamber was crowded with a happy and colorful gathering. Senator Weeks was there, and former Governor Stickney, of Vermont, and Colonel John C. Coolidge and his wife. There too were Grace Coolidge and the two boys, John and Calvin. The Lieutenant Governor, neatly attired in the morning coat and striped trousers to which he was now habituated, seemed to those who watched him impassive, dignified, not at all overwhelmed by the glamour of the occasion. After all, he was among friends — his former colleagues in the House and the Senate; the employees who had nodded to him each morning as he walked through the corridors; Mr. and Mrs. Frank W. Stearns, who must have talked it all over with satisfaction in the Hotel Touraine that evening. They all felt that he was merely moving one step nearer to the executive chamber. "It was no secret that I desired to be Governor," wrote Coolidge at a later date. "Under the custom of promotion in Massachusetts a man who did not expect to be advanced would scarcely be willing to be Lieutenant Governor." It had been the practice for Republicans to give their Governors three terms if they had not blundered and if they could be reëlected. Accordingly for three years Coolidge was unreservedly loyal to Governor McCall, deliberately subordinating his own interests and speaking always five words for him to one for himself. With a fine sense of propriety he also avoided all internal party bickering and contented himself with obeying the wishes of his superior.

The Lieutenant Governor of Massachusetts does not preside over the Upper House, as is the practice in many states, but is *ex officio* a member of the Governor's Council, which consists of eight other persons besides himself, one elected from each district. His title, prescribed by the Constitution, is "His Honor," and he assumes the place of the Governor whenever the latter is out of the state or for any reason unable to perform his duties. On the Council he is Chairman of three important committees: on Pardons, Charitable Institutions, and Prisons; on Finances, Accounts, and Warrants; and on Nominations. The Council operates not unlike a cabinet, meeting at least once a week in a large room across from the Governor's office and having the important function of passing on gubernatorial appointments. It controls a large number of minor positions and also approves of all purchases of bonds and other securities as well as of many contracts for the construction of roads and wharves. It thus now became Coolidge's business to check on expenses, to watch details of state administration, and to visit institutions throughout the Commonwealth.

When he was elected Lieutenant Governor, Coolidge, unlike some of his predecessors in that post, resolved to devote himself entirely to its responsibilities. Because it was apparent that he would be unable for years to attend regularly to his law practice, he persuaded Ralph W. Hemenway,[1] a young Northampton at-

---

[1] Ralph Wilbur Hemenway, born on August 6, 1881, in Hyde Park, Massachusetts, attended Amherst College for one year, 1901–1902, and later, after studying law, was admitted to the Massachusetts bar. He still occupies the original Coolidge offices in the Masonic Building, where he is beset daily by inquisitive Coolidge admirers. He has been very helpful to me in the preparation of this biography.

LIEUTENANT GOVERNOR AND MRS. COOLIDGE

torney, to join him in a nominal partnership. The firm of Coolidge and Hemenway thus created made no division of profits, but Hemenway merely kept the offices open and carried on his own cases during the long periods when Coolidge was absent. In 1920, Hemenway made this statement: —

I had never seen Calvin Coolidge until he sent for me and made the proposition to take up the work of his office as partner. I have been his partner now for five years. He could, no doubt, have made me rich by reason of his influence and position, but I can truthfully say that in those five years Mr. Coolidge has not turned over a dollar's worth of business through political influence or pull. He is not that kind of a man. It is not his idea of the proprieties of a public official.

The secretary for the firm of Coolidge and Hemenway was for some years Mrs. Ernestine Cady Perry, who remembers that he always signed the checks for his bills early in the month, leaving no debt unpaid, and then sent her out to deliver them on foot downtown in Northampton. To her he represented the Man Who Lived Within His Income. When he was back home from Boston over the week-end, he would often ask her to copy speeches which he had written out in longhand. He was always dignified and well-dressed and never failed to appear clean-shaven with his shoes well polished. Once, when he had left his coat and hat in the railroad car at Fitchburg in order to go out and send a telegram, the train went off without him. He telephoned Mrs. Perry to meet his usual train, get his coat and hat from the day coach, and then hold them at the station until he arrived so that he would not have to walk across the street to his office in his shirt sleeves. Mrs. Perry's first salary in the office was seven dollars a week, and she has described humorously the fear which she had in her heart, when she approached the senior partner for an increase. She could not bring herself to ask the fateful question, but he recognized her nervousness and, with a smile, said, "Did you want to ask me something?" Mrs. Perry clung to the desk for support, shut her eyes, forgot all her intended long appeal, and whispered simply, "I want a raise!" "Do you think you deserve it?" he asked, in mock severity. "Yes." "I think you do too, but I hope you will save some of it. Save some, no matter how small or how large your salary may be."

Mrs. Coolidge, continuing to live with the boys at 21 Massasoit Street, made no alterations in her manner of living. She could not have been very extravagant even if she had wished to splurge, for the salary of the Lieutenant Governor was only $2000 a year.

Coolidge was well acquainted with the ways to run a household economically. Once he turned to Mrs. Perry and said suddenly, "Do you put up fruits and vegetables?" She replied, "I don't know a thing about canning, and no one at our house does." Then he went on, "Well, I suppose you are too young to know. We always used to put up a lot of fruit and vegetables at home in Plymouth, and at my grandmother's too. I can't get our housekeeper to do any. I think she should." But he did like to spend money on his wife. Mrs. Coolidge once saw him on a Monday morning before going back to Boston taking the inside measurement of one of her hats with a string. On the following Friday she and the boys met him at Bellows Falls, and all four continued on to Plymouth for their annual summer visit. She noticed in his baggage a large, gayly striped hatbox, which he did not mention until after the twelve-mile drive from Ludlow to the Notch. Then he opened it and uncovered a leghorn hat, faced with dark blue taffeta silk, with a single rose artistically arranged on the brim. She had to wear the hat all summer in order to please him.

Coolidge now found himself much occupied in ways which he could not have anticipated. Governor McCall, sixty-five years old, did not relish the constant strain of public gatherings and delighted in sending his Lieutenant Governor to represent the Commonwealth at dinners and conventions all over the state; consequently Coolidge was shortly inundated with invitations and, for a man generally regarded as inarticulate, did a great deal of talking. He now had a motive and an opportunity for developing his political, social, and economic philosophy; indeed most of the doctrines associated with his name were thought out by him and expounded during these formative years. He made no attempt to be sensational or provocative, but he did reiterate certain beliefs which he had come to regard as basic. That he should be accused of platitudinizing was inevitable, for correctness was more important to him than originality.

Of the numerous speeches which he delivered during his three terms as Lieutenant Governor at least twenty have been preserved in the volume *Have Faith in Massachusetts*. He composed them with care and some pain, committed them to memory, and seldom repeated himself. I recall vividly one of the earliest of these occasions — a dinner of the Amherst College Alumni Association on February 4, 1916, when, according to an exuberant reporter, "a thousand sons of Amherst sang their Alma Mater's praise." It was Coolidge's first appearance as a speaker at an Amherst banquet, and he was by no means the stellar attraction. Chief Justice Arthur P. Rugg, '83, of the Massachusetts Superior Court, was the Toastmaster; and the orators included President Alexander Meiklejohn, of Amherst College, Governor Charles S. Whitman, '90, of New York, and Sir Herbert Ames, '85, as well as Governor McCall, who brought the greetings of Dartmouth. Coolidge's remarks were commendably brief; and he spent most of his time defending business against the charge that it is greedy and selfish and that our economic system is unsound. He closed with the words: —

I appeal to Amherst men to reiterate and sustain the Amherst doctrine, that the man who builds a factory builds a temple, that the man who works there worships there, and to each is due, not scorn and blame, but reverence and praise.

On that evening Mrs. Coolidge, who had seldom heard her husband speak in public, was present by invitation of Mrs. Stearns and sat in a box at the Copley-Plaza Hotel looking down at the assemblage. At one stage in Coolidge's speech he quoted a familiar quatrain from Josiah G. Holland's "Gradatim": —

> Heaven is not reached at a single bound;
>   We build the ladder by which we rise
>   From the lowly earth to the vaulted skies,
> And we mount to its summit round by round.

As the nasal twang rang out through the room, Mrs. Coolidge was so overcome with laughter that she hid herself behind the pillar in front of her in order to conceal her mirth from those at the head table. It would have been impossible to select a quotation better calculated to bring out the peculiar rasping quality of Coolidge's Vermont Yankee pronunciation. Here indeed was the man who, according to the legend, could pronounce the word *cow* in four syllables.

From the Lieutenant Governor's addresses it could be deduced that he believed in the efficacy of private initiative, in the dignity as well as the inevitability of hard work, in the responsibility of each man to and for himself. He deplored the increasing tendency "to run to the government for relief from the consequences of conditions which no act of government causes, and which no device of government can correct." With theories of regimentation tending to reduce the individual to a mere insignificant unit in the governmental machine he had no sympathy. He wanted as little interference with business by the government as possible, and he had become convinced that no legislation could be a substitute for human effort. He was an incessant advocate of what was called "relief measures" for the amelioration of poverty and disease and suffering; he was never a laggard in the support of humanitarian legislation; but he insisted that no statute could offer a lasting remedy for laziness and incompetence. All Calvin Coolidge's experience, from the farm to the State House, had taught him that independence, self-reliance, honesty, and hard work are the virtues of a sound citizenry.

With unflagging emphasis he urged his constituents to take an interest in public affairs — in minor and major candidates, in budgets, in town meetings and political rallies. "A careless, indifferent representative," he asserted, "is the result of a careless, indifferent electorate." It is true that he was a strong partisan, certain that in the Republican Party lay the chief hope for national prosperity and happiness. He declared : —

The Republican Party lit the fire of progress in Massachusetts. It has tended it faithfully. It will not flicker now. It has provided here conditions of employment, and safeguards for health, that are surpassed nowhere on earth.

But he was not exclusively a partisan. He placed his hope ultimately in the moral power of the nation, the combined efforts and ideals of high-minded men and women, regardless of party affiliation. The teachings of the great Garman and his own practical training both pointed to the same conclusion.

When Calvin Coolidge advocated over and over again economy in governmental expenditures, efficiency in administration, fewer taxes and less talk, — doctrines which were within twenty years to be condemned by political wiseacres as old-fashioned if not part of "a creed outworn," — his listeners in Massachusetts applauded. He uttered nothing new, but he restated the moral code as if some oracle had just spoken it. He was not magnetic, he had none of Bryan's or Franklin D. Roosevelt's power to sway great audiences, but the people who heard him remembered who he was and talked over what he had said.

The story of these years as Lieutenant Governor is one of steady, unspectacular devotion to duty and of unostentatious thinking. The Lieutenant Governor's office was connected with that of the Governor and situated in a wing with the clerical force. Mr. Coolidge had no personal secretary or stenographer, but was free to call on the members of the Governor's clerical staff for whatever assistance he required. His correspondence was not heavy and could easily be attended to. Coolidge had no desire to impress voters by some dramatic act, and his name was not often in the Boston newspapers. But he was gaining by experience from day to day, doing some watchful waiting, and equipping himself for a possible promotion. Early in February, 1916, McCall was out of the state giving addresses in Philadelphia and New York, and Coolidge had his first chance as Acting Governor.

On January 10, 1916, Stearns wrote the following letter to Dwight W. Morrow : —

It was a great pleasure to have such a good opportunity to talk with you as I did yesterday. I hope you made connections with Calvin Coolidge. I do not want to be foolish about this matter and especially I do not want to do him harm by being premature in talking about bigger things for him but I do thoroughly believe that more than any man I have known about either personally or by reading, Calvin Coolidge is the political heir of Abraham Lincoln. I think he has in strong development many of Lincoln's best traits and I do believe that he is better fitted even today to be President of the United States than any man, except Senator Root, who is mentioned. We cannot do very much about it now publicly but quietly in the way that you are doing it and in the way that I am trying to do it, we can further the cause a good deal.

Just at the minute I have in mind a degree of LL.D. from Amherst College for Coolidge. I have written to one or two of the Trustees. Talcott Williams is Chairman of the Committee. The Trustees feel that they have made some mistakes in the past few years and therefore they are more cautious than usual but if the right man on the Board can be made to understand about Coolidge I think we can get it through. I think the College may well afford once in a while to give that degree to a man who has made splendidly good, even if he has not wholly arrived. I think the College can afford to help him to arrive. If he can have this degree, I think amongst us we can find some way of giving the fact and the words in which Prof. Olds proposes him for the degree, a good deal of publicity.

Perhaps I told you that immediately after the Amherst Dinner, February 4, Mrs. Stearns and I are going to Washington for about two weeks and expect to have Lt. Governor Coolidge and Mrs. Coolidge as our guests. I hope that there he will meet a good many people who will remember him afterwards. Possibly you will know one or two there who can show him some attention. I will try to see that the Massachusetts Senators do their part. . . .

He wrote his stepmother, February 11, "I am away so much that I do not have the time at home I hoped." On the following day the

Coolidges went to New York and later to Washington with Mr. and Mrs. Stearns, returning to New England on the twenty-first. Mrs. Coolidge had been in Washington in 1912 when she had escorted a group of Northampton High School seniors on a sight-seeing travel tour to the national capital, but this was Coolidge's first visit and he enjoyed staying at the luxurious Shoreham Hotel, where so many of the country's statesmen and near-statesmen were visible in the flesh. He was not, however, particularly demonstrative. Some of his friends guided him around the city and finally brought him to the west front of the Capitol and pointed out the magnificent outlook towards the White House and the Washington Monument. "What do you think of that?" someone expectantly inquired. Coolidge turned and, in a precise and expressionless tone but with a twinkle in his eye, said, "That is a view that would rouse the emotion of any man."

We know that Coolidge did not call at the White House, but he was entertained by Senator Henry Cabot Lodge. Twenty-two years older than Coolidge, Lodge had been in practical politics since the 1880's, had occupied a seat in the United States Senate since 1893, and had acquired national fame not only because of his own ability but also because of his intimate association with Theodore Roosevelt. He had, however, refused to follow Roosevelt in 1912 into the Bull Moose Party, and his conservatism had remained untarnished. Well-to-do, aristocratic, domineering, talkative, rather cynically critical of others, Lodge had little in common with the shy, silent Lieutenant Governor just edging on to the political stage. Lodge belonged to exclusive clubs and moved with the "best people"; Coolidge cared nothing whatever for what is called "Society." Lodge had literally been born on Beacon Hill; Coolidge came from an obscure Vermont hamlet. In 1916, however, the older man was friendly to Coolidge and encouraged him to be ambitious. To Lodge the Lieutenant Governor in 1916 was simply a loyal party worker in Massachusetts, like many another who, during Lodge's long career, had filled state positions and then retired to private life. On October 7, 1918, Lodge wrote to Theodore Roosevelt: —

Calvin Coolidge, our present Lieutenant-Governor, is our candidate for Governor. He is a graduate of Amherst, a very able, sagacious man of pure New England type. He is not only wise and tolerant, but he also has an excellent capacity for firmness when firmness is needed. He has been ardently for the war from the beginning. He has been in thorough sympathy with your views and mine, and in his campaign he has not been talking for himself at all but just making war speeches.

It was not until Calvin Coolidge had emerged as a potential rival to Lodge that the two men, so different in background, temperament, and character, drew apart.

While W. Murray Crane was perhaps his closest adviser among the Republican leaders and certainly the one whom he most admired and desired to emulate, Coolidge retained the respect and friendship of the other important men in the party. The Republican State Committee had organized on January 12 with Edward A. Thurston, of Fall River, as Chairman, and had unanimously endorsed a "favorite son," Senator John W. Weeks, for the Presidential nomination. Within a month, however, four very respectable Massachusetts citizens of Progressive leanings — Grafton D. Cushing, Augustus P. Gardner, Charles S. Bird, and Robert M. Washburn — announced themselves as candidates for delegates-at-large, pledged to the nomination of Theodore Roosevelt. Coolidge himself, although he favored the orthodox unpledged ticket headed by McCall,[2] Lodge, Weeks, and Crane, wisely took no part in the preliminary discussion, but Stearns used all his influence to secure their election. At the primaries on April 25 the unpledged delegates won thirty-two out of thirty-six seats, and Coolidge wrote to his stepmother, "The primaries went to our satisfaction here."

By this date the enthusiasm for Chief Justice Charles Evans Hughes as a Republican candidate for President was running high, and the *Transcript* had already come out for him. Weeks's supporters, however, would not abandon hope, and at least two other Bay State Republicans — Samuel W. McCall and Henry Cabot Lodge — were known to be receptive. At the Chicago Convention Frank W. Stearns was present as an alternate delegate-at-large, acquiring his first experience in national politics. Judge Henry P. Field, according to a frequently repeated story, called on Senator Crane, who was working hard for Hughes, at his Chicago hotel. "I see your friend Frank Stearns is in town," said Crane, who usually knew all that was going on. "Yes, I saw him," answered Field. "Do you know who his candidate for President is?" "Hughes, I imagine." "Judge, you have a poor imagination," answered Crane. "He's for Calvin

[2] In late 1915, after he had been elected Governor, McCall rode with Frank W. Stearns on the train from Pittsfield to Boston. His conversation dealt almost entirely with the coming Presidential campaign, and he finally asked Stearns point-blank, "What do you think of my chances?" Stearns replied, "I don't think there is any chance whatever of your being nominated as a straight-out candidate. The only possible hope you have is in case of a deadlock, and the only way you can help that along is to forget it at present and make the best Governor Massachusetts has had for many years." Weeks was stronger as a candidate than McCall, but even his expectations had to yield when Hughes announced his willingness to run.

Coolidge." This was considered funny in 1916, but its humor had evaporated by 1924. Mr. Stearns was often laughed at by his friends at Amherst dinners. "Here comes Frank Stearns," they would say, and then ask, "What's the news of the next President?" On June 16, Stearns wrote "Charlie" Andrews in part as follows: —

I hope you are as pleased with the result of the Chicago Convention as I am. Please think the matter over carefully. Do not give a hurried decision, but let me know when I return from Amherst what place you think Calvin Coolidge should occupy next. He cannot be President this time but I sowed some seeds for him in various delegations covering the country from Maine to California and from South Carolina to the State of Washington, and most everywhere in between.

When Dwight W. Morrow reminded Mr. Stearns that he might be going too fast in his promotion of Coolidge, Stearns replied: —

With regard to Calvin Coolidge, I realize that I must be careful not to over-push him but with the backing that he already has in Massachusetts, and which is stronger than some folks realize, and with his own qualities, there is no reason why he should not go very high. His friends can help by quietly making his qualities known to those who either do not know him at all, or if at all have only met him once or twice and do not realize that he is one of the biggest men in this country today. What I have said about making him Postmaster General was not a joke. I understand that the Postmaster General is one who can have a large hand in making or marring the administration, according as he is wise or foolish. With the immense amount of patronage in the hands of the Postmaster General I should suppose it would require a man with just the gifts that Coolidge has, — an instinctive judgment of men that is almost as infallible as Senator Crane's, and a courage that is equal to the Senator's. To drop into slang, I do not believe that anybody would "put it over" on Coolidge. That he would care to have a position in Washington, I do not know.

At Chicago, Harding, of Ohio, delivered the keynote speech. On the first ballot Weeks received 104 votes, of which 28 came from Massachusetts. The third and crucial ballot on Saturday, June 10, gave Lodge only seven votes and Weeks only three, and Hughes was at once nominated by acclamation. On that same morning Theodore Roosevelt's amazing letter suggesting Lodge as a compromise candidate was read on the convention floor, but fell like a feather on a block of granite. The Republican delegates knew perfectly well that Colonel Roosevelt would accept Hughes and work for him. In these proceedings Coolidge took no part, but just as the convention was opening, he filed in Boston his papers for renomination as Lieutenant Governor.

During the summer the Coolidge family took a small cottage at Hull, on the seashore — their first holiday near the salt water and the beaches. Coolidge had been designated as Chairman of a Special Commission to adjust the finances of the Boston Elevated Railway and was largely responsible for recommending the appointment of a Board of Trustees with control of the property and the authority to fix fares. With small groups and committees Coolidge, like Crane, always functioned well, for he had a judicial mind and trusted to his reason, not his impulses. Furthermore he gained and held the confidence of laboring men, who felt that they would receive from him a square deal. Because he kept his own counsel, seldom allowed himself the luxury of gossip, and did not make rash promises, he managed to avoid trouble. Some persons were jealous of him, but he made few real enemies.

At the Republican State Convention in October McCall and Coolidge were unanimously renominated; and Coolidge made an excellent speech, tactfully praising all the party leaders, including Lodge, who was that autumn running for the first time for Senator under the system of popular vote. The Democratic nominee for Governor was Frederick W. Mansfield, a Boston lawyer who later became Mayor of that city. Coolidge's opponent was Judge Thomas P. Riley, of Medford, who had sat with him in the House of Representatives in 1908, had been Chairman of the Democratic State Committee in 1912–1913, and was an Associate Judge of the First District Court.

During the active campaign Coolidge was called upon frequently to speak and spent much of his time denouncing the Wilson administration. At Northampton, on November 1, he said, "I appeal to all Americans to rescue our country from the control of expediency and return it to the control of righteousness." On the morning of Wednesday, November 8, nearly every American newspaper supposed that Wilson had been defeated, and the *Boston Herald* came out with tall headlines, "Hughes Wins with 390 Votes." But California had not then been heard from, and slowly during the next few days the tidings spread that Wilson was to be President for another term. In Massachusetts, Senator Lodge was victorious, and McCall and Coolidge were reëlected — the former by a plurality of 46,240, the latter by 84,930. Among the Coolidge papers in his handwriting on Adams House stationery is an analysis of the figures in that election of 1916, with an arrow pointing to Coolidge's vote, which was larger than that for any other candidate for office in the Commonwealth — 283,166 as compared with 276,123 for McCall, 280,910 for the Attorney General, and so on down through the list. Calvin Coolidge obviously was pondering in his heart certain facts and statistics. It must have been clear to him that he was a good vote-getter — that, as William Allen White has phrased it, there was some channel of communication between his soul and the soul of the American people. They liked plain words and straightforward acts, and he knew what they were thinking. Very few political leaders in our history have made such an appeal to the Average Man.

But Coolidge's popularity at the polls did not make him arrogant or dictatorial. He continued to fill the second place well. Once at this period Mr. Stearns said to him, "Young man, you are going to get yourself into trouble. You are backing the Governor in things that you know are unwise." Coolidge answered, "I apprehend that I was elected by the people of Massachusetts to a definite job, second in the administration, a long ways behind the first. I accepted the office and my duty is perfectly clear — to back up the administration to the limit, whether I like it or do not like it. If this position should ever be so bad that I positively cannot do this, then my duty is equally clear — to keep my mouth shut. If any protests are to be made, they must be made by the rest of you."

The declaration of a state of war with Germany on April 6, 1917, presented to the Lieutenant Governor a large opportunity for constructive and patriotic service. He was appointed on committees and headed campaigns for raising money. Governor McCall still left to him the responsibility of representing the state administration. But Coolidge's loyalty to his chief survived his own increasing popularity. On one occasion Henry B. Endicott, Chairman of the Committee of One Hundred in Massachusetts, sent a delegation of three men to ask the Governor to aid them in getting an adequate supply of bait for fishermen. The Governor was away, but Coolidge, as usual, was available. They told him their troubles, and he at once called in the Governor's secretary to ascertain whether anyone was opposing what the Committee desired. He answered, "Yes, a certain obstinate man at Gloucester is trying to block the project." The Lieutenant Governor said, "Get him on the telephone." He talked with the recalcitrant gentleman a few moments and then, coming out of the booth, resumed, "What you want done is arranged for. But remember that a condition goes with it. If you give the matter any publicity, do not forget that the Governor settled the question, not I. I am merely his temporary agent."

During the gubernatorial campaign of 1915, McCall, influenced largely by Charles Sumner Bird, leader of the Progressives in Massachusetts, whose support the Republicans badly needed, had announced himself as favorable to a state constitutional convention and, in his first inaugural address, had introduced the subject with a definite recommendation that such an assembly should be called. No revision of the Constitution had taken place since 1853, and the movement of 1916 was largely an attempt of sponsors of the Initiative and Referendum to get their reform adopted. On April 3, 1916, the Governor signed a legislative act submitting the question of a convention to the people, and on Election Day a considerable majority of those voting declared in its favor. The voting for delegates was held on May 1, 1917, but Coolidge was not a candidate. When the body met for its first session on June 6, in the Hall of the House of Representatives, Governor McCall, attended by Lieutenant Governor Coolidge, was present and, after calling the members formally to order, delivered an address upon their duties and responsibilities. Former Governor John L. Bates was chosen Chairman.

The Convention sat throughout the summer and did not adjourn until November 28. In 1918, it sat from June 12 until August 21; and a final session of two days was held on August 12 and 13, 1919.

While Coolidge had no share in the deliberations or conclusions of the Constitutional Convention, he watched its proceedings with keen interest. Many skeptical persons felt that it was not a genuine deliberative body, not a true constitutional convention, but rather a meeting "packed by the work of an active organization to secure the passage of the Initiative and Referendum." Nevertheless it did accomplish some important results. Although the completely redrafted Constitution as approved by popular vote in 1919 was set aside by the Supreme Judicial Court, certain significant amendments were passed, including the Initiative and Referendum, Biennial Elections, and a measure providing for the consolidation of state commissions. It failed, perhaps, in securing a comprehensive revision of the whole document, but it did open up discussion on several vital topics, and in 1917 and 1918 its debates occasioned some very bitter controversy.[3]

The fact that the nation was at war did not eliminate politics in Massachusetts. On April 27, 1917, the Middlesex Club held a dinner at the Hotel Somerset in observance of the Grant anniversary.

[3] *The Massachusetts Constitutional Convention of 1917*, by Raymond L. Bridgman, Boston, 1923.

Coolidge used his time for indulging in a partisan attack on the national administration, saying : —

I trust that the Democratic Chairman of the House Committee on Military Affairs, the Democratic Leader of the House of Representatives, and beyond him, the Democratic Speaker of the House, may stand rebuked by the Republican Party of Massachusetts for their almost disloyal action in the matter of adequate preparation for our national defense.

In congratulating him on these remarks, Mr. Stearns sent him a significant and rather pathetic letter : —

Morituri salutamus. Nevertheless I hope that I am not to die physically immediately, but last night put a finishing touch to my growing belief that I must be very careful in my activities on your behalf lest I obtrude my personality and injure your political fortunes and therefore injure the Commonwealth and the country more than I can help.

You have such a level head that it may be you appreciate, although I doubt it, the reception that you received last night. I do not refer alone to the hand-clapping and the cheers, but to the restrained and earnest enthusiasm for your speech and for you which dominated that audience. I find the same conviction and sentiment wherever I go about the state, and the fine thing about it is that it is both conviction and sentiment. If my work was ever needed, it is not longer needed, but it is yours just the same as ever.

In spite of this modesty, Mr. Stearns was keeping a sagacious eye on tendencies in state politics, for he very well knew that he could not for a moment relax his efforts. His candidate was deporting himself well, but there were practical matters to be considered.[4] And so, as autumn came around again, all the facilities of the business offices of the Stearns store were at Coolidge's disposal; whenever money was required for such sordid items as letters or circulars, it seemed to be forthcoming from Mr. Stearns's magic hand; and he did not cease to arrange luncheons and dinners where his favorite might meet just the right people. He sent out dozens of framed pictures of Coolidge, carefully autographed, and his correspondence

---

[4] Stearns wrote to W. Murray Crane, August 2, 1917 : —
"You asked if Mr. Coolidge is worrying about the situation. I think not. It is not always easy to find out what is in his mind. The Governor is back in Boston for a day or two because of the reception to the Belgian representatives, but as I understand it, intends to be away most of the month. I am doing what I can to keep Mr. Coolidge in good health during this hot weather. He insists upon staying at night in his little bit of a room, not more than half as large as your library, at the Adams House, but I do get him away for evenings. . . ."

increased amazingly in volume. Coolidge himself was not by any means counting his chickens before they were well hatched out. "One should never trouble about getting a better job," he confided to Dwight Morrow, "but one should do one's present job in such a manner as to qualify for a better job when it comes along." [5] In early September he wrote to his stepmother, evidently in reply to an assumption of hers: —

You do not want to feel too certain about next year or about my being Governor. It is very largely a matter of chance. It is rather an accident that I am Lieutenant-Governor. As I told you, many things may happen in a year, so you do not want to consider anything political as assured beforehand.

There was some opposition to McCall within his own party, and Coolidge was urged by unwise counselors to enter the primaries against him for the Governorship. This he naturally refused to do. Grafton D. Cushing, however, had ambitions and thought the moment propitious for entering the lists. W. Murray Crane refused to support Cushing; Coolidge's friends all wished McCall to win so that their man would not be deprived of the gubernatorial nomination in 1918; and as a consequence McCall, at the primary elections on September 25, defeated Cushing rather badly. No one opposed Coolidge within his party, and on October 6, at the Republican State Convention in Springfield, McCall and Coolidge were named by acclamation. On the same day the Democrats, meeting at Faneuil Hall, nominated Mansfield again for Governor and Matthew Hale for Lieutenant Governor.[6] Hale also received the nominations of the Progressives and of the Prohibitionists, and some of Coolidge's friends were alarmed. But his tranquility was not disturbed. On September 25, he wrote his father: —

You probably saw the primary results. It is said to be due in a large part to me. That is part true probably.

I am confident that the election will go all right. I am well content with the man who is to run against me. He will probably be very abusive, but I feel sure he will not get the votes.

[5] Harold Nicolson, *Dwight Morrow*, 87.
[6] Matthew Hale was born, May 30, 1882, in Albany, N. Y., graduated at Harvard in 1903, a member of Phi Beta Kappa, and, after attending the Harvard Law School, was admitted to the bar in 1907. He was Chairman of the Progressive State Committee in 1912–1913 and was the Massachusetts member of the Progressive National Committee. He purchased the *Boston Journal* in 1913 and ran it for some years as the organ of the Progressive Party.

On November 3, in Tremont Temple, Coolidge spoke principally upon the war, urging the support of McCall on the ground that he and the Republican Party had done an efficient job. He showed that months before hostilities broke out a Public Safety Committee had been formed and had made careful preparations for the impending crisis; that weeks before the United States was officially at war a conference of New England Governors had been called and a million dollars appropriated by the General Court for equipping Massachusetts troops; that the State Guard of over ten thousand men had been in training; and that the production and distribution of food had been handled with a minimum of blunders. He added: —

No one has yet pointed out, no one can point out, any failure on the part of our State Government to take efficient measures for this purpose. More than that, Massachusetts did not have to be asked; while Washington was yet dumb, Massachusetts spoke.

On the eve of election the *Boston Herald* published his picture and declared that he was assured of an easy victory. After reminding its readers that in 1916 Coolidge had received the largest number of votes ever cast in Massachusetts up to that time for a candidate for state office, it continued: —

The silly charges that the present Lieutenant-Governor is a reactionary have proved to be a boomerang. Everybody knows that he has always been independent, that he has been fearless, that he has been impartial. He has championed the cause of the Negro against the power of money, and he has protected invested capital from the unjust attack of prejudice and ignorance with equal vigor and satisfaction. The people of Massachusetts found out long ago that he decided questions on their merits, and they have a confidence in him that no charge can shake.

Throughout the autumn Robert Lincoln O'Brien, the talented and vigorous editor of the *Herald,* had done all in his power to help Coolidge, and the *Transcript,* the *Globe,* and the *Post* were also on his side. At the election, although the vote was relatively light, Coolidge had a majority of 101,956 as compared with McCall's 84,930. He made a superb run in the eastern section of the state, where he was supposed to be the weakest. On November 13, with characteristic caution, he wrote his father: —

My vote was very satisfactory, as you saw, 102,000 over my opponent, and within about 2500 of carrying Boston. I told you the Irish vote would probably be for me. It was the same story in all the cities. This is not to be repeated. No one knows what will happen in a year, but it looks as though I would be nominated for Governor.

Just before Christmas, Coolidge wrote Mr. Stearns: —

At the chance of seeming only to reiterate I must take this holiday season to thank you again for your many favors during the year. Your continued help and approval has made me very proud. I hope you will keep in mind that political action is very uncertain and not so set your heart on it that it can seriously disappoint.

It is the process that is important, let the result be what it may. I want to join you in such action that you and I can feel that we have taken the correct course whether others happen to approve or no.

And so 1918 was ushered in, and Governor McCall for the third time took the oath of office, and Calvin Coolidge was recognized as the heir apparent. Before spring came, McCall had notified Coolidge of his resolve not to run again and had advised the Lieutenant Governor to announce his candidacy for Governor. At precisely that moment Frank W. Stearns wrote Coolidge a letter, dated March 30, 1918, which illustrates the affectionately paternal fashion in which the wealthy merchant, now quite accustomed to the anomalies and vicissitudes of politics, viewed his younger friend: —

A little while ago you made a remark something like this, — "I wonder if I have not a little overdone the plan of taking no position on some public questions?" I do not think so up to this time, and I am not at all sure that the time has come to change. Those who have known you for some time never seem to have any question that when the proper time comes and when it is really incumbent upon you to take a position, you will take it without fear, and it has been part of my work to make the knowledge of this fact known to a steadily increasing number, and I have no difficulty in making people understand that. I suppose the proper time for you to make a change in that regard is after you are elected Governor. It may be necessary in the campaign for the Governorship. Even then, I should suppose it could be largely confined to some such questions as the one raised by Mr. Wood with regard to the defectives in the state, and with regard to the proper attitude for Massachusetts in the management of the institutions; but sometime in the not distant future I think the time will come when you should take positions with the confident expectation that the citizens of Massachusetts will get behind you and accept you as a leader.

There are two or three little things that it is your duty to do in preparation for this leadership. One of them is to go once in six months to Dr. J. P. Sutherland, or some other good doctor, and retain him as a great corporation would retain a lawyer, to take charge of your health. You think you can stand most anything, but you are going to be under a brain pressure greater than almost any man in the country, and this recommendation of mine is just common sense. The other thing is that you must at least twice a year get away from Boston and Northampton for at least a couple of weeks at a time, where you can just vegetate. You cannot do that trick in any other way.

I shall not subject you to letters of this kind often. When I do, it is your part in the conflict that is on, and going to increase, to realize that the one gift I have is an instinct in the selection of men. I think I am not boasting when I say I have that and so you must not treat lightly what I have to say. The occasions will not often arise for such letters, but they will occur once in a while.

Coolidge's friends were doing what they could to make people realize that he was warmhearted. Albert P. Wadleigh, Representative to the General Court, one day met "Tom" White,[7] of Newton, one of Coolidge's most astute advisers on political matters, who said to him, "What do you think of my friend Cal?" "I like him all right," Wadleigh replied, "but he makes me think of a human icicle." White answered, "You've got him all wrong. When you know him, he's not like that." About two weeks later Wadleigh received quite unexpectedly a telephonic invitation to lunch with the Lieutenant Governor at the Parker House; and in the hotel lobby he met Representative Hirsh, of Dedham, who was equally astounded at having been asked to join the party. At 12.30 Coolidge walked unobtrusively through the School Street entrance, accompanied by Frank W. Stearns and Mr. Rideout, of Somerville. The five men sat down to a simple meal of codfish balls, mashed potatoes, and coffee. Coolidge asked Wadleigh how the weather was in the Merrimac Valley, how he liked his work in the State House, and what he thought of political conditions. The others had almost nothing to say, and the repast seemed to Wadleigh painfully embarrassing because of its long intervals of silence. Finally Coolidge looked at his watch and said, "The House comes in at two o'clock. Glad you could take lunch with me." He then rose, shook hands, — very limply, — and, with Messrs. Stearns and Rideout, departed, leaving Wadleigh and Hirsh in a mood of bewilderment. A day or two later Wadleigh met White, who smilingly asked, "Do you still think Cal is an icicle?" Wadleigh's answer was, "I like Mr. Coolidge well enough, but it will take a lot of education to make most people understand him."

During the winter and spring McCall was often out of the state,

[7] Thomas W. White was long Supervisor of Administration, with an office in the State House, and acquired a profound knowledge of practical politics. He is now Secretary to Senator Henry Cabot Lodge, in Washington.

and Coolidge was frequently Acting Governor. It was an exciting period. In January came drastic governmental fuel orders, and manufacturing plants were directed to close for five days. On April 5 Coolidge rode up Bunker Hill in the British tank, *Britannia*. On April 11, he welcomed the Polish Mission on its visit to Boston and, when he was greeted with an outburst of applause, gallantly referred to the demonstration as being entirely for the foreign visitors.

We find him again on July 1 delivering a formal address at the joint memorial service in Faneuil Hall of the Knights of Pythias lodges, ending with a long quotation from *Paradise Lost* and emphasizing throughout the desirability of adapting discoveries in the spiritual world to the practical needs of man. So much occupied was he with the exigencies of war that he was seldom able to return on week-ends to his home, although he did go back in June to the inauguration of William A. Neilson as President of Smith College. In the late summer came the first evidences of the devastating influenza epidemic of 1918, and soon everybody was dwelling in an atmosphere of alarm. At the Republican primaries, held on September 4, when the disease was spreading rapidly, Coolidge was nominated for Governor without opposition. For Lieutenant Governor, Channing H. Cox,[8] Speaker of the House of Representatives, won the nomination over Coolidge's former rival, Guy A. Ham. On the Democratic side there was a spirited contest among William A. Gaston, Richard H. Long,[9] and Edward P. Barry. Long, a shoe manufacturer from Framingham with an open purse, finally was named as the candidate and announced on September 25, somewhat prematurely, "I will be the people's Governor."

The epidemic was then at its height. Theatres, churches, and other places of assemblage were closed, and cautious men and women even wore gauze masks at their work. As Acting Governor, Coolidge issued a proclamation **warning** citizens to take no un-

[8] Channing Harris Cox was born, February 28, 1879, in Manchester, N. H., graduated from Dartmouth in 1901 and from Harvard Law School in 1904, and at once began the practice of law in Boston. From 1910 until 1918 he was a member of the Massachusetts House of Representatives and from 1915–1918 its Speaker. He was later Lieutenant Governor (1919–1920) and Governor (1921–1924). Since retiring from active politics he has been President of the Old Colony Trust Company. He is a man of marked executive ability and unusual oratorical gifts.

[9] Richard Henry Long was born in South Weymouth, Mass., September 4, 1865, and attended the public schools. Entering his father's shoe shop at the age of twenty-four, he built up a plant which employed 4000 men and women. Although he had always been a loyal and consistent Democrat, he had held no public office.

necessary risks. The Fourth Liberty Loan was about to start, and the Republicans agreed to hold no mass meetings until after it had been completed. The Democrats, however, would not follow this policy, but opened their campaign on October 21. Long, a tireless traveler and speaker, moved from town to town about the state, attracting large crowds by his vilifying methods and attempting especially to win the support of organized labor. Seldom has demagoguery been carried farther in the history of Massachusetts. Coolidge, however, did not seem worried, and on October 31 he wrote his father: —

It is my judgment that the campaign is going all right. Of course all elections are uncertain. I feel rather more certain about this one than any in which I have been engaged, — but as I have said before, whether I should happen to be chosen Governor or not, the people of Massachusetts have already shown a good deal of appreciation for me.

As the campaign rushed to a close, the Republicans tried to make up for their previous patriotic inaction by holding in quick succession several well-publicized mass meetings. Long's aggressive tactics had made him a formidable opponent, and it was essential to counteract his abusive speeches.[10] On October 28, ex-President Theodore Roosevelt came out with a helpful statement: —

Mr. Coolidge is a high-minded public servant of the type which Massachusetts has always been honorably anxious to see at the head of the state government; a man who has the forward look and who is anxious to secure genuine social and industrial justice in the only way it can effectively be secured, that is, by basing a jealous insistence upon the rights of all, on the foundation of legislation that will guarantee the welfare of all.

Another ex-President, William H. Taft, also entered the contest by saying: —

It is a great pleasure to come back to an atmosphere where they really discuss a candidate with reference to his fitness for office; and of course with Calvin Coolidge, he fills the bill so fully that I need not further dwell on it.

[10] Stearns wrote his son, Foster, Oct. 25, 1918: —
. . . "After the election is over I think I will 'take to the tall timber.' I never felt better in my life but I think I could stand a few days vacation, and more than that, I can see a throng of people trying to get at me after election to whisper in Mr. Coolidge's ear that they would like an appointment. It has already begun in a small way. Mr. Coolidge seemed to be feeling unusually jovial for him last night and made the remark 'I don't think I could defeat myself if I tried.' He added, 'I don't know just why, but I guess it is partly because I am not all the time doing fool things.'"

On Saturday, November 2, in Tremont Temple, Lodge and Weeks, as well as Coolidge, spoke. The Lieutenant Governor said almost nothing about the impending election but confined himself to a discussion of the situation in the World War, now drawing dramatically to a close.[11] On the following Monday he opened his remarks in Faneuil Hall with a very brief personal statement: —

We need a word of caution and of warning. I am responsible for what I have said and what I have done. I am not responsible for what my opponents say I have said or say I have done either on the stump or in untrue political advertisements and untrue posters. I shall not deal with these. I do not care to touch them, but I do not want any of my fellow citizens to misunderstand my ignoring them as expressing my attitude other than considering such attempts unworthy of notice when men are fighting for the preservation of our country.

On Sunday, November 3, Coolidge had written to his father: "From all I can see I shall be elected. It has been a difficult campaign. The Opposition has been very unscrupulous, but it will not get them any votes." On Monday morning the *Boston Herald* printed a stirring editorial headed, "Coolidge vs. Long," in which it declared that Coolidge completely outclassed his opponent in personal qualifications for the governorship and asserted that Long's candidacy was viewed without enthusiasm even by his own party. The article brought out the contrast, already expressed in many quarters, between "Coolidge, the Constructionist" and "Long, the Profiteer." On that same morning the Republicans carried a large advertisement in all the newspapers under the caption, "Republican Bugle Call to the Colors," and including a characteristic statement by Coolidge: —

My conception of public duty is to face each problem as though my entire record in life were to be judged by the way I handled it, — to keep always in touch with the folks back home, — to be firm for my honesty of opinion but to recognize every man's right to an honest difference of opinion.

The duties of Governor of the Commonwealth are not intricate or burdensome if a man looks upon their discharge as a public function and not as a personal prerogative. If chosen to be your Governor, I shall try to conduct the duties of the office so as to merit the sincere endorsement of men of fair minds in all parties. I can promise nothing more. I

[11] This speech, one of the most emotional and eloquent that Coolidge ever made, is printed in *Have Faith in Massachusetts*, 148–157. In it he said, "We are discussing a league of nations. Such a league, if formed, must not be for the purpose of diminishing the spirit or influence of our Nation, but to make that spirit and influence more real and effective. . . . It is our one desire to make America more American."

would not deem myself worthy of your support if I promised anything less.

Coolidge was to have a closer call than he or his managers had realized. Long had spent a large sum of money and had worked very hard throughout the Commonwealth. Nevertheless before morning dawned on November 6, Coolidge knew that he had won. John W. Weeks had been defeated by David I. Walsh for United States Senator, and there had been other Democratic gains; but Coolidge and Cox were safe.

Some light is thrown on the situation by a letter from Mr. Stearns to his son, Foster, on November 6, a portion of which reads as follows: —

The fight is over and it certainly was a mean one. Walsh beat Senator Weeks by 18,500 votes. Coolidge beat Long by 17,500 votes. Coolidge ran ahead of Weeks about 26,000 votes. I won't attempt to describe in a letter all the intricacies of the campaign, but it was one of the meanest in some ways that I have ever known anything about. There was a time last night when I even feared that Coolidge was defeated. He has suffered from the nature of the campaign. It was assumed that he was sure to be elected and probably overwhelmingly and it was greatly feared that Weeks would be defeated, so the result was that the news items were largely on the Weeks contest, which resulted in "blanketing" the Coolidge publicity. This does not mean that the papers were not nice to Coolidge — they were, and editorially they were very strong for him, but the discussion, which gives publicity, was for Weeks. Then, again, Mr. Coolidge is very unwilling to go into newspaper controversy. There was a dastardly advertisement published in the interest of Mr. Long. I don't remember whether I sent you a copy of it or not. It had at the top "Rebukes the President," then a picture of Coolidge with some black hands pointing at him, and an attack on his lack of record, etc. I had a beautiful advertisement all prepared to answer it, which I proposed to have signed by a large number of prominent people. I showed it to Mr. Coolidge. He said, "It is a good advertisement but I will not get into a controversy of that kind. I will not attack an individual. If the people of Massachusetts do not know me well enough to understand the animus of such an advertisement and are not willing to elect me without my answering every indiscriminate attack, then I would rather be defeated," and the whole campaign on his behalf has been along those lines. I felt all the time that it would have been better for Mr. Weeks if very much more attention had been given to Mr. Coolidge; that he was the best one to get out the vote, but they could not see it. Perhaps it is not strange.

Coolidge's official majority turned out to be 16,773. In view of the exceptional nature of the campaign, this result was not unsatisfactory, but there were moments on the eve of the election when it looked as if he had been defeated. It was a contest overshadowed by the news from the European front. Coolidge went with his wife to Maine for a few days of rest, but while he was there tidings of the Armistice arrived, and he promptly returned to Boston. Tuesday, November 12, was designated by Governor McCall as Victory Day; and Coolidge reviewed a parade at the State House and spoke at the great "Victory and Liberty Meeting" in Symphony Hall that evening. The World War was over, and the boys would soon be coming home.

Never has a Massachusetts man been better qualified by experience and training for the Governorship than Calvin Coolidge. He had sat in both the House and the Senate, and had presided over the latter body. He was familiar with the business of the Governor's Council and had been so often Acting Governor that nothing pertaining to the position of Chief Executive was strange to him. As Lieutenant Governor he had performed admirably the duties of his office and had been a loyal second in command. Mr. Stearns tells the story of how Robert A. Woods, head of South End House in Boston, once urged Coolidge to come out as favoring the expenditure by the Commonwealth of a large sum for institutions in which the mentally deficient could be segregated. Coolidge replied, "This is not a question with which I ought to concern myself now. I am a candidate for Lieutenant Governor, and it would not be wise or effective for me to raise this issue. That is for the Governor to do. If I am ever Governor or a candidate for Governor, I shall be perfectly willing to sponsor your plan." Well aware of what was within the limits of propriety, Coolidge did not propose to go beyond them.

Furthermore Coolidge had built up a reputation for quick and efficient action. He did not make rash promises, he said just what was in his mind, and he never pledged himself to do more than he could perform. When he was asked for some favor, he usually replied, "Well . . . I'll see what I can do about it"; but he seldom disappointed the applicant. If he was pressed to do something in a hurry, he became irritable, and he seldom moved unless he was cognizant of the entire situation. Once when there seemed to be an unusual degree of excitement over a bill, he said to a friend, "We've always got to have a certain amount of hysteria." He was a good executive, who kept cool and calm, and his desk was clean when he left his office in the afternoon.

It had been fortunate for Governor McCall, who cared little for detail, that he had such a reliable Lieutenant Governor. Coolidge, through his acquaintances in the Legislature, could keep in touch with what was going on all over the state. Without doing much talking, he extracted information from others and thus came to have almost as much political acumen as Senator Lodge. When he himself became Governor, he knew precisely where to turn for advice or aid.

Throughout December, 1918, McCall had a severe cold, and Coolidge was again Acting Governor. On the thirteenth, Stephen O'Meara, the Police Commissioner of Boston, died, and within eight days the Governor appointed Edwin U. Curtis to succeed him. Mr. Curtis will later have an important rôle in this narrative. On the fifteenth, Coolidge announced that his secretary would be Henry F. Long, who had held the same position under McCall. Long, then thirty-five years old, had been a businessman until his election to the General Court in 1915. There McCall had become acquainted with him and had discerned his unusual qualifications for secretarial work. His knowledge of State House procedure, his skill in dealing with men, and his tact and discretion, were helpful to both McCall and Coolidge.

From the hour of his election as State Senator until his inauguration as Governor, Calvin Coolidge's progress was virtually uninterrupted. He had not deliberately planned it. From one stage to another he had moved, with the assistance of Frank W. Stearns, doing the day's work as he had urged others to do. So far as he was concerned he had reached the summit of his ambition — indeed had risen higher than he had ever dreamed of doing twenty years before. At about this period his classmates at Amherst held a dinner in New York City, which Coolidge was persuaded to attend. After the meal, when everybody was in an expansive mood, one of the class of 1895 said, "Cal, you weren't very much of a leader in college. Probably you never thought then of going into politics. And yet here you are Governor of Massachusetts. What did it?" Coolidge meditated a moment behind his thin cigar and finally ventured in his nasal voice, "I guess Fortune did it." "Oh come now, Cal," came from several of his friends, "that won't do. Tell us the real secret." And the inscrutable Coolidge, after another puff, responded, "Wal, mebbe I did nudge Fortune some!" . . . Some of the nudging had been done by Frank W. Stearns.

X

Governor of Massachusetts

A FINE product of the "escalator" system by which, in the palmy days of the Republican Party in Massachusetts, a competent and popular officeholder was rewarded by promotion from one position to another, Calvin Coolidge was also an outstanding example of the "local boy who has made good." Accordingly when, on November 15, 1918, he returned to Northampton for the first time after his election as Governor, he was hailed almost as a royal personage. Mrs. Coolidge and he arrived on the "7.22" to be met at the station by the Northampton regiment, a band, and a cheering crowd of citizens. A parade was formed to accompany the Governor-elect to his Massasoit Street home, where Mayor Morse introduced the first Northampton resident to be chosen Governor of the Commonwealth since the days of Caleb Strong in the early nineteenth century. Coolidge replied in part: —

I do appreciate the honor shown me on my return to Northampton. . . . I thought while coming up through this street, with this splendid escort, that I had never appreciated how much Northampton thought of me. . . . It is hard for me to appreciate my own accomplishments. I have often wondered why, from the thousands of persons in the Commonwealth, I should be chosen as a candidate and elected as Governor of the state, the second office in all this nation.

On that evening, at a performance of the Northampton Players in the Academy of Music, Coolidge made one of his rare appearances at the theatre, with his wife and two sons, in a box. As the Coolidge family stepped into the auditorium, Dr. Allen shouted, "Attention! The Governor! Everybody up!" And the audience rose and applauded lustily as the party marched down the aisle. Early in December, the City of Northampton gave its most distinguished citizen an official banquet at the Hotel Draper, presided over by Judge Henry P. Field, who was in one of his wittiest moods. Coolidge met the demands of the occasion, recalling the men whom he had known in his salad days as a lawyer and drawing an amusing picture of the select company which used to meet around the coal stove in the store of Clark and Parsons. In conclusion he said, "I shall send out no invitations to anyone in Northampton to attend the inauguration — everybody come!"

The Great and General Court convened on Wednesday, January 1, 1919, and on the following morning came the inauguration, which took on as usual the aspects of a social event. Calvin Coolidge had watched similar proceedings, and participated in them, but never as the central figure. A Massachusetts inauguration is always a colorful occasion, with much pomp and circumstance and silk hats and gorgeous uniforms everywhere on display. In accordance with custom Coolidge presented himself at the Governor's chambers, where he was greeted by McCall and his aides. There a committee from the joint session of the General Court called upon him to announce that the members were awaiting his pleasure. Before departing, McCall grasped his hand affectionately and wished him Godspeed, at the same time handing to him the ancient keys to the Council Room, the famous Butler Bible, presented in 1884 by Benjamin F. Butler, the bound volume of *Acts and Resolves of the Commonwealth,* transmitted with an inscription from each governor to his successor, and the other traditional insignia of his high position. Then the procession, headed by the Sergeant-at-Arms, with his rosette and mace, and including the Sheriff of Suffolk County, with his resplendent uniform and dress sword, state officials, judges, officers of the army and navy, and a few civilian guests, moved slowly to the Hall of Representatives, where the oath was administered to Coolidge by the President of the Senate. Seated in the audience were Colonel John C. Coolidge, Mrs. Calvin Coolidge, and the two boys. On February 11, Coolidge wrote to his stepmother, who had been too ill to attend : —

I am sending you a picture of what you would have seen had you been at the inauguration.

You will see that it is a good likeness of Father and a very fine likeness of Vilas Moore. You will see the two boys sitting over at the left of father and in front of the desk. The blurred face just at the right of father is the Chief Justice of the Supreme Court, Mr. Rugg, and behind Father is Governor Stickney.

As the words of the oath of office died away, the roar of seventeen guns on Boston Common announced that a forty-eighth Governor was in power on Beacon Hill; and almost at that moment Samuel W.

THE GOVERNOR

McCall slipped out of the State House and walked down the broad steps towards the street, a private citizen again after many years of public service. Channing H. Cox was then inducted into office as Lieutenant Governor, and Calvin Coolidge stood up, amid loud hand clapping, to read his Inaugural Address. Occupying thirty-one minutes to deliver, it was one of his most liberal pronouncements and in some respects as fine a speech as he ever made. A few of its more salient sentences will show its tone: —

You are coming to a new legislative session under the inspiration of the greatest achievements in all history. You are beholding the fulfillment of the age-old promise, man coming into his own. You are to have the opportunity and responsibility of reflecting this new spirit in the laws of the most enlightened of Commonwealths. We must steadily advance. Each citizen must have the rewards and opportunities worthy of the character of our citizenship, a broader recognition of his worth and larger liberty, protected by order, — and always under the law. In the promotion of human welfare, Massachusetts happily may not need much reconstruction, but, like all living organizations, forever needs continuing construction.

Let there be a purpose in all your legislation to recognize the right of man to be well born, well nurtured, well educated, well employed, and well paid. This is no gospel of ease and selfishness, or class distinction, but a gospel of effort and service, of universal application.

In this address, with its vision of a modern Utopia, Coolidge reflected the mood of unselfishness and coöperation which had pervaded a nation united for war; and he was obviously hoping to transfer into times of peace that same patriotic zest and spirit of loyalty. He wished to carry on the state government with the same attention to thrift, to hard work, and to self-sacrifice which had marked the summer of 1918. The difficulty was that no people can maintain that type of emotional exultation very long, and then only under the compulsion of self-interest. The natural reaction after the strain of war was not heroism, but relaxation, as history was again to prove.

Nevertheless the Inaugural Address was well received. In commenting favorably upon its spirit, the *Boston Herald* said: —

Massachusetts has not in years had a Governor who entered his duties with so good an understanding of the state institutions and their needs as the man who was inaugurated yesterday.

It was observed with satisfaction that Coolidge had called attention to the needs of the underprivileged, that he had urged improvement in the rural schools, that he had stressed the desirability of rehabilitating the teacher's calling. The *Springfield Republican* declared that the Inaugural bore abundant evidence of having been composed by "a man helpful in intention, practical in method, and progressive and far-sighted in his conception of public service."

Calvin Coolidge wrote this speech himself, as he did nearly all those of this period. On one occasion, however, he was asked to talk at a dinner given at the celebration of the centennial anniversary of a well-known piano company, and Mrs. Coolidge was amazed to hear him deal with composers and musical compositions in a way indicating wide knowledge of a field which lay wholly outside his experience. After the affair was over, she asked him laughingly where he acquired all his information, but he sidestepped the question and appeared quite shamefaced. He would not permit this musical address to be included among his published speeches. Ordinarily, however, he would scribble his remarks on sheets of foolscap paper, in soft pencil, rewriting and transposing with infinite pains before he would allow them to be copied by a typist. He was seldom pleased at the time with what he had done and usually worried a good deal before the event, but afterwards he would sometimes read what he had said and add, "That was a pretty good speech after all."

Following the inauguration, the new Governor held a reception in the Hall of Flags, and he was the host at a luncheon to his staff. In the evening Mrs. Coolidge led the grand march at the inaugural ball. At all these ceremonies the happiest guest was probably Frank W. Stearns, who was now watching the fruition of his carefully laid plans. Some of his dreams had been realized, but he was far from being content with what had been accomplished. If we are to understand the farseeing and very practical quality of his mind, we must read carefully the following letter sent by him on January 8, 1919, to Dwight W. Morrow, who had just returned to the United States after several months in Europe. It was important, as Stearns saw it, that Morrow should be brought up to date regarding the situation.

I was very sorry that I could not come down and talk with you yesterday afternoon, but I had my passage engaged on the three o'clock train and felt it necessary to get home. The fact is I have to be a little careful not to get too tired. Twice during recent campaigns I have been notified by the doctor that I must pull up, and once he went so far as to tell me that I had not many weeks left if I did not. I think he exaggerated but I want to keep on the job, so I am a little careful.

With regard to money matters, I do not know exactly what I did spend personally, but during the year preceding the election it probably cost me $6000 or $7000 beyond what I collected for Mr. Coolidge's campaign. If you had been in the country I probably should have remembered what you said to me about wanting to take a hand when Calvin ran for Governor and asked if some of his friends not in Massachusetts did not want to help out to the extent perhaps of $2000 or $3000. This is all taken care of now. There were reasons why I did not want to ask very generally for funds, and no funds were received for his personal campaign except from those who insisted on it and were more interested in him than in any other part of the campaign. Sometime, perhaps, I shall explain this a little more, because it has some country-wide political bearing. Incidentally, I may say that one Amherst man contributed $2500.

For the coming year I think funds will be more needed than they were last year even. The Democrats in Massachusetts having had the success of electing Walsh Senator are greatly encouraged. Their candidate for Governor last November announces that he intends to continue to run for at least two years, and he is supposed to be a man of very large wealth and willing to spend without limit. No such expenditure as that is necessary or useful, but there are a good many proper uses for money, especially from day to day through the year. Just as illustrating, Mr. Coolidge decided that it would be a nice thing to send out a greeting card to some of the state employees. He was going to send it one cent postage. I told him that as he had consulted me it was now out of his power to decide, — we would have a good looking card and would send it first class, and we would send it not only to the present members of the Legislature, for instance, but to all who had ever been with him in the Legislature. More than that we would send it to every family in Northampton, and Mrs. Stearns would make him a Christmas present of the transaction. It resulted in a cost of $600, but it was one of the best political moves I have known, and he has been greatly delighted with the reception it received.

One of his greatest assets is Mrs. Coolidge. She will make friends wherever she goes, and she will not meddle with his conduct of the office. I told Mrs. Stearns a short time ago that it was her duty to give a lunch to a carefully selected list of ladies to introduce Mrs. Coolidge here. This was done at a cost of $500.

Another time the University Club gave a reception and dinner to C. To make sure it was a success I had quite a list of guests, — cost $125.

There is a good deal to be done in the way of publicity. So far as I have an idea of his resources, he is not in a position to do these things. His salary for several years while in the Legislature was $1000. As Lieutenant-Governor it was $2000. He has always kept his home in Northampton which, as you know, is one-half of a very small house. He himself has lived most of the time in Boston in a room at the Adams House for which he paid $1.00 a day. He has now taken two rooms at the Adams House. His salary as Governor, I think, is $10,000 a year, but there will be a good many expenses connected with the office, so that I doubt whether he is much better off with his $10,000 than he was with the $2000. Ever since he first ran for Lieutenant-Governor I have tried to see that he was at no personal expense for himself. I have done most of this myself, although I have in the actual campaigns had contributions, as was natural. He is exceedingly independent and would be terribly disturbed if he felt that he was under obligations to anybody, but I have not been able to discover that it frets him that I have assumed some of these bills. I know nothing of the working of his mind, — at least I know nothing by anything he says, — but I think he knows there is nothing I want except to at this time elect him Governor and then keep the road just as clear as I can for him of all sorts of complications so that he may, as he certainly will, make the best Governor that Massachusetts has had since Senator Crane. Of course I think there is very much more in store for him, though any work of preparation for that has to be done very carefully. He feels that nothing queers a man in public life more than to have folks feel that he is using one very high office merely as a stepping stone to get another. We have had a good deal of trouble from that very thing in Massachusetts and he does not intend to make that mistake.

While I am talking about money matters, I am very anxious that he shall take a house in Boston of reasonably good size, if possible on Beacon Hill, but not on the Back Bay, — if possible one of the more or less historic houses; that he move his family there; that he shall have a lady who shall be able to take some care of the boys when out of school, so that Mrs. Coolidge shall not feel anxious about them, and the same person could probably act as a Secretary to Mrs. C. I think they should entertain constantly, but simply, chiefly at lunch. I think that every member of the Legislature, Democrat and Republican, should have an opportunity during the year to invite two or three of his constituents to lunch with the Governor. Just think what a town talk that would make in a little village on the Cape. He makes friends, and she will, just as quickly as he comes in contact with people. The whole scheme is to get him actually known to every citizen in Massachusetts and some from outside. I have told him frankly that it is my job to finance, and I shall be glad to do it. I have not said anything about this to anybody except to two or three of the wisest men I know here, and men who know both C. and his wife. They say I must put this thing through. Following my usual habit with him, when I have something very important, I write it instead of trying to talk with him. It is desperately hard to talk with him about any personal matter. I have as yet not received an answer, though I wrote him about a month ago.

Meanwhile I shall go on pursuing the policy that I did last year, entertaining in a quiet way men from all over the State, though this year I shall probably have to do it myself instead of having the Governor with us, as I generally did last year. He is a working Governor if ever there was one.

You see I am writing you very frankly and in a way that should be strictly between ourselves. It ought not to go to a third party, no matter who he is, but I am taking it for granted that no one else is more genuinely interested in Calvin Coolidge and in his success than you are, and from some things you have said I take it that you sympathize with my estimate of him, — that he is really one of the greatest men of the country. Four years intimate association with him has convinced me that he has many of Lincoln's strongest qualities. I think his courage is extraordinary; his ability to see through a question and to judge what the result of certain action will be, not merely at the time it is taken but in its working out through the years to come, is extraordinary, and so is his judgment of men. I am not a politician in the ordinary sense of the word. I have not political acumen, but I have never wavered in my conviction that I was doing the State and the Country a good turn by doing everything I could to make Calvin Coolidge known. How successful I have been is for others to say. The time has come, as I said yesterday, when you can help wonderfully because quietly and steadily we want to make him known outside of Massachusetts.

I had a talk with Norton yesterday in New York. He said, "Roosevelt is gone. Now there is Coolidge." And he said, "I must devise some way to make him known in the West." Of course the natural answer for me was that he could do that better than I could. I have no acquaintance in the West and I suggested that he do what he could in New York. He seemed to think that C. is quite well known already in New York, but I am sure he can be better known.

I am writing this now so that you may have it in mind. I do not know of anything better that can be done to help human beings and help business than to make Calvin Coolidge the one great leader in the country. I do not think he can leave the State very much. It is possible that he could occasionally if there was some occasion where he could be helpful.

During his first year as Governor I would very much like to see him receive a degree of LL.D. from Harvard, from Amherst, from Princeton, from William and Mary College, and from some Western College. You see I have no small ideas. I think possibly through Mr. Lamont you can help on the Harvard degree, and you certainly can on the Amherst degree. It would be very much better at Amherst that the suggestion does not come at all from me.

This is all very rambling but I have not time to rewrite it and I want to get it to you before you go on your vacation.

Almost at once after perusing this very frank elucidation of Mr. Stearns's plans and hopes, Morrow replied: —

I received your telegram of the 7th, and also your long letter of the 8th. The letter I have read with the greatest interest. I arrived home the last day of the year, and I found the invitation to the inauguration. I at once wired Calvin in accordance with the enclosed copy. I shall certainly write him a good letter.

I want, however, to do more than that. I want to have a very long talk with him about his work. You may look upon me, because of my associations, as a conservative, but I really think I have been all my life something of a radical. I have tried, of course, to be radical along lines that would help instead of along lines that simply threw existing machinery out of gear. This is what I liked about Calvin's fine aphorism when he was made President of the Massachusetts Senate. "Be as revolutionary as science; be as reactionary as the multiplication table."

Now, this has a bearing on the next two years, or ten years, of Calvin's life. I wish he might think carefully about the first half of his maxim. I should like to see him as "revolutionary as science." I should like to see him get the real facts with reference to some of the things that are wrong in the world and take a bold stand on making them right.

For the last year I have been abroad dealing with all sorts of Government officials. Some of them have been socialists like Thomas, the great Socialist leader in France; some of them have come from old conservative families, like Lord Robert Cecil, son of the Marquis of Salisbury. I have about come to the conclusion that the division of the people of the world is not really between conservative and radical, but between people that are real and people that are not. Calvin is one of the fellows who is real. He really wants to make things better, not to pretend to make them better.

Some days after this remarkably frank interchange of ideas Stearns went to New York, at Morrow's request, ostensibly to talk about the affairs of Amherst College. Reaching the Grand Central Station at six o'clock, he was met by the effervescent Morrow, who took hold of his arm and walked him up to the Metropolitan Club, dancing a kind of jig as they went along. As they proceeded, Stearns getting more and more weary from the unaccustomed exercise, Morrow said, "Before we have our talk this evening, I want to make you an explanation or apology. For the past two or three years, when you have talked about Calvin, I have thought you were crazy. I want to say now that I was the one who was crazy. You were not. I could not see the picture; I can now." They spent the evening with hardly a mention of Amherst, discussing how important it was that Calvin Coolidge should become President of the United States.

Stearns's intimacy with Coolidge was still an unusual one. Close though they were in many ways, Stearns still called him "Mr. Coolidge," and the two when together were never very fluent, often sitting for long periods in complete silence. Stearns was able to relieve him by acting as a buffer between him and importunate favor seekers; and he was ready, when asked, to contribute his advice. As soon as he became Governor, Coolidge requested Stearns to resign from two commissions of which he was a member, feeling that the two of them might be subjected to criticism. When Stearns was once asked what his relationship to Coolidge was, he answered, "As an individual, my feeling towards him is that of a father; as a public official, it is much like that of a son." Stearns always had the entree into the Governor's office, but took care not to make his presence too obvious. In every respect he was the soul of discretion, and Coolidge trusted him as he trusted no other man.

As Governor, Calvin Coolidge occupied for two years a somewhat ornate room almost cubical in shape on the southwest corner of the third floor of the old Bulfinch State House — a room now used by the Governor's Council and somewhat altered since 1919. The Governor sat with his back to the fireplace with its black-and-gold Italian mantel and the two tall windows, looking at the portraits of John Hancock and Samuel Adams, the door leading into the corridor, and the circular gilded clock above it. To the west are the quarters occupied by the Lieutenant Governor and the clerical staff; to the east is the entrance for the Secretary, and directly across was what was then the Council Room. The Governor's desk was gigantic in its proportions, with a glass top. Underneath the chair was placed a bell, well-hidden but so sensitive that the slightest touch of the foot would bring Mr. Reed, the colored messenger, to announce, "Your Excellency, the delegation is getting impatient," and thus drive away visitors who were overstaying their time. This device was conceived by McCall but used rarely by Coolidge.

The room is historic, and looks it, with a dignified quality, a massive nobility, that are impressive. Amazing scenes have taken place here, from the time when Governor Increase Sumner first occupied it in 1798. Here have sat a long line of distinguished Governors: Caleb Strong (1800–1807, 1812–1816), a citizen of Northampton; the aristocratic Christopher Gore (1809–1810), with whom Daniel Webster studied law; the scholarly Edward Everett (1836–1839); the crotchety George S. Boutwell (1851–1852), and the stately Nathaniel P. Banks (1858–1860); John A. Andrew (1861–1865), the war Governor; and Coolidge's mentor, the silent W. Murray Crane (1900–1902).

As an executive, Coolidge was very efficient, transacting business with speed and decision. People soon discovered that he was not susceptible to any form of "influence." In the midst of exhortation he remained impassive, but with both ears open, and then did what he thought best. Mr. Stearns tells the story of how once he was approached by three prominent persons who wished him to increase an appropriation by $50,000. One of them delivered an oration on the subject. The Governor asked, "Anybody else got anything to say?" A second presented the same viewpoint at even greater length. Coolidge then said, "I understand you all agree on what you want." The three said, "Yes," almost simultaneously. "Can't be done," replied Coolidge. "Good-bye."

To those who had known him for the past few years, his habits seemed almost unchanged. It is true that he now had rented a suite of two rooms and a bath at the Adams House, and was paying two dollars a day there instead of one. He also was frequently seen at luncheon with leading Boston businessmen at the Union Club, to which he had been elected on February 18, 1918. But his manner of living was as simple as ever, and he still had few connections with Boston's exclusive inner social circle — the circle to which belonged Henry Cabot Lodge and Grafton D. Cushing. Some persons were nettled at his impassivity, but the general public found him dignified and high-minded, a fit representative of the best New England traditions. An unfavorable critic declared that his speeches were those of a crow becoming unexpectedly vocal, and a contemporary magazine article described him as "drab and monochromatic." Keen observers, however, noticed that something about him caught the imagination and had won him the esteem of good judges of men. He knew most of the legislators by their first names, and his acquaintance in political circles was amazingly large. He was generous in his advice to the younger members and was soon rated the most popular Governor with the General Court that Massachusetts had had for many a year.

The leadership of the Republican Party in Massachusetts might have been claimed by either Lodge or Crane, both of whom were veterans compared with Coolidge. George H. Bacon, of Worcester, was Chairman of the Republican State Committee in 1918 and Frank B. Hall, of Worcester, in 1919. Benjamin F. Felt, who continued as Secretary of the Committee, was one of Coolidge's most faithful and sagacious friends, both then and later. Among the other party leaders who were particularly close to him in his gubernatorial days were, besides Lieutenant Governor Cox, William M. Butler, John N. Cole, B. Loring Young, Charles L. Burrill, Joseph E. Warner, John H. Sherburne, and Thomas W. White.

Calvin Coolidge was Governor of Massachusetts for two terms of one year each, in each of which a special session was called. In 1919 also the State Constitutional Convention held its concluding session on August 12 and 13, — while Coolidge was on a vacation in Plymouth, — for the purpose of approving the new draft of the

Constitution; and at the November elections this was ratified by 263,359 votes to 64,978, with 204,146 blanks. Actually less than half of those who went to the polls voted for the rearrangement of the Constitution. Early in 1920 the Justices of the Supreme Judicial Court, requested by the Governor's Council to give an opinion, returned a unanimous reply that the "rearrangement of the Constitution" was not "the Constitution or form of government for the Commonwealth of Massachusetts." In spite of persistent efforts in the Legislature, this opinion, and later a similar more formal decision by the Court, stood. What had been gained by the Convention were a few amendments of some importance, but the effort to revise and rewrite the original Constitution had failed rather miserably. From Coolidge himself came no word of praise or condemnation for what the convention had accomplished; indeed he was almost aggressively neutral towards the entire project.

Of the other important events of Coolidge's gubernatorial term, the Boston Police Strike of 1919, the Republican Convention of 1920, and his election as Vice President are all of the highest significance and must be treated separately. In this chapter attention will be devoted particularly to certain episodes of his first term.

Although hostilities for Americans overseas virtually terminated with the Armistice, the aftermath of the World War presented many puzzling problems. Belated casualty lists were still being published, and soldiers and sailors were discharged daily from camps and ports in the United States. The numerous wartime committees were winding up their correspondence and fading out of existence. Recognizing the difficulties of assimilating and rehabilitating the returning veterans, the Governor issued a message on January 12, advocating an immediate resumption of industrial activities: —

Men entrusted with the grave responsibility of managing the business affairs of Massachusetts are now called upon to decide whether they will continue their activities as usual or wait to see if there is a decline in prices. . . . There are two things to do. One is to wait; the other is to go on with business activity. If everybody waits, there no doubt will be a perpendicular fall, with attending want, distress, and calamity. If people will go ahead with business, while there may be a gradual decline, it can be borne with the least inconvenience.

Measures were passed with rapidity and unanimity for the benefit of the returning soldiers. Among the more important bills were those providing a bonus of $100 from the Commonwealth to each service man; authorizing cities and towns to spend money on "Welcome

Home" celebrations; giving preference in public appointments to veterans and continuing their exemption from poll taxes until their discharge; establishing a commission to find employment for veterans; authorizing towns and cities to lease quarters for local American Legion posts; and creating a new voluntary State Militia with the Yankee, or 26th, Division as a nucleus. For Governor Coolidge, as for nearly everybody else at that moment, nothing was too good for the boys who were coming back.

On February 24, Governor Coolidge welcomed to Boston President Woodrow Wilson, who had landed at Brest, France, on the preceding December 13, and, after participating in the Peace Conference at Paris, was now returning to the United States in order to press his arguments for the Covenant of the League of Nations. The text of the Covenant had been published in American newspapers on February 15, and Lodge, Moses, Borah, Knox, Penrose, Johnson, Smoot, and other conservative Senators had already announced their opposition to what its enemies called "the evil thing with the holy name." Wilson's choice of Boston as the port for his triumphal entrance to his own country was naturally resented by Senator Lodge. The occasion, however, was a notable one, particularly because one President and two future Presidents, Calvin Coolidge and Franklin D. Roosevelt, — who was there as Assistant Secretary of the Navy, — were together on the same platform in Mechanics' Hall. Coolidge, who had prepared a brief and prosaic speech of welcome on three small typewritten cards, read it rather coldly — and then, realizing the inadequacy of his formal remarks and giving one of his rare, friendly smiles to the President, he continued extemporaneously: —

We welcome him as the representative of a great people, as a great statesman, as one to whom we have entrusted our destinies and one whom we are sure we will support in the future in the working out of those destinies, as Massachusetts has supported him in the past.

In the speech which followed, Wilson made a pleasing impression, and the warmth of his greeting helped to confirm him in his feeling that, no matter what the Senate might do, he had the people of the country behind him. The press of the country interpreted Coolidge's words as indicating that he was certainly not hostile to the League. His friend and backer, W. Murray Crane, was from the beginning favorable to the Covenant and strongly critical of Lodge's position, as was also William M. Butler; and it was apparent that Coolidge's philosophy drew him in that direction. At the famous debate on the

League of Nations in Symphony Hall on March 19, the Governor presided and introduced the two speakers, Senator Lodge and President Lowell, in terms eulogistic of both. When asked for his decision, he remarked prudently, "Both men won." On April 15, before the Fall River City Republican Committee, Coolidge, in another of his liberal speeches, led his hearers to believe that he did not share Lodge's aversion to the League. When a reporter asked him at this period, "Governor, what do you think of the League?" he hesitated and then replied: —

I am the Governor of Massachusetts. The State of Massachusetts has no foreign relations. If ever I should hold an office calling for action or opinion on this subject, I shall put my mind on it and try to arrive at the soundest conclusions within my capacity.

Later, as Vice President and President, Coolidge took a position clarified by his words in his *Autobiography:* "The more I have seen of the conduct of our foreign relations the more I am convinced that we are better off out of the League." In theory, however, he was attracted by the plan of an organization for international peace, and in 1919 he was certainly no "bitter-ender." Indeed he was careful to be out of Boston later in the year when Borah and Hiram Johnson spoke there against the Covenant. The *Boston Herald* was right in assuming that Coolidge had chosen to follow Crane, not Lodge.

As the troops disembarked from France each delegation was met down Boston Harbor by representatives of the Governor, and military bands were kept busy playing a welcome on the docks and through the streets. The first bill which Coolidge signed as Governor was one appropriating $10,000 for defraying part of the expense of greeting the famous Yankee Division; and when this unit landed in early April, it was given an inspiring reception. Coolidge wrote on April 10 to his stepmother: —

The men of our old militia are coming home fast. The parade is Friday, April 25. I very much want father to come down. He would like to see me Governor here again, and no one knows what may happen in the fall. . . . I am sending carfare for father.

The battle flags of the Yankee Division were decorated on April 22 at Camp Devens, with all of the New England Governors present. The final parade was a brilliant spectacle as Coolidge reviewed it from the portico of the State House, and it may be doubted whether Massachusetts ever had a prouder day. The six Governors stood together for hours while the companies marched by in an interminable procession. The Governor of New Hampshire recalled later that Coolidge spoke to him just once between the moment when he said, "Good morning," and the time when he muttered, "Well, it's most over." After they had stood for rather more than two hours, Coolidge turned to him and drawled, "Governor, I think you will find that if you put one foot on the rail and lean in my position for a while, then change to the other foot, it will rest you." The New Hampshire visitor confessed later, "I could not, and cannot now, understand a man who could stand five hours and have nothing else to say."

On April 30 the Yankee Division was demobilized at Camp Devens and the men gradually settled back into civilian life. Still one more ceremony remained when, on Flag Day, June 14, the colors of all the Massachusetts military units were massed in front of the State House and finally deposited with the battle banners of other wars in the Hall of Flags.

Meanwhile the Governor had not been remiss in his other executive duties. For the first time in 1919 a budget system was put into effect as provided for by an amendment to the Constitution passed the previous year. When Coolidge had finished with the budget, he had reduced the estimates of department heads by almost exactly four million dollars and by this means had kept the state tax at the same rate as in 1918. This was the same type of economy which he had practised as Mayor and which he was to advocate as President.

Massachusetts had already, on April 2, 1918, ratified the Prohibition Amendment to the Constitution, and when the deciding state, Nebraska, announced its favorable vote on January 16, 1919, the church bells in Boston rang out in celebration of what was then thought to be a triumph for the forces of decency. Boston itself went "dry" on July 1 of that year, and the long, unfortunate era of enforcement was ushered in. Coolidge said nothing on the subject, but let it be known that, while the law was on the statute books, it would be maintained.

The quality of an executive is usually indicated in his vetoes, and Coolidge's vetoes, though not numerous, were significant. On March 31, he sent back to the Legislature without his approval a bill providing for the improvement of the East Boston Ferry service, saying simply that the city authorities had not requested such action and that it was unnecessary. When a measure was passed for the widening of L Street, in South Boston, Coolidge again withheld his sanction, with the pertinent observation, "The functions of the City Hall ought not to be performed by the State House."

Again in May the General Court enacted a measure suspending the Civil Service regulations in favor of veterans. It was a popular act, and the Governor wished to sign it, but some of its provisions might have resulted in the appointment of incompetent men to positions concerned with the protection of public safety and health. Accordingly he returned the bill with the words : —

Men who have been in the service at the risk of their lives to preserve a rule of law will not be pleased if they find on their return that those who have remained at home are lacking in the courage to pursue the same course.

He also, on May 31, vetoed a bill which would have reëstablished the old seniority rule in the police forces of the Commonwealth; and in so doing he paid a compliment to the police, insisting that the existing policy of recognizing and rewarding efficiency should not be superseded.

Perhaps the most publicized veto of the session of 1919 was that of the so-called Salary Grab Bill, increasing the compensation of members of the House and Senate from $1000 to $1500. In this veto Coolidge pointed out that the state of the times required a careful scrutiny of public expenditures; that no man in the Commonwealth was so poor that he could not serve for a session of about five months, five days a week, at a salary of $1000 and a travel allowance of $2.50 for each mile between his home and the State House; and that, in any case, the realities of life are not measured by dollars and cents. Coolidge's veto was sent in on June 6, but the General Court passed the act over his disapproval, as legislative bodies have sometimes been known to do. A few days later the *Boston Herald* said of the gubernatorial vetoes, "No clearer or more admirable veto messages have ever been addressed to the Massachusetts Legislature."

In the spring of 1920 the General Court passed a bill allowing the sale of beer or light wines with a 2.75 per cent alcoholic content — an act directly contrary in spirit to the Eighteenth Amendment. Coolidge's veto message, dated May 6, is marked by cogent common sense. He said : —

It may be that the Eighteenth Amendment and the act under it are null and void. So far as any court has decided I understand the amendment has been sustained. They have been before the Supreme Court for some time, where up to now they stand as law. That which the court hesitates to decide I shall not hasten to declare. It would be extremely improper to undertake to influence that decision by the action of the lawmaking power of Massachusetts. Do not anticipate it. Await it. My oath was not to take a chance on the Constitution. It was to support it. . . .

We have had too much legislating by clamor, by tumult, by pressure. Representative government ceases when outside influence of any kind is substituted for the judgment of the representative. This does not mean that the opinion of constituents is to be ignored. It is to be weighed most carefully, for the representative must represent; but his oath provides that it must be "faithfully and impartially according to the best of his abilities and understanding, agreeably to the rules and regulations of the Constitution and the laws." Opinions and instructions do not outmatch the Constitution. Against it they are void. It is an insult to any Massachusetts constituency to suggest that they were so intended. Instructions are not given unless given constitutionally. Instructions are not carried out unless carried out constitutionally. There can be no constitutional instruction to do an unconstitutional act.

The language of this vigorous veto traveled across the country, and even the *New York Times*, which had opposed all prohibition legislation, congratulated Coolidge on his courage. The bill in question could not be passed over the Governor's veto and did not become law. Still another dramatic veto was that of December 22, 1920, after he had been elected Vice President, in which he refused to concur in a legislative act overruling the findings of the Supreme Court of Massachusetts in connection with the distribution of expense for a stone bridge between Springfield and West Springfield. The Supreme Judicial Court had appointed a Board of Commissioners to apportion the expense among neighboring towns and cities, and the decision of the Commission had been approved by the Court. Now some interested legislators were attempting to bring about a different distribution. The salient sentences in this veto message were : —

The decisions of our courts must not be held in light regard, either by the General Court or by the people. Respect for judicial decisions is essential to the maintenance of law.

Coolidge had the brand of unostentatious courage which distinguishes men of real convictions. Michael E. Hennessy tells the story of a hearing in connection with a bitter controversy between "jitneys" and streetcars in Salem. The Governor, after investigation, directed the railroad trustees to put their cars back in operation and promised to enforce the order with the State Police. "If you do that," declared one of the "jitney" men, "the labor people will go into every town in the state and crucify you politically." After he had continued in this threatening tone for a few minutes longer, Coolidge said quietly, "Don't let me deter you. Go right ahead." A little later one of the committee remarked, "Well, about all we have done so far is to pass the buck." At this Coolidge's eyes flashed and he said, turning to the speaker, "Try it on me. I won't pass the buck." [1]

A Governor's life has few uneventful days, and Secretary Long's Diary indicates that Coolidge's time was well occupied. The legislative session of 1919 was one of the longest in Massachusetts history, lasting 206 days and not proroguing until July 25. During this period Coolidge went back to Northampton only three times, and then for the week-end only. On February 5, he spoke at an Amherst Alumni Dinner at the Boston City Club, and told the guests that the existing industrial unrest was simply an attempt by mankind to maintain the personal relation between men which ought to be permanent and that many labor leaders were honestly trying to work out the salvation of the workingman. As if to emphasize his point, a strike of eight thousand telephone operators held up business in April for several days. Finally Coolidge wired Secretary Burleson requesting permission for the Commonwealth to take over the telephone system as a step essential to the public welfare; and when this news came out, it took only a short time for the conflicting parties to reconcile their differences.

In June Coolidge was the recipient of several of the honorary degrees which, in the United States, are the recognition of certain forms of success. For reasons not easy to explain he was never so honored, even while he was President, by Harvard, Princeton, Columbia, or Dartmouth. The Amherst Doctorate of Laws, which sentimentally he valued the most, was presented on June 18 by President Meiklejohn, with the following appropriate citation: —

Calvin Coolidge, — as you have learned and used the lessons of this college, so she would learn and use in speaking of you a lesson which you teach, — that of adequate brevity. Upon you, sir, shrewd observer of men and affairs, tireless student of the ways of government, fearless without flightiness, leader of men not simply by office but by intelligence and integrity, honored son of Amherst, trusted Governor of the Commonwealth, we confer the degree of Doctor of Laws.

Similar honors came to him during the following week from Williams and Tufts; and on June 20 both he and Senator Lodge spoke at the Harvard Alumni Luncheon. Coolidge enjoyed ad-

[1] Michael E. Hennessy, *From a Green Mountain Farm to the White House,* pp. 112–13.

dressing academic or collegiate gatherings and invariably prepared himself carefully for such occasions.

Of all his accomplishments as Governor, Calvin Coolidge regarded as both the most difficult and the most important what was called the consolidation of state commissions. At the time of the assembling of the Constitutional Convention of 1917, there existed in the Commonwealth one hundred and eighteen separate departments, — the slow accretion of many careless years, — and their clamorous personnel was demanding more and more space in the already crowded State House. Special commissions had naturally been created from time to time to meet emergencies, but the permanent ones had also been increasing in number and in cost. In the Constitutional Convention the matter came up for debate in August 1918, and was thoroughly discussed, one of the most convincing speeches in favor of consolidation being made by David I. Walsh, who spoke feelingly out of two years of experience as Governor.[2] After a prolonged consideration of the various issues involved, during which the advocates of consolidation found themselves frequently outvoted, the suggested amendment was passed by the Convention, August 21, 1918, in the following form: —

On or before January first, nineteen hundred twenty-one, the executive and administrative work of the Commonwealth shall be organized in not more than twenty departments, in one of which every executive and administrative office, board, and commission, except those officers serving directly under the governor or the council, shall be placed. Such departments shall be under such supervision and regulation as the General Court may from time to time prescribe by law.

This new article, numbered LXVI, was submitted to the people on the ballot in the autumn of 1918 and approved by a vote of 158,394 to 81,586, with 189,467 blanks — a result which indicated that not many citizens were really interested. In July 1919, the General Court enacted Chapter 350 of the Acts of that year, giving effect to the Constitutional Amendment. Under this measure many of the old positions were abolished or rearranged so that the Governor had virtually the opportunity of reorganizing the entire state government. The heads of certain departments were granted more authority or broader scope; in some cases where there had been a single commissioner associate commissioners were created; and it was obvious that many people were bound to lose lucrative jobs.

[2] For a more detailed discussion of this subject see *The Massachusetts Constitutional Convention of 1917*, by Raymond L. Bridgman, Chapter IX, pp. 97–101.

While this proposed legislation was pending in the General Court, the Governor notified the chief holders of office under the existing departments that he would not tolerate any activity in opposing the reduction of personnel. Furthermore, after the Reorganization Act had passed, he determined to carry out its provisions himself. It was not obligatory that the changes should be made until January 1, 1921, but Coolidge, with his strong sense of duty, did not intend to evade a responsibility which was morally his. A mere self-seeking politician might have let himself be persuaded that it would be better for his own interests to postpone action as long as possible. Every public official who lost his comfortable job was likely to become an enemy, and the number of friends made in the process would inevitably be much smaller than the foes.

As soon as the November election was over and he was sure of another term, the Governor read his hundreds of congratulatory letters and then set out on November 6 with Frank W. Stearns for Northampton, where he remained, ostensibly on a vacation, until after Armistice Day. On Tuesday, November 12, when he returned to his desk, the news had spread that the Governor was about to make ready the list of new appointments, and he was pursued by office seekers and their friends wherever he moved. What he was doing was to collect all the available information about the incumbents of the existing positions and possible new candidates and to study the qualifications of everybody likely to be concerned. For the next few days his desk was inundated with letters, and his office was literally besieged by political vultures seeking for a hearing. He sent, himself, for many people, but absolutely refused to see any others. He lunched with John W. Weeks, very privately, at the Union Club on November 15, but consulted few of the other party leaders. Once during this period of incubation Mr. Stearns called at the Governor's office, to find him sitting with his chair tipped back and his feet across one of the desk drawers in his favorite pose, evidently in deep meditation. He was clearly in no mood for talk, and Stearns, after lingering for a moment in silence, departed, aware that his presence was not desired.

As usual, Coolidge was resolved to make his own decisions and to rely on the amazing intuition which had stood him in such good stead before. One of his close friends from Springfield called on Mr. Stearns, who was erroneously regarded as all-powerful, and complained that he could not secure access to the Governor in order to urge the appointment of an important Republican from the Connecticut Valley. Stearns said to him, "If anybody could get to the

Governor, you could; but even I haven't been able to talk to him. What you ought to do is to go down to St. Paul's Church and offer up a silent prayer for a man in great distress." It so happened that the appointment was not made, and no explanation whatever was offered to the man's sponsors. Some weeks later, however, when he was passing through Springfield, Coolidge sent for a local newspaper editor and explained that while the candidate in question had been sound in character, he had proved himself incompetent for the work. The editor, who had previously been much annoyed, was eventually convinced that Coolidge knew more about his friend's ability than he did.

It is perhaps unnecessary to add that Mr. Stearns, though very close to Coolidge and more constantly in his company than any other man, did not presume upon their intimacy and rarely submitted suggestions unless asked to do so. Shortly after Coolidge's election as Governor, one of Stearns's acquaintances called at his office and asked his aid in securing an appointment as Judge of the Superior Court. Stearns answered, "I have never made a recommendation for an appointment to the Governor, and I never shall. If you want that place and are fitted for it, you must have some lawyer friends who can speak for you, but I cannot." Later in the day, however, Stearns mentioned the applicant's name in this connection to the Governor, who sat back and said, "Mr. Stearns, what do you know of this gentleman's legal and judicial training?" "I'm afraid that I don't know very much about it except that he's a fine man and a staunch supporter of yours." "Mr. Stearns," said Coolidge, very deliberately, "I don't think that you ought to interfere in matters about which you are so badly informed." That was all! The situation was expressed even more clearly on a similar occasion when Mr. Stearns, in response to somebody who said, "You have great influence with the Governor," answered, "Yes, perhaps more even than you think, but it will last just as long as I don't try to use it, and not one minute longer."

On November 22, when the appointments were nearly all settled in Coolidge's mind and he was very tired, his secretary, Mr. Long, brought him his morning's mail, in which was a pleasant letter from Mr. Stearns, enclosing a check for $5000, and expressing the hope that Coolidge would accept this gift from Mr. and Mrs. Stearns, as from his own father and mother. In a moment the Governor called Mr. Long back and said, "Did you see this check?" "Yes, I did," answered Long. "Mr. Stearns ought to realize that I can't permit that kind of a gift," said Coolidge. Then he scribbled off on a memorandum sheet torn from an envelope the words, "I have no respect for anybody who cannot take care of himself," and directed Long to send it with the check to Stearns by special messenger. That evening Coolidge called on Stearns and voiced his appreciation, but said positively that he could not keep the money; and he added that since he had begun the practice of law he had saved something every year. "Somehow," he concluded, "I'll manage to get along."

On Sunday evening, November 23, Coolidge dined alone with the Stearnses at the Hotel Touraine. As he took up his hat to leave, he almost furtively handed Stearns a document, saying in his dry manner, "Perhaps you'd like to look at this. It has gone to the newspapers." Before examining it, Stearns stifled his curiosity and amused himself by jotting down some of his guesses. Approximately seventy persons had to be appointed, of whom six or eight could be regarded as indispensable or at least reasonably sure of reappointment. Stearns had been present at conferences where candidates had been discussed and had listened to what had been said for and against. Yet he found that, outside of the obvious names, he had been correct in only a few instances.

On the morning of November 24 the list of sixty-four appointments was printed in the newspapers as they were to be submitted to the Council. John N. Cole was Commissioner of Public Works; Payson Smith was Commissioner of Education; E. Leroy Sweetser was Commissioner of Labor and Industries; Alfred F. Foote was Commissioner of Public Safety; Payson Dana was Commissioner of Civil Service; Robert W. Kelso was Commissioner of Public Welfare. Many "old-timers" had been shelved; on the other hand, the various races, religions, and political parties had been adequately recognized. The *Herald* promptly said in an editorial regarding the appointments: —

Nearly all of them are good, some of them altogether admirable. There are exceedingly few, if any, of the scandalous sort which usually creep into any wholesale award of patronage. On the whole the Governor has shown intelligence and ingenuity of a high order. He has recognized the various elements of the state, and he has infused into its service some "new blood." And that will prove in many ways advantageous.

It is interesting to observe how completely the Governor kept his own counsels. Of the predictions of popular discussion how few bear the test of results. Mr. Coolidge, taking pencil in hand, went over the available material, which no man in Massachusetts knows better than he, and has given us results that in many cases occasion as much surprise to the beneficiaries as to the electorate. The Governor's Council should hasten to confirm these nominations as a whole.

The *Evening Transcript,* in an editorial on November 25 headed "The Governor's 'Great Decision,'" was not altogether commendatory of the appointments and declared that the list contained several names "that seem to be poor substitutes for tried and true servants of the Commonwealth." But it also advised the Council to accept the complete slate and not to single out separate appointees for rejection. In only two cases were the protests at all vociferous. Miss Mabel Gillespie had been recommended for the place of Assistant Commissioner of Labor and had the endorsement of several labor organizations. Just before the list was published, two well-known Massachusetts ladies requested Mr. Stearns to urge the Governor to name Miss Gillespie. After at first refusing to be an intermediary, Stearns finally consented to tell the Governor what the ladies had said. Coolidge's answer was, "If these women know as much as they think they do how to handle these questions, they ought to know that Miss Gillespie has traveled all over trying to persuade every tailor in the state to refuse to make uniforms for the new police force. Shan't appoint her." Miss Ethel Johnson became Assistant Commissioner of Labor.

The loudest wail, however, was raised by Charles S. Baxter, — often called "the Sage of Medford," — who had formerly been campaign manager for Samuel W. McCall and had late in the campaign of 1919 come out more than audibly for Coolidge. He had expected to receive one of the choicest plums; but the Governor, apparently with deliberation, gave him only a place as Assistant Commissioner of the Metropolitan District, at a salary of $1000 a year for two years, and also ignored all of Baxter's followers. Baxter declined the appointment and made a vicious attack on Coolidge, asserting that the public had been excluded from the Governor's office. Shortly after, meeting Lieutenant Governor Cox on the street, Baxter said, "You'd better tell Coolidge to resign as Governor and let you appoint him Judge of the Hampshire County Probate Court, because that's the highest office he'll ever hold again." When the Presidential boom for Coolidge began to get under way, Baxter said publicly that it must be a joke. On the whole the incident redounded to Coolidge's credit, and Baxter gained nothing by his foolish conduct.

On Monday, November 24, Coolidge lunched with Lodge at the Union Club, and on the following day he was back in his office, looking much relieved. He told Long that he had not even read the newspapers, but wasn't much afraid of their comment. On November 26 he went back to Northampton for a Thanksgiving dinner with his family.

He had some reason to be thankful. At its next meeting, on December 1, the Council confirmed all of the appointments; and when the Governor shortly made additional nominations to complete the full list, these were also passed without a protest. Of his share in reorganizing these state commissions Coolidge was always proud. He said once to a friend, "They say the Police Strike required executive courage; reorganizing one hundred and eighteen departments into eighteen required a good deal more." Later at the White House he told Governor Channing H. Cox that his reorganization of the state departments was the most important single thing he had ever done and that it gave him more concern at the time than any one task he had to perform in Washington. "I saved you a pretty mess," he added; and this was true, for Coolidge could easily have let the whole matter rest until his term was over and he was out of Boston and Cox was in the State House. The incident reveals several of Coolidge's characteristics: his thoroughness, his independence, his secretiveness, and his courage.

Coolidge's two years as Governor were, to use his own words, "a time of transition from war to peace." It seemed to him a period of much confusion, when nothing was stable and it was impossible to do more than feel one's way along from week to week. In his second Inaugural Address, on January 9, 1920, he said: —

In general, it is time to conserve, to retrench rather than to reform, a time to stabilize the administration of the present laws rather than to seek new legislation.

Nevertheless Coolidge did promote and sign numerous bills for the benefit of labor. A forty-eight-hour working week for women and children was established by the General Court and received his approval. Other measures directed towards the same end provided for weekly payment of compensation in cases of partial incapacity; increased the maximum weekly payments under the Workman's Compensation Law from $14 to $16; required the posting of decrees of the Minimum Wage Commission by the employers affected; and compelled the furnishing of labor specifications to textile workers. All this legislation was contributory to an improvement in economic and industrial conditions.

Michael E. Hennessy gives an impressive list of other measures for the passage of which Coolidge was largely instrumental.[3] They include laws checking profiteering landlords, regulating outdoor advertising, creating a commission to care for the graves of Massachusetts soldiers buried in France, prohibiting rental increases of more than 25 per cent in one year, enlarging the powers and usefulness of coöperative banks, and authorizing the appointment of a commission to investigate and report on the matter of maternity benefits. On the business of the General Court Coolidge's influence was most salutary, for his experience had been extensive and he knew all the technical procedure involved in getting a measure passed. But it was not the moment for planning a comprehensive program of reform. He analyzed the situation accurately in his *Autobiography* when he said of these two years: —

In general, conditions were such that the entire efforts of the people were engaged in easing themselves down. There was little opportunity to direct their attention towards constructive action. They were clearing away the refuse from the great conflagration preparatory to rebuilding on a grander and more pretentious scale. Nothing was natural, everything was artificial. So much energy had to be expended in keeping the ship of state on a straight course that there was little left to carry it ahead.

On all matters of legislation, Coolidge was a realist, who indulged in no illusions. At any given moment he was aware of the trend of public sentiment and of the extent to which it could be changed. Often it was his function to pour cold water on too heated enthusiasm. Once a prominent Bostonian called on him, visibly and audibly excited over a new plan of administration. The Governor listened, but said nothing. Finally the visitor asked, "What do you think of my scheme, Governor?" "Won't 'mount t' anything," replied Coolidge. The caller, who had entered so full of ardor, felt the chill and stammered, "I suppose I'd better be going." "Well," concluded the Governor, "any time you've got anything you think we ought t' hear, come in."

The publicity which Coolidge received before his administration ended focused attention on his peculiarities. The first magazine article about him, written by Bruce Barton in *Collier's,* and prepared at the instigation of Dwight W. Morrow, naturally emphasized the Governor's Yankee background and picturesque qualities. Following the Police Strike in the autumn of 1919, the newspapers had much to say concerning his record. The *Literary Digest* for November 15

[3] Hennessy, 110–11.

printed two pages about him, with a photograph of himself and Mrs. Coolidge; and an even longer article in the same periodical for November 29, headed "Quiet But Convincing 'Cal' Coolidge," was a compilation of biographical and personal detail. Never averse to legitimate publicity, Coolidge rather enjoyed having his photograph taken. Once he said to Mr. Stearns as they posed, "Let's spruce up a bit. And let's talk. It looks more natural and makes a better picture." Soon people all over the United States knew that Calvin Coolidge was a sandy-haired, smooth-faced man, of medium height and slender build, with lines of concentration puckering up his forehead, a long, shrewd nose down which his eyes seemed to glance thoughtfully, and a tight-lipped mouth, dipping in sharp furrows on the corners — a man who seemed serious-minded but much more youthful than his forty-seven years.

It was at this period that the legend of his taciturnity was spread far and wide. The tale was told of the ride which he took with a friend to a place thirty miles inland from Boston, where the Governor had to make a speech. Not a word was exchanged on the way out in the automobile. On the return journey there was also utter silence until they approached the seashore, when Coolidge turned and said confidentially, "It is cooler here." He once rode with John N. Cole from Andover to Northampton, a distance of more than a hundred miles, in the Governor's car. Mr. Cole, acquainted with Coolidge's moods, sat looking out the window at the scenery until the Governor, just as they turned to enter Massasoit Street, said, in all sincerity, "Pleasant ride, wasn't it?" There are many similar stories, some of them authenticated,[4] and it is unquestionably true that complete silence never really embarrassed Mr. Coolidge. At certain unpredictable times he could talk fluently, but such occasions were infrequent. He particularly disliked being "drawn out," and was almost brutally unresponsive when questioned by impertinent people.

People who knew him well observed that he had moods of irritability and that on some mornings he was "snappish" and curt, even with his best friends. He was troubled at certain seasons by asthma, which was aggravated by the straw matting in the Senate Chamber, and he also had some indigestion. Under provocative circumstances

---

[4] Once when a reporter pressed him on the subject of his taciturnity, Coolidge said, "I've usually been able to make enough noise to get what I want." Again, when General Clarence R. Edwards, who had the reputation of being an expansive talker, met him on the street and said, "Hello, Chatterbox," Coolidge replied amiably, "Well, General, I've found out that what I don't say doesn't get me into half as much trouble as what you do say."

he was known to indulge in mild profanity. He greatly disliked pretense or pomposity and enjoyed puncturing an inflated ego. On the other hand, his secretary, Henry F. Long, describes him as the kindest, most understanding man he ever met, deeply considerate of everyone around him. According to Mr. Long, Coolidge gave no signs of "vaulting ambition" but cared most of all about getting his work done with speed and efficiency.

A certain whimsical quality sometimes showed itself in the Governor's conduct. Professor George B. Churchill, of Amherst College, who was serving most acceptably in the Senate, went to the Governor to urge him to take a certain course of action which, in his opinion, was for the benefit of the Commonwealth. Coolidge gave Senator Churchill no satisfaction, and the latter left the office and went back to Amherst, feeling decidedly crestfallen. When he reached his home, he found on his study table a telegram from the State House saying, "The matter you wanted fixed has been fixed." On still another occasion, Churchill called on the Governor to request him to form a special commission. Coolidge suggested that no such commission was necessary and elicited from the Senator a long defense of the plan. As Churchill rose from his seat, thinking that his errand had been futile, the Governor said, "Wait a minute, Senator," and pulled out of his desk drawer a paper with five names on it. Handing it to Churchill, he said, "How would these men do for the committee?" "Fine, of course," replied the Senator. "But I thought there wasn't going to be any committee." Coolidge's answer was, "I've already sent their names to the Council."

Coolidge was never inclined to take advantage of his position as Governor. Once a delegate to the Republican Convention of 1920 from Brooklyn, who was favorably disposed towards Coolidge but had never met him, came to Boston to hear him speak. After the exercises, the Governor asked him to take a ride and they drove to the Arnold Arboretum. On the gate was a sign reading, "Automobiles Not Admitted." The Governor said to the Secret Service man, "Find the Superintendent, and I think he will give us a permit to drive in." The officer came back soon and said, "I cannot find him, but we might as well go in just the same." Coolidge's answer was, "We will not go in until we have a permit. The Governor of Massachusetts does not break a law any more than anyone else."

Coolidge's bodyguard while he was Governor, was a tall, handsome state policeman named Horrigan. On one occasion, as the two were leaving the Parker House after luncheon, Horrigan stopped the passing traffic for the Governor's car. When he had seated him-

A "SILENT DEBATE" BETWEEN "CAL" COOLIDGE AND UNCLE MURRAY CRANE

CARTOON IN THE "BOSTON POST," 1918

self in the automobile, Coolidge said, "Horrigan, if there should be an emergency call for me, I suppose I would have the right to stop traffic. But don't do it otherwise. I am the first person in Massachusetts to obey the law, not the last." When an elaborate reception was being given in Dorchester, just outside of Boston, for the returning veterans and the reception committee was hunting for the Governor, he was discovered standing in the lobby of the theatre, with no escort. "Why, Governor," said the chairman of the committee, "when did you get here? We didn't see your car or any of your aides." "No, I haven't any automobile and there aren't any aides with me. Thought I'd take a night off, so I came out in the streetcar."

In some people such an incident might be regarded as a bid for democratic approval. With Coolidge it was another evidence of his thoroughgoing simplicity. In his literary style he disliked superlatives, preferring always the emphasis of understatement. In his personal habits he avoided ostentation. He always cared more for the realities than for the decorations of office. This attitude was fundamental in his character.

A characteristic story illustrating another Coolidge attribute is told by Tom O'Connor, a newspaperman at the State House in 1920. The Special Session of that autumn was devoted very largely to the approval of the consolidation and codification of the General Laws of the Commonwealth, and few in the Legislature took the business very seriously. Towards the close the matter of extra monetary compensation inevitably was being discussed by Senators and Representatives. The legislators from Western Massachusetts decided to have a "Get Together" dinner on a night just before the session was to prorogue, and a committee representing them called on the Governor at his office to invite him to the festivities. As they trooped in, Coolidge looked up from his desk, mumbled a greeting, and then resumed his writing. During the subsequent loud chatter and hand shaking the Governor continued his pen scratching, as if oblivious of the confusion around him. Then someone made a speech, telling what a great honor it would be to have the newly elected Vice President as a guest; but still he did not lift his head. Finally the group began to file out, obviously disappointed; and as some of them still remained on the threshold, Coolidge looked up, cleared his throat, and said in clear, acidulous tones, "I trust you won't forget to vote yourselves some compensation."

Entirely aside from Coolidge's action in the Police Strike, he was a good Governor, worthy of the best traditions of the Commonwealth. Dignified, earnest, and industrious, he performed his duties in a common-sense fashion which appealed to the average voter. He liked to be called "effective" and was particularly pleased when Benjamin F. Felt congratulated him on his efficiency. He made no serious mistakes, and he impressed observers as being fair-minded. The comment on him was, "He's not brilliant but he's safe."

Mrs. John C. Coolidge, who had been virtually a second mother to Calvin, had attended his wedding and watched his career from the time when he first entered political life. To her he had written his most intimate letters, and she was very dear to him. On January 19, 1920, when her health was rapidly declining, he wrote her from the State House: —

It is very sad to see you suffer so much. I know you are patient. Surely there is some compensation for you somewhere. I hope the rest of your days a kind Providence may deal kindly and gently with you and that you may have the peace which you so richly merit.

On March 7 he wrote her from the Union Club, "We think of you very often and wish we could see you and help you bear your suffering." On April 25 he sent her from the Algonquin Club a very short note, the last letter which she had from him: —

We belong to this club too. It is still cold here. Wonder if it is fit going to go to Plymouth. You must let us know soon as the going is settled so we can come up.

A Mr. Whiting, a newspaper man, may go up a week from to-day. Have father show him around if he comes up.

Mrs. Coolidge was soon mercifully relieved from her suffering and died on May 19, 1920, in her sixty-fourth year, just before her stepson was nominated for Vice President. The Coolidges went to Plymouth and saw her buried in the cemetery at the Notch. In his *Autobiography* Calvin Coolidge paid her a well-deserved tribute.

Although the Governor would not consent to the hiring of a house in Boston, insisting that it was unnecessary, his wife was not infrequently in that city, staying either at the Adams House or with the Stearnses at the Hotel Touraine. The two boys remained in Northampton and attended the public schools. Only on occasions of exceptional importance were they allowed to see their father in all his gubernatorial glory. Mrs. Coolidge's charm and tact, and her winning conversational ability, were just attracting the notice of Coolidge's friends. She had had only a limited opportunity while he was merely one of many legislators; when he became Lieutenant Governor, and later Governor, a wider world was opened for her.

"Although my husband has moved up, it makes no difference in our mode of living," she said. "Why should it? We are happy, well, content. We keep our bills paid and live like anybody else." But although she was unassuming and simple in her tastes, she possessed a social grace which was contributory to her husband's success. She knew how to make a home, but she also knew how to keep everybody around her in a genial mood. Coolidge often referred humorously to her social activities and wrote his stepmother early in 1920: —

I wish you were here to see the dresses my wife has. Folks who see them know why I cannot pay very high rent.

On January 6, 1921, Calvin Coolidge, soon to become Vice President of the United States, stepped down as Governor. The retiring Governor, by tradition, does not attend the inauguration of his successor, and Coolidge, although warmly urged to be present by Channing H. Cox, decided not to break with precedent. At his office that morning he was noticeably in high spirits. He advised Cox to let any visitors to the Governor's office do all the talking and to be careful not to say anything to encourage them to go on when they had stopped. He admired the flowers which were arriving and, picking out one especially beautiful basket, said, "Would you mind if I took that for Grace?" When the guns roared out announcing that Channing H. Cox was Governor of the Commonwealth, Calvin Coolidge was walking down the Beacon Street steps as many ex-Governors had done before him. Within an hour or two, a private citizen, he took with Mrs. Coolidge the familiar train from the North Station to Northampton, riding in a day coach through a country which they both knew well. That night they slept again in the house at Massasoit Street. The next day he felt that he didn't have very much to do.

On January 10, 1921, while going through a pile of papers on his desk, Governor Cox found under the desk blotter a short note reading as follows: —

MY DEAR GOVERNOR COX, —

I want to leave you my best wishes, my assurance of support, and my confidence in your success.

Cordially yours,
CALVIN COOLIDGE

Almost Coolidge's last act before leaving the State House that morning of Cox's inauguration had been to write a letter of courtesy to his successor.

XI

The Boston Police Strike of 1919

IN the career of every successful statesman there is likely to be a moment which, in the retrospect, seems to be a turning point, a choice among roads leading in different directions. It is then that he resolves to do rather than not to do, to act rather than to remain passive, to go to thè left rather than to the right. His behavior at this critical juncture is the result of many converging forces — ancestry, background, experience, environment, and philosophy. His conduct may be explained as sacrificial courage or shrewd opportunism, depending on the theory of the critic. But the decisive effect on the hero's future is obvious to his biographer.

The Boston Police Strike of 1919 was the most significant episode in Calvin Coolidge's progress. He had served two thirds of a term as Governor of Massachusetts in his usual competent, unspectacular way, without attracting attention outside of New England. So far as New York or Washington newspapers were concerned, he was just another governor. Republican leaders in the Commonwealth assumed that he would be renominated and re-elected in due course; but on his own admission he had reached what he regarded as "the summit of any possible political preferment," [1] and he felt as autumn approached that he would be content to round out his public career with one more term of gubernatorial experience. His habit of doing the day's work had kept his mind off any higher aspirations. He cared nothing about running for Congress; and if he had cherished any secret ambitions for national fame aroused by Frank W. Stearns, they would have seemed futile, for Massachusetts was a relatively small state, poorly situated strategically for pressing the claims of a favorite son with only a local reputation. Besides, there was Senator Lodge. . . . And then, mainly because of the Police Strike, wider vistas opened themselves

[1] *Autobiography,* 124.

before Governor Coolidge, and he was unexpectedly offered what Robert M. Washburn has well called "an issue and an opportunity." [2] Almost overnight he emerged as a personality whose doings were good copy from coast to coast and about whom any story was acceptable. Soon he was being mentioned as Presidential material. A political miracle was really to happen.

Following the Armistice of November 11, 1918, ensued a period in the United States of rapidly rising prices, during which wages stood still or moved upward only slightly. These conditions inevitably produced a succession of industrial disturbances, some of them serious. The Plumb Plan for the nationalization of railways was being widely discussed, and the Industrial Workers of the World — known as the I.W.W.'s — were trying desperately to establish "one big union." It has been estimated that the number of labor disputes during 1919 in America was 2665 and that more than four million persons were at one time or another "on strike." [3] Workers everywhere were in a restless and aggressive mood, and agitators were accordingly stimulated to exceptional activity.

During the textile strike in Lawrence, Massachusetts, which came to a head in late January, 1919, Governor Coolidge called to his office F. F. Fuller, then on the editorial staff of the *Boston American*, and said, "Mr. Fuller, I am being urged to send the militia to Lawrence, and before deciding I want to know more about the real situation. So I wish you would go to Lawrence at my expense, take all the time you need, and study the matter thoroughly — not, of course, posing as my representative, but as a natural part of your duty as a newspaper reporter." Mr. Fuller confessed at once that he rather favored the strikers, but Coolidge, knowing that he was an accurate observer, still urged him to go. Fuller made a careful study of conditions and reported to the Governor on the basis of the information which he had uncovered. In consequence, Coolidge notified the American Woolen Company that he did not propose to send in the militia and urged its president privately to settle the strike as soon as possible. Through the Governor's quiet intervention, the American Woolen Company adopted a policy of "appeasement," and the difficulties were adjusted finally on May 20. The incident is

[2] Washburn, 94.
[3] These figures are taken from the *Literary Digest*. *Time* has asserted (March 22, 1937) that in 1919 there were 3630 strikes and 4,160,000 strikers, but quotes no authority. For a vivid picture of these post-war labor disturbances see Mark Sullivan's *Our Times*, Volume VI, "The Twenties," pp. 156–67. The situation was similar to that in the spring and summer of 1937, when John L. Lewis's Committee on Industrial Organization was taking the place of the Industrial Workers of the World.

worth mentioning because it substantiates the opinion already expressed that Coolidge, far from always espousing the cause of the employer, usually preserved a judicial fairness in disputes between capital and labor. James J. Davis, while Secretary of Labor in the Coolidge cabinet, said publicly, "I will place the labor record of Calvin Coolidge against the record of any man who ever held the Presidency of the United States or the Governorship of any state." It was because of his well-known lack of prejudice that Coolidge's position with regard to strikes of any character was so important.

In February a threatened general strike in Seattle was suppressed by the tough-fibred Mayor Ole Hansen. In midsummer, employees of the Boston Elevated Railroad actually held up transportation for several days until an agreement to arbitrate was negotiated and the men resumed work, to receive shortly by adjudication a substantial increase in pay.[4] The most ominous outbreak was among the employees of the United States Steel Corporation, which began on September 22 and reached an unsuccessful termination for the strikers on January 8, 1920. The spirit of revolt was in the air, and workers were demanding, not requesting, their rights. Under circumstances such as these the Boston police made the egregious error of defying the orders of their Commissioner, forming a unit of the American Federation of Labor, and thus precipitating a tragic succession of blunders, the echoes of which were heard for years after.

The Police Commissioner of Boston in 1919 was Edwin Upton Curtis, a graduate of Bowdoin College in the class of 1882, who had been admitted to the bar in 1885 and had settled as a lawyer in Boston. He had been Mayor and Collector of the Port, and had been appointed in December 1918 to succeed Stephen O'Meara as Police Commissioner. He was dignified, handsome, a trifle stiff in his bearing and something of a martinet. Robert M. Washburn has said that Curtis's virtues were a clear head, determination, and efficiency; but he was also absolutely incorruptible, stubborn on a matter of principle, and invincibly courageous — a very fine type of public servant.[5] In his fifty-ninth year, he was suffering, although

---

[4] *Autobiography*, 127. Coolidge felt that conditions fully justified this raise in wages.

[5] Curtis died on March 28, 1922. The sketch of him in the *Dictionary of American Biography* by H. W. Howard Knott is adequate. An excellent likeness of him appeared in the *Boston Evening Transcript* for September 9, 1919. Curtis had a kind of Roman virtue; yet he was beloved by those who knew him well. Although brought up in a strongly partisan school of Republican politics, he was eminently fair-minded.

only his intimates knew it, from heart disease and had been warned to avoid overexertion, either physical or mental. More than once during the period of the strike he temporarily collapsed, and only his indomitable will kept him from breaking down completely.[6]

By the peculiar terms of a legislative act of 1906, intended to be a move in the direction of efficiency, the Police Commissioner was an appointee of the Governor for a period of five years, and could be removed only by the Governor, for cause and with the approval of the Governor's Council. He was also, however, in some degree under the control of the Mayor, without whose authority he could not enlarge the police force or alter the pay of the members. Commissioner Curtis had thus a double responsibility to Commonwealth and to municipality, a dual obligation which might — and did — under some circumstances become embarrassing. In order to secure the best results the Mayor and the Commissioner had to act jointly and in full agreement.[7]

Curtis was, as has been suggested, a lifelong Republican. The Mayor in 1919 was Andrew James Peters, a Democrat elected two years before. After being graduated from Harvard in the class of 1895, — the same year in which Coolidge received his diploma from Amherst, — he had studied law, entered politics, moved through the Massachusetts General Court to Congress, — where he served four terms, — and had then been named Assistant Secretary of the Treasury in 1914, by President Wilson. He was in the autumn of 1919 in his forty-eighth year, three months older than Coolidge, and generally regarded as a public-spirited, high-minded, and trustworthy citizen. He had himself a long line of Yankee ancestors and had married Martha Phillips, of another prominent family. Mr. Peters's record was unblemished, and he was respected even by his political opponents for his reasonable and temperate mind.[8]

On May 10, 1919, responding to the initiative of Commissioner Curtis, Mayor Peters had raised the salaries of Boston policemen and firemen $200 apiece, with a maximum of $1600. At the same time the salaries of other city employees were increased only $100. Nevertheless the police were disgruntled with their living quarters, especially in Station 2 directly behind City Hall, and still complained

[6] Dr. John W. Farlow writes in a letter of June 1, 1935: "Mr. Curtis lived next door to me, and not being well at the time, he required special medical treatment which I was able to give him with considerable relief to his discomfort."

[7] See *Police Administration in Boston*, by Leonard H. Harrison, Harvard University Press, 1934.

[8] Mr. Peters died of pneumonia in June 1938, but I had had the opportunity of consulting him frequently with regard to the Police Strike and he had read this chapter in its first draft and made comments upon it.

of long hours and low compensation. Furthermore events elsewhere were keeping them stirred up. Early in June it was rumored that a nation-wide strike of telegraphers was imminent. On August 2 a cablegram from England announced that a thousand policemen in London and nearly as many in Liverpool had gone out "on strike." A small, energetic group among the Boston police were on the alert, ready to seize almost any means of improving their economic status and getting control in their own hands.

The question of a policemen's union was not a new one. Curtis's predecessor, O'Meara, had issued on June 28, 1918, a General Order vigorously condemning the action of certain members of the department who had discussed the advisability of organizing a union, using as a nucleus what was called the Boston Social Club. When in the early summer of 1919 a similar movement started, Curtis not only authorized a newspaper statement of disapproval, but also posted on July 29 a General Order in which he expressed himself as follows: —

I desire to say to the members of the force that I am firmly of the opinion that a police officer cannot consistently belong to a union and perform his sworn duty. . . . I feel it my duty to say to the police force that I disapprove of the movement on foot; that in my opinion it is not for the best interests of the men themselves; and that beyond question it is not for the best interests of the general public, which this department is required to serve.

The Commissioner thus put himself on record by delivering what amounted to an ultimatum. Peters at once published a statement supporting Curtis in his position. Coolidge had left on July 26 for Plymouth, where he remained until August 18. On his arrival at his office on August 19, he saw several people regarding the police difficulty, including Herbert Parker, General Sherburne, John N. Cole, and Arthur B. Chapin, and issued a statement to the newspapers saying: —

Mr. Curtis is the Police Commissioner invested by law with the duty of conducting the office. I have no intention of removing him, and so long as he is the Commissioner I am going to support him.

Despite the clear warning of Curtis and Peters the members of the Boston Social Club applied on August 10, by telegraph, for a charter from the American Federation of Labor. On the receipt of this news Curtis promptly issued another General Order beginning: —

It is or should be apparent to any thinking person that the police department of this or any other city cannot fulfill its duty to the entire public if its members are subject to the direction of an organization existing outside the department.

Curtis further responded to the challenge by promulgating a new section of the *Department Rules and Regulations* (Section 19, Rule 35), reading as follows: —

No members of the force shall join or belong to any organization, club, or body composed of present or present and past members of the force which is affiliated with or a part of any organization, club, or body outside the department, — except that a post of the Grand Army of the Republic, the United Spanish War Veterans, and the American Legion of World War veterans may be formed within the department.

Every member of the Boston police, it must be noted, had sworn to obey and to be bound by the rules of the department; yet even this unambiguous warning did not cause the agitators to slacken their efforts.[9] On August 11, the day following their application, a charter was granted to Boston Police Union, Number 16,807, American Federation of Labor; and the members, in open defiance of Curtis, met and elected officers. At no time did these men communicate with the Police Commissioner or lay their grievances before him. It was precisely as if a platoon of soldiers had refused to obey a commander. On Sunday, August 12, as if by prearrangement, the Central Labor Union of Boston passed resolutions pledging to the police "every atom of support that organized labor can bring to bear in their behalf." The new union thus formed in disregard of the Commissioner's express prohibition had reason to believe that it would be protected to the limit by the organized labor of Boston. At the time Samuel Gompers, President of the Federation, was in Europe. Before he sailed in the early summer, however, he had discussed the situation with Mayor Peters, who had warned him that the formation of a policemen's union in that city would precipitate plenty of trouble.

Curtis was now bound either to act or to resign, and he was not

[9] The Boston firemen some months earlier had established a branch of the American Federation of Labor without arousing much critical comment. As a matter of fact, policemen's unions affiliated with the A. F. of L. had been formed in thirty-seven cities, including Washington, Fort Worth, St. Paul, Terre Haute, Los Angeles, Vicksburg, and Topeka. It was the resolute action of Commissioner Curtis which made Boston what the *Boston News Bureau* called a "pathological experiment station." He it was who focused the attention of the general public on the serious and fundamental issues involved.

the man to flinch in a crisis. Losing no time in ascertaining the names of the eight leaders and officers of the new union, he charged them with insubordination. The union would not disband. The Commissioner was inflexible, "as stubborn as a horse mackerel." It was obvious to those "on the inside" that the possibility of a compromise was remote. At about this period Governor Coolidge is rumored to have written a letter to his stepmother stating that he realized what the outcome of the dispute would be, that he was determined as to his action, and that he would probably as a consequence be defeated at the next election. Unfortunately, however, no such letter has come to light in his files. It must have been written in longhand and probably was not preserved at Plymouth.[10]

The union now warned the Commissioner that, if its officers were disciplined in any manner, a strike would be called. His response was to place the eight men on trial. Their counsel, James E. Vahey and John P. Feeney, did not deny the facts as alleged, but merely argued that the Commissioner's regulation was "invalid, unreasonable, and contrary to the express law of Massachusetts." Curtis, after the hearing customary in such cases, found them guilty, but to everybody's astonishment postponed sentence for ten days; and when, on August 29, eleven more ringleaders were tried and also found guilty, sentence was again withheld. Curtis himself later declared that this unusual delay was to give the men an opportunity to recant and withdraw from their allegiance to the American Federation of Labor.

Another element was now interjected into the already sufficiently jumbled situation. Mayor Peters, who had been escaping from the August heat for a few days with his family in Maine, hurried back and promptly lined up beside the Commissioner, saying: —

[10] Mr. Stearns's statement in an interview with Theodore C. Joslin is as follows: "I know that he wrote a private letter, during those critical days, outlining the course he intended to follow, — and did, — and saying it would very possibly mean his elimination from public life." It is quoted in Washburn, page 80, and has since been reiterated by Mr. Stearns in a conversation with me. On July 9, 1920, the *Boston Herald's* correspondent said that Frank W. Agan had mentioned this letter to Coolidge, quoting a passage in which the latter declared that he would perform his duty, adding, "Even if it means the sacrifice of all political ambition, I will do it." Coolidge refused at the time to affirm or deny the writing of such a letter and fenced with a question, "Did I write that?" Colonel John C. Coolidge, however, held the letter in his possession and verified the Agan statement. On October 25, 1918, Coolidge wrote to Edwin A. Grozier, of the *Boston Post,* regarding his campaign for Governor: "Of course I want this cause to triumph. I understood perfectly that my attitude in the police matter greatly endangered what at that time appeared to be my certain election. What I did then had to be done. It was of more consequence than my success at the polls. I should not have done otherwise had I known that it would bring my certain defeat."

The American Federation of Labor deserves our coöperation and support in every proper way, but I do not think that the policemen of any of our states or municipalities should become affiliated with it. This, as I understand it, is Commissioner Curtis's position, and in this I think he was right.

The Mayor, however, was temperamentally less uncompromising and rigid than Curtis. Peters did not wish to precipitate, or tolerate the precipitation of, a major municipal disaster without some attempt to reconcile the opposing parties. More than anyone else, he was aware that public opinion could not be disregarded, and he himself at that moment was far from sure that Curtis would receive the backing of the Boston press. Accordingly on August 27 he named a Citizens' Committee of Thirty-Four, headed by James J. Storrow,[11] a partner in the banking firm of Lee, Higginson and Company. For this committee Curtis himself offered a few suggestions; and its membership, clearly nonpartisan, included representatives of various political affiliations, religious preferences, and social backgrounds. It was formally organized, at the Boston City Club, on August 29, with an Executive Committee consisting of George E. Brock, John R. Macomber, P. A. O'Connell, James J. Phelan, A. C. Ratshesky, and Frederick S. Snyder, with B. Preston Clark as Secretary and Storrow, of course, as Chairman. Other prominent figures among the group were Charles G. Bancroft, Charles F. Choate, Charles H. Cole, J. Wells Farley, A. Lincoln Filene, Robert F. Goodwin, and Charles F. Weed. Mr. Storrow lost no time in declaring that "police officers should not join the American Federation of Labor"; but he added also, to Curtis's annoyance, that he could see no objection to their "forming their own independent and unaffiliated organization." To make their official position clear at the outset the Citizens' Committee adopted the following resolution: —

That the Citizens' Committee is opposed to the affiliation by any organization of the Boston police force with the American Federation of Labor, for the reason that such affiliation tends to divide the allegiance of a body of men which in the very nature of its duties can have but one allegiance, and that to the whole community.

While Curtis approved of Storrow's appointment as Chairman of the Citizens' Committee, it soon appeared that a majority of its

[11] James Jackson Storrow (1864–1926), graduate of Harvard in the class of 1885, had been Chairman of the Boston School Committee, had run for Mayor in 1909 against John F. Fitzgerald, had been Chairman of the Massachusetts Committee of Safety in 1917, and later Fuel Commissioner for Massachusetts. He was a gentleman of the finest type, interested in many forms of public service.

members were anxious to avoid any open rupture with the police; [12] and when he became aware of this, the Commissioner lost confidence in them and whatever steps they might take. For five sweltering days, from August 29 to September 2, Storrow, Phelan, and Brock met with John F. McInnes, President of the Policemen's Union, and his associates to discuss the emergency. Their conferences were held in Room 28 of the Parker House, where Storrow was kept so busy that he could not even go home at night to his family in Lincoln. On Labor Day, September 1, the Storrow group had a meeting with Curtis, who came down from Nahant to join them. But all this parley ended inconclusively, and the representatives of the police, although impressed with the courteous treatment which they had received, repeated their intention of calling a strike if, or when, the nineteen patrolmen were punished.

At this point, then, the Citizens' Committee were for some form of compromise, not having any idea of yielding on the charter issue. Mayor Peters had not lost hope that such a solution might be brought about; and Governor Coolidge, with his ear to the ground, had not committed himself and was hoping that the crisis might be passed without his intervention. [13] On August 26, Long recorded in his Diary, "Governor getting tired of seeing people. He is planning to visit institutions." He was in Northampton on August 28, attending a Methodist gathering, and on the next three days did not come to his office, being busy preparing speeches. On Labor Day he spoke at Plymouth, Massachusetts, and on September 3 at Westfield, at the 250th anniversary of that town — in both cases referring rather exultantly to the prevailing prosperity. Outwardly he seemed little troubled, but some farsighted citizens of Boston were so apprehensive that they began the enrollment of volunteer police to be ready for a possible emergency. Curtis had announced that he would pass sentence on the morning of Thursday, September 4; and the *Boston Herald,* in commenting on the sessions of the Citizens' Committee,

---

[12] Several members of the Committee were out of sympathy with what they regarded as Storrow's too conciliatory attitude; and Colonel Robert F. Goodwin actually resigned when he saw the course which the Committee was taking. Goodwin wrote, "I am firmly convinced that the stand taken by Commissioner Curtis is right and that he should have the frank and open support of every citizen who endorses his course."

[13] Robert Lincoln O'Brien, then editor of the *Boston Herald* and to-day one of the best-informed men on the subject of the strike, feels that Coolidge was strongly influenced by W. Murray Crane — that Crane, in fact, was the Hamlet of the Police Strike drama. Coolidge and Crane usually thought alike on public questions, but I have been unable so far to discover specific evidence that the two were in consultation in August or early September, 1919. Mr. Long's Diary shows that Coolidge telephoned Crane on August 22, but the two men apparently did not meet for a conference during this period.

could only say, none too optimistically, "Four Days of Futile Conference Leave Deadlock."

On Wednesday morning, September 3, a letter signed by Storrow and requesting a brief delay was presented at Curtis's office, but his counsel, Herbert Parker,[14] after receiving and reading it, took the responsibility of refusing to transmit it to the Commissioner. On that evening, in desperation, a group from the Citizens' Committee, with Mayor Peters as their spokesman, secured a conference with the Governor after his return from Westfield and asked him to intervene with Curtis. Coolidge was still noncommittal, simply saying in his curt and final fashion, "I feel it is not my duty to communicate with the Commissioner on the subject."

In his *Autobiography* Coolidge justified his position by his conviction that the question of obedience by the police to the rules of the department and the orders issued by the Commissioner could not be arbitrated. As he saw the situation, the police were like mutineers on the high seas; and to a man of his philosophy the issue had no shadows. He had already, we may assume, taken the same stand as Curtis. He himself had, as he said, "no direct responsibility for the conduct of police matters in Boston"; but he did watch the trend of events, keep informed as to developments, and by his open refusal to interfere really helped Curtis. A single word from him would probably have led to a compromise, but that word he would not utter. His attitude was distinguished by legality and discretion, but it was the part of wisdom as well.

Curtis had announced that he would render a judgment on Thursday morning, and the counsel for the unionized police, when asked if they wished a continuance, replied that they were indifferent. Nevertheless when the Mayor sent a letter asking formally for a postponement, the Commissioner yielded and put off his decision again until Monday, September 8. The Citizens' Committee now had a few more hours for patching up a compromise. With only

---

[14] Throughout the events leading up to and following the Police Strike Mr. Parker's advice and influence were potent, particularly with Curtis, whose counsel he was. Then in his sixty-fourth year, he had been graduated from Harvard in 1878 and had later built up a large practice as a trial lawyer. From 1901 until 1905 he had been Attorney General of the Commonwealth under Governors Crane, Bates, and Douglas. Conservative by temperament and training, Parker had much in common with Curtis, and had been intimately associated with him during the Massachusetts Constitutional Convention of 1917-1919, the final session of which had been taking place during that fateful August of 1919. As counsel for Curtis, Parker would accept only a nominal fee of $50. The most conspicuous photograph in Parker's office was that of Curtis, whom he admired only a little this side of idolatry. Parker had read and made comments on this chapter before his death on February 11, 1939, just before his eighty-third birthday.

brief recesses the members of the Executive Committee met on Thursday, Friday, and Saturday, and finally on Saturday afternoon were obliged to fall back on a temporary plan stipulating that the nineteen union officers should not be further disciplined, that no strike should be called, and that the other alleged grievances of the police should be submitted to a neutral board of arbitration.

Peters gave his sanction to the report late on Saturday afternoon, and it was presented to the public in the form of a letter to the Mayor, dated September 6, and signed by Storrow, Clark, Brock, O'Connell, Phelan, Ratshesky, and Snyder. In transmitting it in turn to the Commissioner, Peters wrote: —

The report commended itself to me as a wise method of dealing with the subject, and I recommend it to your favorable consideration. If acceptable to you and the men, it affords a speedy and, it seems to me, satisfactory settlement of the whole question.

With these words of praise the Mayor put himself on record in support of his own committee, as was natural, especially because he had been kept informed almost from hour to hour of the results of the deliberations of Storrow and his associates.

During those confused days when so many public-spirited citizens were attempting to find a legitimate adjustment of conflicting opinions, the Governor was repeatedly urged to declare himself in favor of compromise. A group of friends called upon him at the State House to warn him that, unless he did speak out, he would be defeated in the coming election. His only comment was, "It is not necessary for me to be elected" — after which remark he sat in stony silence staring out of the window until his embarrassed visitors rose and slipped away. On Saturday the Governor fulfilled engagements in Abington and Andover, at "Welcome Home" gatherings to veterans. At Andover he and his old friend, John N. Cole, conversed in subdued tones, but Coolidge showed no outward evidences of worry. On the following morning two gentlemen, one a lawyer and the other a businessman, asked Frank W. Stearns to meet them at the Copley-Plaza Hotel to discuss an important matter. There they solemnly besought him as a moral duty to use his influence with the Governor in favor of the compromise plan. Mr. Stearns, with no less seriousness, thought a moment and replied: —

Gentlemen, I am not a lawyer, but I have heard the matter discussed by eminent lawyers and have arrived at the conclusion that the compromise which you suggest — which amounts to an agreement on the part of the Police Commissioner of Boston to give the deserters a written promise to put the whole matter to arbitration — is not worth the paper on which it would be written. I do not believe that sworn officers of the law can leave a matter of this kind to arbitration, or that it would be effective if they did.[15]

In so speaking we may be sure that the prudent and usually un-communicative Stearns spoke also for the Governor; and I am convinced from this and other available evidence that Coolidge's sympathies throughout were with Curtis and not with the Citizens' Committee. As a matter of fact, Curtis and the Committee were not actually so far apart as has sometimes been supposed, but any com-promise was distasteful to Curtis and to his adviser, Parker.

The Governor was not available on Sunday, September 7, for he had set out by automobile at nine o'clock for Northampton, on his way to Greenfield,[16] where on Monday he was to keep a long-standing engagement for an address before the state convention of the American Federation of Labor. At Northampton on Sunday evening he talked over the telephone with W. Murray Crane, at Dalton, and with William F. Whiting, at Holyoke, both of whom were staunchly for Curtis.

Meanwhile Curtis, exhausted by the strain to which he had been subjected, had left Boston for a peaceful week-end at his home in Nahant. The Citizens' Committee did, however, place their report in his hands by special messenger at nine o'clock on Sunday and also saw that it reached the press in season for comment on Monday morning. All the morning newspapers, including the *Globe,* the *Post,* the *American,* and the *Herald,* bestowed upon it their editorial blessing, the *Herald,* however, rather unenthusiastically. Of the evening papers the *Transcript* alone protested, under the heading, "No Time to Surrender." Its leading article closed with this sen-tence : —

Ours is not a city whose people are willing to surrender in the face of threats from foes without or within, and now is the time and this the place for a finish fight if the Boston policemen make their membership in the American Federation of Labor the price of peace.[17]

[15] The substance of this interview is derived from a memorandum made by Mr. Stearns at the time.
[16] The assertion frequently made that Coolidge stopped at Lancaster for a conference with Curtis and Parker was denied by Mr. Parker in an interview with me before his death, and has no evidence whatever to sustain it.
[17] In this connection gossip was abroad in Boston at the time to the effect that the American Federation of Labor had adopted the policy of fighting out the question of unionizing the police and had selected Boston as the battleground — first, because the labor element in Boston was strong and second because Coolidge was

On Monday morning, September 8, Curtis, counseled in his every move by Parker, sent to Peters an unyielding reply in the third person, reading in part as follows: —

The Commissioner can discover nothing in the communication transmitted to your Honor and relating to action by him which appears to him to be either consistent with his prescribed legal duties or calculated to aid him in their performance. The Commissioner approves necessary betterment in the economic condition of the police force of the City of Boston and had heretofore expressed such approval, but these are not the conditions which require his present action.

Underneath this stilted and technical phraseology, the Commissioner was making it evident that he would not budge. It has been intimated by various commentators that Curtis had been throughout in close touch with the Governor, but this was not the case. Even Parker saw nothing of Coolidge until after the strike had broken out.

On Monday, as had been predicted, the Commissioner suspended the nineteen offending policemen. They were suspended, not discharged, and could under the regulations be later reinstated. Curtis's finding, covering one full page of the *Transcript,* was supported by both precedents and arguments. He declared, with much emphasis, that he had been entrusted with "a very important public duty," which he could not divide with any other official. Later, in his annual report as Police Commissioner, he examined minutely the plan of the Citizens' Committee and declared (1) that the attitude of the unionized police regarding it was "in no way indicated"; (2) that "its merits could properly come up for discussion only after the men on trial had purged themselves of their violation of a rule of the department"; and (3) that if the policemen had been really contrite, they would have severed their connection with the American Federation of Labor. On the other hand, it is clear that Vahey and Feeney, counsel for the union, had earnestly advised its officials to accept the compromise; indeed, in Storrow's judgment, it would have been approved at a general meeting of the men to be held on Monday afternoon. The Storrow Report stresses the point that between Saturday afternoon, when the plan took final shape, and Monday morning, not enough time had elapsed for the members of the union to determine whether or not they would sur-

---

regarded as a weak Governor. It was also felt that the militia and the State Guard would not come out in Massachusetts against a strong labor movement. The evidence for this theory does not seem to me convincing.

render their charter and consent to an adjustment. This question is largely academic, in view of the more important issues involved.

Meanwhile the Governor, having slept on Sunday night in the isolation of his Northampton home, had proceeded on Monday to Greenfield, where at eleven o'clock he entered the hall in which the convention of the American Federation of Labor was holding its sessions. He spoke for half an hour in an uninspired way, declaring that the country had never been more prosperous and urging the delegates to take back to the men and women whom they represented the gospel "that upon all rests the responsibility of doing all that may be done to make the name America stand for mighty endeavor and strenuous effort." Not a word did he utter about the Boston police or the possibility of a strike. The Governor had intended to spend a few days inspecting state institutions, but Mr. Stearns telephoned him at Northampton urging him to return as soon as possible to Boston and Coolidge followed this advice. On his drive back to Boston he stopped at Fitchburg to telephone his office for the latest news, reaching the Adams House shortly after four o'clock. At Fitchburg he picked up Representative Frederick C. Nichols, Treasurer of the Fitchburg Savings Bank, and carried him to Boston in his car. The insinuation that his journey was "mysterious" is absurd, for anybody who read the newspapers could have learned where he was to be. That evening Coolidge dined at the Union Club in a large private room with Wyman, Peters, Storrow, and several members of the Citizens' Committee.

Following Curtis's decision, given out shortly after nine on Monday, Peters and Storrow tried vainly to reach the Governor, but ultimately arranged for a conference at his suite in the Adams House before the Union Club dinner. There they fervently besought Coolidge to defend the compromise plan, but he declined to interfere. Then Storrow and Peters asked him to mobilize at least three or four thousand troops for action in case of a strike; and again the Governor refused, maintaining that the situation could safely be left in Curtis's hands. The issue was now sharply drawn between Peters and Curtis, and the Governor had resolved to stand by. The official, or public, story of these dramatic events can be followed in the newspapers. What is missing is what went on behind the scenes where no reporters were present, in hasty conferences and intimate conversations in club corridors, in telephone messages which no one recorded or can now repeat accurately. The influence of such men as W. Murray Crane, Frank W. Stearns, and William M. Butler undoubtedly was strong with the Governor. A score of people now living were more or less "on the inside," but their recollections are often contradictory and the biographer finds himself compelled to sift and weigh and discard.[18] Even less easy to be certain of are the speculations which went on in Coolidge's mind, behind that mask-like, unexpressive countenance.

On Monday night the Adjutant General, Jesse F. Stevens, and Lieutenant Colonel R. O. Dalton, officer in charge of Intelligence, remained at the Adams House, as did Henry F. Long.

While these conferences were in progress, the police were secretly voting and decided, 1134 to 2, to leave their duties at 5.45 on Tuesday afternoon. A large proportion of them were deluded by the promises of their leaders and did not realize the seriousness of what they were doing. As Tuesday morning dawned, it was obvious to those near the scene that the threatened walkout would probably occur before the day was over. The *Herald* took a firm stand, declaring that "a policemen's strike, particularly if accompanied by sympathetic strikes in other quarters, would be a serious thing for Boston; but in the long run it would be far less disastrous than a complacent surrender of the city's government to an outside authority." Public opinion was gradually forming against the union men; but they, like the victims of a Sophoclean tragedy, seemed unable to avert their doom. The American Federation, still sitting at Greenfield with Calvin Coolidge's words yet ringing in their ears, adopted resolutions denouncing "the Hunnish attitude of Police Commissioner Curtis" and proffering full moral and financial aid to the policemen's union. The chief agitators had apparently no conception of the hostile feeling which a strike would arouse. Unconsciously they had chosen to give battle at a moment when their chances of victory were as slight as those of Burnside at Marye's Heights or Pickett at Gettysburg. But it is easier to be a prophet after the event than before it.

On that same fateful Tuesday the Mayor was early at his office in the City Hall; Commissioner Curtis sat restlessly at his desk at 29 Pemberton Square;[19] and the Governor took his customary slow after-breakfast stroll from the Adams House across the Common up the slope to his room under the Bulfinch dome. All three had forebodings, and no one of them was inwardly very calm. The

---

[18] Perhaps the most authentic information comes from Henry F. Long, who kept a diary throughout this period, with full details as to the Governor's movements and actions. Mr. Long has also prepared an account of the Police Strike which he has permitted me to use.

[19] Curtis was very much afraid of being assassinated and kept an automatic revolver always on his desk within easy reach.

Mayor at one o'clock called upon the Commissioner to ascertain what preparations had been made to preserve order if a strike were to take place. Curtis replied that he had the situation well under control and possessed ample means for the protection of the city. Believing honestly that the men were devoted to him and would never adopt extreme measures, he refused the offered assistance of the State Guard.[20] Baffled in his efforts to help Curtis, Peters suggested that it might be tactful to consult the Governor. While Curtis said frankly that this was not necessary, he finally consented to meet Peters in Coolidge's office; and there, at five o'clock, the three principal figures in the drama came together. The Police Commissioner, queried sharply, reiterated his assertion that he had provided for emergencies and did not need or desire the State Guard. After listening to both Peters and Curtis, the Governor said, "I am going to take the assurance of the Police Commissioner," and again declined to call out troops.[21]

To put himself on record, the Governor, after the conference was over, dictated a letter to the Mayor elucidating his position and stating that "the duty of issuing orders and enforcing their observance lies with the Commissioner of Police and with that no one has any authority to interfere." He did not propose to go over the head of the Police Commissioner until compelled by circumstances to do so; and he was, in fact, quite satisfied with what Curtis had done.[22] He concluded: —

There is no authority in the office of Governor for interference in the making of orders by the Police Commissioner or in the action of the Mayor and the City Council. . . . I am unable to discover any action I can take.

[20] For a more detailed account of this singular interview see the letter from Peters to Storrow, September 25, 1919, published as Appendix 15 to the report of the Storrow Committee. Peters after the conference said to inquisitive reporters, "Police Commissioner Curtis assured me that he was in a position to give the people adequate protection."

[21] See the *Report of Committee Appointed by Mayor Peters to Consider the Police Situation* (Boston City Document 108, 1919). This presents very significant testimony on the Police Strike from men who were in touch with it from the beginning.

[22] On Monday, Arthur B. Chapin, Vice President of the American Trust Company, who knew both Curtis and Coolidge well, went, with Curtis's approval, to call on the Governor and asked him frankly how he would act if an emergency arose. According to Chapin, the Governor thought a moment and then said, "I am very friendly to Ned Curtis. I am told that he feels that enough policemen will remain loyal so that he can handle the situation, but you may tell him from me that if any emergency arises whereby it becomes necessary for me to act, I will stand back of him to the fullest extent." Chapin reported the substance of this talk to Curtis, who said, "While I felt that it would be so, I am glad to know this direct from him."

The guarantee which Curtis thus repeatedly and positively gave to both the Mayor and the Governor undoubtedly restrained them from taking steps to meet the impending crisis. According to the *Boston Post* for September 9, when Curtis was interrogated, he replied indignantly, "I am ready for anything"; and he made the same reply to a representative of the *Traveler*. In defending his inaction Curtis later protested that, even up to the moment when the strike opened, he was uncertain whether the police would desert their posts. He added that the hour fixed by the strikers was "suddenly and secretly determined upon," and that he had been assured, furthermore, that a large proportion of the force would under any circumstances remain loyal. Then, too, he had been advised by counsel that neither he nor anybody else had the authority to call upon the State Guard unless "tumult, riot, or mob" were threatened. His only resource — so he argued — was to appoint special or temporary police who might in an emergency be substituted for the regular patrolmen. The truth is, of course, that he was too sanguine, and relied too credulously on the information furnished by his subordinate officers. If he had not been so certain, Peters, and possibly even Coolidge, might have taken charge, had the State Guard in readiness, and thus have averted trouble. A less obstinate man might have saved money and bloodshed.

As it was, virtually no precautions were taken. Tuesday evening was misty, with the chill of early autumn in the air, and not many people were on the streets for pleasure. Shortly after five o'clock reports began to reach the Intelligence Department that policemen were abandoning their stations. The first warning, at 5.11, came from Station 16, where 90 per cent of the men coming in on the new shift had quit their posts. At 5.35 Station 1 was "practically empty except for officers." The actual number to desert was 1117 out of 1544 — a far larger proportion than Curtis had anticipated. The walkout itself was reported as orderly and peaceful except for some cheering from crowds around the stations. Governor Coolidge, with Attorney General Henry A. Wyman [23] and Lieutenant Colonel Robert O. Dalton, Chief of Intelligence, sat after dinner at the Hotel Touraine with Mr. Stearns, receiving the news. The Motor Corps and the Cavalry Troop held their regular drill that evening at the Armory and were kept there under orders until eleven o'clock, at which hour, there being apparently no emergency, they were dis-

[23] Henry Augustus Wyman (1861–1935), a native of Maine and a graduate of Boston University in 1885, was a well-known director of corporations and trustee of estates in Boston, whose sagacity was much respected in legal circles.

missed. It should be added that the Governor had some days before secured from the Adjutant General full information regarding the units of the State Guard which would be available when called. Shortly after ten o'clock the Governor, somewhat reassured and trusting in Curtis's optimism, went to bed, telling Long not to bother him, and slept undisturbed until morning. In his *Autobiography* he has confessed that he knew nothing of the night's disorder until he went down to breakfast on Wednesday.

As the gossip about the walkout spread on Tuesday evening little groups of irresponsible hoodlums congregated on the street corners and commenced their pranks. Soon the more venturesome, noticing the absence of bluecoats, began removing the spare tires from cars and knocking off the hats of pedestrians. Shortly after eleven o'clock a trolley car was held up and stoned by a mob, and the passengers were forcibly ejected. Rapidly what had originally been a vague spirit of mischief, like that abroad on Hallowe'en Night, turned into rioting. Windows were smashed in stores and the goods on display were seized; fruit stands were overturned; and the primitive instinct to destroy was unexpectedly let loose. Dice games were openly in operation on the Common and round the steps of some of the deserted police stations. The few members of the Metropolitan Police who appeared found themselves outnumbered and virtually helpless.[24] In accordance with the trend of mass psychology, irresponsible mischief-making degenerated into criminality, and a crowd of people individually law-abiding became as a group lawless and even menacing. Spectators on the streets could see with their own eyes how revolutions are engendered and how speedily jeers turn into blows and pistol shooting. The last report of damage came from Avery Street shortly before three o'clock, but there was some noise and disorder until sunrise.[25] All this could have been stopped very early if a regiment of the State Guard had been available to suppress the first attempts at rioting.

On the following morning the *Herald* opened its news article on the events of the previous evening as follows: —

Lawlessness, disorder, looting, such as was never known in this city, ran riot last night in South Boston, the North and West ends, and the downtown sections of the municipality, following the departure of the striking policemen from their station houses.

[24] The loyalty of the Metropolitan Police had evidently been tampered with, and nineteen of them were subsequently dismissed for this reason.

[25] A vivid, although rather overdone, description of that night is to be found in "Anarchy in Boston," by Randolph Bartlett, in the *American Mercury*, December 1925, pp. 456ff.

Editorially every newspaper in Boston condemned the strikers in the most vigorous language, and they found little sympathy. Naturally the question of the responsibility for the pathetically defenseless condition of the city was not ignored, and it has often since been discussed in clubs and around dinner tables by the partisans of the various officials involved. I am myself convinced that neither Peters nor Coolidge can justly be blamed for what happened on Tuesday night. Coolidge in his *Autobiography* said candidly: "I have always felt that I should have called out the State Guard as soon as the police left their posts. The Commissioner did not feel that this was necessary." Peters would also have acted with decision if he had not been informed repeatedly by Curtis that no peril existed. Curtis, it must be remembered, had said not once but again and again, "I am ready for any crisis." As a matter of fact, he was not ready. He deserves the utmost credit for resisting the demands of the unionized policemen, but he was not prepared for the emergency when it arrived.

When the moment came for action, Peters did not delay and was the first to take defensive measures. Reached by telephone at his Brookline home shortly after midnight, he ordered his secretary to summon certain officers of the militia to the City Hall early in the morning. Through the early morning hours he lay awake listening to further telephonic reports as they came in; but in view of his conference with the Governor on the preceding day he felt reluctant to interfere. When he reached his office shortly after eight o'clock he was surrounded by well-intentioned but jittery advisers, and he could not ignore the possibility that railroad men, firemen, and telegraph operators might institute a sympathetic strike. Peters did what he could to restore confidence by conferring at once with Colonel Thomas F. Sullivan, Colonel Decrow, and others, by ordering the Boston State Guard units to report at five that afternoon, and by preparing a formal request that the Governor call out three additional regiments. He also notified the Motor Corps and the Ambulance Corps to be ready for the summons. He then said, "I have hitherto relied upon the statement of the Police Commissioner that he had complete control of the situation" and, proceeding under a special act, sent a letter removing Curtis from authority over the Police Department and placing General Charles H. Cole in temporary command at 29 Pemberton Square. This letter was despatched by messenger from the Mayor's office at 9.45 and delivered before 10. At 10.30 a letter arrived from Curtis to Peters, saying, "I am of the opinion that tumult, riot, or mob is threatened" and suggesting that the Mayor exercise his authority under the statutes of 1917, Chapter 327, Part I, Section 26. Of the effectiveness of Peters's actions there can be no doubt. Curtis, on his part, at once called upon the Governor in much distress, complaining that he had been unjustly superseded and notifying Coolidge that the latter must either remove or sustain him. Under the circumstances the Governor was bound to come to Curtis's rescue.

All day Wednesday arrangements were being hastily made for controlling another night of disorder. The volunteer police force which certain patriotic citizens had been joining was called out under the command of William H. Pierce. The loyal policemen who had been so little in evidence on the previous evening were mustered for the preservation of peace. Meanwhile public resentment was deepening, and even the strikers were realizing the tempest which they had stirred up.

As soon as twilight fell it was apparent that an ugly spirit was abroad. The hoodlums were giving way to professional criminals. The volunteer troopers who ordered the crowds to keep moving were assailed with bricks, stones, and bottles. Four Harvard undergraduates endeavoring to disperse a mob on Brattle Street had a hard fight to escape serious injury. Many of the striking policemen were stationed here and there inciting the throng to violence. When the resistance of the gangs grew stubborn, the troopers in self-protection were obliged to use their pistols and some casualties, including three deaths, resulted.[26] By Thursday morning, however, decency had triumphed, and Scollay Square, which had been the centre of the rioting, was quiet. The underworld had discovered that public opinion was thoroughly aroused, and the dawn saw members of the State Guard patrolling the streets without any untoward incidents. The Citizens' Committee later reported, "By Thursday morning order had generally been restored in the city."[27]

But although the immediate peril had passed, the controversy between the Mayor on the one hand and the Governor and the Com-

[26] Later the unfortunate cases of fatal shooting were investigated by a Court of Inquiry consisting of Colonel Blake, Colonel Gibbs, and J. Duncan Phillips, and the members of the State Guard were completely exonerated. Efforts made through the civil courts and in the Legislature to break down the testimony of witnesses failed in every instance. Probably extreme measures were absolutely essential in order to demonstrate the supremacy of law.

[27] Characteristic excerpts from the press of many cities may be found in the *Literary Digest* for September 20 and 27, 1919, nearly all of them referring to the strikers as "deserters in the face of sworn duty" and often comparing them to Bolshevists. One of the strikers has often told me in picturesque language of his astonishment at finding himself denounced as a foe of law and order. Very few of the strikers had considered the possible consequences of their action.

missioner on the other was getting warmer. On Wednesday morning Peters, in a moment of irritation, had released a statement in which he alleged that the Citizens' Committee, in their attempts to avoid a strike, had "received no coöperation from the Police Commissioner and no help or practical suggestions from the Governor." This assertion from the Mayor's office was not calculated to increase his popularity with the Governor. On Thursday morning Herbert Parker, summoned hastily to Coolidge's office, found there William M. Butler, Henry A. Wyman, and one or two others. The Governor said in his dry manner, "I see the Mayor has taken a hand in this," and then consulted his advisers as to the wisest procedure. The group agreed that a proclamation should be prepared, and Coolidge drafted such a document beginning, "The entire State Guard of Massachusetts has been called out" and asking all citizens to aid him in "the maintenance of law and order." Somewhat later, also with the approval of those present, the Governor issued an Executive Order taking over the direction of the Boston police force, instructing Curtis to return to his duties as Police Commissioner, and notifying him to obey only such orders as the Governor might "issue or transmit." [28]

The controversy between the Mayor and the Governor was now heated, but the Governor possessed the power. On receipt of Coolidge's proclamation, Peters announced that he had been informed of the Governor's "assumption therein of the management of Boston's police force in addition to his powers as Commander in Chief of the military forces of the Commonwealth" and pledged to him his "loyal, earnest, and complete support." Curtis, once more established in authority at 29 Pemberton Square, asserted that no one of the striking policemen would be taken back and set into motion plans for recruiting a new force, with the faithful policemen as a nucleus. He next fixed the minimum salary of patrolmen at $1400 a year, this increase to take effect on September 14. Finally he issued General Order Number 125, dismissing the nineteen patrolmen who had already been suspended, the dismissal to be in full operation on Saturday, September 13, at 5.45 in the afternoon. These vigorous measures left no doubt as to Curtis's policy regarding the deserters.

[28] The full text of this order is printed in *Have Faith in Massachusetts,* page 221. The Governor took charge of the Police Department without notifying Peters of his intention and, when Parker suggested that it might be tactful to let the Mayor know what had been done, Coolidge replied, "Let him find it out in the papers." The proclamation was issued at three o'clock in the afternoon on Thursday and sent by special messenger to the Mayor's office. Several persons who saw Governor Coolidge during the day recall his rage at Peters.

On Thursday the city was peaceful, and even when darkness fell no rioting was reported. The *Transcript* for Friday said, "Boston is quiet and orderly to-day, following an equally satisfactory night." President Woodrow Wilson, speaking in Helena, Montana, on Thursday evening, declared that the action of the Boston police in leaving the city "at the mercy of an army of thugs" was "a crime against civilization" and added significantly, "In my judgment the obligation of a policeman is as sacred and direct as the obligation of a soldier. He is a public servant, not a private employee, and the whole honor of the community is in his hands." The Central Labor Union of Boston, meeting on Thursday evening, was exceedingly cautious and voted that "the time is not now opportune for the ordering of a general strike." Commissioner Curtis on Friday morning sent out another order : —

That none of the patrolmen who failed to report for duty, September 9, 1919, or since that time may report for duty under any circumstances ; nor are they to be allowed to remain or loiter on the premises of the different station houses.

Meanwhile Samuel Gompers, who had returned from Europe on August 26, discerned at once the blunder which his organization had made and attempted to intervene. On September 9 his aged father died in Dorchester, near Boston, but the son, then in the West on a trip, could not reach home to be at his deathbed. He did, however, hasten East, arriving in New York, where the body of the elder Gompers was to be buried, on Friday morning. After consulting with certain labor leaders, he sent identical telegrams, dated September 12, to Peters and Coolidge, requesting that the strikers be reinstated, pending arbitration. The strikers themselves had now been convinced of their tactical mistake ; and at a meeting held on Friday evening voted almost unanimously to accept Gompers's suggestion that they return to work on the status they had enjoyed before the strike started.

This action came altogether too late. Coolidge, talking on Friday to newspapermen, had termed the conduct of the strikers "desertion of duty" and had made it clear that he had no intention of allowing them to resume their jobs. Attorney General Wyman had meanwhile given his opinion to Curtis that the positions formerly held by the striking policemen were vacant both in law and in fact. On Saturday morning the Governor received a delegation headed by M. J. O'Donnell, President of the Central Labor Union, representing 80,000 workers in key industries, but declined to consider their

request that the offenders should be reinstated. If Calvin Coolidge
had been in any doubt as to the attitude of the public, he must have
been cheered by the chorus of approval which greeted each successive utterance he made. Behind him was the press of the city, of
the Commonwealth, and of the nation at large, from coast to coast.
Although he did not know it, Senator Lodge was writing on Friday to his daughter, Mrs. Augustus P. Gardner: —

The situation in Boston is of the gravest kind. I am glad to see the
Governor behaving so well. Andy Peters fluttered a little but I think
is right on the main issue. Policemen are like soldiers and sailors. They
are government servants and they must not have the liberty of striking.
They do not differ essentially from the army and navy. It is a tremendous
issue, and if the American Federation of Labor succeeds in getting hold
of the police in Boston it will go all over the country, and we shall be
in a measurable distance of Soviet government by labor unions. I have
faith to believe that the American people will not stand for it. It is hard
to tell much at this distance but I think public opinion seems right and
will win.

We now reach the dramatic incident which, as the biographer
looks back upon it, helped so considerably to give Calvin Coolidge
national prominence. The *Herald,* on September 12, had lauded the
Governor editorially, saying: —

We are in the eye of the nation. Other cities are looking on. If the
Soviet theory succeeds here, it will spread to other battle grounds and
become nation wide.

There can be no doubt that certain conservatives in Massachusetts, and in other states as well, perceived that the situation
offered an opportunity for rebuking Gompers, who had been assuming too much importance in political affairs.[29] What Coolidge said,
even more than what he did, clarified for Americans everywhere the
philosophy underlying his condemnation of the police strike. When
Gompers's telegram reached the Governor, he replied: —

Under the law the suggestions contained in your telegram are not
within the authority of the Governor of Massachusetts but only of the
Commissioner of Police of the City of Boston. With the maintenance
of discipline in his department I have no authority to interfere. He has

[29] This idea is emphasized by Frank W. Buxton, editor of the *Boston Herald,*
who adds, "I fancy if some of the surviving Republican leaders would talk, they
could furnish a flood of light on these perplexities. Published 'facts' are one thing,
but usually there lie behind these some matters that modify, often explain, sometimes overturn."

decided that the men have abandoned their sworn duty and has accordingly declared their places vacant. I shall support the Commissioner in the execution of his order.

At this period several influential businessmen in Boston were urging Coolidge to make concessions in the interests of harmony. Political managers warned him again that he was endangering his future. But he had no fears. When he was threatened with a general strike, he sent telegrams to Secretary of War Baker and Secretary of the Navy Daniels at eleven o'clock on Thursday requesting them to be ready, if necessary, to send armed forces into the Commonwealth.[30] The essential strength of his character, its capacity for resisting outside pressure, never showed itself to better advantage than during September 1919.

Gompers, while waiting in New York for his father's funeral, now sent one more telegram, which reached Coolidge late in the afternoon of Saturday, September 13. In it he said in part: —

The question at issue is not one of law and order, but the assumption of an autocratic and unwarranted position by the Commissioner of Police, who is not responsible to the people of Boston, but who is appointed by you. Whatever disorder has occurred is due to his order in which the right of the policemen has been denied, a right which has heretofore never been questioned.

Coolidge was thus offered his opportunity and grasped it with unerring sagacity. The Lord had delivered his opponent into his hands. The Governor's reply, carefully phrased, was sent by telegram on Sunday, the precise hour being impossible to discover. The full text, printed in all the Boston newspapers on Monday morning, reads as follows: —

Replying to your telegram, I have already refused to remove the Police Commissioner of Boston. I did not appoint him. He can assume no position which the Courts would uphold except what the people have by the authority of their law vested in him. He speaks only with their voice. The right of the police of Boston to affiliate has always been questioned, never granted, is now prohibited. The suggestion of President Wilson to Washington does not apply to Boston. There the police remained on duty. Here the Policemen's Union left their duty, an action

[30] Green, 142. The telegrams read: "The entire state guard of Massachusetts has been called out. At present the city of Boston is orderly. There are rumors of a very general strike. I wish you to hold yourself in readiness to render assistance from forces under your control immediately on appeal which I may be forced to make to the President."

which President Wilson has described as a crime against civilization. Your assertion that the Commissioner was wrong cannot justify the wrong of leaving the city unguarded. That furnished the opportunity; the criminal element furnished the action. There is no right to strike against the public safety by anybody, anywhere, any time. You ask that the public safety again be placed in the hands of these same policemen while they continue in disobedience to the laws of Massachusetts and in their refusal to obey the orders of the Police Department. Nineteen men have been tried and removed. Others having abandoned their duty, their places have, under the law, been declared vacant in the opinion of the Attorney General. I can suggest no authority outside the Courts to take further action. I wish to join and assist in taking a broad view of every situation. A grave responsibility rests upon all of us. You can depend upon me to support you in every legal action and sound policy. I am equally determined to defend the sovereignty of Massachusetts and to maintain the authority and jurisdiction over her public officers where it has been placed by the Constitution and laws of her people.

To this telegram no reply was ever received.

The *Transcript,* discerning at once the significance of this ringing telegram, gave it strong editorial praise, saying, "It is as admirable in tone as it is unanswerable in terms — a state paper certain to enhance the high traditions of the great office so worthily filled to-day." Its crisp staccato phrases spread beyond New England across the Mississippi and the Rockies. What Coolidge had done was to present in clear, unforgettable language a complete justification for his policy on the police strike. The telegram was not eloquent in a Websterian fashion, but its logic was difficult to refute and the average man could understand it. It appeared, furthermore, at precisely the right psychological juncture to focus attention on the writer and to establish him as a symbol of decency and courage.

The authorship of the famous telegram has been attributed to several of the Governor's advisers, particularly Attorney General Wyman. Mr. Wyman is unfortunately now unable to speak for himself, but in his lifetime he certainly never allowed anyone to quote him on the matter. Secretary Long's clear recollection is that Coolidge drafted the telegram on heavy block paper and that Wyman, at the Governor's request, read it, but made no suggestions. Long then sent it off to the telegraph office by telephone. All the internal evidence of style and structure is sufficiently convincing as to the writer. The crucial sentences, those which etch themselves upon the mind, are unmistakably in the terse, direct, and penetrating manner of Calvin Coolidge. *Aut Caesar aut nihil!*

Although its aftermath was to stretch rather dully over several months, the incident itself was almost finished. The actual damage caused by the strike proved to be slight and was settled by the City of Boston for about $34,000 — not much more than the cost of a small fire. A fund was started on September 20 to aid the "Defenders of Public Safety," — the loyal police and the volunteers, — and a report dated February 1921 showed that $527,119.22 had been collected and more than $380,000 disbursed. The striking policemen too had their advocates. A Women's Committee of Public Safety was formed, which held meetings for the purpose of arousing sentiment in favor of the jobless deserters. Now that the strike itself had failed, every effort was made by the unionized patrolmen to regain their original standing. A typical example of twisted thinking was an editorial in the *New Republic*, which said : —

It is well that the strike of the Boston police has failed. In spite of the substantial grievances of the strikers, their proposal to affiliate with the A. F. of L. was not compatible with the faithful execution of their regular duties. . . . The police did not deserve to win, but as a penalty for having lost, they deserve even less such extremely drastic punishment. The refusal to take them back is harsh, inexpedient, and wrong-headed.

But this viewpoint was not that of the average citizen, on whom the rioting had made a lasting impression. As early as September 10, the *Herald* had said of the strikers, "They never should have been policemen. They never will be again, if the community has an ounce of self-respect." Again on September 15 the same newspaper added, "Much as we pity individuals, no striker should under any circumstances ever again be a policeman." Commissioner Curtis himself would yield nothing, but set immediately at the task of recruiting a new police force, and on January 10, 1920, announced that he had once more his full quota of 1574 men. On September 17 plans for a sympathetic strike of Boston firemen fell through. Finally, on September 23, at the party primaries, Calvin Coolidge was renominated without opposition for Governor by an unusually large Republican vote.

On that evening while sitting with William M. Butler and Frank W. Stearns in the latter's apartment discussing the results, Coolidge, referring to the movement for reinstating at least the more innocent strikers, said quite unexpectedly, "This propaganda is still going on. I think I must say something publicly." Neither Butler nor Stearns answered at the time; but in the morning Stearns called up Butler and said, "I have thought the matter over and I believe the Governor should say something." Mr. Butler replied, "I agree, only tell him to make it strong." At nine o'clock Mr. Stearns dropped in at the State House as usual in the morning, told the Governor of his opinion, and added, "If you do decide to speak, make it strong and, if proper, put it in the form of a proclamation by the Governor, and then you will get the front page of the newspapers for it." Coolidge said, "What does Mr. Butler think about it?" Mr. Stearns answered, "Why not call him on the telephone and find out?" After conversing briefly with Butler, Coolidge turned and said, "If possible, Mr. Butler is stronger than you about it." Stearns went out to his department store, but Coolidge sent for him in an hour, handed him two or three typewritten pages, and said drily, "That has gone to the newspapers. You can show it to Mr. Butler if you want to." Stearns proceeded at once to Butler's office and let him read the proclamation out loud. His comment when he had finished was, "I wanted it strong, but he cannot say that." "There's no help now; the newspapers have it," replied Stearns. Thus it was that the unusual proclamation of September 24, an even more positive statement than the telegram to Gompers, was prepared and published. In it the Governor said: —

To place the maintenance of the public security in the hands of a body of men who have attempted to destroy it would be to flout the sovereignty of the laws the people have made. It is my duty to resist any such proposal. Those who would counsel it join hands with those whose acts have attempted to destroy the government. There is no middle ground. Every attempt to prevent the formation of a new police force is a blow at the Government. That way treason lies.

This statement, coming out on the day following the primaries, helped to clear the atmosphere and to establish the issue for the coming gubernatorial election. Gossip in State Street had been misrepresenting the Governor's attitude. It had been hinted that for political reasons he would not oppose allowing the strikers to be reinstated. This proclamation showed that he had no intention of yielding, even to pressure from Republican leaders, and that he was willing to stand firm on what he had done and said. On September 25, Vahey and Feeney came out with a lengthy defense covering six newspaper columns in an effort to counteract the effect of Coolidge's proclamation, but it was generally disregarded. The public

had already made up its mind, and to this day every recurring movement to vindicate or reinstate the strikers has failed. As recently as
March, 1938, Police Commissioner Timilty refused to listen to their
appeal; and Governor Charles F. Hurley, when they called on him
for help, declared that he would abide by the Commissioner's decision. Many of the strikers have now secured other positions and
are too old for active police duty. The possibility that any of them
will ever regain their former jobs is indeed remote.

It was, and has been, the policy of Coolidge's critics to minimize
or ridicule his share in the Police Strike crisis. Allegations have
been made that, after the rioting was over and order had been
restored, he took charge, thus acquiring prestige through the courageous acts of other men, especially Curtis. This viewpoint is best
summed up, perhaps, in a paragraph from the *Nation:* —

> Governor Coolidge sat discreetly on the fence until he saw on which
> side public sentiment was gathering. When this had manifested itself
> distinctly against the police, and after Boston's danger had been
> averted, Governor Coolidge climbed down from the fence on the side
> with the crowd and issued a proclamation needlessly mobilizing the en-
> tire State Guard.

From the evidence available this interpretation has very little
to sustain it. Calvin Coolidge's temperament was not that of Theodore Roosevelt, and he never in all his life acted impulsively. From
the beginning he felt that Curtis was right in opposing the unioniza-
tion of the police and accordingly declined to interfere with him.
Why should he participate in a controversy in which his man seemed
likely to win? The soundest comment on the Governor's conduct
came later from an obviously unprejudiced source, James J.
Storrow, in a letter written on August 24, 1923, to Professor Charles
E. Merriam of the University of Chicago, in which he said: —

> Coolidge's instinct is in the first place to back up the man who has
> the immediate responsibility, even though his own subordinate. This I
> think is a sound administrative proposition. The Police Commissioner
> was sure he had the matter well in hand, could fully control the situa-
> tion, and so advised the Governor. Coolidge had the right and could
> hardly help relying on his advice, especially as the Commissioner was
> a first-rate man. He happened to be wrong in this case.

Coolidge's chief blunder, as he himself admitted, was in not
mobilizing the State Guard on Tuesday afternoon. In justification
of this apparent inactivity, Storrow declared that Coolidge's theory

as Governor was "to wait a bit, let the issue develop squarely, and then act." While Storrow declared that he personally would doubtless have had the troops ready, he admitted that Abraham Lincoln would probably have met the emergency as Coolidge did. If the Governor had intervened on Tuesday, he would have had to disavow Curtis. Storrow added in his letter: —

Coolidge never is quick on the trigger, but he keeps his mind right on the problem, and it is generally more important in public affairs to be right than quick.

The adherents of the chief actors in the episode — Curtis, Peters, and Coolidge — have often in their enthusiasm forgotten that there is credit enough for all three. Each one in his way proved himself a man, and it is unnecessary and unjust for the friends of any one of them to disparage the others. What Coolidge did was to uphold Curtis, to place himself squarely and courageously in opposition to Samuel Gompers, and finally to crystallize public opinion and reiterate the supremacy of law and order. He himself commented on the affair as follows: —

No doubt it was the police strike of Boston that brought me into national prominence. That furnished the occasion and I took advantage of the opportunity. I was ready for the emergency. Just what lay behind that event I was never able to learn. Sometimes I have mistrusted that it was a design to injure me politically; if so it was only to recoil upon the perpetrators, for it increased my political power many fold. Still there was a day or two when the event hung in the balance, when the Police Commissioner of Boston was apparently cast aside discredited, and my efforts to give him any support indicated my own undoing. But I soon had him reinstated, and there was a strong expression of public opinion in our favor.

It has been hinted by some radical sensation-mongers that Herbert Parker, Robert Winsor, and representatives of the banking firm of Kidder, Peabody, and Company, — rivals of Lee, Higginson, and Company, in which Storrow was an important partner, — had, after consultation with financiers from New York and Pittsburgh, resolved to discredit Storrow and also to bring the national labor controversy to a head by manoeuvring the police into a position where they would be compelled to strike and thus to bring down upon themselves the wrath of law-abiding citizens. The police strike, on this fantastic theory, was a conspiracy, a phase of a feud between two banking firms, like that between the Guelphs and the Ghibellines, the

"The Pilot Who Weathered the Storm"

(*Cartoon in the "Boston Herald," November 4, 1919*)

citizens of Boston being the deluded and unfortunate victims. The leading figures connected with the strike had many motives, some of them noble, some of them selfish, and not all of them obvious. Party feeling between Republicans and Democrats underlay much of what went on. But the explanation just outlined seems preposterous, quite out of accord with the characters of the persons most concerned. The picture of the close-lipped and cautious Coolidge as *particeps criminis* in a project for promoting the interests of Kidder, Peabody, and Company is, to say the least, unconvincing.

It has also been intimated that Coolidge was at heart rather pleased to have the disorder break out on Tuesday evening, believing that because of it the public might be aroused and he might derive some political benefit from the reaction. This theory was sponsored by a newspaperman named Drake, who published in the *Boston American* an affidavit to the effect that Superintendent Pierce of the volunteer police had announced that no call had been made for him and his men on Tuesday and that none would be sent out until Wednesday morning. The implication was that Curtis, and with him Coolidge, was not sorry to have the people of Boston realize by dire experience what a serious calamity they were facing with the police on strike and no protection available. Proof for this accusation seems to be lacking, and neither Curtis nor Coolidge can now testify in his own behalf. But if human character in any way determines human conduct, they were not the men deliberately to subject the city to a night of disorder for the purpose of furthering their private ends or their political fortunes.

For the biographer and the historian the real importance of the Boston Police Strike lies in its consequences for Calvin Coolidge. He may not personally have determined the outcome; he may have been overscrupulous and legalistic; but he did, through his telegram to Gompers and his ensuing proclamation, bring to the attention of men and women in Massachusetts and eventually throughout the United States his own sound views on the relation of government employees to the public good. His political philosophy was consistent, well-organized, and known to his intimate friends; the strike enabled him to influence a larger audience. Edward E. Whiting put the matter succinctly when he said, "The Police Strike did not make Coolidge, it revealed him. . . . The Police Strike provided a theatrical situation. Governor Coolidge plucked from it and gave to the American people a vital truth, the obviousness of which had been forgotten." In the autumn of 1919 the tendency to scoff at or resist constituted authority was growing. Those citizens who believe that in a democracy the law should be supreme were greatly troubled. What Coolidge did was to restore confidence. He rallied the ranks of law-abiding men and women. Without being fully aware of the far-reaching influence of his utterances, he became the advocate of orderly government and remained so to countless admirers until his death.

Meanwhile the excitement caused by the Police Strike slowly subsided, with occasional intervals of revival. The State Guard was continued on emergency duty for several weeks, but no further danger developed. On October 15 women relatives and friends of the strikers assembled in Fay Hall to demand their reinstatement and heard Harold J. Laski declare that it was Commissioner Curtis who was the real deserter. On November 7 Judge Carroll of the Massachusetts Supreme Court denied the petition of the nineteen policemen for a writ of mandamus to compel Curtis to restore them to the force. Vahey, for the petitioners, maintained that Rule 35 of the Police Department, promulgated by Curtis, was "invalid and unreasonable, and contrary to the Constitution of the United States." Herbert Parker was, as formerly, Curtis's attorney. The report of Storrow's committee appeared on October 4, as we have seen; and still another document in the case was Curtis's formal report as Police Commissioner, dated November 30, 1919, and concerned principally with the strike.[31] For months the strikers clung desperately to their organization and did everything possible to block the recruiting of a new police force, and even managed to hold up the manufacture and delivery of new uniforms. But their cause was definitely lost and within a year most of them were absorbed into other occupations. On the very day of Coolidge's second inauguration as Governor, January 8, 1920, Samuel Gompers, speaking at a luncheon of the Boston Chamber of Commerce, denounced Curtis as being directly responsible for the strike and caused much excitement among the guests. Feeney, testifying before the Legislative Committee on Metropolitan Affairs on February 18, 1920, gave Peters the credit for quelling the trouble caused by the walkout and declared that the policemen's union would have accepted the agreement drawn up by the Storrow Committee. After Curtis died in 1922, a memorial was put up to his memory, and Calvin Coolidge, then Vice President, sent a letter of eulogy. And

---

[31] This was printed as *The Fourteenth Annual Report of the Police Commissioner for the City of Boston* (Public Document Number 49).

so the controversy lingered on, indeed still lingers in the memories of many of the participants.[32]

Boston, from this experience, learned how thin the veneer of civilization actually is. For a few hours the instruments of darkness had their way undisturbed, and terror stalked abroad unchecked and unrepressed. It was fortunate for the city, and for the nation, that the issue was raised — and settled.

[32] At least one novel, *Boundary against Night* (Farrar and Rinehart, 1938), by Edmund Gilligan, has been written about the Police Strike, but it presents an incredible Coolidge against a much too lurid background and very much perverts the truth.

XII

In National Politics

IN the autumn of 1919 Calvin Coolidge was by no means sure of the effect which his attitude towards the Boston Police Strike would have on his career. The Democrats, on September 23, nominated for governor Richard H. Long, the aggressive Framingham shoe manufacturer who had been Coolidge's opponent the year before and who now, counting on the support of organized labor, thought he saw the road clear for his success. His running mate was Colonel John F. J. Herbert, of Worcester, an energetic, loud-voiced World War veteran who had been associated with the formation of the American Legion. In their platform the Democrats forced the issue by saying : —

While we do not condone the policemen who left their posts of duty, we condemn Governor Coolidge for his inaction and culpability in failing to protect the lives and property of the city of Boston.

Long himself promptly took the side of the strikers, demanded their reinstatement, and in one address declared, "Governor Coolidge has shown himself to be the weakest, most helpless and incompetent Governor that our state has ever had." President McInnes and nearly a hundred members of the policemen's union were soon to be traveling about the Commonwealth speaking to the employees of industrial plants and urging them to "get Coolidge" on November 4. David I. Walsh, after holding off during the early weeks of the campaign, was persuaded to come out for Long, and the Central Labor Union followed him.

Fortunately not all of the citizens of Massachusetts shared Long's demoralizing views. The Republican State Convention, held on Saturday, October 4, in Tremont Temple, nominated Coolidge, with Channing H. Cox for Lieutenant Governor, by acclamation. Convalescing from a severe cold, Coolidge appeared on the platform to receive a magnificent ovation which reached its climax when he said in a voice obviously weakened by illness : —

The forces of law and order may be dissipated; they may be defeated; but so long as I am their commander-in-chief, they will not be surrendered.

Even Senator Lodge took time enough away from his battle in Washington against Woodrow Wilson and the League of Nations to praise Commissioner Curtis and Governor Coolidge for their attitude on the Police Strike. It was at this convention, however, that Lodge suffered a rather severe reverse, for W. Murray Crane challenged him on the League of Nations issue and, in a midnight meeting of the party dictators, succeeded in writing an endorsement of the League into the Republican platform.[1]

Throughout this campaign one person was working tirelessly in Coolidge's behalf, having made up his mind that it was to be an important preliminary skirmish before the more difficult struggle for the Presidency. Robert Lincoln O'Brien once said that Frank Stearns, in his affection for Calvin Coolidge, had created a mythical character, as Dickens did in *Martin Chuzzlewit*. But Mr. Stearns was undisturbed by such frivolous comments. With leisure and money sufficient for his purpose, he followed his gleam with tenaciousness, hopefulness, and patience. When he required assistance, he called upon influential friends, many of them Amherst graduates like himself, to whose college loyalty he could appeal. At times the Coolidge "boom" resembled an Amherst crusade.

Even before the Police Strike, Stearns, with his usual prescience, had assembled selections from Coolidge's addresses and placed them in the hands of Houghton Mifflin Company for publication. The idea of such a volume came first from Robert A. Woods, Amherst, '86, then connected with the South End House in Boston, who, when asked to prepare a biography, replied, "Let Coolidge speak for himself." Coolidge's answer to those who sought his approval was, "All right, but I'll have nothing to do with it!" As originally planned by Stearns, the book was to contain thirty-one separate items, open-

[1] The first session of the Sixty-sixth Congress lasted from May 19 to November 19, 1919, and Lodge left it to come back to Boston for the Convention. President Wilson had broken down on September 27, during his speaking tour through the West, and was lying almost helpless in the White House. Although Crane was able to thwart Lodge's wishes in Boston, the United States Senate virtually killed the League of Nations on November 19 and adjourned the same day. The difference of opinion between Crane and Lodge on this issue was serious and irreconcilable.

ing with Coolidge's address to the State Senate in 1914, on being elected its President, and closing with his remarks at the Harvard Commencement in 1919. In the preliminary draft the book was called *Bay State Orations*. While the galley proof was being read by Stearns and Felt, the Police Strike broke, and several of Coolidge's utterances dealing with it were hastily set up in type and added. Meanwhile Roger L. Scaife, then of Houghton Mifflin Company, had criticized the drabness of the title and suggested as a substitute, *Have Faith in Massachusetts,* a sentence taken from the speech to the Senate. The book was published on October 10, under a contract with Mr. Stearns, who had been the dominating factor throughout the negotiations. Up to 1939, 7486 copies had been sold in the United States and 250 in England. Under directions from Mr. Stearns, furthermore, 65,465 copies were distributed through one channel or another to libraries, newspapers, and private individuals. In the second, and final, edition, the compilation included forty-three separate items, closing with Coolidge's speech in Tremont Temple on the Saturday before his triumphant reëlection as Governor.

The makeup of the book was calculated to attract the average reader and voter. The selections were brief, the topics were varied, and the contents could be sampled here and there with profit and without too much effort. There were no long pages of dry statistics and no footnotes in fine type. It is a much better book than most persons realize. Although it is not free from self-evident truths of the kind familiar to those who have listened to political orations, it has pithiness and epigrammatic quality. Some of its phrases are worth pondering, remembering, and quoting, and the entire volume will bear reading, even to-day.

Have Faith in Massachusetts, so widely distributed at such a psychological moment, produced a favorable impression; and the enthusiasm for Coolidge doubled and trebled as the campaign drew to a close. One of his speeches before the Associated Industries of Massachusetts ended, "Have faith in your country, have faith in one another, and above all so live and act that you may be able to say, 'I have kept the faith.'" Mr. Stearns brought this address to the attention of the Reverend Edward T. Sullivan, of Newton Centre, and suggested that it offered material for a sermon. Dr. Sullivan's discourse in his church on Sunday morning, October 19, was on the topic "The Heroisms of Common Life" and praised Coolidge for scorning "the fallacy of safety first." It was later extensively circulated as a campaign document.

In his *Autobiography* Coolidge confessed his feeling that the speeches which he delivered that autumn, though few in number, had a clearness of thought and revealed a power with which he had not hitherto been endowed and which confirmed his belief that when a duty comes, strength is given to perform it. In an address on October 27, the birthday of Theodore Roosevelt, he said: —

We are facing an issue which knows no party. It is not new. That issue is the supremacy of the law. On this issue America has never made but one decision.

Throughout the campaign, in fact, Calvin Coolidge conducted himself with restraint, dignity, and good taste. On October 21, he sent out his first Armistice Day Proclamation, in the course of which he declared: —

War is the rule of Force. Peace is the reign of Law. Let war and all force end, and peace and all law reign.

Four days later, while presiding over a meeting at the State House to attack the high cost of living, he praised Mayor Peters for his work during the Police Strike: —

We acted together at that time, as at other times, with the best judgment that our combined advisers of the city and state could furnish us. Whatever results there were were secured through our joint efforts.

Finally, at the very close of the campaign, in Tremont Temple, he said with reference to the subject: —

That the supremacy of the law, the preservation of the government itself by the maintenance of order, should be the issue of this campaign was due entirely to circumstances beyond my control. That anyone should dare to put in jeopardy the stability of our government for the purpose of securing office was to me inconceivable. . . . But the issue arose by action of some of the police of Boston, and it was my duty to meet it. I shall continue to administer the law of all the people.

One must turn over the already yellowing pages of Boston newspapers during those November days to understand the extent to which public opinion was aroused. Coolidge indulged in no personalities, denounced no opponents, but merely stressed principles. He had as little of the demagogue as any man in public affairs. But the Democratic candidate had no such scruples, and did his utmost by abuse and recriminations to fan into a blaze all the smoldering hatreds left over from the Police Strike. Long declared that

Coolidge was responsible for and could have prevented the riots in Boston.[2] The correspondent of the *New York Times* reported that among Long's adherents were "all the Bolsheviki, the Soviet, the I.W.W. . . . . the striking policemen and all their disorderly followers." Newspapers ordinarily Democratic, like the *New York World* and *Times,* the *Boston Post,* the *Springfield Republican,* and the *Worcester Evening Post,* repudiated Long. Long promised to give the veterans of the World War a bonus of $360 apiece; to remove the Police Commissioner of Boston and reinstate the striking policemen; and to abolish the poll tax and compel the rich to make up the difference in revenue. In plain language, Long resorted to all the unscrupulous devices of the demagogue. The inevitable consequence was to bring thousands of intermittent voters to the Republican side on the issue of Law against Mob.

No doubt, as the *New Republic* said, the chief interest for the nation on that election day centred in the contest for the governorship of Massachusetts. In the minds of good citizens it was essential that Coolidge should not only win but win decisively, for a moral principle was at stake. William H. Taft came into the Commonwealth to speak for Coolidge, and the governors of more than a dozen other states consented to be quoted as favoring his election. On the Saturday evening before the election Senator Lodge and Charles Sumner Bird excoriated Long as a profiteer and political agitator. On November 2, sermons were preached in Coolidge's behalf in many Massachusetts pulpits. Full-page advertisements headed, "Remember September the 9th," appeared in all the Boston newspapers. At noon on Monday the Governor addressed a notable gathering in Faneuil Hall. It had been a strenuous, hard-fought contest on a well-defined issue.

From the very first returns it was evident that Coolidge was leading, and the official figures gave him a total of 317,774 to Long's 192,673, a majority of 125,101. Coolidge's vote was actually the largest cast up to that time in Massachusetts for any gubernatorial candidate. Labor to a large extent had stood by the Governor, and the independents went strongly for him. Congratulations came in from Hughes, Harding, Taft, Nicholas Murray Butler, Will H. Hays, and many others; and President Wilson sent from the White House a telegram reading, "I congratulate you upon your election as a victory for law and order. When that is the

---

[2] At a Democratic rally just before the election, Colonel Herbert, candidate for Lieutenant Governor, said, "Calvin Coolidge is morally responsible for the loss of life in Boston in the early days of the Police Strike."

issue all Americans stand together." [3] The *Transcript* editorial on the result was headed, "Shining Triumph for Straight American- ism"; and Senator Lodge was quoted as saying, "You have splen- didly led the great fight for law and American principles and, sus- tained by the people of Massachusetts, have won a great victory for Americanism." The Stock Market showed a perceptible rise in securities. From coast to coast, among the better elements in all parties, it was felt that decency had been sustained and anarchy re- buked. Typical of the comment outside the state was a paragraph in the *Outlook* for November 12: —

The victory shows not only that Massachusetts stands firmly against the revolutionary radical forces that would undermine our system of government, but that the American people can be depended upon to preserve the institutions of law and liberty that their fathers established and for generations at great cost have maintained.

Rather cheerful over the Republican prospects, Governor Coolidge had gone to Northampton to vote, but was back in Boston that evening to receive the returns. As victory became evident, he made a ringing statement, "Three words tell the result. Massachusetts is American." His total personal expense for the campaign had been only $2171.90, of which $1000 had been contributed to the Repub- lican State Committee and $500 to the Republican City Committee in Boston. He had been through a severe illness, was somewhat debilitated, and was very glad to go for a few days into seclusion. Before leaving for Northampton, however, he issued for the United Press his opinion on the verdict, in which he said: —

When this controversy first started, I stated that Massachusetts was determined to maintain its authority over her public officers where it had been placed by her constitution and her laws. That determination has been exhibited in the election. It means exactly that.

The people of Massachusetts have supported their constitution and their laws because under them they have enjoyed a government that has given them ample protection. . . . Knowing these things, they scorned those who denied them and turned to those who declared them.

Calvin Coolidge did not, like Lord Byron, precisely awake one morning to find himself famous. The spread of his name over the country was gradual and cumulative during that autumn of 1919. Immediately after the Police Strike he had been mentioned as Presi-

[3] A certain mystery exists regarding this telegram. The President was appar- ently too ill to answer it, and it has been suggested by a person in the White House at the time that it was drafted and sent by Secretary Tumulty. The words, however, were those which the President might have used if he had been well.

dential material; and on November 4 the *Daily Hampshire Gazette* reflected public opinion in saying, "If Coolidge should be elected Governor by an overwhelming majority, it would give him a big start for the Republican nomination for the presidency." Oddly enough, Carl Ackerman, in the *Transcript* for November 5, did not include Coolidge's name in a list of thirty-eight Presidential possibilities, including Lodge, Borah, Lowden, Wood, Pershing, Harding, and other lesser luminaries. This enumeration unquestionably represented the judgment of the professional slate-makers, who had not yet discerned Coolidge's full potentialities. But in that same issue of the *Transcript* also appeared an article by Charles S. Baxter, who said: —

Governor Coolidge now looms so large before the nation with his wonderful triumph and so impressive a verdict by the Massachusetts electorate behind him that he must be given serious consideration by the Republican Party in the selection of its national leaders for the presidential campaign of next year.

Unquestionably the decisive character of the election focused attention on the quiet Massachusetts Governor. President Edwin T. McKnight of the Massachusetts Senate, in announcing on November 6 his candidacy for district delegate to the Republican Convention, declared himself for Coolidge as the Presidential nominee. On the following day in Springfield, Illinois, Representative William A. Rodenburg, speaking to the Illinois Republican Editorial Association, was loudly applauded when he mentioned Coolidge's name for the Vice Presidency. The Boston correspondent of the *New York Times* said that on every side he heard the prediction that the name of Calvin Coolidge would be presented to the next Republican Convention. Perhaps most significant of all was the fact that the *Literary Digest,* on November 15, printed an article on him, — the first of what was eventually to be a large number, — quoting passages from the daily press, both Republican and Democratic, and saying in summary, "Such an impressive victory in a doubtful state and upon what is becoming a great national issue . . . has naturally thrust Governor Coolidge into the limelight for the Republican nomination for President in 1920."

Indeed the sequence and direction of events were entirely favorable to Coolidge's candidacy. The Police Strike had aroused a curiosity about him which had been further stimulated by *Have Faith in Massachusetts.* With Mr. Stearns's plans Coolidge would have nothing to do, but the volume had been mailed to Congressmen, judges, mayors, state committeemen, editors, to anyone, anywhere, who would be likely to have influence in Republican councils. Coolidge himself had pursued his customary policy of waiting a little, permitting the issue to clarify itself, and then acting. Then, too, his opponent had rashly chosen to attack Coolidge and risk his future upon taking the offensive. By these tactics Coolidge, who was almost invulnerable, had profited; and now he watched with something like philosophic calm the changing eddies of the political current. The distinguished Colonel Henry L. Higginson, Boston's foremost citizen, died on November 14; the United States Senate killed the Peace Treaty on November 19; and Harvard defeated Yale in football on November 22. These matters filled plenty of space in the newspapers, and Coolidge was somewhat neglected. But his interests were being cared for just the same. On November 27, he spoke on "Lord Jeffrey Amherst Night" in New York, in furtherance of the Amherst Centennial Fund, and said, "It seems fairly plain that whether or not our institutions can survive with the aid of higher education, without it they have not the slightest chance." A few days later he sent his father a letter with one characteristic paragraph indicating that he was not oblivious of what was going on: —

Of course you know no one can tell what will happen in the future. It is not probable that anything will happen. It is a great compliment to be mentioned and honorably presented. You and mother better be content with that. From what I hear Vermont seems likely to be for me. Does the Rutland *Herald* say anything?

In his *Autobiography* Coolidge says, "About Thanksgiving time Senator Lodge came to me and voluntarily requested that he should present my name to the national Republican convention. He wished to go as a delegate with that understanding." This interview took place, according to Henry F. Long's Diary, on Monday, November 24, at luncheon at the Union Club. Shortly before this Senator Lodge had asked Frank W. Stearns to call at the home of Dr. William Sturgis Bigelow, on Beacon Street, and there told Stearns that, if Coolidge's name were to be placed before the Republican Convention, he would like to be a delegate and have the privilege of nominating him. In a memorandum dictated after this conversation, Mr. Stearns recorded his impression: —

Lodge told me at the time, possibly in answer to a question from me, that he was for the Governor, not merely as a favorite son, but really for him for the nomination for the Presidency of the United States.

In surveying conditions in Massachusetts, Lodge then hinted to Stearns that in all probability W. Murray Crane, after their disagreement over the League of Nations, would not care to be a delegate-at-large on the same ticket with him. Stearns assured Lodge that the latter was mistaken — an opinion which Crane later himself confirmed. Lodge then requested Stearns to attend to making up the slate for Republican delegates-at-large from Massachusetts, explaining that he himself would be busy with international affairs throughout the coming winter. After this conversation Stearns, not unnaturally, felt that he had Lodge's promise "to work loyally and heartily for the nomination of Governor Coolidge." On November 26, the *Transcript* came out with a news item headed, "Lodge for Coolidge." He was the first prominent Republican to come out for the Massachusetts Governor.

Coolidge soon let it be known that he was not attracted by second place on the ticket. On December 10, when he learned that the South Dakota Republican Convention had proposed his name for the Vice Presidency, he wrote to the South Dakota Secretary of State: —

It was entirely unexpected that my name should have been presented to your convention. It is not, however, my desire to appear as a candidate for the office of Vice-President of the United States. I shall not, therefore, make the declaration which your laws require from a candidate. This in no way detracts from my deep appreciation of the honor that has been given me.

On December 8, Stearns went to Washington to represent Coolidge's interests at the meeting of the Republican National Committee. At Worcester, on December 10, Coolidge was cheered as the next President at a public reception accorded him by the State Grange, but in his address he touched upon nothing but agricultural problems. A few days before, Mr. H. Philip Patey called upon Governor Coolidge, carrying a copy of *Have Faith in Massachusetts,* and said to him after it had been autographed, "I know that the next Chairman of the Republican National Committee will be the Honorable John T. Adams, of Dubuque, Iowa. They don't know much about you out there in the Middle West, and I'm wondering whether it would not be a good plan to send Mr. Adams a complimentary copy of this book." Coolidge replied, "Mr. Patey, I thank you very much for thinking of me but inasmuch as I have never met Mr. Adams, I would not feel quite free to do what you suggest." Patey replied, "I won't say another word. It merely occurred to me that it would be a timely act." When Patey told Mr. Stearns of the incident, the latter's comment was, "The big goose, he should have sent the book. I'll see that it's done at once. Mr. Patey, I can't get that man to lift his little finger to help himself. But then he seems to be making progress, and perhaps his way may be as correct as yours or mine." Adams became Vice Chairman of the Committee and in due course received his copy of *Have Faith in Massachusetts,* presented to him by Mr. Stearns.

Almost in spite of Coolidge, his name was being mentioned more and more frequently. The *Literary Digest* for December 27, 1919, printed an article, "Who's Who in the Presidential Race," putting General Leonard Wood, who had announced himself as a candidate as early as the preceding June, as "the favorite against the field." Lowden and Henry J. Allen were included as desirable contenders, and Coolidge came fourth on the list. Regarding him, the *Digest* said that newspaper interviews and stories had made the public at large well acquainted with "this naturally quiet and retiring man." It was at this period that the *Richmond Journal* maintained that Coolidge was badly handicapped by the support of Lodge! William H. Taft wrote to Gus Karger on January 5, 1920, "Coolidge seems to be really serious in his candidacy. I wonder what Murray Crane thinks of it and how far he is following Murray's advice in what he is doing?"

Early in January the situation reached a new stage. On January 6, 1920, Mr. Stearns wrote Coolidge the following letter: —

Now that your friends (amongst whom you know you can always count me) have taken into their hands the proposition to present you to the country as a candidate for the Presidency, and have very wisely, I think, selected Mr. J. B. Reynolds to have charge of matters, I want to say that every citizen of Massachusetts should make it clearly known that he stands for you without any second choice, and will constitute himself a committee of one to do everything he can for you from now until you are nominated or until you notify us that you think the time has come to make no further effort.

This is my platform, and I hope you will make any use of this letter that you think will be helpful.

But when Coolidge was sounded out by reporters who wished his views on national problems, he issued a statement which disappointed many of his admirers: —

I do not feel that any man could regard himself as qualified to fill the great office of President. If it comes to any man, it should not come of his own seeking, but as a great duty to be met with a knowledge and faith that when duties are sent powers are sent to enable their discharge.

I do not care to express any opinion as to what should be done by men entrusted with affairs at Washington or elsewhere, in regard to matters which have been committed to their decision. . . . I am devoting my energies to administering the affairs of Massachusetts, and that I shall continue to do so long as I am Governor.

Naturally his second inaugural, on Thursday, January 8, was eagerly awaited, especially by those who wished him to express himself on the controversial questions of the day. The occasion was a proud one for the chief figure. Directly in front of the Speaker's desk from which he spoke were his father, his two sons, and many of his friends. In the Speaker's gallery were his wife, Mrs. Channing H. Cox, and their guests. As he began his message he was loudly cheered, and he was frequently interrupted by applause. The address itself did not touch on international problems, such as the League of Nations, but stressed fundamental principles, urging the people to conserve the resources of the state and to seek a remedy for the economic discontent which had followed the World War. "Industry," he declared, "must be humanized, not destroyed. It must be the instrument, not of selfishness, but of service. Let our citizens look not to false prophets but to the Pilgrims; let them fix their eyes on Plymouth Rock as well as on Beacon Hill."

Within a few days Coolidge campaign headquarters had been opened in a six-room suite in the Hotel Raleigh, in Washington, in charge of "Jimmy" Reynolds,[4] who had been since 1912 Secretary of the National Republican Committee — a man with a wide acquaintance among practical politicians and a profound knowledge of the machinery and methods of politics. In mid-January, Stearns arranged for similar headquarters in Chicago, under Mrs. J. L. Bennett; he was prepared to raise the funds necessary to maintain these offices and had, indeed, already received contributions from several sources. On Sunday, January 25, however, Coolidge caused consternation among his active supporters by issuing a statement, without consulting even Mr. Stearns, in which he refused to enter any contest for delegates in Massachusetts. He did not wish, he said, to allow the Governor's office to be used "for manipulative purposes," and he did not propose affirmatively to seek the office

---

[4] James B. Reynolds, born in 1870 in Saratoga, New York, had graduated from Dartmouth College in 1890. He had been a reporter on the *Boston Advertiser,* Assistant Secretary of the Treasury, and a member of the Tariff Board. He knew everybody of any importance in Washington and was highly respected.

of President. The *Boston Herald* promptly declared that it was the duty of Massachusetts Republicans to elect an uninstructed delegation. There was a feeling in some quarters that Coolidge had shown himself to be a master strategist;[5] but Stearns was keenly disappointed and could do nothing but close up the Washington office. When he was interviewed on the subject, Reynolds only said, "Politics is a wicked game."

What was going on in Coolidge's mind is not easy to discover. So far as anyone could tell, his friends were making progress. W. Murray Crane and Senator Gillett had already declared for him, and Senator Lodge had actually given out an interview saying that Massachusetts should support him. It would have been easy for him to leave matters in charge of Frank W. Stearns. But in his *Autobiography* Coolidge said: —

When I came to give the matter serious attention, and comprehended more fully what would be involved in a contest of this kind, I realized that I was not in a position to become engaged in it. I was Governor of Massachusetts, and my first duty was to that office. It would not be possible for me, with the legislature in session, to be going about the country actively participating in an effort to secure delegates, and I was totally unwilling to have a large sum of money raised and spent in my behalf. . . . I did not wish to use the office of Governor to prosecute a campaign for nomination to some other office.

It has been suggested by cynical commentators that Coolidge was actually playing a deep game. If, however, he was really ambitious for the Presidency, he adopted a peculiar method of accomplishing his desire. He completely discouraged those who had gladly come out openly for him. He resolutely refused to discuss the subject. It has been accurately stated that the movement for his nomination was started and carried on without his consent or even his approval. Professional politicians were, of course, unable to account for such conduct except on the theory that Coolidge had subtle motives. It is not remarkable that Lodge, on February 11, told Washington newspapermen that he did not know whether or not Coolidge was out of the running. As a matter of fact, his words

[5] Professor Barrett Wendell, of Harvard, wrote, January 26, to R. W. Curtis: "Coolidge's statement seems to me in any case clever. It should hold the party together, and prevent his candidacy unless he looms larger in Chicago next June than now looks likely. If he does, it does not commit him; but gives him a chance to come forward with far more strength than would otherwise be probable. Whether it is sincere is of course another question. To me it seems so." (Howe, *Wendell*, pp. 322–23.)

and actions are difficult to interpret unless we accept his own very simple explanation.[6]

If Theodore Roosevelt had been living and in good health, his nomination in 1920 would have been inevitable. As it was, General Wood, regarded as the legitimate heir to the Roosevelt tradition, was early in the lead. He had come on January 18 to Boston, where he had spoken at the Old South Meetinghouse and had greeted friends at the Algonquin Club. Wood claimed citizenship in Bourne, Massachusetts, and Congressman William W. Lufkin, who was managing his campaign in Massachusetts, was appealing on this ground for a solid Bay State delegation. It seems clear that Lodge, without openly repudiating his allegiance to Coolidge, reached by early spring the conclusion that Wood was a better prospect.

During the hard winter the people of Massachusetts had their attention drawn forcibly to other matters. In February came a snowstorm of unusual violence and duration, accompanied by a coal shortage and another epidemic of influenza. On February 12 died Henry B. Endicott, the public-spirited citizen of Boston who had been so useful during the World War on numerous committees. The high cost of living was becoming unbearable, and the newspapers made much of the fact that Coolidge's landlord in Northampton had raised his rent from $27 to $32 a month.

The more eager Massachusetts Republicans became to have Coolidge a candidate, the less responsive he appeared to be. On March 3 he spoke at an Amherst Dinner in the Copley-Plaza Hotel. "Above all," he said, "we need to work. . . . We are not so much in need of reforming as performing." But he would not respond to the appeals of his followers. Several men of influence, including, besides Crane and Gillett, General John H. Sherburne and John N. Cole, were prepared to fight for a Massachusetts delegation which would be unequivocally for Coolidge. When he announced, "I have not been and am not a candidate for President," his friends tried to persuade him to insert the single word "active" before "candidate." His answer was, "Statement stands!" On the streets of Boston one could hear Amherst graduates saying to one another, "What can you do with a man like that?" The only hope, as Mr. Stearns saw it, was to send to Chicago unpledged delegates who, in an emergency, could feel free to vote for Coolidge. This idea was voiced by Bruce

[6] Professor Barrett Wendell, writing in January, said of Coolidge: "The chances are, no doubt, that he will not be dreamt of in Chicago. If he is, I incline to think that he may turn out to be a Yankee Lincoln, — a local lawyer large enough to handle things memorably."

Barton, who wrote a sketch of Coolidge for the *Outlook* in which he said, "If things get into a deadlock at Chicago, it seems to me well worth while to keep an eye on Calvin Coolidge." William H. Taft, writing on May 3, thought that "if the convention were to be held on that day the ticket would be Lowden and Coolidge."

The so-called "Unpledged Group" of delegates-at-large included Lodge, Gillett, Crane, and the late Edward A. Thurston, of Fall River, who had never held public office but had been an efficient Chairman of the Republican State Committee. They were opposed by a slate including Samuel W. McCall, Alvan T. Fuller, Thomas W. Lawson, and Russell A. Wood. McCall, on March 2, had attacked the Big Four headed by Lodge, calling it a "machine-made group," and two weeks later he and Louis A. Frothingham declared for Wood first and Hoover second. On April 27, in the Bay State "primaries," the vote cast was ridiculously small, but Lodge led the others on the ticket, receiving 75,428 votes as compared with 62,254 for Gillett, 60,927 for Crane, and 48,947 for Thurston. These four men chosen were elected without pledges of any kind, but with the promise that they would "work for party harmony." Meanwhile the *Boston Herald* had announced with authority on March 5 that Lodge would nominate Coolidge at Chicago; but when Stearns called on Lodge on March 29, the latter, while declaring himself still willing to carry out his promise, added that he had his doubts as to whether such a nomination would be consistent with Coolidge's own statements disavowing an active candidacy.

On the morning after the "primaries," the *Herald* outlined the situation: —

Although Governor Coolidge has formally withdrawn as a presidential candidate, he remains available for dark horse purposes. More accurately, he occupies the middle ground somewhere between that and the status of a favorite son. Most of the delegates from Massachusetts will vote for him on the first ballot. Senator Lodge will present his name. . . . You never can tell what will happen at a convention. The Governor is among the possibilities.

The atmosphere was seething with political gossip, and the opinions expressed were diverse and contradictory. The friends of Coolidge interpreted the returns on April 27 as favorable to their man. On the other hand, it was well known that Senator Lodge was trying to escape from his rash commitment and finding the conflict between duty and desire very annoying.

Among the thirty-one district delegates from Massachusetts were

William F. Whiting, of Holyoke; George V. L. Meyer, of Hamilton; Charles L. Burrill, Gaspar G. Bacon, and Charles H. Innes, of Boston; John H. Sherburne and Thomas W. White, of Brookline; and Louis A. Coolidge, of Milton. Among the alternates was one woman, Mrs. Alexandra Carlisle Pfeiffer, whose part in the convention proceedings was to make her conspicuous. On Monday, May 24, Louis A. Coolidge entertained the Massachusetts delegation at dinner at the Algonquin Club, at which time it was evident that six or eight regarded themselves as pledged to General Wood. To Calvin Coolidge's supporters this situation was sure to be embarrassing, for it was not easy to explain to the Middle West why the Governor should not have the unanimous endorsement of his own state. But a united Massachusetts delegation could have been made possible only through Coolidge's coöperation; and this he would not give.

During the late winter the friends of General Wood were indefatigable and filled the papers with optimistic notes regarding his campaign. A boom for Herbert Hoover, started in January, was halted because his political affiliations were in doubt; but when he announced on March 30 that he would permit the Republicans to use his name, his admirers in Massachusetts, headed by Samuel W. McCall, did some hard, although not very rewarding, work in his behalf. Governor Frank O. Lowden, of Illinois, also a candidate, displayed little strength in New England. Still another was Hiram Johnson, of California, but his affairs were mismanaged and very few prognosticators thought much of his chances. A nation-wide poll conducted by the *Literary Digest* on April 17 indicated that Wood was leading, with Hoover not far behind.

A new element was interjected when, on March 23, Senator Borah called openly on General Wood to reveal the figures regarding his campaign fund. Several of Wood's enthusiastic supporters had unfortunately placed him in a position where he could be criticized because of the large sums being expended in his behalf; and Governor Lowden was vulnerable in lesser degree for the same reason. A Senate investigating committee reported on June 4, just before the convention, that $1,250,000 had up to that date been spent by the Wood committee — nearly one half contributed by Procter, the soap manufacturer — and about $414,000 by the backers of Lowden.

Meanwhile Mr. Stearns, who had by no means abandoned hope, was laboring strenuously through the winter and spring. Some money was supplied by Coolidge's adherents, but the total, as reported by the Senate Committee, was only $68,375, as compared with $200,000 for Johnson and $113,000 for Harding. The largest donors were Frank W. Stearns ($12,500); Andrew Adie, President of the United States Worsted Company ($10,000); William F. Whiting, Treasurer of the Whiting Paper Company, in Holyoke ($10,000); Max Mitchell, President of the Cosmopolitan Trust Company ($6000); W. Murray Crane ($5000); and Ernest B. Dane, President of the Brookline Trust Company ($5000).[7] All the financial arrangements were conducted by James B. Reynolds, who continued to serve as Coolidge's campaign manager, with modest offices in the Parker House not far from Mr. Stearns's store. Clearly the Coolidge campaign was not so well supplied with money as those of active seekers for the nomination. But the Governor, in spite of his unresponsiveness, had amazingly hearty backing, and his admirers were never discouraged. On May 14, when Warren G. Harding and Irvine L. Lenroot came to Boston for a meeting of the Home Market Club, the Ohio Senator referred whimsically to Coolidge's candidacy, saying, "If I lived in Massachusetts I should be for Governor Coolidge for President. Coming from Ohio, I am for Harding."

Dwight W. Morrow, still ardent for Coolidge but fearful that his own partnership in J. P. Morgan and Company might be detrimental to the cause, did very little openly for his classmate; but he and another Morgan partner, Thomas Cochran, were Mr. Stearns's staunch helpers. On June 1, 1920, Morrow wrote to James R. Sheffield, of New York City, a delegate to the Republican Convention and later our Ambassador to Mexico, a letter which expressed clearly his viewpoint. It began quite abruptly: —

Some time ago you asked me to write you my opinion of Coolidge. Here it is. I met him twenty-nine years ago this Fall, when we entered Amherst in the same class. For a year I boarded at the same boarding place with him. It cost us $3.00 a week. He was the son of a country storekeeper in Plymouth, Vermont, and I was the son of a schoolteacher of Pittsburg. If there had been a cheaper eating house at Amherst, we doubtless would both have been there.

The concluding paragraphs of summarization were highly significant, coming from a man of Morrow's ability and judgment: —

I am sure Coolidge would make a *good* President; I think he would make a *great* one. He has had a very unusual experience, but the country

---

[7] Among the other contributors were Frank W. Remick and Frank G. Webster, of Kidder, Peabody and Company; John W. Simpson and Grosvenor H. Backus, both Amherst men and New York lawyers; and Robert W. Maynard, Vice President of the R. H. Stearns Company.

and the world need to utilize the experienced. He has real courage entirely free from bluster. He has faith, — a profound faith in the fundamental soundness of democracy, and that faith has begotten, as it did in Lincoln's case, a great faith on the part of the people in him. He has tolerance, and when we think of the next four years either in our domestic or in our foreign problems, an indispensable quality is toleration. He has knowledge, and there never was a time when it was more true that knowledge is power. Finally, he has character, and not only this country, but the whole world, is hungering for a leader with character.

I am quite conscious that there are other good men whom you must consider in Chicago. I do not share in the general cry that the Republican Party is short of men. In this summary I have tried not to deal with the *Superlative* or even with the *Comparative* but only with the *Positive*. You and your fellow delegates will know whether there is a *better* or a *best*.

Congress ended its session on Saturday, June 5, in time to allow its members, if they desired, to go to Chicago. At 4.45 on Sunday afternoon the special train carrying the Massachusetts delegation pulled into Chicago, there to be greeted by Lodge, Crane, Louis A. Coolidge, and others who had gone on ahead as an advance guard. Under the orders of General Sherburne, the group formed into columns of fours, and, preceded by a brass band, marched up Michigan Avenue singing, to the tune of "John Brown's Body," "We'll all get out and work for Coolidge, on next Election Day!" It was a quaint irony which placed Henry Cabot Lodge in the van of a parade chanting this song.

Calvin Coolidge, although he was not to be in Chicago, was aware of what was going on. Later, when some publicity was being prepared, he wrote, with reference to Edward E. Whiting, "If Mr. Whiting goes to Plymouth, the only thing you can do is to give him such information as he wants and show him the farm and show him the house where I was born. Tell him what I used to do when I was a boy." His duties as Governor were an excuse for keeping him at home during the convention week. At a dinner of the Ancient and Honorable Artillery Company on Monday evening, he smiled enigmatically and responded briefly when he was introduced as the next President. During the remainder of the week he spent his evenings in the Adams House, although he did on Thursday deliver the Commencement Address at the Middlesex School, in Concord. In Chicago, Councillor Harry H. Williams, of Brockton, having been told by various delegates that they were unacquainted with Coolidge's true position, wired him, expressing his solicitude and saying, "Delegates are asking what your attitude is towards nomination. What shall I tell them?" The Governor promptly sent a message back, "Thanks for your good wishes. Tell them the truth." No one could have seemed less concerned than he about what was going on. He could have learned from the newspapers, however, that the odds against his nomination for the Presidency were being quoted at fifteen to one.

But Coolidge's interests were not being neglected. "Jimmy" Reynolds, suave and genial, was in Chicago several days in advance. On the special train to the West were Frank W. Stearns with his son Foster. Benjamin F. Felt, Secretary of the Massachusetts delegation, had gone a day or two before. Already Stearns had arranged with George A. Galliver for the compilation of a little pamphlet of sixty pages, bound in imitation black leather and containing excerpts from Coolidge's speeches. Within eighteen hours of its inception this booklet had been printed and bound. On the outside were the words *Law and Order* in large gilt capitals; and, by a touch of inspiration, each delegate was presented with a copy having his name upon the cover. It was made intentionally thin so that it could be tucked away in an inside pocket, and many of the delegates were later seen perusing it as they sat in their seats waiting for something to happen. "It was," said Mr. Felt, "as neat and effective a piece of political publicity as I have ever seen."

The Coolidge headquarters were in the Congress Hotel, across from the more pretentious and noisier rooms of Senator Warren G. Harding. There could be found at almost any hour of day or evening Frank W. Stearns, known to the delegates as "Stearns of Massachusetts" — an honest, kindly soul, apparently afflicted with mild monomania, it is true, but a very pleasant person to meet. There were some unfortunate, although suppressed, squabbles within the Massachusetts group, and there was considerable jealousy of John N. Cole, who was not a delegate, and the prominent part which he, "Tom" White, and General Sherburne were taking. Stearns, however, kept on good terms with them all and would not budge in his conviction that Coolidge could be nominated. Dwight W. Morrow and Thomas Cochran, both powerful financial figures, were on hand to watch the course of events, and so was Grosvenor H. Backus, of New York, who had been a leader in the preliminary Coolidge campaign. "Tom" White was quoted on Sunday evening to the effect that the Massachusetts Governor had "as good a chance for the nomination as any of the dozen men whose names will go before the convention." Frank A. Vanderlip declared that there had been no crystallization on candidates, that things were in a fluid state, and that the influential people had not actually made up their minds — all of which was probably true. Mr. Stearns's unruffled optimism had to be based on faith, not facts. Out on the shores of Lake Michigan it was plain that Calvin Coolidge was under an almost insuperable geographical handicap. New England had not had a President since Franklin Pierce; Massachusetts not since John Quincy Adams. Any Middle Westerner would have the inside track over a Yankee, especially if New England did not present a solid and unyielding front. Accordingly, although Stearns and his followers aroused sympathy and were respected for their obvious sincerity, very few persons felt that he was undertaking anything but a thankless and futile task.

Oswald G. Villard, writing in the *Nation* for June 19, 1920, called the Republican Convention of 1920 "from first to last one of the dreariest and most discouraging party gatherings ever held." This is, of course, the opinion of a prejudiced thinker. To an impartial observer concerned with personalities rather than platforms, it had many colorful aspects. Henry Cabot Lodge was making his last appearance but one at a national political convention; and when it had been called to order on Tuesday, June 8, by Will H. Hays, Chairman of the National Republican Committee, Lodge was promptly presented and unanimously elected as Temporary Chairman. His slender form, his nervous gestures, his aristocratic beard, his crisp and cultured enunciation, his witty and often caustic oratory, had been familiar to generations of Republican leaders. Now at the age of three score and ten, he was still brisk and positive, elated at the outcome of his recent clash with President Wilson over the League of Nations, in which his younger adversary had broken under the strain. His keynote speech was a bitter attack on the Democratic administration, demanding that Woodrow Wilson and his dynasty be driven from power and office — a speech described by Mark Sullivan as full of "waspish malice." Thomas Carens, writing in the *Boston Herald,* said, "Senator Lodge has made the issue of the coming campaign, and it can be summed up in one word — Wilson." On Wednesday morning Lodge was elected Permanent Chairman, a position which he had filled at Republican conventions in 1900 and 1908. As he stood on the platform, he was depicted by a discerning witness as "the last of the Puritan grandees . . . aquiline, slim, sententious . . . this Brahmin of the Boston Brahmins." Obviously his election as Permanent Chairman, for which he had been manoeuvring for some weeks, gave him an excuse for not nominating

Calvin Coolidge; but Mr. Stearns had already suspected what was going to happen and had made other tentative arrangements. Although Lodge may still have had visions of the Presidency, — which he had on more than one occasion narrowly missed, — he knew in his heart that his day was almost over. The coming man at the convention, even though few perceived it, was Calvin Coolidge.

The platform, not adopted until Thursday evening, declared broadly, but not too explicitly, that the Republican Party stood "for agreement among the nations to preserve the peace of the world," but was obviously a compromise intended to retain the allegiance of the "bitter-enders," like Hiram Johnson. It was opposed with all his failing energy by W. Murray Crane, who unsuccessfully argued for a plank calling for immediate ratification of the League Covenant, with reservations. Crane was at this time an ill man, easily fatigued, and not nearly so impressive as he had been in 1916.

On Friday morning opened the long succession of nominating and seconding speeches, beginning with that of Governor Henry J. Allen, of Kansas, presenting General Leonard Wood. The Coliseum simmered with oratory and applause. Wood's name was cheered for forty-two minutes, Lowden's for forty-six, and Johnson's for thirty-seven. No "old-stager" believed that the volume and duration of noise would decide the choice, and yet the followers of each candidate did not wish to be outdone in endurance by those of his rivals. The *Boston Transcript* said on the following evening, "After reading these nominating speeches, Washington, Lincoln, Grant, Roosevelt, Julius Caesar, and Napoleon feel like pretty small potatoes this morning"; and it is true that eulogy has seldom been less restrained, less tempered with plain common sense. And then, when the chief contestants had been more than adequately praised and the agitation following Mrs. Katherine Philip Edson's seconding speech for Johnson had quieted, Connecticut yielded to Massachusetts, and Speaker Gillett, dignified and scholarly in appearance, rose to speak on behalf of Calvin Coolidge, having been invited to take the place of Senator Lodge. It was about three o'clock in the afternoon, and he talked barely more than five minutes; but his remarks were admirable in their directness, their sincerity, their brevity. In pleading for his fellow collegian he said in part: —

Our candidate is a man of few words, and in that respect I shall imitate him. And I only wish I could imitate his effective use of words. . . .

We have been fed long enough on glittering rhetoric and extravagant novelties and rainbow-tinted dreams. We need an era of hard sense, of old freedom. We need to reinvigorate the homely, orderly virtues which have made America great. . . . Do you want a winner? Take the man who has never concealed his convictions, who has never lowered his standards, and who has never known defeat. . . . '

Such a man is our Governor. He is as patient as Lincoln, as silent as Grant, as diplomatic as McKinley, with the political instinct of Roosevelt. His character is as firm as the mountains of his native state. Like them, his head is above the clouds, and he stands unshaken amid the tumult and the storm.

The Massachusetts delegation cheered Gillett long and lustily, but their demonstration was not equal to that received by Wood, Lowden, and Johnson; and then the sultry afternoon was enlivened by an episode which brought even slumbering delegates back to consciousness. Mrs. Alexandra Carlisle Pfeiffer, who had directed the Hasty Pudding show, *Barnum Was Right,* at Harvard College during the late spring, had been an admirer of Lady Astor's part in English politics and, wishing in a modest way to emulate her, had been chosen as an alternate to the convention, the only woman in the Bay State contingent.

On the train to Chicago, Mr. Stearns, discerning her charm and dramatic quality, asked her to make a seconding speech for Coolidge, and John N. Cole scribbled down a rough draft of what she ought to say. She had seen Coolidge only once, for a minute or two at the Adams House, and had never talked with him. In Chicago she purchased at a department store several nursemaid's white uniforms, with a V collar, long sleeves, one breast pocket, a black patent-leather belt, a black tie, and a sailor hat, white on top and black underneath the brim; and she made arrangements to change her costume three times a day so that, when the moment for her speech arrived, she would look neat and fresh. Thirty-four years old, she was then light-haired, with a round face, attractive features, and a rather plump but pleasing figure. Before the hour for their joint performance, Mr. Gillett and she went outside and sat on soap boxes, munching crackers which they had bought at a corner grocery store. When her call came, Mrs. Pfeiffer was escorted to the platform and began slowly in a rather deep, well-modulated voice with a slight English accent. From her first clearly enunciated sentence she had her audience with her, for she could be heard easily throughout the vast hall and, although she was only five feet four inches in height, her professional bearing made her impressive. What she said was good, but whatever she spoke would have charmed her listeners by the grace of its delivery.

Mrs. Pfeiffer talked a little less than four minutes, in a series of short sentences, each one separated distinctly from the others. She began: —

Calvin Coolidge, a real American, born on the Fourth of July, has endeared himself to every man, woman, and child in the state which he governs because of his steadfast belief in the real things of life — home, people, country.

She ended with a repetition which she well knew how to drive home: —

If you ask what the nation most needs to-day, it is the simplicity in private and in public life of Calvin Coolidge; the fidelity in public service of Calvin Coolidge; the loyalty to American institutions of government of Calvin Coolidge; and the humanity in public deeds of Calvin Coolidge.

As Mrs. Pfeiffer closed, tremendous applause broke out from all parts of the auditorium, and members of the Massachusetts delegation carried flowers to the platform until she was completely surrounded by roses and orchids. She had been in every respect a success, the more so because her staccato phrases ringing out like repeated blows from a hammer were much appreciated after hours of florid and monotonous male oratory.[8]

One by one the other aspirants were presented by their supporters: Judge Peter C. Pritchard, of North Carolina; the veteran Nicholas Murray Butler, of New York; Herbert Hoover, of California; Warren G. Harding, of Ohio; Governor William C. Şproul, of Pennsylvania; Miles Poindexter, of Washington; and Howard Sutherland, of West Virginia — until eleven in all had entered the competition. The first ballot, taken almost immediately, showed Wood with 287½ votes, Lowden with 211½, Johnson with 133½, and the others trailing. Coolidge received thirty-four votes — twenty-eight from Massachusetts, two from New York, two from South Carolina, one from Kentucky, and one from Texas. The other seven votes from Massachusetts, including those of Senator Lodge, Louis A. Coolidge, Gaspar G. Bacon, and Lewis Parkhurst, were

[8] Mrs. Pfeiffer spoke frequently during the Presidential campaign of 1920 for Harding and Coolidge and later had interviews with President Coolidge at the White House. She continued her career as an actress and in 1934 was awarded the gold medal given by the American Academy of Arts and Sciences for the best diction on the American stage for that year. In 1936, in a room in the Hotel Touraine in Boston, she reënacted for me her nominating speech of 1920, dressing as nearly as possible in the fashion which she had employed at Chicago and recalling virtually every phrase. On April 22, 1936, a few weeks later, she was found dead in a New York hotel.

for Wood. The second ballot showed no significant change. Wood and Lowden were clearly deadlocked, and although the former continued to lead for four successive ballots that afternoon, it was evident to those "on the inside" that he could not possibly secure a majority. When the situation became apparent to Senators Smoot and Lodge, the former moved at seven o'clock that the convention adjourn, and Lodge, the Chairman, after putting the motion, deliberately disregarded the obvious preponderance of "Noes" and said, "The Ayes have it and the Convention is adjourned until to-morrow morning at ten o'clock." [9] On that evening the *Transcript* predicted that the choice would be Wood and Johnson, but this was only a guess and a very poor one. The heat in Chicago was almost intolerable, the rates at the hotels were exorbitant, and many of the delegates wished to start back home before the week-end. But no one knew how the deadlock could be broken.

Behind the scenes, however, events were taking place which were to make history. The Great Republican Gods were in more or less solemn conclave. In February 1919, Harry M. Daugherty, "boss" of the Ohio Republican machine, voiced the cynical opinion that no candidate would be nominated on the first three ballots, but that the winner would be selected by fifteen or twenty somewhat weary men sitting around a table "about eleven minutes after two o'clock on Friday morning." [10] This is precisely what happened if we accept the tale told by George Harvey's biographer, Willis Fletcher Johnson, and confirmed from other reputable sources. [11] Harvey, once a Democrat and a sponsor for the political fledgling, Woodrow Wilson, but in 1919 and 1920 a Wilson hater and a Republican convert, maintained in Will Hays's suite, 404–5–6, on the thirteenth floor of the Blackstone Hotel, [12] a headquarters for a little coterie of United States Senators — a group who brought upon the convention the reproach of being "too much Senate." On this momentous Friday evening Harvey and his associates assembled after dinner, aware that the bewildered and perspiring delegates needed guidance and were

[9] The account given by Mark Sullivan of this incident is most vivid (*Our Times,* Vol. VI, pp. 57–8). Sullivan in further comment says, "Every delegate knew that the 'Noes' had far outnumbered the 'Ayes,' but accepted the Chairman's decision calmly, rather smilingly." Sullivan went out with Senator Smoot and asked him why he and Lodge had forced the adjournment. Smoot replied, "Oh, there's going to be a deadlock and we'll have to work out some solution; we wanted the night to think it over."

[10] White, *Masks in a Pageant,* pp. 405ff.

[11] Johnson, *George Harvey, A Passionate Patriot,* pp. 273ff.

[12] Mr. Ernst V. Kung, Manager of the Blackstone Hotel, writes (Oct. 11, 1938) that the suite was engaged and occupied by Mr. Hays, but that Harvey may have occupied the other bedroom. The suite consisted of a parlor and two bedrooms.

in a mood to be stampeded in almost any direction. The leaders present, according to the best testimony, included Frank B. Brandegee, of Connecticut; Charles Curtis, of Kansas, later Vice President; James E. Watson, of Indiana; Medill McCormick, of Illinois; Reed Smoot, of Utah; William Calder and James W. Wadsworth, of New York; and Henry Cabot Lodge, of Massachusetts. Of these, Harvey, Curtis, and Brandegee were not even delegates, but their power was great. Others were doubtless in and out for short periods during the evening. W. Murray Crane, who was indisposed throughout the convention, apparently did not appear. Senator Boies Penrose, critically ill in Philadelphia, was kept informed by telephone of what was going on, but was in no sense a dictator.

Sitting there in a room thick and blue with tobacco smoke, several of them in their shirt sleeves, the Old Guard ruminated and deliberated. They were agreed that Wood, Lowden, and Johnson must be discarded. They next considered other names — Sproul, Will Hays, Knox, Lenroot, Henry J. Allen, and even Lodge himself, who, however, evidently acquiesced in the opinion that he was too old. The merits of Calvin Coolidge were not ignored and, if Lodge had been willing to back him, the Massachusetts Governor might have been declared acceptable. But Lodge during the previous months had grown obstinately indifferent to Coolidge. William F. Whiting, not long before his death in 1936, told me that in May 1920 he went to Washington and pleaded for three hours with Senator Lodge to stand by Coolidge. In reply, Lodge simply said over and over, "I will not do it." During convention week, at a dinner in the Chicago Club, Lodge said to Henry L. Stoddard, "Nominate a man who lives in a two-family house! Never! Massachusetts is not for him!" Later, in an interview with Frank W. Stearns, Stoddard confirmed the substance of this story and added, "That is an exact quotation of what Lodge said to me, but the rest of what he said was so bad that I did not have the courage to repeat it." This is not the time for examining Lodge's motives, which were the compound of various emotions and prejudices. But many members of the convention are still convinced that, if Lodge had come out openly on that evening for Coolidge, the self-appointed senatorial committee would have accepted him.

As the night wore on, the sentiment of the group turned to Warren G. Harding, of Ohio, whose campaign Harry M. Daugherty had been managing but who had thought himself so far out of the race that he had directed an agent, George B. Harris, to file on that very evening a declaration of his candidacy for the office of United

States Senator. The available evidence indicates that he did not really wish to be President but had been induced by Daugherty to permit his name to be used.[13] But when his chances were discussed in Room 404 it was soon discovered that he had no enemies; and certain important state delegations, when sounded, indicated their approval. Finally, about two o'clock, Harding was sent for and appeared, unshaven, with wrinkled clothes and dark circles under his eyes. Harvey took him to a small room attached to his suite and there, with all his immobile impressiveness, said to him substantially as follows, "Senator Harding, you may be nominated to-morrow for the Presidency; and I wish you to assure me and the gentlemen in the next room that upon your sacred honor and before your God you know of no reason arising out of anything in your past life why you should not stand with confidence before the American people as a candidate for the highest office within their gift." Deeply moved, the Ohio Senator requested fifteen minutes by himself and was shown into one of the two bedrooms belonging to the suite. What he thought during that period will never be disclosed; but he did return, "calm and confident," and said to Harvey and later to the entire group, "Gentlemen, there is nothing in my record to make me unavailable."[14] Thus Warren G. Harding was chosen, according to George Harvey "because there was nothing against him and because the delegates wanted to go home." According to a reasonably well-authenticated story, Harvey, some months before at a house party on Long Island, had guessed in a sealed prophecy that Harding would be the next Republican candidate. Nevertheless his final selection was unexpected, both to him and to others, and, indeed, to everybody except Daugherty.

As the delegates straggled into their seats on that sultry Saturday morning, the consequences of the senatorial conspiracy were not immediately apparent.[15] On the fifth ballot, Lowden advanced for

[13] The evidence on this point is assembled by Mark Sullivan in *Our Times*, Vol. VI, pp. 72ff. Sullivan's account of this episode is unquestionably the most accurate yet printed and is an excellent example of how a trained and honest mind weighs evidence and reaches conclusions.

[14] Johnson, *George Harvey*, p. 278. Harry M. Daugherty, in his *The Inside Story of the Harding Tragedy*, regards this account of what happened in Room 404 as mythical, but his evidence and his arguments are untrustworthy. Some of the details may be inaccurate, but the story as related above must be essentially correct. The incident of Harvey's talk with Harding was told to Mark Sullivan within thirty-six hours after it had occurred.

[15] William Allen White, a keen observer, wrote shortly after the convention to Edward D. Duffield, of New Jersey, "There never was any time when the Senate group was not in control of the Chicago Convention. I was a delegate there as you were and I was also a reporter and had the reporter's end of it, and I knew all the time what was going on behind the scenes. I am dead sure that I was not mistaken."

the first time into the lead, with 303 votes to 299 for Wood, Harding being in fifth place. In the sixth trial, Wood and Lowden were exactly even, but Harding, quite significantly, had moved up to third. The seventh ballot showed no material change, except that Harding had increased his total from 89 to 105. Still another roll call gave Harding 133¼ votes. He had been gaining little by little all the morning, and the whispering indicated that the current was setting more strongly in his direction. But the delegates needed luncheon, and a recess was voted, to extend until four o'clock.[16]

The Coolidge vote, meanwhile, had altered only slightly. He received 29 on the fifth ballot, 28 on the sixth, 28 on the seventh, and 30 on the eighth — 24 from Massachusetts, 4 from New York, 1 from Connecticut, and 1 from Alaska. During the recess Crane did his utmost to secure an adjournment until Monday so that the Coolidge forces might confer and push him as a "dark horse." Two of the Coolidge managers, moreover, approached Senator Lodge in a last desperate hope that he would be willing to allow the Massachusetts delegation to go solid on one ballot for Coolidge and thus give him standing as a compromise candidate. Crane, in the retrospect, was insistent that if Lodge, even as late as Saturday afternoon, had come out openly for Coolidge, the latter might have been nominated.[17] In his *Autobiography* Coolidge said: —

My friends in the convention did all they could for me, and several states were at times ready to come to me if the entire Massachusetts delegation would lead the way, but some of them refused to vote for me, so the support of other states could not be secured.

But it must be remembered that Lodge had already agreed that the prize should go to Senator Harding. Even if he had impulsively consented to swing the Massachusetts delegation to Coolidge, his senatorial colleagues would have considered that he had betrayed them. We cannot ignore the fact that Lodge and Coolidge, in the patterns of their lives, were far apart. They had no common meeting ground. Coolidge was a statesman of a type which Lodge had never seen before, and he could not be expected to understand the Massa-

[16] During the recess, according to Henry L. Stoddard, Wood and Lowden drove around in a taxicab, in the hope that a compromise could be arranged, possibly by having one consent to accept the Vice Presidency. Neither one would yield, and the peculiar conference failed. See Henry L. Stoddard, *It Costs to Be President*, pp. 76ff.

[17] On the other hand, Louis A. Coolidge, one of Lodge's adherents, is reported to have said on June 17, 1920, to James B. Reynolds, "There never was the slightest chance that Calvin Coolidge could be nominated for President, or that he ever will be. Just get that out of your mind, no matter what anyone tells you."

chusetts Governor's amazing vote-getting powers. Nor could Lodge at that point have yielded his supremacy in Massachusetts politics to Crane, with whom he had sharp differences of opinion, and to Coolidge, who was sponsored by Crane. Many of the Massachusetts delegation never forgave Lodge for what they believed to be his selfishness and lack of loyalty. Fortunately the outcome, although distressing at the time to both Crane and Stearns, was not permanently detrimental to Calvin Coolidge.

When the convention reassembled at 4.46, after some delay, the program as agreed upon the night before was carried out with smoothness and speed. The word had been passed around during the recess that Harding was the man. Groups of shirt-sleeved men appeared in the galleries as if at the wave of a magic hand, carrying huge pictures of Harding and banners bearing his name. On the ninth ballot, he moved into the lead, and the Wood forces for the first time were broken. When Connecticut was called and thirteen of her fourteen votes — hitherto cast for Lowden — were cast for Harding, the Ohio delegates staged a demonstration; but the real excitement came when Kansas, believed to be loyal to Wood, went over to Harding, and its contingent marched around the hall, with Willis J. Bailey carrying the state flag and a Harding standard. On the tenth ballot, Harding had a clear majority and was nominated. More than 150 delegates — men like Henry L. Stimson — remained staunch for Wood to the very end. According to Nicholas Murray Butler, Harding had announced to him on Friday morning, "This convention will never nominate me. . . . I am going to quit politics and devote myself to my newspaper." On Saturday evening Butler was with him and Lowden behind the platform in the convention hall when Charles B. Warren, of Michigan, brought Harding the news of his nomination, and the latter, with one hand in Lowden's and the other in Butler's, said, "If the great honor of the Presidency is to come to me, I shall need all the help that you two friends can give me."

On the final roll call, Coolidge had only five votes — four from New York and one from William F. Whiting, the only Massachusetts delegate to stand firm until the last. The Bay State gave seventeen to Harding and seventeen to Wood. Among those for Harding were Lodge, Crane, Gillett, Thurston, Bacon, White, and Sherburne.

The nomination of Harding was now, in routine fashion, made "unanimous," although a few dissenters from radical Wisconsin shouted "No" when the motion was put. The delegates in little groups began to saunter out of the auditorium. Those who lingered settled back to the perfunctory duty of naming a candidate for Vice President — apparently perfunctory because the senatorial cabal, meeting hastily among the wooden beams underneath the platform, had agreed on Senator Irvine L. Lenroot, of Wisconsin, whom, like Harding, they knew and trusted. Harding himself had preferred Hiram Johnson, but had been overruled. Meanwhile Crane had conferred with Senator Elon R. Brown, of Watertown, New York, and others of the New York delegation and had been assured that most of them could in an emergency be swung for Coolidge. But events moved too fast for Crane. When Senator Lodge called for nominations, Senator Medill McCormick, of Illinois, secured recognition and, after assuring the delegates that they had selected for the Presidency a man "of ripe experience, of deep learning, and of great power," proceeded briefly to present the claims of Lenroot. Several delegates seconded this nomination — Hert, of Kentucky, Remmel, of Arkansas, Calder, of New York, and Herrick, of Ohio. It looked as if the excitement were over; and Lodge, seeking a well-earned rest after the tension, withdrew, leaving former Governor Frank B. Willis, of Ohio, in the chair. Senator McCormick also left the building and strolled out into the annex at the south end of the Coliseum. At this point an unexpected and dramatic incident proved that the convention could and would rebel against too much dictation.

Wallace McCamant,[18] of Portland, Oregon, a member of the Oregon delegation of ten as a delegate-at-large, had been sent three copies of *Have Faith in Massachusetts* and had read the volume carefully even before leaving the West Coast for Chicago. "I was impressed," he writes, "with Governor Coolidge's sterling Americanism, his fine spirit during the World War, the soundness of his thinking, and the conservative trend of his thought." Pledged originally to Wood, Judge McCamant voted for him on each of the ten ballots. When the Presidential nominee was determined and the edict was sent down from the platform urging the delegations to fall in line for Lenroot for Vice President, the Oregon group, no one of whom liked Lenroot as a candidate, resented this autocratic procedure. An informal conference followed on the floor, in the

[18] McCamant, then in his fifty-third year, had been born in Pennsylvania, and had graduated from Lafayette College. A lawyer by profession, he had been for a short period Associate Justice of the Supreme Court of Oregon; and he had been a delegate to the Republican National Conventions of 1896 and 1900. He was later President General of the Sons of the American Revolution. On March 17, 1926, he was rejected by the Senate as Judge of the Ninth Judicial Circuit, largely because of the animosity of Senator Hiram Johnson, who remembered that McCamant had supported Wood, not Johnson, in the Chicago Convention. McCamant was a wiry, vigorous man of much force of character.

course of which Charles H. Carey, of Portland, whose voice had hoarsened, expressed the wish that McCamant should bring Coolidge's name before the convention. All this had to be done with great rapidity, but there were only eight Oregon delegates left in the hall and their concurrence was soon obtained. Then Judge McCamant, climbing on a chair, secured recognition from the presiding officer, Willis, who undoubtedly thought that the Portland man was rising to second the nomination of Lenroot. The auditorium was at the moment in a state of much confusion, but McCamant's voice was resonant and he managed to make most of his words clear. The official reporters caught his remarks as follows, although different versions, some of them entirely fanciful, have been published: —

When the Oregon delegation came here instructed by the people of our State to present to this Convention as its candidate for the office of Vice President a distinguished son of Massachusetts (Lodge), he requested that we refrain from mentioning his name. But there is another son of Massachusetts who has been much in the public eye during the past year, a man who is sterling in his Americanism and stands for all that the Republican Party holds dear; and on behalf of the Oregon delegation I name for the exalted office of Vice President Governor Calvin Coolidge, of Massachusetts.

The mention of Coolidge's name was greeted with an outburst of applause and cheers, evidently as unplanned as it was unexpected. Villard reported in the *Nation* that Coolidge's name received "a far more spontaneous and enthusiastic roar of approval than Harding got at any time." A veteran newspaper correspondent turned to his neighbor and said, "It's all over. Coolidge is nominated." Judge McCamant had appeared at exactly the right psychological moment and said precisely the most effective words. A sentiment favorable to Coolidge had been created by *Have Faith in Massachusetts,* and now the delegates, repressed and tired, were eager for some relief from the emotional strain. The response was immediate. All over the floor men rose to second the nomination of Coolidge — first from Michigan, then from Maryland, North Dakota, Kansas, Connecticut, and Pennsylvania. Even Remmel, of Arkansas, broke all precedents by withdrawing his second for Lenroot and turning it over to Coolidge. It was the first real stampede for many years in a Republican convention. Allister Murray, meeting Senator McCormick in the annex, remarked, "Well, they're nominating." "Yes," replied McCormick, indifferently — "Lenroot." "No," responded Murray, "Calvin Coolidge!" Galvanized into precipitate action, McCormick turned and rushed for the platform, but arrived too late. Nothing then could have stemmed the Coolidge tide.

A Colorado delegate attempted to have the nominations closed, but Willis J. Bailey, of Kansas, held up the proceedings by insisting on the presentation of Henry J. Allen, governor of his state; and still one more candidate, Henry W. Anderson, of Virginia, was brought before the convention. While the speeches in behalf of these men were going on, however, the hall was echoing and reëchoing to Coolidge's name, and cries of "We want Coolidge!" arose from the benches. When at last the roll call was taken, Coolidge was far ahead, the final result being 674½ for him as against 146½ for Lenroot. He was nominated at exactly 7.05, Chicago, or Central, time.

Mark Sullivan, in the *Boston Herald* for June 6, had predicted that if Coolidge failed to get the Presidential nomination, he had the best chance of anybody for second place on the ticket. The truth is that in those closing hours the convention escaped from its "bosses" and expressed the will of the people. Through his shrewd management Frank W. Stearns had made Coolidge's achievements and character known to the persons whose influence counted. It was *Have Faith in Massachusetts,* with its common-sense philosophy, which won the support of Judge McCamant and countless others like him. It was noticeable at the convention that the delegates seemed to be interested in Coolidge and particularly in his identification with Law and Order. He certainly had few enemies, and most of those were from his own state. In an absolutely unbossed poll on the convention floor he would probably have received more votes than Warren G. Harding.

The long and weary day drew to a close in Chicago. Some routine business, the thanking of various committees, the customary passing of votes, had to be completed in an almost deserted hall, and the convention adjourned at 7.30. Mr. Stearns, rather tired and much disillusioned, went to bed, not sure whether he ought to be glad or sorry. When he had been asked by the Massachusetts delegation whether they should support Coolidge for the Vice Presidency, he had replied that he considered it inadvisable, first, because he felt that Coolidge might thus be shelved politically, and second because, as Vice President, he would have so little to do that the idle life might kill him. Later, after reflection, Mr. Stearns wrote, "Of course at the time I was greatly disappointed, but I have come to feel that there was a Providence that controlled things and that for Mr. Coolidge and the country it was better that he should come into the Presidency as he later did." Coolidge himself had much the same view and wrote in his *Autobiography* regarding his failure to receive the nomination for President : —

While I do not think it was so intended, I have always been of the opinion that this turned out to be much the best for me. I had no national experience. What I have ever been able to do has been the result of first learning how to do it. I am not gifted with intuition. I need not only hard work but experience to be ready to solve problems. The Presidents who have gone to Washington without first having held some national office have been at a great disadvantage.

One bit of prophecy must be recorded as it first appeared in print. In a report of the convention in the *Outlook,* June 12, 1920, Frederick M. Davenport mentioned a remark made to him during the convention by a close friend of Coolidge, who said, "If Calvin Coolidge were nominated for the Vice Presidency, I wouldn't take the Presidency for a million dollars." "Why?" asked the astonished Davenport. "Because I would die in a little while. Coolidge has always been lucky politically. Everything comes along to him in a most uncanny and mysterious way. Excuse me from the Presidency with him in the vice-regal chair." Many people have claimed or been assigned credit for this statement or one of similar tenor. Its oracular quality was perhaps more apparent later than it was in Chicago in the spring of 1920.

Calvin Coolidge was not immoderately excited by the course which events had taken. On Friday afternoon he was with Mrs. Coolidge at the Belmont Spring Country Club, and in the evening his secretary arranged for a long-distance telephone call from Mr. Stearns, who told him from Chicago what had been going on. On Saturday evening about 7.30 he received the news of Harding's nomination and then went out for a short walk across the Common and through some of Boston's downtown streets. He had not been sanguine about his prospects, and his face as he strolled along was observed to be as expressionless as ever — certainly without a trace of disappointment. Returning to his suite of rooms on the fourth floor of the Adams House, he sat there with his wife placidly smoking his long cigar. Shortly after eight the telephone bell rang and he answered it personally, as was his habit. After listening to what was being said, he turned to Mrs. Coolidge and remarked, "Nominated for Vice President!" She thought that her husband was joking, as he sometimes did, and replied nonchalantly, "You don't mean it!" "Indeed I do," was the response. Mrs. Coolidge said, "You are not going to accept it, are you?" There was not even a shadow of a smile around his lips as he answered, "I suppose I shall have to."

Within ten minutes the Coolidges were besieged by reporters, so many that he had to retire to his bedroom and there, with pencil and pad, scribble off a brief statement: —

The nomination for the Vice-Presidency, coming to me unsought and unexpectedly, I accept as an honor and a duty. It will be especially pleasing to be associated with my old friend, Senator Warren G. Harding, our candidate for President. The Republican Party has adopted a sound platform, chosen a wise leader, and is united. It deserves the confidence of the American people. That confidence I shall endeavor to secure.

Naturally Massachusetts was glad. For the first time since Henry Wilson ran for Vice President under Grant, one of her citizens was a standard-bearer on the national Republican ticket. The *Herald* said in its headlines, — none too accurately, — "Crane's Power Chose Coolidge." The bells rang out in Boston and North-ampton. Coolidge slept, he told the reporters, very soundly on Saturday night and announced on Sunday, June 13, that he would fill out his term as Governor. On Monday morning his desk at the State House was stacked high with telegrams and letters, among them one from Chauncey M. Depew: "I have been present at every Republican Convention beginning with 1856, and I have never seen such a personal tribute paid to any individual, by any convention, as was paid to you in the spontaneous nomination for Vice-President." With them also was a message from Vice President Thomas R. Marshall, a recognized wit, reading, "Please accept my sincere sympathy."

When the special train conveying the weary Bay State delegates pulled into the South Station at three o'clock Monday afternoon, hundreds of steam whistles blew a greeting. The members, several of whom had not distinguished themselves by loyalty to the Governor, marched nevertheless to the State House, where he had a chance to meet his friends and receive their congratulations. What passed between him and Senator Lodge during the next few weeks is not recorded. So far as their official relations were concerned, the two men remained friendly. Lodge, a staunch party man, supported the entire Republican ticket in 1920; and two years later, on September 23, 1922, Coolidge responded to a personal appeal from Lodge and went to Pittsfield to speak in his behalf during his campaign for reëlection to the United States Senate.[19] Early in 1924, when Robert M. Washburn published his book, *Calvin Coolidge, His First Biography,* the proof was shown to President Coolidge, who suggested certain alterations and excisions. In connection with the Police Strike and Coolidge's part in it, Washburn had commented, "Then Mr. Lodge, a master of diction unexcelled, said of him, 'Here's to the pilot who weathered the storm,' " and Coolidge excised this sentence. On May 10, 1924, Louis A. Coolidge, who disliked Calvin Coolidge, wrote to Senator Lodge calling his attention to the expurgation and saying : —

The Administration has made up its mind to eliminate you as far as possible in all Massachusetts political activities. They distrust you and some of them hate you. They dislike you for what you did not do in the convention of 1920, and they dislike me for the same reason.

To this unfortunate attempt to create trouble Lodge replied in excellent temper : —

There is only one thing that I ought to say in reply to what you tell me about my being eliminated from Massachusetts politics. That is something that does not trouble me at all. I cannot be eliminated by anybody, because I have no desires for appointments or for running Massachusetts politics or anything of that sort. I have no further career ahead of me, except to finish my present term with reasonable credit if I can. I think, however, that it is only fair to say this, and I believe I ought to say it. The President has treated me ever since he came in with the utmost consideration and friendliness. I have never had any personal request to make of him, but I should not hesitate to make one if I desired to. He has been most friendly. He has consulted me about everything of importance, not only the affairs I have especially to do with but the political situation generally, and has shown a confidence in me which I value. I should not say what I am about to say, except in confidence, but he sends for me a great deal, and I could not ask that any man could be more friendly and considerate, occupying the position which he now occupies. I have a great deal of faith in him. He has done very well in a trying and responsible position, and I am perhaps fairly familiar with some of the difficulties which he has been obliged to meet. . . . I am satisfied of one thing and that is that there is no one in this country with any chance of being nominated or elected to the Presidency who is comparable to Coolidge at this time in either

[19] On their return from Pittsfield, Lodge and others of the party stepped out of the train at Springfield to buy some newspapers. Lodge purchased a paper which had in large headlines, "Coolidge Receives Ovation at Pittsfield," and, turning to a man near him, said, "Look at this, will you? *Coolidge* receives ovation, and it was *my* meeting." And with other remarks of a similar nature, he tore the paper to pieces and threw them out on the track.

character or ability, and I am going to give him the best support I possibly can. I only say this much, not for the purpose of arguing with you about what you say in your letter and which I know is entirely friendly, but simply to tell you what my own experience has been and I, after all, have been in public life a good while and have known a good many men, and I am very sure that I am not mistaken in what I say about the President.

Whatever Senator Lodge may have thought or said or done or left undone in 1920, it is pleasant to know that before he died he changed his mind regarding Coolidge. As for Coolidge, he could afford to be generous. His failure to secure the Presidential nomination in 1920 was no great blow to him. Furthermore the gods, after all, were on his side.

XIII

Election as Vice President

As soon as he could with propriety escape from the throng at the State House on the Monday following his nomination for the Vice Presidency, the indefatigable Coolidge, like a dutiful Amherst alumnus, set out from Boston to attend his twenty-fifth reunion. On his arrival in Springfield, he was greeted by his classmates Lucius R. Eastman and Charles A. Andrews, and escorted to the Colony Club, where the banquet was held. Deering, his roommate, was a candidate for Governor of Maine and could not be present; but forty-six out of the seventy living members were on hand, and there were the usual cheering and reminiscing and singing of the familiar melodies — "Paige's Horse is in the Snowdrift," "Cheer for Old Amherst," and other favorites of the '90s.

That night he slept in Northampton. Dwight W. Morrow and his nephew, Richard B. Scandrett, called at 21 Massasoit Street just after breakfast the next morning and were greeted by Coolidge himself at the front door. The early newspapers were on the porch, not yet looked at, and Morrow, picking them up as he entered, said, "All the country is talking about you to-day, Calvin." "Are they?" replied Coolidge nonchalantly. "Well, by to-morrow they'll have found something else to talk about."

At Amherst, where he received a continuous ovation, he was elected unanimously as President of the General Alumni Association. The Phi Gamma Delta fraternity gave him an impromptu but very enthusiastic reception, and he submitted himself patiently to laudation. It was the beginning of a very busy period, for he presented diplomas at Holy Cross College, in Worcester, on Wednesday; on Sunday he was at Williams College; on the following Monday he was awarded the honorary degree of Doctor of Laws at Wesleyan; on Tuesday he received a similar honor at Bates College, in Maine; on Thursday he attended the Harvard University Commencement;

and on Saturday he went to the University of Vermont, Mrs. Coolidge's college, and there was given another degree. Coolidge was always at his best on academic occasions, enjoyed wearing the gown and mortarboard, and could be persuaded to accept such invitations even when he was much occupied with affairs of state. He often said that he felt at home before a collegiate audience.

Still Governor of Massachusetts, Coolidge had no intention of taking any extended vacation. He did, however, go to Washington at the end of June and had a conference lasting most of one day with Senator Harding. A strange contrast the two candidates presented — Harding, the handsome, easy-going, voluble Middle Westerner, a perfect Babbitt type, and Coolidge, the spare and uncommunicative Yankee, ascetic in his personal habits, irreproachable in his private life, cautious even in his minor vices. Accompanied by James B. Reynolds and Frank W. Stearns, he sat listening while Harding explained his plans; and records to be used on the phonograph were made for campaign purposes, Coolidge speaking for five minutes on the inevitable topic of "Law and Order." In a statement to the press, Harding said : —

Governor Coolidge breakfasted with me this morning, and we have agreed that we will base the campaign on an appeal to restore party government as a constitutional substitute for personal government.

The Governor and I each served as Lieutenant-Governor in our state, and we have both learned from personal experience how possible it is for a second official in a state to be a helpful part in a party administration. I think that the Vice-President should be more than a mere substitute in waiting. In establishing coördination between the executive office and the Senate the Vice-President ought to play a big part, and I have been telling Governor Coolidge how much I wish him to be not only a participant in the campaign but a helpful part of a Republican administration. The country needs the counsel and the becoming participation in government of such men as Governor Coolidge.

Coolidge arrived on Sunday, July 4, his birthday, at the homestead in Plymouth; and the quiet hamlet became, what it was to be for more than a decade, a spot on which the eyes of a curious nation were focused. Reporters camped in the vicinity, interviewing the older inhabitants and resurrecting bits of Coolidge lore. They wrote picturesque stories about the homestead, with its primitive plumbing, its Victorian furniture, its lack of all the modern luxuries and most of the modern comforts, its simple rural atmosphere and isolation. Miss C. Ellen Dunbar, who taught the youthful Calvin in the old stone schoolhouse at the Notch; Miss Jessie Hopkins, one of his classmates who lived as an invalid in Ludlow; Albert W. Goddard, manager of the Goddard Hotel in the same town; Mrs. Don C. Pollard, Coolidge's aunt in Proctorsville — all these were persuaded to talk and contributed to the accelerating Coolidge legend. The *Boston Herald* published a series of articles in which local gossip was used to build up the figure which soon the whole country was to know. Newspaper readers became acquainted with Colonel John C. Coolidge, with his housekeeper, Miss Aurora Pierce, and with Miss Florence Cilley, who kept the store — good honest Vermont "folks," a little bewildered by their sudden notoriety but entirely dignified as they faced the camera. The photographers were very busy around the Notch in those days. They induced Calvin to let them take pictures of him milking a cow, but the animal had always been accustomed to being milked in the barn, and when the Governor approached with pail and wooden stool, she started for the barn door. It took several minutes of coaxing before she could be induced to return and stand in the open while Coolidge assumed the conventional pose of the true milker. He felt obliged to enter into the spirit of the publicity mongers and did his best to satisfy them, even to the extent of dressing up in his grandfather's smock or allowing the camera men to accompany him when he went fishing. Aside from this, he changed his habits very little. He did not even install a telephone in the homestead but kept in touch with his office through a neighbor's telephone a hundred yards away or through trips to the Woodstock Inn and its pay station.

A day or two after his arrival, Coolidge had a slight attack of indigestion, one of the early precursors and warnings of the disease from which he eventually died. He attributed his *malaise* to "an overload of Commencement addresses." He was well enough on July 17, however, to greet more than two thousand Vermonters, who came on a hot summer morning with their picnic luncheons to meet the Coolidges, listen to speeches full of good Republican doctrine, and drink lemonade made by Miss Pierce. Four days later, following a conversation with Crane, Frank W. Stearns wrote to Coolidge commenting on Harding's speech of acceptance, a copy of which had just been sent to them. After saying of it, "I am afraid it is going to prove a great disappointment. Words, words, words, seem to be the characterization," Stearns went on: —

The Senator and I talked about what you should say a great deal, and he seemed to be well, for him, and to have his mind very clearly on the question. You are in an uncomfortable position. I can realize that, so far as possible, I suppose it won't do for you to contradict the statements of the candidate for President. Nevertheless I feel that the most important thing that is going to be said or done in the campaign is going to be your speech. I think it will be read almost as much as Harding's speech, and I think it will have more effect than his.

There is no use of trying to get away from it, the country will follow you more than they will follow any man alive today, and they look for some clear-cut statements from you at this time. On the League of Nations business, won't it be possible for you to make some much clearer statements than he has and yet not statements that are wholly contradictory to his position? . . .

The President chose to demand a treaty and a league, so mixed with one another that it is hard to settle it. We must take conditions as they are, and the thing to do now is for the Republican President, as soon as he takes office, to call a special session of the Senate to act on this matter with great promptness and pass the present treaty and league with such reservations as are necessary to maintain the absolute independence of the United States and put the country in a condition to always be able to take care of itself, and, having taken care of itself, to be in a position to help others. These two things are of equal importance and the order in which they come is of vital importance.

It should be made perfectly clear in any statement that the Republicans do not intend to discuss the mistakes that have been made, but as quickly as possible make the best of a bad situation. I do not suppose there is anything helpful in what I have written, but I am very clear what the country expects from you, and I am very sure it will expect a speech of some length and addressed as little as possible to the past, but clear-cut as to the future. . . .

I cannot be fooled all the time. I am not over-estimating the position you hold in the minds and hearts of the people. There is no doubt of this. This is not anti-Harding but pro-Coolidge. If I were to give some of my reasons for being sure of this, I suppose you would turn up your nose at them, but you would be mistaken if you did, and the confidence is growing. Do not make any mistake about it.

This letter, conveying delicately the wishes of W. Murray Crane, reached Coolidge as he was preparing his own speech of acceptance. He had always been a "mild reservationist" on the League, completely out of accord with Moses, Borah, Lodge, and the other "bitter-enders," and needed no exhortation from Crane and Stearns. The ceremony of notification took place at an outdoor gathering held on July 27, on the grounds of Smith College, in Northampton. The presiding officer was an old friend of Coolidge's, former President L. Clark Seelye, of Smith College. The Chairman of the Committee of Notification had been William Allen White, but he was not enthusiastic about Harding and desired to be free during the campaign; consequently his place was taken by Governor Edwin P. Morrow, of Kentucky, whose remarks were mercifully brief. In his response Coolidge was careful to say nothing which would conflict with the already expressed views of Senator Harding. He advocated no startling reforms or novel doctrines, but spoke without equivocation of the rights of the individual, the necessity of the elimination of extravagance, obedience to law, and the importance of the home. He reserved almost to the last the question of the League of Nations, saying : —

The proposed League of Nations, without reservations, as submitted by the President to the Senate met with deserved opposition from the Republican Senators. To a League in that form, subversive of the traditions and the independence of America, the Republican Party is opposed. But our Party, by the record of its members in the Senate and by the solemn declaration of its platform, by performance and promise, approves the principle of agreement among nations to preserve peace, and pledges itself to the making of such an agreement, preserving American independence, and rights, as will meet every duty America owes to humanity.

The *Outlook,* in comment, said of this address, "The spirit is not that of a candidate seeking for votes, but that of a public teacher seeking to promote the acceptance of certain political principles." It was not a speech comparable in epigrammatic power with some of his earlier utterances, but his good taste kept him from enunciating any policy which might be embarrassing to Harding. When the crowd had somewhat dispersed and the Coolidges were standing by themselves, a friend said to Mrs. Coolidge, "I suppose that you will both take a little rest now. This must have been a tiring day for both of you." Mrs. Coolidge laughingly replied, "Calvin says it is about like any other day. We are going right back to Boston." On the next morning the Republican candidate for Vice President was at his desk in the State House, resuming his routine. A reporter for the *Boston Herald* saw Colonel John Coolidge standing apart looking over the crowd, and said, "This has been a wonderful day, Colonel. We are all proud of this occasion. We expect great things of your son." The only reply was, "I hope you'll never be disappointed."

Among those present at these ceremonies were Senator Lodge and former Senator Crane, the latter a very ill man who was to die within a few weeks. Rather feebly, he called Mr. Stearns aside and asked, "Who invited Senator Lodge to come on this occasion?"

Mr. Stearns replied, "I do not know, sir." Crane then asked petulantly, "Did you do it?" "Certainly I did not." "Well," continued Crane, "I should like to know who did it. He has no business here — he is not wanted." It was not in Coolidge's nature to cherish grudges, and he had no intention of causing a split in the Republican Party. He did not trust Lodge, but his greeting to him was courteous, and even the people close at hand could not have detected any antagonism between them.

On October 2, Crane died, and Coolidge attended the funeral in Dalton. For Crane he felt an affection which he had for very few men, and some days later he wrote his father at Plymouth: —

You must have seen Mr. Crane was dead. I never saw him after he was at my house. I often talked with him. He had had those spells for a long time. I went to Albany with him five years ago and he had a spell there but not bad. Had he been his old self at Chicago I feel the result there would have been different. We did not know until too late that he had been physically unable there to do what we had expected of him. He was a great man. I shall always remember he voted for me until the last.

It was at Crane's funeral that Coolidge, when photographers insisted that they wanted a picture of him and Lodge together, said, with his usual sense of propriety, "I came to bury my friend. It is no time for photographs!" The incident was interpreted by watchful newspapermen as indicating a formal breach between the two, but, as a matter of fact, they continued to meet on amicable terms and neither ever spoke an openly hostile word to the other. In private conversation where he could not be quoted, Coolidge occasionally dropped remarks not very flattering to the Senator from Massachusetts, but officially he was the embodiment of discretion.

On September 25, he wrote Mrs. W. Murray Crane: —

As near as I can judge the campaign looks all one way. I don't think I ever saw any such condition as appears to be developing. It has all the appearance of something more than a landslide.

At the Republican State Convention, held on September 18, Channing H. Cox, who had been an able Lieutenant Governor, was nominated for Governor without opposition, and Alvan T. Fuller, an automobile distributor of marked ability, was named for the second place on the ticket. In his speech at the convention Coolidge described the Democratic administrations of Woodrow Wilson as "a mirage of false hopes and false security" and pointed out that the

World War, by making America the great source of food supply and of munitions for Europe, had relieved the preceding business depression but that it had not provided a permanent remedy for the destructive policy that had damaged American prosperity.

In October, at the request of the Republican National Committee, Coolidge headed a group of Republican spellbinders on an invasion of the so-called Solid South. Before leaving he wrote his father, in a mood of pithy irascibility: —

I did not want to go on a trip. I do not think it will do any good. I am sure I shall not enjoy it. A candidate should never be sent on a trip of that kind.

The other members of the party were Governor Frank O. Lowden, of Illinois, Governor Edwin P. Morrow, of Kentucky, and the Honorable Job E. Hedges, of New York, a veteran wit and platform orator. They went by special train, stopping at strategic centres in Kentucky, Tennessee, Virginia, West Virginia, and North and South Carolina. Coolidge's addresses were usually brief, many of them being delivered from the rear platform of the train, but he spoke fifty-six times in six days. He was particularly effective in denouncing "the rising tide of radicalism," which he urged his Southern hearers to help stem. The speakers had much amusement, among themselves, for everyone had a sense of humor, and diverting incidents occurred at almost every stop. On the whole the trip was successful. It had been predicted that no one would come to listen to Republican oratory; but in Richmond, where almost no advance publicity had been arranged, a hall capable of holding six thousand people was packed to the doors, with many hundreds outside. On October 29, after he was back at the State House, he wrote his father: —

I have been away and too busy to write. We are all well. I feel sure we shall carry the election by a good margin. It would have been a little bigger three weeks ago, but it will be enough.

One picturesque contribution to the Republican campaign literature was a little pamphlet entitled *His Excellency, Calvin Coolidge, Governor of Massachusetts,* prepared by Robert M. Washburn, of Boston, with the subtitle, "His First Biography." This volume, which underwent many additions, excisions, and modifications during the next few years, contained in its original form only twenty pages, including illustrations. It was witty, spicy, and unusual in style, and it contained the implied prediction that Coolidge would be President of the United States from 1929 to 1937. The booklet had eleven chapters, of which the ninth, headed "The Weak Links in His Armor," was totally blank, like the famous chapter on "The Snakes in Ireland." Washburn's brochure, ready for distribution on Notification Day, — July 27, — went rapidly through several editions and was used extensively by the Republican National Committee.[1]

On the day before election, the Governor sent his father a final message of assurance : —

The campaign is over. Some mistakes were made, always are I suppose, but the ones this year were so foolish I do not see how they could have been made by men really trying to elect the ticket.

I am at home today. Came home yesterday.

Boys are well. Your dog is growing well. She has bitten the ice man, the milk man, and the grocerman. It is good to have some way to get even with them for the high prices they charge for everything.

In the morning Mr. Stearns will try to find out how to telephone returns to you. I shall be passing the evening at my headquarters in the Touraine.

Tell Aurora I hope she is well.

On that day, Coolidge's secretary, Henry F. Long, wrote also to Colonel Coolidge : —

The Governor is in Northampton today, having gone up over the road yesterday in order to be ready to cast his vote bright and early tomorrow morning with Mrs. Coolidge for the Republican ticket from top to bottom. He is feeling a good deal better, although I think he is quite tired out, but cheerful and hopeful.

The Coolidges voted shortly after nine o'clock on election morning, and were greeted by a cheering crowd as they passed up the stairs at the City Hall. The Republicans were filled with confidence, and the betting in Wall Street was decidedly in their favor. Back in Boston in the early afternoon, the Governor went to the state suite in the Hotel Touraine, listened to the reports, and greeted his friends, who came in throngs as soon as the result was evident. In the late evening Coolidge went out for a few minutes to the American House, where the Republican State Committee had gathered, and

---

[1] Holman Day, the novelist, had been asked by Mr. Stearns in the early winter of 1920 to prepare a campaign biography of Coolidge, but the manuscript seemed unsatisfactory to several of Coolidge's friends, and it was never published. Day, however, was paid the full price agreed upon for his labor. Washburn's book was, of course, unsubsidized.

made a short speech. The result had really never been in doubt. James M. Cox, the Democratic nominee, had been a weak candidate, in spite of an aggressiveness which increased as November drew near; and his long campaign trips brought him no reward. The nation was in a mood when it longed for the kind of conservatism which Harding embodied. The League of Nations was made by Cox a major issue, and the country wanted none of it. As it turned out, the popular vote was sixteen millions for Harding and only nine millions for Cox. In the Electoral College the triumph of the Republicans was even more decisive, for Cox had only 127 votes against Harding's 404. The result indicated that the people of the United States were tired of reforms, bored by international affairs, and quite willing to settle back in peace and enjoy prosperity. Coolidge himself, when it was clear that he had been elected, issued a statement saying, "It means the end of a period which has seemed to substitute words for things, and the beginning of a period of real patriotism and true national honor." The outcome was to give this sentence a tinge of irony.

The victors had a good time enjoying the victory. On the following day, Coolidge wrote his father in longhand: —

I hope you got our message last night about the election. I am wondering how the vote of Plymouth stood. Perhaps I shall get a letter from you in the morning.

We are all well. I was home Sunday and Monday, returning here Tuesday after voting. Northampton went very strong for us.

I hope you are well. Does James say there are no beechnuts?

All Northampton, including the young ladies of Smith College, was out to celebrate on Election Night, with parades and bands and fireworks. The official outburst of local satisfaction, however, came on the following Friday evening, when a dinner was given at the Draper Hotel, followed by a large gathering at which Dr. L. Clark Seelye presided, and Governor Sproul, of Pennsylvania, did the eulogizing. As he concluded, Governor Coolidge entered, in the midst of a tumultuous demonstration. His speech was heartfelt, full of references to his early experiences in Northampton and packed with "Thank yous!" The climax came when he said, "It has been a great honor to be Governor of the Commonwealth of Massachusetts — the greatest honor I ever had. But the greatest satisfaction that ever came to me was when my fellow citizens in this town chose me to be Mayor of the City of Northampton."

Northampton was not the only spot where jubilation reigned.

The Boston City Club staged a Victory Luncheon to which the Governor was escorted from the State House by five hundred elated members; and that evening the University Club held a reception for Coolidge and the Governor-elect, Channing H. Cox. On October 14, Stearns had written Coolidge a very thoughtful letter: —

Your remark last night about a house in Washington brought two or three things to my mind.

1. I will be glad to take a lease for four years of any house that suits you (not Louis Coolidge's house) and be responsible for the rental. This I should like very much to do. It can be taken first in my name if that simplifies matters at all, or any way you choose.

2. If you plan to get a little vacation soon after election, Mrs. Stearns and I would like to have Mrs. Coolidge and you and your father our guests, either with or without us, at Poland or Woodstock or anywhere else you choose.

3. If after your term as Governor is over, it is possible for you to go away for a somewhat extended vacation, either to the Pacific Coast or somewhere in the South like Asheville, or some such place, again we should like to have Mrs. Coolidge and you our guests, either with or without us.

None of these things requires any answer at this minute. Everybody is going to be so busy the next two or three weeks that the time may come suddenly when you have to decide some of these things. Any or all of these suggestions hold good.

Fond though he was of Mr. Stearns, Coolidge could accept none of his generous offers; indeed he announced soon after election that he proposed to remain in Boston and permit Cox to take a recuperative trip to Porto Rico. Inevitably nearly every organization in New England planned congratulatory luncheons and dinners, and he was seldom free for an evening during the rest of his term. It was observed, however, that he did not appear at a dinner given on November 20, by the Roosevelt Club, to honor Henry Cabot Lodge. Coolidge's dry appreciation of the praise which he was receiving was expressed in a note to his father: —

I wonder if any one sends you the *Boston Globe*. They are running a life of me. Most of it is fiction, of course, so you might like to read it.

Amherst College was preparing to observe her one hundredth anniversary and, in connection with this, to raise a Centennial Fund of three million dollars. At a meeting in Amherst on November 20, Coolidge pledged his allegiance to his Alma Mater, incidentally sitting on the bleachers in the afternoon watching with immobile countenance while Amherst defeated Williams in their annual football contest. On Saturday evening, November 27, dinners were held simultaneously in twenty-one district centres, to commemorate the birthday of the college's patron saint, Lord Jeffrey Amherst; and Coolidge, speaking in New York City, took as his subject, "The Supports of Civilization," saying, in his crisp manner: —

The process of civilization consists of the discovery by men of the laws of the universe, and of living in harmony with these laws. . . . Those who want a continuation of stability and confidence must seek it by supporting the efforts of our colleges and universities. . . . We justify the greater and greater accumulations of capital because we believe that therefrom flows the support of all science, art, learning, and the charities which minister to the humanities of life, all carrying their beneficent effects to the people as a whole.

Early in December the Governor escaped to Pennsylvania, primarily to attend a conference of governors, but incidentally to deliver a succession of addresses in other cities. On December 8, he wrote his father: —

We are home from Pennsylvania. We had a good time. I spoke in Harrisburg, Philadelphia, Chester, and New York.

I was home yesterday to vote. The boys are well. John got your letter while I was there.

I have a very great deal of work to do and can't get much rest. I have had to speak at three dinners tonight. I get invitations from all over the U. S. and from Canada. You must plan to come down Christmas. Do you want to come here or Northampton? I rather think we shall be at Northampton. You must come and see the boys.

On December 17, the Coolidges went for a short visit to the Hardings at Marion, Ohio, where Harding invited Coolidge to sit at cabinet sessions. The two men were plentifully photographed and actually enjoyed little privacy; but Coolidge was consulted on some of the Presidential appointments and policies. He was back in New England in time to attend, on December 21, at Plymouth, the three-hundredth anniversary celebration of the landing of the Pilgrims. The principal speaker was Senator Lodge, who occupied the position which Daniel Webster had filled so eloquently just a century before. Lodge's address, a scholarly and intellectual utterance of the highest order, was profoundly pessimistic in tone, a masterpiece of sophistication and disillusionment. Coolidge, sitting on the chilly stage of the Old Colony Theatre in the chair of Governor

Bradford, wore his overcoat and muffler until he rose to speak. In his brief remarks, without perhaps intending to counteract Lodge's pessimism, he struck quite a different note, especially when he said: —

Plymouth Rock does not mark a beginning or an end. It marks a revelation of that which is without beginning and without end — a purpose shining through eternity with a resplendent light, undimmed, even by the imperfections of men; and a response, an answering purpose, from those who, oblivious, disdainful of all else, sailed hither seeking only for an avenue for the immortal soul.

Two days before Christmas Mr. Stearns unburdened his heart again in one of the many letters in which he showed how warmly he felt towards the younger man whose political fortune he had helped so much to make. It is too long for full quotation, but a few paragraphs reveal what was in the writer's mind: —

You do not know Owen D. Young as I hope you will come to know him, — intimately. I know him, and it means a great deal to me to have him say, as he did walking down from the State House last Sunday, "The country has great cause for thankfulness that that man is to have a strong influence in the coming administration. I wish he were to have control but even the fact that he is to be in a position of influence is cause for gratitude." . . .

One day Mrs. Stearns said to me of one of the children, "She seems to be very dependent on picking other people to do things for her." I replied, "That is no small gift, and she must have inherited it from her father. I am no piker as a picker myself, — I picked you and you have done very well." I think that you yourself are quite a success in the same line, for you must have foreseen coming events fifteen years or more ago when you choose Mrs. Coolidge to be your helper in the work for others that you have done and are destined to do.

It is clear from his correspondence that Coolidge was relieved to have his second term as Governor draw to a close. Before it was ended, he appointed his secretary, Henry F. Long, as Commissioner of Corporations and Taxation, thus rewarding a faithful and efficient servant. On January 5, 1921, when the Republican State Committee met, Frank H. Foss was elected Chairman over Frank B. Hall, who was heard afterwards excoriating the "Coolidge Machine," of which "Tom" White, State Supervisor of Administration, and "Charlie" Innes, well-known as a successful lobbyist, were regarded as the directors. On that evening, Coolidge attended a dinner at the Somerset Hotel in honor of Benjamin F. Felt, who had been for seven years Secretary of the Republican State Committee and had furnished invaluable aid to both Stearns and Coolidge. An ivory elephant and a purse of $500 in gold were presented to Mr. Felt, and then Coolidge, introduced by Hall, made one of his most graceful speeches in appreciation of all that Felt had done.

On the next morning, in accordance with precedent, Coolidge received his successor in the Executive Chamber. Then the slow procession started off to the Hall of Representatives, leaving Calvin Coolidge behind with his faithful friends. Again following tradition, as we have seen, he walked down the steps to the Hall of Flags, outdoors and down the granite steps to Beacon Street, followed several paces behind by Stearns, Butler, Arthur B. Chapin, Robert W. Maynard, Robert S. Weeks, Charles M. Davenport, and Benjamin F. Felt.[2] Often that exit has been a sad one. It was sad for Samuel W. McCall, who left the State House a broken and disappointed man. It has marked for many others the termination of a political career. For Coolidge, however, it was but another episode in his progress onward and upward. The *Transcript* that evening published a brilliant editorial headed, "As Coolidge Goes Down the Steps," summarizing the record which he had made during his two years as Governor and showing that his name would long "be associated with constructive legislation in the Commonwealth." The *Herald* on the following morning headed its editorial columns with the words, "Calvin Coolidge, Citizen."

The long wait between actual election and the taking of the oath as Vice President was by no means over. Coolidge went back to the double house on Massasoit Street and relative peace, but he could not, of course, keep out of the public eye. On January 18 he spoke before the Vermont Historical Society, in the Hall of Representatives at Montpelier, saying, in a mood which indicated his deeper philosophy : —

Disintegration begins within. We are possessors of tremendous power, both as individuals and as states. The great question of our institutions is a moral question. Shall we use our power for self-aggrandizement or for service? It has been lack of moral fibre which has been the downfall of the peoples of the past.

Those who study Coolidge's utterances and blend them with his political and personal conduct are likely, if they are unprejudiced,

---

[2] The idea of having a few personal friends remain with Coolidge until he left the State House was entirely Senator Butler's. Butler said that he had never forgotten seeing Governor Crane leave the State House absolutely alone and made up his mind that Governor Coolidge should not depart in the same fashion.

to reach the conclusion that he was entirely consistent in his motives and his action. A noteworthy example of what he felt is to be found in his address, on January 23, before the Women's Roosevelt Memorial Association, many passages of which indicate that his mind was concerned with national problems. Especially significant was a paragraph early in the speech: —

The greatest peril to our institutions does not lie in a direct assault upon them, nor will it come from those who, with evil intent, strive for their destruction. Disaster will come from those who probably with good intentions seek the private control of public action. . . . The great contests in our government have partaken of the character of an effort to substitute for this public will some form of private will, for the public welfare some private interest.

Using Lincoln and Roosevelt as illustrations of men "who broke the menace of monopoly," he continued regarding the latter: —

He stood for a great principle impartially applied. He declared and enforced the supremacy of the public law alike against those who opposed it in the name of capital or in the name of labor. In that he was the true friend of both, the benefactor of employer and employee, and the defender of the republic of the United States.

At this period, as well as at many others, Coolidge was accused, particularly by literary "smart alecks," of taking refuge in platitudes. But statesmen of the best type are more concerned with being right than with being brilliant. Coolidge's attitude towards public service was high-minded and honest. He emphasized the fundamental virtues, but only because they always need emphasizing. Truth was more important to him than originality. During January and February, 1920, he meditated to some purpose on the new responsibilities which were to be his, little realizing how far removed the Harding administration of which he was to be a part was to be from the theory on which his own action had always been based.

On the same visit to New York, Coolidge was awarded the gold medal given by the National Institute of Social Sciences for his behavior during the Boston Police Strike. In replying to the presentation, he paid a tribute to Edwin U. Curtis: —

If it had not been for the clear insight and the determination of Edwin U. Curtis, a former Mayor and then Police Commissioner of the City of Boston, the question that came to me would never have come. It was because he decided that question right in the first instance that I had the opportunity of supporting him in the second.

A few days later the Coolidges were in Atlanta, where he spoke before the Southern Tariff Association; from there they went to the Grove Park Inn, at Asheville, North Carolina, for a real rest. They returned to Northampton just before Washington's Birthday, and on February 28, early on a raw and chilly morning, set out on their journey to the capital. At New Haven they met Frank W. Stearns and a party from Boston, who joined them on their train. Vice President and Mrs. Thomas R. Marshall greeted them at the station in Washington and, taking them to the New Willard Hotel, did everything to put them at ease in their changed surroundings.

Coolidge took especial pains to see that his elderly father made the trip with the minimum of discomfort. After spending the night in Northampton, Colonel John went on March 3 to Washington with Benjamin F. Felt and Professor George D. Olds as traveling companions. Calvin had even purchased a silk hat for the old gentleman and had insisted that he should wear it. He was able to attend all the exercises and actually made two brief speeches.

Once settled at the New Willard, Coolidge worked intermittently over his address, chatted with the friends who called upon him in vast numbers, amused himself by opening boxes of flowers, and accustomed himself to the new political climate. On the evening of March 3 he dined in his suite with his father, his wife, his two sons, Mr. and Mrs. Stearns, and Mayor Fitzgerald, of Northampton. Those who talked with him noticed that he was calm and unexcited. After all, he had been through inaugural ceremonies before.

The following morning was clear and crisp, with plenty of sunlight. The President-elect and the Vice-President-elect left the New Willard at 10.20 for the White House, Mrs. Harding and Mrs. Coolidge following in another automobile. At the White House, after some delay, the invalided President Wilson, in one supreme effort of courtesy, joined Senator Harding and escorted him on the traditional drive down Pennsylvania Avenue to the Capitol. Wilson was able to enter his office for a few minutes and sign some bills, but he did not feel strong enough to attend the exercises and soon drove back with his wife to their new home in the city. As it was, he had risked his life in doing as much as he did.

As was customary, the oath of office was administered to the incoming Vice President in the Senate Chamber, before the usual gathering of dignitaries. Coolidge then called the Senate to order and delivered the shortest Inaugural Address ever given before that body. In a few words he described the importance of the Senate as "the citadel of liberty." "Its greatest function of all," he declared, "too little mentioned and too little understood, whether exercised in legislating or reviewing, is the preservation of liberty." He added that no legislative body in the world had used its powers "with more wisdom and discretion, more uniformly for the execution of the public will, or more in harmony with the spirit of the authority of the people which has created it." The newspapers agreed that this speech indicated a desire to mind his own business and to leave everything else alone. Coolidge was later to modify somewhat the high opinion of the Senate expressed on Inauguration Day.

Coolidge's address covered about ten minutes. When it was over and friends stepped up to offer their congratulations, he said, in reply to a question, "I don't feel half as important as I did on the day I graduated from Black River Academy." The guests then moved out to the East Portico, where Chief Justice White administered the oath to Harding. Coolidge was particularly impressed by the "lack of order and formality that prevailed" and felt that the Massachusetts inaugurations were much more dignified. The new President spoke for about forty minutes. It was probably the first important occasion at which an amplifying apparatus was used; and one of the vast throng standing between the Capitol and the Library of Congress and listening to the vague and ambiguous sentences of the speaker said to his neighbor, "The amplifier is all very well, but what Harding needs is a condenser!"

When Harding's address was over, Coolidge returned to the Senate Chamber and swore in the new members. He and his wife then went back to the White House for a late luncheon. With a gesture of economy, Harding had declined to sponsor an Inaugural Ball, but the "Ned" McLeans held a dance in their town house to which all Washington was invited. The Coolidges, however, did not attend. In the evening Calvin's former associates in the Massachusetts Senate gave him a dinner. By ten o'clock the new Vice President was in bed and probably asleep. He was glad, as he told one of his friends, to have once again "a regular job."

Later Coolidge incorporated in his *Autobiography* his interpretation of what had happened because of the change of administrations. He wrote: —

When the inauguration was over I realized that the same thing for which I had worked in Massachusetts had been accomplished in the nation. The radicalism which had tinged our whole political and economic life from soon after 1900 to the World War period was passed. There were still echoes of it, and some of its votaries remained, but its power was gone. The country had little interest in mere destructive criticism. It wanted the progress that alone comes from constructive policies.

This statement represents Coolidge's opinion almost a decade after the event and, as such, is not one of his most judicious utterances. The Harding administration was certainly not to go down in history for its "constructive policies," and there were moments before it was over when most honest and fair-minded men welcomed as salutary a considerable amount of "destructive criticism." But in 1921 the Republicans were very happy. President Harding, with a characteristic gesture, at once opened up the White House grounds to the people. It was felt that the austerity, the frigidity, of the Wilson administration was gone, and that a New Era of ease and graciousness was about to begin. Unfortunately there was trouble ahead.

When he took the oath as Vice President, Calvin Coolidge knew very little about Washington. His visits there had been infrequent, and he had never been entertained at the White House until he lunched with the Hardings following his inauguration. His speeches during the campaign of 1920 had taken him to the South and the Middle West, but his acquaintance with national figures in the Republican Party was not large or intimate. He had now to meet new people and become accustomed to new ways. He was careful "not to be obtrusive," but he kept his eyes and ears open, as he had done when he first moved to Boston. His own comment on the situation was simple : —

Aside from speeches I did little writing, but I read a great deal and listened much. While I little realized it at the time, it was for me a period of most important preparation. It enabled me to be ready in August, 1923.

XIV

Vice President

To not a few of those who saw Calvin Coolidge for the first time at his inauguration he appeared to be, as he seemed not long before to Professor Barrett Wendell, "a small, hatchet-faced, colorless man, with a tight-shut, thin-lipped mouth; very chary of words, but with a gleam of understanding in his pretty keen eye." A keen observer, Sherwin Lawrence Cook, commented on his "unimpressive physique, his reticence, his lack of florid speech, his utter want of social attributes, his entire aloofness," and asked how such a man could ever have been elected to a municipal council. Not many of the Washington inner circle had met him, and he was certainly different from the ordinary back-slapping politician so often found in the lobbies of the Capitol. Even the newspapermen were puzzled and could not understand how he happened to be where he was. Mark Sullivan, who had had wide experience, in commenting on a photograph of Harding and Coolidge together, declared that Harding, "except for a fatal streak of softness, was the bigger man, the larger personality," but this will not be the verdict of history. As had been the case in Amherst, in Northampton, and in Boston, he made little impression on those who took a hasty glance and moved on; but he had a quality which improved on acquaintance, and before long people began to talk about him and his quaint remarks.

Coolidge was physically and temperamentally the antithesis of President Harding, who has been described by Charles Willis Thompson as having "a perpetual smile and meaningless geniality." Harding was an orator of the Old School, with a "vague and fuzzy mind," who loved to hear himself talk. Gullible, soft-hearted, and tolerant, he had few enemies, and his unscrupulous friends found him easy to manipulate. Edward S. Martin said of him, "He had modesty, humility, and a desire to do right"; but he was hampered by unfortunate personal loyalties. The troubles of the Harding administration were largely due to the President's uncritical amiability. Although addicted to several of the pleasant vices, he was fundamentally without guile, but his susceptibility to the influence of his satellites was perilous to effective government. He could never, as Woodrow Wilson did, have sacrificed friendships for what he conceived to be the larger good. Under him, Washington seemed to be holding a continuous Old Home Week, and he brought to the White House the viewpoint of the small-town man. Standing beside Harding, Coolidge looked like the embodiment of the Yankee virtues, — caution, thrift, and shrewdness, — the qualities which the President most lacked.

As Vice President of the United States, Coolidge occupied a position which paid him a salary of $12,000 a year. In addition to this, he was allowed his own automobile and chauffeur, his own secretary, page, and clerk, and his private telegraph operator. His chief duty was to preside over the Senate; and he was entitled not only to a room in the Senate Office Building but also to one in the Capitol, directly behind the Senate Chamber. In the Senate proceedings he had no vote except in case of a tie. He was also *ex officio* President of the Smithsonian Institution. His actual duties, beyond these, were not numerous, and he had plenty of time to himself.

Until a few days before he was to set out for Washington, Coolidge had not chosen his secretary. He had thought intermittently of Henry F. Long and of Benjamin F. Felt, with whose methods he was familiar, but neither had had any experience in the national capital. Finally Mr. Stearns suggested Edward T. Clark,[1] of the Amherst Class of 1900, — known to his college generation as "Ted," — who had been secretary to Senator Lodge from 1900 to 1916 but had later taken a position with Stone and Webster, in Boston. When Stearns mentioned Clark's name over the telephone to Coolidge, the latter replied, "All right. Suits me. See him and make the arrangements." At a short conference a day or two afterward, Coolidge definitely engaged Clark, who turned out to be an admirable selection. He was intelligent, loyal, and close-mouthed, and remained with Coolidge as his personal secretary throughout his Presidential period. The hurried manner in which this important detail was settled indicates how useful Mr. Stearns was in countless unrecorded ways.

[1] Edward Tracy Clark, born in Kingston, New York, in 1878, prepared for Amherst at Howard University, and later attended Columbia Law School. After 1929, Clark became Vice President and Manager of Drugs, Inc., with an office in Washington. He died on December 16, 1935. Coolidge's stenographer while he was Vice President was Miss Ethel E. Peck.

When Mrs. Coolidge was talking over the responsibilities of her position as wife of the Vice President, she said, "More hotel life, I suppose." And so it turned out to be. Coolidge obviously could not accept Mr. Stearns's munificent offer of a house, but eventually engaged Suite No. 328, consisting of two bedrooms, a dining room, and a large reception room, in the New Willard. In commenting later on this decision, he said, "There is no dignity quite so impressive, and no independence quite so important, as living within your means." He also advanced the opinion that an adequate residence with suitable maintenance should be provided for the Vice President. "The great office," he declared, "should have a settled and permanent habitation and a place, irrespective of the financial ability of the temporary incumbent."

The Coolidges found their new life not unpleasant. Mrs. Coolidge did not, it is true, have a home of her own where she could preside as hostess. But her radiant charm made itself felt almost at once. Calvin wrote of her to his father on May 10: —

Grace is home as you may know from the papers. She is wonderfully popular here. I don't know what I would do without her.

Until she came to Washington, Mrs. Coolidge's social opportunities had been limited both by her lack of money and by her environment. Life in Northampton, while agreeable, was simple in every way, and the Coolidges had not been addicted to giving or receiving elaborate entertainments. Even after her husband became prominent in state affairs, she was seldom in Boston, and her acquaintance with families in the Back Bay was slight. She attended large official functions as a duty. In Washington, however, the situation was different. The Vice President and his wife were social as well as political personages, entitled to precedence at dinners and regarded as "lions" to be secured, if possible, for important functions. At once Mrs. Coolidge's attractiveness, tact, and sense of humor ensured her popularity and everyone wanted to make her acquaintance. She herself enjoyed meeting people, and made up by her graciousness for her husband's habitual reticence. In society Coolidge was certainly an "odd stick," but Mrs. Coolidge was soon as much a part of it all as if she had been brought up in Boston's Junior League and Vincent Club.

Behaving as he had done when he was Lieutenant Governor, Coolidge was consistently loyal to his superior. On the evening of March 5 when the Bay State delegation at the inauguration had a dinner for the Vice President at a Washington hotel, Coolidge's speech was a plea for support of the Chief Executive. Everyone familiar with contemporary affairs was aware that the new administration had a multiplicity of problems. Business was generally bad; strikes were still prevalent; and the number of unemployed on January 1, 1921, was estimated at 2,225,000 — a large number in those pre-Depression days. The leading article in the *Literary Digest* for January 8, 1921, was headed, "When Will Good Times Return?" In the face of trouble, Harding's conduct was such as to inspire confidence, as a rereading of contemporary newspapers will prove.

He began by holding a conciliatory White House conference with the leaders of his party. As we have seen, he had already broken a precedent by requesting Coolidge to sit with the cabinet; and for the first time in American history, a Vice President was thus to be "on the inside" of both executive and legislative matters, a situation which a few critical Senators rather resented. On election night Harding had wired Coolidge, "You are to expect to play a full part in the coming Republican administration." Harding had great confidence in Coolidge, consulted him frequently, and was influenced by him to a marked degree. The cabinet itself had been accurately predicted as early as February 23, and the names were ratified one after one in ten minutes, following the inauguration. Of these appointees, three were indubitably strong — Charles E. Hughes, in the Department of State, Andrew W. Mellon, in the Treasury, and Herbert Hoover, in the Department of Commerce. John W. Weeks (War), James J. Davis (Labor), and Henry C. Wallace (Agriculture) were also highly respected. Albert B. Fall (Interior) and Harry M. Daugherty (Attorney General), to the latter of whom Harding was paying a heavy political debt, were to be the vulnerable members; and Edwin N. Denby (Navy) was also to be more of a liability than an asset. Will H. Hays, the Postmaster General, retired after exactly a year in office, and was succeeded by Dr. Hubert Work. Later, after Fall sent in his resignation to take effect on March 4, 1923, Work was made Secretary of the Interior and Harry S. New was designated as Postmaster General. These were the only changes. The cabinet did rather effectively tie together several groups and factions, and Harding showed a will of his own in choosing Hoover and Daugherty. On the whole, it was a cabinet well above the average in ability, and Coolidge was to be glad that he had accepted the President's invitation to join them.

The first meeting of the cabinet was called at eleven o'clock on Tuesday, March 8, and in the official photograph taken at that time,

© *Harris and Ewing*

GRACE GOODHUE COOLIDGE

Coolidge was placed at the President's left with Hughes on Harding's right. When reporters inquired what chair he occupied at the cabinet table, he replied noncommittally, "All information will have to come from the President." [2] To other questions which followed, he remained as unresponsive as the Sphinx. His associates have reported that he seldom participated in the cabinet discussions, but found no difficulty in listening and in conducting himself with discretion under circumstances which might have proved embarrassing.

Coolidge's high position naturally increased his prominence in his own state, and the *Boston Herald,* on March 9, declared, "The Republicans of Massachusetts are fast dividing into what might be described as a Coolidge group and a Lodge group." The leaders then classified as "Coolidge men" included Louis K. Liggett, Charles H. Innes, Clarence W. Barron, Channing H. Cox, and others. Coolidge, however, took pains to deny that he was giving aid and comfort to any political machine and added, "I'm minding my own business and keeping my mouth closed." A possible contest for National Committeeman was averted when John W. Weeks agreed to continue in that position.[3]

From March 4 until March 15 the Senate remained in Special Session, and indeed it was to sit with three or four brief recesses for the next two years. Its President *pro tempore,* reëlected on March 7, 1921, was Albert B. Cummins, of Iowa, then in his seventy-second year. The Massachusetts members were the aging but still dominating Henry Cabot Lodge, who had been in the Senate since 1893, and his Democratic younger colleague, David I. Walsh, who was serving his first term. Hiram Johnson was there from California, George H. Moses, from New Hampshire, and

[2] His seat was actually at the far end of the table next to Secretary Davis. Coolidge's caution was unnecessary, for official photographs had already been taken of the cabinet in session.

[3] In commenting on this peculiar situation, Mr. Stearns wrote to his son, Foster, April 8, 1921, in part: —

"I have kept busy assuring friends of Mr. Coolidge that all this talk in the Boston papers is sheer newspaper talk and so far as it indicates anything it indicates that two men in Washington are very much disturbed and are doing what they can to dig themselves into a pit and they need have no anxiety that it will do Mr. Coolidge any harm. I tell folks that I do not believe there is any serious commotion in the Senate over the fact that Mr. Coolidge sits with the Cabinet; that it is a Massachusetts trouble almost entirely. I rather made up my mind that at the bottom of this connection is the old three-cornered row between McCall, Weeks and Lodge. The Republican party has been torn asunder by this row for many years. We had, practically, peace so long as Mr. Coolidge was here because the people in the Senate were united behind him. Now that Senator Crane is gone they are trying to see if they cannot open the row and side-track Mr. Coolidge. Unless all experience and all present signs fail it will only strengthen his position."

William E. Borah, from Idaho — all Republicans and bitter opponents of the League of Nations. Oscar W. Underwood, of Alabama, Joseph T. Robinson, of Arkansas, Claude A. Swanson and Carter Glass, of Virginia, were able Democrats, but considerably outnumbered. The radical element had a courageous voice in Robert M. La Follette, of Wisconsin. Boies Penrose, of the Republican Old Guard, died on December 31, 1921, and was succeeded by George W. Pepper, from Pennsylvania. Other prominent members were Charles Curtis, of Kansas, John S. Williams, of Mississippi, James W. Wadsworth, a young man then in his second term from New York, and Reed Smoot, of Utah. It was a group of strong personalities, of hard fighters and forceful speakers.

The Senate Chamber itself is familiar to millions of Americans, and Coolidge soon became accustomed to his environment — to the green carpet; to the mahogany desks, each with its cuspidor, its waste-paper basket, and its chair with leather seat and back; to the sofas in the corners for the pages; to the galleries with the niches above containing busts of Vice Presidents; to the clock on the rear wall over the door. He occupied the centre chair on the rostrum, with the Sergeant-at-Arms on his right and the Doorkeeper on his left, and the Secretary of the Senate and various clerks at a long table in front of and below him. On his right were the Senators rated as Democrats; on his left were the Republicans. It was an interesting body, very jealous of its prerogatives and inclined to be suspicious of newcomers. In his capacity of presiding officer Coolidge behaved with impartiality, but could do very little, of course, to influence or direct legislation. His own comments on the Senate and its procedure are not illuminating, but he did say in his *Autobiography:* —

Presiding over the Senate was fascinating to me. . . . It may seem that debate is endless, but there is scarcely a time when it is not informing, and, after all, the power to compel due consideration is the distinguishing mark of a deliberative body. . . . I was entertained and instructed by the debates. However it may appear in the country, no one can become familiar with the inside workings of the Senate without gaining a great respect for it. The country is safe in its hands.

The accomplishments of the Harding administration, such as they were, cannot be attributed to Calvin Coolidge and properly deserve only a small space in this narrative. A Special Session of Congress, called for April 11, lasted until just before Thanksgiving, with a recess of four weeks in August and September. The administration was especially interested in economy measures, including a national budget and other legislation affecting taxation and the tariff. Harding's first message, dated March 9, urged the settlement of the long-standing dispute with Colombia over damages caused by the loss of the isthmian strip and the payment of an indemnity of $25,000,000. The necessary treaty was ratified in April. On July 2, Congress ended formally the state of war with Germany and Austria, and treaties of peace, negotiated some weeks later, were shortly signed and ratified.

One of Harding's most significant accomplishments, with which the Vice President was openly in sympathy,[4] was the Budget and Accountancy Act, signed on June 20, creating a Budget Bureau, of which the colorful Charles G. Dawes, of Chicago, was soon appointed Director. On June 26, Dawes addressed the President, the cabinet members, and more than five hundred bureau chiefs on the broad question of constructive economy. The time was soon to come in the late spring of 1923 when Coolidge, during Harding's illness, was to preside over this gathering. He had himself helped to make out such a budget in Massachusetts, and he thoroughly approved of the system as a practical means of eliminating waste.

On November 12, the day following the impressive dedication of the Tomb of the Unknown Soldier in Arlington National Cemetery, Harding opened a Conference on the Limitation of Armaments in which the Great Powers had been invited to participate. Before this assembly had adjourned on February 6, 1922, it had produced seven treaties and had, to use Coolidge's words, "reached an epoch-making agreement for the practical limitation of naval armaments."[5] The significance of what was accomplished at this conference seemed greater at the moment than it did fifteen years afterwards, but it was at least a noble gesture, for which Harding and Hughes deserve much credit. Harding himself was not an advocate of the League of Nations, but he did in a somewhat vague fashion favor international understanding such as might be gained through a World Court, and recommended to the Senate in February 1922 that the United States adhere to it; but his well-intentioned efforts were futile. The United States in the early 1920's was spiritually worn out, tired of Wilson's idealism, exhausted by the nervous tension of war times. What President

---

[4] Interviewed in May by Charles S. Groves for the *Boston Sunday Globe*, Coolidge, with unusual loquacity, had said that the most important problems facing the country were taxation and finance.
[5] See Mark Sullivan, *The Great Adventure in Washington* (1922).

Harding called Normalcy really had its appeal to a majority of the American people, and they welcomed his invitation to them to get back to everyday living, to quiet and repose. Harding — friendly, undiscriminating, a trifle vulgar when he was off guard — symbolized the aims of those small businessmen who wanted their taxes low, their profits reasonably large, and their proceedings untroubled by insistent governmental scrutiny. The Harding administration was in its mood a natural, perhaps an inevitable, after-war reaction from the strain of 1918, when most citizens were giving until it hurt. Now that the crisis was past, they wanted to be let alone.

Before the Sixty-seventh Congress had expired on March 3, 1923, taxation had been reduced and payments of considerable size had been made on the large national debt; an Emergency Tariff Bill, superseded a year later by the Fordney-McCumber Tariff Act, with its broad revision upward, had been put through, but none too enthusiastically; the Veterans' Bureau had been organized; some farming legislation had been passed, but not enough to satisfy the chief demands of the agricultural interests. A Soldiers' Bonus Bill, passed by the House and the Senate in 1922, was courageously vetoed by the President on September 19 of that year. Although Harding himself did not comply with the Prohibition Amendment and actually tolerated drinking surreptitiously in the White House,[6] he outwardly approved of enforcement measures. Of this Congress Coolidge declared, "It would be difficult to find two years of peace-time history in all the record of our republic that were marked with more important and far-reaching accomplishment." That this opinion is exaggerated will seem apparant to most American historians, but the period was not so altogether barren as it has sometimes been assumed to be. The autumn elections of 1922 had seen the defeat of many of the key men in Congress, and the Democrats and Farmer-Laborites together made inroads on the Republican majority in both Houses. It was obvious that the Western farmers were restless, and that the groups of Insurgents represented a protest against Republican domestic policies. When the Sixty-seventh Congress broke up, Harding declined to call another Special Session. At a period when many different factions were aggressive, but could agree on almost no settled program, the President thought it best to seek relief from Congressional debate. By that time he had plenty of trouble on his mind — most of it as yet unrevealed to the public — and was a completely frustrated and disillusioned man.

[6] For an interesting comment on what went on in the White House, see Alice Roosevelt Longworth, *Crowded Hours,* pp. 324–25.

To those of Coolidge's Massachusetts admirers who had expected great things of him in Washington, it seemed as if he had sunk into relative obscurity. The anonymous *Mirrors of Washington,* a cynically scurrilous volume published in the late spring of 1921, did not even include Coolidge, although there were chapters on Harding, Wilson, Hughes, Hoover, Lodge, Root, and others. The degree to which the new Vice President was unknown is indicated by the fact that he was even given a middle initial to his name, as in the complimentary pass issued to him by the National Baseball League which designated him as Calvin G. Coolidge and in that from the American League which called him Calvin C. Coolidge. The Washington news for many months is singularly devoid of mention of Coolidge, except as a guest at dinner parties, and it might almost be said that politically he was a Forgotten Man. In the autumn of 1921, however, Edward G. Lowry, a well-known journalist, prepared a book called *Washington Close-Ups,* which included sections on both Harding and Coolidge. Originally Lowry had culled most of his details from Robert M. Washburn's pamphlet biography, — then the only book on Coolidge in existence, — but Mr. Washburn was not pleased with the procedure which Lowry had followed and threatened Houghton Mifflin Company, the publishers, with suit. Eventually Lowry rewrote his article, without any reference to Washburn's work,[7] and the sketches attracted some attention. The country was to know Coolidge better before very long.[8]

Although Coolidge's publicity value had temporarily fallen off, he was far from idle. The relative calm of the Vice Presidency offered him an opportunity not only for meditation on the lessons of the past and on the promise for the future, but also for the revaluation and enlargement of his political creed. He had been for several years primarily a legislator and an executive — a man of action. Now he had leisure to read, to observe, to reflect, and to reach conclusions. Events had rushed rapidly on one another in his career; he needed now to refresh his mind, to go back to first principles. Every statesman requires interludes like these when he can lie

[7] In a letter to Coolidge, September 29, 1921, Mr. Stearns said, in this connection, "I have always had a sneaking regret that I did not use Washburn's pamphlet in some parts of the country during the campaign. I think it would have been a good document, but every one whom I talked with opposed using it. I have just been looking it over again today, and I still think it was a remarkable campaign document."

[8] Lowry's article, headed "Coolidge: Foster-child of Silence," portrays the Vice President as "the official diner-out of the Administration," and says in conclusion, referring to his majestic silence, "He is a type entirely new to Washington."

fallow and equip himself for further exertions. Consequently we find him reading Wells's *Outline of History,* following carefully what was being said in the Boston, New York, and Washington newspapers, and taking books on economics and finance out of the library. In his *Autobiography,* Coolidge said of this period: —

> During these two years I spoke some and lectured some. I was getting acquainted. Aside from speeches, I did little writing, but I read a great deal and listened much. While I little realized it at the time, it was for me a period of most important preparation.

The many addresses which Coolidge made while he was Vice President may be regarded as the outpourings of an active, searching mind compelled for reasons beyond its control to seek another channel for its energy. One or two early successes made him popular, and he was soon overwhelmed with invitations. He would go early to his office in the Capitol and spend the morning hours at his desk; and even after the Senate began its session, he would frequently call some Senator to the chair and resume his work. Until he became President, and even afterwards, he continued to draft his speeches in longhand and then have them copied in double-space by his stenographer.[9] He took great pains with whatever he had to say and was careful not to let himself lapse into indiscretion. Wishing to be sure that he would not be misquoted, he shunned extemporaneous speeches. "It is not difficult for me to deliver an address," he once wrote. "The difficulty lies in its preparation." In his talks over the country he never told amusing stories, never made fun of anybody, but was dignified, straightforward, unquestionably sincere. When one considers the various audiences that he faced, the different topics that he chose or were inherent in the occasions, one must credit him with unusual versatility. The same principles and attitudes recur, of course, but the phrasing is different. If any reader of this biography is willing to spend a few hours with *The Price of Freedom,* printed in 1924 and including twenty-eight of his selected addresses, their high quality will become apparent. They have none of the faulty logic, the starchy vagueness, the wordiness, which characterize Harding's utterances. Coolidge was accused of talking platitudes, but they were only such in the sense that all basic truths have been uttered, indeed must necessarily be uttered, again

---

[9] The story has often been told of Coolidge's visit to Emily Dickinson's house in Amherst, in June 1920, when he was shown several of her manuscripts and, evidently bored, said, "She wrote with her hands. I dictate." I can find no evidence whatever for this tale and can only believe that it is the invention of some fertile genius. Most of Coolidge's writing was done "with his hands."

and again. What he said always had some bearing on his essential theme.

Heywood Broun has declared dogmatically that Calvin Coolidge was "the least gifted author the White House has known in many generations." This sweeping verdict is an illustration of how, even in literary criticism, opinion can be affected by prejudice. Charles Willis Thompson, in his book, *Presidents I've Known* (1929), has a chapter entitled "Coolidge the Stylist," which, after examining Coolidge's published writings, reaches the conclusion that he was "one of the very few Presidents who can be thought of as literary men." Coolidge's style, as Thompson sees it, is based on the short, crisp sentence — a sentence which is "the distillation of a long process of thought." He was skilled in condensed expression, in epigram and antithesis, and his phrasing attracted attention.

The fact is that attacks on Coolidge's speeches from the smart-aleck group have resulted in an underestimation of their quality. People who have never read them have been undiscriminating in their condemnation. Coolidge himself was modest enough on the subject, and, on December 29, 1924, wrote Mr. Thompson in part: —

I am not conscious of having any particular style about my writings. If I have any, it is undoubtedly due to my training in the construction of legal papers, where it is necessary in the framing of a contract, or the drawing of a pleading, to say what you mean and mean what you say in terms sufficiently clear and concise so that your adversary will not be able to misinterpret them, or to divert the trial into a discussion of unimportant matters. The rule is to state the case with as little diffusion as possible.

Another influence on my writings has been the fact that most of that which is published was composed when I was Lieutenant-Governor and Vice-President. Quite naturally, I left to the Governor and to the President, during those times, comment on current political problems, and dealt myself in more general and fundamental principles. While this did not create so much interest at the moment, it has, perhaps, lent a more permanent value to some of the addresses which I have made.

A short review of his speaking activities during his term as Vice President will not be unrewarding and will justify the view that Coolidge was inferior to few Presidents in felicity and vigor of expression. On April 28, 1921, he spoke at the Founders' Day Celebration of Carnegie Institute, in Pittsburgh, on Andrew Carnegie, whom he portrayed as a man who represented American ideals and "put his trust not in force but in reason." One paragraph of this address is a perfect example of Coolidge's effective use of short sentences. Referring to Carnegie's benefactions, he said: —

He was always seeking out the realities. He offered opportunity. He knew it was all his beneficiaries could profitably receive. If they were to have life more abundantly he knew it could come only through their own effort. He could not give the means by which others could provide these for themselves. He did not pauperize. He ennobled.

At the annual meeting of the American Classical League, in early July, at the University of Pennsylvania, Coolidge extolled the merits of the Greek and Latin masterpieces which he had studied at Amherst and maintained that our national will to endure and our ideals have been derived largely from them. In this unusually able presentation of the value of classical study he employed many of the oratorical devices of Webster, particularly the curt, snappy sentences, opening in the same phrasing and bursting out like a succession of pistol shots. The following is a good example: —

We believe in our republic. We believe in the principles of democracy. We believe in liberty. We believe in order under the established provisions of law. We believe in the promotion of literature and the arts. We believe in the righteous authority of organized government. We believe in patriotism. These beliefs must be supported and strengthened.

Throughout this address the words are simple, the sentence structure is never involved, the thought is never confused. While Coolidge sometimes utilized quotations effectively, he did not rely on concrete illustrations to win the attention of his audience but moved chiefly in the realm of abstract ideas. Yet every once in a while he produced a sentence which caught the imagination. He did not lower himself for his listeners, but tried to bring them up to his own level of serious purpose.

In October he spoke at a Community Chest Dinner in Springfield, Massachusetts, on "The Power of the Moral Law," — one of his favorite themes, — and in Kansas City, at the annual convention of the newly formed American Legion, whose members he warned that their glory for posterity would lie in what they had given, and would give, to their country and not in what their country had given, or might give, to them. In the winter and spring of 1922 he was again at his best in commemorating at different places four great Americans — Alexander Hamilton, Abraham

Lincoln, George Washington, and Ulysses S. Grant. In a speech on July 6, at Fredericksburg, on "Great Virginians," Coolidge summarized his political philosophy: —

The world today is filled with a great impatience. Men are disdainful of the things that are, and are credulously turning toward those who assert that a change of institutions would somehow bring about an era of perfection. It is not that a change is needed in our Constitution and laws so much as there is a need of living in accordance with them. . . . It is not our institutions that have failed, it is our execution of them that has failed. . . . There have been criticisms which are merited, there always have been and there always will be; but the life of the nation is dependent not on criticisms but on construction, not on tearing down but on building up, not in destroying but in preserving.

It is passages like this, unquestionably worked out with much care, which place Coolidge among the conservatives, with statesmen like Webster and Lincoln and Cleveland rather than with Jefferson and Franklin D. Roosevelt. Other things being equal, he preferred to keep the old customs and institutions and work through them to a better era. It was always a reform which he sought and not a revolution. As he saw it, the trouble was not so much with the governmental machinery as with the men who were operating it. His philosophy was temperamental, deep-seated, and thoroughly consistent. He did not vacillate with the changing winds of popular sentiment.

On August 2, he addressed the Industrial Conference at Babson Institute, in Wellesley Hills, Massachusetts, on "The Meaning of Democracy"; and eight days later he was in San Francisco telling the members of the American Bar Association that we have too many laws. At the Massachusetts Republican Convention, on September 23, in Boston, he paid a deliberate and eloquent tribute to Senator Lodge, who was running again for the Senatorship and meeting with strong opposition. Those who conceive of Coolidge as revengeful should remember that, in spite of what Lodge did in the Convention of 1920, the Vice President came to his rescue in the hour of need. He ended: —

The people of this Commonwealth can bestow honor and confidence upon Senator Lodge. But if benefits are to be conferred, he will not only receive; he will bounteously give. Think not of his interests, but do not fail to think of your own.

On Memorial Day the Vice President was back in Northampton, delivering a patriotic address which was packed with informatory remarks on the development of our country. On this occasion, Coolidge spoke with praise of the Washington Conference and with hope regarding our participation in the World Court. On June 12 he was the speaker at the one hundred and fiftieth anniversary of the settlement of the city of Burlington, Vermont, and paid a tribute to his native state; and five days later he was at Wheaton College, Norton, Massachusetts, receiving a degree of Doctor of Laws and talking on the subject "The Things That Are Unseen." Here again he set for his hearers a lofty standard in what was to be his last formal address before he became President:—

We do not need more material development, we need more spiritual development. We do not need more intellectual power, we need more moral power. We do not need more knowledge, we need more character. We do not need more government, we need more culture. We do not need more laws, we need more religion. We do not need more of the things that are seen, we need more of the things that are unseen.

It is a bitter irony which has led to the charge that a man who spoke habitually in this tone was a materialist. Those who honestly maintain that he was a materialist must also believe that he was a conscious and scheming hypocrite, pretending to be one type of man when he was actually at heart quite another — the Tartuffe of American politics. His references to spiritual values are not casual or occasional; they are intentional and frequent. In one oration he says:—

The age of science and commercialism is here. There is no sound reason for wishing it otherwise. The wise desire is not to destroy it, but to use it and direct it rather than to be used and directed by it, that it may be, as it should be, not the master but the servant, that the physical forces may not prevail over the moral forces, and that the rule of life may not be expediency but righteousness.

Again he declares, with a sincerity which seems to me convincing:—

Civilization is always on trial, testing out, not the power of material resources, but whether there be, in the heart of the people, that virtue and character which come from charity sufficient to maintain progress.

No open-minded person can read these speeches carefully without concluding that to Calvin Coolidge life was really more than meat and the body more than raiment. Indeed many paragraphs smack more of the preacher than of the statesman. From them, too, a man emerges, with a working creed not too rarefied or ethereal for the average citizen to comprehend — a man of conservative tendencies, distrustful of radical movements and relying on the better instincts of human nature; an optimist, confident that all things do, in the end, work together for good; a patriot, proud of his country and its history and hopeful of its future; an idealist, who put his faith in the salutary power of truth and freedom. The Calvin Coolidge of these speeches is, in his moral standards, in his sense of responsibility, in his dignity, in his vision, and in his gift for leadership, a man of noble character.

The earliest radio broadcasting station in the United States — KDKA — was opened on November 2, 1920, in East Pittsburgh, on Election Night, but Coolidge did not speak over the air until December 10, 1923, from the White House, at the Harding Memorial Service. When radio transmission and reception had been perfected, Coolidge's nasal voice, penetrating and clear in its enunciation, came through the air unblurred and gave him a manifest advantage over rival statesmen.

Because of these addresses the hitherto rather provincial Coolidge learned to know his country, moving across the continent with the same ease that he had once felt on the slow "accommodation train" from Northampton to Boston. Gradually he became acquainted with the leading politicians of the Middle West and the South and found them very much like those whose propensities he had known in the corridors of the Massachusetts State House. The American people, furthermore, came to know him, grew accustomed to his Yankee twang, caught something of his personality. Coolidge's critics still continued to describe him as a nonentity, who had been carried upward by a succession of lucky accidents. But a nonentity does not get talked about as Calvin Coolidge did. By the spring of 1923, after he had been in Washington two years, he was recognized in the Capital as having a quality all his own.[10]

Many of the best stories, authentic or legendary, about his peculiarities originated in this Vice Presidential period. Night after night, accompanied by his gracious and witty wife, he went out to dinners from which, because of his official rank, he could escape as early as ten o'clock. On one Sunday shortly after his inauguration the Coolidges breakfasted as the guests of Miss Mabel Board-

[10] Mrs. Harding never really liked the Coolidges. President Butler, of Columbia, was at the White House in 1922, just after Congress had declined to buy the John B. Henderson house for a Vice Presidential residence. Mrs. Harding said, "I defeated that bill. I just couldn't have people like those Coolidges living in that beautiful house."

man at Grasslands, the most exclusive of the Washington clubs. They then attended the service at the First Congregational Church and afterwards held a reception for friends at the New Willard. They were out for luncheon, and in the evening dined with forty other guests at the home of Senator and Mrs. Thomas J. Walsh. Why he continued to accept invitations one after another no one could explain; and even his succinct, "Got to eat somewhere!" did not clarify the mystery. Unembarrassed he could sit between two lovely ladies and answer only in monosyllables, and the most alluring hostesses tried their wiles on him without success. Some bright Washington belle discovered that he would talk on Vermont, and from that moment it was the favorite topic of those who sat on his left and right. He almost never laughed, and even his faint smiles were rare. Never before in his life had he been an habitual "diner-out," and he was probably at first rather ill at ease. He had become notorious for his lack of "small talk," and it was too late in life to develop it, even if he had desired to do so. His wife joked about his reticence, but even she could not unloose his tongue. Beside him, William the Silent, Von Moltke, General Grant, all the other uncommunicative heroes of history, were garrulous.

At dinners Coolidge did listen when something worth while was being discussed. But he did not care to be directly queried; furthermore the inquiry most frequently made of him by dinner partners in 1921 and 1922 was, "How do you like Washington?" and this banality, generally regarded as a legitimate conversational opening, only made him shrink more deeply into his shell. Some clever lady was responsible for the tale that every time he opened his mouth, a moth flew out. But the best story — probably authentic — is that of the prominent society woman who said as she sat down next to him, "Oh, Mr. Coolidge, you are so silent. But you must talk to me. I made a bet to-day that I could get more than two words out of you." "You lose," was the Vice President's reply. One suspects that very often his reticence was a form of defensive armor, to protect him against inquisitiveness and even impertinence.

Every once in a while, when he did say something its wit traveled through Washington social circles, and the rumor spread that the silent man was really quick-witted. It was reported that he had said, in speaking of his dinner engagements, "Sometimes I don't know whether I'm having food or soda mints, I have to mix the two so often." The famous *bon mot,* attributed to Alice Longworth, that Coolidge looked as if he had been weaned on a pickle, was not really hers, but originated from an anonymous patient of her physician's; but by constant repetition she gained the credit for it. When the Coolidges went with the Longworths to Bath, Maine, by private car for Senator Walter E. Edge's wedding, on December 9, 1922, Mrs. Longworth found that the Vice President, instead of going to his Pullman berth at ten o'clock, apparently enjoyed sitting up and watching the poker games and occasionally interjected a word of dry humor.[11]

Probably Coolidge was often bored. Yet, outside of the dinners, it was in many respects the life which he had known for some years in Boston. He had been the Lieutenant Governor of a sovereign state, had presided over and controlled its Senate, had been loyal to the Governor of the Commonwealth, as he now was to President Harding. He took the same walk each day from a hotel through a park to a domed capitol. The politicians whom he saw chattering ceaselessly in the committee rooms and on the street corners were of a type which he knew only too well. The horizon in Washington may have been wider, but human nature was just the same, and he could hear the familiar questions, "What is there in it for me?" and "What's the best way to approach him?"

In June 1921, Mrs. Coolidge went to Mercersburg to look at the famous Pennsylvania Academy, and the Vice President wrote, "I rather think that I shall put the boys up there next fall." The enrollment of John and Calvin in Mercersburg was duly accomplished, and they entered in the following September. In June 1922, Coolidge spoke at the breaking of ground for a new chapel at the school, and urged the students to direct their attention to obedience, honesty, industry, thrift, and faith.

In mid-June Coolidge was back in New England for the Centennial Celebration at Amherst — the most momentous event in the history of the college. At the chief meeting he delivered an address, representing Amherst men in public affairs, and stressing "the foundation of Western civilization which asks not whether it will pay, but whether it is right." Nearly half of the living graduates were there, and speeches of many different types were delivered — no one any better, however, than that of Calvin Coolidge. It was a crowded time of pageants and parades, of concerts and reunions, and the Vice President, who had just been elected a Trustee, was the most conspicuous figure on the campus. Times had changed since the days when Alpha Delta Phi and Psi Upsilon had not found in him the human material which they wanted.

[11] Longworth, 325–26.

Conscientious as usual, the Vice President did not feel warranted in taking a vacation while Congress was in session. When it took a recess for four weeks, however, he did slip away in late August to Plymouth, motoring all the way to Vermont. In answer to queries, he simply said, "I'm loafing, just rusticating," and he managed to arrive without having reporters or photographers around to harass him. He was too late for the haying, and the fishing season had closed, but he found plenty to do just sitting on the porch, going for the mail, talking with his neighbors, and occasionally motoring to the Woodstock Inn for luncheon. For him Plymouth, with all its lack of comfort, was home.

During the following autumn and winter, as we have seen, the Vice President was often away from Washington on speaking tours; and occasionally a picturesque incident attracted the attention of the press. It was noteworthy, for example, when, in May 1922, the Coolidges attended the Devon Horse Show in Philadelphia and saw the Corinthian Challenge Race for the most famous hunters in America. Incidentally the Vice President paid a quarter for a spin at the wheel of fortune and won a box of a hundred cigarettes. "That's the first time I ever won anything," he commented.

Calvin Coolidge was clearly not happy during the spring of 1922. He felt that he had powerful enemies who were trying to undermine him in Massachusetts, and he found the Vice Presidency decidedly boring. On March 16, Mr. Stearns, troubled after a visit which he had made to Coolidge in Washington, wrote him a letter to cheer him up. He said in part: —

I came away from Washington quite a little disturbed by your statement that you were getting suspicious of everybody. If it is merely that you let out your temporary feelings, that is all right, that is a healthful process, but if the feeling is deep-seated with you, it is an awful pity, and I do not believe there is any substantial ground for it. Of course, between us, we know a few people who are not friendly. There is no occasion to be suspicious of them. We know their attitude, but they are a very small number, I am sure. I take it that it is true in the case of every public man who has come to high position that there are some folks who are jealous. . . . It makes me a little sick at heart that you should not get more comfort out of your success, which really has been extraordinary, and the beauty of it is that the confidence in you the country over grows, not only among those who know you personally but very widely among others. . . .

Why not be glad to see folks, let them know that you are glad to see them and try for six months to take it for granted that just plain common folks, the backbone of the country, feel it an honor to meet the

Vice President of the United States. . . . I know how folks feel, and I am not making any mistake whatever. It is of enormous importance to the country that you assume your position of leadership, which you certainly have. Nobody can destroy it but yourself. I cannot imagine any way in which even you can destroy it unless you persistently for years make folks feel that you are not interested in them. I know you are. Let them know it.

In reply all Coolidge could say was: —

Your letters all received. I do not think you have any comprehension of what people do to me. Even small things bother me. But that is no matter. I can't go to New York for Mr. Mott or anyone else. I have been there *eight* times.

Most of the letters which he wrote at this period have this note of uncertainty, of irritation, and of pessimism.

Meanwhile President Harding was losing his complacency. The large-hearted Rotarian who had opened the White House grounds to the public on March 4, 1921, was now being betrayed by his native kindness, his trustfulness, his inability to think evil of anybody. Soon the first evidences of corruption appeared among the little coterie of men around the President. Colonel Charles R. Forbes, a glib and plausible adventurer whom Harding had too hastily appointed head of the Veterans' Bureau, became enmeshed in a net of scandal and eventually, on February 15, 1923, resigned, leaving a trail of graft behind him. His closest assistant, Charles F. Cramer, committed suicide less than three weeks later. The notorious Jess Smith, Attorney General Daugherty's parasite and handyman, also fell into difficulties and took his own life on May 30.[12] For Harding, who was personally honest, these disillusionments, one upon the other, were devastating, and he showed his despondency in his manner. As yet the newspapers had not realized the full significance of what had happened, but the President was well aware that more revelations were to come.

Meanwhile information was leaking slowly out regarding the Teapot Dome oil scandals, and Harding reluctantly perceived that he had been betrayed by some of those in his own cabinet. The full story has been told by other writers and does not need repetition here; the important fact is that Albert B. Fall, Secretary of the In-

---

[12] For a picturesque and accurate account of Jess Smith's career, see Mark Sullivan, *Our Times,* Volume VI, pp. 226ff. Daugherty's own defense of Smith may be found in his *The Inside Story of the Harding Tragedy,* pp. 245ff., but is completely untrustworthy.

terior, was clearly involved in a conspiracy with a group of men interested in oil to steal America's oil reserves. Denby, the Secretary of the Navy, had been persuaded to induce the President — who was quite ignorant of the sinister influences behind the move — to sign an executive order transferring the control of the Naval Petroleum Reserves to the Department of the Interior. Then, by various ingenious devices and with the assistance of Fall's authority, leases were signed for the exploitation of the oil reserve lands, and Fall was duly rewarded for his share in the plot. Out of sheer loyalty to his official family, Harding, on June 7, 1922, announced that Denby's action in transferring control of the oil lands to the Secretary of the Interior had his approval. But the Senate investigating committee, with the austere and just Thomas J. Walsh, of Montana, as Chairman, went at once to work, and soon disquieting rumors drifted out to be whispered in club dining rooms and private gatherings. Although Walsh's first public hearing was not held for eighteen months, — on October 25, 1923, — the President had been aware before his death of the indefensible acts which were being uncovered.[13]

To add to these misfortunes the President had his own private troubles, for some of his indiscretions were returning to plague him. It is not strange that his face looked drawn and his eyes seemed puzzled, and that he was restless and distraught. He had thought that the Presidency would be a pleasant experience. Now he found himself betrayed by supporters who were using him for their own selfish aggrandizement. No one will ever reveal all the worries which the President had to face during the spring of 1923. But he was far from well. His blood pressure was high and getting higher under the strain, and other symptoms had appeared which had caused his physician, Dr. Sawyer, to warn him. When he set out on June 20, 1923, in the private car "Superb" for a trip to the West Coast and Alaska, he was a disappointed, debilitated, and tense man who could not, even on what was called a vacation trip, escape from his troubles.

It was obvious on the railroad journey across the continent that the President was not in a relaxed mood. Preoccupied and irritable, he insisted on playing bridge at every leisure moment, and he could not sleep. The whole trip was, indeed, a mad performance, for Harding, physically ailing though he was, made eighty-five public speeches from June 20 to July 31, an average of more than two a day. On the

[13] Frederick L. Allen's *Only Yesterday*, Chapter VI, has an interesting narrative of the scandals of the Harding administration. Samuel Hopkins Adams's novel, *Revelry*, presents in fictional form, very much exaggerated, the current gossip about Harding's private life. Another more careful version is to be found in the same writer's biography of Harding, *The Incredible Era*.

some dentistry done at an office in Woodstock. He attended a conference of New England governors held at Poland Spring, where Channing H. Cox urged him to run for the Senate. "No," replied Coolidge. "If I don't run for Vice President again I won't run for anything." As the news of Harding's illness became serious in tone, newspapermen settled down at Ludlow to be near at hand in case of a crisis. On Monday, July 30, Mr. Stearns wrote from Swampscott to Foster: —

There is a great deal of anxious excitement here today. It seems that President Harding in Alaska was taken with what seemed to be ptomaine poisoning. He seemed to be getting the better of it, but when he arrived at San Francisco the attack came on again, complicated, as near as we can find out, with a heart attack. The rumor has been flying around all day today that the President had died. The last and most authentic report we have is that he is very seriously sick, but not critical. I think there is a good deal of anxiety about him. . . . The Coolidges are still at Plymouth. We rather expect them to arrive at Swampscott Sunday or Monday.

Coolidge saw no Sunday newspaper and actually did not learn of the President's serious illness until Monday morning, incredible though this may seem.

On Wednesday, August 1, the Vice President had his picture taken driving a hay rake and also pitched some hay in rather amateurish fashion. He told the lingering newspapermen that he might go to Swampscott the next morning or might possibly linger in Plymouth until Saturday.

On Thursday the reports of the President's condition were reassuring, and Coolidge spent the afternoon doing a job of tree surgery, cleaning out the dead wood of an old maple with a hatchet and expecting on Friday to fill the cavity with cement. The day had been bright and warm, and the sun had gone down with hardly a cloud in the sky. The Coolidges both went to bed at nine o'clock without any premonitions. Coolidge himself wrote later, "I believed all danger past."

President Harding had already died at seven-thirty that evening, but because of the difference in time the telegram from his secretary, George B. Christian, Jr., did not reach Washington until some hours later; and the message was at once sent over the wires to White River Junction and from there telephoned to Bridgewater, the nearest station to Plymouth. W. A. Perkins received the momentous message and made two copies. He then went out with the news to find one of Coolidge's party. William H. Crawford, a news-paperman, had come to Plymouth to secure an interview with Coolidge and was spending the night in a boarding house in Bridge-water, awaiting an appointment for the following morning. He was awakened shortly after midnight by Erwin C. Geisser, Coolidge's stenographer, and Joseph N. McInerney, his chauffeur, who told him excitedly that the President had died. The three dressed with great speed and went tearing in the Vice President's car through the night over the winding road through the woods to the Notch. A small group of reporters staying at the hotel in Ludlow received the news at about the same time and also started in an automobile for the Coolidge homestead, but McInerney won the race by about three minutes. He and his companions knocked at the door, and Colonel Coolidge, a poor sleeper, lighted a kerosene lamp and came to greet the unexpected callers. Coolidge himself continued the story: —

I was awakened by my father coming up the stairs calling my name. I noticed that his voice trembled. As the only times I had ever observed that before were when death had visited our family, I knew that some-thing of the gravest nature had occurred . . . . He had been the first to address me as President of the United States. It was the culmination of the lifelong desire of a father for the success of his son.

There was a stark simplicity about the scene which followed that accentuated its natural dramatic quality. Colonel Coolidge slept in a room on the first floor, off the dining room, at the back of the house. The Vice President, after reading the official telegram handed him by his father, washed in the china bowl, took about fifteen minutes to dress carefully in a dark suit with a black tie, and knelt there in the bedroom to pray. Then he walked slowly down the narrow stairs, with Mrs. Coolidge following close behind him, to the dining room. This room, soon to become so notable in American history, was about seventeen feet in length and fourteen feet wide. At the opposite end from the stairway were three bay windows. One door opened out to the piazza, and other doors led to the kitchen, to Colonel John's bed-room, and to the little used parlor. It was a low-studded room, only about eight feet in height, with a wallpaper of embossed gilt, some-what faded by time. It was the room which the family used most, the natural place of assembly, the room in which Calvin's sister and step-mother had died, and in which, as Calvin recollected, his own mother had sat or reclined during her invalid years. In the centre was the dining-room table covered with a red tablecloth. At the moment it was

CALVIN COOLIDGE REPAIRING A TREE AT PLYMOUTH NOTCH
ON THE DAY BEFORE HE BECAME PRESIDENT

illuminated rather dimly by a kerosene lamp.[14] The other furnishings were unimpressive — a piano, a large wood stove, a small side table bearing a few old books and magazines, two rocking chairs and two straight chairs with fretted backs, and a well-worn reddish Wilton rug. On the walls were a few simple pictures inherited from previous generations. It was like the dining room of many a well-to-do farmer in that section of Vermont — and, as a matter of fact, better furnished and better arranged than any in that vicinity. As a setting for the events which were impending, it was perfect.

Meanwhile several newspapermen had arrived from Ludlow, and the room was filling up. Coolidge read a second official telegram, meanwhile making no remarks. The telephone company had hurriedly sent a crew to set up a temporary wire so that communication could be established direct with Washington. Mrs. Coolidge was seated on the arm of a chair, with her hands clasped over her knees, and Colonel Coolidge was tiptoeing around the room. Soon the Honorable Porter H. Dale, Congressman from Vermont,[15] entered accompanied by Joseph H. Fountain, editor of the *Springfield Reporter,* representing the Associated Press. Suddenly Coolidge said, as if he had just made up his mind, "I will dictate a statement," and went out into the parlor with Geisser, who took the words of the President down directly on his typewriter. After writing a few lines of condolence in longhand to Mrs. Harding, the President dictated another message and soon came back with several copies for the press. It was the first act of his administration and read as follows: —

Reports have reached me, which I fear are correct, that President Harding is gone. The world has lost a great and good man. I mourn his loss. He was my Chief and friend.

It will be my purpose to carry out the policies which he has begun for the service of the American people and for meeting their responsibilities wherever they may arise.

For this purpose I shall seek the coöperation of all those who have been associated with the President during his term of office. Those who have given their efforts to assist him I wish to remain in office that

[14] Miss Aurora Pierce, the housekeeper, was much annoyed when the newspapers announced that the lamp was "old and greasy." It was, she said, old, but certainly not greasy. She and her helper, Bessie Pratt, slept through all the excitement and knew nothing of what had happened until they came down to get breakfast.

[15] Porter Hinman Dale, born in 1867, was admitted to the bar in 1896 and began the practice of law in his native village of Island Pond, Vermont. He served in the House of Representatives from March 4, 1915, until August 11, 1923, when he resigned and was elected the following autumn to the United States Senate. He and Coolidge were on intimate terms.

they may assist me. I have faith that God will direct the destinies of our nation.

It is my intention to remain here until I can obtain the correct form for the oath of office, which will be administered to me by my father, who is a notary public, if that will meet the necessary requirement. I expect to leave for Washington during the day.

Even those who were present at that dramatic scene differ in their recollection of precisely what happened. The reporters took the message as it was handed to them and made their way to Ludlow to file their stories. Soon the telephone was ready, and Coolidge talked both with his Secretary, "Ted" Clark, and with Mr. Hughes, the Secretary of State, who advised him of the form which the oath should take. Attorney General Daugherty also sent a telegram requesting Coolidge to take the oath immediately. Meanwhile Colonel Coolidge, after some seaching, had found a copy of the Constitution of the United States and had read Article II, Section 1, Paragraph 8, which gives the wording of the oath or affirmation, but does not specify by whom it shall be administered. Finally, however, Coolidge reached a decision. "Father," he asked, "are you still a notary?" "Yes, Cal," was the reply. "Then I want you to administer the oath." Colonel Coolidge, who meanwhile had gone out to the kitchen to shave and put on a collar and tie, returned and stood erect with his back to the porch, facing his son across the marble-topped table, which had been cleared except for two oil lamps and the copy of the Bible which had belonged to Coolidge's mother. The Vice President stood directly beneath a framed picture of himself on the wall. Between them was Mrs. Coolidge, and in the background were Dale, Geisser, Fountain, McInerney, Crawford, and L. L. Lane, a railway mailman who had accompanied Dale. Then Colonel Coolidge, adjusting his spectacles and clearing his throat, read the prescribed oath, "I do solemnly swear that I will faithfully execute the office of President of the United States and will, to the best of my ability, preserve, protect, and defend the Constitution of the United States." Calvin Coolidge repeated the words in a firm voice, with his right hand raised, added, "So help me God!" and then, by the glow of the lamps, signed the oath in triplicate. The time was precisely 2.47 A.M. As he laid his pen aside, and his father affixed the seal, he raised his head and glanced at Mrs. Coolidge, who still stood near by. Speaking no word, he nodded, and the two left the room. He was President of the United States.[16]

[16] The artist, Arthur Keller, went to Plymouth, painted the interior, made a sketch of Colonel Coolidge, and afterwards came to the White House and sketched

Colonel John Coolidge, now thoroughly awake, sat up all night, but the President went back to bed for a few hours of rest, and actually, according to his testimony, went to sleep. He had been struck by the fact that never in history before that time had a father administered to his son the qualifying oath of office which made him the chief magistrate of a nation. The scene might well, in its simplicity, have been contrasted with Napoleon's coronation or the elaborate ritual which accompanies the crowning of an English monarch in Westminster Abbey. It was indeed a solemn moment when so much power and obligation fell unexpectedly on the shoulders of a single man. A candidate elected in normal course to the Presidency has ample time in which to adjust himself. Calvin Coolidge had none. Some years later, when the artist, Charles Hopkinson, was painting the President's portrait, he was discouraged by the lack of animation in his face and finally asked, "Mr. Coolidge, what was the first thought that came into your mind when you were told that Mr. Harding was dead and that the Presidency was yours?" Thinking a moment, Mr. Coolidge, without changing his expression in the slightest, said, "I thought I could swing it."

Mr. Coolidge may well have thought that he could "swing it." He had served a long apprenticeship in subordinate offices, had learned the science of government, both theoretical and practical, and had mastered the technique of effective administration. As he repeatedly said later, "I was ready." His emotions through that August night and morning must have been mingled — some pride and some humility, some faith and yet a little natural timidity, some satisfaction and perhaps some regret. But everything about the scene was honest. Calvin Coolidge had won the prize which had never come to Clay and Webster and Calhoun and Blaine and Hughes and Root. Of course it might have been overwhelming. Instead he conducted himself with perfect dignity, with no hypocrisy or arrogance or impropriety, and moved with definiteness and certainty from the moment when he decided to have the oath administered then and there. Democracy has never had a finer triumph than when great power was conferred under such plain surroundings.

On the evening of August 2, the Coolidges had planned to make a visit to Frank W. Stearns, at Swampscott. On the morning of

---

the faces of the other participants. Coolidge said that although the likenesses were not good, everything in relation to the painting was correct. Guido Boer also has painted the scene, rather badly, and the *Boston Sunday Post* published a composite photograph which is not accurate in detail. An excellent account of the incident appeared in the *Ladies' Home Journal* for April 1924.

August 3, he was President of the United States. He rose at seven, as usual, packed hurriedly, and then motored with Mrs. Coolidge thirty-seven miles to Rutland, where they took a train for Troy. But before he left the Notch, the President stopped for a moment at his mother's grave and said a short prayer. In his *Autobiography* he wrote: —

It had been a comfort to me during my boyhood when I was troubled to be near her last resting place, even in the dead of night. Some way, that morning, she seemed very near to me.

When the train reached the Grand Central Station, Frank W. Stearns, who had been in New York at the Commodore Hotel attending a meeting of the Amherst College Trustees, was on the platform to greet the President, and so were "Ted" Clark, who had come on from Washington, and Benjamin F. Felt. Mr. Felt, who had heard the news and telephoned Mr. Stearns about it at four o'clock that morning, received later a telephone from Mrs. Stearns telling him that Mr. Coolidge wished him to go to a clothes closet in the Hotel Touraine, get his silk hat, and bring it with him to New York. Mr. Felt found the hat in a leather box, guarded it carefully all the way, and handed it to Mr. Coolidge as soon as the train arrived. It was the one which the latter wore throughout the subsequent proceedings. Felt was rewarded by an invitation to join the Presidential entourage and proceed with it to the capital.

As soon as the train pulled into Washington, the Coolidges were greeted by the members of the cabinet who were in the city and went at once to their customary suite in the New Willard. On the following morning, Calvin Coolidge, whose motto, according to the *Transcript*, should have been *Semper Paratus,* was busy with the responsibilities of his high office. There had been a general feeling that, under Harding, the Republican Party had been sinking lower and lower into the mire. As Calvin Coolidge took his place, a mood of quiet optimism prevailed. The American people were prepared to trust him and to accept his leadership.

XV

The First Term As President

MORE than once as Vice President, Calvin Coolidge, frankly bored, had complained to Frank W. Stearns of his "barren life." The formal dinners and social gayety which Mrs. Coolidge so much enjoyed gave little thrill to her husband, who had no compensating functions in government to keep him diverted. With his accession to the Presidency, however, monotony vanished, and he found himself confronted with innumerable obligations. The man who the week before had been carrying his mail in one hand back from the Plymouth Post Office was soon to receive more than four thousand letters a day. He was to be called upon for decisions, harassed by petitions, and beseiged by office seekers and "publicity hounds." Whatever he said or did was indelibly recorded. Thomas Hardy once wrote, "When the eyes of a multitude beat like waves upon a countenance, they seem to wear away its individuality." Coolidge's emotions had always been masked, but he soon learned under the White House limelight to avoid even a smile which might get him or someone else into trouble. Only under strong temptation did his impish tendencies break through his routine conventionality.

To some observers Coolidge may have seemed, as he did to Mark Sullivan, a "fragile figure," with his still boyish features, blue eyes, and blond head. But the head was a wise one. Those who had been intimate with him read the newspaper stories on the morning of Friday, August 3, with the feeling that he would not be bewildered, that he would conduct himself with discretion, and that the nation was safe under his guidance. On Saturday morning the President met some two hundred newspapermen in the New Willard Hotel to tell them that everything must await the plans for Harding's funeral; he had already requested Mrs. Harding to remain in the White House as long as she cared to do so, and he shortly prepared a proclamation ordering the usual period of mourning. General Pershing was astounded to have the President send for him and issue instructions regarding the funeral procession. To an officer who had been in the habit of directing troops the experience was unique, but he commented on it with great good humor. William H. Taft, after a call on August 7, reported that the President "looked cool and self-possessed." As the train carrying the body of the dead President moved across the continent, the mood of the nation was one of unrestrained grief, for Harding had been a friendly, generous soul, and the full extent of the administration delinquencies had not yet been brought to light.[1] After the body had lain in state in the rotunda of the Capitol and services had been held in the East Room of the White House, the coffin was taken to Marion, Ohio, for interment. The Coolidges accompanied the funeral party and paid their last respects to the dead President in his home town. The burial took place on August 10.

On the following afternoon, Mrs. Harding returned to the White House to attend to the packing and moving of her possessions, and the Coolidges dined with her that evening. Five days later she left to spend a week or two with her friends, the "Ned" McLeans, just outside of Washington, but some cleaning had to be done in the Executive Mansion and the new President and his wife did not move in until the afternoon of August 21. During this interval, they continued to make their headquarters at the New Willard, and a vivid contemporary account of what went on there is found in a latter of August 28, from Mr. Stearns to his son: —

We had a suite of rooms next to the Coolidges. The hallways were filled with newspaper men from early morning until late at night. They tried to make me talk about Mr. Coolidge. At first I refused to say anything, but finally was persuaded by Ted Clark, Jimmy Reynolds, and others that they certainly would write something and that I had better try to get them to paint a true picture rather than an imaginary one. I also found out that the one thing they wanted to know was who controlled Mr. Coolidge. The only person they could think of was myself. They seemed to have no other person in mind, so I set about convincing them that I did not control him. I think the public has the picture quite correctly and they understand that if I do not control him nobody does, and that therefore he comes to the Presidency freer of entanglements than any man who has ever come into that office.

Mr. and Mrs. Coolidge at once notified Mrs. Harding that the White

---

[1] George B. Christian, writing in *Current History* for September 1923, said, "The accurate historian will rank Warren G. Harding as one of the really great Presidents of the United States." I recall attending a memorial meeting in Dublin, New Hampshire, at which Harding was hailed by highly intelligent persons as a statesman of the first rank, and actually compared with the martyred Lincoln.

House was hers as long as it was convenient for her to use it to pack up her belongings and move out. A few days before I came away they moved into the White House and I was their first guest, taking dinner with them that night. The next morning your mother arrived, and we spent two days and two nights at the White House as their first guests. Their next guests were Ambassador Harvey and his wife.

One of Coolidge's first acts after reaching Washington was to have Justice A. A. Hoehling, of the Supreme Court of the District of Columbia, administer to him a second oath of office. This ceremony took place in the hotel, without any publicity. The validity of the original oath had been questioned by Attorney General Daugherty, on the ground that Colonel John C. Coolidge, who was merely a state official, had authority to swear in only officers of the State of Vermont. The President also seized a few minutes to write in longhand, on black-bordered mourning stationery, a letter to his old friend, James Lucey, the shoemaker of Gothic Street, in Northampton, with whom he had talked so much in his early days as an aspiring local politician. The letter, afterwards much publicized, read as follows: —

Not often do I see you or write you but I want you to know that, if it were not for you, I should not be here, and I want to tell you how much I love you.

Do not work too much now and try to enjoy yourself in your well-earned leisure of age.

It was like Calvin Coolidge, with his deep underlying vein of sentiment, to think at the moment of his rise to great power of those who had been nearest to him when he was obscure.

Although Coolidge had not hitherto joined any church, he had attended services with some regularity in Northampton and also in Washington, at the First Congregational Church, of which the Reverend Jason N. Pierce, Amherst, '02, was the pastor. During his Vice Presidential period, Coolidge had occupied by invitation the minister's pew, not very far forward and therefore inconspicuous; he had also seen much of the Pierces in the capital and had been able to extend to them many courtesies. Once, after an Amherst gathering at the Cosmos Club, the Vice President talked to Gilbert H. Grosvenor, President of the National Geographic Society, about Dr. Pierce's church and urged him to attend it, saying that the sermons were the best in Washington.[2] Before leaving Rutland,

[2] "President Coolidge As I Knew Him," in the *Congregationalist*, January 19, 1933. This article contains several interesting stories about the President.

Coolidge had telegraphed to Dr. Pierce to meet him at the station, and the two had a conference shortly afterward. On the Sunday after he had taken the oath as President, Coolidge went to the familiar church on the corner of 10th and G streets, in the heart of the downtown business section, and remained for the holy communion service. When Coolidge had done this, Dr. Pierce invited the President to unite with the church, received his acceptance, and then persuaded the members to vote him into their fellowship without making a public profession of faith.[8] Mrs. Coolidge was elected an associate member at the same time. In his *Autobiography* he said regarding this incident : —

Had I been approached in the usual way to join the church after I became President, I should have feared that such action might appear to be a pose, and should have hesitated to accept. From what might have been a misguided conception I was thus saved by some influence which I had not anticipated.

Coolidge's frequent references to his being but "an instrument in the hand of God" confirm the impression derived from other sources that he was a sincerely devout man. Although his beliefs may not have been entirely orthodox, he did have faith in some Divine Power controlling the destinies of the universe. He said in an address, October 20, 1925, before the National Council of Congregational Churches, "I do not know of any source of more power other than that which comes from religion . . . except through the influence of religion." Dr. Pierce noted particularly, after Coolidge's elevation to the Presidency, a deepening of his sense of dependence on God. When J. Richard Sneed asked him, "Do you pray in every crisis?" he nodded affirmatively. Gamaliel Bradford, in his thoughtful and penetrating essay on Coolidge, comments particularly on this phase of his character : —

Turn over his writings and speeches, and on page after page you will come across religious allusions of some kind. . . . It is impossible to question the absolute sincerity and profound conviction of his religious attitude. It is not only believed but lived, and no man ever carried his convictions into his life with more fervor and reverent piety than Calvin Coolidge. But the attitude is simply that of the Christian, not to say Fundamentalist, orthodoxy of the middle nineteenth century, or earlier. It is the unshaken belief in an anthropomorphic God, who

[3] On October 18, 1923, the delegates of the National Council of Congregational Churches, meeting in Springfield, unanimously elected Coolidge as Honorary Moderator.

THE PRESIDENT

guides the destinies of nations and also the petty affairs of individuals, and to whom it is of real importance what you or I or Calvin Coolidge may do or not do. . . . Now this matter of religion, with Calvin Coolidge, is not a side-issue. It is vital.

I find myself unable to agree with Bradford in his insistence that the "theological fabric" meant so much to Coolidge. A certain kind of mysticism, perhaps the survival of earlier memories, perhaps the natural consequence of meditation on the universe, did influence his thoughts and writings; but he had little of the unreflective evangelicalism of a man like William Jennings Bryan. Nor was he inclined to dogmatism. Like so many men who have attained leadership, — like Webster and Lincoln and Woodrow Wilson, — he had an acute sense of his personal responsibility to God. On the other hand, I cannot discover that creeds or rituals ever claimed his attention. He approved of the Church as an institution, but his own religion was primarily a matter between his God and him.

Rather against his will, Coolidge found himself compelled to accept certain forms and ceremonies surrounding his high office. His pew was moved far enough to the front so that Secret Service men could watch him from all parts of the church. The congregation stood when he arrived, and the pastor invariably escorted him from his pew to the door when the benediction had been pronounced. But even a church did not repress his sense of humor. Once he said to Dr. Pierce, "I attended the dedication of All Souls Church last week and heard your namesake preach." "I know you must have heard a fine sermon," Pierce replied. As the clergyman turned to speak to Mrs. Coolidge, the President stopped, nudged his arm, and chuckled, "It was two sermons!"

The confidence in Calvin Coolidge felt by his close friends was reflected in the undisturbed attitude of Wall Street, — that sensitive seismograph of national business psychology, — in the optimistic comment of conservative leaders, and in the praise even of Democratic newspapers. He was called "a quiet, unobtrusive man, trained through two decades of public service for this emergency"; and the *Philadelphia Public Ledger* said, "It is almost as though he had schooled himself for the Presidency from the very start of his career." William Allen White's *Emporia Gazette* described him as "this runty, aloof, little man, who quacks through his nose when he speaks." Here and there in the radical press a discordant note was sounded. The socialistic *New York Call* characterized him as "probably the man of smallest calibre who has ever been made President of the United States." The *Nation* published an article on August 15, headed "Calvin Coolidge: Made by a Myth," in which were the following sentences: —

And now the Presidency sinks low indeed. We doubt if ever before it has fallen into the hands of a man so cold, so narrow, so reactionary, so uninspiring, and so unenlightened, or one who has done less to earn it, than Calvin Coolidge. . . . Every reactionary may today rejoice; in Calvin Coolidge he realizes his ideal, and every liberal may be correspondingly downcast.

But such prejudiced comments were conspicuous because they were so rare. On the other side, a Socialist meeting in New York on the first Sunday of his administration howled down an anti-Coolidge resolution with cries of "Give him a chance!" Naturally his career was reviewed in newspapers and magazines with special reference to "Coolidge luck." He was pointed out as a Favorite of Fortune, a Child of Destiny. But the real answer to the *Nation's* attack was the justly famous editorial in the *Boston Herald* for Friday, September 14, written by Frank W. Buxton, which was awarded the Pulitzer Prize for the best editorial of the year 1923.[4] It is worth printing in full: —

Who made Calvin Coolidge?

Margaret Foley, of course. When Levi H. Greenwood was President of the Massachusetts Senate, he opposed woman suffrage. She opposed his reëlection in his district and prevailed. Senator Coolidge became President Coolidge on Beacon Hill, and the signals were set clear for the road to the Governorship.

Who made Calvin Coolidge?

Edwin U. Curtis, of course. When he was a sick man in that old brick building at the dead end of Pemberton Square, the heedless policemen went out on strike to the refrain of "Hail, hail, the gang's all here!" The sick man showed the strength of the stalwart, until finally Governor Coolidge sent a telegram to Samuel Gompers that tapped its way into national prominence and is today a sort of magna carta of the people's rights.

Who made Calvin Coolidge?

James Lucey, the Northampton cobbler, of course. No explanation or argument is necessary here, but merely a reminder. The *Herald*

---

[4] This editorial was reprinted in the *Literary Digest* for May 31, 1924, and has been frequently quoted since that time. In commenting on it Mr. Buxton writes me, too modestly, "I didn't think it was much good, and was tempted to throw it away."

published a facsimile a few days ago of President Coolidge's letter to him, which said, "If it were not for you, I should not be here."

Who made Calvin Coolidge?

Frank W. Stearns, of course. With as close an approximation to second sight as we now expect in these days, and with an ability to see around the corner years before Einstein told us how rays of light are bent, this substantial, self-made, self-respecting Boston merchant, with his quiet sense of obligation to the community, discerned qualities which hardly anybody else glimpsed. To go to the Republican Convention he left a Governor, only to come back to pay his respects to a potential Vice-President.

Who made Calvin Coolidge?

Senator Crane, of course. He made Coolidge, by showing him, in precept and practice, the way of wisdom and by vouching for him in high places where his chance say-so was as good as his oath and bond. To the younger man he gave that mixture of personal attachment and respect of which he was none too prodigal, but always of mighty advantage to the few who won it.

Who made Calvin Coolidge?

The Republican Party of Massachusetts, of course, a canny organization, with some Bourbonism, some democracy, some vision, some solid traditions, and no end of genuine appreciation of the merits of trustworthy men. It always lined up behind him solidly, even when he displayed that reticence which to the unknowing was some evidence of ingratitude, and to the knowing was merely Coolidgeism.

Who made Calvin Coolidge?

The people of Massachusetts, of course. They took him at more than his own modest valuation, whether he wanted to be a town officer or Governor. They had that which thousands call a blind faith in him. More thousands called it a passionate intuition.

Who made Calvin Coolidge?

His mother, of course, who endowed him with her own attributes; a father that taught him prudential ways with all the quiet vigor of the old Greeks who preached moderation in everything; his school and his college; his classmate, Dwight Morrow, and his guest of a day or two ago at the White House, William F. Whiting.

Who made Calvin Coolidge? Calvin Coolidge, of course! From the reflective shoemaker and furious Miss Foley to the complacent Frank W. Stearns and the watchful and discerning senator from Dalton, came some of the makings, but the man himself had the essentials of greatness. Give another man those same foes and friends and he might still be as far away from the White House as most sons of Vermont.

The American people, in so far as their views could be expressed, were well satisfied. He was called by the *Literary Digest* the "High Priest of Stability," and it was stated that his prescription for the country's ills was confidence, reassurance, and optimism. The ordinary citizen, the mythical Man in the Street, liked what he was able to learn about Coolidge, and believed him to be honest, able, and well-equipped for the Presidency.

In Massachusetts, Coolidge had always been given what is professionally known as a "good press." At the first regular conference in the White House office, he greeted the newspapermen seated at his desk, wearing a dark blue, double-breasted suit, with a mourning band on the arm. His desk was clear, as it usually was, for he was a quick and easy worker, quite different from Harding. When the correspondents had gathered four or five deep around him, Coolidge stood up and told them that the executive offices would always be open to provide them with information. He then picked up the little pile of written questions which had been handed to him and answered each one briefly. He was completely master of the situation, as if he had been replying to similar interrogations all his life,[5] and even paused to tell an amusing story of something that had happened at the cabinet meeting. One of the old-timers who called for a cheer for the President had his suggestion vetoed by others who realized that such action would be in poor taste with Mrs. Harding still in the White House. Coolidge, who overheard phases of the whispered debate, commented, "Seems to be opposition to my administration already." The applause did come later.[6]

Coolidge set out too hurriedly for Washington to bring with him any attendants or clerks. Instead of choosing either Mr. Felt or Mr. Clark, as had been expected, he appointed as his Secretary Campbell Bascom Slemp, of Virginia, long a Congressman (1909–1923), and a practical politician, with a wide acquaintance in Washington and a background of legal training and experience. To

[5] Stearns wrote his son, Foster, August 28, "It was interesting to see the President after he had been on duty five minutes. No one seeing him would have supposed he had not been there fifty years in the same place. He was unusually cordial to everybody but said little more than he usually says. Everything he said took the form of orders."

[6] George McAdams published an interesting account of this first newspaper conference in the *New York Sunday Times*. See Green, 188ff. One enthusiastic correspondent rushed up to General Sawyer, Harding's physician, who had a gray Van Dyke beard, exclaiming, "How do you do, Senator Lodge?" This brought from the President "a cough and two loud chuckles."

Coolidge, still politically a provincial, Slemp was of much assistance, for he had been called, with some justice, "the Republican patronage boss of the South." The hostile *Nation,* commenting on the choice, said : —

So far as the President is concerned we are not surprised by the appointment. Our guess is that Mr. Coolidge will not be found lacking in knowledge of, or skill in, the political game, and that he will be an exceedingly astute candidate for the Presidential nomination next year unless his own mistakes and the trend of the times compel the leaders to seek a new "leader." Mr. Coolidge rose as a Massachusetts politician through the party machine. Any one who has done that need never be accused of being a tenderfoot or an idealist in politics.

During the relatively peaceful months of the late summer and early autumn, with no Congress on his hands, Coolidge was able to survey the situation, to make the necessary selection of people for his personal staff, to call in advisers from various groups and sections, and to talk with Frank W. Stearns, William M. Butler, and others about the future. His first appointment was that of Lieutenant Colonel Clarence O. Sherrill to be his Military Aide; and he soon requested Dr. Sawyer, who had been Harding's physician, to remain with the new administration in the same capacity. Before very long General Sawyer resigned and was replaced by Major, later Colonel, James F. Coupal, who had attended him when he was Vice President. In general Coolidge hated to be rushed. He was in a new and somewhat unfamiliar position, and he did not wish to make mistakes.

The President at once notified the members of Harding's cabinet that he desired to retain them. He had been sitting around the cabinet table with them and knew them well — their weaknesses as well as their strength. Hughes and New were in Washington to greet him, and Denby appeared within a few days. As they met, Hughes said, "Mr. President, there is nothing to do but close the ranks and go ahead."

Weeks, as Secretary of War, presented something of a problem, for, although he came from Massachusetts, he had not been close to the Coolidge group of Republicans. When the President consulted Stearns on the matter in the summer of 1923, the latter advised that Weeks be retained. Coolidge then said, "All right — but if he is to stay in the cabinet, Mr. Butler and you must pay him such attention as is proper to a Massachusetts cabinet member." Stearns and Butler lost no time in calling on Weeks. As they rose to go, Weeks remarked, "Sitting here as I do, I meet a great many people and have a chance to do a good deal. What I say to people is, 'If Mr. Coolidge makes good, he will be the logical candidate.'" At this point Stearns noticed that Butler was about to explode, but he finally calmed himself and replied, "Well, John, when you have made up your mind whether he is making good, let me know, won't you?" [7]

The two vulnerable members of the cabinet were Denby, who was slow-witted and gullible, and Daugherty, whom few people trusted. But the storm was not to break over their heads until some months later. Denby was not called by the Senate Investigating Committee until October 25; Doheny was not summoned until December 3 and did not actually appear until January 24, 1924; Fall did not testify until February 2, 1924 — an ill and broken man; and not until that same day did Congress pass a joint resolution calling on the President to appoint special counsel for prosecuting the oil scandals independent of the Department of Justice. Just how fully Coolidge was aware when he became President of the blunders and indiscretions of Denby and Daugherty will probably never be known.

Although the cabinet for the moment remained intact, the control of affairs changed with startling rapidity.[8] The senatorial leaders who had dictated Harding's nomination had no means of approach to Coolidge and could not understand how to deal with him. The "Ohio Gang," easy-going, vulgar, and even sinister, no longer had access to the White House. They had paid little attention to Coolidge while he was Vice President, and now they were completely out of the political picture. It was obviously impossible to adopt with Coolidge, who was almost frigid in his rectitude,[9] the tactics which had seduced his predecessor. The only man on the inside was Frank W. Stearns, who was almost as noncommittal and fully as incorruptible as his chief. It is not strange that the grafters and political manipulators who had flocked to Washington under Harding now saw that their day of glory was over. Someone looked over the books that Coolidge had been reading in the New Willard: the Bible, works on history, economics, the tariff, and our insular possessions; Norton's *Constitution of the United States;* a two-volume life of Whitelaw Reid

---

[7] Since 1915 Weeks had suffered from serious heart trouble, and he was far from a well man in 1923. He retired on October 13, 1925, and died in the following year.

[8] One member of the cabinet is reported to have said after their first meeting under Coolidge, "For the Lord's sake, how could we have sat twice a week with this man for two years and never have known him? We can see that it is up to us to get right out and hustle."

[9] A New England newspaper editor who dined with Coolidge in December reported that it was a relief to have in the White House a man with convictions.

— all of them solid and substantial treatises. This was a man who took his job seriously.

Although Mr. Stearns was in Washington until August 24, and, after that, returned frequently to what came to be regarded as his suite in the White House, the President did not, it seems, discuss everything with him. Coolidge received as a gift in 1926 a copy of Colonel House's *Intimate Papers,* and glancing through it said, "Mr. Stearns, an unofficial adviser to a President of the United States is not a good thing and is not provided for in our form of government." Stearns replied, "Did I ever try to advise you?" "No," was the answer, "but I thought I had better tell you." The humor in this conversation could have escaped neither of the participants. Once the President said nothing to Stearns for almost two weeks, even at meals. On the morning when he first took possession of the White House, he sent five times for his friend to come to the executive offices. Each time Mr. Stearns obeyed promptly, went into the inner sanctum, walked around the room once or twice, and then went out, without eliciting a word from the President. "A dog would have done equally well," said Mr. Stearns. "The President was lonesome in his new quarters and just wanted somebody familiar around." When Stearns had returned to New England, he wrote: —

I take it Mrs. Coolidge and you understand that the house at Swampscott is at your disposal whenever it is your pleasure to come, — all of you. I don't want to interfere with your plans in any way, but I don't want you to think that we have any other plan than to be ready for your family whenever it is your pleasure to be there.

There can be no doubt that, even when paying little attention to him, Coolidge liked to have Mr. Stearns near by; and Mr. Stearns was also the perfect "buffer" against unwelcome intrusion. Nobody was more familiar to the reporters than that sturdy figure, with his deliberate speech and inevitable cigar, and he kept in touch with nearly everybody of influence in the vicinity of Washington. He saved the President no small amount of trouble, for Mr. Stearns was a realist whose judgment could be relied upon.

The whole mood of the White House may be said to have altered within two or three weeks. The Hardings had been "just folks," accustomed to having old friends "drop in," and during their residence the Executive Mansion, accustomed to changes, had an atmosphere like that of Sinclair Lewis's Zenith. Harding had not abandoned his Marion habits and was usually ready to play golf in his favorite four-ball match, to join in a quiet poker game over which his wife, known to her intimates as the Duchess, presided, or even to sip a highball in the privacy of his White House bedroom. Coolidge, although he tried riding horseback and even experimented with a mechanical horse for mild exercise,[10] had almost no parlor recreations and no fondness for games of either chance or skill. His charming wife was there to relieve the tension and put visitors at their ease, but she, like him, had too much native dignity to lapse into the casual tolerance of the Hardings.

The new First Lady, adapting herself with facility to the exigencies of her absorbing occupation, was a universal favorite and played her part as well as any previous mistress of the White House. The Chief Justice kissed her hand on the funeral train going out to Marion, Ohio, — to show his "foreign training," — and found her "very nice." From her early morning interview with Mrs. Elizabeth Jaffray, the housekeeper, until her final word later in the day with her secretary, Miss "Polly" Randolph, she was busy — meeting callers by appointment, planting trees, laying cornerstones, attending the scores of more or less official functions. The domestic staff in the White House goes along from generation to generation, and the Coolidges retained, as a matter of course, Irwin H. ("Ike") Hoover, the Chief Usher, Brooks, the colored valet, and other personages familiar with the daily routine.[11] The Coolidges were the first beneficiaries of a new law, passed under the Harding administration, by which the government defrayed the expense of all official entertaining; and the staff was accordingly much enlarged. In all their personal expenditures the Coolidges were careful, although not penurious, and the accounts were systematically checked. Mr. Coolidge paid all his bills himself and probably saved money while he was in the White House — possibly as much as $50,000 a year. It was rumored that when a messenger brought him his first salary check, he pondered it carefully, put it in his vest pocket, and said drily, "Call again."

Unlike the second Mrs. Wilson and Mrs. Harding, Mrs. Coolidge did not discuss government affairs with her husband and certainly

[10] On February 14, 1924, Representative Vinson, a Democrat from Kentucky, insisted on reading to the House of Representatives some ridiculous doggerel verses on "Cal's Hobby Horse." Representative Luce, of Massachusetts, objected to this ridicule of the President, but Bertrand H. Snell, temporary presiding officer, would not prevent the reading.

[11] Mrs. Jaffray published in 1927 her *Secrets of the White House;* Irwin H. Hoover's *Forty-two Years in the White House* came out in 1934, after his death in the previous year; and Miss Randolph's *Presidents and First Ladies* appeared in 1936. All three volumes have a gossipy flavor, but each one has interesting items to contribute to the story of Calvin Coolidge.

PLOWING AT THE COOLIDGE FARM

made no attempt to influence him in his decisions. She took pains to keep her own social life separated from his business, and often did not know until the last minute what his plans for her were. Never has a First Lady been more discreet, more content to remain in the background, more removed from political intrigue.

Mrs. Coolidge occupied the southwest corner suite on the third floor of the White House; and the President's bedroom, dressing room, and bath were next to it on the south side. In Mrs. Coolidge's own personal sitting room was the famous Lincoln bed, with its massive gold crown, but the Coolidges always slept in another bed in the President's chamber. On the same south side, overlooking the gardens, were the President's study, the Oval Room, — known as the library, — and the suite on the southeast corner always reserved for Mr. and Mrs. Stearns.

The President fell readily into an established routine, from which he seldom deviated. Although he was an honorary member of the Chevy Chase Club, the Columbia Country Club, and others in the suburbs, he never utilized the excellent golf courses at these clubs. He was out of bed at six-thirty each morning, shaved himself, strolled for a few minutes around the grounds,[12] and returned for breakfast with Mrs. Coolidge in their bedroom at eight o'clock. When he first arrived in Washington as President, he alarmed the Secret Service men by taking early morning walks but, finding himself mercilessly beset by crafty patronage seekers who offered themselves as companions, was compelled to abandon the practice. According to the newspapers, he once gave William Wrigley, Jr., and Fred Upham, Treasurer of the National Republican Committee, more strenuosity than they had bargained for on one of these excursions. But Coolidge had seldom since his boyhood walked more than one or two miles a day, and had not accustomed himself to heavy exercise or even to "daily dozens." It was not long before he had fallen back into his customary program of very moderate exercise, light eating, and plenty of rest and sleep.

After breakfast, Coolidge proceeded directly to his office, where he examined his mail, dictated the necessary correspondence, and remained until shortly before one o'clock, meeting appointments and sometimes shaking hands with a long line of visitors, — a process which he said that he enjoyed, — feeling that their greeting was

[12] On one snowy Sunday Dr. Pierce said to him, thinking of the broad walk around the White House grounds, "If there was a custom that every man had to shovel his own walk, some people who envy you, Mr. President, would hesitate to have your job." His reply was, "It's just one mile around the grounds. I paced it off last week."

"often a benediction." [13] After luncheon, if nothing official interfered, the President took a nap, sometimes for more than two hours. When by themselves, the Coolidges dined at seven o'clock. Mr. Coolidge rarely retired later than ten o'clock, — frequently somewhat earlier, — and often slept eleven hours a day. This practice was undoubtedly the survival of a habit formed at Plymouth, but it was also a wise attempt to conserve all his energy for what was important. With his lack of diverting avocations, it was hard for the President to keep away from business, and even on Sunday he was likely to step into the executive offices to glance at mail and see what was going on. As spring came on the Coolidges formed the habit of boarding the *Mayflower* each Sunday after church and going for a short cruise down the Potomac. When they went for the week-end, church services were held on the yacht.

"Ike" Hoover, an inveterate gossip, did not like Coolidge, and showed his animus in his somewhat ill-natured volume, *Forty-two Years in the White House*. In his survey of Presidents from Harrison to Franklin D. Roosevelt, he considered Coolidge the "least interesting" and complained that he never had a real conversation with him — a fact which perhaps explains the Head Usher's marked prejudice. According to Hoover, the President was often irritable and occasionally startled the household by his rages over matters of trifling significance. He was inclined to be autocratic in his manner, and had the reputation of being difficult to please. Having no "kitchen cabinet," no inner circle of advisers, he "went it alone in all things," and was consequently regarded by the people in the White House as a man of mystery. He was still indifferent to the attractions of the theatre, and looked positively unhappy when obliged to sit through a concert. The servants thought that he was "up to many odd things." They noticed that he permitted no one except Mrs. Coolidge and his son John to ride in an automobile with him and often set out for church alone in one car with Mr. Stearns by himself in the one following; that he called members of the staff by funny names which they often resented; that his whimsical humor took shape in practical jokes; and that he even sometimes rose from the dinner table after his dessert before all the guests had been served, thus embarrassing Mrs. Coolidge greatly. He showed an active interest in many of the small details of the White House, even inspected the ice boxes and criticized the menus, and actually once voiced a mild objection be-

[13] Coolidge once set a record at an Army and Navy Reception by shaking hands with 2096 persons between 9.05 and 10.00 in the evening, an average of about thirty-eight a minute.

cause Mrs. Jaffray had provided six hams for one dinner of sixty covers.

Many of the traits considered by the White House retinue to be eccentric were the result of habits acquired in the rural life of Plymouth Notch. Nobody there would have thought Calvin Coolidge queer because he liked to know what was going on in the kitchen. As for his irritability, it was principally due to the strain of the Presidential office on a sensitive nervous system. It should be added that, no matter what he felt, he simply did not possess the gift of saying a kind word here and there as he moved along or of expressing appreciation of special efforts made for his comfort. After attending a White House reception in December, Taft wrote, "Mrs. Coolidge looked very pretty and was most gracious. Coolidge is Coolidge, and he does the pump-handle work without much grace and without a great deal of enthusiasm." He did understand his own frailties and tried to guard against fatigue, never hurrying or allowing himself to be driven too hard by insistent Congressmen. When he felt jaded, he dallied with a jigsaw puzzle or even read a detective story. He was an abstemious eater and, during Prohibition, drank neither wine nor distilled liquors. His only self-indulgence was tobacco, and he smoked cigars, often of high-priced brands, in paper holders costing a cent each. Mr. Coolidge was an individualist, but the chatter of servants should not lead to any misconception.

Mrs. Jaffray has described Mr. Coolidge as "a silent and rather austere man with little or nothing to say." But the fact that he did not converse with the White House staff does not mean that he could not talk. John Bassett Moore, in discussing Coolidge's taciturnity, says rightly that it was characteristic rather than calculated, more often due to preoccupation or shyness than to deliberation. Many persons who sat down with him at this period found him almost garrulous, particularly on topics in which he was interested. Because he maintained a reserve with people who wanted to get something from him, they often left him chilled and disappointed. But he was always dignified and never failed to claim the respect which was due his position. When Will Rogers in an advertising program imitated his nasal voice over the radio so well that listeners actually thought it was the President's, Coolidge was much offended and refused to accept the humorist's apology. He dressed exceedingly well, with the proper attire for every occasion, and did not like it when some newspaperman spread the story that he had only two pairs of shoes. Whenever he appeared in public, he was highly conventional and knew precisely what was expected of him. Never cheap or vulgar or clumsy, he could be trusted to meet the demands of any occasion. Very few Presidents have mounted the national stage with more poise than he.

From the moment he arrived in the capital, Coolidge was besieged by important persons who wanted to see the new President. On Monday, August 6, he had appointments with Samuel Gompers and Frank Morrison, of the American Federation of Labor, with John T. Adams, of the National Republican Committee, and with John Hays Hammond, of the Coal Commission; and William M. Butler, whom Coolidge trusted, sat in at each of these conferences. For the remainder of the week the President devoted himself to the Harding funeral, but on Saturday he met the cabinet quite informally at the New Willard, and he called the first regular meeting for Tuesday, August 14. Meanwhile he had stopped at the executive offices and greeted the members of his staff. As soon as practicable he summoned various Republican leaders and learned their views. From Senator Lodge, at Nahant, he had some friendly letters, to which he responded with frankness tinged with discretion. Lodge even offered his assistance, volunteering to come to Washington if that seemed essential. On August 15, he wrote: —

I want to congratulate you on your success so far, which seems to me very marked. I think you have made a most excellent impression on the country in all ways. I have not a word of criticism or advice or suggestion in that respect.

The President had one immediate emergency to meet — a legacy from the previous administration. The *Boston Herald* had already pointed out that Coolidge would confront in his first weeks in office the biggest test of his career — the impending strike of the anthracite coal miners in Pennsylvania. Harding had appointed a Federal Coal Commission, headed by John Hays Hammond, with George Otis Smith, Thomas R. Marshall, Charles P. Neill, and Clark Howell as other members; and Coolidge promptly called a conference of coal miners and coal operators to meet with them on August 15, in New York City. The miners' group, headed by John L. Lewis, and the operators, with Samuel D. Warriner as spokesman, came together for an inconclusive discussion. Meanwhile the President kept very much in the background and refused to allow himself to be quoted on the subject. The country was getting alarmed; people in New England were beginning to experiment with bituminous coal; and a second conference, at Atlantic City, broke up without agreement. On August 21, when the President learned of this second failure, he said to reporters, "Tell the people there will be fuel." Three days later he summoned Governor Gifford Pinchot, of Pennsylvania, to the White House and designated him as Special Coal Strike Mediator, and other conferences were called by him at Harrisburg. After a plan of settlement suggested by Pinchot was rejected by both sides, the strike opened, as planned, on September 1, with 150,000 miners refusing to work. Throughout these negotiations Coolidge had been optimistic; but he did announce that he had been advised that he had no power to seize and operate the mines.

At last, after more deliberation and sounding out of public opinion, an agreement was reached on September 8, under a make-shift plan lasting for two years. The miners ratified the contract on September 17 and the mines were reopened two days later. The President, who was kept informed of every move, step by step, was not apparently much troubled. He emerged from the controversy without discredit, but the victory was really with the miners, who obtained the substance of their demands. One gets the impression that Coolidge throughout held the whiphand, but did not choose to exercise his power openly.

Even though Congress was not in session, the President had his difficulties. On Thursday, August 9, just before they were both setting out for Marion, Ohio, George Harvey, then Ambassador to Great Britain, had called on Coolidge and, in what Harvey called "quite a rapid-fire conversation," had answered many questions regarding the political situation. This was the beginning of a rather close relationship between the two men, both natives of Vermont [14] and both conservative in their philosophy. Harvey was frequently a guest at the White House during the next two or three years, sometimes "for days together." While he, like most other persons with whom Coolidge consulted, was inclined to exaggerate his influence on the President, the latter was always glad to get Harvey's realistic advice.

On August 13, Harvey rather unexpectedly resigned, and Coolidge, after Elihu Root had declined the appointment, sent Mr. Stearns with a letter to Frank O. Lowden, offering him the Ambassadorship to Great Britain; but Mr. Lowden could not be persuaded to accept. [15] In October, after careful consideration, the President resolved to appoint Frank B. Kellogg, who had just

[14] See *George Harvey, A Passionate Patriot,* by Willis F. Johnson, pp. 393ff. Harvey was born January 16, 1864, and attended as a boy the Caledonia County Grammar School, not far from St. Johnsbury Academy and of the same general type.

[15] Information supplied by Frank W. Stearns.

completed a term as United States Senator from Minnesota.[16] Kellogg, a St. Paul lawyer, had been special counsel for the Government in cases against several alleged monopolies and also for the Interstate Commerce Commission in the investigation of the Harriman railroads. In late October Mr. Stearns, returning from one of his visits at the White House, spent an evening in Dwight W. Morrow's apartment in New York City, with Colonel Charles H. March, who had been Chairman of the Minnesota delegation to the Republican Convention in 1920, and Thomas Cochran, a native of St. Paul and a member, like Morrow, of the firm of Morgan and Company. Both March and Cochran were distressed at the appointment of Kellogg, who was regarded by them as a "radical," and said that Minnesota, the Dakotas, and other adjacent states might as a result be lost to the Republican Party. Cochran said repeatedly, "I am heartbroken." In his letter to Coolidge describing the meeting, Mr. Stearns said: —

I have been disturbed at the attitude of both Morrow and Butler in one respect. They seem to be in mortal dread that they will be "butting in" if they say anything to you unless you ask them, and seem to be afraid to talk frankly to you. I have read the riot act to both of them and told them that no matter how great a man may be, no matter how wise he may be, he is entitled to have the opinions, information, and advice from such men as they are, even if it is not always asked for. They may know something that would be important to you on some subject where you might not even suspect that any information was needed. I don't know whether I have had any effect on them or not. No President ever had two more valuable or more unselfishly devoted friends than they are. . . .

When I was in Washington a few weeks ago, I picked up a book. The author said, "No man can tell the whole truth to the President of the United States. I have tried it. It can't be done." If that is true, the Lord help a President.

[16] See David Bryn-Jones's *Frank B. Kellogg* (1937). Born in Potsdam, New York, December 22, 1856, Mr. Kellogg had moved to Minnesota with his parents in 1865. Admitted to the bar in 1878, he settled down to practice in Rochester, and eventually, during the Roosevelt administration, became known as a "trust buster," particularly because of his work as prosecutor of the Union Pacific Railroad and the Standard Oil Company. Elected to the United States Senate, as a Republican, he took his seat on March 4, 1917. He supported Wood in 1920 for the Republican nomination and had been a "mild reservationist" on the League of Nations. He was defeated in 1922 for reëlection to the Senate, but had been appointed by Harding in March 1923 as a delegate to the Fifth Pan-American Conference in Santiago, Chile. Coolidge and Kellogg held similar political views and were temperamentally very congenial. Coolidge asked Kellogg to dine with him in early October, when the latter was arguing a case before the Supreme Court, and was much impressed by his sound judgment. A few days later, after Kellogg had returned to Minnesota, the President summoned him to Washington and offered him the Ambassadorship to Great Britain.

I think this is all I have to say, but I have hardly a free moment today. I will leave the balance for a second edition but do want this to go forward.

To this very candid expression of opinion, Coolidge replied in one of his most revealing statements: —

I have received your two or three letters, and am sorry that you have had any discomfort. It is my impression that the matter to which you refer will work out all right. That is the impression of the man here who is the best informed man there is in Washington on the situation to which you refer. I want to suggest to you again that everything I do is going to be criticized oftentimes by my very best friends. Of course I am going to make a large number of mistakes. I am unable to account for the reason for it, but those things do not worry me any more. I trust that you may come into that frame of mind yourself. I am going to do what seems best for the country, and get what satisfaction I can out of that. Most everything else will take care of itself.

It will have been observed that Mr. Coolidge's caution led him to omit the mention of any names in his letter. In his reply, Mr. Stearns was less reticent: —

I do not always expect to be "comfortable" and there was nothing in the "discomfort" of that meeting in New York that did me any harm. I have little doubt that the matter will work out all right, even in Minnesota, and I did not for a minute look on the appointment as a "mistake." I thought from the field that was left, after the two best men were not available, one because of age and sickness and the other because he would not accept, your selection was the best you could get and that it is a reasonably good one. Moreover, that seems to be the way the country has taken it.

I know that you are going to be criticized. That goes with the position. If it does not worry you, it certainly will not worry me. Up to date, whether as Governor or President, you seem to thrive on criticism. We could afford to pay Pinchot to act just as he is acting, and if Johnson's last remarks are correctly quoted, we could afford to pay him. The country does not want any superman and as you are human, you will make mistakes, I don't doubt. I do doubt your making a "very large number of mistakes." If these things do not worry you, they certainly won't worry me.

Naturally enough, as Coolidge had prophesied, he was subjected from the opening of his administration to close and critical scrutiny, from which he emerged with no loss of prestige. He was very careful not to make enemies unnecessarily, and remarked in his *Autobiography*, "Perhaps one of the reasons I have been a target for so little abuse is because I have tried to refrain from abusing other people." He certainly knew how to keep his own counsel, and he never indulged in those vindictive comments on his contemporaries which have so frequently damaged the careers of statesmen. Out of a sense of propriety he refused all invitations to make speeches, although he did address five hundred postal clerks on September 5 and in October presided for a few moments at the annual convention of the American Red Cross.

Aside from the coal strike, there was very little business to be transacted. The Five-Power Naval Treaty was signed on August 17, in Washington, with no unfavorable reactions. The oil scandals, following the public hearing called on October 25 by Senator Thomas J. Walsh, filled the newspapers with unedifying material and brought Denby and Fall into the limelight. But the President, although he must have followed the testimony with deep concern, said nothing in public about it. Even to Mr. Stearns he did not really unburden himself on this subject. He could tell, from the turn which events were taking, that there was trouble ahead — trouble for which he was in no sense responsible but for which he and his party would have to bear part of the blame. It was during this autumn that Senator Borah, who had already made a statement in Spokane, Washington, to the effect that Coolidge was the logical candidate for 1924, called on the President and, in response to a request for suggestions, simply said, "Get rid of Daugherty." [17] Coolidge was impressed, but declared, with characteristic common sense, that the removal of Daugherty would be regarded by the general public as his repudiation of the Harding administration and would be resented by large numbers of citizens. The incident, as we shall see, had its proper sequel.

On December 4, what some critical newspapers had begun to call "an air of mystery and silence" was at last broken by the President's message to Congress,[18] which, although not long, omitted no important phase of governmental affairs and impressed unbiased listeners and readers as straightforward, clear, unevasive, and courageous. In his references to the League of Nations he had been influenced in some degree by George Harvey, who had prepared for him a long memorandum on the subject; and recognizing the prevailing mood of the country, Coolidge declared that the con-

[17] See *Borah of Idaho,* by Claudius O. Johnson (1936), pp. 288–89.
[18] This was the first President's message ever broadcast over the radio and was an event of national significance. Radio listeners a thousand miles from Washington reported the reception to be so good that they could hear the speaker turn his manuscript. Six days later Coolidge was persuaded to broadcast his views on national issues direct from the White House. See Gleason L. Archer's *A History of Radio* (1938).

troversy over it was closed. He did, however, still favor America's participation in a permanent World Court of Justice. Although he felt that the war debts of European countries to us should not be canceled, he had no objection to adjusting them.[19] He was not altogether in sympathy with those who wished to recognize the Soviet Government of Russia. He urged, though not fervently, a strengthened army and navy. With a bravery for which he has not always been conceded credit, he discussed the aggressive program of the American Legion and ended with the significant words, "I do not favor the granting of a bonus."

Naturally he introduced his favorite theme of economy, dwelling on the desirability of immediate tax reduction and putting himself on record as opposed to tax-exempt securities. Insisting that both local and national taxation must be lowered, he reiterated, "Of all services which the Congress can render to the country, I have no hesitation in declaring this one to be paramount." On the perennial problems of the farmer, Coolidge displayed both fearlessness and wisdom. He was familiar with the dirt farmer's difficulties, but he was sure that agriculturists should not rely on any complicated system of relief, any governmental fixing of prices, any raid on the public treasury. "Simple and direct methods put into operation by the farmer himself," he said, "are the only real sources for restoration."

Coolidge concluded this able state paper with three noble paragraphs expressing his fundamental philosophy: —

We want idealism. We want that vision which lifts men and women above themselves. These are virtues by reason of their own merit. But they must not be cloistered; they must not be impractical; they must not be ineffective. The world has had enough of the curse of hatred and selfishness, of destruction and war. It has had enough of the wrong use of material power. For the healing of the nations there must be good-will and charity, confidence and peace. The time has come for a more practical use of moral power, and more reliance on the principle that right makes its own might.

In its terseness and simplicity Coolidge's message was favorably contrasted with Harding's florid utterances. It proposed no idealistic or constructive program, but Coolidge had no intention of posing as

---

[19] One of the remarks most frequently quoted as having been made by Calvin Coolidge is his statement on the war debts of European countries to us, "They hired the money, didn't they?" I have tried in vain to ascertain the source of this quotation and must, under the circumstances, regard it as belonging to the Coolidge apochrypha. Mrs. Coolidge's comment is, "I don't know whether he said it, but it is just what he might have said."

a crusader. Nature had not cast him for that part. What the nation needed most at the moment was recuperation and peace, a sedative and not a stimulant; and it was because Calvin Coolidge fitted so perfectly into this mood that he was so highly regarded by his contemporaries. The message was very favorably received; indeed he himself said later, "No other public utterance of mine has been given greater praise." It was felt that he had taken the helm with a firm hand and had been "resolute, downright, and forthright." While it was hailed too effusively by the *Minneapolis Journal* as "unequaled among the public utterances of a generation" and by the *Los Angeles Express* as "among the most remarkable contributions to the philosophy of statecraft," other more restrained judges agreed that it had met the test. William H. Taft, in a letter to his daughter, described it as "great in its comprehensiveness and style, great in the soundness of its economic statesmanship, and great in the courage that it took to say what he has said, and great in its absence of all evasiveness and in its very quiet directness." Businessmen were especially gratified, and Coolidge was hailed as "the nation's advance agent of prosperity." Chauncey M. Depew heard some of the railroad workingmen discussing it and saying, "We understood every word of it and it is all right. We've got a leader for President."

Even while President Coolidge was on his way to Washington, certain of his friends began to consider the matter of his nomination in 1924. Senator George H. Moses came out publicly for him almost as soon as Harding was in his grave; and of the cabinet members, Mellon, Work, and Davis were all on record for Coolidge before the month of August closed. The President himself said to Mr. Stearns early in September, "I shall be very much distressed if my friends talk at this time about 1924. If they are as friendly to me as they profess to be, they will spend their energies in backing me up in the work I now have in hand and let 1924 take care of itself." To William H. Taft, who saw him on September 25, he seemed "very keen in his desire for the nomination." Taft told him that the country would be delighted to have a rest before Congress came together and that the great majority of the people wanted to be let alone. Many callers at the White House pledged him their support, and the sketches of him in the current press could not ignore the coming campaign.

On November 30, Mr. Stearns wrote his son to keep him in touch with what was going on: —

When I was last in Washington, it became very evident that people all over the country were anxious to know who was to represent the

President in the pre-convention and convention campaign. All sorts of people were suggested, and many of the people seemed to think I was to be the lucky person. That, of course, would be a great mistake; so I put it up to the President. I told him I thought some one should be selected quickly, and I should like to have him authorize me to ask Mr. William M. Butler to take that place. He said he would be very much pleased if Mr. Butler was willing to undertake it. I am sure this is a wise choice because there will be less jealousy to have the National Committeeman from the President's own state selected than for a man to be selected from any other one state. Moreover Mr. Butler understands better than any other one person the President, the President's political ideals and methods of working, and can speak for him more safely and wisely than any other one person. Of course it makes it much easier for me. Whatever I am able to do I can do in conjunction with Mr. Butler better than with anyone else. I can see that it means lively work from now on.

The entire program was carried out as planned. It had been assumed by astute observers that Coolidge was ambitious, and in its issue for August 23 the *Literary Digest* assembled information indicating that he was "already an avowed and formidable candidate for the next Republican nomination." It was a relief, but no surprise, when Mr. Stearns, speaking for the President, made the formal announcement and when Coolidge himself, at a dinner of the Gridiron Club on December 8, confessed that his hat was in the ring. The public statement was timed for the annual meeting of the Republican National Committee on December 11, and an informal poll of that group showed that 46 of the 53 members present favored Coolidge. Mr. Stearns wrote: —

Mr. Butler and I had a hectic time in Washington last week at the meeting of the National Committee. I don't think either one of us got to bed before one A.M. for eight successive nights, but the results of our work were very satisfactory. . . . One thing we made a point of was that the Convention should not go to Chicago but go to Cleveland, and on that point we won. This I think is greatly to our advantage. Mr. Butler is to be the President's personal representative in the pre-convention campaign and will devote practically all his time to that work until after the Convention. Then if Mr. Coolidge is nominated, as there is every evidence now that he will be, Mr. Butler will probably be a candidate for U. S. Senator, in which event he will not be Chairman of the National Committee in the campaign. We understand the present Chairman, Mr. Adams, does not wish to be Chairman in the campaign. Probably the right man will develop in the next six months.

The opposition rapidly faded away. On December 14, William H. Taft wrote, "It looks now as if Coolidge were going to be nominated without much real opposition." Senator James E. Watson, of Indiana, and Governor Gifford Pinchot, of Pennsylvania, had been willing to be wooed, but now saw that a challenge to the Coolidge supremacy would be hopeless. The only other avowed candidate of any importance was Senator Hiram Johnson, of California; and on December 22, the *Literary Digest,* summarizing the newspaper opinion from coast to coast, concluded that Coolidge was far ahead of any possible rival. Indeed the National Committeeman from California, William H. Crocker, declared, "I wish my chances of Heaven were as good as the chances of President Coolidge to carry California against Hiram Johnson." Nearly everybody now decided to get aboard the Coolidge bandwagon. Charles G. Dawes wrote Stearns, December 21, "I know how delighted you must be with the magnificent record which President Coolidge is making. I got his measure long ago through Dwight Morrow. His nomination and reëlection are certain." Three days before, by prearrangement, Henry Ford, who had been talked of as a possible candidate, came out with a ringing statement endorsing the President and saying, "The country is perfectly safe with Coolidge. Why change?" On January 2, 1924, the President himself wrote, "We cannot now see that anything can prevent my nomination on the first ballot at the Republican Convention, but one never knows what will happen in politics."

In its issue for January 5, 1924, the *Literary Digest* had an article headed, "Three Men Who Work for Coolidge," with excellent character sketches of Stearns, Butler, and Slemp. Butler, a sturdy self-reliant figure with gray hair, gray moustache, and iron jaw, had risen from modest beginnings in New Bedford, Massachusetts, to wealth and power. He had been in the State Legislature and had been elected President of the Senate, but his strength in politics was based on the fact that he had been for twenty years W. Murray Crane's personal counsel. At times inclined to be dictatorial, he was not without enemies, but he was unswervingly loyal to Coolidge, who, as Governor, had often consulted him. Butler was more disposed to use force than Stearns, who was always the diplomat and preferred subtler methods of gaining his point. The two combined made an admirable combination, for they were accustomed to success, respected one another, and would never admit defeat.

The Coolidges had been in official mourning during the autumn, but the two boys had come for a few days in early September. A few days later they took their first cruise down the Potomac in the *Mayflower*, with the Irwins of Northampton and the "Ted" Clarks as their guests. Other friends had been invited from time to time, but no formal entertaining had been carried on. At Christmas, the Coolidge boys were again in the White House for a week or two, and the entire family helped to join in carol singing around the community Christmas tree behind the Treasury Building.

The Sixty-eighth Congress, which held its first session from December 3, 1923, to June 7, 1924, was nominally Republican, but the party itself was split on many issues, and there was a marked tendency, especially in the Senate, to disregard the President's wishes. It is evident now that many of the so-called Republican leaders were not heartily for Coolidge and were not pleased that a younger man was forging ahead of them. Furthermore they were aware that they could not control him or his actions. During the spring of 1924, after securing reports from all over the country, Mr. Stearns reported to the President that everybody was against him — that is, "everybody except the voters." On the other hand William H. Taft wrote on February 16, 1924, to his brother Horace, "I share your amazement at the development of Coolidge's character. His capacity for cogent, brief statement, the quickness with which he acts, the hardheadedness that he displays, and the confidence that he is stirring in the people are all gratifying." As usual in battles between the Executive and the Legislative branches of government, popular sentiment favored the Executive.

The House had 225 Republicans against 206 Democrats, with a few members unclassified; but whenever Republicans of progressive views declined to follow the more conservative leaders, the working majority for the party could not be relied upon. The Speaker, Frederick H. Gillett, was Coolidge's friend of long standing, a fellow Amherst man, who had nominated him for the Vice Presidency; and another leading figure on the floor of the House was Bertrand H. Snell, who had been in college with Coolidge. The two Senators from Massachusetts were Lodge and Walsh, the former having been reëlected in a close fight, with Coolidge's backing; and other conspicuous members of the Upper House were Johnson, Underwood, Borah, Curtis, Moses, and La Follette. A small but aggressive group of Westerners, including Capper (Kansas), Norris (Nebraska), Ladd (North Dakota), and Brookhart (Iowa), constituted what was to be known as the Farm Bloc, who were united for legislation favoring agriculture and usually voted with the Insurgents. Although Coolidge had only recently swung the gavel over their deliberations, the more powerful Senators seemed inclined to ignore him. The story of the ensuing proceedings was summed up by the *Philadelphia Public Ledger:* "The things the President has approved Congress has disapproved; those things he disapproved, Congress has approved."

On December 10, the President transmitted to Congress a budget message, in which he again emphasized the desirability of cutting down on government expenditures and reiterated his uncompromising antagonism to the veterans' bonus. As one commentator put it, he "made fiscal integrity the keynote of the Administration's progress." He virtually notified Congress and the country that they must choose between tax reduction and the bonus, thus showing that his interest in economy was more than theoretical.

As we have seen, Coolidge, through no fault of his own, had inherited some odoriferous scandals for which the lax and irresponsible Harding administration could scarcely escape the blame. It was impossible to deny that Secretary of the Navy Denby had permitted and President Harding had carelessly approved the transfer of certain valuable oil tracts from the Navy Department to the Interior Department; that Secretary of the Interior Fall had then accepted a large sum of money from Edward L. Doheny and Harry F. Sinclair, to whom he had leased the American Navy Oil Reserves, in California, and the Teapot Dome Reservation, in Wyoming; and that Attorney General Daugherty had connived at these and other forms of mismanagement. The efforts of the Democrats in Congress to incriminate leading Republicans represented good party strategy in the spring of 1924. Their primary aim was to hold Coolidge responsible for Harding's erring appointees, and his position was frequently embarrassing, for, with his high standards of private and public morality, he was revolted by each new bit of evidence implicating important officials.[20]

When the flagrancy of Fall's misconduct was brought to light, the President announced in late January, 1924, that every law would be enforced and every right of the people and the Government protected. On February 11, however, when the Senate tried to force his hand by requesting him to remove Secretary Denby from the cabinet, he made a firm and indignant reply, telling the Senate to mind its own business and saying at the close: —

[20] The story of the oil scandals is told, with proper attention to both accuracy and dramatic effect, by Mark Sullivan, *Our Times,* Vol. VI, pp. 272ff.

The President is responsible to the people for his conduct relative to the retention or dismissal of public officials. I assume that responsibility, and the people may be assured that as soon as I can be advised so that I may act with entire justice to all parties concerned and fully protect the public interests, I shall act.[21]

Denby's participation in the oil scandals indicated stupidity rather than corruption, but he could not resist the popular clamor, well promoted by Democratic leaders, and resigned in late February, thus greatly relieving the President.[22] All this did the Republican Party little good, and Frank R. Kent declared, "The smugness and serenity of the Coolidge counselors have vanished overnight." At the same period came attacks on Attorney General Daugherty, and one Washington correspondent asserted that everybody in the administration circles shivered when that cabinet member's name was mentioned. On January 29, Senator Wheeler had introduced his resolution calling upon the President to ask Daugherty to resign for his failure to prosecute corruption in high places. A day or two later, Coolidge sent for Senator Borah, "on urgent business," and the latter hurried to the White House. He had been there only a short time before Daugherty entered, and Borah was at once aware that

---

[21] After sending the President a congratulatory telegram on February 12, Mr. Stearns wrote him a letter reading in part as follows: "The words in the telegram sound cold. I do not know whether or not sentiment seems weak to you. If it does, then this is one of my weak days, because I am filled up and overflowing with it today. I do not want to seem boastful or lacking in humility. I did not learn anything new from your message to the Senate or your speech. I mean new in the sense of learning anything about the certainty with which the country can rely upon you in every emergency; but I think that back when you were President of the Senate I must have been struck by lightning, as Saul of Tarsus was said to have been, and seen a new light. I do not claim any credit for it. It was not carefully thought out. I had no way of proving I was right, but at that time I predicted just what has now happened, and I have done it every day and night since then, and you will have to let me take a little satisfaction in that every right thinking, intelligent person in the United States now agrees with me."

[22] On February 19, 1924, Dwight W. Morrow wrote Stearns: —

"I have felt a very deep sympathy with the President in the trying time he has been going through during the past few days. I hesitate to bother him by even a note.

"I assume it is possible that Mr. Daugherty may resign. While I think it will be better for the whole situation if he should do so, at the same time I feel that the president is wise in not forcing his resignation under the present excitement.

"I am wondering what the next step is to be. If Mr. Daugherty should resign, the new appointments to the two vacant Cabinet positions will be of very great importance in allaying public feeling. Character — and well known character — will be of the first importance. Not in my time has the country been so startled by the act of public servant as it has been by the disclosure that Secretary Fall actually took money in a satchel. It has quite demoralized men's thinking and acting. I think the ideal solution would be to get Secretary Hughes to resign as Secretary of State and take the Attorney Generalship, and to put a man of the type of John Bassett Moore in the position of Secretary of State."

the President had planned a meeting between him and the Attorney General. Daugherty said, "Well, don't let my presence embarrass you"; and Borah replied, according to one story, "I think I should be the least embarrassed person here." As the conversation developed, Daugherty finally said to Borah, "I don't know why you want me to resign. I have never had to turn you down. You have never asked me for anything." Borah and Daugherty talked for about an hour on the situation created by the Wheeler Resolution, but the President said nothing until, after the Attorney General had left, he turned to the Senator and said briefly, "Senator, I reckon you are right." [23]

Coolidge went about as usual during the winter, seemingly unperturbed, and had no intention of letting himself be manoeuvred into a false position. Taft wrote of him on February 29, "Calvin is having a hard time, but he has a wonderful composure and great common sense, great patience and courage, and he towers above everybody in Washington in the political field in this respect." Coolidge himself was not vulnerable, but he watched a campaign of "character lynching" in the course of which man after man was accused of depravity, often on the flimsiest testimony. What had actually happened was bad enough, but not bad enough for the scandalmongers. The Democrats combed Coolidge's record with systematic regularity without uncovering anything which connected him in the slightest way with Teapot Dome. Under the strain, as Dr. Paxson well puts it, the President "showed great capacity for silence and for taking political abuse without retort." In March he appointed Chief Justice Curtis D. Wilbur, of the California Supreme Court, to succeed Denby as Secretary of the Navy. As is usual in such situations, opinions differed regarding the choice, some newspapers calling him a man of high standing as lawyer and judge, while others, particularly those dominated by Senator Hiram Johnson, described him as well-meaning but intensely narrow and prejudiced.

After several weeks of whispering regarding Daugherty, the President finally asked for his resignation, and it was offered and accepted on March 28, the reason assigned being the Attorney General's refusal to allow the Congressional Investigating Committee access to certain files. To fill the vacancy, Coolidge on April 7 appointed Harlan F. Stone, an Amherst man of his own age in the

[23] *Borah of Idaho,* 289, gives the most authentic account of this significant interview. Two or three writers on Coolidge had allowed their imaginations full play in dealing with it.

class of 1894, who had been Dean of Columbia Law School from
1910 to 1923. "Doc" Stone, as he had been called in college, had
been perhaps the outstanding undergraduate of his generation at
Amherst, and his record as lawyer and jurist was not only unblemished but distinguished.[24] The appointment was received everywhere with satisfaction and promptly confirmed.[25]

Meanwhile Congress had been thwarting the President in every
way possible. In his first Message he had called attention to thirty-
three items of suggested legislation; four months later not one of
these executive proposals had been acted upon favorably. Even
Coolidge's cherished economy measures had been ignored or rejected. On May 13 he had been compelled to veto the Bursum Pension Bill appropriating $58,000,000 for increased pensions to
veterans of earlier wars. When he vetoed a Bonus Bill for veterans
of the World War, it had rapidly been passed over his disapproval,
— in the House, on May 17, by a vote of 313 to 78, and in the
Senate, on May 19, by a vote of 59 to 26, — with such Old Guard
Republicans as Lodge and Longworth leading the assault on the
Treasury. The Mellon Plan for taxation recommended by the President had been rejected by Congress for a compromise measure, —
the so-called Simmons-Longworth Bill, — and although Coolidge
signed it on June 2, he did so declaring that some of its provisions
"were not only unsatisfactory but harmful to the future of the
country." Everything considered, his efforts for wise economy had
met with failure. The Bonus Bill in itself had apparently wrecked
his program.

The famous Rogers Bill reorganizing the Diplomatic and Con-
sular Service was passed in May, signed by the President, and
went into effect on July 1, 1924. As the result of a long struggle to
take the foreign service out of politics, this measure was most important, and Coolidge was delighted. But in other respects his wishes
were thwarted.

He had advised our joining the World Court; whereupon the
Republicans on the Senate Committee on Foreign Relations had
disregarded his suggestions and reported a compromise which the

---

[24] Coolidge had already sought Stone's advice on the oil scandals and had
been much impressed by him. Counseled by Stone, the President had appointed
Senator Atlee Pomerene, of Ohio, and Owen J. Roberts, of Pennsylvania, as special counsel to investigate the situation. As Stone was leaving the White House
and still talking about the Attorney Generalship, Coolidge suddenly said, "How
about your taking it?" Stone demurred, but finally said that, if it were offered
to him, he would regard it as a call to public service.

[25] William H. Taft wrote to his wife, April 3, 1924, "Coolidge's appointments
to succeed Denby and Daugherty have been real helps to him."

President acidly declared to be "unworthy of America." Despite
all that Coolidge and Hughes could do, Congress added to the
Selective Immigration Bill a clause providing specifically for the
exclusion of the Japanese; and again, in signing this unfortunate
act, the President appended a statement of protest. Senator Lodge
had openly defied him on the Bonus, the World Court, the Bursum
Bill, and the Japanese Exclusion Act. One editor said that "a Republican Congress has devoted itself to bloodying the President's
nose, boxing his ears, and otherwise maltreating him." But public
opinion was with the President, and Congress — particularly the
Senate — was bitterly attacked in the press for both its inaction
and its wrong actions. Although it was weeks behind its normal
schedule, nobody in the Capitol seemed to be troubled. The complaint was everywhere heard, "Too much talk!" When Congress
finally did adjourn, out of sheer necessity, just before the Cleveland
Convention, a cartoon appeared by Evans, in the *Columbus Dispatch,*
headed, "Congress Passes a Real Relief Measure. Public Rejoices
at Congress Passing Its Resolution to Adjourn."

In general the newspapers, both Republican and Independent,
were behind the President and strongly critical of Congress; and
keen observers noticed that Coolidge was winning the confidence
of the nation. One well-known newspaper described the session as
"particularly noteworthy for its activities based on political motives." The *St. Louis Globe-Democrat,* in a mood of irritation,
burst out: —

The people are sick of Congressional inefficiency and turmoil, they
are sick of the lack of cohesion and purpose, they are sick of the
Senate's usurpation of the control of foreign affairs, sick of the domination by blocs and cliques, sick of its mistakes and its failures.

And yet, though so unpleasantly rebuffed by Republican leaders
in Congress, Coolidge was politically getting stronger. The *Omaha
Bee* pictured him in a cartoon as tied to a stake, with a fire blazing
under and around him, menaced by the ominous figures of Scandal-
monger and Political Savagery and Partisan Democracy, but with a
thermometer in his mouth indicating a normal temperature. Those
who had thought of him as a nonentity, a mere fleeting phenomenon,
were having their eyes opened. Whatever he said or did seemed to
be "good politics," and he won his following, not by making
promises, but by earning their respect. The skill which he had revealed as an administrator, the sensitiveness which he had shown
to the reactions of the average man, the complete devotion to duty

which marked his every act — these were virtues which the voter could appreciate. Furthermore they liked the purity of his life, his simplicity and reticence. In the primaries he was successful in state after state, and on April 10 William M. Butler announced that Coolidge had a sufficient number of delegates to ensure his nomination on the first ballot. In May, the President selected Butler as Chairman of the National Republican Committee. It had become apparent even to the Old Guard that Coolidge was the only hope of the Republican Party.

In late April, at a luncheon of the Associated Press in New York City, Coolidge seized a favorable opportunity for outlining his own platform, and in so doing stressed again the need for economy, indicated his intention of punishing the oil malefactors, and praised the so-called Dawes Plan for adjusting the disputes over the war reparations. He spoke hopefully of the World Court and of the possibility of an international arms-limitation conference. It was a speech in which, without cant or hypocrisy, he emphasized what he called "the law of service." While a very realistic and opportunist Congress was frustrating his expectations, he did not hesitate to voice a political philosophy based on idealism.

The Republican Convention which opened on Tuesday, June 10, at Cleveland, was one in which the senatorial clique so prominent at Chicago four years before exercised very little influence, and everything moved smoothly from beginning to end. The delegates-at-large from Massachusetts were Channing H. Cox, Henry Cabot Lodge, Frederick H. Gillett, William M. Butler, Anna C. Bird, and Jessie A. Hall, but Senator Lodge was ignored on the committee appointments, and he who had three times been Permanent Chairman of previous conventions was throughout very much in the background.[26] Senator Moses and others had warned Lodge of what was likely to happen, and the result was even more humiliating than had been predicted. The room assigned him in the hotel was so poor that he actually sought refuge and comfort with his former secretary, Louis A. Coolidge. Frank W. Stearns was not a delegate. Just before the primary elections, as he was sitting with several friends in Butler's Washington headquarters, someone asked him

[26] The newspapers made the most during the spring of 1924 of what they called the "rift" between Lodge and Coolidge, but the two men continued to meet on friendly terms. The situation at Cleveland was perfectly natural. Coolidge preferred to entrust his affairs to men who represented his own viewpoint, and Lodge was not one of them. Lodge himself was a veteran who could understand the fortunes of war. Taft wrote to his wife, "Coolidge's secret thoughts of Lodge are not fit to print." It is certain, however, that Coolidge never wrote a word derogatory to the older man.

if he was to be a delegate. In a jocular mood he replied, "No, I'm not, but my feelings have been hurt. I thought that at least one person would suggest that I be a delegate and give me a chance to decline." One of those present thought Stearns was in earnest and urged Butler to press the matter. That evening in the President's study Stearns told the story, and Coolidge said, "If you want to decline something, I now name you Secretary of the Navy. Now where is your declination? I want it now. I don't want to run any risk of your accepting." Stearns answered, "Thank you, sir, I decline, but I will make a record of this offer to hand down to my grandchildren."

But although Stearns was not officially a delegate, he was in Cleveland and in full control of the proceedings; and he must have observed with some pride the change which had taken place in his status since the convention of four years before. Stearns, with his outward innocence and good-will covering a shrewd, almost uncanny knowledge of men's motives and ambitions; Slemp, with his tact, his geniality, his political experience; Butler, with his quiet strength, his firmness, and his gift for leading others — these three worked well together in partnership. The Temporary Chairman, Theodore E. Burton, of Ohio, delivered an unusually able keynote speech, in which he reviewed the achievements of the Republican Party and dealt courageously with the scandals of the Harding administration. While admitting that "unworthy motives and a grasping avarice" in high places had been uncovered and should be punished, he protested against the impression that there was "widespread corruption" in the government. He also said, "With some disappointment as one whose public service has been in a legislative position, truth compels me to say that by far the greater share of our citizenship looks to President Coolidge rather than to Congress for leadership," and this statement was followed by a long and enthusiastic demonstration.

Frank W. Mondell, of Wyoming, was made Permanent Chairman without opposition. The platform, read by Charles B. Warren, of Michigan, contained nothing startling or original.[27] On Thursday, when nominations for President were called for, Alabama yielded to Massachusetts, and Channing H. Cox moved that President Marion Le Roy Burton, of the University of Michigan, be accorded the privilege of placing in nomination the candidate of

[27] Chief Justice Taft wrote to his wife, "The old Senatorial gang, Lodge, Brandegee, Watson, and Curtis, seems not to have had much to do with the platform." He was right.

Coolidge's own state.[28] When his excellent, but decidedly too long address was over,[29] the delegates picked up their state standards and began marching down the aisles, everybody participating except the delegations from Wisconsin and North Dakota. The demonstration lasted for eighteen minutes. Seconding speeches were made by Miss Florence C. Porter, of California, Martin B. Madden, of Illinois, William W. Stickney, of Vermont, — who said of the Coolidges that "they never wasted any time, never wasted any words, and never wasted any public money," — Judge Charles H. Carey, of Oregon, Miss Minnie J. Grinstead, of Kansas, Dr. George E. Cannon, of New Jersey, Mrs. Frank E. Humphrey, of Nevada, Mr. Isaac M. Meekins, of North Carolina, and Mr. N. A. Elsberg, of New York. No further nominations were made, but on the first roll call Robert M. La Follette, of Wisconsin, received 28 votes from his own state and 6 from North Dakota, and Senator Hiram Johnson 10 from South Dakota. Out of 1209 votes, Calvin Coolidge was given 1165. Way, of South Dakota, moved to make the nomination unanimous, but when the motion was put, "Noes" were heard from the Wisconsin and North Dakota delegations, followed by hisses from the other delegates and loud cries of "Put them out!" The Chairman then announced, "With the exception of a very few voices the nomination of Calvin Coolidge for President of the United States is made unanimous."

Several men were put into nomination for Vice President — William S. Kenyon, of Iowa, Frank O. Lowden, of Illinois, James E. Watson, of Indiana, Charles G. Dawes, of Illinois, Charles Curtis, of Kansas, William P. Jackson, of Maryland, Arthur M. Hyde, of Missouri, and Frank T. Hines, of Utah. Borah was suggested from many quarters, but refused with indignation. There is some evidence that Coolidge would have preferred him as a running mate and that he actually gave out from the White House his instructions to Butler to that effect. According to one story, Coolidge once asked Borah to run with him on the ticket, and the latter replied by asking, "For which position?" When he declined, Borah meant what he said. Although Oglesby, of Illinois, warned the Convention that Lowden would not consent to be a candidate, the latter received on the first ballot the largest number of votes and

[28] Dr. Burton had been President of Smith College while Coolidge was living in Northampton and knew him very well.
[29] Colonel John C. Coolidge, sitting in the room in the Plymouth homestead where Calvin had taken the oath of office less than a year before, heard Burton's speech over the radio and carefully timed each round of applause. It was in the days of head sets, and he had to keep the receiver to his ears.

on the second was given 766, sufficient for the nomination. At this point the Secretary of the Convention read a telegram from Lowden declining the honor. After some discussion, it was decided to ask him once more to reconsider his decision, and the Convention adjourned until evening. Then another telegram was read from Lowden, which had to be accepted as final. On the third ballot, General Dawes received the votes of 682½ delegates, and this nomination was at once made unanimous.[30] The convention then adjourned at half-past ten, Thursday evening, June 12. Henry W. Taft, who was present, felt that it was a convention of many minds, but little centralized authority, either in thought or in management. It was certainly a Coolidge convention from start to finish.

The Democratic Convention, held in New York City, turned out to be a prolonged and increasingly bitter contest between Alfred E. Smith, from "the sidewalks of New York," and William G. McAdoo, son-in-law of Woodrow Wilson, from California. The religious issue was prominent, for Smith was a Roman Catholic, and bigotry had its say on the floor of the convention. After 103 ballots, the tense situation resulted in the choice of a compromise candidate, John W. Davis, of New York City. Mr. Davis, an honest and high-minded man, was hampered from the opening of his campaign by the fact that he had been attorney for Morgan and Company. The Democratic theme was, of course, the corruption which had been uncovered during a Republican administration. "The Republican Party is impotent," declared Senator Thomas J. Walsh, and added that the real peril to free government lay in the "easy tolerance of turpitude in public office."

The shelving of the Old Guard at Cleveland led some commentators to fear that the Republican Party might again be split asunder, as had been the case in 1912. It was indisputable that there had been a certain amount of friction and maladjustment at the convention and that Butler had antagonized several important members of the party. But shrewder observers noted that there had been a gradual but perceptible transfer of power since Harding's death, that the old pilots had been quietly dropped, a new captain had seized the helm, and a fresh crew had been taken on board. William H. Taft wrote on June 14 to his wife, "I went to the White House

[30] Stearns wrote, June 14, 1924, to his brother-in-law, Atherton Clark, "There was a mix-up over the Vice Presidency. It is a long story but has turned out reasonably satisfactorily. In confidence, there are some things about Dawes's positions that may cause a little trouble. On the other hand, he will add to the strength of the actual campaign and he is personally very agreeable to the President. They are warm friends, and Dawes will be personally loyal to him."

to say good-bye to the President and to congratulate him on his nomination. He was in fine humor and said that matters had satisfied him. He smiled with satisfaction when I expressed pleasure that the Senatorial gang with Lodge at the head were relegated to the back benches." If there had been any wounds at Cleveland, however, they were soon healed. The Democratic platform could assert, "A vote for Coolidge is a vote for chaos," and say, "The Republican Party has proved its inability to govern even itself," but no one believed this kind of campaign propaganda. Some people could see little difference between the Old Guard and the Young Guard, but it was explained by Henry L. Mencken that what had happened in the Republican Party was the shifting of control "from professional politicians to businessmen who are political amateurs" — a reference to Stearns and Butler. To Samuel Blythe, however, President Coolidge appeared as trying to "reshape and remodel the obsolete Republicanism of the Old Guard into a new, fresher, and timelier Republicanism."

Both Coolidge and Davis were conservative by temperament, and thoroughgoing radicals did not like to choose between them. For this reason a group of disaffected men and women met on July 4, at Cleveland, and nominated for President Senator La Follette, who appealed to the disgruntled independent voters of both parties. While La Follette probably at no time hoped for election, he did think that he might secure enough votes to throw the decision into the House of Representatives, where he and his followers would hold the balance of power.

During the campaign the President avoided partisan meetings or strictly political speeches. He even declined the offer of a degree of Doctor of Laws from Yale, made to him through the intervention of ex-President Taft. He regarded any attempt at "swinging around the circle" as undignified, and made up his mind very early to remain quietly in Washington. In speaking on June 30, for the first time in public after the Republican Convention, at the seventh regular meeting of the Business Organization of the Government, he said with vigor, "I am for economy. After that I am for more economy. At this time and under present conditions, that is my conception of serving all the people." To these remarks popular sentiment responded with frank enthusiasm. The *Philadelphia Record* voiced a popular opinion when it said, "If the President's speech to the thousand or more Federal officers who spend the public money is a campaign speech, we respectfully congratulate him on a good opening." On August 14, in Memorial Continental Hall in

Washington, he was formally notified by the Honorable Frank W. Mondell of his nomination and, in his acceptance speech, said: —

We are likely to hear a great deal of discussion about liberal thought and progressive action. It is well for the country to have liberality in thought and progress in action, but its greatest asset is common sense. In the commonplace things of life lies the strength of the nation. It is not in brilliant conceptions and strokes of genius that we shall find the chief reliance of our country, but in the home, in the school, and in religion. . . . The people know the difference between pretense and reality. They want to be told the truth. They want to be trusted. They want a chance to work out their own material and spiritual salvation. The people want a government of common sense.[31]

A stinging attack on this speech was published in the *New Republic,* which was supporting La Follette: —

These are the words of a pigmy at a great task. They are the records of a mind utterly incapable of understanding many of the problems that confront it. They are the inconsistent and inconsequent flounderings of a man who deserves all pity. Fate had pitchforked him into a place beyond his intellectual power. A merciful defeat is what his best friends should wish for him. Mr. Coolidge has stood pat. He and his party are without that vision for lack of which a party perishes.

While Calvin Coolidge failed to achieve perfection, either as man or as statesman, he did not need to convince the American people that he was undeserving of such bigoted criticism. Another attitude, perhaps no less biased in the other direction, was expressed by Senator Lodge from the Charlesgate Hospital, in Boston, where he was seriously ill: —

It is with profound satisfaction that I have read your speech of acceptance. It seems to me admirable, clear and strong, and it leaves no doubt as to the policies which you advocate and which the party follows you in supporting. I am very glad you made that very strong and terse review of what has actually been accomplished since March, 1921. It is an unusually fine record, and yet the party has been assailed and assaulted, as if we had more than three years of absolute emptiness. I think that what you say cannot but have a very marked effect on public opinion throughout the country.

I noted what you said about accomplishments in foreign affairs. It has been very remarkable. In the one session of Congress which we have had since you became President we have reported to the Senate

[31] William H. Taft wrote his brother Henry, August 19, 1924, "Coolidge's speech was exactly like his policy, — direct and common sense, — and I think it has given the country, and especially the business portion of it, something upon which to chew and be convinced."

and ratified thirty-two treaties. No such record, I venture to say, has ever been made by any administration. That in itself is complete proof of the great activity and energy shown by your administration from the day when you took the reins of power. . . .

The conference called by President Harding and the work thus far done by your administration in regard to reparations have been successful and substantial in their result far beyond anything that the league has achieved or that could in my opinion be achieved by a combination loaded down with the inheritance and hatreds of a thousand years. It is our freedom of action that makes us so powerful for good, as is illustrated in the way you have managed the question of reparations.

In reply to Lodge's congratulations, Coolidge, then on a short vacation in Plymouth, wrote a short and perfect example of the completely noncommittal letter. The text read as follows: —

I very much appreciate your fine letter of August 14, and wish to thank you for all that you are good enough to say in it. I hope you are feeling better as the days go by and that your improvement will continue. I am taking a few days rest and enjoying every moment of my stay here. The fine bracing air will I am sure be very beneficial.

In this, as in other respects, Lodge and Coolidge were precise opposites. Lodge delighted in putting his ideas down on paper in an entertaining fashion; Coolidge never said anything of importance in a private letter. The correspondence between the two men is so one-sided as to be almost ridiculous. Lodge's notes are packed with opinions, suggestions, comments, and prophecies; Coolidge's are courteous but not intended to be the vehicles of self-expression. No one will ever publish a volume of the Letters of Calvin Coolidge. They are too few in number and tell too little about the essential man.

Mr. Davis, in the meanwhile, had been forced into the policy of denouncing his opponent and the Republican Party. In his speech of acceptance he made his proposed course of action clear: —

I charge the Republican Party with corruption in administration; with favoritism to privileged classes in legislation. I charge it also with division in council and impotence in action. . . . I indict the Republican Party in its organized capacity for having shaken public confidence to its very foundations. . . . An Executive who can not or will not lead a Congress that can not and will not follow — how can good government exist under such conditions?

The exigencies of partisanship drove the Democrats to laud this speech and the Republicans to belittle it. It would have had much more effect if Warren G. Harding had been the opposing candidate.

But in the eyes of the people Coolidge was in no degree responsible for the gross delinquencies of the Harding administration or for the irrationalities of Congress. Whatever might be said about his party, the President was known to be honest, and the public liked what he had said and was saying. The oil scandals had almost no influence in the campaign; what seemed most important was Coolidge's own character. Several Democratic newspapers, including the powerful *Boston Post*,[32] turned temporarily Republican. George Harvey wrote an effective article for the *North American Review,* headed "Coolidge or Chaos!" It was obvious from the opening of the campaign that Davis would find it difficult to make an issue out of what Calvin Coolidge had done or not done since August 3, 1923. The good sense of the American people kept them from blaming the scandals of the Harding administration on his successor.

Early in the summer occurred what was undoubtedly the enduring tragedy of Calvin Coolidge's life. His second son, Calvin Coolidge, Jr., was a boy who in many respects resembled his father. Like him in facial expression and physique, he also had something of his dry wit and sententious utterance. The Coolidges made their plans to spend most of the summer of 1924 in the White House, with frequent trips down the Potomac on the *Mayflower.* On June 4, Mrs. Coolidge went with Mrs. Stearns to Mercersburg Academy to see her older son, John, graduate, and the entire family returned afterward to Washington. Two weeks later, young Calvin, after playing tennis on the White House courts, developed a blister on his toe. For some inexplicable reason the blister became infected, and the poison rapidly spread into the bloodstream. On July 4, the President addressed the National Education Association on "Education: the Cornerstone of Self-Government," but his heart was at his son's bedside, and he wrote, "Calvin is very sick so this is not a happy day for me." Despite everything that medical science could do, despite the ministrations of specialists from Eastern cities, the virus spread. On July 6 he underwent an operation as a forlorn hope, but he grew weaker and weaker and finally died at 10.30 on the evening of July 7. "When he went," wrote Coolidge in his *Autobiography,* "the power and the glory of the Presidency went with him." [33] To some of his

[32] In an editorial on September 12, 1924, the *Post* announced this policy, saying, "The *Post* proposes to support Calvin Coolidge for the Presidency. Not because he is a Republican but in spite of it. . . . Time will show that President Coolidge is as good a democrat as Mr. Davis and as honest a liberal as Senator La Follette."

[33] Many of the stories told of young Calvin indicated that he resembled his father in temperament and character. When the boys first settled in the White House, Mrs. Coolidge thought that they should take dancing lessons. "Did my

friends the President, after this loss, seemed a changed man; and he once said to Richard B. Scandrett, "Mr. Scandrett, when I look out that window I always see my boy playing tennis on that court out there." William H. Taft wrote of him at this time, "He is a man who does not evoke sympathy because he suffers in silence." But even Coolidge could not help saying something about his loss.

From all over the nation came a spontaneous outpouring of sympathy at the death of the first child of a President to die in the White House since the time of Abraham Lincoln. There was a quiet service in the White House. Then the body was brought to Northampton for funeral services in the Edwards Church on July 10 and taken that afternoon for interment to Plymouth, where Mrs. Coolidge pathetically placed the boy's Bible on his coffin. When the party returned to the homestead from the cemetery, the President went with his remaining son, John, to the back porch. There he asked the boy to stand up to his full height, and then made a pencil mark there and wrote, "J. C. 1924." Then he asked, "How tall was Calvin?" "Just an inch shorter than I am." To one side of the mark he had made for John and about an inch below, the President drew another line and wrote, "C. C. 1924"; and, as if an afterthought had struck him, added, "If he had lived." Commenting later on his loss, he said, "The ways of Providence are often beyond our understanding. It seemed to me that the world had need of the work that it was probable he would do."

To both Calvin and Grace Coolidge the loss of their younger son was the major tragedy of their lives. On the fifth anniversary of his death Mrs. Coolidge wrote a poem, which was later printed in the magazine, *Good Housekeeping,* under the title, "The Open Door" : —

> You, my son,
> Have shown me God.
> Your kiss upon my cheek
> Has made me feel the gentle touch
> Of Him who leads us on.
> The memory of your smile, when young,
> Reveals His face,
> As mellowing years come on apace.

---

father ever take dancing lessons?" asked Calvin. The mother confessed that he never had. "Well, if my father never did, I don't need to," said his namesake. On the very day that Coolidge became President, young Calvin started work in a tobacco field. When one of his fellow laborers said to him, "If my father was President, I would not work in a tobacco field," Calvin replied, "If my father were your father, you would." The fullest story of Calvin's illness and death is told in Mary Randolph's *Presidents and First Ladies,* pp. 77ff.

And when you went before,
You left the gates of Heaven ajar,
That I might glimpse,
Approaching from afar,
The glories of His grace.
Hold, son, my hand,
Guide me along the path,
That, coming,
I may stumble not,
Nor roam,
Nor fail to show the way
Which leads us home.

Following this tragic event, the Coolidges went to Swampscott for a few days with the Stearnses. On July 21, the President wrote his father: —

Of course I am busy here. There are many things to do. Grace seems to thrive in this climate. It is lucky we left Washington, for it is the hottest summer they have had there for a long time. Here I wear winter clothes. If you feel you need another nurse, let me know, and I will get you one.

To the campaign itself the President seemed to give little attention. After a few days in Washington in early August, he returned with his family to Plymouth for a brief visit. While he was there he received as guests a notable party, including Henry Ford, Thomas A. Edison, and Harvey Firestone, and presented to Mr. Ford a sap bucket used by several generations of Coolidges. According to the story told by the newspapermen present, the ceremony was very simple. Taking the bucket in his hand, the President said, "My father had it, I used it, and now you've got it!" When Congressman Allen T. Treadway called at the Notch, he asked the President for a photograph, saying, "I have one, but it was taken when you were Lieutenant Governor." "I don't see what you want another for," observed Coolidge. "I'm using the same face."

On August 31, the Coolidges were again back in the White House to receive the Prince of Wales, who came to Washington very informally for luncheon, with the President, Mrs. Coolidge, and their son, John. According to "Ike" Hoover, the Prince seemed to be ill at ease and the President, seeing his embarrassment, quite outdid himself as a conversationalist. Later in the afternoon members of the cabinet and their wives came in to meet His Royal Highness. The nervousness of the foreign visitor was not calculated to put his hosts at ease.

PRESENTATION OF A VERMONT SAP BUCKET BY COOLIDGE TO HENRY FORD

Throughout the autumn the President barely mentioned his candidacy for reëlection, not caring to prostitute his high office in order to gain votes. His only response to attacks made upon him was complete silence. On September 1, he spoke to a group of labor leaders on "The High Place of Labor." He worked very hard over an address on "Ordered Liberty and World Peace," delivered at Baltimore on September 6, at the dedication of a monument to General Lafayette, at the close of which he urged his fellow countrymen to give their aid to the peoples of Europe. One sentence is most significant: —

If we want France paid, we can best work towards that end by assisting in the restoration of the German people, now shorn of militarism, to their full place in the family of peaceful mankind.[34]

Before the Holy Name Society, on September 21, he spoke on "Authority and Religious Liberty"; five days later he was talking at Philadelphia, on the anniversary of the First Continental Congress; on October 1, he welcomed the victorious Washington baseball team. in some humorous remarks; on October 4, he took part in the dedication of a monument to the famous First Division of the American Expeditionary Force; on October 15, at the unveiling of a statue to Bishop Francis Asbury, he took as his topic, "Religion and the Republic"; to a delegation of foreign-born citizens who came to the White House on October 16, he spoke on "The Genius of America"; and finally, on the evening of November 3, just before the election, he talked over the radio, urging all citizens to cast their ballots on the following day, and closing his speech by saying "Good night" to his father in Plymouth. While the contest was going on, he conducted himself with dignity and quiet confidence. He had good reason to do so, for everything was going his way.

His campaign managers, however, were not idle, and had discovered some picturesque methods of publicizing the Vermont Yankee. As early as April, the Home Town Coolidge Club of Plymouth, Vermont, was formed, and adopted an official song, "Keep Cool and Keep Coolidge." A little later, Herbert L. Moore, who had roomed for a year with Coolidge at Black River Academy, formed a Coolidge-Dawes Caravan and made a trip across the continent, with the Plymouth dance orchestra to attract the crowds. As the summer went along, Coolidge was clearly gaining week by week, and it was evident that he would gain nothing by "swinging round

[34] *Foundations of the Republic,* 100. It seems certain that Coolidge wrote all the speeches in this volume himself.

the circle" in a whirlwind of speechifying. William H. Taft, calling on him in early October, found him "very cheerful" and "quite confident of election." On October 23, he wrote from Washington to his father: —

The outlook appears to be promising, but as I have often told you, elections are very uncertain. I hope this is the last time I shall ever have to be a candidate for office.

Actually it was an unimportant, uninteresting, and unexciting campaign. The poll conducted by the *Literary Digest* indicated almost from the start that Coolidge was far in the lead. Its final report to its readers, dated November 1, 1924, showed that he had received more ballots than all his opponents together, with La Follette actually somewhat ahead of Davis. The result of the election was never in doubt, and no one was astonished when it was found that the popular vote gave Coolidge 15,718,789, Davis 8,378,962, and La Follette 4,822,319 — the largest Republican plurality in history. Davis and Bryan carried only the eleven states of the Old Confederacy and Oklahoma; and in the Electoral College Coolidge had 379, Davis 139, and La Follette 13. On the receipt of the pleasant tidings, the President made a very modest statement: —

I can only express my simple thanks to all those who have contributed to this result and plainly acknowledge that it has been brought to pass through the works of a Divine Providence, of which I am but one instrument. Such powers as I have I dedicate to the service of all my country and of all my countrymen.

Coolidge made it perfectly clear that he was under obligation to no one person or group of persons. William V. Hodges, Treasurer of the Republican National Committee, was told that contributions to the party finances carried no implication of possible reward. Three points were emphasized by Coolidge's representatives: no obligation must be incurred; all bills must be paid promptly; and the letter and spirit of the law must be observed. No contributions were accepted from corporations, and great care was taken to protect the party managers from criticism.[35] Anything like the publicized CIO contribution to the Roosevelt campaign of 1936 would have been rejected summarily by Calvin Coolidge.

"Calvin Coolidge was the issue, and to the President belongs the victory," announced the *Boston Transcript;* and it was universally acknowledged that the President was much stronger than

[35] Memorandum from William V. Hodges, July 19, 1939.

his party. The attitude of Congress in rejecting his proposals had probably helped his candidacy, and he now stood in a position where he had complete control of the Republican councils. Senator Lodge, who had tried more than once to block Coolidge's progress, died on November 9, a few days after the election, a broken and disappointed man.[36] Mrs. Warren G. Harding died on October 21. The old order was rapidly passing, and in its place Calvin Coolidge, supported by Frank W. Stearns and William M. Butler, ruled the nation. George A. Plimpton telegraphed Stearns, "I cannot imagine anybody being happier than you are to-day unless it is Coolidge himself. You have certainly demonstrated your ability as a king-maker, so to speak. Warwick isn't in it. He had only a handful of people to deal with and you have 120 millions." The attitude of the public was revealed immediately in the Stock Market, which had during November and December the greatest boom on record up to that time. Congress was to be decisively Republican, with a majority in both houses over Democrats and La Follette liberals combined. The Republican Old Guard had disintegrated, and the *New York Evening Post* rightly said: —

The President has won 382 votes on his own strength. The Old Guard contributed less than nothing. He can pick his aids on Capitol Hill. They will be his lieutenants. He will give the orders.[37]

Once again we must ask ourselves why Calvin Coolidge appealed, as he did in 1924, to people of all classes and grades of intelligence. He was not magnetic, like the two Roosevelts, or ingratiating, like Harding and Taft, or intellectually dazzling, like Wilson. He had none of the plausibility of the natural vote-getter, no showy or shining qualities, no engaging audacity, no gift for self-dramatiza-

[36] The last interchange of letters between Lodge and Coolidge was on the subject of a political appointment for Theodore Roosevelt Robinson, "Teddy" Roosevelt's nephew. Lodge wrote on September 24, asking for the President's help. Coolidge replied that he would do what he could. The final letter, written by Lodge on September 30, suggested that young Robinson might perhaps be made Assistant Secretary of the Navy, and said, "I have been coming along well and should have been over my trouble some time ago if it had not been for something which happens not infrequently after operations, a slight threatening in the veins of one leg, and therefore I have been made to keep my legs straight out before me, a very tiresome performance, and I am only just getting on my feet to walk, but all is going well and the doctors seem to think that everything is as propitious as possible." Within a few weeks he was dead. Governor Channing H. Cox, of Massachusetts, at once appointed William M. Butler to fill the vacancy as United States Senator.

[37] William H. Taft wrote on November 12, "It was a famous victory and one most useful in the lessons to be drawn from it, one of which is that this country is no country for radicalism. I think it is really the most conservative country in the world."

tion. During that summer he was ridiculed by the intelligentsia as a "jellyfish," a "small-town statesman," "just a figurehead"; and he was accused of being platitudinous, dull, and humorless. There was nothing imposing or awe-inspiring about him, and Coolidge jokes in those days were as common as those about the new-model Ford automobile. But the American people had just passed through a period of tension, of unusual nervous excitement, followed by one of notable corruption. Calvin Coolidge appeared without any premonitory omens before a nation which welcomed a return to the fundamental, unspectacular virtues. He had worked hard, he had been faithful to duty, he could be trusted as being safe and honest. The voters respected the purity of his private life, his simplicity, his freedom from sham and pretense. In 1916 Theodore Roosevelt had said, "The country ought not to take me unless it is in an heroic mood." In 1924, the United States was not looking for either heroism or romanticism. What it wanted was plain ordinary common sense. Calvin Coolidge had character — and in the long run character outlasts what is temporarily spectacular.

The result for the country was decidedly beneficial. Following the election of 1924 a spirit of optimism was in the air. Psychologically everything indicated a period of confidence, of increasing industrial production, of high prices for farm products, of expanding exports, of easy money — all the familiar factors making for prosperity. Coolidge's message to Congress on December 3, reiterating the need of even more economy in government, had behind it a mandate from the nation. He declared: —

We have our enormous debt to pay, and we are paying it. We have the high cost of government to diminish, and we are diminishing it. We have the heavy burden of taxation to reduce, and we are reducing it.

It was the general verdict that Congress, in its final session, could undertake little constructive lawmaking. What the country desired, according to one Representative who seemed to echo the President, was "less legislation and more efficiency, economy, and honesty in government." Even Congress, impressed by the Coolidge triumph, seemed to have caught his mood and to have been converted to his philosophy; but the few weeks remaining before the inauguration offered little opportunity for putting it into operation. The "Lame Duck" Session of the Sixty-eighth Congress produced very little in the way of constructive legislation. The question of the disposition to be made of the government power plants at Muscle

Shoals was the subject of much heated debate; and the Underwood Bill, providing for leasing the waterpower rights to a private corporation and sponsored by the administration, was actually adopted by the Senate on January 14, 1925. When it was amended by the House, however, the differences of opinion proved to be irreconcilable, and even the President's influence could not achieve a final decision. In spite of a lengthy report prepared by the unofficial Agricultural Commission and endorsed by the President, Congress took no legislative action, and no relief was offered to the farmers.

On the whole, the Sixty-ninth Congress had done very little to deserve praise. It had rather successfully thwarted Coolidge in some of his cherished plans, but this negative accomplishment brought it no credit in the eyes of the nation.

In September, John Coolidge, now the only son, had entered Amherst College, where, following his father's example, he joined the Phi Gamma Delta fraternity. The President wrote on December 22, referring to him, "I think he has done fairly well in his work there and has been a good boy. Of course many people have called upon him for outside diversions." In the same letter he added, "If only Calvin were with us, we should be very happy," and a day later he wrote, "Now John is home I miss Calvin more." Christmas in 1924 was a rather sad period for the President. Except for John and the Stearnses, there were no guests in the White House. The Coolidges had a quiet dinner, walked in the evening to the national community Christmas tree, and then listened to carols sung from the White House portico. The President seemed always to be thinking of his dead younger son.

On January 3, 1925, following the holiday season, the President wrote, with a trace of his old humor: —

To-day is the birthday of Grace. She is 46 I believe.

John has been home almost two weeks. He returns Sunday. While here he has been constantly engaged in a life of frivolity.

On January 5, after the retirement of Associate Justice Joseph McKenna, of the Supreme Court, Coolidge appointed Attorney General Harlan F. Stone to the vacancy, and his choice was warmly approved by the journals of both parties. In choosing men for important positions, Coolidge seldom played politics, but tried honestly to select the best available candidate. A careful study of his appointments will show that he was seldom influenced by partisan motives, party man though he was.

Somewhat later in the month, on January 17, 1924, the President delivered before the American Society of Newspaper Editors, in Washington, a speech from which sections have often been quoted to prove that he was a complete materialist. The passage most frequently cited is probably the following paragraph: —

After all, the chief business of the American people is business. They are profoundly concerned with producing, buying, selling, investing, and prospering in the world. I am strongly of the opinion that the great majority of people will always find these are moving impulses of our life. . . . In all experience, the accumulation of wealth means the multiplication of schools, the encouragement of science, the increase of knowledge, the dissemination of intelligence, the broadening of outlook, the expansion of liberties, the widening of culture. Of course the accumulation of wealth cannot be justified as the chief end of existence. But we are compelled to recognize it as a means to well-nigh every desirable achievement. So long as wealth is made the means and not the end, we need not greatly fear it. And there never was a time when wealth was so generally regarded as a means, or so little regarded as an end, as to-day.

The words just cited have only too often been torn from their context to enable critics of Coolidge to support their thesis. What the President was suggesting was that it takes money to build hospitals, to equip libraries, and to found and maintain schools and colleges — in which contention he was perfectly right. And he went on in this same address to carry his argument to the proper conclusion: —

It is only those who do not understand our people who believe that our national life is entirely absorbed by material motives. We make no concealment of the fact that we want wealth, but there are many other things that we want very much more. We want peace and honor, and that charity which is so strong an element of all civilization. The chief ideal of the American people is idealism. I cannot repeat too often that America is a nation of idealists. . . . No newspaper can be a success which fails to appeal to that element of our national life.

Furthermore, in this same utterance, Calvin Coolidge dwelt with unusual emphasis on the necessity for a free press, on the importance of newspapers as "a great educational and enlightening factor," on the desirability of their serving honestly the public interests. Those who are attempting to form a just estimate of Coolidge and his political philosophy ought to consider a speech like this as a well-ordered whole and not isolate single phrases or sentences. Those who call him a materialist must deliberately ignore the fact that he was himself almost completely indifferent to monetary rewards or to what money will and can buy; that he refused again and again from Mr. Stearns and others large gifts which would have added to his comfort and security; and that while, like a true Vermonter, he had no objection to earning an honest dollar or being paid for work that he had done, he was never governed by material motives. Only a very prejudiced critic is likely to condemn him for maintaining that the average American is occupied chiefly, not with reveries or crusades, but with earning a living for himself and his family.

In late January Colonel Charles R. Forbes, once head of the Veterans' Bureau, was convicted of defrauding the government and sentenced to a fine and two years in the penitentiary.[38] As the depths of corruption to which the Harding administration had sunk became more and more apparent, Coolidge's disgust increased, and on two or three occasions he expressed himself forcibly on the subject to Frank W. Stearns. But he did not feel that it was his duty to denounce the appointees of the President with whom he had been so closely associated. That Coolidge himself was not fully informed regarding the scandals around him cannot be doubted. Not even those most zealous to uncover his weaknesses have been able to find even a hint of his connivance with the "Ohio Gang." Many of his friends wished then, and have wished since, that he had moved more vigorously against the "grafters" who had surrounded Harding. But that was not Calvin Coolidge's way.

By the time of the election of 1924, Calvin Coolidge needed no further introduction to the American people. They had become familiar with his appearance, his manner, his methods of speech. They knew what he stood for and what he was likely to do. Some of them thought that he was ultraconservative, illiberal, provincial, and even stupid — but these were in the minority. By others he was regarded as the chief hope for the preservation of American institutions. His popularity was based almost entirely upon the confidence which he inspired. Franklin D. Roosevelt's charm of personality has magnetized many a voter who fundamentally disagreed with him; Calvin Coolidge's native qualities of rectitude and courage made citizens respect him who found little in him to arouse affection. It was comforting to Democrats as well as to Republicans to be sure that the man in the White House for the next four years, even though he might make mistakes and stir up hostility, would be dignified and incorruptible. Generalizations are always dangerous, but it is fair to say that few Presidents of the United States have been as popular in and out of office as Calvin Coolidge.

[38] *Our Times*, Vol. VI, 239ff. *Literary Digest*, Feb. 14, 1925.

XVI

President in His Own Right

A MERE inauguration was, for Calvin Coolidge, no novel experience, and on March 4, 1925, he did not impress observers as being either nervous or elated. Young Calvin's death was still vivid in his sensitive mind; indeed something of his inner melancholy was an undertone in a letter written to his father on February 26: —

Of course I want you to do what will give you the most pleasure. If you do not feel like coming to the inauguration, I am not going to urge you about it, or urge you to stay after you get here. You and John and I are all that is left. You have worked hard for me, and I do not want to put any more burdens on you. The House is open and the invitation given; every medical or other attention are at your disposal.

Colonel Coolidge actually did leave the Notch on March 2, with towering snowdrifts almost shutting in the homestead, and reached Washington amid brilliant sunshine, with a winter nip still in the air. Other guests, too, had gathered in the White House: Mrs. Andrew I. Goodhue, Grace Coolidge's mother; Mrs. Hills, of Northampton, and Miss Laura Skinner, two of Mrs. Coolidge's close friends; the Stearnses, of course; and young John Coolidge, who came down on the previous night from Amherst College and went back that evening at seven o'clock. The inauguration ceremonies, at the President's request, were as unostentatious and inexpensive as they could possibly be made. Taft wrote his wife on February 3, "The effort seems to be to have as much show as they can if it can be called republican and simple."

An interesting chapter in "Ike" Hoover's *Forty-two Years in the White House,* headed "An Inauguration That Fell Flat," pictures what happened in the Coolidge household on that day. The President, unmoved by pageantry, would have preferred to keep to his customary routine, and did so as far as he politely could. Up as usual before seven o'clock, he went for a short walk around the grounds at seven-thirty and at eight had breakfast with his wife in

A COOLIDGE LETTER FROM THE WHITE HOUSE

their suite. He then proceeded to his office to look at the mail, returning at ten for a last glance at his Inaugural Address. Just before eleven o'clock he welcomed Charles G. Dawes, the Vice-President-elect, and his wife, and the party set out for the Capitol, escorted by a military company from Vermont. On the route he said very little, and to the cheering crowds seemed apathetic and unresponsive. In the President's room off the Senate Chamber, Coolidge lingered long enough to sign numerous bills passed during the last hours of the Sixty-eighth Congress, including one of which he really did not approve, increasing the compensation of Congressmen, cabinet members, and the Vice President. Then he marched into the Senate Chamber, where he listened with poorly veiled indifference to Dawes's unexpected and ardent attack on the Senate's time-honored right to filibuster, in the course of which the new Vice President pointed his finger, shook his fist, and waved his right arm in denunciation of Senate Rule Number 22. It was so sensational that everybody was still murmuring about it when the President stepped out on the balcony to take the oath administered by Chief Justice Taft.

Coolidge's Inaugural Address, the first to be broadcast over the radio, had been a matter of much concern to him but turned out to be one of his ablest utterances. William H. Taft declared that the President had acquired "great aptness of expression and brevity and force." Some listeners thought it seemed too complacent. He declared that the United States was leading the world in the rapidity with which it was adjusting itself to the results of the World War; that "under the helpful influences of restrictive immigration and a protective tariff, employment is plentiful, the rate of pay is high, and wage earners are in a state of contentment seldom before seen"; and that, while we should adhere to the Permanent Court of International Justice, we should maintain our position "of political detachment and independence." Asserting that the election had shown the American people as favoring "economy in public expenditure with reduction and reform of taxation," he continued, with epigrammatic felicity: —

I favor the policy of economy, not because I wish to save money, but because I wish to save people. . . . Economy is idealism in its most practical form. . . . The wise and correct course to follow in taxation and all other economic legislation is not to destroy those who have already secured success but to create conditions under which everyone will have a better chance to be successful. The verdict of the country has been given on this question. That verdict stands. We shall do well to heed it.

Coolidge did not advocate any major reform or notable shift in policy. Like Daniel Webster, whom in several respects he resembled, he was engaged in the task of defense and preservation, and his attitude was expressed in one sentence, "We are not without our problems, but our most important problem is not to secure new advantages but to maintain those which we already possess." In this and similar reflections the President found "ample warrant for satisfaction and encouragement." In closing his appeal for economy and peace, Coolidge reached a high level of eloquence: —

America seeks no earthly empire built on blood and force. No ambition, no temptation, lures her to the thought of foreign dominions. The legions which she sends forth are armed, not with the sword, but with the cross. The higher state to which she seeks the allegiance of all mankind is not of human but of divine origin. She cherishes no purpose save to merit the favor of Almighty God.

It was a long speech for Coolidge, covering more than forty-seven minutes, and he was tired when it was over. When the party returned to the White House, he swallowed a quick luncheon, walked to the glass-enclosed stands to review the parade, — meanwhile maintaining a noticeable reserve, — and at three-forty retired to his room and threw himself on his bed, utterly exhausted. He did emerge again at four-thirty to greet several visiting delegations, but looked to them far from happy. After a dinner with his guests at the White House he went out for a few minutes to attend a banquet at the Cairo Hotel, given by members of the Massachusetts Legislature. He did not speak there, explaining that his voice was strained; and he was back in bed before ten o'clock.

Despite the President's boredom, all the omens for the administration seemed propitious. An article by Robert Lincoln O'Brien in the *Boston Herald* on March 5 said, "The Democratic Party lies in a state of hopeless collapse," and was headed, "Coolidge Logical Candidate to Succeed Himself in 1928." On July 5, David W. Mulvane, National Committeeman from Kansas, made a similar statement, apparently with the approval of Everett Sanders. It would have been difficult for anybody to believe in 1925 that within a very few years the nation described as prosperous would be in the midst of a financial and spiritual depression so deep that to some people emergence from it seemed unlikely. But to Calvin Coolidge on Inauguration Day the possibility of national disaster appeared remote. The tone of his address indicated absolute confidence and faith in the future.

The personnel immediately around the President changed somewhat from 1925 to 1929. On January 15, C. Bascom Slemp announced his retirement from the position of President's Secretary and was succeeded on March 4 by Everett Sanders, a Republican Congressman from Indiana, who had declined to be a candidate for renomination in 1924.[1] Sanders, whom Coolidge already knew rather intimately, turned out to be tactful, shrewd, and loyal, and was far more successful in the position than his predecessor had been. "Ted" Clark was retained on the President's staff, and Mary Randolph continued to be White House Secretary. Charles E. Hughes had notified the President in November 1924 that he could not remain in the Department of State; and early in January it was announced that Frank B. Kellogg, then Ambassador to Great Britain, would succeed him on March 4.[2] Mr. Kellogg suggested the name of Dwight W. Morrow for Undersecretary of State, but the President, after thinking the matter over, said, "No, I don't think that would do" — perhaps feeling that Morrow's financial connections might injure his value to the State Department. Joseph C. Grew was finally retained in that office, to be succeeded in 1927 by Robert E. Olds. When Henry C. Wallace, Secretary of Agriculture, died following an operation for an infected gall bladder, on November 4, 1924, Coolidge promoted Howard M. Gore, then Assistant Secretary of Agriculture, to the vacant place, until the following March 4, when he was succeeded in the cabinet by William M. Jardine, President of the Kansas State Agricultural College. Jardine, an authority on crop production, coöperative marketing, and other phases of the farm problem, was opposed to the McNary-Haugen Bill and therefore a man after Coolidge's own heart. Already Curtis D. Wilbur, of California, had succeeded Denby as Secretary of the Navy; and

[1] Everett Sanders, born March 8, 1882, near Coalmont, Clay County, Indiana, was admitted to the bar in 1907 and practised his profession in Terre Haute, Indiana, until elected to Congress as a Republican in 1916. He had been Director of the Speakers' Bureau of the Republican National Committee in 1924. Sanders was, and is, a man well over six feet in height, with chubby face and spectacles, rotund but vigorous. Mr. Sanders has been of much assistance to me in preparing this biography.

[2] See *Frank B. Kellogg*, by David Bryn-Jones, pp. 163ff., which gives interesting details regarding this appointment. Coolidge's opinion of Kellogg was very high indeed. Chief Justice Taft in a letter dated March 9, 1925, commented as follows: "I am very sorry to have Secretary Hughes leave the State Department. He was a great Secretary, one of the ablest we have ever had, as he was a great Judge and a great Governor. Mr. Kellogg is by no means his equal, but Mr. Kellogg is a hard-working, clear-headed lawyer, with some experience on the Foreign Relations Committee of the Senate, and with his recent experience as Ambassador to England, and I doubt not he will make a very safe adviser for the President, though he will not be the brilliant representative of our Nation in the State Department that we have had in Mr. Hughes. Mr. Hughes retires for the purpose of amassing a competence for his wife and family."

Dwight F. Davis, of Missouri, after having been Assistant Secretary of War, was advanced to the Secretaryship, October 13, 1925, on the resignation of John W. Weeks because of illness. Mellon in the Treasury, New as Postmaster General, and James J. Davis as Secretary of Labor carried over from the Harding period and remained throughout the Coolidge administration. When Hubert Work, of Colorado, resigned on July 24, 1928, as Secretary of the Interior, his place was taken by Roy O. West, a Chicago lawyer who had been Secretary of the Republican National Committee. Herbert Hoover withdrew in 1928 some weeks after he became the Republican nominee for President, and Coolidge named in his place William F. Whiting, of Holyoke, a friend of long standing. Not all these appointees had marked distinction, but in each case the man was competent, and the Coolidge cabinet was free from the scandals which had so marred the administration of Warren G. Harding.

In one case, however, largely because of an unfortunate accident, Calvin Coolidge had to meet the most humiliating defeat of his career. On January 10, 1925, after appointing Attorney General Harlan F. Stone to the Supreme Bench, the President named Charles B. Warren, of Detroit, to the vacant place in the cabinet, and on February 24 the Senate Judiciary Committee ordered a favorable report on the appointment. Then the storm broke. Warren was a gentleman of considerable national distinction, who had occupied important positions under the government and had been Chairman of the Platform Committee at the Republican Convention in 1924.[3] Coolidge apparently consulted nobody, not even his adviser, William M. Butler, on the subject of Warren's qualifications; and it was soon obvious that there was to be opposition. Warren's conduct as President and Counsel of the Michigan Sugar Company led to the charge that he had violated the antitrust laws, and the Progressives and many Democrats promptly lined up against him. When the President was notified that it would be difficult to have the nomination confirmed before the close of the session, action was postponed, and the President issued a statement defending Warren against the accusations which had been made. When the vote was actually taken in the Senate on March 10, it was well known that the result would be close. At the critical moment, when the roll was being called, following a heated debate, the Vice President, having been assured that it was safe to leave the Capitol, was in his room at the New

[3] Warren, a lawyer by profession, had been Ambassador to Japan and later to Mexico.

Willard Hotel enjoying an afternoon nap. Hastily summoned by special messenger, he arrived too late to break a tie, and Warren was consequently rejected, 41 to 39. If Dawes had been presiding at the time, he could have settled the question in Warren's favor. As it was, when the administration leaders attempted to press the matter, Senator Overman, of North Carolina, the only Democrat who voted originally for confirmation, rejoined his party associates and changed his vote. Coolidge, indignant and obstinate, decided, in spite of excellent advice, to force the issue and resubmitted Warren's name, only to have it rejected on March 16, this time by the decisive vote of 46 to 39. Warren was the sixth Presidential cabinet appointment to be turned down by the Senate, and the first since the days of President Andrew Johnson. In his anger, the President announced that he would offer Warren a recess appointment which would keep him in the office of Attorney General until the assembling of Congress in December, but Warren wisely refused the proposal. On March 17, the President sent in the name of his friend and neighbor, John Garibaldi Sargent,[4] of Vermont, and it was unanimously accepted. Warren's rejection naturally aroused much discussion at the time, and the Coolidge supporters were temporarily disconcerted by the unexpected opposition to his wishes. But the damage to the President's prestige was not permanent. He may have said to Chief Justice Taft, "The Senate is a lot of damned cowards," but he wrote in his *Autobiography:* —

The Congress has sometimes been a sore trial to Presidents. I did not find it so in my case.

On the other hand, the *Autobiography* also makes the point that the President must "resist any encroachment upon his constitutional powers" — one of the most important of which is the power of appointment; and Coolidge adds: —

While I have always sought coöperation and advice, I have likewise resisted these efforts, sometimes by refusing to adopt recommendations and sometimes by the exercise of the veto power.

As a matter of fact, Coolidge was entirely satisfied with Sargent, who had preceded him at Black River Academy and who was known

[4] John Garibaldi Sargent (1860–1939), born in Ludlow, Vermont, had graduated from Tufts College in 1887, where he was known as "Jumbo" on the football team, and was admitted to the bar in 1890. He had practised law in Ludlow and had been Attorney General of Vermont from 1908 to 1912. Tall, ungainly, and picturesque, Mr. Sargent was a first-class country lawyer, and turned out to be a competent Attorney General of the United States.

to everybody in the Plymouth region as "Gary." He soon became popular in Washington, where everybody recognized his shambling gait and careless dress. The truth is that Sargent, through his general practice in a country town, had acquired a wide knowledge of human nature which made him a first-class judge of men. Chief Justice Taft once said that the Department of Justice was in better shape under Sargent than at any time before within his knowledge.

No public official with an extensive appointing power can possibly hope to please everybody. In Chief Justice Taft's correspondence covering this period are many complaints regarding the appointment of federal judges. On August 20, 1928, he wrote on this subject: —

If Coolidge had any independence on the subject of judicial appointment, I would hope to have some influence, but I haven't any. It is discouraging to one interested in maintaining the high personnel of the federal inferior judges.

Again on February 11, 1929, we find him writing to Charles C. Burlingham: —

I have been laboring on this business ever since I have been in office, and find confidentially the trouble to be with the President in not resisting the pressure of the Senators, and in the failure of the Attorney-General and others interested to search for competent candidates. . . . Let us hope that the next Administration will be convinced that the selection of good judges is one of the most important functions that the Executive has.

All the evidence indicates, however, that the President spent a great deal of time thinking over men qualified for certain positions and was ever willing to listen to those who were pressing the claims of their candidates, as Taft frequently did; but that Coolidge invariably made the final decision himself, often without seeking the counsel of even such close advisers as Stearns or Butler. Few Presidents have set for themselves higher standards for appointees or acted more independently of solicitors. It has been alleged that he was "controlled" by financial figures like Andrew W. Mellon and Thomas Cochran, but I do not find that they suggested or dictated appointments. Although Coolidge did not neglect the usual courtesies to Senators and department heads, he was skillful in resisting the importunities of organized minorities. Politicians actually found him exceedingly difficult to manage, for he saw through all their subtle wiles. He felt, as he says in his *Autobiography,* that "the public service would be improved if all vacancies were filled by simply appointing the best ability and character that can be found." Some of his appointments were not regarded as good, but I have come across virtually no cases in which he was susceptible to pressure or grossly deceived by corrupt counselors. He did not get himself into the difficulties from which President Harding suffered throughout his administration and which eventually caused his breakdown. Coolidge was honest in his intentions. He made mistakes, but not because he yielded to the solicitations of self-seeking men.

Contrary to a widespread impression, the Coolidges while in the White House were most hospitable, and had more guests than had been invited during any administration up to that time. Excluding relatives, intimate friends, and officers of administration, the President had 102 house guests in five years and seven months. In four years Taft had 32 house guests; in eight years Wilson had 12; and Harding had only five. The Coolidges observed a reasonable formality in their entertainment and liked to know in advance how long visitors were to stay, but they were both courteous hosts.

With the more distinguished guests there was always a little nervousness around the White House, although the Coolidges did not often share in it. The Prince of Wales came for luncheon on August 31, 1924, dressed most informally and apparently ill at ease. On October 21, 1926, Her Majesty, the Queen of Rumania, an inveterate publicity seeker, caused plenty of excitement, and her visit required a careful study of diplomatic etiquette. Some of the plans went awry, and the Queen's efforts to engage the President in conversation were little more successful than those of other visitors who had tried the same experiment. "Ike" Hoover felt that Mrs. Coolidge, in her beautiful simple gown, practically without ornamentation, was superb.[5] Will Rogers was in the White House on January 17, 1927, but was obviously ill at ease; and later he offended Coolidge by imitating his voice over the radio. Colonel Lindbergh's visit, in June 1927, was made to the temporary White House, in Dupont Circle, but probably aroused more enthusiasm in Washington than that of any Prince or Queen. Mrs. Lindbergh, the Colonel's mother, came with him, and the program during their visit was very full, with cheering crowds calling constantly for the gallant young aviator. Among other notables were the Premier of France, Princes from Japan and Sweden, and the Presidents of

[5] For a gossipy account of this visit see Mary Randolph, 49ff.

the Irish Free State, Cuba, and Mexico. Among the house guests were Howard Chandler Christy, who stayed for some days painting portraits of President and Mrs. Coolidge; Frank O. Lowden; Mr. and Mrs. John D. Rockefeller; Colonel House; Dr. William M. Irvine, Headmaster of Mercersburg Academy; and several of his Massachusetts friends, including Channing H. Cox. Chief Justice Taft was often there for meals, and a popular guest at tea was Charles Moore, Chairman of the National Commission of Fine Arts. On three successive days in 1928, Jane Cowl, Douglas Fairbanks and Mary Pickford, and Ethel Barrymore lunched with the Coolidges, and "Buster" Keaton, Madge Bellamy, and Ina Claire were also registered in the White House Guest Book at that period. Under Coolidge a foreign ambassador, like Alanson B. Houghton or Myron T. Herrick, was likely to spend several days at the White House on his return to this country. When Lord Willingdon, Governor General of Canada, came with Lady Willingdon to Washington, much excitement was aroused over the question of precedence between him and the British Ambassador, Sir Esme Howard, but the diplomatic tangle was finally straightened out to everybody's satisfaction. The last formal dinner given by the Coolidges was to the President-elect and Mrs. Hoover, Mrs. Gann, and Senator Charles Curtis.

Mr. Coolidge's quaint habits continued to puzzle the White House staff. Miss Ellen A. Riley, who was in charge of domestic affairs in the White House at that period, remembers that it had a refrigerator the size of a small room. Just before a state dinner it was filled with salads, hors d'oeuvres, and entrées, and also on the shelves were two or three pans of rations for the dogs. The President came in, opened the refrigerator door, surveyed the contents slowly, and then paused to say, "Mighty fine-looking dog food." On the evening of May 2, 1924, to "Ike" Hoover's intense disapproval, Coolidge had his chair taken to the north porch, in full view of passers-by, and sat there for twenty minutes. But Coolidge was just behaving in a natural fashion, as did Mrs. Coolidge when, with Rebecca, her tame raccoon, in her arms, she mingled with the throng at the White House egg rolling. The Coolidges instituted some pleasant customs, including the singing of carols on Christmas Eve from the north portico and the New Year's salute from the White House roof.

Coolidge extended much hospitality at the famous White House breakfasts, to which guests were invited for eight-thirty in the morning. At seven such meals in January 1929, 129 guests were entertained, including many enemies of the administration. In his *Autobiography,* Coolidge speaks with much satisfaction of these events, saying that they "were productive of a spirit of good fellowship which was no doubt a helpful influence to the transaction of public business." "Ike" Hoover, however, regarded these breakfasts as having less significance and records the painful fact that many members of Congress, not liking the early hour, would plead all sorts of excuses for declining. The President said very little, but the guests always enjoyed the food, even though the host seldom made any effort at arrangement and never seemed to care where or how people were seated.[6]

The Coolidge administration was expensive, and the White House staff was considerably increased during that period. Furthermore, for the first time in some years a President took a long vacation during the summer, and a full staff was maintained wherever the Chief Executive went — to Swampscott, to the Adirondacks, to South Dakota, or to Wisconsin. The new law providing the President with a fund for official entertaining also made it possible to keep a larger number of servants throughout the year. The President had no objection to the expenditure of money in order to maintain the dignity of his position.

The Special Session of the Senate was over on March 18 and, with no Congress on his hands for several months, the President breathed easier. He and Mrs. Coolidge were now regular attendants at the First Congregational Church, sitting off the centre aisle in the fourth pew from the front. Throngs of sight-seers gathered in front of the church edifice as the Presidential automobile drove up, and Secret Service men were scattered throughout the congregation. The regular pew holders so filled the seats that few outsiders could secure admission. The President, it was noticed, did not join in the singing and usually looked a trifle bored by the service, but Mrs. Coolidge took part in everything. According to the newspaper stories, the President wore at the Easter service that spring a hat which had been reblocked, cleaned, and retrimmed with a new ribbon at a cost of $2.50.[7] He astonished everybody by appearing with Mrs. Coolidge, in late May, at a performance of *La Traviata* by the Washington Opera Company.

In general, Coolidge seemed to be in good health, with the excep-

---

[6] Hoover, *Forty-two Years in the White House,* pp. 126ff.
[7] Coolidge's economy policy was criticized in the spring of 1925 by manufacturers who complained that it was affecting business, actually causing a small buyers' strike.

tion of an occasional stomach upset. His excessive fondness for peanuts was often commented upon by those who knew him best and he paid a mild penalty for overindulgence. In May 1925, however, he had a more severe attack, which may have been the first warning of the heart trouble from which he eventually died. He wrote his father on May 26: —

You apparently saw in the paper that I had a little pain in the stomach the other morning, which lasted about an hour but was of no consequence. I suppose I had eaten something that didn't happen to agree with me.

When Everett Sanders spoke to him about it, the President replied, "Just had the bellyache!" and he was able to go on the *Mayflower* the next day as if nothing had happened. It was an evidence of the popular confidence in Coolidge that the news of even this slight indisposition alarmed the financial world and would probably, if the Stock Exchange had been open, have caused a sharp break in the market.

From time to time at special ceremonies the President set forth his views on current topics, both in public speeches and in official statements. Although famous for his taciturnity in private life, he surpassed most of his predecessors in the number of his addresses and the amount of his oratory. Charles Merz, in an article in the *New Republic*,[8] pointed out that Coolidge, in 1925, delivered 28 speeches as compared with 17 for Woodrow Wilson in 1917. Mr. Merz also catalogued 61 "official statements" during the same period and 179 "unofficial statements." Coolidge's speeches, furthermore, covered a wide range. According to Merz, he addressed the Germans on March 12, the Norwegians on June 8, the Negroes on June 25, the Swedes on July 1, the Irish on July 21, the Latin-Americans on October 28, and the Italians on November 24. Among the groups to which he talked were automobile men, contractors, trust-company officers, investment bankers, newspaper editors, motion-picture magnates, marine engineers, mining engineers, mechanical engineers, and farmers. Mr. Merz, a rather amused critic, did not add that Coolidge seldom spoke in a perfunctory fashion, but tried to say something fitted to each occasion — and usually succeeded.

On Memorial Day, at the Arlington National Cemetery, in an address which he later entitled "The Reign of Law," he lamented the decay of self-government, especially the prevailing tendency of

[8] Quoted in the *Literary Digest,* June 19, 1926.

Calvin Coolidge in the Black Hills

local communities to shift their responsibilities on Washington.[9]
In sentences which aroused much comment, most of it favorable,
he said: —

What we need is not more Federal government, but better local
government. . . . From every position of consistency with our system,
more centralization ought to be avoided. . . . The individual and the
local, state, and national political units ought to be permitted to assume
their own responsibilities. Any other course in the end will be subversive both of character and liberty. But it is equally clear that
they in their turn must meet their obligations.

In this speech Coolidge rather courageously declared himself
opposed to experiments in state socialization and federal bureaucracy, and even objected to the practice of national contributions
to state projects, such as road building. With this was the warning
that, unless local communities could and would settle their problems
themselves, the Washington authority would inevitably step in.
Even before his death, he was to see the national government doing
precisely this and adopting policies which were directly opposed to
his philosophy of the old American theory of local self-government
on the part of individuals, of counties, of cities, and of states.

As an illustration of his practical side, we should not neglect
his talk in late June to the assembly of administrative officers
charged with preparing the national budget. After pointing rather
proudly to what had been achieved in reducing appropriations and
paying off the national debt, he seized the occasion to deplore the
prevalent tendency to turn to the federal government for aid towards
projects which should be paid for by the individual states. He also
promised that the next Congress would effect a considerable revision downward in taxation; and to this end he conferred during
the summer with many leading members of the Senate and the
House.

On June 22, the Coolidges went to Swampscott, Massachusetts,
on the Atlantic coast not far from Lynn, where a residence called
White Court became the summer White House. It was a large
comfortable house, perched on a knoll above granite crags and owned
by the family of the late Frederick E. Smith, of Dayton, Ohio. Not
for nine years had a President established a seat of government away
from the capital. Offices were arranged on the seventh floor of the
Security Trust Company Building in Lynn. There the President

[9] *Foundations of the Republic*, 221ff.

had his portrait painted again and enjoyed a rest from urgent domestic and foreign affairs. He had been there only a few days, however, when he was called to Plymouth because of the serious illness of his father. An operation was performed on June 28, for an abscess of the prostate gland, and Colonel John rallied, but never fully regained his health.[10] When he returned to White Court, the President wrote his father nearly every day — little notes, full of sympathy, never effusive but saying a great deal. One of these, written on August 2, has about it an exceptional interest : —

It is two years since you woke me to bring the message that I was President. It seems a very short time. I trust it has been a great satisfaction to you. I think only two or three fathers have seen their sons chosen to be President of the United States. I am sure I came to it largely by your bringing up and your example. If that was what you wanted, you have much to be thankful for that you have lived to so great an age to see it.

It was the summer of the notorious trial of John Thomas Scopes, in Dayton, Tennessee, for teaching evolution to school children, with the dramatic clash of the two lawyers, Clarence Darrow and William Jennings Bryan, followed by the death of the latter on July 26. It was the period also of the Florida land boom, with the hectic excitement as real-estate values in Miami and other Florida cities soared

---

[10] The following item from the *New York World* for June 30, 1925, entitled "Colonel John Fights for Life," is a comment on Colonel John C. Coolidge's character : —

"There is the flint of an earlier, almost forgotten, stock in old John Coolidge. It was a stock which bred pioneers, hardy men who faced elemental things and survived, though they grew gnarled and seamed in the struggle. And it was a stock that found, through bleak blizzards and hardship, a curious philosophy, a sort of American stoicism. These men spurned the luxury of soft civilization. They loved beauty, for they made homes that were beautiful, but it was simple beauty that they loved, and simple living. They could feel deeply, but they believed that to betray feeling was weak and womanish, and they learned to hide what they felt under salt Yankee humor. John Coolidge is blood and bone of this lean and lanky race. It was in keeping with his philosophy that when his son became President of the United States he should make no fuss about it. He might take a few days off to see the boy inaugurated, but no silly demonstrations. And it was in keeping with his philosophy that when he was taken ill he should make no fuss about that. After repeated urgings from Washington he went to Boston to see the doctors, but when a friend asked him what the trouble was he replied he 'guessed he would have to read the papers to find out.' A lovable bit of irony — the mild assertion of his own simplicity, and a neat poke at the gabbling curiosity of the rest of the world. And it was in keeping with his philosophy that when things grew serious he should refuse to be weak and let his grandson call the doctor ; and that, when the operation was ordered, he should walk to the operating table unassisted ; and that he should go through with it under only local anaesthetic, and that he should joke with the surgeons. Altogether a fine old fellow, with simple taste and iron nerve which put most of us to shame in a blatant and hysterical age. May he pull through and live to be a hundred."

to incredible heights. Business was good, and stocks were rising, and nobody was worried much about the future or about a possible decline in prosperity. The Coolidges lived a quiet life, taking short cruises on the *Mayflower,* which was anchored at Marblehead.

In mid-August the Coolidges motored to Plymouth, hoping to persuade Colonel John, now an invalid, that he should come to Washington for the winter; but the old gentleman wanted to remain and die in his own house, and nothing could induce him to leave. Dr. Coupal did, however, go occasionally to the Notch and make a report on the patient's condition. The President continued to send little notes, some of them very moving, and a few with humorous touches. On October 21 he wrote from Washington: —

We are having some cool weather here now, so that I imagine you are getting the usual late October chill at home. We have discontinued sending flowers, and I have sent a check to James Blanchard for what he has done in caring for them. I told Mr. Sargent that, if you were coming down here, he had better see if you couldn't dispose of the horse. I also told him that we would send Aurora some cats and dogs to keep her company during the winter. I don't expect to hear from her as to any she would like to have. We are having a Congregational Convention in this town, so that our house is full of ministers. It will last for most of this week. I hope you are still keeping comfortable.

On January 1, 1926, the President sent the most revelatory letter that he ever wrote — plainly under the stress of much emotion: —

It is a nice bright day for the New Year, but rather cold. I wish you were here where you could have every care and everything made easy for you, but I know you feel more content at home. Of course we wish we could be with you. I suppose I am the most powerful man in the world, but great power does not mean much except great limitations. I cannot have any freedom even to go and come. I am only in the clutch of forces that are greater than I am. Thousands are waiting to shake my hand to-day.

It is forty-one years since mother lay ill in the same room where you now are. Great changes have come to us, but I do not think we are any happier, and I am afraid not much better. Every one tells me how cheerful you are. I can well understand that you may be. So many loved ones are waiting for you, so many loved ones are daily hoping you are comfortable and are anxious to know about you.

In late January the President had installed in the Plymouth house a direct telephone between there and Washington, and each day he talked with his father. The end came on March 18, 1926, so suddenly that Calvin Coolidge arrived at Plymouth too late to see his father alive. For the first time in American history a President's father had died while his son was in office, and the newspapers made much of the picturesque qualities in Colonel John's career and personality. He was in his eighty-first year and had survived his second wife by almost six years.

The President's first important appearance in the autumn was at Omaha, on October 6, before the national convention of the American Legion.[11] After discussing the World War and its aftermath, he turned to the broad question of tolerance, saying: —

Whatever tends to standardize the community, to establish fixed and rigid methods of thought, tends to fossilize society. . . . It is the ferment of ideas, the clash of disagreeing judgments, the privilege of the individual to develop his own thoughts and shape his own character, that makes progress possible.

Amplifying this liberal theory, the President spoke out vigorously against racial antagonisms and fears, against national bigotry, arrogance, and selfishness. "We must," he declared, "mobilize the conscience of mankind." It was a strong and noble utterance, which made a profound impression upon the delegates.

But the address which aroused the most comment, favorable and unfavorable, was delivered on November 9, in New York City, before the State Chamber of Commerce, under the title "Government and Business." [12] It was a long and carefully prepared presentation of government policy at the close of a year which, as he said, could "justly be said to surpass all others in the overwhelming success of general business." It was his thesis that "economic effort ought not to partake of privilege, and that business should be unhampered and free." Our country was "in a state of unexampled and apparently sound and well-distributed prosperity"; the attempts to eliminate waste had led to economy in production; the national debt was being rapidly liquidated, and taxes would soon be considerably reduced. He really thought then that the sums due us from foreign nations would ultimately be paid in their entirety.

Probably Calvin Coolidge saw no reason why the current prosperity should not continue for an indefinite term of years. He forgot what his study of history should have taught him — that periods

---

[11] *Foundations of the Republic,* 287ff. See also the *Literary Digest,* October 17, 1925, for contemporary comment. Coolidge's remarks were generally felt to be aimed at the Ku Klux Klan.
[12] *Foundations of the Republic,* 317ff.

of expansion and depression have alternated like the swings of a pendulum, in accordance with laws which economists are just beginning dimly to perceive and understand. He failed to discern certain significant factors in the situation — the disorganized and restless condition of Europe, the perils of the speculative spirit in an industrial age, the fluctuations of mood to which human nature even at its best is subject, and the enormous possibilities for disaster in the confusion following the World War. He summed up admirably the principles of the doctrine of *laissez faire* as they were evident in the capitalistic setup of the 1920's. We see now, in the wisdom which follows the event, that he was dwelling happily in a world of illusions. But it is unjust to blame him for not comprehending what so many better-equipped authorities never saw until they were caught in the whirlpool. The failure of his theory is not attributable necessarily to its illogicality or irrationality, but rather to the intrusion of elements completely beyond the control of any group of businessmen or even of the President of the United States.

The Coolidge philosophy was in 1925 that of the nation as a whole, and it seemed to be working well.[13] The prosperity by which it was apparently justified has been treated in various ways by different authors, and is still well remembered, although it seems nowadays to belong to a remote Elysium. The average man's condition was steadily improving. In 1919, according to the best available statistics, there were not far from seven million passenger automobiles in the United States; in 1929 there were more than twenty-four million. The buying power of the nation measured by this standard had increased more than three times. It is true that many families bought an automobile before they purchased a house, and that people were beginning to care less about what they ate or where they slept than how they could move from spot to spot. Nevertheless the prosperity of the Coolidge era was actual, and Frederick L. Allen is right in calling it, for the large majority of persons, a period of "unparalleled plenty." It was not merely that the number of millionaires in this country increased from 4500 in 1914 to 11,000 in 1926. It was not merely that the prices of stocks were high and dividends large. The wage earner also was far better

---

[13] The most thoughtful and scholarly study of urban conditions in the United States under Coolidge is *Middletown* (1929), by Robert S. and Helen M. Lynd, describing the results of research made by the authors in Muncie, Indiana, a city of about 40,000 people. Sinclair Lewis's *Babbitt*, although it appeared in 1922, is a first-class satire on the period; and his *The Man Who Knew Coolidge* (1928) moves into the realm of burlesque.

off. The six-day, or five-and-one-half-day, week and the eight-hour day were well established. Savings banks and life-insurance companies reported large increases in their assets, and wages improved in their buying power. The laboring man had more comforts, even more luxuries, than he had had a decade before.[14]

Figures on unemployment for this period are difficult to secure, but even at the height of Coolidge prosperity perhaps 5 per cent of the whole body of workers were without jobs. In general, however, those who really wished to work were offered the opportunity, and the average laboring man, outside of the farming class, was doing very well. Farmers, lumbermen, and tobacco workers apparently did not share in the general prosperity, and had a legitimate reason for complaint. But it is significant that the leaders of the nation in the 1920's were not much concerned with the problem of the unemployed — the problem which ten years later was to be constantly on the minds of American statesmen.

This was the golden age of advertising, sales pressure, and installment buying, accompanied by an unprecedented amount of what cynics called "bunk." Before Coolidge went out of office, the average family had acquired not only its own car, but also a radio, an oil heater, an electric ice chest, a washing machine, a vacuum cleaner, a telephone, and numerous other mechanical devices calculated to save labor in the house and give pleasure to its occupants. Luxuries of which Daniel Webster and Ulysses S. Grant had never dreamed were now within the buying power of workmen in factories. Women especially felt the effect of the rise in consumer credits and spent more time and money on the creation and preservation of attractive physical qualities. The radio was beginning to blare forth the merits of cosmetics and perfumes, of rouge and lipstick, of drugs which would increase weight or reduce it. "Beauty Shoppes" were opened on every Main Street, and magazines displayed advertisements of devices for accentuating feminine "allure." The publicity given to "movie stars" helped to introduce an era of bobbed hair and skimpy gowns, in which corsets and high shoes were as archaic as the bustle. People were being made conscious of personal defects, — of halitosis and pyorrhea, of deficiencies in reading or of speech, — and directed to the proper places where, at some expense, these could be corrected. The influence of fashion, of what is vaguely called society, was perhaps stronger than it had

[14] For a more detailed discussion of Coolidge Prosperity see Preston William Slosson, *The Great Crusade and After,* especially Chapter VI, "The Ways of Prosperity."

ever been before in this country — largely because of the motion pictures.

Of all the decades since the signing of the Constitution, that during which Calvin Coolidge was President was probably the most picturesque. It is true that there was no war, with its attendant and consequent excitement. But the national mood was ebullient, extravagant, high-strung, with a craving for "something doing." The heroes of sport — "Red" Grange in football, "Bobby" Jones in golf, "Bill" Tilden in tennis, "Jack" Dempsey and "Gene" Tunney in prize fighting — lived in their own special world of promoters, sports writers, press agents, radio broadcasters, and other parasites, who exploited their accomplishments. In May 1927 came Colonel Charles A. Lindbergh's dramatic solo flight across the Atlantic, which seized and held the imagination of the two continents and made him a national idol. Naturally his success induced others to emulate him through similar exploits, and Commander Richard E. Byrd, Amelia Earhart, and many others all had their official welcome in New York City, with the accompanying ballyhoo. Everything for a few years was geared "in high"; every emotion was somewhat overplayed; pictures were too brilliant and language was too much adorned with superlatives.[15]

The fever was accentuated by the evils accompanying Prohibition. The Eighteenth Amendment to the Constitution went legally into effect on January 16, 1920, and almost before the average citizen of Middletown could believe it the country was technically "dry." Aided by the moral uplift of the World War, persistent reformers saw the adoption of their "noble experiment" and prophesied a country completely sober. But the amendment proved impossible to enforce. In certain sections the most high-minded leaders of public opinion condemned the act and in some cases violated its provisions. President Coolidge, who obeyed the law implicitly, — as President Harding had not done, — believed that it should be enforced and did his best to see that its provisions were carried out. Soon the country was infested with bootleggers and speak-easies, with racketeers and night clubs, accompanied by a prodigious amount of hypocrisy and lawbreaking. In a period when the activities of the underworld were stimulated and gangsters enjoyed a heyday, "Al" Capone and his spectacular career were characteristic phe-

[15] *Books and Battles, American Literature, 1920–1930* (1937), by Irene and Allen Cleaton, describes picturesquely the kaleidoscopic features of the decade — the young intellectuals (who hated Coolidge), the New Humanism, the Lively Arts, the Vogue for Vogues, the bawdy shockers, the trend from limbs to legs, the exposers and reformers.

nomena. The moral sense of the community underwent a progressive and perceptible deterioration.

Compared with their fathers and mothers of the Gay Nineties, people wanted their lives highly spiced and adventurous. It was the period of the "flapper," the tabloid, the rum-runner; of "necking" and "jazz babies"; of the Leopold-Loeb case and the notorious "Peaches" Browning. Mr. Frederick L. Allen, in *Only Yesterday*, heads one of his chapters, "The Younger Generation Runs Wild." Exotic dances were becoming popular, and bathing beauties were being exploited for the edification of a vulgar public. The American people ran rapidly through one craze after another — mah-jongg, miniature golf, crossword puzzles, and other strange forms of diversion. There was a great deal of bravado, of bad manners, of exhibitionism, — shown by marathon dancers and flagpole sitters and automobile racers, — and also much unhappiness and disillusionment when the excitement was over.

Into the causes of this hysteria it will be impossible to enter here. The post-war psychology, with its survival of war neurosis, undoubtedly had much to do with it. The apparent futility of a life which might before morning be terminated by a bullet or a bayonet led to a glorification of the *carpe diem* philosophy — to the singing of the refrain, "A short life and a gay one!" The old fundamentals of morality had disappeared, and sophistication was regarded as an evidence of culture. In the retrospect, it all seems tawdry, crude, vulgar, and cheap, but in 1925 Flaming Youth was having its innings.

The most amazing fact about this indecorous and extravagant era is that the Man in the White House was the embodiment of all that the age itself was inclined to disparage and deride. Calvin Coolidge illustrated all the old-fashioned virtues — thrift,[16] industry, decency, dignity, and morality, frugal living and simple piety and good manners; and he was the popular President of a nation that was running wild. He was like a high priest who had been pushed into the van of a Bacchic Procession. He was far removed in his quiet family life from the improprieties all around him. In a period when vast numbers of people seemed to live in domiciles on wheels, he stayed at home. An advocate of temperance and prudence and early rising, he seemed to be an anomaly.

[16] When, in December 1924, he had to go to Chicago, he refused a special train but was willing to take a special car until he found out that the cost would be $90 for the car and an additional charge of 25 fares. The President then engaged space for himself and his party in an ordinary sleeper — thus saving about $1700 of public money.

Certainly he was in no sense responsible for what had happened to the social order. Nothing that he had said or done had encouraged the revelry, and nothing that he could say or do could possibly stop the riot. He continued to make speeches saying, "The nation with the greatest moral power will win," and his audiences applauded him, but he stopped nobody from dancing along the Primrose Path. Fortunately the great body of the American people remained relatively sane. The noisy and vulgar and criminal groups continued to "make" the front page of the tabloids, but millions of respectable people kept on living decent lives. But they, like the President, felt affronted by what was going on and wondered where it would end. The world around Calvin Coolidge was dancing and drinking and "petting," and he was doing none of these things.[17] His only modern vice was the jigsaw puzzle, to which he was inordinately addicted.

For explicable if not convincing reasons Calvin Coolidge had less opportunity than most of his predecessors to lead in constructive legislation. After all, he was a majority President, and most of his constituents were satisfied. The pressure of discontent, except among the farmers, did not reach the White House. Some Chief Executives have come into office with a mandate to restore confidence and prosperity; Coolidge had only the function of keeping the country confident and prosperous. He could, of course, restrain public officials from undue extravagance, insist on the economical management of government affairs, and relieve men and women from the burden of taxation — and this he did. But he found the American people, on the whole, contented and hopeful, and he was glad enough to observe the principle of "Let well enough alone." It did actually seem at times from 1925 to 1929 as if unemployment, poverty, and human misery, although still existent, were on the decline under the capitalistic system. Furthermore it would have been difficult, if not impossible, for Calvin Coolidge, or any other national leader, to resist the spirit of the age. Professor Samuel E. Morison, in commenting on the Coolidge period, said in 1929: —

The United States has evolved from a country of political experiment, a debtor to Europe, a radical disturber of established government, the

---

[17] Among the books read most widely during his period were Anita Loos's *Gentlemen Prefer Blondes*, Cabell's *Jurgen*, Hemingway's *The Sun Also Rises*, Arlen's *The Green Hat*, Marks's *The Plastic Age*, Hull's *The Sheik*, Erskine's *The Private Life of Helen of Troy*, and Dreiser's *An American Tragedy* — but Coolidge read none of these. Nor did he like H. L. Mencken's periodical *The American Mercury*, which was then in its prime, ridiculing the "booboosie." His own reading was still largely biography, economics, and history — books like Bowers's *Jefferson and Hamilton* and Sandburg's *Lincoln*.

hope of the oppressed and an inspiration to all men everywhere who wished to be free, into a wealthy and conservative country, the world's banker and stabilizer, the most powerful enemy to change and revolution.

Of this evolution, Calvin Coolidge was, in his generation, a symbol. By temperament he was no crusader; but there were few voices crying for a crusade. Even Franklin Delano Roosevelt was then saying very little about reform. The time did not seem to be "out of joint," and therefore Calvin Coolidge was not impelled to try to set it right.

In spite of the rejection of Warren for the cabinet, the new administration started out harmoniously. Coolidge had overcome his opponents, dispersed the Republican Old Guard, and won the support of the common people. He was now the acknowledged leader of his party, with unquestioned prestige and influence. Furthermore the Republicans had a narrow or nominal majority in both branches of Congress. Senator Lodge, Coolidge's Massachusetts rival, was gone, and Senator Charles Curtis, of Kansas, was the new Republican leader in the Senate; while Lodge's successor, William M. Butler, occupied a strategic position as the President's personal spokesman on the floor. On the basis of party affiliation, the Republican Senators numbered fifty-five, — six more than a majority, — but among them in the Sixty-ninth Congress were William E. Borah, of Idaho, George W. Norris, of Nebraska, Smith W. Brookhart, of Iowa, and Robert M. La Follette, Jr.,[18] not to mention such liberals as Lynn F. Frazier and Gerald P. Nye, of North Dakota, and Peter Norbeck and William H. McMaster, of South Dakota. These men were Independents, unpredictable in their attitude on controversial problems, and they sometimes joined with the Democrats to bring about embarrassing situations for the dominant regular Republicans. As a matter of fact, the party leaders, when committee assignments were being made, treated a few of the insurgents as if they were not Republicans but members of a *tertium quid;* and Brookhart and Frazier were, on that basis, rather ostentatiously ignored. Nye and the younger La Follette, on the other hand, were treated in committee assignments as if they were identified with the party organization. Coolidge himself was on excellent terms with Senators like Borah and Capper, and there were moments when he preferred the society of the Independents to that of the

[18] The older La Follette, after polling a popular vote of more than 4,000,000 in 1924, died on June 18, 1925, and his elder son was at once elected to succeed him as Senator from Wisconsin.

Regulars. At heart he always had a kindly personal feeling for the more liberal group of his own party — a fact which his radical critics often forget.

When the House of Representatives was organized, Representative Nicholas Longworth, son-in-law of Theodore Roosevelt, was elected Speaker, but thirteen insurgents and independents voted for Henry A. Cooper, of Wisconsin — the Democratic candidate, Finis J. Garrett, of Tennessee, receiving 173 votes to Longworth's 229. Although they were nominally Republicans, the party leaders removed twelve of the rebels from their places on important committees and transferred them to minor assignments. This act of discipline showed that, to Longworth and his group, the insurgents were fully as dangerous as the avowed Democrats. We can see now as we look back that these Independents, treated so cavalierly in 1925, were the forerunners of a movement which was later to be known as the New Deal.

Calvin Coolidge's Message to Congress of December 1925, if read to-day, seems remarkable because of the topics which he did not discuss — unemployment, for example, and child labor and old-age pensions and slum clearance and the relief of the underprivileged. His reticence on these matters was not due to indifference. No one had spoken more vigorously than he on the need for social justice. But according to his philosophy such problems should be settled by local communities and not by the federal government. Perhaps the most significant paragraph in his message emphasized the desirability of checking the tendency towards federal paternalism. In elucidating one of his favorite doctrines, he said: —

The functions which the Congress are to discharge are not those of local government but of national government. The greatest solicitude should be exercised to prevent any encroachment upon the rights of the states or their various political subdivisions. Local self-government is one of our most precious possessions. It is the greatest contributing factor to the stability, strength, liberty, and progress of the nation. It ought not to be infringed by assault or undermined by purchase. It ought not to abdicate power through weakness or resign its authority through favor. It does not at all follow that because abuses exist it is the concern of the federal government to attempt their reform.

Of course Coolidge was accused in some quarters of reversing the historic attitude of the Republican Party; but the more thoughtful Republicans were aware that the strengthening of the federal government, once so vital to the preservation of the republic, had gone far enough, and that the real need in 1925 was to check its authority and resist its encroachment. The Coolidge position, as stated here and elsewhere, is particularly significant in view of the later tendency, under Franklin D. Roosevelt, towards centralization. What Coolidge was stressing was the importance of individualism, of an alert, self-reliant community spirit as opposed to the dominance of a socialized state. The philosophy which he was advocating was that which he had learned in the Vermont hills and to which he had adhered all his life.

Aside from this fundamental issue, the President reiterated his familiar views on economy and tax reduction, urged citizens to "observe the spirit" of the Prohibition legislation, spoke of the advisability of our joining the World Court, and commented on such matters as the registration of aliens, the report of the Morrow aircraft inquiry, and the possible reorganization of governmental departments. It was clear that he contemplated nothing revolutionary, that he was to continue to be sane and safe.[19]

The Coolidge policy of economy was having visible results on the well-being of the average citizen. On the previous October 19, Secretary Mellon had suggested that the Treasury could afford tax cuts amounting to $300,000,000; and in February 1925, Congress passed a measure reducing very considerably the rates of taxation for both large and small taxpayers, and relieving approximately two million persons from the need of paying an income tax. The act was criticized on the ground that it was primarily intended to help the wealthy, but this charge was not supported by unprejudiced students of government finance. It is worth noting that the interest-bearing national debt at the close of 1926 stood at $19,300,000,000 as compared with $26,300,000,000 in the summer of 1919. It had decreased at the rate of about a billion dollars a year — an accomplishment regarded in those times as worthy of high praise.

Not everybody, however, was satisfied, and the farmers in particular had their grievances, especially when they compared their condition with that of those engaged in industry or finance. Over the preceding twenty-five years farming efficiency had increased, and despite a reduction in acreage and a general drift to the city, crop production was relatively larger. But the Western agriculturist could prove by statistics that the gradual drop in prices after the World War, due to deflation, had affected him more than any other class of worker. While the value of his crops had declined, he had

[19] For a summarization of the message see the *Literary Digest*, December 19, 1925.

been obliged to pay higher prices for machinery and supplies. Consequently the Middle West was again in opposition to the industrial East. It was the old story of agrarian impatience with manufacturing and banking interests — the same type of rebellion which formerly had been headed by William Jennings Bryan and the Populists and the various farm blocs which had superseded them. One of the immediate problems was that of controlling and marketing surplus crops. Each individual farmer naturally based the size of his acreage on the possibilities of sale. When prices rose, the acreage was likely to increase, with the result that the market was glutted with superfluous, and often with perishable, products. It is true that this unbalanced situation tended to correct itself through the laws of supply and demand, but only after wastefulness and suffering over broad areas. What was required was some scientific method of prediction and adjustment so that the fluctuation of prices could be minimized and production limited to reasonable needs.[20]

The problem was really a serious one, and Coolidge, who had been brought up among dirt farmers in Vermont and could speak on the subject from first-hand experience, naturally felt that they were entitled to all the sympathy and help which a generous government could legitimately give them. On December 7, 1925, at the annual convention of the American Farm Bureau Corporation, in Chicago, he spoke on the subject,[21] saying, with great courage, that he did not believe that the federal government should directly or indirectly fix prices or engage in buying and selling farm produce. The original McNary-Haugen Bill, first introduced in the Senate on January 16, 1926, sponsored by Senator Charles L. McNary, of Oregon, and Congressman Gilbert N. Haugen, of Iowa, had been an attempt to control surpluses and stabilize farm prices by creating a Federal Board which in big-yield years could purchase the surplus and either hold it for a time off the market or dispose of it abroad. For this bill the President had no enthusiasm. He declared that agriculture must rest "on an independent business basis," and kept returning to his fundamental doctrine, "Government control cannot be divorced from political control." Consequently he was opposed to the McNary-Haugen Bill, or any similar measure based upon that

[20] For an interesting treatment of this situation see Slosson, especially Chapter VII, "The Changing Countryside."
[21] At the luncheon directly after his speech the President was served with eggs from Utah, milk from Illinois, maple syrup from Vermont, cheese from Wisconsin, fruit from Florida, nuts from California, and cigars from Kentucky. For newspaper comment on the speech see the *Literary Digest* for December 19, 1925.

principle, but he did approve of a plan by which the government could assist farmers to improve their status through coöperative marketing. At the same time he defended the protective tariff, saying that protection was "a great benefit to agriculture as a whole." At this statement there was some resentment from Democrats and Independents; indeed one prominent newspaper asserted that the President's principal mission in Chicago was "the defense of the protective tariff which every primer economist knows is a curse to American agriculture."

Coolidge concluded this carefully reasoned speech by raising the plane of his argument to something higher than mere financial considerations. In one vigorous paragraph he said: —

In all our economic discussions we must remember that we cannot stop with the mere acquisition of wealth. The ultimate result to be desired is not the making of money, but the making of people. Industry, thrift, and self-control are not sought because they create wealth, but because they create character. These are the prime product of the farm. We who have seen it, and lived it, know.

Here once more we have Calvin Coolidge relating one phase of political action to a broader and consistent philosophy — the philosophy of individualism, of independent action and opportunity. Coolidge felt that it was better for a man to keep his freedom, even though failing to secure all the benefits he desired, than to be dependent on the government for his well-being. The estimate which historians will make of Coolidge as time marches on will depend largely on what philosophy proves to be in the long run best for mankind. In his public acts and speeches Coolidge was no opportunist but an honest and brave thinker.

Nevertheless discontent among the farmers was spreading during the winter and spring of 1926. They were contrasting their own condition with that of the prosperous mill workers of the industrial area and declaring that something must be done to help them. Senator Capper announced that the West would be swept by a political tornado unless the tariff were revised in the interests of the farmer. Nevertheless the McNary-Haugen Bill was defeated at the close of the session in the late spring of 1926. What really settled its fate was a letter from Secretary Mellon stating that it was economically unsound; that its enactment would raise the cost of living and lower the purchasing power of wages; and that one disastrous result of its passing would be to increase production and decrease consumption. The net result of several months of debate was merely the establishment of a Division of Coöperative Marketing in the Department of Agriculture and the appropriation of $225,000 for its maintenance.

When the session came to a close on July 3, nearly a thousand laws and resolutions had been passed, of which only two — both private measures — were vetoed by the President, although five were disposed of by "pocket veto." Among the genuine accomplishments was the Watson-Parker Railroad Labor Act, creating a new Board of Mediation to serve in cases of dispute between railways and their employees and signed, with some reservations, on May 20, by the President. The Public Buildings Act, approved on May 25, appropriated $165,000,000 for the construction of certain badly needed federal buildings. In the passage of this law Mrs. Coolidge was tremendously interested, and she talked often with Charles Moore, Chairman of the National Commission of Fine Arts, regarding the beautification of the capital city.

Nevertheless, when the session was over, commentators remarked that much had been left undone. No measures had been passed regarding Muscle Shoals, the coal-strike quandary had been evaded, and no relief had been offered to alien owners of sequestered property. The Rivers and Harbors Bill had been passed by the House but neglected by the Senate. The President and Congress had gone along peaceably, without any open clash, and the machinery of government had rolled along without the need of brakes or lubrication.[22] In one case, however, the President's wishes had been rather dramatically thwarted. Wallace McCamant, of Portland, Oregon, who had nominated Coolidge in 1920 for the Vice Presidency and who had been a lifelong Republican, was given a recess appointment by Coolidge in September 1925 as Judge of the Ninth Circuit Court. When the Judiciary Committee of the Senate reported favorably on the nomination, Senator Hiram Johnson caused it to be sent back for reconsideration. McCamant had been opposed to Johnson as a Presidential candidate in 1920, and the Californian had made up his mind to "get him." Eventually McCamant was turned down, and Johnson had his petty revenge. The incident is indicative of the extent to which spite is sometimes carried in American politics, and the President was much annoyed by the result.

[22] William H. Taft wrote on January 10, 1926, "Coolidge's influence in Congress is asserting itself, and I think he is giving more body to the Republican Party in Congress than it has had for a long time." Later, on July 7, he added, writing to Charles D. Hilles, "I quite agree with you that Coolidge has lost some ground, not as much, I think, as a good many people say or think, and continued good business will wipe out the slips."

On July 5, in Philadelphia, the President delivered an address in commemoration of the one hundred and fiftieth anniversary of the Declaration of Independence, in the course of which he made a clear statement of his conservative faith: —

Under a system of popular government there will always be those who will seek for political preferment by clamoring for reform. While there is very little of this which is not sincere, there is a large portion that is not well informed. In my opinion very little of just criticism can attach to the theories and principles of our institutions. There is far more danger of harm than there is of hope of good in any radical changes.

In the same address, as he drew to a close, he warned his countrymen not to sink into a pagan materialism, saying: —

We live in an age of science and of abounding accumulation of material things. These did not create our Declaration. Our Declaration created them. The things of the spirit come first. Unless we cling to that, all our material prosperity, overwhelming though it may appear, will turn to a barren sceptre in our grasp.

In a succession of speeches like this, each on a different theme but each constituting a phase of a philosophy, Calvin Coolidge made it clear that he was no stupid or uninformed executive, evading issues or guessing at the truth. We may not agree with his way of thinking and acting; we may feel that he was reactionary, slavishly bound to tradition, opposed to rational progress; but we cannot, I think, doubt his consistency and honesty. He seldom reached a decision without a good reason, and he was always able to justify his conclusions by arguments. Those who picture him as a helpless fumbler simply do not comprehend his nature. He may have been wrong, but he always knew what he was doing and why he was doing it. He sometimes took more time than even his friends could have wished, but it was not laziness or procrastination which caused the delay. He wanted to be sure of his ground.

Immediately after the Philadelphia address the Coolidges went to White Pine Camp, fourteen miles from Saranac Lake, in the heart of the Adirondack region, with the nearest railroad station four miles off. The camp was offered to the President by Irwin R. Kirkwood, a newspaper owner of Kansas City, who owned in the depths of the forest a very comfortable summer "cabin," equipped in the most luxurious fashion. No motors could get close to it, and it was completely isolated from inquisitive visitors, on Lake Osgood, one of the loveliest bodies of water in the mountains. An occasional item of news drifted out, — how the President caught a three-pound pike within a few hours after his arrival, how arrangements had been made for motion pictures three times a week, — and the executive offices opened in a cottage near Paul Smith's hotel were in charge of Everett Sanders, who kept the press informed as to what was going on. The President spent his time fishing and strolling around the trails. He inspected a Plattsburg camp and also went for a few days in August to Plymouth. It was a peaceful vacation, although a number of guests found their way to the lake — Frank B. Kellogg, Owen D. Young, Julius Rosenwald, General Lord, Secretary Jardine, James R. Sheffield, John G. Sargent, and others, including Bruce Barton, who secured from him a noteworthy interview printed in the *New York Sun* for September 22.

The Coolidges returned on September 19 to a White House glistening with white paint and improved by the installation of a new electric elevator. Many minor repairs had been carried through to make it more comfortable. The autumn elections were not altogether favorable to the Republicans. The Republicans lost seven seats in the Senate, including one in Massachusetts, where the popular David I. Walsh, a Democrat, defeated William M. Butler, Coolidge's friend and close adviser as well as Chairman of the Republican National Committee, by more than fifty thousand votes. In support of Butler, Coolidge wrote a public letter summarizing his good qualities, and the Coolidges furthermore returned to Northampton in order to cast their ballots for him; but their candidate was not magnetic, and he had made many enemies in his own party. The Democrats, with proper partisan fervor, declared that Coolidge was done for, but unprejudiced observers could see no real blow to the President's prestige. Although the Republican majority in the Lower House was to be only forty, it was still sufficient for all practical purposes.

Coolidge's most important address during the autumn was at Kansas City, on Armistice Day, where, after dwelling on the horrors of war, he finally abandoned all hope of American adherence to the Permanent Court of International Justice. His preoccupation with internal problems was also evident in his Annual Message on December 7, 1926, in which his two chief topics were tax reduction and farm relief. When it became evident that the Treasury would have a surplus of not far from $400,000,000 for the year, he advocated temporary reduction in the tax schedules as a further encouragement to business. With reference to the agricultural situation, he again voiced his disapproval of any plan which would bring the government into producing or marketing but did hope that a "sound solution of a permanent nature" could be brought about. Seldom has a President's message contained so few recommendations for legislative action. His remarks on foreign affairs were very general, confined to the statement that our policy is one of peace. The tone of the message can be expressed in the somewhat complacent observation that "what the country requires is not so much new policies as a steady continuation of those which are already being crowned with such abundant success."

During the short session the advocates of the McNary-Haugen Bill again brought pressure to bear on Congress, and in the following February it was passed by both Houses, with a vote cut squarely across party affiliation. Within a week, on February 25, the President returned the bill with his disapproval and a long and very vigorous message justifying his veto — a message which William H. Taft called a "sockdolager," and rightly, for it minced no words on a subject which had always irritated him. Coolidge pointed out that the bill was intended to facilitate governmental price fixing and that its "equalization fee" was actually a tax for the benefit of special groups. Attached to the veto was an opinion of the Attorney General to the effect that the measure as passed was unconstitutional. The President declared that the bill was chiefly objectionable because it would not really help the farmer and would end by establishing an enormous government bureaucracy. Those who knew political currents felt that the major struggle for the year would centre in this "thumping veto," but no serious attempt to override it was made in Congress and the man in the street believed that Coolidge was right. When Senator La Follette in February introduced a joint resolution against a third term, Curtis succeeded in having it tabled, and it would have had little support. The truth is that many Congressmen voted for the McNary-Haugen Bill hoping that the President would kill it and that, furthermore, Coolidge's display of courage gained him the respect of people who had hitherto regarded him as spineless.

The Sixty-ninth Congress terminated automatically on March 4, 1927, in the midst of a contemptible filibuster which had held up several important measures, including the Deficiency Appropriation Bill, and which aroused popular indignation against Senator David A. Reed, of Pennsylvania, who was mainly responsible,[23] and also

[23] Senator James A. Reed, of Missouri, was trying to extend the life of a Select Committee for investigating campaign expenses, and Senator David A. Reed organized the filibuster against the Missouri Senator's plan.

against the ridiculous Senate rules which did not allow majority cloture. In summing up the achievements of the short session of only sixty-seven legislative days, the *Literary Digest* mentioned the Dill-White Radio Control Bill, placing the regulation of radio transmission under the direction of a Radio Commission of five members and establishing the authority of the government over a new and increasingly important means of communication; the Prohibition Reorganization Bill, placing enforcement officers under the Civil Service and establishing the Prohibition Unit as an entity in itself; and the McFadden-Pepper Banking Act, which extended the scope of the reforms of the Federal Reserve Act of 1913 and gave national banks for the first time the legal right to open branch subsidiaries. On several important matters the Congress was unable to take action, but the President declined to call a special session, feeling that the country could get along without further legislation over the summer.

Calvin Coolidge had no great cause to be pleased with the Congress which "petered out" on March 4, 1927. Early in the year he nominated as a member of the Interstate Commerce Commission Cyrus E. Woods, of Pennsylvania, on the recommendation of Senator Reed of that state. Several hearings were held, at which Mr. Woods appeared and was questioned, and it became evident that the hostility of Kentucky, Tennessee, and West Virginia to such a sectional appointment was ineradicable. Woods was rejected on January 25, by a vote of 49 to 28. Coolidge was more successful in a dispute with the House of Representatives over the Naval Appropriation Act on the matter of three battle cruisers which the President did not wish to have constructed. The Big Navy group took issue with the Chief Executive, who explained the reasons for his opinion and finally had the appropriation reduced, by the close vote of 183 to 161.

Generally speaking, the President's popularity did not wane perceptibly during the spring of 1927, and the prevailing prosperity made him seem the logical Republican candidate for 1928. In late February, before a Republican organization in New York City, President Nicholas Murray Butler of Columbia University, a prominent figure in the party councils, expressed the opinion that common sense would lead Coolidge not to be a candidate in 1928. He added, "The Republican Party is going to have a hard enough time in 1928 without inviting certain defeat through injecting the third-term issue into the campaign." Dr. Butler's speech found almost no support in the national press and was regarded as a somewhat premature indication of his own receptivity as a candidate. Even when Senator Norris came out in May against a third term, Coolidge remained silent and gave no intimation as to his plans,[24] but it is certain that William M. Butler and Frank W. Stearns were proceeding on the assumption that, when the hour came for making a decision, he would allow his name to be used.

For the summer of 1927, at the recommendation of Senator Peter Norbeck, of South Dakota, the Coolidges decided to go to the Black Hills of that state, about two thousand miles from the national capital. The state game lodge, formerly used as a hotel for tourists, was assigned as the summer White House. It comprised more than twenty rooms, with a number of rustic log buildings for guests and servants, and had in the living room a massive stone fireplace which invited relaxation. Twelve miles of trout streams were promised for the sole use of the Presidential party. According to a well-authenticated story, local residents, knowing the near-by stream was short of trout, released about fifteen hundred good-sized fish near the Coolidge camp, keeping them within a five-hundred-yard stretch with nets.

The Coolidges arrived in the Black Hills on June 15, having left the temporary White House in Dupont Circle [25] immediately after entertaining Colonel Charles A. Lindbergh and his mother on Saturday, June 11. On the trip out the President stopped at Hammond, Indiana, to dedicate the Wicker Memorial Park and make a plea for the "unskilled workers," who had not enjoyed their full share of the national prosperity. Although the little hamlet and railroad station of Hermosa is the nearest railroad point, the President chose Rapid City, thirty-two miles from the lodge, as the place for the executive offices — a city of about 8000 inhabitants, one of the most important in the state. Telephone wires had to be strung over the slopes and peaks of the Black Hills from Rapid City to the

[24] According to J. Fred Essary, of the *Baltimore Sun,* the Washington correspondents put up a game on Coolidge in the spring of 1927, by each handing him the same query, "Shall you run in 1928?" When the hour of the press conference came, they all filed in, and the President was standing at his desk as usual with the written questions in his hand. Solemnly he said, "I have here a question about the condition of the children in Poland," and proceeded to talk for ten minutes on a subject which no one had brought up.

[25] During the spring of 1927 the White House was undergoing some renovation, and the Coolidges were installed for some weeks in a temporary residence. The attic of the White House was transformed into an entire new floor of eighteen rooms, for guests and servants, at a cost of $400,000. Taft wrote, February 6, 1927, "The Coolidges are going into the Taft house (the house of Mrs. Patterson, daughter of Joseph Medill, of *Chicago Tribune.* They took it furnished) down next to the Boardmans. That is a fine house and admirably adapted, I should think, to Presidential occupancy."

lodge. Newspapermen maintained headquarters in Rapid City and saw the President there on Tuesdays and Fridays.

Once arrived in the forest, the President was up early and came back with a good-sized catch of trout. "Did you use a fly?" asked one of the newspaper correspondents; and Coolidge precipitated an anglers' controversy by answering candidly, "No, I used a hook and worm." Horrified piscatorial statesmen, like Senators Borah and Reed, protested that it was highly unethical to use worms for trout, and the issue was thus raised between democracy and aristocracy among fishermen. High authorities were invoked, from Izaak Walton to Bliss Perry, to justify the disputants, and much amusement was stimulated in the press at a time when it was thought that news would be scarce.

It turned out that plenty of good stories were to emanate from the Black Hills that summer. A group of Wyoming visitors presented Coolidge with a ten-gallon hat, which he wore for the photographer. On his fifty-fifth birthday, on July 4, a group of cowboys appeared to greet him, and he, at their request, wore a fancy cowboy costume, with CAL in large letters on the "chaps." [26] He was adopted by the Sioux Indians as technical chief of their tribe, and on August 17 addressed more than ten thousand of them, speaking as their Leading Eagle.

Newspaper editors were insisting in the spring of 1927 that political considerations had determined the President's choice of a summer residence — that he had selected the Northwest in order to win back the farmers' vote which he had presumably lost through his veto of the McNary-Haugen Bill.[27] Indeed cartoons appeared over the legend, "The Winning of the West." But very few well-

[26] Mrs. Dwight W. Morrow recalls that many of Coolidge's friends were perplexed when he permitted himself to be photographed in cowboy costume. At last one of them, as tactfully as possible, entered a protest to the President. "But I don't see why you object," said Coolidge. "The people have sent me this costume, and they wouldn't have sent it unless they expected me to put it on. Why shouldn't I have my picture taken with it on to please them?" "It's making people laugh," said his friend. "Well, it's good for people to laugh," replied the President. Mrs. Morrow continues, "I believe that, even supposing he did not want to wear the costume, he was really doing it out of courtesy and consideration for those who had offered him a gift." (*Good Housekeeping*, February 1935.) When a group of Boy Scouts called on him, Coolidge put on a similar costume, and even mounted a horse. Mrs. Coolidge has written, "I believe he knew that he was making those boys happy at the cost of future criticism from friends who would remonstrate with him for appearing to act a part in order to curry favor with our summer neighbors."

[27] This view has been publicized in "Ike" Hoover's *Forty-two Years in the White House*, which states that the trip to the Black Hills was planned "with every intention of making political capital out of the stay." But Hoover, always a prejudiced witness on matters connected with Coolidge, was not in the President's confidence and was not taken to State Lodge.

informed persons had any doubt that Calvin Coolidge could be nominated and elected in 1928,[28] whether he took his vacation in the West or the East. William Allen White declared that the President would have no serious opposition, adding, "Coolidge represents something definite in the American heart." And then, at precisely the moment when his friends were perfecting their organization and even his opponents were reconciling themselves to defeat, he made the most dramatic move of his career.

Regarding Coolidge's decision not to be a candidate in 1928, various stories have been told, many of them half-fanciful and several marred by insinuation and innuendo. The truth can easily be ascertained from persons still living who were on the spot at the time and knew the President best. He himself has offered testimony in an article published October 3, 1931, in the *Saturday Evening Post:* —

When I announced my determination not to run for President in 1928, my decision had been made a long time. While I wanted the relief that would come to Mrs. Coolidge and me from the public responsibilities we had held for so many years, my action was also based on the belief that it was best for the country.

With this clear statement available, it would seem unnecessary to lend the ear to mere gossip or to seek for more devious motives. Another witness of undisputed veracity is Everett Sanders, Secretary to the President, who is still alive and has recounted his version. The account which follows is based largely upon his own carefully prepared narrative of events, checked by Mrs. Coolidge's recollection.

In late July, 1927, the President summoned Sanders to his improvised office in the southeastern corner of the high-school building in Rapid City, invited him to sit down, and then said in a perfectly natural voice, "Now — I am not going to run for President." Sanders was too much astonished to reply, and Coolidge continued, "If I should serve as President again, I should serve almost ten years, which is too long for a President in this country." Sanders answered, "I think the people will be disappointed." Coolidge then handed Sanders a slip of paper on which was written, in blue pencil, the sentence, "I do not choose to run for President in nineteen twenty-eight," — twelve words, — and inquired, "What do you think of that?" After some casual comment on the phraseology,

[28] William M. Butler, Chairman of the Republican National Committee, and William V. Hodges, its Treasurer, made a trip to the West in the spring of 1927 and were convinced that Coolidge's nomination was certain and his reëlection as sure as such an event could be. (Letter from William V. Hodges, March 10, 1939.)

to which the President paid little attention, Sanders ventured to ask, "You feel sure that you have reached a definite decision about the matter?" "Yes," was the reply. "Well," commented Sanders, "since there is no occasion for speaking now, I do not see why

I do not choose to run for President in nineteen Twenty eight

FACSIMILE OF ORIGINAL NOTE

there should be any hurry about making the announcement." In his memorandum, Sanders has said: —

No one can recall after a lapse of time the substance of such a conversation, but the impression frequently remains very vivid. The one impression that I had, and which still remains, was that he had not called me in to seek my advice as to whether he should run. After we discussed the phraseology of the note which he had submitted to me, I knew that he had not the slightest idea of heeding my advice about that unless I should agree.

Coolidge next arranged with Sanders to have the announcement made public on August 2, the fourth anniversary of his entering upon the Presidency. On that fateful Tuesday morning, after finishing breakfast at the Lodge, he said casually to his wife, "I have been President four years to-day," and then stepped into the automobile for the ride alone with the chauffeur to Rapid City, thirty miles down the valley.[29] Sanders, who was waiting when the President arrived at eight-thirty, greeted him in his office and asked, "Do you still intend to make your announcement to-day?" "Yes," was

[29] Senator Capper's statement that, as a guest at the Lodge, he rode down with the President that morning is not in accord with Mrs. Coolidge's recollection. The Senator went to Rapid City in another car later in the day. William Allen White, who makes the distance from the Lodge to Rapid City ten miles instead of thirty, also describes the President as, during the ride, "composing his renunciation." The truth is, as we have seen, that the renunciation had been composed several days before.

the reply. Then Sanders went on, "I think it would be well if you made it at twelve o'clock instead of nine o'clock. There is three hours difference in time between Rapid City and New York, and if the announcement is made at twelve o'clock, it will come after three there, and the stock market will be closed. News of this kind is sure to affect the stock market. It is always best to have the news break at a time when the effect of it can be digested while the stock market is closed." Coolidge quickly agreed to this and, at the end of his regular nine-o'clock conference with the newspapermen, remarked casually, "If you will return at twelve o'clock, there will be an additional statement."

About eleven-thirty, after attending to his routine mail, Coolidge called Sanders into his office, picked up his pencil, and wrote in a neat hand on a small sheet from a memorandum pad the same words that Sanders had already seen, "I do not choose to run for President in nineteen twenty-eight." "Take this," he said, "and about ten minutes before twelve call in Mr. Geisser, have him run off a number of these lines on legal-sized paper, five or six on a sheet, with carbons enough to supply the newspapermen, and some to spare. Then bring the sheets to me uncut." [30] Sanders retired to his own quarters and summoned Erwin C. Geisser, the President's personal stenographer, who, although visibly very much affected, followed implicitly the instructions. Sanders took the sheets to the President, who picked a pair of shears out of the desk drawer and cut painstakingly through the paper, making neat little slips, perhaps two inches in width. He then said, "I am going to hand these out myself; I am going to give them to the newspapermen, without comment, from this side of the desk. I want you to stand at the door and not permit anyone to leave until each of them has a slip, so that they may have an even chance."

Walking back to his office, Sanders found there Senator Capper, who had arrived not long before from the Lodge, and said to him, "Senator, we do not usually permit anyone to come into the newspaper conferences except regularly accredited newspaper corre-

[30] William Allen White's story that the President dictated the famous sentence to "one of his personal stenographers" is obviously incorrect, based on Senator Capper's inaccurate recollection. Mr. Sanders has kept in his possession the original slip containing the twelve words, — not "ten cryptic words," as Mr. White describes them, — and has kindly allowed me to reproduce it in facsimile. Erwin C. Geisser, who is also still alive, after reading Sanders's account of the incident, confirmed its general accuracy and wrote on November 22, 1938, "I have read the foregoing. I was President Coolidge's personal stenographer at the time indicated and was in Rapid City. The President did not dictate the statement. The description of the event so far as my part of it was concerned is accurate."

spondents, but since you are a journalist and publisher, I think you will be interested in going in with the boys." Senator Capper took his place with the others, entirely unaware of what was to happen. The President told the newspapermen that the line would form on the left, and then handed to each in turn a slip of paper. When Sanders opened the outer door, there was a wild scramble for the nearest telegraph office and long-distance telephone. The excitement which ensued did not die out for many months.[31]

After the reporters had escaped to spread the news, the President turned back to his desk, stared absent-mindedly for a moment at some documents, called for his hat, and joined Senator Capper in a walk to the Presidential limousine. Calvin Coolidge was smiling broadly as he entered the car, realizing, perhaps, that he had caused a sensation which was spreading around the globe. Although Mrs. Coolidge felt intuitively that something had been on her husband's mind, she knew nothing whatever in advance of the decision or the announcement. After the President had retired to his room for a nap following the luncheon, Senator Capper, always a reserved man, said cautiously, "That was quite a surprise the President gave us this morning." When Mrs. Coolidge professed ignorance, he told her what had happened, and she broke out, "Isn't that just like the man! He never gave me the slightest intimation of his intention. I had no idea!" Later she wrote, "I am rather proud of the fact that after nearly a quarter of a century of marriage, my husband feels free to make his decisions without consulting me or giving me advance information concerning them."[32]

Why did he do it? In the first place, it was not an impulsive or hasty resolve, but, as he himself said and as Sanders's evidence proves, a deliberate and carefully planned decision. He never allowed his emotions to dominate his reason, and he knew precisely what he was doing when he prepared the statement which precipitated so much controversy. By nature he was prudent and logical, and his acts were the consequence of long meditation. In his *Autobiography,* Coolidge included a chapter headed, "Why I Did Not Choose to Run," in which he presented a number of reasons, not all of them equally convincing, to explain his conduct. A man's motives are seldom absolutely clear-cut, even to himself,

[31] William Allen White, in *A Puritan in Babylon,* describes this incident as taking place on August 3, and says that the news reached Wall Street shortly after the close of the stock market ticker for the week, adding, "On Monday the market fell." As a matter of fact the statement was issued on Tuesday, August 2, and the stock market drop naturally took place on Wednesday.
[32] *American Magazine,* September 1929.

and I have no doubt that he was actuated by complex considerations, some obscure and some deep-seated. With full appreciation of these facts, he wrote: —

I had never wished to run in 1928 and had determined to make a public announcement at a sufficiently early date so that the party would have ample time to choose some one else. An appropriate occasion for that announcement seemed to be the fourth anniversary of my taking office. The reasons I can give may not appear very convincing, but I am confident my decision was correct.

In the second place, he meant what he said. The theory that he was trying to test out public sentiment is, with a person of his temperament, simply not plausible.[33] On August 2, 1927, he was aware that he would be unopposed if he agreed to accept the nomination for another term. All he had to do was to nod an affirmative, or even to say nothing, and thousands of enthusiastic supporters would open a campaign for him. Why, if he really desired another term, should he needlessly run the risk of having his ambition thwarted? Furthermore Calvin Coolidge was not only an honest, straightforward man, but he had a gift for saying just what he meant. He could, under the right circumstances, be a most astute politician; but surely he had nothing to gain and everything to lose by a direct renunciation a year before the Republican Convention would meet. To assume that he was playing a trick on his party and on the American people, at a considerable risk to his own career, is attributing to him motives which do not fit his character. In default of convincing evidence that he was insincere, he is entitled to our confidence.

What were his reasons? The third-term issue did not trouble him, for he did not feel that it was applicable to a man who had succeeded to part of a term as Vice President.[34] "Others might argue that he does," he said, "but I doubt if the country would so consider it." It has been intimated by William Allen White that he was remorseful because of his discharge a few weeks before of James Haley, a Secret Service man who had accompanied Mrs. Coolidge on a walk and had returned with her late to luncheon,

---

[33] Colonel J. F. Coupal, former White House physician, issued a copyrighted story in July 1931, saying Coolidge did not intend, when he made his statement, to remove himself unconditionally from the Presidential field. "Instead he merely wished, in compliance with his sense of justice, to cast aside any advantage his position might give and permit the people to choose another man if they preferred." Coolidge's own words make this interpretation untenable.

[34] *Autobiography*, 240.

to the President's great agitation and annoyance;[35] but this explanation is not far from preposterous. In his explanation in his *Autobiography,* he spoke of the "heavy strain" of the office, adding that "it is hazardous to attempt what we feel is beyond our strength to accomplish." There is some reason for believing that the President knew at least as early as 1928 that there was something wrong with his heart. Brigadier General Sherwood Cheney, once a White House military aide, speaking in 1938, declared that Coolidge had been warned by his physician of this weakness and knew that he ought not to subject himself to the burden of four more years in the White House. This theory is substantiated by other evidence, some of it contributed by persons who knew him very well. He had also been much concerned over the heavy responsibility which Mrs. Coolidge was obliged to bear, and doubted whether she could carry it much longer "without some danger of impairment of her strength."

Among his motives was the consciousness that his work as President was almost done. Mrs. Coolidge recalls that, in a talk with a member of the cabinet, her husband said: —

I know how to save money. All my training has been in that direction. The country is in a sound financial position. Perhaps the time has come when we ought to spend money. I do not feel that I am qualified to do that.[36]

In his *Autobiography* Coolidge pointed out that "the chances of having wise and faithful public service are increased by a change in the Presidential office after a moderate length of time."[37] When a former member of the cabinet expressed the conviction that the country would undergo within the next few years a serious economic and financial convulsion, Coolidge replied tersely, "It's a pretty good idea to get out when they still want you."[38]

Hubert Work, formerly Secretary of the Interior and Postmaster General and a good friend of Coolidge, declared in 1936 that he had little patience with those who would insinuate that the President expected renomination in 1928. Only a few days after the statement of August 2, 1927, Work said to him, "You would be renominated without opposition and would assuredly be reëlected."

[35] Those who wish to learn in detail of this incident should read White's *A Puritan in Babylon,* pp. 353ff. The matter was a trivial one, but some Boston newspapers, lacking other more important news, put it into the headlines.
[36] *Good Housekeeping,* May 1935.
[37] *Autobiography,* 241.
[38] *Good Housekeeping,* May 1935. The story is told by Mrs. Coolidge.

To this he responded, "Yes, I believe I could be. But ten years is too long for one man to be President. Four years more in the White House would kill Mrs. Coolidge." . . . And so, with the conviction that Calvin Coolidge felt conscious of the "weariness, the fever, and the fret" of the Presidency, and also of the danger that he would have little more to contribute to the office, we can perhaps understand why he did not choose to run. The decision is less mysterious than some biographers have made it seem.

There were people, of course, who scrutinized the phrasing, especially the word "choose," and tried to evolve from it some occult meaning. Humorists went back to *Through the Looking-Glass* and quoted : —

> The eldest oyster winked his eye,
> And shook his heavy head, —
> Meaning to say he did not choose
> To leave the oyster-bed.

Etymologists and stylists wrote to the newspapers to prove that the President meant this or meant that. But the Man from Vermont was only using the idiom of the men and women from whom he had learned to talk, and no native Vermonter had any doubt what Calvin Coolidge meant when he said, "I do not choose." In his *Autobiography* Coolidge wrote : —

In making my public statement I was careful in the use of words. There were some who reported that they were mystified as to my meaning when I said, "I do not choose to run."

Although I did not know it at the time, months later I found that Washington said practically the same thing. Certainly he said no more in his Farewell Address, where he announced that "choice and prudence" invited him to retire.

William H. Taft's interpretation, on August 16, 1927, is as follows : —

We have been all excited here over Coolidge's declaration that he does not "choose" to run for the Presidency. . . .

With reference to Coolidge, I think he really wishes to avoid running for the Presidency, that he has had enough, but the peculiar form which his declination takes seems to me to be an indication that while he wishes really to avoid a renomination, he does not care to put himself in a place where by the unanimous demand of the party he may feel under obligation to run and will not be confronted with a previous statement by him that he would not run.

A 1928 CAMPAIGN CARTOON BY HERBERT JOHNSON

Frank W. Stearns had not gone to Rapid City. His physician had told him that the altitude would not be good for his health, and accordingly he had remained in Boston, making plans with Butler for the campaign of 1928.

As soon as possible after the President issued his announcement, however, Everett Sanders sent a special wire to Stearns telling him what had happened. The news came to him as a complete surprise, for which he was far from prepared, and he took some days to think it over. Finally, on August 8, he wrote the President as follows: —

I have tried every day since your announcement was made to write you a letter and each day I have backed off. I shall not make any thorough attempt now. I would rather talk with you some time. If I say that I am glad you made the statement, it might sound as though I had changed my mind about you as President. If I say that it leaves you in a wonderful position in case you are drafted, it might sound as if I questioned your genuineness in making the statement. Of course neither of these things is true. But the more I think about it, the surer I am the statement was wise, could not be improved upon in its wording, and was timely.

As I understand it, you have announced that you had a choice, that is to say that you could have had the nomination if you wanted it. That is certainly true. You have announced that you do not expect any contingency which will make it necessary for you to accept the nomination. You have not said that under no circumstances would you accept the nomination. I don't think you would have a right to say that unless there was something in your health that made it obligatory. Whether such a contingency will arise is not a question worth considering right now. It very well may occur. But in any event one thing seems to be certain. It removes all question of a campaign for delegates for you, and your real friends will be loyal to what amounts to orders from you. If the contingency suggested should arise, it will then be perfectly evident to every honest person that it is a case of being drafted.

The feeling with regard to the position you have taken is quite unanimous so far as people I have met are concerned, and some of these are people naturally critical, who have been critical of various positions you have taken, for example, the cancellation of the debts. One of the most critical along such lines that I have met was almost in tears the other day and said that it was a catastrophe. A Salem man perhaps expressed it as well as any one. He is a man of high business standing. He said we should feel as if we had notice from the doctor that a member of our family was at the point of death, and that it was a member of the family on whom we all lean for guidance. We should pray that the Lord will save his life, and that the people of the country will find some way of making their real desires effective. This is sketchy, but the best I can do.

Mr. Stearns obviously had not abandoned hope, feeling that the country would demand that Coolidge run again. But when Mr. Sanders expressed some such opinion, the answer came quickly back, "Mr. Stearns is not the man who would have to serve as President." Furthermore, when Mr. Sanders hinted that certain citizens of Massachusetts felt that he did not really mean what he said, Coolidge replied, "Do people in my own state think that I'm guilty of political trickery?" At any rate, on August 3, at the regular morning conference, the President left no doubt in the minds of the newspapermen present as to the meaning of the previous day's statement. When questioned, he indicated that he had no plans as to what he would do after his retirement, but that work would probably come his way. Men who were present have told me of their conviction that the President meant exactly what he said. He himself refused to interpret or amplify the published statement, declaring that it was quite sufficient.

During the remainder of the summer delegations came and went, guests appeared and disappeared, and Coolidge, more irascible than usual, fished and said very little. Probably he was worried about his health, but to those around him he seemed despondent, and he certainly derived only a glum enjoyment from the recreations which the Black Hills afforded. He continued to attend church on Sundays in the little wooden chapel at Hermosa, conducted by the twenty-two-year-old student preacher, Rolf Lium, and the congregation thought he looked gloomy and tired. Herbert Hoover came up for a day or two and outlined to his chief what he had done to aid the sufferers from the devastating Mississippi flood of the preceding April.[39] The reporters in Rapid City gleaned what stories they could pick up, but nothing comparable with the Big Story came their way. Meanwhile back East the Republican leaders, thwarted in the plan to send their most successful vote-getter back to the White House for another term, considered new alignments and discussed possible candidates. They were stunned

[39] This flood of April 1927, in the valley of the Mississippi, was described by Hoover as "the greatest peace-time calamity in the history of the country." Going himself to the stricken area, Hoover took charge of rehabilitation, and the American Red Cross raised over seventeen million dollars to aid the sufferers. Many persons felt that the President should have called an extra session of Congress to render the necessary assistance, but Coolidge felt that such a session would involve a great deal of unedifying and useless political discussion.

and bewildered, and realized that nothing could or should be done until the President was back in the capital.

On August 31, the Coolidges left for a trip to the Yellowstone National Park. The President was ill for a day before they started, but recovered in time to take the journey. Mrs. Coolidge and John watched the geysers, mingled with the guests at the lodges and hotels, and spent some busy days in sight-seeing. Mr. Coolidge seemed uninterested in the beauties of nature and preferred to fish in the lakes while his family walked and rode and pleased their hosts. The party returned to State Lodge on August 28.

On September 2, Colonel Lindbergh, on a cross-country trip, caused much excitement by flying low over Rapid City in tribute to the Coolidges, whose guest he had recently been. The Presidential party returned, tanned and clear-eyed, to Washington on September 11, and the President was glad to be at his desk on the following morning for a conference with Secretary Kellogg. Even though he had announced his abdication, he still had his job to do. Not for a year and a half would he be free.

XVII

The Close of Public Life

DURING Calvin Coolidge's five years and seven months as President, the United States engaged in no wars and its pacific intentions were emphasized in statement after statement by the Chief Executive. Nevertheless the situation in foreign affairs was confused, for the Department of State had inherited several difficult problems, not only in Europe but also in Mexico, Nicaragua, the Philippines, South America, and China.[1] Coolidge himself had never been abroad, and lacked the experience with other nations and statesmen possessed by such a wanderer as Herbert Hoover. Furthermore, until he became Vice President he had attended rather strictly to his local "day's work," and his attitude towards international controversies had been that of a provincial who refuses to become excited over events for which he has no direct responsibility. Fortunately he was advised and supported by two excellent Secretaries of State — Charles E. Hughes, who had been in Harding's original cabinet, and Frank B. Kellogg, who took Hughes's place on March 4, 1925. William E. Borah, who became in December, 1924, Chairman of the Senate Committee on Foreign Relations, was less predictable and, although honest and straightforward, caused the President some embarrassment. Coolidge was, however, on good personal terms with Borah and respected his opinions. Most of the actual burden belonged to Kellogg, who, in spite of some temperamental peculiarities which led Washington gossip to style him "Nervous Nellie," was really a man of high intelligence and resourcefulness.

The foreign policy of the Coolidge administration continued at first the program already laid down by President Harding and Secretary Hughes. Coolidge himself, as we have seen, had at one time, particularly in 1919 and 1920, leaned towards the League of

[1] Voicing the opinion of one "on the inside," Chief Justice Taft wrote, April 4, 1927, "Frank Kellogg has certainly had a hard time with Mexico, Nicaragua, and China. The Chinese situation seems obscure and hopeless."

Nations, following W. Murray Crane as opposed to Henry Cabot Lodge. Early in the Harding administration, however, it became evident that public sentiment in the United States did not favor our entrance into what its more savage opponents denounced as "the evil thing with the holy name," and that the isolationists had a strong majority in Congress. Quite informally but with the enthusiastic approval of the League, we had joined in the work of many of its committees, especially those concerned with humanitarian projects. Following the Locarno Conference,[2] Germany was admitted to the League of Nations, and there was good reason for believing that the power and influence of the Geneva body had been enhanced.

Nevertheless the persistent refusal of the United States to join the League prevented our participation with European nations on several important matters. Coolidge was in favor of our joining the Permanent Court of International Justice, — better known as the World Court, — and in his first Presidential message urged the Senate to consider our adherence, with the so-called "Hughes reservations." On March 3, 1925, the House, by a vote of 302 to 28, passed a resolution expressing approval of this plan, and a few days later the Senate agreed to consider the question in December. When the subject was brought up at the opening of the next session, Senator Borah was in opposition, maintaining that the World Court reintroduced his old bogey of political entanglements with foreign powers;[3] and he and his little group of isolationists resorted to filibustering tactics in order to thwart the manifest will of the Senate. The administration leaders then invoked the cloture rule, and the Senate decided on January 27, 1926, by the overwhelming vote of 76 to 17, to accept membership in the World Court. Unhappily, however, our acceptance was encumbered by five reservations, and the League of Nations did not feel inclined to revise completely the organization of the World Court in order to ensure our joining. When the decision of the League was announced in the following summer, Coolidge, abandoning hope, stated in his annual message that the issue, so far as he was concerned, was closed.[4]

[2] The Locarno Conference, held in October 1925 at the town of Locarno, in Switzerland, resulted in a number of treaties, in which Germany was included, aimed at "a relaxation of the moral tension between nations" and a strengthening of peace and security in Europe. The ensuing treaties, signed in London, on December 1, 1925, were hopefully regarded by many as steps toward permanent European security and a resulting world-wide disarmament.

[3] Johnson, *Borah of Idaho*, pp. 369ff. Borah regarded his fight against the Court as a continuation of his previous battle against the League, and he was supported by many of his comrades of 1919.

[4] Subsequently, however, under the leadership of the elderly Elihu Root, the League consented to a revised Protocol of Adherence, which was accepted by the

As for the debts owed to the United States by European nations as a consequence of the World War, the Coolidge administration was disposed to regard them as obligations some day to be settled, but which might be adjusted in amount on the basis of "the present and probable future ability of each debtor to pay." When the debtor countries did ask for consideration, it was the policy of the State Department to make sweeping reductions under new contracts over a long period. As inflation brought Germany to the verge of disaster, Secretary Hughes's plan of a committee of experts to make an economic approach to world problems took shape, and the Dawes Commission was appointed in December 1923. Its comprehensive plan was ready in the spring of 1924, and the so-called Dawes Conference met on July 16, in London, with Prime Minister Ramsay MacDonald presiding over a gathering composed of delegates from nine powers. Frank B. Kellogg, then our Ambassador to England, and James A. Logan represented the United States. After some discussion, Germany was invited to participate. The negotiations which ensued had to be conducted delicately and would have failed if Kellogg had not himself cleverly arranged to have M. Herriot and Herr Stresemann dine with him at Crewe House and discuss their problems informally. The success of the plan depended ultimately on a loan of $200,000,000 to the impoverished German Government; and Coolidge himself was able through Thomas Cochran of J. P. Morgan and Company to place $110,000,000 of the amount with that firm.[5] The President followed the proceedings day by day from Plymouth Notch, and on August 17 instructed Hughes to send a cablegram to Kellogg, as follows: —

Message received with great satisfaction. I congratulate you on your skill and success. You have greatly contributed to the welfare of the world.

Towards the middle of August, when agreement was still dubious, Kellogg received a cable message from the President, stating that if the Conference seemed likely to break up without adopting the Dawes Plan, he wished Kellogg to ask that it remain in session for a day or two longer until he could submit a proposal. Kellogg re-

---

Hoover administration and resubmitted to the Senate. This body, after delaying action for some years, finally, early in 1935, declined to approve it by something short of a two-thirds vote, in spite of the avowed support of President Franklin D. Roosevelt. See Jessup, *Elihu Root,* Volume II, pp. 435ff.

[5] Mr. Cochran at this time made his first visit to Plymouth and was taken by the President on a long tour of the Notch and its surroundings. His comment was, "I never saw the Boss so genial."

plied that all danger was over. Later, when Kellogg had become Secretary of State, he asked the President what the mysterious proposal was. Coolidge smiled and replied, "The Conference did not break up, did it?"[6] As matters turned out, the Dawes Plan was made almost obsolete because of the Great Depression and the repudiation of most of the international war debts, but it was the first step towards helping Germany out of her post-war difficulties by reducing her obligation to a definite sum.

In 1925 many of the debts owing to us from smaller nations were placed on a revised contract basis; but when such a new agreement, very favorable to his country, was signed by the French Ambassador in Washington in April 1926, the French government did not dare to submit it to Parliament, so violent was the popular disapprobation. It is only just to add that the United States in no case pressed actively for payments on these war obligations.

The President and Secretary Kellogg were also prepared to take the lead and make large concessions in furtherance of additional reduction of armaments, supplementing those carried through at the Washington Conference of 1922. If the United States had been a member of the League of Nations, a world-wide disarmament program might have been practicable, but under the circumstances public opinion in other countries was not altogether sympathetic to proposals emanating from Washington. A plan for a conference on the limitation of the building and armament of submarines and cruisers was rejected summarily by France and Italy; and when delegates from Great Britain, Japan, and the United States met at Geneva in June 1927, to consider the subject, the discussion between the British and American representatives became heated, and its final plenary session, on August 4, had to close with a confession of failure. It was in reference to this fiasco that Coolidge, in his Armistice Day address in 1928, referred caustically to the proposals of the British as "a tentative offer which would limit the kinds of cruisers and submarines adapted to the use of the United States but left without limit the kind adapted to their own use." Seldom before had a President indulged in such sharp criticism of a friendly power.

Coolidge did not often use language so vigorous in discussing foreign affairs. While Elihu Root's comment that the President "did not have an international hair in his head" was undoubtedly too severe,[7] it is certain that Coolidge rarely took the in-

---

[6] Bryn-Jones, 155.
[7] Quoted in Jessup, 433.

itiative in matters involving other countries. During one of the not infrequent crises in our relations with China during the 1920's, Joseph C. Grew, who for the moment in the absence of his chief was Acting Secretary of State, crossed the street to the executive offices to consult the President on a matter of policy. "I don't know anything about this," said Coolidge. "You do, Mr. Grew, and you're in charge. You settle the problem, and I'll back you up." After Grew had acted and the expected publicity ensued, the press appeared with sensational headlines; and he was summoned to the White House to confront an obviously irate President with a morning paper in his clenched hand. "What does this mean?" he asked, glaring at Grew. "How can a thing as important as this happen without my knowing about it?" "Mr. President," answered Grew, "this is the matter regarding which I consulted you day before yesterday, and that article is only the perfectly natural reaction of the American press." Coolidge drummed on the desk with his fingers and looked out the window for what seemed to the Acting Secretary at least five minutes. Then, turning again to his work, he said, "All right. I guess you know what ought to be done and can take care of it." [8]

It is true that Coolidge had not been a careful student of foreign affairs; but he did try patiently to learn about them and, shrewd administrator that he was, he came to rely on authorities in their respective fields. He did not originate or define to any marked degree the foreign policy of his administration, although he of course approved of the decisions which Hughes and Kellogg felt it wise to make, and he exercised a guiding rein when negotiations were being carried on. It could never have been said of him, as it was of Woodrow Wilson, that he was his own Secretary of State. On the other hand, he was not ignorant of what was occurring, and he sometimes surprised his assistants by his mastery of obscure detail.

Another of his admirable traits was his attitude towards those whom he selected for responsible duties. After endeavoring to choose competent men, he left them to do their jobs in their own way, without petty interference, giving them complete authority and unqualified support. He was seldom inquisitive or fussy or jealous or dictatorial. His appointees felt that they could, in emergencies, use their own judgment and be sure that he would not desert them. The final decision in major problems had to be his, but he was usually guided by the advice of those whom he had picked. They, in turn, appreciating their freedom and his confidence, had their

[8] Summarized from a conversation with Joseph C. Grew in July 1939.

loyalty strengthened. Two fine illustrations of this relationship are available in the cases of Dwight W. Morrow and Henry L. Stimson.

Throughout Coolidge's administration our relations with Mexico were precarious, chiefly because of the oil and ore properties in that country controlled by capital from the United States. The Mexican Constitution adopted in 1917 was the result of a nationalistic movement aimed partly at preserving Mexican resources for the Mexican people; [9] indeed one article, the famous Number 27, stated categorically that the ownership of lands and waters in Mexico was vested in the nation and that foreigners holding concessions must agree to be considered Mexicans in respect to such property, subject to Mexican laws and regulations. But Article 27, even as late as March 4, 1925, had not yet been put into actual effect, pending the necessary legislation. Meanwhile the confusion and misunderstanding between the two countries had continued. American capitalists who, in good faith, had invested their money were crying for protection; and on the other side, idealists like Senator Borah were insisting that we should not intervene for any economic or imperialistic purpose.

James R. Sheffield, who had been appointed American Ambassador to Mexico by Coolidge,[10] was not sympathetic with the existing Mexican Government, under President Plutarco Elías Calles, and, with conditions as they were, could do little to foster understanding between the two countries. But he was right in predicting that the Mexican Congress would soon pass the long-delayed legislation for putting Article 27 into effect, as it proceeded to do in December 1925. Secretary Kellogg naturally entered a diplomatic protest, and a long exchange of notes followed. Chief Justice Taft, after seeing Kellogg on New Year's Day, 1927, wrote that the latter was having "a very hard time with the Mexican situation, because it is almost impossible," and was losing sleep in his anxiety to have it settled. A few days later, the Senate, under Borah's leadership, by an almost unanimous vote urged the administration to arbitrate the quarrel.

Coolidge, however, had another point of view. On February 12,

---

[9] For a fair summary of the conditions leading up to the adoption of this constitution, see *United States and Mexico*, by J. Fred Rippy and others, published by the University of Chicago Press, and *Mexico and Its Heritage*, by Ernest Gruening.

[10] Sheffield's appointment was confirmed on January 25, 1925. On July 2, after a conference with Sheffield, Secretary Kellogg issued a vigorous statement declaring that conditions in Mexico were unsatisfactory and that the United States would expect the Mexican Government to indemnify Americans for property illegally seized.

1924, in a speech before the National Republican Club, he had announced that he intended to see that American rights and lives were protected; and in another speech, on April 25, 1927, he advanced the doctrine that any foreign power was bound to extend to aliens the safeguards generally recognized by the law of nations. Charles E. Hughes and Frank B. Kellogg agreed with the President in this policy, and sustained him in the conviction that the question, involving as it did a fundamental right, ought not to be opened up to arbitration. Many critics accused the administration of being too defiant in its defense of "capitalistic interests," and Senator Borah especially was opposed to protecting American businessmen who, with their eyes wide open to possible consequences, had made investments in Mexico. In the last analysis, however, Coolidge did not want war with Mexico. He had no great confidence in the existing Mexican government, felt that it had been unnecessarily hostile to American businessmen, and was resolved to maintain our national dignity. But the situation had reached a hazardous point, and Coolidge, with characteristic common sense, made up his mind to see what a friendly gesture could do to allay suspicion and reestablish amicable relations. It was obvious that negotiations could be carried no further by Sheffield, and that someone less suspected by the Mexicans must take his place.

The smoothing over of the difficulties between the two neighboring countries was due chiefly to Dwight W. Morrow and what his biographer describes as the impact of his "precise but visionary mind upon a situation in which fact and theory had become inextricably entangled." It will be recalled that Morrow, the most prominent and promising member of Coolidge's college class, had become in 1914 a partner in J. P. Morgan and Company, had contributed to the financing of early Coolidge campaigns in Massachusetts, and with his dynamic Morgan associate, Thomas Cochran, had worked tirelessly for Coolidge in Chicago in 1920. Short in stature, with a magnificently modeled head, Morrow was impressive because of his intellectual power, his determination, and his versatility and resourcefulness. Excellent judges of men saw in him a perfect harmony between imagination and intellect, a union between soul and mind.[11] In any company he was sure eventually to dominate because of his exceptional personal qualities.

Morrow, nervous, vibrant, and magnetic, was very different from Coolidge in temperament; furthermore, despite his identifica-

[11] The words are those of Montagu Norman, Governor of the Bank of England, quoted in Nicolson's *Dwight Morrow*, p. 52.

tion with Wall Street, he had strong liberal inclinations, and on March 10, 1920, sent to Governor Coolidge four volumes of the works of Professor William Graham Sumner, largely in advocacy of free trade. In reply, Coolidge had written: —

I have read most of the four volumes of Sumner. I regard his arguments on the whole as sound. I do not think that human existence is quite so much on the basis of dollars and cents as he puts it. He argues in one place that the enunciation of great principles has had little to do with human development; that America became democratic through economic reasons rather than the reasons that came from the teachings of philosophy and religion. He nowhere enunciates the principle of service. That principle so far as I know has never been applied to protection. My observation of protection is that it has been successful in practice, however unsound it may appear to be in theory. That must mean that the theories have not taken account of all the facts.

One evening just before the Chicago Convention of 1920, Morrow had thrust into Herbert Hoover's hands a copy of *Have Faith in Massachusetts,* saying, "Calvin Coolidge is the man best fitted to be President of the United States" — this at a moment when Hoover was himself an avowed candidate for the Presidency. Morrow had arrived at this conclusion through a careful study of Coolidge's public utterances, and he was greatly disappointed when his candidate had to accept the second position on the Republican ticket. As soon as Harding died, on August 2, 1923, the news was telephoned to Morrow at his home in Englewood, New Jersey. When he came back to his dinner guests after receiving the message, he seemed to be in a trance. Roused by the queries of his friends, he woke with a start to realities and said slowly and impressively, still a little bewildered, "Calvin Coolidge is President of the United States!" [12] On the following day, while on a train to Chicago, Morrow wrote Coolidge a personal note which must be quoted in full: —

Three years ago in Worcester I told you in all sincerity that I was convinced that you were better equipped in character and in training to serve this nation as its President than any of the other possible candidates that were being discussed. That conviction was based upon your character as I knew it and your long training in public affairs. I have never changed that belief. The greatest responsibility that rests upon any man in the world has now come to you. No former Vice President who succeeded to the Presidency by the death of the President was confronted with responsibilities as great. Your whole life's train-

[12] This story is told by Robert Frost, the poet, who was a guest in the Morrow home on that evening. See Nicolson, 267.

ing fits you for your mighty task; and the faith that you expressed in the closing line of your short statement made in Vermont is the faith that all your real friends will share. May God bless and keep you strong and well.

On the same day Morrow sent to the new President a longer dictated letter on foreign affairs, urging him to call an international conference on the reparation question, to adopt a consistent policy towards Latin America, and to replace Colonel Harvey in London by Elihu Root. He also requested him as a favor to release the persons still imprisoned for sedition during the World War. Unfortunately the answers are lacking, but Morrow's influence was not destined to be paramount during the Coolidge administration. The President, always a little afraid of a possible Power behind the Throne, did not choose to avail himself immediately of Morrow's loyalty and wide experience. The latter, on his part, never resented what a less devoted friend might have regarded as neglect, and the relations of the two college classmates continued to be amicable for the remainder of their lives. If Morrow was disappointed at not being called at once to the White House, he concealed his chagrin and attended to his own business — which gave him plenty to do.

In September 1925, however, Morrow was quite unexpectedly designated by the President as a member of a board instructed to report on the best means "of developing and applying aircraft in national defense," and appointed specifically to examine the sensational charges made by Colonel William Mitchell, head of the Army Air Service, who had asserted that our air equipment was antiquated and inadequate. Coolidge, who almost never employed first names in correspondence, called "Mr. Morrow" to Washington on September 17; and at the first meeting of the Board, on motion of Senator Hiram Bingham and General James G. Harbord, Morrow was elected Chairman. It sat for eight "congested weeks" and summoned ninety-nine witnesses, including Orville Wright, many "experts," and several cabinet officers. The business was admirably managed by the astute Morrow, who kept everybody in a good humor while exposing Colonel Mitchell's exaggerations and extracting from authorities the opinion that the United States was not menaced from the air by any foreign power.[13] After the vigorous

[13] As Morrow studied the personnel of the Board, he decided that seven of the nine were first-class for the purpose intended, but that two Democratic members of Congress — Carl Vinson and James S. Parker — were relatively unimportant. Later he discovered that these two members of the Lower House — who also proved to be valuable counselors — were helpful in getting the report

report, drafted by Morrow and signed by all the members of the Board, it was generally felt that he would be offered another government position, possibly a diplomatic post, but nothing happened for many months. When the subject was introduced in his presence, he declared that he could not accept an "honor" from Coolidge, but was ready to take a "job"; and he was especially interested in China, Russia, and Mexico.

The President himself made no move for many months. In the early spring of 1927, it was evident that Ambassador Sheffield ought not to remain much longer in Mexico. In a letter to William H. Taft, May 13, 1927, Sheffield said: —

I wrote the President a personal note some weeks ago with reference to my giving up my post, to which he has never replied. It is a pretty good example of the "silence of Cal." However we are packed up with the expectation that we will not return, but I am saying nothing about it, lest the Mexican Government learn of my plans and immediately have a *jubilate*.[14]

With his mind on this problem, Coolidge said one day to Senator Butler, at the White House, with Mr. Stearns present, "I am considering the appointment of Mr. Ratshesky as Ambassador to Mexico." Abraham C. Ratshesky, one of the most prominent Jewish citizens of Boston, was President of the United States Trust Company in that city, formerly Assistant Food Administrator for Massachusetts during the World War and member of the Massachusetts Public Safety Committee — a man of unquestioned business ability and probity but entirely inexperienced in dealing with critical international situations. Senator Butler said nothing at the moment, but when he departed, Mr. Stearns, for one of the few times during his relationship with Coolidge, spoke up and suggested that Mr. Ratshesky, although possessing admirable qualities, would not be the best man to go to semi-hostile Mexico. He added, "I think Dwight Morrow might accept the appointment." Direct as usual, the

---

of the Board through Congress, and realized that Coolidge, in appointing them, had been very farsighted.

[14] *Vide* the Taft papers. On April 15, 1927, Taft wrote to Sheffield: "This morning I went down to see the President on another matter, and I talked with him about the situation. I asked him how you were doing, and he said that no man could do better than you had done, that he was very well satisfied. 'Of course,' he said, 'they don't like him particularly in Mexico, but how could a man decently act in such a way that they would?' I thought what he said would have gratified you and I venture therefore to repeat it." But even then Coolidge must have known that it was time to relieve Sheffield.

President asked, "Have you any good reason to believe he would?" "Yes," answered Mr. Stearns, "I have some reason, although I am not absolutely sure about it." "I would appoint him in a minute if I thought he would go," was Coolidge's succinct comment.[15]

Not long afterwards, in June, on his return from a trip to Spain, Morrow stayed for two nights with the Coolidges at the temporary White House in Dupont Circle, at the same time that Colonel Charles A. Lindbergh was there as a guest,[16] and on that occasion the President virtually offered Morrow the Mexican post — and he gave a tentative acceptance. On July 14, in a note written in longhand from Rapid City, South Dakota, Coolidge formally requested him to serve as Ambassador to Mexico, ending with a sentence which, in view of the date, is highly significant: —

I would prefer to trust you with this place above anyone else I know, but I want you to consult your own wishes. You will be greatly serving your country wherever you are. I do not wish you to think of me personally at all but only of yourself, and make your decision without reference to whether I run again or not.

The Mexican mission was from many aspects a thankless task, involving much hard work, some inevitable physical discomfort, a definite possibility of failure, and not much opportunity for reward, particularly as Coolidge had more than hinted to Morrow that he would not run again. But Morrow, who would doubtless have refused to go to London or Paris, was attracted by the Mexican adventure and by the President's restrained suggestion that, through undertaking it, he could "prevent a good deal of harm." On August 19, he visited the Coolidges in the Black Hills and there completed the final arrangements. He wrote his wife: —

The President wants me very much to go to Mexico, — and I am going, — that is to say I am going if you stick to your bargain and go with me. . . . As I talked with him, I thought more and more that it was up to us to go and that I and probably you would regret it always if we didn't do it.

[15] From a memorandum made by Mr. Stearns at the time. Secretary Kellogg always believed that he himself had suggested Morrow; indeed he wrote William R. Castle, Jr., "Mr. Coolidge never thought of sending Morrow to Mexico until I proposed it." (Bryn-Jones, 183.) Coolidge probably heard of Morrow from both Stearns and Kellogg, and possibly from others, but kept his own counsel in each case. That was his way.

[16] Colonel Lindbergh had landed in Paris on his non-stop flight across the Atlantic on May 21, and Coolidge had dispatched a United States cruiser to bring him and his plane back from Europe.

On the morning of October 23, 1927, the Morrows arrived in Mexico City.[17] Coolidge's parting words to his new Ambassador had been, "My only instructions are to keep us out of war with Mexico." The story of Morrow's amazingly successful experience as a diplomat has been related with literary skill by Harold Nicolson, and the episode is a familiar and proud one in our history. Viewed on his arrival with suspicion because of his financial connections, he captured the hearts of the Mexicans, high and low. He had no pretense, no pomposity, no deceit. With sympathy for Mexico's perplexing problems, with tact and persuasion and engaging frankness, he accomplished by conciliatory methods what threats and the use of force had failed to do. Because he understood the Latin temperament and paid proper respect to Mexican pride, he won over a people who were prepared to meet him with resentful faces. By bringing Colonel Lindbergh, in December, on a non-stop solo flight from Bolling Field to Mexico City, Morrow introduced an element of romance; and he was able to gain the confidence of President Calles, a rather solemn, sensitive, and realistic man, but also a capable statesman, who discovered that he was dealing with a gentleman.

Morrow's method of approaching a problem has been described by his partner, Thomas W. Lamont, as follows, "A careful study of the history of, and factors in, the situation; a stripping away of all unessentials, and then a rebuilding and presentation in a way both simple and convincing." Through the tortuous and sometimes discouraging negotiations which ensued, Morrow moved with discretion and patience. On the question of the oil concessions, both governments yielded something. The United States, in return for recognition by Mexico of all rights in oil lands acquired before 1927, abandoned its previous objection to the issuance of confirmatory concessions by that government. Through this compromise the United States maintained the principle of vested property rights in oil lands; and Mexico upheld to her own satisfaction the theory of national ownership of the sub-soil. Thus by friendly negotiation an irreparable breach was avoided. The indefatigable Morrow even brought about a temporary agreement between the Roman Catholic

---

[17] Because Congress was not in session, there was no opportunity before Morrow left for the confirmation of his appointment. Borah, who was at first opposed to the President's designation of a Morgan partner as Ambassador to Mexico, was converted by reading a speech of Morrow's before the New York Chamber of Commerce. Morrow himself had feared that Borah would oppose his confirmation by the Senate, and was not willing to be exposed to such humiliation. It was Colonel Raymond Robins who persuaded Borah that Morrow was the right person for the position; and Borah was much pleased with Morrow's notable success. See Johnson, 339ff.

Church and the Mexican Government; and on Sunday, June 30, 1929, after Calvin Coolidge was out of office, the church bells rang out again in Mexico after a silence of three years.

Morrow's mission to Mexico has been accurately described as "one of the most instructive episodes in modern diplomatic history." He did far more than keep us out of war, as he had been instructed to do; he softened hatreds and introduced a conciliatory spirit into our relations with Latin-America. His work was not permanent, — probably could not have been, — but he did apply to jaded nerves and sensitive emotions the soothing touch which was so badly needed. What he did reflected great credit on himself as well as on the Coolidge administration. He returned in December 1929, in order to go as an American delegate to the London Naval Conference. After playing a brilliant and decisive part in framing the London Naval Treaty, he came back to the United States in April 1930, and was elected in the following November as Senator from New Jersey.

He died, worn out by hard work and worry, on October 5, 1931.

For dealing with the situation in Nicaragua, the President was fortunate in enlisting the services of a man of much the same idealistic and conscientious type as Dwight W. Morrow, and of even wider experience. In that Central American republic, the United States, in order to protect its interests, had maintained a troop of marines from 1912 until 1925, when they had been withdrawn. As soon as they had left, turmoil broke out, and revolutions and counter revolutions followed, until, in 1926, the United States Government recognized General Adolfo Diaz, whose title seemed to be the most legitimate, as President. This action was followed by protests from various factions in Nicaragua, including those who favored Juan B. Sacassa, a claimant openly recognized, encouraged, and aided by Mexico. Finally, in December 1926, marines were again landed at Diaz's request, and American warships were stationed in Nicaraguan ports. Our policy in Nicaragua was being denounced, not only in Europe and Latin-America, but also on the floor of the United States Senate, for its imperialistic tendencies and its alleged "Dollar Diplomacy." As a matter of fact, the total investment of Americans in Nicaragua was not over twelve million dollars, of which ten million dollars was involved in bananas and timber on the east coast. What is technically called Wall Street was hardly concerned at all. Actually Coolidge had no object except to restore tranquillity as soon as possible. Both Kellogg and Coolidge were reluctant to intervene, but could discover no other alternative, particularly as a successful Mexican-aided revolution would be a serious blow to American prestige in Central America.

In the spring of 1927 the President asked Henry L. Stimson, formerly Secretary of War under President Taft, to come to Washington. After 1913, Stimson had returned to his law practice in New York City, but had later entered the military service and seen action in the field during the World War. He was regarded as a statesman of liberal tendencies who could be counted upon to approach any complicated issue with courage, intelligence, and tact. Called in to aid the State Department in connection with the Tacna-Arica dispute, he had been of much assistance to the harassed Secretary Kellogg, who accordingly kept him in mind as the dangerous Mexican influence became more apparent in Nicaragua. When Stimson had his preliminary talk with Kellogg, the latter was vague and indefinite as to what ought to be done, and Stimson, who had an important law case on his hands, was prepared to decline. Later in the day, at the White House, after the President had approached the subject in the same tentative fashion, Stimson asked, "What is it you want, Mr. President? Do you want me just to be your eyes and ears, and come back to report to you?" "No, no," replied Coolidge, "I want you to do a good deal more than that. I want you to go down there, and if you can see a way to clean up that mess, I want you to do it." "That's different," answered Stimson. "Of course I'll go." And so Stimson, who knew nothing about the history of Nicaragua and could not even have bounded the country, came back into public life. Coolidge was again following out the practice which he advocated in his *Autobiography* of assigning to the various key positions under the government "men of sufficient ability so that they can solve all the problems that arise under their jurisdiction."

On April 9, Stimson and his party, which consisted only of his wife and secretary, sailed from New York and, on their arrival at the west coast of Nicaragua, proceeded at once to the capital, Managua, where, with the assistance of the American minister, Eberhardt, and the American Admiral Latimer, he busied himself in getting in touch with all available sources of public opinion. A well-organized and bitter war was in progress between the army of the Conservatives, who, under President Diaz, were in possession of the government, and the army of the Liberals, headed by the able General Moncada; but a virtual deadlock had resulted, and both contestants were receptive to American intervention in the establishment of law and order. The presence of a small body of American marines, far from being resented by the noncombatants, had for many years been regarded as the only prospect of future peace. Nearly everybody was sick of fighting and eager to find a way out before the next planting season; moreover the people of both parties were ready to look to the United States for active assistance in bringing about a cessation of hostilities.[18]

After frequent consultations with representative citizens, Stimson, on May 4, met General Moncada at Tipitapa, between the lines of the opposing armies, for a conference held picturesquely under a large blackthorn tree near a dry river bed, and secured his coöperation. Under Stimson's guidance, both sides agreed to an immediate and complete disarmament; to a peace which would permit the planting of a new crop in June; to an amnesty for all persons in rebellion or exile; to the return of all occupied or confiscated property to its original owners; to the organization of a Nicaraguan constabulary on a nonpartisan basis, to be instructed and temporarily commanded by American officers; and to American supervision of the coming election of 1928. To these stipulations everybody acquiesced except Sandino, one of General Moncada's minor lieutenants, who started northward with a small band of followers, refusing to join in the truce. He was promptly repudiated by Moncada himself. Stimson left Managua on May 16, after a remarkably rapid and altogether acceptable adjustment of what had been a bitter rivalry. Even Senator Borah, the outspoken Republican critic of the Coolidge foreign policy, expressed himself as approving a settlement which assured to the people of Nicaragua an opportunity, in a fair and free election, to choose their president.[19]

When Sandino's forces, augmented to nearly five hundred and aided by Mexico, attacked in mid-July a little band of thirty-seven American marines and forty-seven native constabulary and were repulsed with great slaughter, critics of the administration again became vociferous. Secretary Kellogg, on his part, declared quite rightly that Sandino and his company were "nothing more than common outlaws," who had the support of none of the decent Nicaraguan leaders. Once more from the opposition in the Senate came the familiar cries of "Selfish Imperialism!" but the sound judgment of those acquainted with the situation regarded the incident, though deplorable, as being contributory to permanent peace.

[18] *American Policy in Nicaragua* (1927), by Henry L. Stimson. For a survey of contemporary opinion regarding the settlement, see the *Literary Digest*, May 21, 1927.
[19] Chief Justice Taft, who tried to keep Ambassador Sheffield in Mexico well-informed, wrote him on May 25: "Stimson seems to have settled the present difficulties in Nicaragua. Of course an election held under the auspices of the United States is hardly nonintervention, but it is certainly the best we can do."

The President shortly named General Frank R. McCoy as Chairman of the National Board of Elections to be created by the Nicaraguan Government.

Colonel Stimson's mission was an effort on the part of the United States to perform an unselfish service for a troubled Central American country and leave it with its sovereignty and independence unimpaired. The policy of leaving the republics of Central America to enjoy autonomy but of protecting them against external interference and aiding them to control, in emergencies, internal disorder was never better justified. When the election took place on November 4, 1928, Moncada was chosen president without any disturbance at the polls, and the Conservatives, who had enjoyed the support of Washington for twenty years, were defeated. No more convincing proof could be supplied of the fairness of the American supervision.

Unfortunately the other nations of Central America did not fully understand the terms of the Stimson settlement, and the policy of the United States continued to meet with criticism, especially from Mexico, which had prematurely aligned itself with one Nicaraguan faction.[20] Realizing this, Coolidge accepted an invitation from President Machado, of Cuba, to attend the Sixth International Conference of American States, to be held at Havana on January 16, 1928. The President went to Havana in a battleship, accompanied by Kellogg, Wilbur, Hughes, Morrow, and several members of Congress, and opened the proceedings with a speech, very conciliatory in tone, which made a profound impression. Later Hughes, in a discussion on the theory of intervention, spoke extemporaneously in reply to attacks by South American delegates and explained the American policy of what he called "interposition of a temporary character" for the purpose of protecting the lives and property of American citizens.[21] The speech disclaimed any hidden motives or any desire for territorial expansion, but did point out the difficulties which arose when, in a country like Nicaragua, government was unable to function; and Hughes candidly declared that, under such lamentable conditions, any country was justified by international law in taking action to protect the lives and property of its nationals.[22]

[20] The *Literary Digest*, October 22, 1927, pp. 16–17, presents an interesting symposium of Latin-American newspaper opinion regarding President Coolidge and his policies, the preponderance of opinion being hostile. The Mexico City *Libertador*, for example, said, "No decent man, no true patriot, could shake hands with the man responsible for the crime against humanity, committed in Nicaragua, by the President of the United States and his Secretary of State." This appeared, of course, before Morrow arrived in Mexico.

[21] Toynbee, *Survey of International Relations*, 1927, pp. 406–7.

[22] Coolidge, in one of his later syndicated articles, under date of April 27, 1931, said: "It will do no harm to emphasize the duty of the United States to

Hughes's remarks were listened to with much attention, and the Conference finally agreed to postpone for two years further discussion of the vexing problem.

One other matter, in which the Harding administration had accepted the difficult position of arbitrator, troubled the State Department during the 1920's. Chile and Peru had for many years disputed the possession of two almost barren provinces, Tacna and Arica, and in 1922 the United States volunteered its good offices. Harding's death made Coolidge the official arbitrator, and his award provided for a plebiscite in the disputed territory. A Plebiscite Commission, with General Pershing at the head, tried to carry through the decision, but the coöperation of the two contending nations was impossible to secure. In 1926, General Lassiter, who had succeeded Pershing, recommended that the plebiscite be abandoned. Kellogg then opened negotiations for a reconciliation between Chile and Peru, and the two countries in 1928 resumed diplomatic and commercial relations. The original cause of altercation was finally ended on May 17, 1929, when President Hoover announced that Tacna would go to Peru and Arica to Chile — a perfectly just settlement suggested on several occasions by Secretary Kellogg.[23] What the Coolidge administration had done in this case, as in the others before discussed, was to do its best to remove the reasons for misunderstanding between and with the Central and South American peoples. That the President and his advisers did not fully succeed is entirely too obvious. They did believe, however, that somehow in the near future a plan could and should be worked out for conciliation and arbitration throughout the American continent.

The American policy towards the Philippines outlined in 1900 by Elihu Root,[24] and carried out, in general, with tact and skill by a succession of Republican Governor Generals, had given to the Filipinos a common language; a modern system of communication; sound and stable finance; a sanitary program which was rapidly transforming a disease-stricken country into the most wholesome region in the tropics; and a promising start on the difficult art of

---

protect its citizens in Nicaragua or any foreign country. . . . We have helped Nicaragua establish a government, hold two elections, and organize a military force. We want her to walk alone, not always lean on us. Her government should deal with bandits. We have not set up a protectorate but in a neighborly way tried to help Nicaragua provide her own law and order."

[23] Vide *Tacna and Arica*, by W. J. Dennis, Yale University Press, 1931.

[24] This policy had been summarized in a letter to the First Philippine Commission signed by President McKinley, but actually drafted by Root as Secretary of War. The first civil governor at Manila was William H. Taft, who was installed on July 4, 1901.

self-government. When the Wilson administration came into power in 1913, however, a policy of immediate Filipinization of the entire insular government was adopted by the Democrats, who had always, on principle, opposed American occupation. The consequence of too great haste in turning the direction of affairs over to the Filipinos had been disastrous: epidemics of tropical diseases had returned; the insular government was on the verge of bankruptcy; severe criticism had emanated from American residents and visitors to the islands; and there was a widespread relaxation in honesty and efficiency.

When the Republicans regained control of the United States Government in 1921, Harding promptly appointed a commission including General Leonard Wood and W. Cameron Forbes to investigate whether the Filipinos were ready for independence, as their leaders were claiming. The report of this commission indicated that the islanders were not yet prepared for self-government; and the President then designated Wood as the logical man to carry out as Governor General the recommendations which he had suggested. Wood, because of his rich experience and accomplishment in Cuba, had a well-earned reputation for constructive service — a reputation which was enhanced by his work in the Philippines. He did restore fidelity and honesty in the Filipino Government and brought back efficiency in sanitation and financial management. This was not accomplished, however, without inevitably antagonizing many of the Filipino leaders, who resented the necessary measures of reform and refused to coöperate with Wood. In the summer of 1926, at Wood's invitation, Henry L. Stimson visited the Philippines and, although holding no official status, studied conditions and assisted Wood with counsel and advice. Struggling against external obstacles as well as continued ill-health, General Wood, with characteristic courage, had kept tenaciously at the business of reform, but finally, worn out by his onerous duties, returned to the United States in the late spring of 1927 and died, after a brain operation, on August 3.

In selecting Wood's successor, Coolidge naturally turned to Stimson, who, following his trip to the Philippines, had published significant articles in the *Saturday Evening Post* and *Foreign Affairs* on the situation in the Far East. In the autumn of 1927, at the request of Dwight F. Davis, Secretary of War, Stimson went to Washington, and the President asked him to take the position of Governor General of the Philippines.[25] As Stimson rose to leave, after having

[25] On September 26, the President, Taft, Forbes, and Davis met at the White House and had what Taft described as "a very satisfactory talk." "I don't know whether the President will follow us," he added, "but we did the best we could

accepted the place, Coolidge said, "Now about instructions. When I pick out a man to do a job, I don't generally instruct him, but if you wish instructions, you draw them up and I'll sign them." Stimson's task, aside from continuing the broad policy originally instituted by Root and the long line of Republican generals, was to persuade the Filipino leaders to coöperate with the United States, and in this he was notably successful.[26] Coolidge himself was opposed to granting immediate independence and vetoed a bill passed by the Philippine Legislature authorizing a plebiscite on the question. He adopted the view of both Wood and Stimson that the Filipinos were not yet prepared for full self-government and that the granting of it under pressure from Filipino politicians would be disastrous for the natives as well as unfortunate for the United States. Here again Coolidge relied implicitly on men whom he trusted. As a matter of fact, Stimson was in favor of conceding independence to the islanders when they were ready for it, although he hoped that they would then prefer to remain as part of the United States. He said, "I should be glad to have the Philippines decide to be connected permanently with this country, but it must be a marriage of free will, not a rape." In this view Coolidge concurred.

Stimson remained in Manila from March 1, 1928, until he was appointed Secretary of State by President Hoover. Because he could not arrive from the Philippines until March 26, 1929, Kellogg continued to serve as Secretary of State for several weeks under the Hoover administration.

During the early part of Coolidge's administration there had developed in China a strong nationalist feeling, displayed in hostility towards the foreigners who had settled in that country; and the trouble was intensified by a civil war between conflicting factions. The Department of State, although entirely willing to modify the so-called "unequal treaties" which denied China tariff autonomy and retained the principle of extraterritoriality, could not discover which Chinese groups were really in authority. Under the circumstances the United States was obliged to maintain a naval force in Chinese waters to guard the lives of its citizens. When, however, Great Britain requested the other signatories to the Washington

---

for him." It was at this meeting that Stimson was recommended highly by the three Presidential advisers.

[26] Writing on January 13, 1928, to Taft, George W. Wickersham, who had just been attending a dinner given to Stimson, wrote: "Stimson was in good form, and spoke very well, largely about Wood and his work, and his, Stimson's, intention to mould his course by Wood's record. I think it was a great thing for Coolidge to brush aside all political nominations thrust upon him and take Stimson, who is a man of the highest character and very distinguished abilities."

Treaty to join her in coöperative and compulsive action, Secretary Kellogg, on January 27, 1927, issued a "Statement of Policy," saying that, while the United States would join with the other powers when such a course seemed desirable for her own interests, she reserved the right of independent procedure whenever that was necessary. Following the Nanking incident in March 1927, when British and American residents were threatened by the Chinese Nationalist Army, the United States joined other foreign nations in demanding apologies and reparations, but finally declined to participate with the Treaty Powers in military and coercive measures against the Nanking Government. In July 1928, the United States took an even more independent course by signing a treaty agreement with China, thus recognizing the Nanking Government and granting it the long-sought tariff autonomy. What Kellogg did was virtually to help the Chinese Nationalists by refusing to join in what was known in diplomatic circles as a "gunboat policy." Although our troops were still on Chinese territory, the President made it clear that they were there solely as a precaution and not to control or direct Chinese politics. His sane attitude helped to preserve friendly relations between our country and the Far East.

From the administration viewpoint the Pact of Paris, — commonly known as the Kellogg Pact, — by the terms of which sixty-two nations promised to renounce war as a means of settling disputes, was its supreme achievement in foreign affairs, and Kellogg's share in bringing it about earned him the Nobel Peace Prize in 1929. The series of informal and formal statements leading up to the signing of the Pact on August 27, 1928, have been discussed in detail in other volumes. Influenced largely by Professor James T. Shotwell, of Columbia University, Briand, the French Prime Minister, had addressed to the American people, on April 6, 1927, a message suggesting that France and the United States agree to "outlaw war." Mr. Kellogg felt that it would be wiser to extend the idea to embrace other nations, and accordingly on December 28, after securing the coöperation of Senator Borah, prepared a note — which was read and sanctioned by Coolidge — suggesting a multilateral treaty to include all the nations of the world.[27] The proposal was received with some skepticism, both at home and abroad, but the power of public opinion was strong, and, after much negotiation, general agreement was reached. The ceremonies connected with the signing

[27] Kellogg's own account of the events leading up to the Pact of Paris may be read in Bryn-Jones, 230ff. For the documents see *The Pact of Paris, with Historical Commentary,* by James T. Shotwell, International Conciliation, No. 243, October 1928.

of the Pact at the Quai d'Orsay were well staged, and by January 1929, sixty-two states had accepted its provisions. The Treaty was presented to the United States Senate on December 4, 1928, with the request of the President that it be ratified before the expiration of his term of office. Although such die-hards as Senators Moses and Reed grumbled, Borah was for it and spoke eloquently in its advocacy. It was eventually ratified by a vote of 85 to 1, and signed by Coolidge and Kellogg on January 17, 1929.

Within a decade the philosophy of the Pact of Paris was abrogated by many of the signers. Japanese action in Manchuria in 1931, the Italian invasion of Ethiopia, and other more recent aggressions by Germany and Italy have, of course, violated the spirit and text of the Pact of Paris and have made its fate similar to that of many another "scrap of paper." That the Pact of Paris was intended to bind its signatories and to pledge them to call violators to account cannot be doubted.[28] It is equally true that even the United States has not always recognized this responsibility. Henry L. Stimson, Secretary of State in 1932, did invoke the Kellogg Pact in protesting against the Japanese invasion of Manchuria, but to no avail.[29] On the other hand, Italy's equally deplorable attack on Ethiopia was not condemned officially by Secretary of State Hull.[30] The noble aims of the Pact of Paris have not been achieved, and the agreement of which Coolidge and Kellogg were so proud seems to-day to be almost as futile as the League of Nations. But the Pact did at least reassert in no perfunctory fashion the anarchical nature of war, and to that extent blazed a path which may later become a highroad to international peace.

In his *Autobiography,* so strangely reticent on many important matters, Calvin Coolidge said nothing about the foreign policy of his administration, perhaps feeling that little of significance had been accomplished. But while the period from 1923 to 1929 was marked by no spectacular event, the Department of State did preserve a friendly attitude towards the rest of the world and reiterated the

[28] See Henry L. Stimson, *The Pact of Paris — Three Years of Development,* U. S. Government Printing Office, 1932. Stimson said of the Pact, "On its face it is a treaty containing definite promises." This view is sustained by other high authorities.

[29] Stimson relied on the second article of the Pact, which consisted of a covenant by the signatory nations never to attempt to solve their controversies except by pacific means. See Stimson, *The Far Eastern Crisis,* 1936, pp. 61ff.

[30] In a speech delivered in St. Paul, in 1935, Kellogg said forcefully, "When Italy invaded Ethiopia, it violated the Pact of Paris, and therefore a treaty with the United States. . . . The United States, in common with other countries, should designate Italy as the aggressor in the present Italo-Ethiopian conflict and denounce the former country's violation of international treaty obligations."

idea that arbitration, not armaments, should settle disputes between independent powers. The President had favored the World Court until he had been convinced that further advocacy would be useless; and while unwilling, like most of his countrymen, to cancel the money obligations due us from foreign nations, he did make generous concessions to the debtors. American intervention in Nicaragua, requested and welcomed by all factions in that country, had resulted in a more stable government; and as the American marines were gradually withdrawn, the reasons for hostility towards us also disappeared. It is true that the United States felt obligated to protect its citizens in China, but the Department of State had led all other foreign powers in offering concessions to the Nationalists in Nanking. Mexico was temporarily placated under the beneficent influence of Dwight Morrow, and a more satisfactory basis for understanding had been established. As for the Pact of Paris, visionary and unauthoritative though it turned out to be, it represents one more advance in the long and difficult quest for world peace. Calvin Coolidge could write, in all sincerity, on July 31, 1930: —

At the present time the foreign relations of the United States are in a particularly satisfactory condition. . . . With but one exception our war debts with Europe are adjusted, all misunderstandings have been removed from the Pacific Ocean area, Central and South America are quiet, our claims in Mexico are being adjudicated, the revolution in China involves us but slightly, and the naval limitation treaty has taken our armaments from the field of international friction. . . . Our position towards all other people is neutral and impartial. Our chief motive is a great desire to be friendly. No foreign government regards us as a menace. We hold the respect of the world sufficiently to be usually sought as the arbitrator of its disputes.

Following the return of the Coolidges to the capital on September 11, 1927, life in the renovated White House resumed its normal course. Everybody in Washington had been startled at the President's suddenly announced decision not to run again, and many refused to accept his words as final; but when he was told over and over, by people from all sections and classes, that he must let his name be used, he said simply, "I've been here about long enough" or, "There are plenty of other good men around." [31] Senator Simeon

[31] The reactions of Chief Justice Taft are very illuminating. As early as May 22, 1925, he felt that the party "could probably not do any better than renominate Coolidge." On October 10, 1927, he wrote, "My impression is that before they get through the Convention, they will find that they need Coolidge and will demand his service." In November, he said, "I am very certain that there will be an attempt to nominate Coolidge, but I really think he is quite

D. Fess, of Ohio, one of his staunchest supporters, had had three hours alone with him at State Lodge, at the close of which he had "no further doubt" that Coolidge did not wish another term. Later in the autumn, however, he reached the conclusion that the President should be forced to run and expressed this opinion to some reporters. Coolidge then called Fess to the White House and said, "Really, Senator, you're causing me some embarrassment, and if I were you, I should stop mentioning a third term." The report was circulated that Fess had been "spanked," but this did not stop the discussion, and the *Literary Digest,* in its issue for November 12, reproduced a number of contemporary cartoons on the subject of the "Coolidge Puzzle." The gossipy White House usher, "Ike" Hoover, in substantiation of his conviction that the President was eager to be drafted by a spontaneous popular call, declared that those of Coolidge's guests that autumn who went away predicting his eventual nomination were always invited back, while those who, like Nicholas Murray Butler and George Harvey, accepted his statement as final were from that moment on neglected. On December 6, however, when the Republican National Committee met at the White House, Coolidge inserted a paragraph in his prepared speech reading as follows: —

My statement stands. No one should be led to suppose that I have modified it. My decision will be respected.

After I had been eliminated, the party began, and should continue, the serious task of selecting another candidate from among the numbers of distinguished men available.[32]

This time most newspapers admitted that his refusal must be regarded as final, and the Republican leaders, including Dawes, Curtis, and others, confessed that they would take him at his word.[33]

---

determined to suppress it. He may not be able to withstand it. I think he would sweep the country." On May 26, 1928, he wrote, "Coolidge will not run. I don't think his wife is in good condition, and I don't think he is, and he does not want to run, and he is a man who ordinarily does not do what he does not want to."

[32] Stearns wrote Morrow, December 16, 1927, "You probably saw in the papers that the President made a supplementary statement that didn't differ much from his first one. Personally I think it would have been better if he hadn't, but it did no very great damage. The National Committee got into what might have become a very serious row. This was not, as the public thought, because of the place where the convention would be held, but the real row was an attempt to damage Senator Butler."

[33] On March 20, 1929, Coolidge refused the request of the Wyoming Republican Committee that he reconsider his decision; and in April he issued a statement requesting Massachusetts voters not to write his name on the ballot in the coming state Presidential primary. It annoyed him exceedingly to have the Senate, on February 10, 1929, adopt by a vote of 56 to 26 the La Follette Resolution against third terms for Presidents.

Even those stalwarts, Stearns and Butler, realized that the President would not alter his decision.[34] The *Philadelphia Inquirer* voiced a strong public sentiment when it declared, "It is impossible now to talk of drafting Mr. Coolidge, however much his decision may be regretted." Receptive candidates, accordingly, opened their campaigns, with the odds at the start in favor of either Hoover or Dawes. Neither then, nor later, did Coolidge show any disposition to name his possible successor, and Herbert Hoover's friends were much chagrined at the President's persistent silence on the subject.

The Seventieth Congress, meeting for its first regular session on December 5, 1927, was organized with Nicholas Longworth as Speaker of the House and Senator George H. Moses as President *pro tempore* of the Senate. The Republicans possessed a working majority in the House, but in the Upper Chamber the "insurgents" had a sufficient number to control legislation by throwing their strength at will to either party. In his annual message the President spoke with vigor and confidence, saying that "the country as a whole has had a prosperity never exceeded" and adding that "if the people maintain that confidence which they are entitled to have in themselves, in each other, and in America, a comfortable prosperity will continue." He renewed his plea for constructive economy, and objected to the reduction of taxes for the benefit of selfish interests. He wished to relieve the farmers, — although not by means of the objectionable McNary-Haugen Bill, — and he felt that the tariff ought not to be altered. It was a document devoid of anything new or startling, but the people of the United States were not ready for a reform program and would have been unresponsive if one had been suggested. Why give medicine to an apparently healthy body politic?

Largely because of the impending party conventions, Congress adjourned in late May, without putting through any very important measures. A bill authorizing appropriations amounting to $325,-000,000 for flood control was approved on May 15 by the President. The McNary-Haugen Bill, slightly modified, was again passed by both Houses and again vetoed, not without some display of feeling, by the Chief Executive; [35] and the effort to override the veto

[34] On January 13, 1928, Butler wrote Stearns, "Our friend Coolidge has sadly mixed up things. That he is out for good and all I am convinced, and I am troubled; but where are we going? We must go somewhere. We may hesitate at Hoover, but who else? I think you had better run. I will support you vigorously."

[35] All conservatives, and a considerable group of liberals, were with the President in this veto. George W. Wickersham wrote Taft on May 28: "I am glad you feel as I do about Coolidge's message on the McNary-Haugen Bill. I think it is the best thing he ever did, and if a farmer who otherwise was tempted

failed, as had been the case before. A joint resolution for the federal operation of Muscle Shoals was pushed through Congress, but the President administered the *coup de grâce* through a pocket veto. The "Lame Duck" amendment, later to be passed under Franklin D. Roosevelt, failed again in the House, although it had Coolidge's support. During the session, Coolidge vetoed thirteen bills and smothered three others by declining to affix his signature within the stipulated time.

Returning to Massachusetts for the first time in almost two years, the President and Mrs. Coolidge attended, on May 18, the sesquicentennial celebration of Phillips Academy, Andover, the Headmaster of which was Alfred E. Stearns, whom he had known at Amherst. In preparation for his address, which dealt entirely with education, Coolidge spent two weeks familiarizing himself not merely with the history of Phillips Academy, the oldest endowed and incorporated secondary school in America, but also with the development of secondary education in this country. He said to the Andover boys, in words which some of them have never forgotten: —

Two great tests in mental discipline are accuracy and honesty. It is far better to master a few subjects thoroughly than to have a mass of generalizations about many subjects. The world will have little use for those who are right only part of the time. Whatever may be the standards of the classroom, practical life will require something more than 60 per cent or 70 per cent for a passing mark. The standards of the world are not like those set by the faculty, but more closely resemble those set by the student body themselves. They are not at all content with a member of the musical organization who can strike only 90 per cent of the notes. They do not tolerate the man on the diamond who catches only 80 per cent of the balls. The standards which the student body set are high. They want accuracy that is well-nigh complete.

From Andover, the Coolidges proceeded in their special train to Northampton, where Mrs. Coolidge's mother had been seriously ill in the hospital, and from there returned to Washington to see Congress end its session and make their plans for the summer.

As is always the case in a Presidential year, the chief excitement, in and out of Congress, centred in the coming Presidential election.

---

to think that those eminent gentlemen, McNary and Haugen, are offering him anything of value will read this message, or even a few of the salient parts of it, he will come to a realization that what they are handing him was not even a gold brick — nothing but a plain unvarnished clay brick! I understand all the leaders of the farm crowd, that is the fellows who are fabricating bogus gifts for the farmers, are in a state of wild indignation, first, against Coolidge, and more directly against Hoover."

The Republican Convention, opening on Tuesday, June 12, in Kansas City, had only two outstanding candidates, Lowden and Hoover, with the latter in the lead almost from the beginning. With Coolidge definitely out of the contest, state after state had declared itself during the spring for Hoover, who, even without the President's support, had built up a large following and a well-oiled machine. Many party leaders had not abandoned hope that at the last minute Coolidge would yield to solicitation and quietly permit the use of his name. If he had done so, even by a simple gesture, he could have been nominated, but he gave no such sign.

The theory that Coolidge "hoped to be the nominee, expected to be the nominee, and was disappointed and distressed when he was not chosen by the Convention," [36] is still occasionally expressed, but is, in the opinion of those in the best position to know, entirely untenable, and is in direct contradiction to all the President's private and public statements on the subject. Chief Justice Taft wrote in late March, "I don't know what Hilles has in mind when he is continually talking of drafting Coolidge, for I do not think Coolidge has the slightest idea of running, and I think there will be quite enough men in the Convention who have assumed that he will not run, and will therefore not yield to a sweep of enthusiasm." [37] Everett Sanders, the President's Secretary, went to Kansas City as his personal representative, with explicit instructions that Coolidge's name was not to be presented. Before leaving Coolidge, Sanders asked, "Shall I see Mr. Mellon?" to which the President replied, "Mr. Mellon will support Mr. Hoover." On the convention floor, Mellon sent for Sanders and asked whether the President had sent any message. Sanders answered that, while Coolidge had given no orders, Mellon could assume that he was not to lend the President any support. [38] It was Sanders's distinct impression at the time that Coolidge did not wish to have anyone bring up his name; and this is also the conviction of both Mr. Stearns and Mrs. Coolidge, who knew him better than anyone else. What he would have done if he had been nominated unanimously by the Convention he had not decided. [39]

At Kansas City, Coolidge's untiring supporter, Senator Fess,

---

[36] *Vide* "Ike" Hoover, pp. 167 ff.

[37] William H. Taft, to Moses Straus, March 20, 1928, in the Taft papers.

[38] "Ike" Hoover, by implication, suggests that Everett Sanders was a "traitor" to Coolidge, but the charge, in the opinion of those most in touch with events at that period, is absurd.

[39] Conversation between William V. Hodges and President Coolidge, December 7, 1928, as incorporated by Mr. Hodges in a memorandum immediately afterward.

delivered a rather commonplace keynote speech. The platform was duly presented and adopted, after which the candidates were nominated one by one with the traditional flow of oratory. The President had intended to take a train on Monday evening for Brule, Wisconsin, but Mrs. Coolidge was ill, and they could not leave until Wednesday night. While the balloting was going on in the Convention Hall, the President was in his drawing-room on the special train fast asleep. During the proceedings, after Hoover had been placed in nomination, followed by Norris and Watson, an Ohio delegate, Ralph D. Cole, secured the floor and nominated Calvin Coolidge, hoping undoubtedly for a stampede. But it was much too late. The leaders had already agreed on Herbert Hoover, and at that moment nothing could have altered them. Senator Moses, who was presiding, merely requested the Secretary to continue calling the roll of states, and everything went along without interruption. On the first roll-call, Herbert Hoover received 837 votes out of 1089 and was declared the Presidential nominee of the Republican Party. Eighteen votes, in spite of all that he had said, were cast for Calvin Coolidge. Under Borah's direction, Charles Curtis, of Kansas, was chosen as the Vice Presidential candidate, and the Convention was over.

The President had arranged to spend the summer of 1928 at Cedar Island Lodge on a small island in the Brule River, about thirty-five miles from Superior, Wisconsin, where the executive offices were located in a high-school building. The estate, which belonged to the heirs of H. C. Pierce, comprised almost five thousand acres, with seven lakes and many miles of dim forest and balsam-scented trails, and was known as an Anglers' Paradise. The news of Hoover's nomination did not reach him until he appeared at breakfast on the morning of Friday, June 15, just before reaching Superior, and he promptly dispatched a telegram of congratulation to the nominee. He seemed to be in fine spirits when he stepped off the train, and even laughed outright in chatting with the newspapermen, but he was really tired and nervous, and Mrs. Coolidge, herself a convalescent, was much worried about him. A gold fishing license had been presented to him by the State of Wisconsin, and soon, dressed in a red striped mackinaw, ten-gallon hat, khaki trousers, and high boots, he was out on the river with his Chippewa Indian guide, John La Roque, casting flies. Before evening of the first day he had brought in several steelhead trout, and he had many good catches before the season was over.

It was impossible, of course, to keep away from politics. In late June, in the sultry heat of Houston, Texas, the Democrats nominated

Alfred E. Smith for the Presidency, and the campaign was on. A third candidate, Norman Thomas, named by the Socialist Party, was already in the field. Coolidge, isolated though he was, did what he could to bestow his pontifical blessing on Herbert Hoover, who came with his wife to Brule on July 18. There the two men were photographed together. When Hoover was officially notified on August 14, Coolidge telegraphed him, "Your speech of acceptance ranks very high in political discussion. I congratulate you upon it and upon the reception which has been given it by the country." The question of race and religion was unfortunately raised early in the campaign, for Smith was a Roman Catholic, and intense opposition to him developed in certain quarters, even in the ordinarily Democratic South. Both Coolidge and Hoover, however, called for fair play on this issue, and neither one brought up the question in his statements or speeches.

The President was on a vacation, which he badly needed, and spent most of his time in recreation and rest. The staff on this trip included eighty-eight persons and composed a small community in itself, with Colonel Starling, of the Secret Service, Colonel Latrobe, the Military Aide, and Colonel Coupal, the President's physician, to be with him as companions. In early July Secretary Work presented his resignation, in order to become Chairman of the Republican National Committee. Coolidge fulfilled some speaking engagements, especially a fine address delivered at Cannon Falls, Minnesota, on July 29, in dedication of a Civil War monument. He visited mines and attended county and state fairs and greeted friends when they were near by. For the first time in his life he took up trapshooting, and enjoyed it immensely. When the Coolidges returned to Washington on September 12, to be welcomed by the Hoovers and several cabinet members, they were both brown and healthy, looking as if the summer had done them good.

On Wednesday, September 19, the President and his wife, accompanied by Attorney General Sargent, left Washington for Northampton, where they registered for the coming election and called on Mrs. Goodhue, who was still in the hospital, a hopeless invalid. They then moved on to Plymouth, where they spent Thursday night in the homestead, with Miss Aurora Pierce to wait upon them. From there they made a rapid tour around Vermont, having a look at places which had been damaged by the recent flood. It was at Bennington, just before leaving his native state, that the President, responding at last to an ovation from the crowd at the station, recited the short speech quoted at the opening of this biography. It was spontaneous, poetical, unprecedented in his career, and throbbed with childhood memories. He was still, after all those years of absence, a Man from Vermont.

In his last conference with Coolidge before the election, Hoover was visibly worried — needlessly, however, for the gods were on his side, and the victory was so decisive that good Republicans believed the Democratic Party to be not only moribund but dead forever. For the first time the radio had been used extensively to broadcast political speeches; and the number of mass meetings and party demonstrations was exceptionally large. So efficacious a political argument was Coolidge Prosperity that it would probably have been a Republican year no matter who was running. The electoral vote of 444 for Hoover and Curtis against 87 for Smith and Robinson was overwhelming in its appreciation of the Republican policies, and Hoover had a popular majority of 6,423,612. The conservatives never seemed surer of their ground.

Coolidge took no active part in the campaign and indicated no excitement regarding it. At the very end he allowed himself to be photographed with Hoover at the White House, and he did, on the eve of election, make a radio speech for his party candidates. He was well aware that his help was not needed. On one occasion "Ike" Hoover heard him remark, "The people have been so prosperous for eight years and have made so much money, they may wish to go on a spree and elect Governor Smith," [40] but the facetiousness of this observation is sufficiently evident. When the result was known, the President sent the President-elect a telegram and shortly afterwards congratulated him in person. Again "Ike" Hoover, presumably to prove that Coolidge was disturbed by the outcome of the election, says that, at the cabinet dinner on November 8, the President left the table before the dessert had been all served, to the great embarrassment of guests, waiters, and musicians. [41] It is not improbable that Coolidge at this time had some form of attack of a kind which he had suffered from before and which had led him to be concerned about his health. That he should be nervously wrought up by Herbert Hoover's election to the Presidency is, to say the least, neither plausible nor probable.

The President's attention to his health led him to leave in late November for the Swannanoa Country Club, near Waynesboro, in the Blue Ridge Mountains of Virginia, where Mrs. Coolidge and he spent several days in rest and quiet, seeing almost nobody. While

[40] Hoover, 179.
[41] *Ibid.*, 131–32.

they were there, public announcement was made of the engagement of Miss Florence Trumbull, daughter of the Governor of Connecticut, to John Coolidge. The engagement had been suspected and hinted at by the press for some months, even while the boy was still in Amherst College, but any statement regarding it had been postponed until after he had graduated and secured a job. The Coolidges were back in the White House on December 2 to receive congratulations.

In late December, the President and his wife went still farther south to Sapelo Island, off the coast of Georgia, as the guests of Howard E. Coffin, the famous consulting engineer. The place itself was almost inaccessible, with only one telephone line which had been hastily installed for the emergency. While he was there, Coolidge took up shooting and made some very respectable bags of quail. The English artist, Frank O. Salisbury, was also one of the party and painted portraits of both Mr. and Mrs. Coolidge. They returned to Washington shortly after the opening of the new year, for the closing weeks of power.

As Calvin Coolidge's administration drew to the end, the prosperity of the country was apparently not only unimpaired, but even increasing. Hitherto 1926 had stood out as a peak year in American industry, but 1928 set a new record not only for the production of goods but also for profits, especially in the larger corporations.[42] Secretary of Labor James J. Davis, in a letter to a newspaper in Cardiff, Wales, had pointed out that "no country can be considered Utopia when 86 per cent of its people are poor"; and official statistics indicated that 13 per cent of the population of the United States owned 90 per cent of its wealth. But it was also a fact that, in 1928, the American laboring man was much better off than the worker of any country on the globe, and that his real wage, measured by purchasing power, was twice as high as that of a worker in London and more than four times as high as that of a worker in Brussels, Rome, or Madrid. It is no wonder that optimism and complacency were in the air. Herbert Hoover, in his speech of acceptance in August 1928, had said, "We in America are nearer to the final triumph over poverty than ever before in the history of any land. . . . We shall soon, with the help of God, be in sight of the day when poverty will be banished from this nation." Calvin Coolidge, in his last annual message in December, declared that "the great

---

[42] *Literary Digest*, January 26, 1929, pp. 66–68. There were no widespread labor troubles. According to Dun and Company's annual review, both production and consumption "attained unexampled levels in certain channels."

wealth created by our enterprise and industry, and saved by our economy, has had the widest distribution among our own people, and has gone out in a steady stream to serve the charity and business of the world." At Christmas time it was asserted that the President had made to the American people a gift of continuous prosperity.

Unfortunately this very real improvement in the condition of the average man and woman had been accompanied by an unprecedented and inexplicable outbreak of speculative mania. The Florida real-estate boom of 1925 and 1926 had run its humorous and tragic course, leaving the usual disasters in its wake. But the gambling instinct, always latent in the mob, had been aroused and, with the stock market easily available, even persons with relatively small incomes were obsessed by a passion to get rich overnight. People who had never before owned a share of stock suddenly decided to purchase, often on a margin. Men ordinarily conservative, staid, and unimaginative citizens joined in the hysteria, and everybody at the same time was hoping to get something for nothing. For this strange manifestation of mass psychology there was no explanation on any rational basis.

During the latter part of Calvin Coolidge's administration the increase in speculation on the New York Stock Exchange became so startling as to arouse comment in the financial journals, and the rise in security prices was correspondingly amazing. Every morning brokers asked one another, "What next?" The number of shares dealt in for the year 1920 was 223 million; by 1926 this had expanded to 452 million, and it was obvious that things were going well in Wall Street. In 1927, however, it rose to 527 million, and the Great Boom was on. So far as the tendency can be expressed in mere statistics, it is worth noting that the volume of trading in 1928 was 920 million, and in 1929 it was 1124 million. This was the period when members of the Stock Exchange were swamped with orders, and the white-headed boys just out of Yale and Princeton turned automatically to investment banking, with the alluring prospect of owning yachts and maintaining strings of polo ponies within a few lucrative years.

The advance in prices, even in supposedly conservative securities, was completely irrational. Available figures show that the average for common stocks rose from the so-called "norm" in 1926 to 114 in June 1927, to 148.2 in June 1928, and to 191 in June 1929. Hundreds of thousands of people, many of them in hamlets and villages far removed from Wall Street, felt as they read the reports that they had more money to spend — and spent it. Some of them gave a consid-

erable proportion of their profits to schools and hospitals, and lived
to see the time when the credit for these donations was all that was
left to them from the Golden Age. The proportion of those who
bought stocks on margin was large, and brokers' loans, which in 1922
amounted to less than two billion dollars, had increased in 1927 to
four and a half billion dollars, and in 1928 to six and a half billions.
It was obvious that many self-respecting people — clerks and school-
masters and physicians and clergymen — had forgotten Calvin Coolidge's doctrine of thrift and were actually borrowing considerable
sums in the expectation that the advance in prices would continue,
enabling them to sell eventually at a profit.[43] Even those who sold,
however, usually bought other stocks with the proceeds, and few had
the good sense to invest in government bonds and be safe.

Some conservative advisers felt, as 1928 opened, that common
stocks were altogether too high in relation to their earnings, both
actual and potential, and that the outlook for business was not
bright. Bankers of a cautious disposition counseled their clients to
be prudent. But prudence was not the national mood. When the Federal Reserve Board, in August 1927, had lowered the rediscount rate
from 4 per cent to 3½ per cent, it had stimulated the rush towards
speculation; and when the President in early January, 1928, in response to a direct question, made a statement to the effect that brokers'
loans were not too high, he helped to encourage further inflation.[44]
This statement, so curiously unlike any which the ordinarily uncommunicative Coolidge had made before, aroused widespread interest and comment, and was deplored by those conservative financiers
who felt in their secret hearts that the future was being discounted to
an unwarranted extent by those who were willing to pay excessively
high prices for securities.[45] It was the one important occasion when

[43] Mr. John T. Flynn feels that security speculation has never been practised
by more than 1 per cent of the population — certainly not over a million people.
(*Security Speculation*, pp. 54ff.) But they are a group whose influence, for various
reasons, is very powerful and widespread.

[44] Judson Walliver is responsible for a story, related by William Allen White
(*A Puritan in Babylon*, 392), that Coolidge, queried at a press conference about
brokers' loans, held the question over, took it to one of his secretaries, and said,
"What about this?" The young man promised to prepare a reply and produced
the statement which the President gave to the press on January 6. When Coolidge
heard about the results, he attempted to correct the blunder, but it was too late.
This explanation may be correct, but it needs further proof, which I have been
unable to obtain. It is more probable that, after consultation with Secretary Mellon,
Coolidge thought it unwise to check a movement which, he thought, would naturally
and inevitably subside.

[45] *The Literary Digest*, January 21, 1928, printed a symposium of comments
on the President's statement, some of them favorable. Coolidge had attributed
the sharp rise in brokers' loans to larger bank deposits and a longer list of security
issues handled by the Stock Exchange.

Coolidge did not keep his mouth shut, and his untimely utterance proved to be the most unfortunate blunder he ever made.

The President's reassuring statement was followed by the most active Saturday's trading Wall Street had ever seen. And then, in March, began a succession of advances in prices, wholly unjustified by the condition of business or by promise for the future, and an even more feverish boom was under way. The story of what happened during the next few exciting months has been related in popular fashion by Frederick L. Allen, in his *Only Yesterday;* but a crowd of living witnesses can add their own impressions of a period when the opening of the Stock Exchange each morning saw them hundreds or thousands of dollars richer — on paper. It was all very thrilling. A jump of eight or ten points in a single day came to be regarded as not abnormal; indeed on March 12, Radio opened at 120½ and closed eighteen points higher.

The Federal Reserve Board, with some discernment, did what it could to restrain the madness, raising the rediscount rate in February to 4 per cent, in May to 4½ per cent, and in June to 5 per cent. At the time of the party conventions, the speculative hysteria was less violent, but the lull proved to be only temporary. There were other brief intervals in 1928 when prices declined for a day or two and wiseacres predicted that the bull market was arrested; but always the ticker resumed its march, and a new peak was reached after Hoover's election in November. On November 23, the volume of trading on the Stock Exchange reached seven million shares, and a seat on the floor sold for $580,000. By the close of the month Radio was selling for 400 — a preposterous price in view of the earnings of the company. In December, when the market broke once more, Radio dropped seventy-two points in a single day, but the slump was only an intermission, and the year closed with prices higher than ever.

On February 2, 1929, a few weeks before Calvin Coolidge retired to private life, the Federal Reserve Board issued a warning, stating that the resources of the Federal Reserve Banks were not intended for "the creation or extension of speculative credit"; and it seemed as if the Board might get the situation under control. Stocks fell off significantly in late March, as the new administration got under way, and money rates rose sharply. By summer, however, the newly formed investment trusts were absorbing great blocks of securities, and prices were soaring. Six months after Coolidge had left office his "prosperity" was still enduring; indeed Radio had risen from 94½ on March 4, 1929, to an adjusted high of 505 on September 3.

Then, with all the suddenness of a far-flung avalanche, came a succession of "breaks," culminating in the Great Crash of Thursday, October 24, which swept thousands of people down to ruin. Despite all that could be done by the most dominating figures in Wall Street, — Morgan and Baker and Lamont and Wiggin and Whitney, — the plunge could not be more than temporarily blocked. On Monday, October 28, a record of almost sixteen and a half million shares was dealt in, and the prices of fifty average shares had fallen off almost forty points. Holders could not meet their margin requirements, and huge blocks of securities were dumped on the market to be sold for whatever they would bring. Fortunes were swept away in a few hours, and small holders lost all their savings. President Hoover did what he could through calming words; Secretary Mellon predicted a revival of industrial activity in the spring of 1930; Julius H. Barnes declared that American business was "steadily coming back to a normal level of prosperity." By the close of October the worst of the panic had passed and the victims were contemplating the wreckage; but the aftermath lasted on for many years. The Golden Age was over. The logical consequence of the Great Bull Market was the Great Depression, with all its unhappiness. But the Great Depression does not come strictly within the scope of a biography of Calvin Coolidge.

And yet, after all, it does! The rank of a statesman in the Hall of Fame is determined ultimately by many factors — his influence and gift for leadership, his personal character, his political and economic policies and their consequence, his constructive program, his farsightedness, and his conduct during crises. Often the judgment of contemporaries is revised by posterity, as in the cases of John Tyler and Andrew Johnson. Most of what Woodrow Wilson strove for in his lifetime has since been abandoned or nullified; yet his admirers are convinced that he will be vindicated by future generations. Calvin Coolidge is identified with no great cause, like the abolition of slavery or the League of Nations or the elimination of social injustice. It can be claimed for him, however, that he administered public affairs with intelligence, wisdom, and integrity — that his job as President was well done. The charges most frequently brought against him are materialism and ultraconservatism, joined with the specific accusation that he failed to abate or stop the speculative mania of the late 1920's. The first two of these indictments will be taken up later, but something must be said here in reply to those who have attributed to him all our economic ills subsequent to his administration.

Until the storm broke in the autumn of 1929, Calvin Coolidge had been regarded by a majority of the American people as the haloed genius of prosperity. His relentless insistence on a balanced budget, on thrift and honest management, was presumably contributory to sound financial conditions. But when the disaster occurred, the sufferers tried to blame Coolidge for not setting the brakes. Unquestionably the President had blundered when he needlessly announced that nearly four billions of brokers' loans represented "merely a natural expansion of business in the securities market." If he was not able to control events, he should have followed his usual practice of saying nothing. William Allen White draws a graphic picture of Coolidge "there in that place of great power basically uninformed about either the source or the direction of the great tides that were washing around him, the resistless undertow that was dragging his country and the world out of the old times into the new." [46] Let us admit that the President was being swept along, like nearly all of his fellow countrymen, by forces beyond his or any other man's control. Go back and read the newspapers during 1928 and 1929! Where were the admonitory voices, and if, in the midst of the din, they had whispered words of warning, who would have listened to them? Is there any evidence that the well-informed journals which mold public opinion attempted to send out danger signals? The testimony is ample that Coolidge was troubled by the trend towards extravagances and speculation and that he warned the nation of the perils of prosperity.[47] But it is not strange, although it is unfortunate, that, when financial experts assured him that all was well, when he saw people with more money to spend and laborers getting higher wages, when he discovered that American citizens wanted to speculate, he was willing to forget his own doubts.

Furthermore we are told on excellent authority that "many distinguished and hitherto conservative economists were persuaded that a New Era had indeed begun." [48] Unscrupulous insiders were profiting by methods which were simply larceny on a stupendous scale, but thousands of gentlemen who prided themselves on their sense of honor were also buying and selling for profit and, with their bank balances perceptibly mounting, had no misgivings as to the propriety of the system which permitted them to get and spend. If Coolidge had raised his voice over a "nation-wide hookup," — assuming that he had possessed an intuition and a prophetic gift which he never claimed, — he would have been denounced as a modern male Cassandra by countless imprecatory throats and possibly might have precipitated for the

[46] White, 391–92.
[47] Coolidge once told H. Parker Willis that, in his opinion, "any loan made for gambling in stocks was an 'excessive loan,'" but he differentiated between his personal view and his responsibility as representative of the government. (*A Puritan in Babylon*, 391.)
[48] Allen, *The Lords of Creation*, p. 361.

moment an even worse calamity. As it was, he watched the mad carnival with misgivings, — himself no part of it, — and hoped that all might be well. He was wrong, no doubt, and a President cannot afford to be wrong on an important issue. To that extent he must share the responsibility for the grim tragedy that followed. But nobody could have checked that speculative madness — not J. Pierpont Morgan nor Andrew W. Mellon nor Calvin Coolidge.[49] Forces were operating bigger than any one man or group of men, forces which even now professional or practical economists do not clearly comprehend. Something was defective in our social and financial structure, but something was also wrong with the minds and hearts of the human race.

It was Fate's colossal jest that Calvin Coolidge, the advocate of hard work, who never believed in getting something for nothing and who felt that Earth gets its price for what Earth gives us, should have headed the nation during that era when gambling was as natural as breathing. He worshiped thrift as a Zulu does his idol; he had never made a bet in all his life and had placed his savings in banks or high-grade bonds; and he cared nothing for the luxury that money makes possible. Temperamentally he was far removed from the stock-market manipulators who were piling up fortunes which were later to vanish like thistledown in a wind. All Coolidge's Vermont training, all of his later experience, had been the negation of "get rich quickly." It was his misfortune as a statesman that he should, by his own personal example, have been exemplifying one type of living at a period when the trend was in another direction.

Coolidge's farewell message to Congress, on December 4, 1928, was primarily a warning against extravagance. Once again he made prosperity and peace the pillars of his political philosophy, and his recommendations were aimed at their firm establishment. He spoke about the navy, farm relief, Boulder Dam, Muscle Shoals, and Prohibition, but these were only ephemeral phases of larger issues. Within a day or two he nominated Roy O. West, of Illinois, to succeed Hubert Work as Secretary of the Interior, and William F. Whiting, of Massachusetts, to take the place of Herbert Hoover, now President-elect of the United States. Both appointments were promptly confirmed. To the fiftieth anniversary number of the *St. Louis Post-Dispatch* he contributed a letter suggesting that Congress provide for the President a country White House, — much like Chequers in

---

[49] "Even had any one group of men in Wall Street had the time to think steadily about the possible economic and social effects of what was going on . . . this group would have been virtually powerless to stop the mad rush toward the edge of the abyss." (Allen, 348.) This is the opinion of every authority on financial matters that I have consulted, including members of the Federal Reserve Board.

England, — where the Chief Executive could find a refuge from heat and visitation. He referred to the heavy burden which every President must bear and pointed out the need for him to secure occasionally "a complete change of atmosphere." Congress at once seized upon the suggestion, and a bill appropriating $48,000 for the purpose was passed and signed by the President on the last day of his term. In commenting on the matter, Coolidge said, "The Congress has shown an inclination to treat a President with the same kind of consideration it extends to our birds and other wild life."

When the "Lame Duck" Session of Congress came to an end on March 4, 1929, it had ratified the Kellogg Pact, passed the necessary legislation for the building of Boulder Dam, voted an appropriation for fifteen new cruisers of ten thousand tons each, and arranged for a new customs treaty with China. It had done nothing with farm relief, with Muscle Shoals, or with the suggested change in the immigration ratio. Like most Lame Duck sessions, it rather quietly "petered out," leaving much to be done by the Seventy-first Congress and the new administration.

The closing weeks were uneventful for the Coolidges. On February 1, the President was at Mountain Lake, in Florida, dedicating the beautiful Bird Sanctuary and Singing Tower which Edward W. Bok had presented to the nation; and in his speech he counseled the American people, then seemingly intent on financial gain, to devote more attention to moral and spiritual values. He still played his rôle well. Mrs. Ashurst, wife of the Senator from Arizona, said to him at dinner, "Mr. President, you have been very fortunate in your administration — no wars, no strikes, no panics." Coolidge stared thoughtfully at his plate and then replied, "I never thought of it that way. I did my duty as I saw it." That was his attitude to the very end. He was still the Man from Vermont.

The person most disturbed by the impending change was probably Frank W. Stearns. Then in his seventy-third year, he had watched a man sixteen years younger than he move from humble political beginnings to the foremost office in the world. Now he was to see him voluntarily renounce further honors and return to the simple home from which he had started. The Stearnses were still frequent guests at the White House, — although it was suggested by some observers that his influence had slightly waned, — and on Mr. Stearns's birthday, November 28, 1928, the President gave him *The Intimate Papers of Colonel House,* in four volumes, with an inscription, "To Frank W. Stearns, with Best Wishes for His Birth-

EN ROUTE TO THE INAUGURATION OF PRESIDENT HOOVER IN 1929

day." Later Colonel House wrote these words, "May I add my good wishes to those of your distinguished friend, [signed] E. M. House." On February 23, 1929, Stearns sent to the President a letter, written in the White House, to put on paper his strangely mingled emotions: —

I do not know that the near approach of March 4th makes it incumbent upon me to say anything. There are many things which I would like to say if I knew how. I imagine you know what they are without my saying them. If you do not, words will not help out, and yet it seems to me a little brutal to remain entirely silent. I am not so much a believer in crises as I am in epochs. I am not quite so modest as I sometimes assume to be. I have the very greatest confidence in my judgment on some subjects. There are some subjects on which all the people in the world differing with me could not change my mind.

I do not regard March 4th as an ending, but a beginning. One epoch will close. The glory of that epoch is that its requirements have met with marvelous success. As I wrote you once when I was going to Europe, I believed then and I believe equally now, that at the time you took control of the government in some ways the country was in the most dangerous position that it has ever been in my day. I do believe that the Lord is in control, whether we can understand it at the time or not. I believe that just as in the case of Washington. or Lincoln your coming to the command turned back a tide which I would not care to describe with adjectives.

When you were Vice-President you will remember that you spoke at the banquet given in celebration of the 100th anniversary of the building of the first Chickering piano. I sat beside Mrs. Coolidge and she said to me, "Do you still believe that Calvin will be President some day?" I have often thought of my reply, which was, "It is common opinion that a man holding the office of Vice-President is in the worst possible position to become President, but whether he becomes President or not, I believe as much as I ever have believed that if he lives his natural life and keeps his health, the time will come when in some emergency the men, women, and children of this country will follow him, and the country will be saved from disaster." It is in this sense that I say March 4 is not an end but a beginning.

As I said in that other letter, it is a terrible responsibility, and it means that the man on whom that responsibility is laid must, from the necessity of the case, be the most lonely man in the country.

Robert Lincoln O'Brien once said in his cynical way to me, "You have created a character just as truly as Dickens ever did." I told him that I had created no character — a character was the product of inheritance, self-discipline, and Divine Providence. If I had been so fortunate as to see a vision of that character and to the measure of my ability had been able to draw a picture of that character so that others might see it, I had reason to be deeply grateful.

I am given much more credit than I deserve for my part in saving the country from disaster. That I have been permitted to have some part in it is not a cause for boasting — it is, as I have said above, cause for deep gratitude. For the association that has existed, in which Mrs. Coolidge, you, the boys, Mrs. Stearns, and I have had such an intimate part, I am very grateful. I hope you will not think me lacking in humility if I hug the comfort that it is sufficient to be an excuse for having lived.

Wherever you are and whatever you do after March 4th, I hope and believe that you will not hesitate to call if I can be helpful in any way, big or little, to you or yours.

I will conclude by signing as I have always signed my letters to you,

Sincerely,

FRANK W. STEARNS

Two days later the President sent his reply: —

My DEAR MR. STEARNS:

Your beautiful letter has been received. I shall always treasure it. It is most gratifying to know that you are still loyal to your idols. I should like to think that I was in some way worthy of the things you are always saying about me.

With kindest regards, I am
Cordially yours,

CALVIN COOLIDGE

Clearly it was difficult for these men, both of them shy and reticent, to express what they felt on an occasion which meant so much to them both. In an effort to avoid sentimentality, each relapsed into conventional phrases. But the tie that bound them was there, and was never broken while they were both alive.

Seldom, perhaps never, has a President gone out of office with his popularity less diminished. Wherever the Coolidges appeared during their last weeks in the capital, crowds gathered to cheer them. "Ike" Hoover felt that the President, still chagrined at his failure to be reëlected, had no interest in the erection of a reviewing stand for his successor and behaved "like a prisoner who had to watch the noise and bustle attendant on the building of a scaffold for his execution." But this was not the impression which others gathered, and many felt that Coolidge was more and more relieved as the end drew near. He went punctiliously through the rather elaborate

routine which custom prescribes when one Chief Executive succeeds another; and "Polly" Randolph has reported that when the
Coolidges walked for the last time from their rooms to the elevator
they were cheerful and smiling.[50] Importuned to say something at
the Union Station as he departed, Coolidge would speak only one
sentence, "Good-bye, I have had a very enjoyable time in Washington." Then, turning to the radio representative, he added, rather
sadly, "I'm not getting much private life." It is significant that the
coach next to the parlor car which the Coolidges occupied on their
way back to Northampton was filled by twenty or more newspapermen, who had been instructed not to let a good news item escape
their vigilance.

Naturally gossip had been busy speculating what Calvin Coolidge would do and where he would go. Chief Justice Taft wrote his
son on February 17: —

We don't know what the Coolidges are going to do. They announce
that they are going back to Northampton, but I should think they
would buy a house here and live in more comfortable quarters. All
sorts of suggestions are made as to what he will do. I saw there was
one suggestion made by a minister, not by a lawyer, that he be appointed to the Supreme Bench. There is one difficulty about it, and
that is that there is no vacancy on the Bench, and the second is I don't
think he would regard himself as quite prepared for that place, though
he certainly would make as good a Judge as some whom he has appointed.

It was reported that he was to become a college president, that
he was to head a large life-insurance company, that he was to run
for United States Senator. He himself, however, had no plan except
to go back home. When he and his wife stepped out of the train
at Northampton at eight-thirty in the morning, there was a gray sky
overhead and slush underfoot, made more unpleasant by a light
drizzle of rain. But the throng of more than three thousand at the
station did not mind standing in the wet. The Mayor greeted the
Coolidges, the ex-President replied briefly, and the auditors cheered.
In what the press called a "big blue sedan," they drove through
avenues lined with men, women, and children, including Smith College girls four deep, to the house on Massasoit Street, where it
seemed as if the photographers would never cease taking pictures.
At last one of them remarked, "What else is there we can get?"

---

[50] Perhaps the best-known Coolidge cartoon is that by Gluyas Williams, in *Life*,
reproduced on page 446.

and the ex-President said wearily, "You've got enough." Soon the crowd trudged away, and Calvin and Grace Coolidge were back in their own house, in private life. In his *Autobiography,* he wrote: —

We draw our Presidents from the people. It is a wholesome thing for them to return to the people. I came from them. I wish to be one of them again.

XVIII

The Twilight Years

HE had almost four years more of life, years when he was to see the resplendent structure of national prosperity called by his name topple and, "like an insubstantial pageant faded, leave not a rack behind." He had, he thought, built so well, on a foundation of economy and thrifty management, and yet within a few months most of his work had crumbled. Millions of discouraged workmen were walking the streets; the bread lines grew longer and longer; large fortunes vanished, and even those who had a little were soon to have less. Calvin Coolidge's vision of a nation permanently contented had evaporated. At first "hard times" seemed only temporary, and jokes were printed on the subject; then wages dropped lower, jobs disappeared, industry sank into the doldrums, and despair followed. Coolidge had left the White House at a moment when the Great Bull Market was flourishing, but now he was being blamed for the Great Depression. No wonder he was disturbed and bewildered, unable to discern what had precipitated such a sudden shift in human affairs. Once again he and countless others were the victims of world conditions over which they had no control. He lived long enough to see a political party which in 1928 had been described as moribund sweep the country in 1932, and the once complacent Republicans go down to catastrophic ruin.[1] It hurt Coolidge, for he was a proud and sensitive man; and once in a while he confided something to a friend which indicated how much he was troubled. It is the story of these concluding three years and ten months — a tragic anticlimax — which remains to be told.

Never in American history has the relinquishment of the Presidency been more truly democratic or involved a more striking contrast. Grover Cleveland became the Sage of Princeton. Theodore

---

[1] Samuel G. Blythe described the Republican Party in 1935 as "a dead whale stranded on the beach."

Roosevelt, after an interval of hunting and travel, returned to his comfortable home at Oyster Bay. William H. Taft, following his defeat in 1912, accepted a professorship in Yale Law School. Woodrow Wilson drove from the White House to a dignified residence in the national capital, where he lived in secluded invalidism until his death. Warren G. Harding died in office. But Calvin Coolidge went direct from Washington to Northampton, to his seven-room apartment in a commonplace two-family house, for which he had been paying rental at thirty-two dollars a month throughout the period of his Presidency. It was not obscurity, for he could never again be obscure. If it had been, he would have liked it better. But Massasoit Street was sought by a continuous procession of sightseers; indeed Dr. Plummer, who still occupied the other side of the house, estimated that, in May, an automobile passed on the average every six seconds, and later in the summer the street was sometimes blocked with cars. The Coolidges did their best to lead a normal life. Mrs. Reckahn continued to act as housekeeper, and the flower garden was turned into a runway for the dogs brought from Washington. The ex-President tried to sit on the porch in the evening as he used to do. But whenever he appeared in public a crowd was sure to gather, and the unceasing demonstrations of popularity wore on his nerves. The house was altogether too near the street, and he soon found his conspicuous position highly distasteful.

When he finally realized that people would not leave him to himself, he purchased in the spring of 1930 the Morris Comey estate, known in Northampton as The Beeches. To the reporters who insisted on full information, he said, "It is a modest place with a little land. It will give my doggies a place to exercise and will enable us to entertain our occasional guests from out of town more comfortably." Actually it was a shingle-sided house of twelve rooms, standing in nine acres of lawn and woodland, with a view out over the famous Ox Bow of the Connecticut River to the Holyoke Range beyond.[2] The situation was particularly advantageous because it could be reached only from a side street and had imposing stone pillars at the entrance with iron gates which could be guarded against inquisitive visitors. Here too he could install his large library in the spacious bookshelves and be at peace. He notified the newspapermen of Northampton that he desired to be "let alone," and they,

[2] The house was built by Dr. Henry N. MacCracken, later President of Vassar College, while he was Professor of English in Smith College. The estate included an outdoor swimming pool, a tennis court, and a billiard room. Coolidge paid for it not far from $40,000. After his death it was sold by Mrs. Coolidge, but sight-seers still hunt it out.

respecting his wishes, rarely asked him for an interview except in an emergency. His troubles were chiefly with reporters and photographers from out of town, who often forced themselves upon him.[3]

As they left Washington, Mrs. Coolidge said of her husband to Mr. Stearns, "What can I do with him?" Fortunately he was to have enough to occupy his mind. When he issued on August 2, 1927, in Rapid City, his famous statement that he would not run again, Ray Long, editor of the *Cosmopolitan,* immediately wrote suggesting that the President prepare for publication the story of his life, but the latter then professed to have no confidence in his ability as an author. Mr. Long's persistence, however, was rewarded by a summons on January 25, 1929, to the White House. When he met the appointment at eight-thirty in the morning, Coolidge remarked, "Mr. Long, you're an early bird." "Mr. President," was the audacious reply, "beneath this business suit beats the heart of a Canadian mounted policeman. . . . I've come down to get my man." Then Coolidge, handing Long a sheaf of typewritten manuscript, told him to go into the cabinet room and read it, adding, "If you're not pleased with it, none of the things we've said need bind you." The *Autobiography* thus produced was published in regular magazine installments through the ensuing spring and summer [4] and eventually printed in a volume of 250 pages by the Cosmopolitan Book Corporation, with a Harris and Ewing photograph of Coolidge as a frontispiece and a reproduction of his signature on the outside of the green cover.

The *Autobiography* had an excellent sale at the price of three dollars and brought Coolidge a considerable revenue in royalties. Later, in Northampton, he had an arrangement with the local bookstores by which, for a dollar additional, he would autograph each copy sold; and the extra money was turned over to the Missionary Society of the Edwards Congregational Church, of which Mrs. Coolidge was a member. It is not a great book, for it tells too little of the author's inner thoughts and emotions and is reticent on many matters which a biographer must regard as significant, but it is readable and has interesting revelatory passages.

Before going out of office, Coolidge also completed three articles on "Peace," which appeared in the issues of the *Ladies' Home Jour-*

[3] "You cannot realize how much I long for peace and privacy," he wrote Henry L. Stoddard on April 10, 1930.
[4] The *Literary Digest,* March 30, 1929, quoted an article from the *New York World,* describing the manner in which the first installment was secretly set up in type, and how copies of the April issue of the *Cosmopolitan* were distributed to the 1,850,000 subscribers.

nal for April, May, and June. They were based on the President's Armistice Day Address on November 11, 1928, in which he had said: —

For the cause of peace the United States is adopting the only practicable principles that have ever been proposed, of preparation, limitation, and renunciation.

Once back in private life, Coolidge established for himself a regular and agreeable routine, finding some relief from the fatigue of the Presidential years by lying abed until eight o'clock each morning. He had purchased the Lincoln limousine which he had used during his last year in Washington and had also engaged a chauffeur, John Bukosky, on whom he could rely,[5] for neither he nor Mrs. Coolidge could, or cared to, drive an automobile. When he first settled down in Northampton, his secretary was Herman C. Beaty, a former Associated Press man. He was superseded in May 1931 by Harry Ross,[6] who was with him until Coolidge died. Ordinarily the secretary would go down early to the offices of Coolidge and Hemenway, still in the Masonic Building but enlarged, with Coolidge's return, to include five rooms. Besides the lobby there were two rooms for the stenographers; beyond these was Mr. Hemenway's private office; and separated from this by a thin partition was Mr. Coolidge's own sanctum, with a plain flat-top desk of oak set across one corner. To his left was a door by which the former President could, in an emergency, escape into the outer hall and thus down the stairs into the street.

To avoid being stared at, Coolidge usually drove to his office in his automobile, arriving there about nine o'clock, to find his mail, already sorted by his secretary, lying on his desk. His correspondence was numerous and varied, consisting of appeals for aid, suggestions for articles, requests for opinions on books, applications for political jobs, advice on an infinite range of subjects, and notes of gratitude from admiring citizens. Before attending to his dictation he glanced through the *New York Herald-Tribune* and the *Boston News Bureau,* — both orthodox Republican papers, — smoking as he turned the pages. In the course of the morning he would consume two or three cigars, using paper cigar holders which he

[5] Mr. Coolidge often called him "Johnny-jump-up." He remained with Mrs. Coolidge after the death of her husband and became almost an institution in the family.

[6] Mr. Ross was regarded by Coolidge as the ideal personal secretary. He is still alive and has contributed to me many details of the ex-President's life in Northampton.

MR. COOLIDGE REFUSES POINT-BLANK TO LEAVE THE WHITE
HOUSE UNTIL HIS OTHER RUBBER IS FOUND

frugally saved from one day to another. About noon he was driven back home for luncheon, which he followed with his customary afternoon nap. Shortly after two-thirty he frequently returned to his office to sign his letters and keep appointments. By four he was home for a walk with the dogs — a white collie, named Beauty, and a red chow called Tiny Tim.

For diversion, he did not resort to exciting pastimes. Occasionally during the spring of 1929 he went fishing in Goshen, with City Clerk James R. Mansfield, but he was careful to make his plans in secret and thus avoid publicity. In the winter of 1929–1930, after the death of Mrs. Coolidge's mother, the Coolidges went to St. Petersburg, Florida, to attend a conference of the New York Life Insurance Company, taking with them no secretary or maid. They spent four weeks at the Lakeside Hotel, at Mount Dora, going from there to New Orleans and eventually to California, where they visited Hollywood and lunched with Mr. and Mrs. Douglas Fairbanks. When Coolidge threw away a cigar butt in Los Angeles, there was almost a riot while men and women scrambled for the unusual souvenir. For a week they were the guests of William Randolph Hearst, at San Simeon, and on the way back they stopped for the opening of the Roosevelt Dam near Globe, Arizona.

After settling in The Beeches the following spring, Coolidge selected his favorite chair on the porch, where in warm weather he could rock through the evening, smoking and looking out across "the meadows," the low-lying grassy flats of the valley of the Connecticut. Three canaries in cages sang until darkness fell. Mrs. Coolidge sewed as long as she could see the stitches, and the two often sat there together, saying nothing except a quiet word now and then. Just a few years before submerged in social engagements, they now chose to see only a few intimate friends. By ten o'clock the ex-President was usually in bed, sleeping the untroubled slumber of a middle-aged man who knows that his allotted work is done.

During the summer heat, often oppressive in Northampton, Coolidge still liked to go back to Plymouth for a few weeks, but living conditions there were very primitive from the standpoint of people who had become accustomed to the comforts of the White House. Accordingly he arranged for an addition to the homestead, equipped with all the modern conveniences, and directed its construction. While it could not be admired as an architectural masterpiece, it proved to be livable and he could rest there in some degree isolated from the throngs of people who drove up every day to the door to see his birthplace and the unspoiled room in which he took the oath of office as President. He still, however, sat on the verandah when the weather was good, watched the actions of the visitors, and received the calls of his friends.[7] Now and then he went fishing, especially at Lake Mitchell, north of Woodstock, and he frequently lunched at the Woodstock Inn with guests.

On June 30, 1930, Coolidge began the writing of a series of daily articles for the McClure Newspaper Syndicate,[8] each about two hundred words in length, — the average for the series was 198 words, — over a period of exactly a year. Each article was headed "Thinking Things over with Calvin Coolidge," and he was left absolutely free to select his own topics. At first he was rather diverted by their preparation. Every evening he made a rough draft in pencil, and on the following morning brought it to the office and dictated it to his secretary. It was then revised and recopied and sent off by his secretary by Western Union telegraph not later than three in the afternoon. He seldom prepared more than one in advance, and he was never late.

In these short articles over his signature, Coolidge had naturally to be restrained and cautious, remembering always the far-reaching influence which he still exerted. Although they sometimes had to be composed on trains, he never left himself unguarded in his statements or endangered himself by originality. He did not often employ the first personal pronoun, and said very little about himself or his experiences. Critical readers complained, with some justice, that he was platitudinous, and sometimes an article would seem incoherent — merely a succession of scattered and not very well-knit observations. He deliberately repressed his sense of humor, relying for his effect on a certain sententiousness, in the manner of Sir Francis Bacon or Poor Richard. One has the feeling as he reads these essays one after the other that Coolidge was now and then bored by the whole business.

The topics which he chose were largely related to government,

[7] Once Coolidge was sitting on the porch with an acquaintance when some visitors passed by and one of them said in a voice loud enough to be overheard, "I don't think much of this place." The ex-President turned to his companion and muttered, "Democrats!" He often amused himself by counting the number of automobiles and the states represented by their license plates. He would never allow himself to be imposed upon, and his manner to strangers was not over-cordial.

[8] Coolidge had been approached on the question of a series of syndicated articles as early as 1928, by Richard H. Waldo, but had then declined the offer, although it included a guarantee of $3000 a week. Some later conversations led to his decision, in April 1930, to try the arrangement for a year. Nearly a hundred newspapers subscribed at the highest price ever paid for feature articles, the *New York Herald Tribune* heading the list with $900 weekly. The total subscriptions for the period of fifty-two weeks amounted to $203,045.

economics, and politics, — as might have been expected, — and rarely dealt with music, art, or literature. The first one, dated July 1, 1930, had definite reference to the financial depression which had descended upon the country: —

We need more faith in ourselves. Largely because of some decline in trade we have set about finding fault with everybody and everything. We are told the President is wrong, the Congress is wrong, the Supreme Court is wrong, and the Cabinet departments, the Federal Reserve Board, the chain stores, the power companies, the radio, and even the religious bodies are all wrong.

Yet our government, our physical properties and our industries have changed very little from a year or two ago when people were fairly content. We have the same country in charge of almost entirely the same people, with substantially the same laws and administration. The most casual consideration shows us that this whole structure could not turn sour over night. But our estimate of it has changed.

Our country, our people, our civil and religious institutions may not be perfect, but they are what we have made them. They are good enough so that it has been necessary to build a high exclusion law to prevent all the world from rushing to possess them.

My countrymen, it is time to stop criticizing and quarreling and begin sympathizing and helping.

This initial article is in most respects typical of those which followed. Coolidge reiterated the familiar doctrines which he had expressed in speech after speech while he was still in active public life. During the early months of 1930, for example, he discussed Thrift, the American Red Cross, Old Age Pensions, Banking, the Boy Scouts, the Radio, the Town Meetings, Reforestation, Child Welfare, the Veto Power, and the Art of Politics. Occasionally he ventured into other fields, on such subjects as the death of Brother Dutton (the missionary to the lepers), on Easter, on the Blind, on Gardening, and on Vacations. He even contributed essays on the value of Greek and Latin, and on the Purpose of a College Education. Here and there an incidental comment helps to throw light on his conservative philosophy: "Sound finance calls for payment of debt and making the revenues of each year meet the expenditures"; "One of the most astounding spectacles is the complacency with which people permit themselves to be plundered by extravagant governmental expenditures under the pretense of taxing the rich to help the poor"; "It will do no harm to have a reminder that when Congress passes laws requiring the expenditure of money the people will have to pay for it"; "The management of Muscle Shoals demonstrates the utter hopelessness of having any considerable enterprise conducted by the Congress."

Underlying these syndicated articles was a firm belief in the so-called capitalistic system, in the doctrine that the only help and hope for man lies within himself, in the theory that self-respect is better than a parasitic dependence on the state, and in hard work, sobriety, and independence. Calvin Coolidge really liked such phrases as the Dignity of Labor, the Fruits of Toil, and Honest Sweat. On the verge of the mighty popular movement which was to manifest itself in the measures of the New Deal and find expression in the speeches and messages of Franklin D. Roosevelt, Coolidge voiced the opinion that the socialized state was perilous in the long run to the individual citizen. For collectivism he had nothing but dislike and distrust. His was almost the last powerful utterance of the forgotten philosophy of *laissez faire*.

In Calvin Coolidge's nature were certain tendencies towards preaching and teaching which show themselves in these articles. In whatever he said the ethical element was likely to be stressed. Those who have called him hypocritical have utterly mistaken the man and his motives. He was practical, but his practicality was mitigated by mysticism and sentiment, and he was not afraid of idealism. He was a clever politician, — shrewd, calculating, and ambitious, — but he never would have chosen the kingdoms of this world if the Devil had presented them to him. Something of the grim Calvinism of his ancestors kept his eyes on heaven as well as on earth. One of the few passages of poetry which he ever quoted was taken from some verses by Edwin Markham: —

> We are all blind until we see
> That in the human plan
> Nothing is worth the making if
> It does not make the man.
>
> Why build these cities glorious
> If man unbuilded grows?
> In vain we build the world unless
> The builder also grows.

Coolidge started on his project with enthusiasm, but before many weeks he had reached a point where the monotony of daily composition left him tired. Furthermore he felt hampered by the restriction which expediency placed upon his frankness, and regarded himself as virtually gagged by his position. During the last few weeks before the contract ran out he counted the hours until the burden was lifted, and he was like a boy released from school when the last essay was on the wires. He had finished what turned out to be a rather disagreeable "chore." [9]

Under the persuasion of his friend Thomas Cochran, Mr. Coolidge accepted an appointment as trustee of the estate of Conrad Hubert, whose property had been left for distribution to various philanthropic causes. He was chairman of the Board, with Julius Rosenwald and Alfred E. Smith as his associates, and the three men usually met in the Bankers' Trust Company at times when Coolidge was obliged to be in New York for the regular meetings of the New York Life Insurance Company Board. Mr. Coolidge was able to get his colleagues to assign a considerable amount to Mrs. Coolidge's favorite charity, the Clarke School for the Deaf.

Coolidge found a far keener satisfaction in his connection with the New York Life Insurance Company, of which he was elected a director in the spring of 1929; and he attended regularly the meetings of the Board held in New York on the twelfth of each month. Mr. Ross, his secretary, who invariably accompanied him, recalls engaging for Mr. Coolidge and himself a drawing-room on the train leaving Northampton for New York about 3.30 in the afternoon. The ex-President would lie down on the divan, while Mr. Ross sat with his feet across the door so that no intrusive visitor could blunder in. At New Haven, where the dining car was attached to the train, the two would go out on the platform and proceed promptly to a table so that they could eat by themselves. In New York, they spent the night at the Vanderbilt Hotel, occupying Suite 801–2–3, where Mr. Ross could be on guard. The price of this suite, by special arrangement, was ten dollars, and when Mr. Coolidge received his envelope containing fifty dollars, — the fee allowed each director, — he turned it over at once to Mr. Ross, who paid all the bills. As a traveler, Coolidge had his idiosyncrasies. He carried a large sponge, his own shaving mug, brush, and old-fashioned razor. Once, when by mistake he had left his razor behind, he had the hotel barber come to his room and lather him, and then shaved himself with the barber's razor, saying to Mr. Ross, "I wouldn't let anybody

[9] "No one who has not endured the ink enthralldom can estimate the intellectual pressure which accompanies the necessity of daily composition — and especially if such composition is carried on within the narrow limit of words. Therefore I was not surprised to have been told only this winter by one of President Coolidge's most intimate friends that the preparation of his daily article became to him an obsessionate dread; and that the constant thought of it wore upon him more grievously than the most arduous of his labors in the Presidency." (George H. Moses, address delivered March 15, 1933, before the New Hampshire Legislature.)

shave me for a hundred dollars." His tips were ordinarily on the frugal side, but he did give the elevator boy ten cents each time they went up and down. Naturally he could not escape the advances of reporters, who attempted to extract statements from him on various topics, but his only answer, repeated over and over, patiently and monotonously, was "Nothing whatever to say."

The criticisms occasionally brought against Mr. Coolidge for sponsoring a commercial enterprise seem to me completely unjustified. He regarded insurance as of the utmost importance because of its encouragement of saving. When he publicly commended it, as was frequently the case, he did so because of his conviction that it was contributory to thrift. Obviously the nominal compensation which he received for his services as director was unimportant to him. He was lending his name to a company which, as he saw it, was helpful to mankind.

On October 6, 1931, he delivered a radio talk, prepared by one of his company's publicity men, in which he advised his listeners to beware of that type of insurance agent who is always trying to induce them to alter their policies. To his astonishment, a St. Louis insurance man, Lewis B. Tebbetts, sued him and the New York Life Insurance Company for $100,000 each, alleging that his reputation as an "honest insurance agent" had been injured by the remarks of the ex-President, which had been printed and distributed by the Company in pamphlet form. After papers had been served on Mr. Coolidge on February 8, 1932, he asked his former secretary, Everett Sanders, to go to St. Louis with the Company's counsel and confer with the plaintiff. As a consequence of the meetings, Mr. Tebbetts agreed to abandon the action, provided Coolidge would reimburse him for his legal expenses. Accordingly the ex-president, averse to publicity but with no sense of guilt, sent Mr. Tebbetts a letter enclosing a check for $2500 and explaining that he meant no offense to him or anybody else.

Coolidge was besieged during these years by well-meaning persons wishing to identify him with some movement or gain his support for a worthy cause. To most such requests he turned a courteous but unlistening ear, but he could not resist one or two which especially appealed to him. Since 1925 he had been a member of the famous old American Antiquarian Society, which had its headquarters at Worcester, Massachusetts; and in 1930, after the death of Dr. Charles L. Nichols, its president, the opinion was expressed by Chief Justice Arthur P. Rugg, of the Massachusetts Supreme Court, that Coolidge might accept this somewhat unusual office. He was duly approached and, after considering the matter a fortnight, agreed to the proposal. At the meeting in Boston, in April 1930, he delivered a graceful speech of acceptance, in which he said, with a personal touch, that he could now still be addressed as Mr. President without anyone's feeling that it was a misnomer. During his three years as president Mr. Coolidge did not miss a single meeting of the Council, and he seemed to enjoy chatting with the members, many of whom were distinguished in their own fields. Usually he arrived at the home of Clarence S. Brigham, in Worcester, in time for luncheon and thus had half an hour afterwards to smoke and talk before the Council assembled. At the time of the annual meetings in 1930 and 1931 he stayed at Mr. Brigham's house and sat up until midnight talking in a reminiscent mood; and in both years he himself wrote and read the Council's report. In the Society's large collection of rare books and documents, Mr. Coolidge displayed much interest, and presented to it some important items.[10]

Another source of recreation for the ex-President was the North-ampton Literary Club, better known in the city as the Wednesday Club — an organization which dates back to 1862 and has never ex-ceeded its original membership of twelve. The practice is for the club to meet twice a month at the home of one of their number for a formal dinner and an evening of discussion conducted by the host. Even before he left the White House some of his friends had pro-posed him for membership, and the minutes of the meeting on April 3, 1929, show that a committee had been appointed to inter-view him on the subject. His first appearance as a member was at the meeting held on May 6, 1929, at the home of Clifford A. Rich-mond. The minutes contain the following paragraph: —

Two reasons made this meeting an outstanding event in the life of the club. First we welcomed to membership neighbor Calvin Coolidge and it would be less than human did we not enjoy a thrill in having in our club one who has with marked sincerity served the people in the highest office in the world. Secondly this is the first time, so far as the records show, that a meeting was ever held in Easthampton.

In the business of the club, Coolidge took an active part. After dinner, the records were read, and there was often a considerable amount of banter, in which the ex-President had a share. Every other meeting was devoted to "Topics," one from each member, and Coolidge invariably had something out of his personal experience to

[10] *Calvin Coolidge, President of the American Antiquarian Society*, by Clar-ence S. Brigham (1934). Reprinted from the Proceedings of the American Anti-quarian Society for April 1933.

contribute. On April 23, 1930, again at Richmond's home, Coolidge talked at some length on his recent trip through the South and West, describing Tarpon Springs and its sponges, New Orleans, a day at the motion-picture studios in Hollywood, and a visit to Hearst's ranch. The minutes say, in comment: —

He smiled at the popular characterization that he is a silent man and a great fisherman and said that he had made more speeches than any other President and had done less fishing.

On January 28, 1931, at the home of Ernst H. Mensel of Smith College, he spoke on "Royalties and Representatives of Foreign Nations," giving his recollections, often very humorous, of Queen Marie of Rumania, the Prince of Wales, the Crown Prince and Crown Princess of Sweden, and the Crown Prince of Japan. On February 17, 1931, he talked briefly of Cartotto, the Italian artist to whom he was sitting for his portrait; on March 18, he spoke on the competition which the railroads were having from bus lines; and on April 23 he described the Folger Library, in Washington. On November 10, 1932, following the Presidential election, the Club met at The Beeches, and the minutes of the meeting are recorded in his own clear handwriting. On that evening there was a general discussion of the election results, led by the host, and the guests did not leave until the relatively late hour of 10.30. His last meeting was on November 30, at the home of Lawyer Walter L. Stevens, where he discussed "Buying Domestic Manufactures." He was not present at the meeting on December 14, and before the January meeting he was dead. Among the other members of the Wednesday Club at that period were John A. Houston, Superintendent of the State Hospital; Edward A. Shaw, President of the First National Bank, who had studied law with Coolidge; Gerald Stanley Lee, the writer; George B. McCallum and Oliver H. Bradley, both of the McCallum Hosiery Company; Dr. Elmer H. Copeland; and Archibald Galbraith, Headmaster of Williston Seminary.

Mr. Richmond has contributed some interesting recollections of the Wednesday Club's most famous member. Nobody at the meetings, even his old friend Shaw, ever called him "Cal," but always "Mr. President" or "Mr. Coolidge." He had a rather uncomfortable way of scrutinizing anything that was offered to him as if it required minute inspection. When he was offered a cigar, for example, he usually examined it rather critically and then drew from his upper vest pocket a Corona. At the last meeting in his home he brought out a box of super-Coronas, nearly twelve inches long, and smoked three of them himself. Whenever he had occasion to speak about his experiences as President, he introduced his remarks with the clause, "When I was in Washington," which became a humorous byword among the members. Mr. Richmond, when writing, stood at a draftsman's table, where he could have his body free. Mr. Coolidge looked at it, shook it, leaned against it. "You write here?" he asked. "I do," replied Mr. Richmond, thinking that he had contributed an idea to an ex-President. Turning on his heel, Mr. Coolidge simply said, "I dictate." It was difficult to open up an avenue of conversation with him by the method of direct questioning, but he could easily be drawn into a discussion by those who knew how it should be done.

After his withdrawal from political life, Coolidge did very little speechmaking, even when it was scheduled to be of a nonpartisan nature. On April 6, 1929, he wrote to William H. Taft, "I am trying to avoid making speeches or attending public gatherings and have so replied to very numerous requests that have come to me." In the autumn of 1929, he wrote President John G. Hibben, of Princeton, in reply to an invitation to speak at that college, as follows: —

It was a great pleasure to hear from you again and I realize the compliment you have paid me in asking me to address your coming conference. I have tried, however, to avoid making speeches in part because I do not like to speak and in part because I doubted if it did much good. Then, I have the feeling that it is more appropriate for those who are charged with the responsibility of authority to take part in the discussion of public questions than it is for one who has retired.

I suppose we all believe in the theory of an independent executive, legislature, and judiciary but there is a difference between being independent and being obstructive. When I presided over the Senate, I came to have a wholesome respect for it, but when one is on the outside of it the impression gained from reports of the press tends to minimize its good qualities and emphasize its bad qualities. Since I have been away from Washington, it has been a relief not to be obliged to follow the action of the government, so that I do not know much about the details of what has been taking place. I think you could get some member of the Senate to speak with much more authority than I could.

During 1930, the year of the Massachusetts Tercentenary Celebration, he was invited to speak in more than two hundred towns and cities in the Commonwealth, but refused all but one. He did appear at the exercises in Boston and later attended luncheon at the Women's Republican Club, on Beacon Street, where he sat next to Miss Katharine Parker, the President, and seemed unusually loquacious.

In the autumn of 1930, he went with Mrs. Coolidge to the national convention of the American Legion, in Boston, spending the night of his twenty-fifth wedding anniversary at the Wayside Inn, in Sudbury. The principal speaker at the great gathering of Legionnaires in Mechanics' Building was President Herbert Hoover. After his speech, however, the crowd began calling for Coolidge, who rose three or four times to bow an acknowledgment. Finally, after an ovation of ten or twelve minutes, he stepped to the amplifier and said simply, "Gentlemen, I charge you to be true to the laws and Constitution of the United States"; and these words made more of an impression on the audience and were received with more genuine enthusiasm than the carefully prepared address by the President.[11]

Mr. Coolidge returned to Washington only once as ex-President and then to attend a luncheon for sixty-six persons on July 24, 1929, given by President Hoover in honor of the signing of the Kellogg Pact. Standing beside President Hoover in the East Room of the White House were Secretary Stimson and former Secretary Kellogg, who had helped write the Pact, and the diplomats of forty-three nations were present. The President, forgetting that the microphones had been temporarily removed to get photographs, began his speech too soon, with the result that what was intended as a solemn ceremony turned into confusion. In the afternoon Coolidge called punctiliously upon Mrs. Hoover, and then took the night train back to New England. In accordance with his sense of public duty he went in June 1931 to Marion, Ohio, to attend the long-delayed dedication of the memorial to President Harding. His own remarks, on June 16, were brief and not effusive. President Hoover, however, described Harding as "a man of delicate sense of honor, of sympathetic heart, of transcendent greatness of soul." Coolidge also was chairman of a non-partisan National Transportation Commission appointed by President Hoover to study the railroad problem. Two other members were Alfred E. Smith and Bernard M. Baruch. Several meetings were held in New York City, but the report of the Commission was not presented until after his death. Coolidge accepted the place at the insistence of Republican friends who felt that he should lend the weight of his still great prestige to the somewhat battered Hoover administration.

[11] During Coolidge's visit to Boston he was in charge of Leverett Saltonstall, then Speaker of the House of Representatives. Mr. Coolidge expressed a wish to call on President Hoover, and Saltonstall said suddenly, "I don't believe I have a pass." "Guess maybe I can get you in," replied the ex-President drily. It was certainly the emphasis of understatement.

THE COOLIDGES AND THE HOOVERS

One interest of an absorbing nature was Amherst College, of which he was still a life Trustee. It was, of course, hinted by many alumni that he might accept the presidency of his college, but he would make no comment on such suggestions. He attended with regularity the meetings of the Board of Trustees and followed even minor details with care. One member recalls that, when a proposal for a new building or the establishment of a new professorship was brought up for discussion, Coolidge usually asked, "Where you going to get the money?" He motored over each June for the Commencement exercises, but refused to speak, preferring to be regarded as an ordinary graduate back with his fraternity brothers and friends. The death of his classmate, Dwight W. Morrow, on October 5, 1931, was a shock to him, and he went to Englewood, New Jersey, to attend the funeral. When President Arthur Stanley Pease resigned early in 1932 in order to resume his teaching as Professor of Latin in Harvard College, Coolidge took an active part in choosing his successor, Stanley King. At King's inaugural on November 11, 1932, Coolidge sat in the front row on the platform with the other Trustees, looking very worn and tired. With President King, with Charles A. Andrews, Treasurer of the College, and with Frederick S. Allis, Chairman of the Alumni Fund, Coolidge had very pleasant relations, and they were frequently guests at The Beeches. Another Amherst friend who lived near by was Judge Henry P. Field, in whose office he had begun the study of law. Judge Field, a bachelor, was always glad to have an invitation to Sunday-night supper with the Coolidges in the good old New England fashion.

Events since he left the White House had not made Calvin Coolidge very cheerful. The terrific drop in the stock market, the onrush of the Great Depression, the criticism of the Hoover administration, the feeling that perhaps he himself had been partly responsible — all these had discouraged him and created a mood of pessimism.[12] A newspaperman described him in the summer of 1930, waiting at the door of the Masonic Building for his chauffeur. He wore a gray suit, well pressed, without a waistcoat, a blue necktie, and a straw hat with stiff brim, and carried a brief case under his arm. As he looked down the street, several persons passed; he did not speak or even nod, but stood there solitary, his thin lips pinched closely together, an expression of seriousness on his face. Perhaps

[12] On April 29, 1932, Frederick C. Nichols called on him in his office and found him "quite embittered and obviously in poor health." He said to Nichols, "I have been ignored and forgotten," and compared his office furniture in Northampton with his former surroundings in the White House.

he was lonely, and certainly he had his unhappy hours. Never physically very strong, he had always conserved his resources and had seldom allowed himself to get overtired; but for years he had suffered from what he called "pollen fever," — probably a form of asthma, — which was at times quite exhausting. Furthermore, although his Northampton physician, Dr. Brown, could discover nothing the matter with his heart, Coolidge had had warnings and premonitions, and Mrs. Coolidge noticed that he often surreptitiously took his pulse. His own health as well as the state of the nation weighed heavily on his mind. But he still, like his Vermont ancestors, trusted in home remedies and patent medicines, and did not tell his doctor all his troubles.

Something of his mood is revealed in an interview given to Raymond Clapper early in 1932: "I feel fine, but I suppose I am all burned out now. . . . If I travel, courtesy requires that I make speeches, sometimes, and there is always the danger of saying something that will cause embarrassment. I couldn't go to Europe without accepting honors and seeing people. I know that when I was in Washington I wouldn't have wanted an ex-President poking around Europe. I had enough trouble with amateur diplomats. I don't want people to think I am trying to run the country." The truth is that he was both ill and tired, and knew that there was something the matter with him.

It had been urged during the spring that he be drafted for the Presidential nomination, and he had some difficulty in curbing the good intentions of overenthusiastic friends. When William F. Whiting wrote him on this subject, Coolidge replied, April 30, 1932: —

When you get to Chicago I am depending on you to see that nothing of this kind happens to me. It won't do.

Later, when Whiting sent him a newspaper editorial commending the idea, Coolidge replied on May 21: —

Your note and clipping received. The suggestion would not work.
I hope you will not take any action anywhere that involves me. Perhaps you will talk with Mr. Charles D. Hilles of New York. It would be easy to make much trouble for a distracted country. I have done all that I can do. Others must now carry on the government. Just drop me.[13]

[13] Later in the summer, when the Coolidges were lunching with the Otis Skinners at Woodstock, Vermont, Mrs. Skinner said to him, "Oh, Mr. Coolidge, I wish it were you that we were to vote for in November. It would be the end of this horrible depression." The blue Coolidge eye twinkled as he replied, "It would be the beginning of mine."

On June 17, 1932, following the Chicago Convention which renominated Hoover for President, Coolidge wrote from North-ampton to Everett Sanders, congratulating him on his election as Chairman of the Republican National Committee. In the course of the letter, he said : —

You know I should be glad to do anything I can to help. My throat, you will remember, always bothers me, and it is in such shape that I do not think I could do much of anything in the way of speaking. Just at present I am having some trouble with my breathing again. I am going to Vermont tomorrow for an indefinite stay, where I can be out of doors, and think I shall be all right when I get a little exercise.

It was obvious from the opening of the campaign that Hoover would have a hard time running against the magnetic and liberal Franklin D. Roosevelt. The people, rightly or wrongly, blamed the prevailing depression on the Republican administration, and Hoover was under a heavy handicap. Naturally enough, the party managers wished to have the open support of Calvin Coolidge, and great pressure was brought to bear on him by Henry L. Stoddard, Thomas Cochran, and others. When Everett Sanders went to see Coolidge in late July, he was much disturbed by the ex-President's appearance, for he was thinner than usual and looked very pale. A photograph taken at this time offers sufficient evidence of his poor physical condition.[14] He was, however, able to prepare an article for the *Saturday Evening Post* in which he declared of Hoover, "We know that he is safe and sound," and explained that the depression would have occurred no matter which party was in power. The *Philadelphia Record* ridiculed Coolidge's "parroty reiteration of an outworn political credo," but the article was widely read and quoted.

On September 21, in response to another appeal from Mr. Sanders, at a time when the Republican campaign was going badly, Coolidge wrote from Plymouth : —

Everybody that has a cause wants me to make a speech. I have said all I know in the article which I have already prepared. If I should start to make speeches the public would expect them to be of the same character and substance as when I was in Washington. I am off here in the country where I do not have any sources of information and have purposely kept out of politics. I cannot for the life of me think of anything important to say that I did not put into the article I have already written, nor is there any one to take care of my throat, which

[14] The writer saw him on August 6, 1932, at Plymouth, and found him genial and cheerful, but plainly worn and tired. He seemed then noticeably lacking in physical vitality.

I do not think would last ten minutes. The last time I tried to make a speech was at Marion, Ohio. I am telling you these things to indicate that while I want to help I do not know how I can do much in the speech-making line. Do you know of anything to talk about that I did not discuss in the article I prepared?

Mr. Henry L. Stoddard wants me to make a speech in New York. I suppose no one knows how I hate making speeches.

What we need to win this election is organization. Talking is all right, but the side that organizes and gets the vote to the polls is the side that wins. Every campaign is hard, but I think we can win.

Sanders had wished Coolidge to speak in Indiana or Illinois, but Coolidge did not care to go that far from New England. The question of a radio address from Plymouth was also considered. The Republicans were increasingly worried, and Sanders wrote Coolidge, September 23, "I . . . believe that if our election is won, it has to be from now on; it would be against us to-day." At last Coolidge yielded to cumulative importunity and told Mr. Stoddard, who came again to Plymouth in late September, that he would talk in Madison Square Garden on October 11. Coolidge made his headquarters at the Waldorf, and Stoddard, meeting him there, escorted him to the Garden. He was soberly dressed in a cutaway coat and pin-striped trousers, and unusually serious in his manner. When the 19,000 people in the audience insisted on cheering him, he took out his gold watch and held it up to remind them that he was on a radio schedule. He was not well on that day or evening and felt at one time that he would not be able to finish the address; and Mrs. Coolidge, listening over the radio in the back room of the Cilley store, at Plymouth Notch, also had her apprehensions. The speech was praised by Republicans and belittled by Democrats. The *New York Times* spoke particularly of "the plaintive and half-apologetic note which was struck again and again," but it did for the moment inject new vitality into a hopeless cause.[15]

Although Coolidge had partly agreed to speak in Chicago, he was obliged to abandon the project. Herbert Hoover writes me under date of August 22, 1938: —

I do know that in the campaign of 1932 Mr. Coolidge generously undertook to make two addresses — one in New York and one in Chicago. After the New York address he sent word to me that he

[15] After this address a woman rushed up to Mr. Coolidge and burst out, "Oh, Mr. Coolidge, what a wonderful address! I stood up all through it." The weary ex-President merely replied, "So did I." For a full discussion of the events leading up to this speech, see Henry L. Stoddard's *It Costs to Be President*, pp. 136ff.

had found the excitement and effort of that occasion was more strain
than he should rightly put on his heart. I of course at once asked that
he should not undertake the Chicago speech. It was my first intimation
that his heart was affected.

The ex-President did, however, talk for fifteen minutes over
a nation-wide hookup on the night before election, but his last-
minute effort did not affect the result. On November 25, following
the Republican catastrophe, Coolidge wrote Sanders from Northampton: —

Since we did not win, the natural reaction will be to begin to blame
each other for the defeat. That is no doubt going on, but I have seen
or heard no suggestion of a criticism of your conduct of the campaign.
I feel sure that you will find nothing but gratitude and praise for the
work you did and the sacrifices you made.

You will recall our victory with the aid of the dissatisfied in 1920,
and how near it came to wrecking our party. You will see the same
difficulty much enlarged after March 4 for our successors.

I want you to know how grateful I am for your public service.[16]

Following his return to Northampton that autumn, Mr. Coolidge was more depressed than usual, and the result of the election
left him despondent. On December 14, he went to the monthly
meeting of the New York Life Insurance Company, — the last trip
he was to take, — and there, from the Vanderbilt Hotel, called up
his old friend, Henry L. Stoddard, who had been ill with the influenza in Stamford, Connecticut. Weak though he was, Mr. Stoddard
got up out of bed and took the train for New York, arriving in
Coolidge's rooms after luncheon. There the two "old-timers," in
the presence of Harry Ross, had a conversation which Stoddard
took some pains to recall in detail. In substance Coolidge said: —

I have been out of touch so long with political activities that I feel
I no longer fit with these times. Great changes can come in four years.
These socialistic notions of government are not of my day. When I
was in office, tax reduction, tariff stability, and economy were the
things to which I gave attention. We succeeded on those lines. It has
always seemed to me that common sense is the real solvent for the
nation's problems at all times — common sense and hard work. When
I read of the newfangled things that are now so popular I realize that
my time in public affairs is past. I wouldn't know how to handle them
if I were called upon to do so.

[16] The letters between Mr. Sanders and Mr. Coolidge are reprinted, by permission, from an article in the *Saturday Evening Post* for March 25, 1933 — "Last
Letters of Calvin Coolidge," by Everett Sanders.

That is why I am through with public life forever. I shall never again hold public office. I shall always do my part to help elect Republican candidates, for I am a party man, but in no other way shall I have anything to do with political matters. . . .

We are in a new era to which I do not belong, and it would not be possible for me to adjust myself to it.

These new ideas call for new men to develop them. That task is not for men who believe in the only kind of government I know anything about. We cannot put everything up to the government without overburdening it. . . .

I am through with public life. You cannot state it too positively. Nothing would induce me to take office again.[17]

On December 21, he wrote to his former secretary, "Ted" Clark, a very significant letter indicating his wearied state of mind and body: —

Of course a new man is new. Ordinarily he can wait a little. The difficulty is that everything is in an emergency requiring immediate action. I would be glad to tell anybody anything I know, and I think it is a time when partisanship ought to be laid aside.

I should not want to serve on any bodies or commissions. The fact is I feel worn out. No one can tell these days what a short time or three or four years may bring forth, but, of course, I know my work is done.

I could not pick it up again. I imagine that was one trouble Cleveland had in trying to administer a second term. Any time you hear anybody talking of me, just tell them to stop it.

On Sunday, January 1, Charles A. Andrews had supper with the Coolidges at The Beeches and found his classmate in a gloomy mood. The world, said Coolidge, was in a perilous state. Nothing was permanent or enduring except religion, which fortunately outlasted elections and depressions. Mr. Andrews left the house with the feeling that the Democratic landslide had been a sad blow to the ex-President.

On Monday, January 2, Mr. William F. Whiting gave a luncheon in Holyoke for the Coolidges and Mr. and Mrs. Morgan B. Brainard, of Hartford, Connecticut. Mr. Brainard made shortly afterward a detailed memorandum of what took place. Mrs. Coolidge told Mr. Brainard that her husband had something on his mind

---

[17] This interesting interview, originally printed in the *New York Sun,* January 6, 1933, was later republished in a small pamphlet, under the title, "I do not fit with these times." See also Stoddard, 143ff. Stoddard felt in the retrospect that Coolidge had been making "a kind of political will," and that he had been called in as a lawyer to draft it.

which was bothering him terribly and that she was trying to learn what it was. She had been afraid that he had read a scurrilous volume called *The Rise of Saint Calvin*,[18] which had recently appeared, and laughingly said, "You know there is an element of truth in that book." After luncheon, Coolidge smoked a cigar, sitting beside Mr. Brainard on the sofa, and talked with him regarding his Connecticut friends, including Senators Roraback and Bingham. The ex-President told Brainard that the Railroad Commission had not yet started to formulate their report but that a great deal of work had been done in the gathering of material and they would shortly be in a position to make a recommendation. More than once, and with emphasis, he spoke of his concern over contemporary business conditions. Nevertheless Mr. Brainard was amazed that a man could have gone through what Mr. Coolidge had endured and show the effects of it so little. Mr. Brainard added, "He seemed in perfect health, both physically and mentally, except for the indefinable worry which Mrs. Coolidge has described and which was occasionally apparent in his conversation."

Probably Coolidge's last caller was Charles B. Hayes, Field Director of the American Foundation for the Blind, who was with him for an hour on Wednesday morning and found him in an exceptionally jolly mood. His last words as the conversation closed were, "I'm coming to New York later this month and will see you then."

On Wednesday morning, January 4, after his talk with Mr. Hayes, Coolidge drove home early from the office and walked slowly around the grounds with Mr. Ross. As they came back to the verandah, he said, "Mr. Ross, I guess I'm getting to be an old man. I have an idea that we might stop going down to the office each day and do our work up here. Then we can go out and walk in the open air whenever we choose." On Thursday morning, however, he seemed to be in good spirits, although he had been doctoring himself with cooking soda for what he called another attack of indigestion. No one was much troubled about that, for he often swallowed a teaspoonful of Eno's Fruit Salts during a meal. After his customary breakfast, he rode down about eight-thirty to his office, read the newspaper, and dictated a few letters. At ten o'clock, much earlier than usual, he said, "Mr. Ross, I guess we'll go up to

[18] *The Rise of Saint Calvin*, by Duff Gilfond, Vanguard Press, 1932. The subtitle is "Merry Sidelights on the Career of Mr. Coolidge." The book is in the "smart aleck" manner, in the debunking mood, and belongs for the most part under the category of malevolent fiction.

the house." As they entered the gate at The Beeches, Mrs. Coolidge was just starting out on a shopping trip, and her husband asked, "Don't you want the car?" "No," she replied, "it's such a fine day I think I'll walk." Mr. Coolidge sat talking with Ross for a few moments, strolled to the kitchen for a glass of water, and even stepped down cellar to see the furnace man shovel coal. About noon he went upstairs to his bedroom, presumably to shave, and there, a few minutes later, Mrs. Coolidge found him lying on his back on the floor in his shirt sleeves. Death had come instantly and painlessly from a coronary thrombosis. He was in his sixty-first year.

Plain man that he was, he died as simply as he had lived; but the sad news flashed from the house at Northampton around a saddened world. At Plymouth Notch, Allen Brown tapped on the window of the Coolidge homestead and, when Miss Pierce lifted the sash, cried, "Calvin's dead, Aurora." She went back to a chair and buried her face in her hands. At the White House, the President was at luncheon with the Secretary of State, Mr. Stimson. "Ike" Hoover — who was later so unnecessarily to malign his chief — leaned over and whispered, "Mr. Coolidge has just died of heart failure"; and Herbert Hoover went at once to send a special message to Congress and issue the order for thirty days of public mourning. The Senate and the House adjourned almost immediately. Soon the flags were at half-mast across the continent. When the blow came to Frank W. Stearns as he sat at his desk in his store, the old man could not speak for many minutes. He went to Northampton that very evening, and the next morning people saw him sitting all by himself in the hotel, silent, phlegmatic, meditating, and waiting for the funeral of his friend.[19]

Saturday, the day of the funeral, was gray and overcast with a chilly drizzle in the late morning. At the services held in the red brick Edwards Congregational Church which the Coolidges had attended for many years, it was so dark inside that the lights had to be turned on. The honorary pallbearers were old friends: Frank W. Stearns; William F. Whiting; William M. Butler; Charles A. Andrews; former Governor Trumbull, of Connecticut, John Coolidge's father-in-law; Judge Hammond; R. B. Hills; Clifford Lyman; and Walter L. Stevens. Such a group of mourners had gathered as Northampton had never seen before. The President and Mrs. Hoover had come from the capital by special train with

---

[19] The best newspaper accounts of the funeral and burial were written by W. A. Macdonald for the *Boston Evening Transcript,* on which I have relied for many of the details.

Chief Justice Hughes, Associate Justice Stone, and three members of the cabinet — Stimson, Adams, and Chapin. Mrs. Franklin D. Roosevelt, wife of the President-elect, was there with her son James. Vice President Curtis came, with twenty-five Senators and a similar number of Representatives. There also were Everett Sanders and Rudolph Forster and Bernard M. Baruch and Mrs. Morrow.

As the body lay in state in the church from eight-thirty to nine-thirty, thousands passed by the coffin. Richard H. Waldo, who stood there for a moment, said later, "I have never seen such weariness in a face." The services were simple, without any eulogy. The Chopin Funeral March was played and also "Going Home," from the *New World Symphony*. Two hymns were sung, selections from the Bible were read by the Reverend Albert Penner, the young pastor, and the service closed with a benediction. It was all over in a little more than twenty minutes. President and Mrs. Hoover and Mr. Hughes called at The Beeches and then went back to Washington.

In a light, cheerless rain the coffin was taken to the hearse to be carried one hundred miles north to Plymouth Notch, where Sexton Azro Johnson had already dug a new grave in the cemetery where all the Coolidges — including Calvin, Jr., and Colonel John — had been buried. Twenty cars in procession made the trip through sleet and mist, while at every crossroads little knots of people were gathered to pay the dead man reverence. Six Vermont deputy United States marshals bore the heavy bronze casket up the steep embankment, and the mourners followed in single file. Meanwhile the cold rain had changed to hail, and someone held an umbrella over Mrs. Coolidge. Everything was quiet except for an icy wind sweeping down from the surrounding hills. Mr. Penner, his head bare, said a few words at the grave, and then all that was mortal of Calvin Coolidge was lowered into the earth, to rest between his father and his son. That night a snowstorm came, and on the next morning all traces of what had happened were hidden by a blanket of white.[20]

Memorial services took place from time to time during the ensuing winter. On January 15, in the Washington Cathedral, more

[20] Probably the finest account of Calvin Coolidge's death and burial is to be found in Clarence Day's *In the Green Mountain Country,* printed first in the *New York American* and afterwards published in a small pamphlet by the Yale University Press (1934). It is a masterpiece of accurate description and genuine feeling. Another excellent account was printed in *Time* for January 16, 1933. See also "The Death of a President," by Achilles Holt, in *The Magazine,* Vol. I, No. 1, December 1933.

than two thousand people gathered to hear an address by the Right Reverend James E. Freeman, Bishop of Washington. Two days later the Legislature of Vermont, at a joint assembly, paid honor to the state's most famous son. On February 7, Chief Justice Arthur P. Rugg, of the Massachusetts Supreme Court, spoke before a large assembly in the national capital. On March 1, the General Court of Massachusetts gathered in joint convention to listen to former Governor Channing H. Cox, who delivered a masterly eulogy, a friendly interpretation of Coolidge's character spoken with most impressive eloquence. The Honorable George H. Moses was the orator on March 15 at a joint convention of the New Hampshire Legislature. Northampton did her share on April 30, when Justice Harlan F. Stone, in John M. Greene Hall, admirably summed up the achievements of the dead statesman.

The instinct of the American people has been sound. Plymouth Notch is a place of pilgrimage, and all through the long summer days visitors park their automobiles and walk up to the piazza and into the sitting room, where they listen eagerly to a description of what happened on the early morning of August 3, 1923. As many as two thousand persons have been known to come in a single afternoon. Many of them wander over to the cemetery a short distance away and gaze silently on the simple tombstone which marks the grave of Calvin Coolidge. He needs no other memorial — no massive monument or temple. It is all just as he would have desired.

XIX

An Attempt at Appraisal

ABOUT few Americans who have attained political distinction have there been more honest divergences of opinion than regarding Calvin Coolidge. Gamaliel Bradford, who never saw him, wrote in his *Journal*, July 7, 1929: —

In the hammock, probing the dry and unprofitable soul of Coolidge. Suppose I shall later be able to get at something of the man; hope so at any rate. I certainly shall not do it from these dreary speeches, as a whole mere masses of desolate emptiness unrelieved, a waste of commonplace and convention such as I could hardly believe in, if I did not read it.[1]

This was while Coolidge was still alive, indeed barely out of the Presidency; and even before this date, Walter Lippmann, representing an openly skeptical attitude, had said: —

Mr. Coolidge's genius for inactivity is developed to a very high point. It is far from being an indolent inactivity. It is a grim, determined, alert inactivity which keeps Mr. Coolidge occupied constantly. . . . Inactivity is a political philosophy and a party program with Mr. Coolidge.[2]

Criticism of him, both ironical and denunciatory, was common enough while he was President; and since his death all the Bright Young Men have had their turn in disparaging Coolidge. The Revolt against Respectability, so widespread in some quarters during the Great Depression, did his reputation temporary damage. In an age when assertive literary groups made Decency synonymous with Dullness, Calvin Coolidge was a proper target for ridicule. He had never been unfaithful to his wife or come home blind drunk or betrayed a friend. Furthermore it was impossible for potential hero

[1] *The Journal of Gamaliel Bradford*, p. 486.
[2] Lippmann, *Men of Destiny*, pp. 12–13.

worshipers to make Coolidge dramatic, like Disraeli, or magnetic, like James G. Blaine, or soul-stirring, like Woodrow Wilson at his best. He was no Great Lover or Great Actor or Great Sinner. His heroisms and renunciations were unspectacular, not advertised for the benefit of the public. He had no trace of Bohemianism, but was a man of slow pulse, guarded emotions, and restrained impulses. Whatever he did was calculated, direct, safe, and sure, and such a type is not understood in Hollywood or Greenwich Village. Then, too, in the inevitable swing of the political pendulum from Republican to Democratic, he was blamed for nearly all our current economic ills. To upholders of the New Deal he seems like a troglodyte, the symbol of an age which can never be revived. Thus the years following his death have not been favorable to a calm estimate of his good and bad qualities or of his right niche in history.

On the other hand, he has had and still has his staunch defenders, men better acquainted with him than Gamaliel Bradford was, who have testified to his admirable traits. To those who called him cold, Channing H. Cox, associated with him over a long period, replied : —

Few public men have had a more individual quality of speech, of manner, or of thought. His extreme reserve which appears in his written words and his silence upon formal occasions became a legend. Yet the people of the country had come to feel the warmth and sensitiveness that lay behind those tightly compressed lips and the deep-lined face.

Clarence S. Brigham, an unbiased witness who knew him well from 1926 to 1933, has written : —

I think Mr. Coolidge's outstanding trait was his kindness and sympathy. He never forgot a friend and had a surprising habit of remembering trivial happenings, if they concerned those whom he liked and trusted.

Countless simple, unpretentious people, hearing that I was at work on a biography of Calvin Coolidge have written me of their own volition to tell me stories of his generosity. Like Lincoln, Coolidge was underestimated in his time by university groups, — the High-Brow Element, — but something about him appealed to the average citizen. Furthermore the tradition of his political acumen and influence still persists among a large body of the electorate. "Oh, for a few years of Calvin Coolidge!" is a heartfelt cry heard to-day among the great and neglected middle class whose spokesman he was. Perhaps among the Vermont hills may be found farmers who are still voting for him, as Confederate veterans used to cast their ballots year after year for Jefferson Davis.

To different observers, Coolidge presented different aspects. To his father and his wife, to Frank W. Stearns and Dwight W. Morrow and Everett Sanders, he did not appear the same as he did to Samuel Gompers or La Follette. Stearns, as we have seen, regarded Coolidge as belonging with Washington and Lincoln, although he good-naturedly added, "Of course I'm not sane on the subject." Radical critics denounced Coolidge as stupid, cold, and reactionary. One cannot expect fair-mindedness from them. Somewhere between lies the essential truth, and it is difficult to find. Even a skilled psychologist like Gamaliel Bradford reached the point in his study of Coolidge when he feared that he "could not arrive at any satisfactory synthesis whatever."

Another difficulty is that, except in his *Autobiography* and in rare interviews and letters, he said little that was significant about himself. He did not choose to unlock his heart, nor was he a Cellini or a Rousseau to bare his soul for posterity. His letters, so far as I have been privileged to examine them, are lacking in the allusiveness and versatility which distinguish those of Henry Cabot Lodge, who could, while fighting the League of Nations in the Senate, carry on a correspondence with Mrs. Winslow on Greek tragedy. Coolidge never commits himself, seldom hazards an opinion, rarely indulges in gossip, and makes no attempt at literary finish; in fact, his secretiveness is almost unparalleled among American statesmen. Thus his biographer is hampered by a lack of confessional material; but fortunately there is what Bradford described as "a vast amount of personal anecdote, deplorably unreliable and diverse in its manifestations, but decidedly significant if you know how to use it." [3] Luckily, too, trustworthy reminiscences have helped to clarify the picture and restrain the tendency towards myth-making. Underneath what was superficial, behind Coolidge's baffling facial mask, was the real man, the man we wish to know.

In this case, then, the biographer has to steer his delicate way between those who regard Coolidge as a dull and negative personality pushed into power by Lady Luck and those who would place

[3] Bradford (August 31, 1929), 491. Many examples could be quoted to illustrate his epistolary brevity. On June 7, 1928, in reply to a letter a page and a half long, Coolidge wrote to Robert S. Weeks, of Boston, "Check enclosed. No receipt required. Assumption correct." To George E. Booth, of Worcester, Coolidge wrote, April 23, 1932, in response to a declaration that Booth was unaware of an important statement by Senator Butler, "I did not know it either. If you will not mistrust me, I will not mistrust you."

him among the truly great. I do not hope to pronounce the final verdict, but I shall try to discount what has been said by both encomiasts and vilifiers and, by weighing evidence, reach something of the truth.

One key to Coolidge's character lies in his shyness. His own statement, already quoted, "I'm all right with old friends, but every time I meet a stranger, I've got to go through the old kitchen door, back home, and that's not easy," is a most significant self-revelation. Judge Henry P. Field said again and again, "Calvin is shy. He dislikes the limelight." Large crowds were to Coolidge rather impersonal and unembarrassing, and he never objected to being photographed, but even a single human soul too close to his was disconcerting. For this reason he maintained a kind of formality with all those around him, and few ventured to cross this intangible barrier. His attitude was well known among his associates and invariably respected.

Oddly enough, however, he never liked to be alone, and walking by himself gave him what he once described as "a sort of naked feeling." When he had around him people whom he already knew, he did not feel obliged to be on his good behavior; this explains why he was so eager in the White House to have close at hand the trustworthy Frank W. Stearns and why he had an agreement with the New York Life Insurance Company that traveling expenses were to be paid not only for himself but also for his secretary. He never wanted to get off by himself. Even in his office he preferred to think with somebody familiar around.

The coldness in Coolidge often resented by visitors was partly an external mannerism, a form of defense created by his shyness. Mr. Stearns was at first amused by it, as is indicated in a letter to his sister, September 30, 1916: —

I should like to have Coolidge and you meet some time and see if you could make him speak. You could, if anybody could, but there is no record of anybody, man or woman or child, who has been able to make him say anything in conversation. We had a military ball in Newton previous to a dinner. Mr. Coolidge was put beside the brightest and most attractive lady in the bunch. After it was over, she was asked how she got along. "Well," she said, "I tried my very best. In the first place, I tried to be serious. Not a word from Mr. Coolidge. Then I tried to be frivolous, and you know I can be very frivolous when I try. Not a word from Mr. Coolidge. Finally, as the dinner was about over, I said to Mr. Coolidge, 'There is only one of those macaroons left, and they are good.' Not a word from Mr. Coolidge. I turned to speak to a gentleman on the other side, and when I looked back my macaroon was gone. I charged him with having taken it. He said, 'Oh, that is yours, is it? Well, you may have half of it.' And that was the total result of the evening."

Later Mr. Stearns's amusement turned to anxiety, and he was very sensitive to criticism of his candidate's reserve.[4] On May 3, 1918, he had a talk with him on the subject and later wrote him frankly: —

Just one word more about what I said this morning. I did not offer it in criticism, nor did those who spoke about it. They are all your strong friends, and all men who realize that your way of meeting folks is a strong asset. I don't believe one of them would think of changing it materially, but when you do meet people, and especially when they are invited to meet you, if you could give them a pleasant smile, even without speaking, it would make the trick complete, and you can do it because you sometimes do.

On still another occasion, when the intimation was made that Coolidge, as Governor, was not easily accessible, Stearns wrote: —

There is another suggestion that has been in my mind for some time, and that is the suggestion that every one in the country has a feeling that Lincoln was one of themselves, and that anybody could get at him without red tape. I wonder if Henry Long, in his great loyalty to you and his desire to save you, is not saving you a little too much. I sometimes think so.

As early as 1910, Dwight W. Morrow, in talking with Coolidge about the latter's political prospects, stressed the point that his reputation for reticence might become an asset at the polls, and this undoubtedly was the case, to Mr. Stearns's astonishment. The fact that he kept his own counsel and did not antagonize others by talk-

4 Benjamin D. Hyde, Amherst, '94, attempted to help Coolidge in the campaign of 1916, and arranged to have him meet two influential gentlemen, Eldredge, of Chatham, and Clark, of Harwich, in his office. After Coolidge went out, Eldredge turned to Hyde and said, "Ben, you say you don't know anything about politics. You have demonstrated it. When you ask us to take hold and help this man, we will do it if you insist, but if you ever dip in the game again, for heaven's sake pick out a live one." In the earlier campaigns, Stearns was constantly writing letters like one sent on October 15, 1915, to Mrs. Arthur H. Lowe, of Fitchburg, in which he said: "I hope I did not leave a wrong impression of Mr. Coolidge. I have come to know him intimately. He is very far indeed from being 'cold.' He is reserved, but he is full of enthusiasm. He said to me one Sunday when he was staying at my house in Newton, 'They tell me I have a poker face.' He said he supposed he knew what they meant. How he acquired it, he did not know, unless from the fact that as a child it was nothing less than torture for him to walk into a room where there was a stranger and that he still has very much the same feeling, but he early made up his mind that if that was the way he felt about it, then it was the thing for him to do whenever occasion offered, and he supposed the 'poker face' came as a result of these two feelings."

ing spitefully of them behind their backs did Coolidge no harm. Taciturn by temperament, he also profited by the example of Senator Crane, who was himself no babbler.[5] He had almost a genius for the concealment of his opinions and although he enjoyed listening to gossip, he seldom took part in it. Except in the absolute seclusion of an inner room he did not comment unfavorably even on Senator Lodge, whom he always regarded as hostile.

And yet, under favoring circumstances, he could talk with fluency and facility, as many of his friends have testified, but he never learned to regard talking as a form of pleasant exercise. On nonpolitical subjects, when he was in the right surroundings and in the proper mood, he sometimes became almost garrulous. Beaty, his secretary for some months in Northampton, came to recognize a certain moment when Coolidge would recline far back in his swivel chair, clip meticulously a new cigar, roll it between his fingers, insert it in one of his famous paper cigar holders, and then be ready to talk. But he had to be with people whom he knew and trusted before he felt free to speak. In his own family he was a "moody intermittent talker."

The stories told of his long and disconcerting silences furnish additional proof of his shyness. With strangers he simply did not know at first how to establish relationships.[6] It is also true, however, that, when his reticence had become legendary, Coolidge found it very useful. His successor in the Governor's chair, Channing H. Cox, noticed that he was spending far more time in the executive offices than Coolidge had done and remarked to the latter on the subject. "You talk back," Coolidge replied.[7] About the Coolidge silences there was something overwhelming, even unnerving. An

[5] A cartoon in the *Boston Post* in 1918 pictures a "silent debate" between "Cal" Coolidge and "Uncle Murray" Crane. It is here reproduced on page 198.

[6] Valentine Williams, the English detective-story writer, was admitted to a conference with the President and has thus recalled the meeting: "We both took chairs, and there ensued the most embarrassing silence I have ever experienced. For a full two minutes you could have heard a pin drop as the President, with a perfectly expressionless face, gazed straight in front of him. Once or twice I felt his glance flicker in my direction, but I did not meet it — I kept my eyes resolutely fixed upon the carpet. At last, heralding his intention with a little grating cough, Coolidge broke the unbearable silence. His voice had a nasal New England ring, but was deliberate and quite unembarrassed. 'That's quite an interesting situation you have over there in England,' he remarked casually." From then on, all went well, and Williams added, "Whether his taciturnity was instinctive or deliberate, there was poise and authority behind it — you realized it as soon as he began to speak."

[7] Stearns asked Coolidge whether in his office he had a button which he could press for calling in his secretary to say that there was important business he must attend to and thus suggest to a caller that it was time to go. "Yes," said Coolidge, "I have a button, but I have never had any occasion to use it. There has never been anybody here yet who, when it was time for him to go, didn't realize it!"

office seeker, eager to present his cause, would burst into voluble solicitation, only to find himself addressing a figure as unresponsive as a mummy. Eliciting only monosyllabic replies, he would usually rise and depart, thankful to escape from the ordeal. A long period of muteness never seemed to trouble Coolidge, who behaved as if it were fully provided for in the social code.[8] One evening on the *Mayflower,* Mrs. Dwight W. Morrow and Mrs. Frank B. Kellogg sat on either side of the President at dinner when he was in one of his least communicative moods. The next morning as Mrs. Morrow entered the dining room, she heard Mr. Coolidge say to his wife, "And where are my fair ladies?" "Exhausted by your conversation of last evening," was Mrs. Coolidge's answer.

Beneath Coolidge's impassiveness was a depth of feeling which occasionally rose to the surface. When Edward K. Hall, President of the New England Telephone and Telegraph Company, lost a son just as he was coming into a promising manhood, Coolidge sent him a book with this inscription: —

To E.K.H.

Whose boy, and my boy, by the grace of God,
Will remain boys through all Eternity.

Among his letters are many in the tone of this one, sent when he was Vice President: —

It was most kind of you to think of associating some of our friends to make a bust of me. But you know the many and constant calls on every one now for relief work that is so much needed. I can better get along without having this done and let them render some needed relief where it is so much in demand.

You have been a long and faithful and indulgent friend. Friendship is beyond price; yours is very precious to me.

[8] Coolidge's philosophy of silence is well illustrated in Walter Hard's poem, "Talk," printed in his volume, *Vermont Vintage,* in which a "man of few words" says to a garrulous hired man at dinner: —

"Sol, did you ever stop to think
Every time a sheep blats it loses a mouthful?"

Many stories are told showing Coolidge's point of view. Former State Senator John P. Brennan once met him as they were nearing the Massachusetts Senate Chamber. Coolidge said, "Haven't made a speech yet?" "No," answered Brennan. "They tell me you're a great talker," continued Coolidge. "Well, Mr. President," answered Brennan, "I'm following a good example, so I'm learning to keep my mouth shut." "That's a pretty good way to keep out of trouble," said Coolidge. "Can't hang you for what you don't say." He once remarked to Dwight F. Davis, "You know, Mr. Secretary, I have found in the course of a long public life that the things I did not say never hurt me." His advisers soon learned that they gained nothing by talking too much.

Mrs. Coolidge herself has written, "Mr. Coolidge had deeper sentimental feeling than most people whom I have known, but he did not reveal it in outward manifestations." On one occasion when she and Mrs. Stearns were going through the lobby of the Hotel Touraine, he handed her a package which looked as if it might contain a toothbrush. She thought it was one of his jokes, but when she opened it, she found a flexible gold-and-platinum bracelet — and remembered that it was a wedding anniversary. Even more typical, perhaps, was his gift at Christmas to Mrs. Coolidge of five twenty-dollar gold pieces, accompanied by a card engraved with Mr. Stearns's name and bearing the words, "Compliments of the Season." Mrs. Coolidge recognized it as the card which had come with a box of neckties from Mr. Stearns a day or two before. In each case we have a man strongly moved by sentiment but uncertain and embarrassed as to how it should be expressed.

Coolidge was always glad to greet members of his family and friends of his college days. In 1928, when the Secretary of the Navy sent him in the customary fashion a list of persons to be appointed on the Board of Visitors to the United States Naval Academy, the President, as he was looking it over, happened to think that one of his fraternity brothers, C. Green Brainard, Amherst, '96, might enjoy the experience. Accordingly he scratched out one prospective appointee, substituted Brainard's name, and then invited the latter to stay at the White House during the sessions of the Board. Brainard, who lived in a small village in Central New York and had seldom seen Coolidge since leaving college, found him a most attentive host, who watched out for his welfare and even in little matters was a good companion. When Brainard departed, the President said, "We try to run a good hotel here. Come down any time." [9]

People who worked with and for Calvin Coolidge, with a few exceptions like "Ike" Hoover, were fond of him and speak of him with affection. His woman secretary for three years in Northampton has characterized him as "the kindest man I have ever known." When he discovered that Brooks, the colored valet in the White House, had a serious heart ailment, he insisted that he must never go up over the stairs but should use the family elevator. Many stories indicate how considerate he was of the feelings of others. [10]

[9] Letter from C. Green Brainard, January 16, 1933. Brainard found him a fluent talker about old times at Amherst, but on Sunday afternoon following his customary nap, when the two were together in the family room, Coolidge worked on a picture puzzle for three quarters of an hour without saying a word.

[10] J. Pierrepont Moffat, of the Department of State, was once assigned for a time to social duties in the White House and found himself shortly almost worn

A Vermonter who displayed a bundle of letters from him said: —

There isn't a note in there that isn't packed with kindness, thoughtfulness, with messages to the home folks and with numerous reminders of his strong affection for the people of these hills. . . . Nobody could read these letters and think Calvin Coolidge a cold man.

Like most men who have done well in life, Coolidge was fully aware of his success and displayed in some of his letters and in his *Autobiography* an obvious satisfaction in his achievements. One passage in his syndicated newspaper articles has clearly a reference to himself: —

The great fact seems to be that when a man dedicates his whole soul to his work, when he fully determines to meet the responsibilities that he incurs, in the time of need some power outside himself directs his course and gives him strength to prevail. To such men comes revelation. They do better than they know. Therein lies the hope of the world.

The borderline between self-confidence and complacency is not always easy to establish, and in his case a too assertive humility would have betrayed the hypocrite. Coolidge never lacked assurance in his ability to measure up to an emergency. Again and again in his *Autobiography* we come across the statement, "I was ready," set down in no boastful spirit but merely as a fact.[11] One of the last sentences in the book has the same tone: —

It was therefore my privilege, after seeing my administration so strongly endorsed by the country, to retire voluntarily from the greatest experience that can come to mortal man.

It is remarkable that such an uncommunicative man should have acquired a reputation for wit, but his mind had naturally a humorous bent which could not be repressed. Some of his most amusing remarks are actually the literal statements of a man who appreciated, as Dr. Samuel Johnson had done before him, the salutary effect of common sense. When he returned to Northampton for the first time after becoming Governor, an elderly gentleman who had not kept

out by the pressure of self-seeking people. One morning he was summoned to the Executive Offices and greeted with the words, "Well, Mr. Moffat, are you learning a lot about human nature?" The President had noticed his strained look and was trying to cheer him up.

[11] On the other hand we have Coolidge's remark made to Mr. Stearns in 1918, after he had had a good many people to luncheon at the Parker House, "I guess this is a pretty good idea after all. These men seem to appreciate it. I am apt to forget that I am Lieutenant Governor, but they don't seem to. The fact is that I don't feel any different to-day than when I was a barefoot boy on the farm."

up with the news said to him on the street, "How d'ye do, Mr. Coolidge. I ain't seen ye about lately." "No," replied the Governor, "I've been out of town." At the observance of a Bryant anniversary at the poet's birthplace in Cummington, Massachusetts, the Coolidges listened to an address by Walter Prichard Eaton. After the ceremonies, a woman who had just been introduced to him bubbled over effusively, "Wasn't that a wonderful speech!" "No," responded the ex-President, "only pretty good." A Southern Congressman once somewhat condescendingly asked Coolidge if he had ever done any hunting. "Shot a sparrow once," was the reply. Utterances like these, to have the maximum of effectiveness, require the nasal drawl, the unsmiling features, the complete immobility of the Vermont Yankee.

That Coolidge had a rich fund of wit was well known to all those who had intimate dealings with him. That he tried deliberately to suppress it is proof of the stern discipline to which he subjected himself, but it broke out repeatedly in quaint comments, of the kind which Vermonters call "tart," on various aspects of life as he saw it. His humor was never Rabelaisian and he did not laugh with full-blooded gusto, but his thin, puckerish smile indicated his appreciation of a well-timed retort. Sometimes his mischievous tendency was expressed in practical jokes. Charles D. Hilles, writing to Chief Justice Taft on February 25, 1926, describes one such experience in which Mays, the White House valet, was the victim: —

I had an amusing experience with Mays. . . . He came up Sunday morning to barber me and talked all the while about Presidents with whom he had been associated. He is not quite sure that he has the key to the President Coolidge brand of humor. He said that Judge and Mrs. Hughes were at the White House recently, and that early in the morning the President rang for him and told him to knock at the door of Judge Hughes and see if the Judge was ready for a shave and a haircut. The President did not move a muscle of his face, and Mays submitted the matter to Mr. Stearns, expressing the opinion that the Hughes chin had always been sacred from the touch of steel. Mr. Stearns said that he could not interfere with the execution of an executive order. Mays confided to me that he then knocked at the door of Judge Hughes, but that he knocked very softly and was relieved when he was not admitted to the room.

Will Rogers insisted that Coolidge wasted more humor on people than anybody he ever knew. With those immediately around him he had many little jokes. He would occasionally press violently the bell on the White House elevator and then walk rapidly off down the stairs, to the consternation of the Secret Service men, who did not at first realize that he was amusing himself at their expense. Major Coupal, the President's physician, was sure to be greeted with some jesting remark, especially if he was a minute or two late for his daily appointment. One story, perhaps apocryphal, insists that once in his office as Vice President, when his stenographer had seated herself for dictation, Coolidge looked out the window and said, "Miss Peck, you're a very comely young lady." A trifle alarmed, she waited to see what would come next. "Yes, you certainly are attractive," continued Coolidge. By this time Miss Peck was wondering whether her employer had suddenly turned Don Juan. Then, addressing her again, Coolidge went on, "I'm telling you this, young lady, to get you cheerful, because I'm going to make a few remarks about your punctuation."

In 1924, Harrison G. Dwight, Chief of the Division of Publications, found in the archives two pre-Revolutionary maps which had been borrowed from the Massachusetts Historical Society in 1826. When Secretary Hughes informed the President of this discovery, the latter replied : —

Your note of December 20 and accompanying papers bring me a reminder of that splendid fidelity for which our Department of State has always been so distinguished. It is, however, even more impressive in its suggestion of the promptness and dispatch with which the official duties of your eminent branch of the government are so uniformly discharged.

Another Coolidge anecdote, resurrected by the *New Yorker*, recalls the time when Ruth Hanna McCormick was trying to persuade the President to name a prominent Chicago gentleman of Polish antecedents to a federal judgeship. Finally she induced him to receive a delegation of Chicago Poles, who appeared in his office and, not knowing precisely what to say, said nothing. Coolidge was also silent, and merely stared rather gloomily at the floor. At last he spoke, "Mighty fine carpet there." The Poles all nodded and smiled expectantly. "New one — cost a lot of money." The smiles of the visitors grew more expansive. The President continued, "She wore out the old one, trying to get you a judge." This clearly terminated the interview, and the Poles went out disappointed, hardly realizing what had happened.

Unlike Lincoln, Coolidge was not a raconteur and, although he enjoyed listening to a good story, rarely used one to illustrate a point. Mr. Edgar J. Rich, the Boston lawyer, remembers a luncheon at the Union Club just after the Police Strike, when someone in Coolidge's presence declared that the new police just taken on the force were exceptionally efficient. The Governor said, "That reminds me of the mouse which happened to find in the cellar a liquor barrel with a leak in it. The mouse began lapping, and lapping, and pretty soon he sat up, looked around, and squeaked fiercely, 'Where in hell's that cat?'" Anecdotes of this type, in the nature of set pieces, are rare in Coolidgiana. Much more common are remarks of the country grocery-store type — dry and whimsical and curt. When the late General Edward L. Logan called to pay his respects at the White House, the President greeted him cordially and then said, "Won't you come to lunch?" "As a matter of fact," answered Logan, "I'm going to be here only to-day and to-morrow." "We lunch on both days," replied Coolidge, without the vestige of a smile. When Rupert Hughes's so-called "debunking" biography of George Washington was published, a group of visitors were discussing it at the White House. During a pause in the conversation, the President looked out the window and said, "I see his monument is still there." Characteristic, too, is the response which he made to a newspaperman at Brule, who asked him how many fish there were in the river. The President answered that the waters were estimated to contain about 45,000 trout. "I haven't caught them all yet," he confessed, "but I've intimidated them."

To certain people, like Lincoln and "Uncle Joe" Cannon and "Tom" Reed and Chauncey M. Depew, good stories seem to attach themselves and turn up generation after generation. Calvin Coolidge also has been made responsible for many clever remarks which he did not utter. A small volume was published in 1933, entitled *Coolidge Wit and Wisdom* and containing "125 short stories about 'Cal.'" Several of the anecdotes in this book are apparently not authentic, but have been invented by resourceful newspapermen and attributed to him.[12] Indisputably credible, however, is one about

[12] Perhaps the most familiar anecdote is that purporting to give a conversation after church, when Coolidge had attended service and Mrs. Coolidge had been unable to go. "What was the sermon about?" she asked at luncheon. "Sin." "Well, what did the preacher say about sin?" "He was against it." Mrs. Coolidge declares that this story is not authentic, but must be attributed to some ingenious but anonymous reporter. Robert M. Washburn is responsible for another famous classic which describes Coolidge as looking out the White House window and saying, "There goes Borah, on horseback, and he's going in the same direction as the horse!" The original version, printed under Washburn's signature in the *Springfield Union*, in 1925, read, "The Titan, Borah, in his only avocation, rides regularly in Rock Creek Park, his only regret that he must proceed in the same direction as the horse." Another story, probably based on truth, has appeared in various

the dinner at the White House for a new member of the cabinet, who arrived with his wife inexcusably late, after the others had sat down. The lady turned to Mr. Coolidge and said, "Mr. President, I knew my husband and I would do something perfectly awful before we'd been very long in Washington." "You have," was the unexpected and disconcerting reply. Once on the *Mayflower,* according to Mrs. Coolidge, a young society matron whom Coolidge liked sat down opposite him on deck. At that time fashion dictated that women's skirts should be short, and hers was entirely in the mode. As she took her chair, she tried to arrange her skirt to cover her knees and was obviously in difficulty. Finally the President said, "What you need, young lady, is a rug!"

There is also the story of the evening walk which the President took with Senator Selden P. Spencer, of Missouri. As they came back to the White House, Spencer said jocularly, "I wonder who lives here?" "Nobody," answered Coolidge. "They just come and go!"

Coolidge was an unusually shrewd judge of men and their motives and saw through all those who attempted to exploit him. His secretary while he was Governor, Henry F. Long, believes this to have been one of his most distinctive qualities and was constantly impressed by his chief's sagacity in ascertaining what selfish purpose each caller had in mind. Once Coolidge said regarding the visitors who secure admission to the White House merely to gain publicity for themselves, "You know a lot of people come into my office just to use it as a sounding board." [13] Many people have let it be inferred that they controlled Coolidge and influenced his actions. The truth is that he listened, more or less patiently, to each one and then decided for himself. Experience had formed in him the habit of disinterested scrutiny and critical judgment. He was never in any sense the tool of business corporations or of financial groups or of organized politicians, and he saw to it that none of them had any claims upon him.

In 1918, when his first campaign for Governor was starting, he told Mr. Stearns that there were certain prominent men who would

---

versions. Shortly after Coolidge was elected Governor, a visitor appeared at his room in the Adams House to congratulate him, and the host pulled a bottle of Scotch whiskey out of a trunk, poured out a modest drink into a tumbler, and handed it to his guest. A little later another visitor appeared, and Coolidge went through the same ceremony. The newly arrived gentleman pointed to the first visitor as if to say, "What about him?" Coolidge caught the idea and merely said drily, "Bill's had his!"

[13] Coolidge once said to Henry L. Stoddard, "I never knew so much meanness existed in the world as I listened to in Washington." See Stoddard, 124ff.

undoubtedly offer money freely and instructed him to notify them that no contributions were needed. They were persons whose intentions were probably not sinister, but who were so closely connected with corporations which might ask for legislation that he wished to be absolutely without obligation to them. William V. Hodges, Treasurer of the National Republican Committee, has furnished me with a memorandum pointing out that, during the 1924 campaign, Coolidge insisted that those working for the party, or contributing to it, must understand that he would not consider that such service entailed any right or preference to Presidential favor. In one case it was discovered that a well-known Republican had solicited a subscription and promised the donor a diplomatic appointment. He was advised that no contribution would be accepted on that basis, and the check — a large one — was returned. Whenever Coolidge acted to please business corporations, he did so because it seemed also best for the country. They have sometimes claimed the credit for guiding his deliberations. As a matter of fact, no President has been more free from domination by pressure groups or more quietly, but decisively, his own master.

It has been alleged that, in his early days in state politics, Coolidge was the tool of a keen and bold Democratic lobbyist, Guy W. Currier, who assisted the young Republican for his own purposes. In those days, as later, Coolidge had the confidence of many local leaders of both parties and did not disdain their support. Furthermore Mr. Currier had an admiration for Coolidge and at one time offered him a lucrative post with a life-insurance company. But the theory that a "Grand Vizier of Massachusetts politics" was responsible for Calvin Coolidge's rise to power on Beacon Hill is rejected by nearly every well-informed witness — and I have consulted many.[14] If Currier and Coolidge had never met, the latter's career would not have been materially altered.

Frank W. Buxton, editor of the *Boston Herald,* writes, "Mr. Coolidge, as you know, kept a great many things to himself. Neither his wife nor Mr. Stearns knew what he was thinking of, planning, or doing." With this opinion I fully concur. W. Murray Crane, Frank W. Stearns, William M. Butler, Henry F. Long, Channing H. Cox, Thomas Cochran, and Everett Sanders were all close at one time to Calvin Coolidge; yet each of them is on record as be-

---

[14] Among those who concur in this opinion are Channing H. Cox, James A. Bailey, Mrs. Calvin Coolidge, Frank W. Buxton, Henry F. Long, Thomas W. White, Charles H. Taylor, and others. One who knew Coolidge intimately during those early years writes, "I should never have thought of mentioning Mr. Currier's name in connection with the Coolidge career."

lieving that he kept his own counsel and, in the end, made his own decisions.

It should be added that Coolidge was a shrewd politician. Chief Justice Taft wrote of him, June 7, 1925, "He is nearly as good a politician as Lincoln." Even as a fledgling statesman, he knew how to keep party workers cheerful and enthusiastic and seldom neglected to give the chairman of each Republican town committee a word of commendation. He remembered all the little personal details which count so much. An extraordinary number of extant letters, all brief, give evidence of his essential humanity, of his interest in birth and marriage and death, in all that people say and do. He was never too busy to acknowledge and discuss family relationships, no matter how remote, and would send long letters packed with genealogical information, indicating that he was acquainted with every branch of his family tree. When a friend lost his aged father, Coolidge offered sympathy; he sent a congratulatory note to a woman of ninety-six — presumably a Republican — who came out to vote before seven o'clock on election morning; when he declined an invitation to speak in some isolated spot before some unimportant organization, he did so with gentleness and tact; when a child was named after him, he said just the right thing to gratify the proud parents. The professionals in Boston soon discovered that they could teach him very little regarding politics as a fine art.[15] He had a sleuth's instinct for learning what was going on, and he knew how to keep his fences mended.

Nor was he ignorant of the unsavory phases of politics — the tacit conspiracies, the subtle flatteries, the seductive temptations, the ingenious wiles by which unscrupulous men try to accomplish their purposes. Practical experience had shown him that deception and double-dealing and betrayal were to be found in unexpected quarters; and when he was called ungrateful, it was often because he turned his back on knaves and self-seekers. He knew the political game and how to play it, but he wanted to play it according to the accepted ethical rules. He could have told strange stories of human weakness, of that bargaining and compromise and logrolling which, even when not illegal, are so much resented by any high-minded citizen. Calvin Coolidge was an astute politician, a hard man to overreach or delude, but the Devil never bought his soul. Mr. Stearns

[15] Judge Henry P. Field said of Coolidge, "As a neighbor he was conservative, close-lipped, and solitary. Men respected him, but he did not encourage their friendship. His greatness did not lie in his contacts with men. But as a politician he was brilliant. He seemed to know what people were thinking and how they would act."

was often exasperated because his candidate would be, from his viewpoint, over-scrupulous. On November 13, 1918, for example, Stearns wrote his son Foster regarding Governor Coolidge: —

He is shrewd enough to know that he needs publicity, and at times says so, but at other times he comes as near a pose as anything in throwing cold water on it. My job is to keep myself well-protected by whatever it is that protects a duck and let the cold water pass over me without damage and then go at it again.

Coolidge was a first-class executive, who accomplished his routine duties with speed and precision. Usually calm and cool-headed, he could not understand how Theodore Roosevelt could be so "restless." [16] President Harding's desk had always been piled high with letters and documents, and he himself was in a chronic state of confusion; [17] but those who visited the White House after Coolidge was settled there found him sitting, his correspondence carefully sorted, apparently at peace with the world. He knew how to distribute responsibility and trust subordinates. In his job he was neat, punctual, definite, and expeditious — a good "boss" to work for. Furthermore he did not keep late hours, and he took longer and more frequent vacations than any Chief Executive in our history.

In making appointments Coolidge was conscientious and tried to avoid prejudice. In 1920, when he was about to appoint a Judge of the Superior Court in Massachusetts, he summoned his friend Charles M. Davenport and asked him about a prospective candidate. He went on, "If I appoint him as a judge, can he see the issues of the case over the heads of the parties? I do not intend to appoint any man to the Superior Court, or to any court, who cannot do that." Mr. Davenport feels that this question epitomizes the qualities which a judge should possess. Coolidge's appointments were sometimes criticized, but he always gave them careful study.

As compared with Theodore Roosevelt or Woodrow Wilson or Herbert Hoover, Calvin Coolidge had a limited outlook. Never having traveled abroad, he knew very little first-hand of conditions in

[16] Once when Dwight Morrow was a week-end guest at the White House, he went with Coolidge to his office on Sunday morning. Morrow sat and looked over the paper while the President worked at his desk. Knowing the President's church-going habits, Morrow became a little perturbed as the clock ticked around. Finally, when Coolidge made no motion to go, Morrow said, "You're going to be late." "No hurry," was the answer. "Takes just seven minutes from upstairs."

[17] President Nicholas Murray Butler, of Columbia, called on Harding and found him sitting with bowed head before a great pile of letters. "I knew that this job would be too much for me," was his first remark. Coolidge would never have said anything like that.

European or Asiatic countries. When the Dean of Lincoln Cathedral dined at the White House, the President opened their conversation by asking, "Where is Lincoln?" Certain fields of knowledge, like romantic poetry or physical and chemical science, were outside his range. According to his secretary, Harry Ross, he read short stories in the *Saturday Evening Post* and knew the exact date of issue of several popular magazines which Ross was instructed to bring to the office as soon as they appeared on the newsstand. Like several other Presidents, he relieved the strain of his position by an occasional detective story, and he spent some time each day looking over selected clippings from the daily papers.

On the other hand, Coolidge was exceptionally well-informed in biography and history and read far more than his acquaintances suspected. While he was in Northampton, his library was chiefly on legal subjects, but later he accumulated more than five thousand volumes, among which will be found nearly every important work on American political biography published since the World War. The list of books sent by his order from the Library of Congress to the White House is sufficiently impressive, and includes such volumes as Spender's *Public Life*, Stuart Chase's *Your Money's Worth*, and authoritative texts on economics and finance.

In 1926, the thoughtful Frank W. Stearns wished to present his friend with a bookplate, but Sidney L. Smith, to whom the commission had been entrusted, died before the design was finished. In 1929, however, Timothy Cole engraved for him a plate on wood, showing the Plymouth homestead, with two white dogs in the foreground and the bust of Washington above against a background of stars and stripes; and Coolidge used it from that time on.

Coolidge told Clarence S. Brigham that he had read all of Dante's *Divina Commedia* in the original Italian, adding, "It was years after I graduated from college, and I did not finish it until after I was married." Mr. Brigham lunched at the White House in May 1928, bringing with him the original manuscript of *Alice in Wonderland*, which he had just purchased. Finding that *Alice* was one of Coolidge's favorites, Brigham explained to him that the first edition, issued in 1865, not being entirely to the author's liking, had been suppressed. "Suppressed?" inquired the President. "I did not know there was anything off-color in *Alice!*" [18] When he was presiding over a meeting of the American Antiquarian Society, a member told him of the magnificent Gutenberg Bible recently purchased by

[18] "Libraries of the Presidents," by Clarence S. Brigham, in *Publications of the American Antiquarian Society*, October 1934.

Congress for a fabulous sum. "I should think," he commented, "that an ordinary copy of the King James version would have been good enough for those Congressmen."

Occasionally Coolidge attended the theatre, usually to please his wife, but he seldom sought it deliberately for recreation, as Woodrow Wilson had done. He once said to Bruce Barton, "A good show tires me so much that I feel the effects all the next day." But that was not always the case. While he was Governor, he saw a play with a group of members of the Legislature, remaining silent throughout and giving no intimation as to what he thought. About a week later another theatre party was arranged, and someone said, "We ought to let the Governor select the performance this time. He didn't have much fun at the other one, judging by the expression on his face." Accordingly he was asked to make his choice, and named the same drama they had seen the week before. "But you didn't like it!" exclaimed one of the group. "Yes, I did. I liked it. I've been back by myself twice since!"

Music Coolidge never understood, either as a performer or as a listener, and he seldom attended a concert except when one was offered as part of the entertainment in the White House. James E. Gregg, Principal of Hampton Institute, wrote to Chief Justice Taft, April 20, 1928: —

I was surprised to see the President sitting in solitary grandeur in his pew and was amused to notice the slight impression which the music evidently made upon him. He had the air of having been compelled to attend by his wife.

He did, however, like martial or patriotic airs, especially when played by the Marine Band. We find in his letters no references to art or architecture, and I can discover no instance of his having sought out a gallery for pleasure. On one occasion, nevertheless, he was escorted through an exhibition of modern painting in Pittsburgh and afterwards, in an interview with the English author, Beverley Nichols, expressed himself as follows: —

As I looked at those pictures, I felt that I could see through them, into the minds of the nations which had created them. I could see the torment out of which they had been born. If that nation's psychology was diseased, so was its art. The traces of neurosis were unmistakable.[19]

[19] Beverley Nichols, in the *London Sketch*, quoted by the *Literary Digest*, October 13, 1928. The interview up to that point had been unsatisfactory, with Nichols "muttering inanities" — his own phrase — and the President merely saying, "Oh!" Coolidge was apparently roused by Nichols's remark that Europe's young men were still overshadowed by the possibility of future wars.

It has already been suggested that Coolidge was unaffected by beauty, except that which he met in nature; and even there he was unimpressed by aspects which moved others. When he visited the lovely flower garden of Mrs. Homer Gage, in Worcester, Massachusetts, he addressed only two remarks to his hostess. As he entered the gate, he said, "How do you do?"; and when he walked out, he said, very politely, "Good-bye." The story has often been told of his strolling in silence through the unsurpassed tropical gardens on the Dupont estate in Delaware and finally pausing in front of a plant and uttering the single word, "Bananas!" He was at last confronting something that he knew. He seems to have paid little attention to the spectacular beauty of the Yellowstone National Park, but he was fond of the Vermont hills, although his emotion was probably more nostalgic than esthetic.

In harmony with the other phases of his character, Coolidge had simple tastes. The living conditions under which he had been brought up were good enough for him, and he was in no danger of being corrupted by self-indulgence. His critics accused him of playing up life on the farm for political purposes, but he really liked being back in the somewhat primitive homestead of his ancestors, shaving in the kitchen and eating with only one servant to prepare and pass the food. He was not trying deliberately to be a Spartan. To him matters of that kind were not very important. Whenever in the White House he had a headache or a bruise, he would ask, "Where's Aurora's liniment?" This was an ill-smelling compound of various pungent ingredients, including ammonia and arnica, blended by Miss Aurora Pierce, Colonel Coolidge's housekeeper. Mrs. Coolidge always kept a bottle of this homemade remedy on hand to meet her husband's needs.

Coolidge had himself no affectations and despised people who, as he said, "put on airs." Once at a White House luncheon the only guest besides Mr. Stearns was an American diplomat home on leave, who easily dominated the conversation, describing his intimate social relations with the rich and aristocratic classes in the country to which he was an ambassador. When he had paused, the President looked over to his wife and said, "Mother, those dogs have crossed the end of the room four times in the last ten minutes." The guest collapsed like a punctured balloon and was restrained in his talk for the remainder of the meal.[20]

The President owed much of his popularity to the fact that he

[20] This story was told to me by Frank W. Stearns, who was greatly troubled by the obvious discomfiture of the guest.

seemed to millions of so-called "common people" to be just one of themselves established temporarily in a position of great power. As the *New York Times* said of him after his death, it did not occur to him to surround himself with official pomp or mystery. He was an entirely natural man and, as such, sometimes made mistakes. He amused the sailors on the *Mayflower* by responding "Aye, Aye!" on the wrong occasions; and when his son John was at a summer military camp and sprang smartly to salute his father, the President looked very miserable and finally, in comical despair, just removed his hat. As Chief Executive, he "put on no side," and he went back to the place from which he had come entirely unspoiled. An editorial comment from the *New York Herald* brings out this important element in his nature: —

He was one of the common people whom Lincoln said God loved. There was something about him that all of us wanted to be like. We loved his humor. We adored his silences. There was something in his makeup that reminded us of ourselves, in the old days when the country was young.

But Coolidge also possessed a very strong sense of the dignity of office and was well acquainted with details of precedence and etiquette. When he visited Phillips Academy, Andover, Governor Fuller of Massachusetts and his wife were by some mistake seated in the second row on the outdoor platform. Suddenly the President's forefinger beckoned to one of the committee, who approached and, as he bent over, heard a whisper, "Governor of the Commonwealth belongs in the front row." Coolidge was absolutely right, and the necessary change of position was accomplished immediately by the withdrawal of a member of the cabinet. When the President brought his "Aunt Sarah" Pollard, his mother's sister, on board the *Mayflower* for a short cruise, the usual ceremony was observed, with the officers drawn up smartly in dress formation; and as the President escorted Mrs. Pollard aft, Dr. Boone heard him say, "Aunt Sarah, personally I do not like all this attention. But it is for the President of the United States, and I have great respect for the office." He dressed with scrupulous care for every occasion, and his clothes, with which he was well supplied, were made by an excellent tailor. Coolidge was much disturbed when Colonel Lindbergh, as a White House guest, appeared dressed for church in a noticeably light-colored suit. After the President tactfully inquired whether dark blue clothes would not be more appropriate, the aviator rather reluctantly made the change. When John Coolidge intimated on one busy afternoon that he was not planning to dress for dinner at the White House, his father informed him in vigorous terms that the customary procedure would be observed.

Although conscious of the respect due to his office, Coolidge never abused its privileges. Both as Governor and as President, he insisted that his chauffeur should obey the traffic regulations and never ask for special consideration. He would not go inside the Arnold Arboretum when he arrived there unexpectedly and found that a special permit was required for admission.

His sense of propriety and his good taste in matters of this kind were far above those of most men who are "drest in a little brief authority."

Always preaching economy in government business, Coolidge was thrifty in his private finances and instilled the same doctrine in his children.[21] To the end of his life he kept a series of small memorandum books in which he entered all his personal expenditures, and he himself made out his federal and state income-tax blanks. His bills, even when his resources were small, were paid on the first of each month, and he was never in debt. Although he could not answer all the appeals made to him for help, he was not ungenerous in his charities and did his best to select those which were most deserving.

Many stories, most of them apochryphal, have been told of Coolidge's economical habits. He had been taught as a child the evils of waste, and the lesson persisted. In July 1925, he went to Camp Devens to review the 26th Division, and thorough preparations were made for his reception. In his washroom General Logan had placed two immaculate towels for the President's personal use; but just before he arrived a hot and dusty aide dashed into headquarters, visited the lavatory, and naturally dried his hands with one of the special towels. When the President was escorted to the washroom, his companion noticed that one of the towels was streaked with dirt, and proffered him the remaining one, but Coolidge waved him aside, saying, "Why soil it? There's one that's been used. That's clean enough." The story would hardly be worth relating if it were

---

[21] Once young Calvin had been given five dollars by Mr. Stearns, and the boy's father insisted that the youngster should make out a statement as to what he had done with the money. A week later, on a hot Sunday, the family went to church. On the way home, Governor Coolidge asked, "Mother, what was the sermon about?" "Mercy," she replied, "don't ask me." "John, what was the sermon about?" "I don't know," was the reply. Then it was Calvin's turn, but the boy said nothing. The question was repeated. "You know all right," said his father, and kept at the interrogation until at last, with a shrug of his shoulders, the boy murmured, "Aw, spending money!"

not for the light which it throws on Coolidge's early training and its resultant instinctive reaction.

Mr. Coolidge, although he was usually impassive, had an unpredictable temper and sometimes flew into rages over matters ordinarily regarded as trivial. The supposition that he was always phlegmatic and self-controlled is shattered by many anecdotes proving that he was capable of explosions almost volcanic in their fury. "Ike" Hoover wrote of him: —

Those who saw Coolidge in a rage were simply startled. The older employees about the White House who had known Roosevelt used to think he raved at times, but in his worst temper he was calm compared with Coolidge.

The President once summarily transferred a Secret Service man, James Haley, for coming back an hour and a quarter late with Mrs. Coolidge from a walk in the Black Hills of South Dakota, although the delay was quite unavoidable.[22] Little things like the misplacement of an overcoat enraged him even more than real causes for anger. On long campaign trips he was likely to become irritable — "testy," as they say in Vermont. Edward E. Whiting recalled that, in 1920, when Coolidge was making a speaking tour through the border states, Colonel Lockwood telegraphed him asking him to write a column summary of the campaign to date. When Coolidge read the message, he banged his first down on the table and exploded, "Damn it! They're always having me writing things. I won't do it!"

Coolidge's irritability was due in part to his lack of physical robustness. He did not possess the aggressive vitality of Theodore Roosevelt, and he had to conserve his nervous energy as much as possible. It is significant that physical exercise either bored or fatigued him and that he gradually abandoned all forms of it except short walks. Fortunately he slept well, and the only recorded period of insomnia occurred when he was worried over the sins of Harding's administration. At that time he said to his wife, "How I hate that sunrise gun!" — referring to the early morning salute from Fort Meyer. Several of his peculiarities — his wish to have somebody always with him, his dislike of long personal interviews, his impulse to leave the dinner table before the others had finished — can be explained on the theory that he did not always feel well. He was not the man to complain of his indigestion or of his hay

[22] William Allen White, in *A Puritan in Babylon*, devotes several pages to this incident, 353ff.

fever, but he unquestionably had warnings of weakness long before the ultimate attack.[23]

In women Calvin Coolidge had little interest, much preferring the society of men, and he lived aloof from feminine wiles. He had no love affairs until he met Grace Goodhue, and he was embarrassed when left for even a short period wholly in the company of the other sex. They in their turn were puzzled by him, for he belonged to a strange male species, apparently impervious to their charms. At dinners they practised their beguilements upon him, only to meet with stolidity or with a reaction so ironical that it was equally discouraging. "Ike" Hoover, who described Taft, rather mischievously, as "a ladies' man, pure and simple," contented himself with saying, "Coolidge had nothing to do with the ladies." His was emphatically a man's world, the world of masculine politics and party intrigue, of shirt sleeves and strong cigars, which flourished before suffrage was secured by women. Coolidge did not dance or know any parlor tricks; he had none of the small talk, the mild banter, so essential for the smooth running of social functions; he never looked happy at a tea. Worst of all, he made no effort to adjust himself to such occasions. For him, as for his father and grandfather in Vermont, woman's place was in the home, and it was man's proud privilege to carry on the routine work of the universe.

This biography has dwelt too little on Grace Coolidge and the assistance which she gave her husband. In 1926 the President said to Bruce Barton: —

A man who has the companionship of a lovely and gracious woman enjoys the supreme blessing that life can give. And no citizen of the United States knows the truth of this statement more than I.

For a man of his type Grace Coolidge was the ideal helpmate, free from vanity or gossipy tendencies, willing to subordinate her wishes to his, and endowed with all the magnetism that he lacked. He used to say of her in his affectionate joking way, "She has kept me running for political office ever since I married her." Actually she never inquired about or interfered with public affairs. In commenting on this phase of her relationship to her husband, Mrs. Coolidge has remarked, "If I had manifested any particular interest in a political matter, I feel sure I should have been properly put

[23] See "The Calvin Coolidge Nobody Knew," by Herman Beaty, in the *Cosmopolitan*, April 1933. Beaty, who was Coolidge's secretary for some time in Northampton after his retirement, had an excellent opportunity of observing him and maintains that he showed outward indications of impaired health.

in my place." In their early days in the White House she found that the President was making appointments for her without her knowledge and that consequently she was not fully informed about her social program. One day at luncheon she said, "Calvin, I think I shall have your secretary prepare for me a list of our engagements for the next two weeks." His reply was, "We don't give out that information promiscuously." In discussing Mr. Stearns's relationship to her husband, Mrs. Coolidge has written, "He and I were in the same class as recipients of Presidential confidence. Many a time we have put our heads together and figured out that two and two made four only to learn later that we had been adding the wrong numbers."

Mrs. Coolidge brought to her duties an unfailing sense of humor and a conviction that her field was the direction of social functions in the White House. The Executive Mansion has never had a more gracious mistress, one more amply endowed with tact and charm, one who knew better just what to say and do as well as what not to do and say. That Coolidge was proud of her — even at times jealous of her — was apparent to everyone around them. Malign Washington gossip, which spares nobody, once or twice whispered that there was a rift between them, but it was all slanderous and baseless rumor.

Coolidge was particularly interested in what his wife wore, sometimes bought her hats and gowns, and was critical of her choices. Once as he was walking along F Street with French Strother, he said, "That's Mr. Blank. He costs me lots of money." "How's that?" "He sells women's fixin's." When her portrait was being painted by Howard Chandler Christy, with a white collie in the foreground, the artist requested her to wear a red gown for purposes of color contrast. Mrs. Coolidge asked her husband's advice, and he, liking one of her white dresses better, replied, "If it's contrast you want, why not wear white and paint the dog red?" At times he was inquisitive about what she was doing, and she kept him amused. Coolidge's last letter to his wife, when he was on a short trip to New York in the autumn of 1932, concludes, "I have thought of you all the time since I left home." That, for a man of his type, was an outburst of powerful emotion.

It was the Vermont tradition that the human male should be master in his own household, and Coolidge was a martinet in his family affairs. Believing thoroughly in discipline, he brought up his two sons to be implicitly obedient; but, although he sometimes reproved them for extravagance or what he vaguely called "foolishness," he was proud of their progress and boasted of it in letters to his father. One characteristic illustration of the control of the President over his family is told by Mrs. Coolidge. When the White House stables were at her disposal, she saw no reason why she should not learn to ride and, aided by Dwight F. Davis, then Assistant Secretary of War, secured an outfit and went to Fort Meyer for her first lesson. The newspapermen, learning what was going on, printed a story the next morning under large headlines, "Mrs. Coolidge Takes up Riding." When Coolidge saw it at the breakfast table, he said disapprovingly, "I think you will find that you will get along at this job fully as well if you do not try anything new." Mrs. Coolidge's adventures in equitation ended there and then.

It would be wrong to create the impression that Calvin Coolidge was always brusque or silent or domineering. It was his essentially human traits which started him on a political career, and these persisted to the end.[24] Bernard N. Baruch, one of his colleagues on the National Transportation Committee, has written of him: —

He handled everything with such rare good taste and judgment, and with so much consideration for everybody, that he won the real affection of us all. . . . Many people thought this sweetness and consideration, as shown in his latter days, were due to his approaching illness, but my contacts with him in other matters made me believe that he always was the human being — very shy, but always considerate of his associates.

Coolidge was patient with photographers and did not object to posing, feeling that it was part of his job. He also had a wide experience in sitting for portraits and proved to be a docile subject. In 1924, Hanatschek made a portrait which now hangs in the Amherst College Library. In the same year Howard Chandler Christy executed full-length portraits of both Mr. and Mrs. Coolidge, now preserved in the Forbes Library in Northampton. The late Edmund C. Tarbell painted in 1925, at Swampscott, a full-length portrait now in the Senate Chamber in the Massachusetts State House, and a copy was later commissioned for the Algonquin Club, in Boston.

[24] Mrs. Dwight Morrow has recalled that in 1918 she and her husband, with their daughter Anne, called on Governor Coolidge at the Hotel Touraine, in Boston. On the train going back to New York, several people came into their drawing-room, and Coolidge's name was introduced. Morrow said that Coolidge had Presidential possibilities, but several men disagreed, and one broke out, "No one would *like* him." Then Anne spoke up, holding out a finger bound with adhesive tape, "*I* like him. He was the only one that asked about my sore finger." Morrow looked pleased and said, "There's your answer."

Portraits of Mr. and Mrs. Coolidge by Joseph de Sigall were also produced at this period. Frank O. Salisbury, the English artist, accompanied the Coolidges to Sapelo Island, Georgia, in 1928, and there did the portrait now hanging in the building of the New York Genealogical and Biographical Society. A copy, with alterations suggested by Mrs. Coolidge, is in the possession of the American Antiquarian Society at Worcester, Massachusetts. De Laszlo painted in 1926 a portrait which belongs to Mrs. Coolidge. Ercole Cartotto made, perhaps, more likenesses of Coolidge than any other artist. He has left a record of what happened when, in the autumn of 1927, he went to the White House to make preliminary sketches : —

The President came to the room in which I was waiting and instantly began to question me. He posed for a preliminary drawing, and he talked at the same time. For three hours, divided into two period sittings, he put me through the most uncomfortable time I had ever experienced. My procedure differed from that of other artists who had painted his portrait. He wanted to know why. He questioned me on citizenship, politics, forms of government, religious institutions. I endeavored to answer the avalanche as intelligently as possible while working. Literally "punch drunk," I was drawing the President. It did not occur to me at the moment that he was taking my measure.

Both Mr. Cartotto and Mrs. Coolidge felt that the result was highly successful, and the President said, "Mr. Cartotto is the first artist who did not *create* a mouth for me." Later Mr. Cartotto saw the President every week-day for eleven weeks, sometimes for only a few minutes, while his sitter dictated or held conferences. After the first portrait, commissioned by Coolidge's fellow alumnus, George D. Pratt, for Amherst College, was completed, Cartotto did others for the Phi Gamma Delta Fraternity and for the State House in Montpelier, Vermont. DeWitt Lockman painted a likeness in the autumn of 1930 for the New York Historical Society. Finally, in 1932, Charles Sydney Hopkinson, of Boston, came to The Beeches and painted the official portrait authorized by Congress and now hanging in the White House — a portrait which gives the impression of a tired and introspective old man.[25]

As Coolidge became more and more the centre of national attention, various writers felt impelled to choose him as a subject. Robert M. Washburn, who had been during the campaign of 1920 Coolidge's

[25] Other artists painted Coolidge from sketches or photographs, but the above list includes all authorized portraits.

earliest biographer, amplified his original paper-bound pamphlet through changing formats and phases into a red-covered volume of 169 pages published in 1923, still under the title, *Calvin Coolidge, His First Biography*. A man of keen intelligence, ready wit, and epigrammatic felicity, Washburn had submitted the text to friends of Coolidge, who insisted on certain alterations, thus betraying an almost incredible caution and lack of a sense of humor. Whenever Washburn had used *Fate,* referring to the Great Power which presumably had assisted Coolidge, the censor substituted *Destiny.* All mention of the Bonus issue was deleted as politically dangerous, and Senator Lodge's name was ruthlessly expunged. Two sentences were arbitrarily stricken out: "A great police commissioner, Edwin Upton Curtis, gave wings to his feet," and "Even Death rode before him and cleared the way." The watchful censor altered the words *tobacco plantation* to *farm,* apparently on peculiar moral grounds, and eliminated entirely Coolidge's famous answer to the question, "What part did you take in college athletics?" — "I held the stakes!" In all, some thirty-six revisions were made, a few because the passage might be regarded as flippant, tinged with cynicism or irreverence, and others because their implications were thought to be dangerous. The tone of the book was friendly throughout, and its whimsicality was never malicious. Furthermore its fresh and homely touches certainly set it apart from any previous campaign biography in American history. Frank W. Stearns thought highly of Washburn's book and would have liked to distribute it more widely; and Coolidge himself once showed the first chapter to Bruce Barton, rather proudly, saying, "Pretty good, isn't it?"

Of the other biographies of Coolidge which appeared at this period, nearly all were hastily prepared and carelessly proofread. The most pretentious was *President Coolidge, A Contemporary Estimate,* by Edward Elwell Whiting, a well-known Boston journalist and columnist, who had received from the White House every facility for acquiring information. Finished as it was before the convening of Congress in December 1923, it could only conclude, "He is of the material from which great things may come. Events will try him." In 1924, Mr. Whiting edited another volume, entitled *Calvin Coolidge, His Ideals of Citizenship,* containing classified selections from Coolidge's public addresses. Much less formal and better calculated to attract the attention of the man in the street was *Calvin Coolidge, From a Green Mountain Farm to the White House,* by Michael E. Hennessy, another Boston newspaperman. The author was not, like Robert M. Washburn, a deliberate stylist, and the book was hastily thrown together, but it contains some fresh and picturesque material. A much more satisfactory production was *The Preparation of Calvin Coolidge,* in the autumn of 1924, by Robert A. Woods, of the Amherst class of 1882. Woods was helped by Frank W. Stearns in preparing his manuscript, and other Amherst men offered suggestions. Still another biography was Horace Green's *The Life of Calvin Coolidge,* also published in 1924. Mr. Green took pains to collect first-hand information and made excursions into early Coolidge folklore, with the result that he produced the most accurate account of the President's career up to that date. A thinner, less substantial volume, *Cal Coolidge, President,* was by the versatile Roland D. Sawyer, a former colleague of Coolidge in the Massachusetts General Court. Kenneth L. Roberts's *Concentrated New England,* of approximately the same period, contained some excellent stories which other later biographers have occasionally borrowed. William Allen White's *Calvin Coolidge, The Man Who Is President,* did not appear until November 1925, too late to be used as a campaign document but far more complete than the biographies which had preceded it. It was to be superseded by the same author's *A Puritan in Babylon* (1939), but the earlier work has many illuminating passages. In 1928, as the Coolidge administration was drawing to a close, Cameron Rogers, an editor and later a screen writer, published *The Legend of Calvin Coolidge,* but it added very little to the source material already in existence.

The more one studies Calvin Coolidge, the more apparent it becomes that, although he gained steadily in power and influence, he changed very little in external appearance, in his attitude towards life, and in his general philosophy, from youth to middle age. His habits, his manners, and his opinions were much the same in 1932 as they had been in 1902. His character, under the beneficent guidance of Garman and Morse, was formed by the time he left Amherst, and his future growth was not in kind but in degree. In my last interview with him, on August 6, 1932, he spoke substantially as follows, with a delightfully ironic touch in the last sentence: —

Senator Lodge has been accused of being inconsistent, but he had a long public service, and it is not to be wondered at that he sometimes did not make his actions harmonize. Now my career was meteoric, and I didn't have time to alter my views. That was one difference between Senator Lodge and me. There were others.

The qualities which Coolidge displayed as a young legislator were faithfulness to duty, reliability, discretion, tolerance, integrity, and common sense. The same qualities were his as President. Throughout his career we find in him a deep-seated regard for law, for authority, for tradition. Joined with this was a belief in what may be called individualism — the doctrine, which seemed so obvious in Plymouth, Vermont, that each man must achieve his own salvation. In his personal and governmental philosophy, Coolidge was conspicuously old-fashioned. He wrote, November 24, 1920, to H. W. Gibson: "There are two things necessary for the enrichment of life, mentally, physically, socially, and spiritually. They are very simple and are known of all men. One is hard work and the other is a determination to do right." He told a group of young people who called on him in March 1924 that "there are only two things necessary for boys — to work and behave themselves." In our later days of educational psychology, with its emphasis on fixations and complexes, Coolidge's formula seems antiquated. But even in our troubled civilization, the principles of discipline and self-respect cannot be altogether obsolete.

Edward E. Whiting, in his book called *Calvin Coolidge — His Ideals of Citizenship,* published in 1924, assembled passages from Coolidge's public utterances to show what he had been thinking about. Mr. Whiting's quotations reveal certain basic concepts — faith in democracy, trust in the Constitution, belief in law and order, confidence in our traditional economic system, reliance on education and religion, respect for duty as a motive in human conduct, and an ineradicable hope that hard work would continue to be a test of manhood. Mr. Whiting said of Coolidge that his conservatism was "that of one who believes that things worth preserving should be preserved." Although quite aware of the tremendous social and economic transformations going on around him or prophesied by collectivist thinkers, he felt "that the great principles of life do not change; they are permanent and well-known." He was sure, even in the midst of the Great Depression, that the sanest and most enduring forward movements in government, industry, public welfare, and religion have been evolved out of what already existed. To phrase it platitudinously, it was not revolution, but evolution, that interested him. He did not wish to sweep everything aside and begin again. He said to Henry L. Stoddard, "Government is growth — slow growth."

Was he blind to the needs of the poor, the disabled, and the old? I think not. In Massachusetts, as we have seen, he displayed an unusual interest in social legislation and earned the respect of the labor leaders. That he was deeply sympathetic with the workingman and his problems is evident from many things that he said and did as Senator and Governor. He did not, however, believe that it was the function of the federal government to handle questions involving the relief of the underprivileged. His conscience was no less sensitive than that of many a self-styled reformer of a later generation; indeed he sponsored much legislation intended to improve conditions for the laborer. On the other hand, he felt that each local community should care for its own destitute, and he was well aware of the enormous danger inherent in any policy of placing the responsibility in the hands of political appointees in Washington. He enlarged upon this theme in a notable speech before the Daughters of the American Revolution on April 17, 1928, saying: —

Whenever some people find that abuse needs correction in their neighborhood, instead of applying a remedy themselves, they seek to have a tribunal sent on from Washington to discharge their duties for them, regardless of the fact that in accepting such supervision they are bartering away their freedom.

Coolidge was aware that he had not been a constructive statesman, and his answer was that he was living in a period when constructive statesmanship was not demanded or required. He declared again and again that it was essential for administration to catch up with legislation, and he behaved accordingly. "When things are going along all right," he wrote to Mr. Stearns, "it is a good plan to let them alone." Chief Justice Taft, in a letter dated September 19, 1925, probably expressed the viewpoint at that moment of a majority of his fellow citizens: —

The situation in the country seems to be as good as we could expect it to be. We haven't had a tremendous boom, but business on the whole is good and the people are fortunate in having at the helm a man who is not disposed to interfere in any way with the even flow of events, and is striving to let the people work out for themselves the prosperity they deserve.

His accomplishment, then, was chiefly negative. He checked the Boston Police Strike and made its malignant influence abortive; he kept the nation from extravagance and waste; he blocked unwise legislation in Congress at times when he was warned by most of his advisers that he would lose his popularity. Not enough emphasis has been laid on his courage. He had reason to believe that, if he antagonized the American Federation of Labor, his political future would be ruined; yet he sent the famous telegram to Samuel

Gompers. In making appointments in Massachusetts under the Re-organization Bill, he deliberately — and unnecessarily — incurred the risk of being actively opposed by a large number of ambitious politicians. In vetoing the Bonus Bill and the various McNary-Haugen Bills, he defied two formidable groups — the veterans and the farmers. This is, of course, a kind of negative courage, more akin to stubbornness than to audacity; but it is courage none the less. When Coolidge's mind was made up, neither threats nor pleas could move him. A newspaper editor said of him, "In a great day of Yes-men, Calvin Coolidge was a great No-man."

His task was to keep the Ship of State on an even keel before a favoring wind — not to reconstruct the hull or install new motive power or alter the course. He was a safe pilot, not a brilliant one. Under him the nation was not adventurous, but it was happy. He won no battles, challenged no traditions, instituted few reforms. What he would have done with a war or a depression on his hands is a fascinating subject for speculation.

The younger Theodore Roosevelt went to him after the election in 1924 and, declaring that the Prohibition Law was not being obeyed, suggested that the President advocate a special tax which would provide a billion dollars a year and could be used exclusively for the enforcement of the Eighteenth Amendment. When Roosevelt had finished his vigorous argument, the President said, without any great excitement, "Colonel, never go out to meet trouble. If you will just sit still, nine cases out of ten someone will intercept it before it reaches you." In his practical way, Coolidge preferred to let sleeping dogs lie. He was a far better man to do the day's work than to plan a program for to-morrow.

Calvin Coolidge was no inspired dreamer. I do not discover in his speeches any evidence of broad vision stretching into the shadowy future. He lacked originality, the power to re-create and re-organize human society. He was deficient in imagination, that quality which belonged to Sir Francis Bacon and William Pitt and Thomas Jefferson and Abraham Lincoln and Woodrow Wilson, men of superlative genius who have looked far ahead in the hope of eventually improving a disorderly world. Coolidge's range was limited. He took no voyages into strange seas of thought. He planned no Utopias. His viewpoint is expressed in a sentence from a letter to a friend, "Let us all work together to get out of the present crisis and not cloud the issue or use up our energy thinking of other things."

The frequently expressed opinion that Calvin Coolidge was the

Child of Fortune is not altogether tenable, and he himself answered it in one of his syndicated articles, for August 29, 1930: —

There are people who complain that they do not have any luck. These are the opportunists who think that their destiny is all shaped outside themselves. They are always waiting for something to happen. . . . Our real luck lies within ourselves. It is a question of character. It depends on whether we follow the inner light of conscience. . . . If we cannot entirely control our environment, we can control ourselves and our own destiny. The man who is right makes his own luck.

To each successive position which Coolidge reached he was elected by a considerable majority of votes in accordance with democratic practice; each place was a preparation for the one which followed; and in each he may be said to have justified the confidence of those who supported him. Furthermore he had no dazzling qualities but won the respect of his contemporaries by sheer merit. No "third-rater" could have deluded a critical public over more than a quarter of a century. He was long on the political stage; he spoke many words and did many deeds; yet he could have been elected again as President and have had the longest period in office of any American Chief Executive. Some quality in Calvin Coolidge made people trust him as they never trusted La Follette or Norris or Borah or "Al" Smith. In the course of reaction against his political philosophy people have forgotten how popular Calvin Coolidge was, up to the very moment of his death. If this is being lucky, Coolidge was a very lucky man.

Because he blew no stirring blast upon the trumpet, because he did not arouse his party to make great social and economic changes, it has been said that he makes no appeal to young men. It is probably true that his caution, his practicality, and his respectability do not stir romantic youth. Even in the 1920's, in the Age of the Flapper, he was an anomaly, badly adjusted to the seething atmosphere of *This Side of Paradise* or *Dancers in the Dark*. The average boy or girl of the 1940's may regard his philosophy as irreparably obsolete. But this is not the conclusive test of a statesman's usefulness. He did instill confidence in thoughtful men and women, to whom he was a symbol of tranquillity and security — two blessings which any adult American, following the World War, was in a mood to appreciate.

In trying to anticipate the verdict of history, we can be sure that Calvin Coolidge will not be remembered as a great constructive

President, like Washington and Jackson and Lincoln and Wilson. Nor does he belong with the weaklings, with Pierce and Buchanan and Grant and Harding. His place is with John Quincy Adams and Rutherford B. Hayes and Grover Cleveland — with strong Presidents who had few great issues to settle but whose integrity and sterling character have made them stand out more for what they were than for what they did.

What does he represent in the judgment of his countrymen? Chiefly, I think, the fundamental virtues which he so fully exemplified in his own way of living — thrift and faithfulness and honesty. To him duty and loyalty and responsibility were more than ordinary dictionary words. They were infallible guides to conduct. He was essentially a moral force. There are those who maintain that he was at heart a self-seeker, willing to utilize anybody to attain his ambition.[26] To me this is not a just rendering of his motives. I see him from the beginning resolutely doing the day's work, maintaining always his dignity and self-respect, and proving false to no man; playing politics with the skill of a master and slowly winning the confidence of a wider and wider community; accepting each new position with a resolve to do his duty as he saw it. This interpretation has its proof in his career.

Calvin Coolidge was no nonentity. Nonentities do not arouse so much discussion. I do not agree with Bradford that Coolidge's soul was "dry and unprofitable," or with Lippmann that he had a "genius for inactivity." Coolidge had a personality which was distinctive and different from that of other American statesmen. We cannot compare him with Webster or Sumner or McKinley or Bryan, for he was unlike each one of them. That unimpressive physique, that thin, pinched countenance, that indifferent manner, that unresponsive smile — these were all his own. And the miracle is that, in spite of them, in defiance of all the rules laid down for winning friends and influencing people, he gained and held the confidence of hardheaded voters. Whenever he was pitted against a demagogue, Calvin Coolidge won.

The Man from Vermont who sat rocking back and forth on the porch of his family homestead in the summer of 1932, watching the pilgrims who came there in droves to see the place where he was

---

[26] Gamaliel Bradford, in his illuminating essay, "Calvin Coolidge, the Genius of the Average," in his book *The Quick and the Dead*, quotes a remark by Mark Sullivan that Coolidge was a man who had come to be head of a corporation by starting in as an office boy—"but an office boy with his eye fixed, from the very first day, on the big mahogany desk of the president with the definite intention of going upward step by step." I do not agree with this interpretation, nor did Mr. Bradford.

born, must have dwelt much in the past. Out of that obscure Green Mountain hamlet he had emerged and moved steadily towards fame and the White House. Around him were the upland meadows where he had pitched hay as a boy, the grass-flecked roads and wooded hills — everything unaltered while he had gone away and come back. As the smoke curled up from his cigar, he may have thought of his school days at Black River Academy and the long happy walks up and down the valley; of his lonely hours at Amherst College, when he was a homesick country lad; of his humble adventures in local politics in Northampton; of the blessings which had come to him through his charming wife; of the friends who had helped him along the way — Judge Field and Murray Crane and Frank Stearns; of the Boston Police Strike, which had offered him his major opportunity; and of that June evening in Boston when he had received the news of his nomination for Vice President. Only a few feet away was the room where, before the dawn on an August morning in 1923, he had so hurriedly and so simply taken over the highest office in the land. His had been a notable career, almost uninterrupted in its successes, unmarred by any shameful episode or discreditable incident. It must have occurred to him, with his knowledge of history, that he had attained a goal for which Clay and Webster and Calhoun and Blaine and many others had vainly striven. He had been a perfect example of the rise to power in a republic.

Among Calvin Coolidge's fine qualities, two stand out above the others — common sense and sound character. He embodied the spirit and hopes of the middle class, could interpret their longings and express their opinions. That he did represent the genius of the average is the most convincing proof of his strength. Perhaps, in a democracy, such men make the most trustworthy leaders.

BIBLIOGRAPHY

ADAMS, SAMUEL HOPKINS, *The Incredible Era.*
Houghton Mifflin, 1929.
ALLEN, FREDERICK L., *Only Yesterday.*
Harper, 1931.
——, *The Lords of Creation.*
Harper, 1935.

BEARD, CHARLES A. AND MARY R., *America in Mid-Passage.*
Macmillan, 1939.
——, *The Rise of American Civilization.*
Macmillan, 1930.
BOWERS, CLAUDE G., *Beveridge and the Progressive Era.*
Houghton Mifflin, 1932.
BRADFORD, GAMALIEL, *The Quick and the Dead.*
Houghton Mifflin, 1931.
——, *The Journal of Gamaliel Bradford.* Edited by Van Wyck
Brooks. Houghton Mifflin, 1933.
BRYN-JONES, DAVID, *Frank B. Kellogg.*
Putnam, 1937.
BUTLER, NICHOLAS MURRAY, *Across the Busy Years.*
Scribner, 1939.

CARPENTER, ERNEST C., *The Boyhood Days of Calvin Coolidge.*
Tuttle, 1925.
CLEATON, IRENE AND ALLEN, *Books and Battles, American Literature,
1920–1930.* Houghton Mifflin, 1937.
COOK, SHERWIN LAWRENCE, *Torchlight Parade.*
Minton, Balch, 1929.
COOLIDGE, CALVIN, *Foundations of the Republic.*
Scribner, 1926.
——, *The Price of Freedom.*
Scribner, 1924.
——, *The Autobiography of Calvin Coolidge.*
Cosmopolitan, 1931.
——, *Have Faith in Massachusetts.*
Houghton Mifflin, 1919.

DAUGHERTY, HARRY MICAJAH, AND DIXON, THOMAS, *Inside Story of the Harding Tragedy*. Churchill Company, 1932.

DAY, CLARENCE, *In the Green Mountain Country*. Yale, 1934.

DENNIS, A. P., *Gods and Little Fishes*. Bobbs-Merrill, 1934.

EVANS, LAWRENCE B., *Samuel W. McCall*. Houghton Mifflin, 1916.

FLYNN, JOHN T., *Security Speculation*. Harcourt, Brace, 1934.

FUESS, CLAUDE M., *Amherst, The Story of a New England College*. Atlantic–Little, Brown, 1935.

GILFOND, DUFF, *The Rise of Saint Calvin*. Vanguard, 1932.

GREEN, HORACE, *The Life of Calvin Coolidge*. Duffield, 1924.

GRIFFIN, SOLOMON BULKLEY, *W. Murray Crane, a Man and Brother*. Little, Brown, 1926.

HARD, WALTER, *A Mountain Township*. Harcourt, Brace, 1933.

———, *Salt of Vermont*. Stephen Daye, 1931.

———, *Vermont Vintage*. Stephen Daye, 1937.

HART, ALBERT BUSHNELL, ED., *Commonwealth History of Massachusetts, Colony, Province, and State*. N. Y., The States History Company, 1927–30.

HAWORTH, PAUL L., *The United States in Our Own Times, 1865–1931*. Scribner, 1931.

HENNESSY, MICHAEL E., *Calvin Coolidge*. Putnam, 1924.

HOOVER, IRWIN H. (IKE), *Forty-two Years in the White House*. Houghton Mifflin, 1934.

HOWE, M. A. DE WOLFE, *Barrett Wendell and His Letters*. Atlantic–Little, Brown, 1924.

JAFFRAY, ELIZABETH, *Secrets of the White House*. Cosmopolitan, 1927.

JESSUP, PHILIP C., *Elihu Root*. Dodd, Mead, 1938.

JOHNSON, CLAUDIUS O., *Borah of Idaho*. Longmans, Green, 1936.

JOHNSON, WILLIS FLETCHER, *George Harvey.*
Houghton Mifflin, 1929.

LINDLEY, ERNEST KIDDER, *Half Way with Roosevelt.*
Viking, 1936.
LINGLEY, CHARLES R., *Since the Civil War.*
Century, 1935.
LIPPMANN, WALTER, *Men of Destiny.*
Macmillan, 1928.
LONGWORTH, ALICE ROOSEVELT, *Crowded Hours.*
Scribner, 1933.
LOWRY, EDWARD G., *Washington Close-Ups.*
Houghton Mifflin, 1921.
LYND, ROBERT S. AND HELEN MERRELL, *Middletown.*
Harcourt, Brace, 1929.
———, *Middletown in Transition.*
Harcourt, Brace, 1937.

MCBRIDE, MARY MARGARET, *The Story of Dwight W. Morrow.*
Farrar & Rinehart, 1930.
MCKEE, JOHN HIRAM, *Coolidge Wit and Wisdom.*
Stokes, 1933.
Mirrors of Washington. Anonymous.
Putnam, 1921.

NICOLSON, HAROLD, *Dwight Morrow.*
Harcourt, Brace, 1935.

PAXSON, FREDERICK L., *Recent History of the United States, 1865–1929.* Houghton Mifflin, 1929.
PEARSON, DREW, AND BROWN, CONSTANTIN, *The American Diplomatic Game.* Doubleday, Doran, 1935.
PEARSON, HENRY GREENLEAF, *Son of New England, James Jackson Storrow, 1864–1926.* Privately printed, 1932.
PEPPER, GEORGE WHARTON, *Men and Issues.*
Duffield, 1924.
PRINGLE, HENRY F., *The Life and Times of William H. Taft.*
Farrar & Rinehart, 1939.

RANDOLPH, MARY, *Presidents and First Ladies.*
Appleton-Century, 1916.
ROBERTS, KENNETH L., *Concentrated New England.*
Bobbs-Merrill, 1924.
ROGERS, CAMERON, *The Legend of Calvin Coolidge.*
Doubleday, Doran, 1928.

SAWYER, ROLAND D., *Cal Coolidge, President.*
Four Seas, 1924.
SHIPPEE, LESTER BURRELL, *Recent American History.*
Macmillan, 1930.
SIEGFRIED, ANDRÉ, *America Comes of Age.*
Harcourt, Brace, 1927.
SLEMP, C. BASCOM, ED., *The Mind of the President.*
Doubleday, Doran, 1926.
SLOSSON, PRESTON W., *The Great Crusade and After, 1914–1928.*
Macmillan, 1930.
STIMSON, HENRY LEWIS, *American Policy in Nicaragua.*
Scribner, 1927.
STODDARD, HENRY L., *As I Knew Them.*
Harper, 1927.
———, *It Costs to Be President.*
Harper, 1938.
SULLIVAN, MARK, *Our Times,* Vols. V and VI.
Scribner, 1935.

THOMPSON, CHARLES W., *Presidents I've Known.*
Bobbs-Merrill, 1929.

WASHBURN, ROBERT M., *Calvin Coolidge, His First Biography.*
Small, Maynard, 1923.
WATSON, JAMES E., *As I Knew Them.*
Bobbs-Merrill, 1936.
WHITE, WILLIAM ALLEN, *Calvin Coolidge.*
Macmillan, 1925.
———, *Masks in a Pageant.*
Macmillan, 1930.
———, *A Puritan in Babylon.*
Macmillan, 1938.
WHITING, EDWARD ELWELL, *Calvin Coolidge, His Ideals of Citizenship.* Wilde, 1924.
———, *President Coolidge.*
Atlantic–Little, Brown, 1923.
WOODS, ROBERT A., *The Preparation of Calvin Coolidge.*
Houghton Mifflin, 1924.

INDEX

INDEX

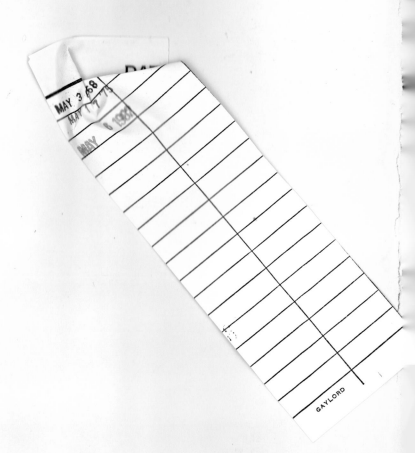